Principles and Applications of Adaptive Artificial Intelligence

Zhihan Lv
Uppsala University, Sweden

A volume in the Advances in Computational Intelligence and Robotics (ACIR) Book Series

IGI Global
PUBLISHER of TIMELY KNOWLEDGE

Published in the United States of America by
IGI Global
Engineering Science Reference (an imprint of IGI Global)
701 E. Chocolate Avenue
Hershey PA, USA 17033
Tel: 717-533-8845
Fax: 717-533-8661
E-mail: cust@igi-global.com
Web site: http://www.igi-global.com

Library of Congress Cataloging-in-Publication Data

Names: Lv, Zhihan, editor.
Title: Principles and applications of adaptive artificial intelligence / edited by: Zhihan Lv.
Description: Hershey, PA : Engineering Science Reference, [2024] | Includes bibliographical references and index. | Summary: "This book covers the latest and cutting-edge application technology of Adaptive AI in various fields. It can provide relevant practitioners with ideas to solve problems and have a deeper understanding of Adaptive AI. At the same time, guide and help Adaptive AI and related industries to deepen their understanding of the industry and enhance their professional knowledge and skills"-- Provided by publisher.
Identifiers: LCCN 2023025868 (print) | LCCN 2023025869 (ebook) | ISBN 9798369302309 (hardcover) | ISBN 9798369302316 (paperback) | ISBN 9798369302323 (ebook)
Subjects: LCSH: Adaptive control systems. | Artificial intelligence.
Classification: LCC TJ217 .H365 2024 (print) | LCC TJ217 (ebook) | DDC 006.3--dc23/eng/20230719
LC record available at https://lccn.loc.gov/2023025868
LC ebook record available at https://lccn.loc.gov/2023025869

This book is published in the IGI Global book series Advances in Computational Intelligence and Robotics (ACIR) (ISSN: 2327-0411; eISSN: 2327-042X)

British Cataloguing in Publication Data
A Cataloguing in Publication record for this book is available from the British Library.

For electronic access to this publication, please contact: eresources@igi-global.com.

Advances in Computational Intelligence and Robotics (ACIR) Book Series

Ivan Giannoccaro
University of Salento, Italy

ISSN:2327-0411
EISSN:2327-042X

Mission

While intelligence is traditionally a term applied to humans and human cognition, technology has progressed in such a way to allow for the development of intelligent systems able to simulate many human traits. With this new era of simulated and artificial intelligence, much research is needed in order to continue to advance the field and also to evaluate the ethical and societal concerns of the existence of artificial life and machine learning.

The **Advances in Computational Intelligence and Robotics (ACIR) Book Series** encourages scholarly discourse on all topics pertaining to evolutionary computing, artificial life, computational intelligence, machine learning, and robotics. ACIR presents the latest research being conducted on diverse topics in intelligence technologies with the goal of advancing knowledge and applications in this rapidly evolving field.

Coverage

- Natural Language Processing
- Fuzzy Systems
- Adaptive and Complex Systems
- Computational Intelligence
- Agent technologies
- Computational Logic
- Machine Learning
- Evolutionary Computing
- Pattern Recognition
- Artificial Life

The Advances in Computational Intelligence and Robotics (ACIR) Book Series (ISSN 2327-0411) is published by IGI Global, 701 E. Chocolate Avenue, Hershey, PA 17033-1240, USA, www.igi-global.com. This series is composed of titles available for purchase individually; each title is edited to be contextually exclusive from any other title within the series. For pricing and ordering information please visit http://www.igi-global.com/book-series/advances-computational-intelligence-robotics/73674. Postmaster: Send all address changes to above address.

Titles in this Series

For a list of additional titles in this series, please visit: www.igi-global.com/book-series

AI and Blockchain Applications in Industrial Robotics
Rajashekhar C. Biradar (Reva University, India) Geetha D. (Reva University, India) Nikhath Tabassum (Reva University, India) Nayana Hegde (Reva University, India) and Mihai Lazarescu (Politecnico di Torino, taly)
Engineering Science Reference • © 2024 • 414pp • H/C (ISBN: 9798369306598) • US $300.00

Emerging Advancements in AI and Big Data Technologies in Business and Society
Jingyuan Zhao (University of Toronto, Canada) Joseph Richards (California State University, Sacramento, USA) and V. Vinoth Kumar (Vellore Institute of Technology, ndia)
Engineering Science Reference • © 2024 • 320pp • H/C (ISBN: 9798369306833) • US $270.00

Advanced Applications of Generative AI and Natural Language Processing Models
Ahmed J. Obaid (University of Kufa, Iraq) Bharat Bhushan (School of Engineering and Technology, Sharda University, India) Muthmainnah S. (Universitas Al Asyariah Mandar, Indonesia) and S. Suman Rajest (Dhaanish Ahmed College of Engineering, India)
Engineering Science Reference • © 2024 • 481pp • H/C (ISBN: 9798369305027) • US $270.00

Artificial Intelligence in the Age of Nanotechnology
Wassim Jaber (ESPCI Paris - PSL, France)
Engineering Science Reference • © 2024 • 299pp • H/C (ISBN: 9798369303689) • US $300.00

Impact of AI on Advancing Women's Safety
Sivaram Ponnusamy (Sandip University, Nashik, India) Vibha Bora (G.H. Raisoni College of Engineering, Nagpur, India) Prema M. Daigavane (G.H. Raisoni College of Engineering, Nagpur, India) and Sampada S. Wazalwar (G.H. Raisoni College of Engineering, Nagpur, India)
Engineering Science Reference • © 2024 • 320pp • H/C (ISBN: 9798369326794) • US $315.00

Handbook of Research on AI and ML for Intelligent Machines and Systems
Brij B. Gupta (Asia University, Taichung, Taiwan & Lebanese American University, Beirut, Lebanon) and Francesco Colace (University of Salerno, Italy)
Engineering Science Reference • © 2024 • 503pp • H/C (ISBN: 9781668499993) • US $380.00

IGI Global
PUBLISHER of TIMELY KNOWLEDGE

701 East Chocolate Avenue, Hershey, PA 17033, USA
Tel: 717-533-8845 x100 • Fax: 717-533-8661
E-Mail: cust@igi-global.com • www.igi-global.com

Table of Contents

Preface xiv

Chapter 1
A Comprehensive Framework for Hyperheuristic Algorithms for Berth Allocation and Scheduling at Marine Container Terminals 1
Bokang Li, FAMU-FSU College of Engineering, USA
Zeinab Elmi, FAMU-FSU College of Engineering, USA
Marta Borowska-Stefańska, University of Lodz, Poland
Szymon Wiśniewski, University of Lodz, Poland
Yui-yip Lau, The Hong Kong Polytechnic University, Hong Kong
Qiong Chen, Jimei University, China
Maxim A. Dulebenets, FAMU-FSU College of Engineering, USA

Chapter 2
Adapting Teaching and Learning in Higher Education Using Explainable Student Agency Analytics20
Ville Heilala, University of Jyväskylä, Finland
Päivikki Jääskelä, University of Jyväskylä, Finland
Mirka Saarela, University of Jyväskylä, Finland
Tommi Kärkkäinen, University of Jyväskylä, Finland

Chapter 3
Adaptive AI for Dynamic Cybersecurity Systems: Enhancing Protection in a Rapidly Evolving Digital Landscap 52
C. V. Suresh Babu, Hindustan Institute of Technolgy and Science, India
Andrew Simon P., Hindustan Institute of Technology and Science, India

Chapter 4
Adaptive Learning in IoT-Based Smart City Applications 73
Nawaf Abdulla, Gazi University, Turkey
Sedef Demirci, Gazi University, Turkey
Mehmet Demirci, Gazi University, Turkey
Suat Özdemir, Hacettepe University, Turkey

Chapter 5
Beyond Surface Linguistics: Assessing the Cognitive Limitations of GPT Through the Long Memory Test 102
Matej Šprogar, Faculty of Electrical Engineering and Computer Science, University of Maribor, Slovenia

Chapter 6
DeepSlicing: Collaborative and Adaptive CNN Inference With Low Latency 123
Shuai Zhang, Nanjing University, China
Yu Chen, Nanjing University, China
Sheng Zhang, Nanjing University, China
Zhiqi Chen, Nanjing University, China

Chapter 7
Improving Live Augmented Reality With Neural Configuration Adaptation........ 151
Ning Chen, Nanjing University, China
Sheng Zhang, Nanjing University, China
Sang Lu Lu, Nanjing University, China

Chapter 8
Interactive Causality-Enabled Adaptive Machine Learning in Cyber-Physical Systems: Technology and Applications in Manufacturing and Beyond........ 179
Yutian Ren, University of California, Irvine, USA
Aaron Yen, University of California, Irvine, USA
Salaar Saraj, University of California, Irvine, USA
GuannPyng Li, University of California, Irvine, USA

Chapter 9
LSTM With Bayesian Optimization for Forecasting of Local Scour Depth Around Bridges and Piers........ 207
Ahmed Shakir Ali, University of Memphis, USA
Saman Ebrahimi, University of Memphis, USA
Muhammad Masood Ashiq, University of Memphis, USA
Ali R. Kashani, University of Memphis, USA

Chapter 10
Phase Unwrapping Method Using Adaptive AI Model for the Application of Industrialization and Precision Metrology Field........ 222
Zhuo Zhao, Xi'an Jiaotong University, China
Bing Li, Xi'an Jiaotong University, China
Leqi Geng, Xi'an Jiaotong University, China
Jiasheng Lu, Xi'an Jiaotong University, China
Qiuying Li, Xi'an Jiaotong University, China
Tao Peng, Soochow University, China
Zheng Wang, Xi'an Jiaotong University, China

Chapter 11
Self-Adaptive ReLU Neural Network Method in Least-Squares Data Fitting 242
Zhiqiang Cai, Purdue University, USA
Min Liu, Purdue University, USA

Chapter 12
The Study of Ecosystem and Vendor Management in Hyper-Automation Across Select Industry Verticals 263
Akshata Desai, Symbiosis Institute of Digital and Telecom Management, Symbiosis International University (Deemed), India
Giri Gundu Hallur, Symbiosis Institute of Digital and Telecom Management, Symbiosis International University (Deemed), India
Natraj N. A., Symbiosis Institute of Digital and Telecom Management, Symbiosis International University (Deemed), India
Abhijit Chirputkar, Symbiosis Institute of Digital and Telecom Management, Symbiosis International University (Deemed), India

Compilation of References 273

About the Contributors 311

Index 315

Detailed Table of Contents

Preface xiv

Chapter 1
A Comprehensive Framework for Hyperheuristic Algorithms for Berth Allocation and Scheduling at Marine Container Terminals 1

Bokang Li, FAMU-FSU College of Engineering, USA
Zeinab Elmi, FAMU-FSU College of Engineering, USA
Marta Borowska-Stefańska, University of Lodz, Poland
Szymon Wiśniewski, University of Lodz, Poland
Yui-yip Lau, The Hong Kong Polytechnic University, Hong Kong
Qiong Chen, Jimei University, China
Maxim A. Dulebenets, FAMU-FSU College of Engineering, USA

Maritime transportation is the main transportation mode for the delivery of cargoes between different continents across the world. Container ships carrying valuable goods are served at marine container terminals (MCTs). Berth allocation and scheduling is one of the primary decision problems that have to be addressed by MCT operators when planning seaside operations. The berth allocation and scheduling problem (BASP) has high computational complexity and cannot be solved using exact optimization algorithms in acceptable computational time for large-scale problem instances. Therefore, many types of heuristic and metaheuristics have been proposed in the BASP literature. However, hyperheuristics still have not been explored for the BASP decision problem, despite their promising performance in other settings. Hence, this study proposes a comprehensive framework for hyperheuristic algorithms for berth allocation and scheduling at MCTs that could be further used to guide the future research in this area.

Chapter 2
Adapting Teaching and Learning in Higher Education Using Explainable Student Agency Analytics20

Ville Heilala, University of Jyväskylä, Finland
Päivikki Jääskelä, University of Jyväskylä, Finland
Mirka Saarela, University of Jyväskylä, Finland
Tommi Kärkkäinen, University of Jyväskylä, Finland

This chapter deals with the learning analytics technique called student agency analytics and explores its foundational technologies and their potential implications for adaptive teaching and learning. Student agency is vital to consider as it can empower students to take control of their learning, fostering autonomy, meaningful experiences, and improved educational outcomes. Beginning with an overview of the technique, its underlying educational foundations, and analytical approaches, the chapter demonstrates the synergy between computational psychometrics, learning analytics, and educational sciences. Considering adaptive artificial intelligence in the context of adaptive learning and teaching, the chapter underscores the potential of these approaches in education. The chapter serves as a brief guide for educators, researchers, and stakeholders interested in the convergence of AI and education.

Chapter 3
Adaptive AI for Dynamic Cybersecurity Systems: Enhancing Protection in a Rapidly Evolving Digital Landscap 52
C. V. Suresh Babu, Hindustan Institute of Technolgy and Science, India
Andrew Simon P., Hindustan Institute of Technology and Science, India

This chapter offers a concise roadmap for navigating the dynamic cybersecurity landscape using Adaptive AI. Beginning with a comprehensive introduction that sets the stage, it delves into the intricacies of the cybersecurity landscape and categorizes common threats in topic two. Topic three showcases the transformative potential of Adaptive AI, focusing on real-time threat detection, proactive defense, and continuous learning. Topic four provides enlightening case studies, offering practical insights. Topic five addresses the practicalities of implementing Adaptive AI, covering considerations and best practices. Topic six explores AI's future in cybersecurity. Lastly, topic seven summarizes findings, emphasizes key takeaways, and recommends utilizing Adaptive AI to enhance dynamic cybersecurity. This book is a valuable guide for safeguarding digital assets in the evolving cyber landscape.

Chapter 4
Adaptive Learning in IoT-Based Smart City Applications 73
Nawaf Abdulla, Gazi University, Turkey
Sedef Demirci, Gazi University, Turkey
Mehmet Demirci, Gazi University, Turkey
Suat Özdemir, Hacettepe University, Turkey

Internet of things (IoT) based smart city applications rely on constant data collection and accurate data analytics, yet the fast-changing nature of such data often causes the performance of machine learning models to deteriorate over time. Adaptive learning has been increasingly utilized in these applications in recent years as a viable solution to this problem. Moreover, IoT applications are vulnerable to various security threats due to their large-scale deployment, resource-constrained devices, and diverse protocols. This has led to an increased interest in efficient security and intrusion detection mechanisms tailored for IoT environments. In this chapter, the authors first focus on methods to address the issue of concept drift in time series streaming data for IoT-based smart city applications, such as weather, flood, and energy consumption forecasting, through adaptive learning. Furthermore, the authors examine adaptive learning-based security solutions to various attacks in different domains of the dynamic smart city landscape.

Chapter 5
Beyond Surface Linguistics: Assessing the Cognitive Limitations of GPT Through the Long Memory Test 102
Matej Šprogar, Faculty of Electrical Engineering and Computer Science, University of Maribor, Slovenia

Contemporary artificial intelligence has advanced markedly toward mimicking human intelligence. Despite linguistic proficiency, machines remain bereft of genuine text comprehension, leading to perceived, albeit superficial, intelligence. This chapter introduces a straightforward test that highlights the non-human-like cognition of machines such as ChatGPT. Eschewing the prevalent approach of progressively complex testing, the long memory test highlights ChatGPT's inability to function at a human level. Central to this assessment, the test mandates reliable information retention, a feat the transformer architecture of GPT fails to achieve.

Chapter 6
DeepSlicing: Collaborative and Adaptive CNN Inference With Low Latency 123
Shuai Zhang, Nanjing University, China
Yu Chen, Nanjing University, China
Sheng Zhang, Nanjing University, China
Zhiqi Chen, Nanjing University, China

Convolutional neural networks (CNNs) have revolutionized computer vision applications with recent advancements. Extensive research focuses on optimizing CNNs for efficient deployment on resource-limited devices. However, the previous studies had several weaknesses, including limited support for diverse CNN structures, fixed scheduling strategies, overlapped computations, and high synchronization overheads. In this chapter, the authors introduce DeepSlicing, an adaptive inference system that addresses the above challenges. It supports various CNNs and offers flexible fine-grained scheduling, including GoogLeNet and ResNet models. DeepSlicing incorporates a proportional synchronized scheduler (PSS) for balancing computation and synchronization. Implemented using PyTorch, the authors evaluate DeepSlicing on an edge testbed of 8 heterogeneous Raspberry Pis. Results showcase the remarkable reductions in inference latency (up to 5.79 times) and memory footprint (up to 14.72 times), demonstrating the efficacy of this proposed approach.

Chapter 7
Improving Live Augmented Reality With Neural Configuration Adaptation.................................... 151
Ning Chen, Nanjing University, China
Sheng Zhang, Nanjing University, China
Sang Lu Lu, Nanjing University, China

Instead of relying on remote clouds, today's augmented reality (AR) applications send videos to nearby edge servers for analysis to optimize user's quality of experience (QoE). Lots of studies have been conducted to help adaptively choose the best video configuration, e.g., resolution and frame per second (fps). However, prior works only consider network bandwidth and ignores the video content itself. In this chapter, the authors design Cuttlefish, a system that generates video configuration decisions using reinforcement learning (RL) based on network condition as well as the video content. Cuttlefish does not rely on any pre-programmed models or specific assumptions on the environments. Instead, it learns to make configuration decisions solely through observations of the resulting performance of historical decisions. Cuttlefish automatically learns the adaptive configuration policy for diverse AR video streams and obtains a gratifying QoE. The experimental results show that Cuttlefish achieves a 18.4%-25.8% higher QoE than the other prior designs.

Chapter 8
Interactive Causality-Enabled Adaptive Machine Learning in Cyber-Physical Systems: Technology and Applications in Manufacturing and Beyond.......... 179
Yutian Ren, University of California, Irvine, USA
Aaron Yen, University of California, Irvine, USA
Salaar Saraj, University of California, Irvine, USA
GuannPyng Li, University of California, Irvine, USA

This chapter describes an adaptive machine learning (ML) method for the utilization of unlabeled data for continual model adaptation after deployment. Current methods for the usage of unlabeled data, such as unsupervised and semi-supervised methods, rely on being both smooth and static in their distributions. In this chapter, a generic method for leveraging causal relationships to automatically associate labels with unlabeled data using state transitions of asynchronous interacting cause and effect events is discussed. This self-labeling method is predicated on a defined causal relationship and associated temporal spacing. The theoretical foundation of the self-supervised method is discussed and compared with its contemporary semi-supervised counterparts using dynamical systems theory. Implementations of this method to adapt action recognition ML models in semiconductor manufacturing and human assembly tasks as manufacturing cyber-physical systems (CPS) are provided to demonstrate the effectiveness of the proposed methodology.

Chapter 9
LSTM With Bayesian Optimization for Forecasting of Local Scour Depth Around Bridges and Piers.......... 207
Ahmed Shakir Ali, University of Memphis, USA
Saman Ebrahimi, University of Memphis, USA
Muhammad Masood Ashiq, University of Memphis, USA
Ali R. Kashani, University of Memphis, USA

Scour is a critical issue that impacts the safety and strength of bridges. Precise scour forecasts around bridge piers can provide useful data for bridge engineers to bring preventive actions. This study uses long short-term memory (LSTM) neural network with Bayesian optimization to forecast the scour around the bridges and piers. The LSTM network was trained and tested using only scour depth data from a calibrated numerical model. The outcomes indicate that the proposed LSTM model provides precise scour depth forecasts. The study presents the performance of the LSTM model for predicting scour depth around bridge piers, which can help enhance the safety and stability of bridges. The model has shown acceptable outcomes, with a rank correlation equal to 0.9866 in the training stage and 0.9655 in the testing stage. Moreover, the LSTM model was used to forecast the scour depth for 11 minutes.

Chapter 10
Phase Unwrapping Method Using Adaptive AI Model for the Application of Industrialization and Precision Metrology Field.......... 222
Zhuo Zhao, Xi'an Jiaotong University, China
Bing Li, Xi'an Jiaotong University, China
Leqi Geng, Xi'an Jiaotong University, China
Jiasheng Lu, Xi'an Jiaotong University, China
Qiuying Li, Xi'an Jiaotong University, China
Tao Peng, Soochow University, China
Zheng Wang, Xi'an Jiaotong University, China

Phase unwrapping method based on Residual Auto Encoder Network is proposed in this chapter. Phase unwrapping is regarded as a multiple classification problem, and it will be solved by the trained network model. Through training and validation stages, optimal network models can be served as predictors of wrap count distribution map of wrapped phase. Then merge the wrapped phase and count together to complete unwrapping. Software simulation and hardware acquisition are the sources of training dataset. To further improve accuracy of unwrapping, image analysis-based optimization method is designed that can remove misclassification and noise points in initial result. In addition, phase data stitching by Iterative Closest Point is adopted to realize dynamic resolution and enhance the flexibility of method. Point diffraction interferometer and multi-step phase extraction technique is the foundation of proposed method. It can be concluded from experiments that the proposed method is superior to state-of-art ones in accuracy, time efficiency, anti-noise ability, and flexibility.

Chapter 11
Self-Adaptive ReLU Neural Network Method in Least-Squares Data Fitting.......... 242
Zhiqiang Cai, Purdue University, USA
Min Liu, Purdue University, USA

This chapter provides a comprehensive introduction to a self-adaptive ReLU neural network method proposed. The purpose is to design a nearly minimal neural network architecture to achieve the prescribed accuracy for a given task in scientific machine learning such as approximating a function or a solution of partial differential equation. Starting with a small one hidden-layer neural network, the method enhances the network adaptively by adding neurons in the current or new hidden-layer based on accuracy of the current approximation. In addition, the method provides a natural process for obtaining a good initialization in training the current network. Moreover, initialization of newly added neurons at each adaptive step is discussed in detail.

Chapter 12
The Study of Ecosystem and Vendor Management in Hyper-Automation Across Select Industry Verticals 263
Akshata Desai, Symbiosis Institute of Digital and Telecom Management, Symbiosis International University (Deemed), India
Giri Gundu Hallur, Symbiosis Institute of Digital and Telecom Management, Symbiosis International University (Deemed), India
Natraj N. A., Symbiosis Institute of Digital and Telecom Management, Symbiosis International University (Deemed), India
Abhijit Chirputkar, Symbiosis Institute of Digital and Telecom Management, Symbiosis International University (Deemed), India

This proposed chapter aims to present a study on RPA leaders and understand the parameters for improving Power Automate's position amongst industry leaders by formulating a SWOT analysis for the company. The work presented starts with scrutinizing various literature on RPA, followed by a detailed analysis of Microsoft's RPA efforts. Gartner published a report on robotics process automation, placing Microsoft's Power Automate lowest in the Leader's magic quadrant. This chapter provides recommendations that could help Power Automate move up the ladder. The research method adopted is a qualitative analysis of the company in focus. As the chapter progresses, it unfolds various offerings of Power Automate that either empower its growth or could be a concern compared to RPA leaders like Uipath, Automation Anywhere, and Blueprism. Power Automate has made its footprints in the RPA space, and with aggressive innovation and restructuring, it can be a prominent player across industries.

Compilation of References 273

About the Contributors 311

Index 315

Preface

Welcome to *Principles and Applications of Adaptive Artificial Intelligence*. This book represents a comprehensive effort to distill the latest concepts, technologies, and applications in Adaptive AI while presenting unique perspectives from the author. Its purpose is to offer readers a profound comprehension of this burgeoning discipline.

This work embarks on an all-encompassing journey through Adaptive AI, delving into fundamental concepts, core technologies, technical architectures, and application scenarios. By engaging with this text, readers will acquire a profound understanding of this evolving field.

Spanning across various sectors, this book explores cutting-edge applications of Adaptive AI, providing practitioners with innovative problem-solving strategies and deeper insights. It serves as a guiding light for industries associated with Adaptive AI, fostering a heightened understanding and bolstering professional expertise.

Grounded in real-world scenarios, this book elucidates theories through practical cases, rendering it a valuable resource for educators and students specializing in Adaptive AI, Internet of Things, Artificial Intelligence, and related disciplines in academic institutions.

Additionally, this compilation touches upon frontier technologies in Adaptive AI, serving as a catalyst for fresh research endeavors. It merges theoretical underpinnings with mathematical formulations to present a comprehensive exposition of Adaptive AI theory.

The relevance of Adaptive AI is undeniable, especially in an era where deep learning models replace traditional business logics, shaping the landscape of service offerings. Yet, the challenges of automation and industrialization persist. This book highlights the significance of solving the AI system self-adaptation problem, unlocking immense cost-effectiveness and operational stability.

Adaptive AI's agility in responding to unforeseen real-world conditions, continuously learning, and dynamically adjusting goals based on real-time feedback, positions it as a pivotal technology. As recognized by Gartner in their 2023 Emerging Technologies and Trends Impact Radar Chart, Adaptive AI stands among the top ten influential technologies.

While the rapid evolution of Adaptive AI sees mentions in various media, comprehensive references are scarce. This book endeavors to bridge that gap, aiming to deepen the understanding of technical personnel within Adaptive AI industries and serve as a guiding compass for educators and enthusiasts alike.

As a handbook tailored for senior undergraduates, postgraduates, researchers, and professionals across academic and business domains, this book aims to illuminate the intricate landscape of Adaptive AI.

Thank you for embarking on this enlightening journey into the world of Adaptive AI.

ORGANIZATION OF THE BOOK

Chapter 1: "A Comprehensive Framework for Hyperheuristic Algorithms for Berth Allocation and Scheduling at Marine Container Terminals" by Bokang Li et al. This chapter embarks on addressing the complexity of berth allocation and scheduling at marine container terminals (MCTs). Despite numerous proposed heuristic and metaheuristic approaches, hyperheuristics remain unexplored in this domain. The authors present a comprehensive framework offering promising prospects for future research in this critical area of maritime transportation.

Chapter 2: "Adapting Teaching and Learning in Higher Education Using Explainable Student Agency Analytics" by Ville Heilala et al. Focusing on the paradigm of student agency analytics, this chapter explores its foundational technologies and implications for adaptive teaching and learning. By empowering students to steer their learning journey, the chapter aligns computational psychometrics, learning analytics, and educational sciences, offering educators and researchers a brief guide in merging AI and education.

Chapter 3: "Adaptive AI for Dynamic Cybersecurity Systems: Enhancing Protection in a Rapidly Evolving Digital Landscape" by C.V. Suresh Babu et al. This concise roadmap navigates the dynamic cybersecurity realm using Adaptive AI. Addressing threats, real-time detection, proactive defense, and practical implementations, the chapter offers insights and best practices. It culminates in emphasizing the role of Adaptive AI for bolstering cybersecurity defenses.

Chapter 4: "Adaptive Learning in IoT-Based Smart City Applications" by Nawaf Abdulla et al. Focusing on adaptive learning in IoT-based smart city applications, this chapter tackles the challenge of concept drift in data analytics. It also explores adaptive learning-based security solutions, aiming to fortify IoT environments against diverse threats, thereby enhancing the resilience of smart city applications.

Chapter 5: "Beyond Surface Linguistics: Assessing the Cognitive Limitations of GPT through the Long Memory Test" by Matej Šprogar This chapter introduces a unique assessment, the Long Memory Test, shedding light on the cognitive limitations of contemporary AI models like ChatGPT. By emphasizing information retention, it challenges the text comprehension capabilities of these models, revealing their inherent shortcomings.

Chapter 6: "DeepSlicing: Collaborative and Adaptive CNN Inference with Low Latency" by Shuai Zhang et al. Addressing the optimization challenges in CNNs for resource-limited devices, this chapter introduces DeepSlicing. The authors present a novel adaptive inference system, showcasing significant reductions in latency and memory footprint through fine-grained scheduling strategies.

Chapter 7: "Improving Live Augmented Reality with Neural Configuration Adaptation" by Ning Chen et al. Focusing on Augmented Reality applications, the chapter introduces Cuttlefish, a system utilizing reinforcement learning for video configuration decisions. By considering network conditions and video content, Cuttlefish dynamically adapts to enhance user experience, showcasing substantial improvements in quality of experience (QoE).

Chapter 8: "Interactive Causality Enabled Adaptive Machine Learning in Cyber-Physical Systems: Technology and Applications in Manufacturing and Beyond" by Yutian Ren et al. Describing an adaptive ML method for utilizing unlabeled data in continual model adaptation post-deployment, this chapter leverages causal relationships for self-labeling unlabeled data. It explores applications in semiconductor manufacturing and assembly tasks, demonstrating the effectiveness of the proposed methodology.

Chapter 9: "LSTM with Bayesian Optimization for Forecasting of Local Scour Depth around Bridges Piers" by Ahmed Shakir Ali Ali et al. This chapter focuses on forecasting scour depth around bridge piers using LSTM and Bayesian optimization. By leveraging neural networks, the study presents precise scour depth forecasts crucial for ensuring the safety and stability of bridges.

Chapter 10: "Phase Unwrapping Method Using Adaptive AI model for the Application of Industrialization and Precision Metrology Field" by Zhuo Zhao et al. Proposing a phase unwrapping method based on Residual Auto Encoder Network, this chapter introduces a sophisticated approach for enhancing accuracy, time efficiency, and flexibility in precision metrology applications. The proposed method outperforms existing techniques in various aspects.

Chapter 11: "Self-Adaptive ReLU Neural Network Method in Least-Squares Data Fitting" by Min Liu This chapter introduces a self-adaptive ReLU neural network method for scientific machine learning tasks. It elucidates a method for minimal neural network architecture, dynamically adapting to achieve prescribed accuracy while providing a natural process for network enhancement.

Chapter 12: "The Study of Ecosystem and Vendor Management in Hyper-Automation Across Select Industry Verticals: Ecosystem and Vendor Management in Hyper-Automation" by Akshata Desai et al. Focusing on Power Automate's position in the RPA landscape, this chapter offers a detailed analysis, comparing it with industry leaders. It provides recommendations to elevate Power Automate's standing, making it a prominent player in various industries.

IN SUMMARY

In concluding this comprehensive exploration of adaptive artificial intelligence, this edited reference book stands as a testament to the multifaceted landscape of AI applications and advancements. Each chapter within this compendium illuminates distinct facets of adaptive AI, elucidating its role and impact across diverse domains.

From the pioneering frameworks for hyperheuristic algorithms in maritime transportation to the nuanced analyses of adaptive learning in IoT-based smart city applications, this collection encapsulates the breadth and depth of AI's adaptive capabilities.

The convergence of AI and education, as portrayed in the discussions on student agency analytics, highlights the transformative potential of adaptive approaches in fostering meaningful learning experiences. Likewise, the revelations regarding AI's limitations, as showcased through cognitive tests and methodologies, provide critical insights into the ongoing evolution of AI systems.

The applications in cybersecurity, computer vision, augmented reality, and industrial automation underscore the pivotal role of adaptive AI in fortifying security measures, optimizing performance, and facilitating real-time decision-making.

Moreover, the methodologies presented within these chapters—ranging from LSTM models for scour depth prediction to self-adaptive neural networks for scientific machine learning—demonstrate the innovation and adaptability inherent in contemporary AI research.

As the editor(s) of this volume, it is our sincere hope that this collection serves as a guiding beacon for researchers, educators, practitioners, and enthusiasts navigating the ever-evolving landscape of adaptive artificial intelligence. By embracing the insights and methodologies outlined herein, we collectively propel the trajectory of AI innovation, fostering a future where adaptability remains at the core of intelligent systems.

Zhihan Lv
Uppsala University, Sweden

Chapter 1

A Comprehensive Framework for Hyperheuristic Algorithms for Berth Allocation and Scheduling at Marine Container Terminals

Bokang Li
https://orcid.org/0000-0002-5383-8195
FAMU-FSU College of Engineering, USA

Zeinab Elmi
FAMU-FSU College of Engineering, USA

Marta Borowska-Stefańska
https://orcid.org/0000-0003-2448-4778
University of Lodz, Poland

Szymon Wiśniewski
https://orcid.org/0000-0001-5488-5949
University of Lodz, Poland

Yui-yip Lau
The Hong Kong Polytechnic University, Hong Kong

Qiong Chen
Jimei University, China

Maxim A. Dulebenets
FAMU-FSU College of Engineering, USA

ABSTRACT

Maritime transportation is the main transportation mode for the delivery of cargoes between different continents across the world. Container ships carrying valuable goods are served at marine container terminals (MCTs). Berth allocation and scheduling is one of the primary decision problems that have to be addressed by MCT operators when planning seaside operations. The berth allocation and scheduling problem (BASP) has high computational complexity and cannot be solved using exact optimization algorithms in acceptable computational time for large-scale problem instances. Therefore, many types of heuristic and metaheuristics have been proposed in the BASP literature. However, hyperheuristics still have not been explored for the BASP decision problem, despite their promising performance in other settings. Hence, this study proposes a comprehensive framework for hyperheuristic algorithms for berth allocation and scheduling at MCTs that could be further used to guide the future research in this area.

DOI: 10.4018/979-8-3693-0230-9.ch001

1. INTRODUCTION

1.1. Background

Maritime transportation is viewed as the most popular transportation mode for the delivery of cargoes between different continents across the world (Elmi et al., 2022; Rodrigues and Agra, 2022). Approximately 80% of international trade volumes are transported by ships and handled at ports across the globe. Container ships carrying valuable goods are served at marine container terminals (MCTs). There are three major types of MCT operations, including the following (Bierwirth and Meisel, 2010; Bierwirth and Meisel, 2015): (1) seaside operations that mainly focus on the service of arriving ships by sea-to-shore cranes, generally referred to as "quay cranes" (see **Figure 1**); (2) marshaling yard operations that deal with the storage of containers delivered from the seaside and the landside; and (3) landside operations that entail the pick-up and/or drop-off of the containers delivered by outbound trucks, generally referred to as "drayage trucks". Berth allocation and scheduling is one of the primary decision problems that have to be addressed by MCT operators when planning seaside operations (Carlo et al., 2015). The berth allocation and scheduling problem (BASP) aims to determine the assignment of arriving ships to the available berthing positions. Furthermore, the service order of arriving ships at each berthing position is determined as a part of the BASP as well. Effective berth allocation and scheduling plans are essential for the MCT performance and timely service of arriving ships.

The solution approaches that have been used for the BASP decision problem can be classified in the following three groups (see **Figure 2**): (1) exact optimization methods; (2) heuristic methods; and (3) metaheuristic methods. Exact optimization methods (e.g., branch-and-bound, branch-and-cut, CPLEX, MOSEK, GUROBI, BARON, CONOPT, DICOPT, etc.) are able to obtain global optimal solutions for different variations of the BASP decision problem (Issam et al., 2017; Jos et al., 2019; Kallel et al., 2019; Dkhil et al., 2021). The BASP problems generally have high computational complexity, as they can be reduced to the unrelated machine scheduling problem. Due to the computational complexity, exact optimization methods are not able to produce good-quality solutions for large-scale problem instances of the BASP. Therefore, many types of heuristic and metaheuristics have been proposed in the BASP literature. Heuristic algorithms are approximate solution algorithms that do not produce optimal solutions for a given BASP decision problem but can return solutions of a good quality within reasonable computational time. Heuristic algorithms are typically customized for a specific BASP variation (Nishi et al., 2020; Ankita and Mathirajan, 2021; Mnasri and Alrashidi, 2021; Fernández and Munoz-Marquez, 2022).

As an example, Ankita and Mathirajan (2021) proposed a heuristic algorithm for the BASP, which was based on the early-to-finish principle. The heuristic was compared to the exact method (LINGO) and was found to be efficient. In particular, the developed heuristic obtained optimal solutions that were identical to the LINGO solutions for the 7 out of 10 problem instances. More recently, Fernández and Munoz-Marquez (2022) presented several new formulations for the strategic berth template problem at MCTs. A heuristic algorithm was developed to generate feasible solutions for the problem and consisted of three steps, including the following: (a) determine a subset of ships to be served considering the mother-ship constraints; (b) determine the allocation of ships to the berthing positions that satisfies the cycle duration; and (c) develop a ship service sequence at each berthing position.

Figure 1. Berth allocation and scheduling at an MCT

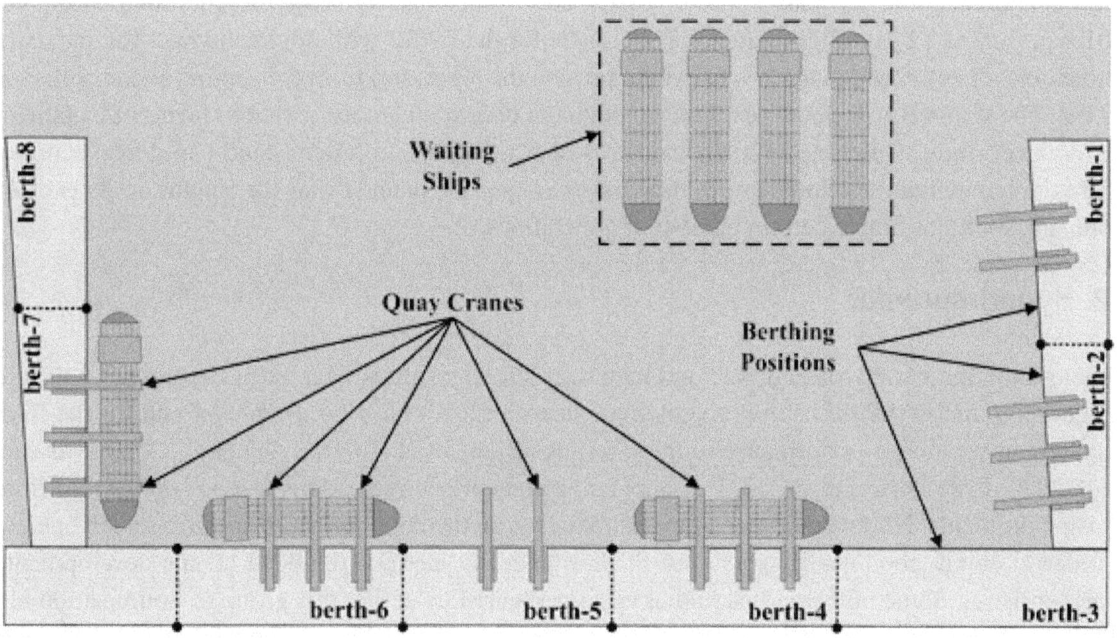

Figure 2. Common solution methods for the BASP decision problem

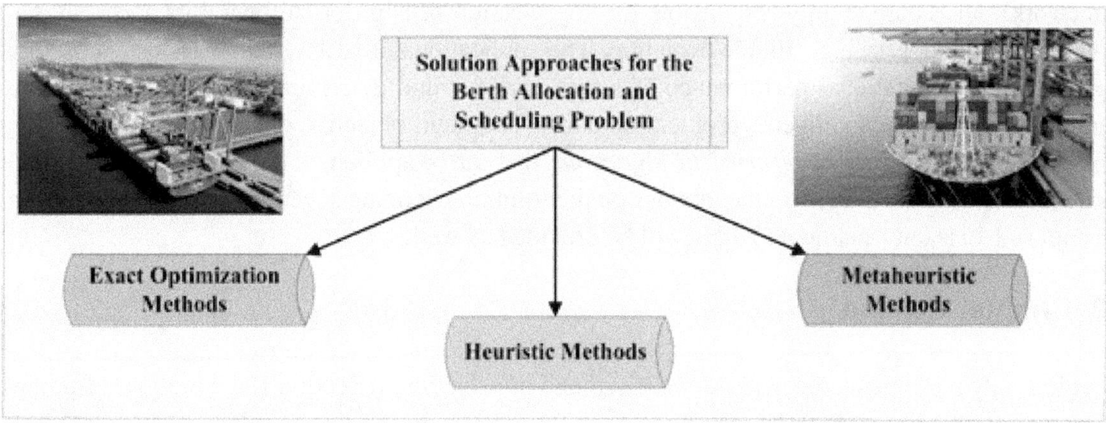

Similar to heuristic algorithms, metaheuristic algorithms (such as evolutionary algorithms, variable neighborhood search, simulated annealing, grey wolf optimizer, particle swarm optimization, ant colony optimization, lion optimization algorithms, red deer algorithm) are approximate solution algorithms that do not produce optimal solutions for a given BASP decision problem but can return solutions of a good quality within reasonable computational time. However, metaheuristics are generally viewed as a much broader group of algorithms and can be used to different decision problems, not just the BASP decision problem (Bacalhau et al., 2021; Peng et al., 2021; Prencipe and Marinelli, 2021; Barbosa et al., 2022; Wang et al., 2022). For instance, Schepler et al. (2019) studied berth allocation and scheduling in stochastic settings where ship arrival times were not known with certainty. The authors presented a solution approach that was based on the iterated tabu search and dynamic programming. Wang et al. (2019) presented a Levy Flight-based metaheuristic for the BASP with tidal windows. The purpose of introducing a Levy Flight random walk was to prevent the algorithm from converging at one of the local optima. The recent BASP studies explore the potential of new and more advanced forms of metaheuristics. As an example, Dulebenets (2020) and Kavoosi et al. (2020) proposed island-based metaheuristics, where the population individuals were distributed among the islands, and the islands could exchange promising solutions after a certain number of generations.

1.2. Hyperheuristics

Although a large variety of heuristic and metaheuristic algorithms have been deployed for different categories of the BASP decision problem, hyperheuristics still have not been explored for the BASP, despite their promising performance in other settings (Leng et al., 2018; Leng et al., 2020; Mosadegh et al., 2020; Cruz-Duarte et al., 2021). Canonical metaheuristic algorithms can be applied to different decision problems. However, certain domains may require the deployment of specific search operators in order to obtain good-quality solutions. Such a tendency justifies the need for the development of hyperheuristics. Some of the earlier studies on hyperheuristics define this group of optimization algorithms as "heuristics to choose heuristics" (Cowling et al., 2000; Wang et al., 2020). Hyperheuristics are typically based on the deployment of low-level heuristics (LLHs) and high-level heuristics (HLHs). LLHs represent a pool of candidate search operators that can be used by the algorithm (e.g., different types of recombination and mutation operators that can be applied within the evolutionary algorithm framework). HLHs are mainly responsible for the selection of appropriate operators and solution acceptance throughout the algorithmic evolution. The applications of LLHs and HLHs can substantially augment the computational performance of hyperheuristics and determine good-quality solutions in complex search cases and diverse problem domains. The main objective of this study is to develop a *generalized framework for hyperheuristic algorithms* that can be applied for the BASP decision problem. Furthermore, constructive recommendations on the solution encoding schemes, candidate operators for the pool of LLHs, and candidate HLHs will be provided as well.

1.3. Chapter Outline

After formally introducing the necessary background information in Section 1, the proposed framework for hyperheuristic algorithms that can be applied for the BASP decision problem is described in Section 2. Section 3 provides a set of constructive recommendations with respect to the solution encoding schemes that would be appropriate for the common BASP variants, candidate heuristics for the pool of LLHs along with illustrative examples of their application, and potential alternatives for HLHs that can be embedded within the proposed hyperheuristic framework. Section 4 discusses how different adaptive and hybridized mechanisms can be incorporated within the proposed hyperheuristic framework. Section 5 summarizes the outcomes of this research and provides some final remarks.

2. PROPOSED HYPERHEURISTIC FRAMEWORK FOR THE BASP

The hyperheuristic framework for the BASP designed in this study is inspired by the principles of population-based evolutionary algorithms. The main difference between the proposed hyperheuristic and typical evolutionary algorithms consists in the fact that the proposed hyperheuristic periodically updates recombination and mutation operators (i.e., these operators serve as LLHs) based on their performance, and HLHs are used to select recombination and mutation operators as well as solutions for the next generation. The overall hyperheuristic framework is presented in **Figure 3**. Before the beginning of the search process, the necessary input data for the BASP decision problem and algorithmic parameter values should be specified in step 1. Then, the counters of generations g and g^* are initiated in step 2. Counter g is used to count all consecutive generations, whereas counter g^* is used to determine generations when LLHs will be updated. As mentioned earlier, the proposed hyperheuristic does not update the search operators in every generation, since it can increase its time complexity. Moreover, the performance of LLHs is difficult to judge based on just one generation. The LLH performance assessment over a set of generations (i.e., *Epoch*) would be more accurate.

Figure 3. An illustration of the proposed hyperheuristic framework

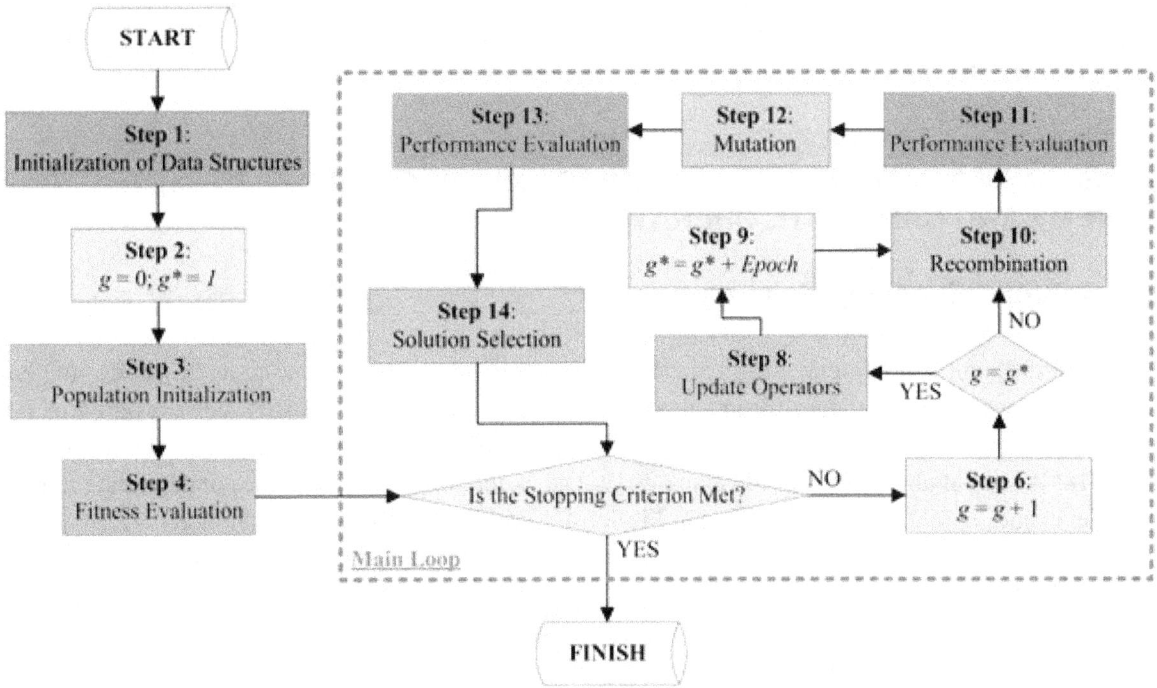

In step 3, the population of solutions is initialized to begin the search process. After that, the fitness of all the population solutions is estimated in step 4. After completing steps 1-4, the proposed hyper-heuristic algorithm enters its main loop represented by steps 5-14. In step 5, the termination criterion (e.g., maximum number of generations) is checked. If the termination criterion is not met, the proposed hyperheuristic moves to step 6 and updates the counter of generations $g=g+1$. Then, if $g=g^*$, the currently deployed recombination operator and mutation operator are updated from the pool of available recombination and mutation operators in step 8. At the beginning of the search process, the performance scores of all the considered recombination and mutation operators are set equal. However, at the consecutive generations, the performance scores of recombination and mutation operators are updated based on the adopted performance metrics (e.g., average solution quality over one *Epoch*, average computational time over one *Epoch*). HLHs are used to select the best performing recombination operator and mutation operator after *Epoch* generations. After updating the recombination and mutation operators in generation g^*, the proposed hyperheuristic updates g^* as $g^*=g^*+$ *Epoch* to ensure that the operators will be updated after *Epoch* generations again (step 9).

After that, the recombination operator selected in step 8 is deployed for the existing solutions (or parental chromosomes) to generate new solutions (or offspring chromosomes) in step 10. The performance of the selected recombination operator is assessed accordingly in step 11 based on the results obtained in step 10. Then, the mutation operator selected in step 8 is deployed for the offspring solutions to generate the mutated solutions in step 12. The performance of the selected mutation operator is assessed accordingly in step 13 based on the results obtained in step 12. In step 14, the proposed hyperheuristic algorithm applies the adopted HLHs to select solutions that will be further used in the following generation. The hyperheuristic exits its main loop once the termination criterion has been satisfied. The following section of the manuscript provides more information regarding the solution encoding schemes that could be potentially used within the proposed hyperheuristic, candidate heuristics for the pool of LLHs, and candidate heuristics for the pool of HLHs.

3. RECOMMENDATIONS FOR THE SOLUTION ENCODING SCHEME AND CANDIDATE OPERATORS

3.1. Solution Encoding Schemes

There are different solution encoding schemes (which are commonly referred to as "chromosome encoding schemes" in evolutionary computation) that can be adopted for the BASP decision problem. An integer solution encoding scheme is viewed as the most popular in the BASP literature (Dulebenets et al., 2018; Pereira et al., 2018; Barbosa et al., 2019; Dai et al., 2023). The examples of candidate integer solution encoding schemes are presented in **Figure 4**. In particular, **Figure 4**(a) shows an example of a two-dimensional integer solution encoding scheme, where the upper row corresponds to berth identifiers, and the bottom row corresponds to ship identifiers. Based on the provided example, ships "2", "4", and "3" are scheduled for loading and unloading operations at berth "1", whereas ships "1", "7", "9", and "6" are allocated to berth "2". The remaining ships (i.e., ships "5" and "8") will be served at berth "3". The service order of ships can be determined based on the solution encoding scheme as well. More specifically, ship "1" will be serviced as the first ship at berth "2", followed by ships "7" and "9". Ship "6" will be serviced last at berth "2" after the service completion of ships "1", "7", and "9".

The solution encoding alternatives illustrated in **Figure 4**(b) and **Figure 4**(c) do not require the upper row for berth identifiers, as the assigned berthing positions can be determined based on the genes with "0" alleles. In particular, ships "1", "4", and "6" will be serviced at berth "1", since the "0" allele(s) are placed after the gene with ship "6" in both **Figure 4**(b) and **Figure 4**(c). Note that the term "allele" is commonly used in evolutionary computation to denote the value of genes (the "genes" refer to individual components of a chromosome/solution), whereas the term "locus" represents the location of a gene along the chromosomes (Eiben and Smith, 2015). The decoding of the second part of the solution can be conducted in a similar fashion (i.e., ships "3", "2", and "5" will be assigned for service at berth "2"; ship "3" will be served first, and ship "5" will be served last). If m and n represent the number of berths and ships, respectively, then the solution dimensions for the three solution encoding schemes will be $2 \times n$, $n+m$, and $n \times m$, respectively. Although the third solution encoding scheme can be effective for small-size instances with a small number of berths and ships (as such encoding can be more convenient for certain types of recombination and mutation operators), the first and second solution encoding schemes might be the most compact representations for large-size instances. More compact solution representations are favorable from the computational time standpoint.

Figure 4. Candidate solution encoding schemes

Berths →	1	1	1	2	2	2	2	3	3
Ships →	2	4	3	1	7	9	6	5	8

(a) Encoding scheme #1

Berths →	1				2			
Ships →	1	4	6	0	3	2	5	0

(b) Encoding scheme #2

Berths →	1						2					
Ships →	1	4	6	0	0	0	3	2	5	0	0	0

(c) Encoding scheme #3

3.2. Candidate Heuristics for the Pool of LLHs

LLHs in the proposed hyperheuristic framework are mainly represented by pools of recombination and mutation operators. Recombination and mutation operators are widely used in evolutionary algorithms to guide the search process (Eiben and Smith, 2015; Kavoosi et al., 2019). Recombination operators aim to explore various domains of the search space and ultimately identify the most promising ones. On the contrary, mutation operators perform the function of a local search, aiming to determine good-quality solutions within the discovered domains of the search space. The selection of suitable recombination and mutation operators largely depends on the solution encoding scheme adopted. Based on the proposed solution encoding scheme alternatives (see Section 3.1), the following sections of the manuscript elaborate on the groups of LLHs that are proposed for recombination and mutation operations.

3.2.1. LLHs for Recombination

The proposed hyperheuristic framework relies on three types of recombination operators, including the cycle recombination operator, order recombination operator, and partially-mapped recombination operator. An example of a cycle recombination operation in showcased in **Figure 5**. The cycle recombination operation starts with the identification of the allele in the first locus of parent "P1" (i.e., ship "2"), and ship "2" is appended to the cycle. Second, the cycle recombination operator checks the first locus of parent "P2" and identifies ship "3". Ship "3" is appended to the cycle. Third, the cycle recombination operator determines the gene of parent "P1" that contains ship "3", which is the gene placed in locus "3" of parent "P1". Then, the cycle recombination operator checks locus "3" of parent "P2" and identifies ship "9". Ship "9" is appended to the cycle. Fourth, the cycle recombination operator determines the gene of parent "P1" that contains ship "9", which is the gene placed in locus "6" of parent "P1". Then, the cycle recombination operator checks locus "6" of parent "P2" and identifies ship "5". Ship "5" is appended to the cycle. Fifth, the cycle recombination operator determines the gene of parent "P1" that contains ship "5", which is the gene placed in locus "8" of parent "P1". Then, the cycle recombination operator checks locus "8" of parent "P2" and identifies ship "2". However, ship "2" has been already appended to the cycle, and, therefore, the cycle recombination operator terminates the procedure. The genes of parent "P1" belonging to the cycle are used to create offspring "O1". The genes with missing ship identifiers (i.e., ships "4", "1", "7", "6", and "8") are copied from parent "P2" to complete offspring "O1". Offspring "O2" is developed following a similar procedure.

Figure 5. Cycle recombination operation

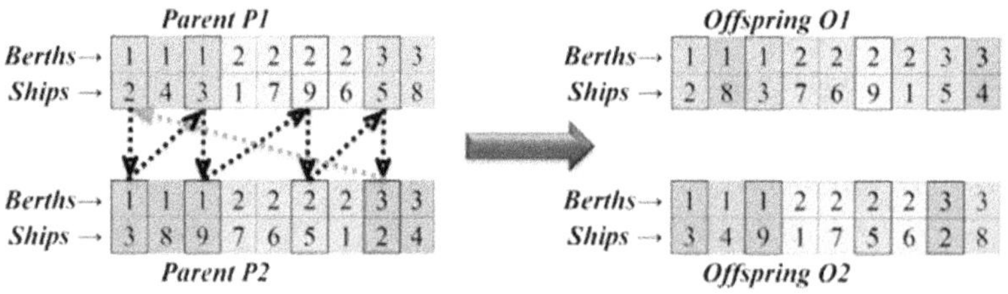

An example of an order recombination operation in showcased in **Figure 6**. First, the order recombination operator selects a group of genes from parent "P1" and copies the selected genes directly to offspring "O1". Based on the presented example, a group of genes with ships "1", "7", "9", "6", and "5" are copied from parent "P1" to offspring "O1". Note the number of genes to be copied from "P1" to offspring "O1" is determined on a random basis and can change from one recombination operation to another. Second, the genes with missing ship identifiers (i.e., ships "2", "4", "3", and "8") are copied from parent "P2" in the order they appear in parent "P2" to complete offspring "O1". Offspring "O2" is developed following a similar procedure. More specifically, a group of genes with ships "3", "5", and "1" are copied from parent "P2" to offspring "O2". Then, the genes with missing ship identifiers (i.e., ships "2", "4", "7", "9", "6", and "8") are copied from parent "P1" in the order they appear in parent "P1" to complete offspring "O2".

An example of a partially-mapped recombination operation in showcased in **Figure 7**. First, the partially-mapped recombination operator selects a group of genes from parent "P1" and copies the selected genes directly to offspring "O1". Based on the presented example, a group of genes with ships "1", "7", "9", "6", and "5" are copied from parent "P1" to offspring "O1". Note the number of genes to be copied from "P1" to offspring "O1" is determined on a random basis and can change from one recombination operation to another. Second, the partially-mapped recombination operator checks whether all the parent "P1" genes belonging to the selected group, which is located in loci "4" through "8", can be found in parent "P2". Based on the considered example, it can be observed that the gene with ship "3" is present in locus "4" of parent "P2" but cannot be found in loci "4" through "8" of parent "P1". Hence, the partial mapping operation should be performed for the gene with ship "3" of parent "P2" as follows. Since the gene with ship "3" occupies locus "4" of parent "P2", the partially-mapped recombination operator has to check locus "4" of parent "P1", which is occupied by ship "1". Ship "1" is placed in locus "7" of parent "P2". Then, the partially-mapped recombination operator has to check locus "7" of parent "P1", which is occupied by ship "6". Ship "6" is placed in locus "1" of parent "P2". Since locus "1" of offspring "O1" did not contain any genes prior to the partial mapping procedure, the gene with ship "3" of parent "P2" can be placed in locus "1" of offspring "O1", and the partial mapping procedure is terminated. The genes with missing ship identifiers (i.e., ships "2", "4", and "8") are copied from parent "P2" to complete offspring "O1". Offspring "O2" is developed following a similar procedure.

Figure 6. Order recombination operation

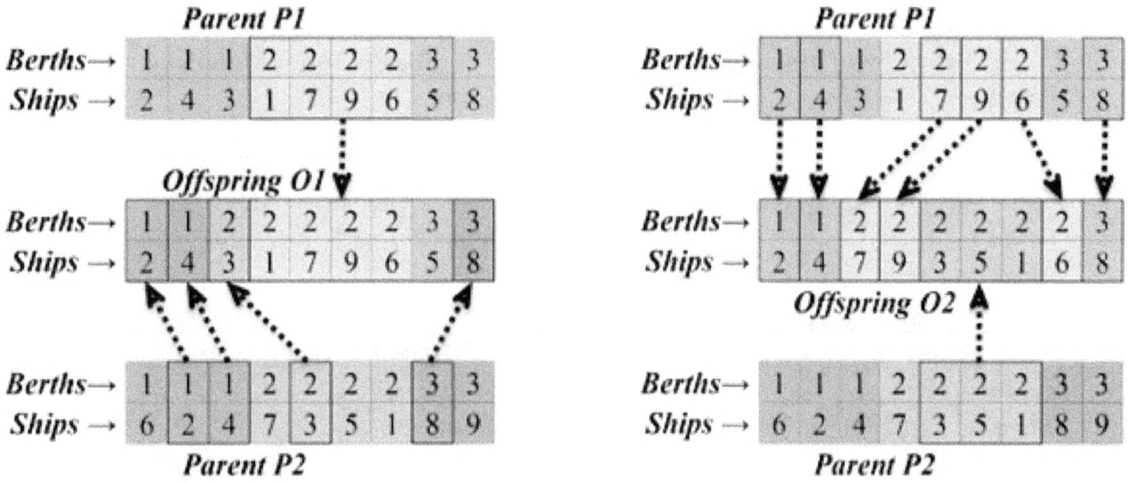

Figure 7. Partially-mapped recombination operation

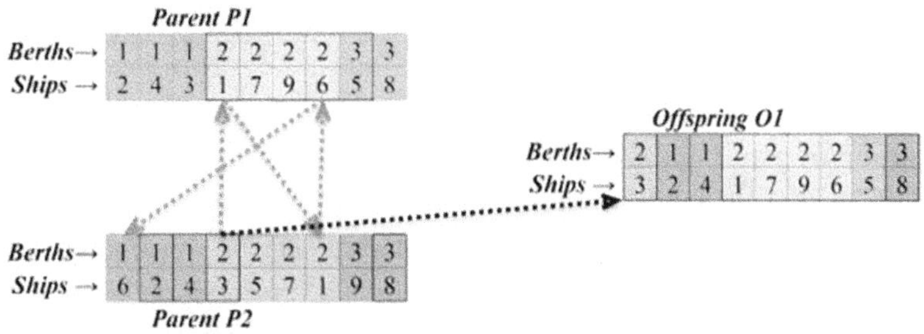

3.2.2. LLHs for Mutation

The proposed hyperheuristic framework relies on four types of mutation operators, including the swap mutation operator, insert mutation operator, invert mutation operator, and scramble mutation operator. An example of a swap mutation operation in showcased in **Figure 8**(a). As a result of the swap mutation operation, ship "4" originally scheduled for service after ship "2" at berth "1" is reassigned for service after ship "9" at berth "2". In the meantime, ship "6" originally scheduled for service after ship "9" at berth "2" is reassigned for service after ship "2" at berth "1". **Figure 8**(b) depicts an example of an insert mutation operation, where ship "8" originally scheduled for service after ship "5" at berth "3" is inserted in locus "7" right after ship "9". Therefore, after the insert mutation operation, ship "8" will be serviced after ship "9" at berth "2".

Figure 8. Candidate LLHs for mutation operations

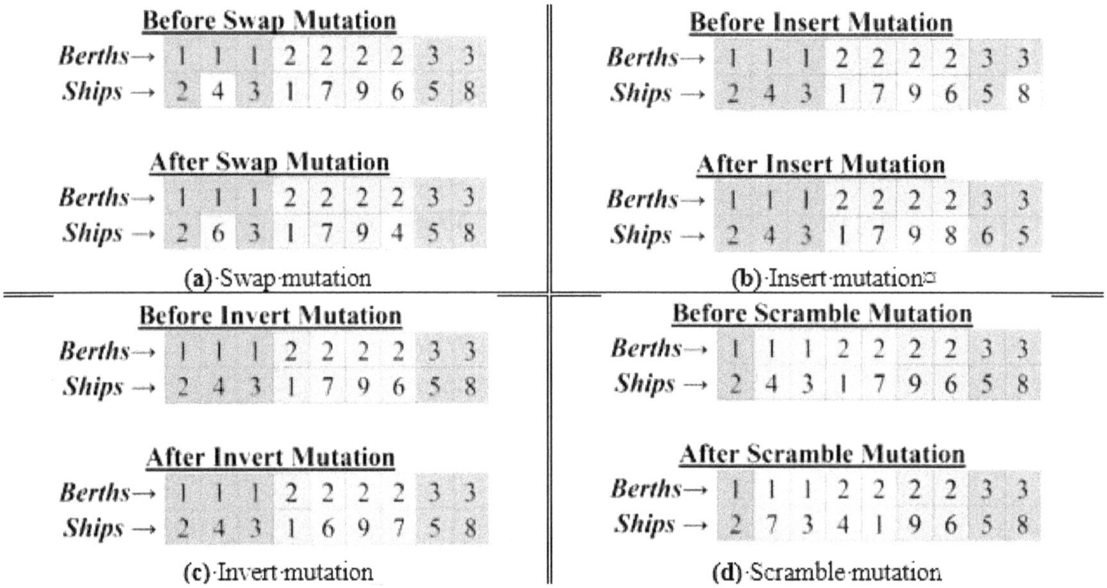

An example of an invert mutation operation in showcased in **Figure 8**(c). First, the invert mutation operator selects a group of genes and then inverts their loci. In the presented example, the genes with ships "7", "9", and "6" were selected for inversion. Before the inversion, ships were served in the order of "1" → "7" → 9" → "6" at berth "2", and the order of ship service was changed to "1" → "6" → 9" → "7" after the inversion. **Figure 8**(d) depicts an example of a scramble mutation operation. Unlike the aforementioned mutation operators, the scramble mutation operator alters the solutions on a random basis without following any specific patterns. In the presented example, a group of genes with ships "4", "3", "1", and "7" were selected for the scramble mutation operation. As a result of the conducted scramble mutation operation, ship "4" was shifted for service as the first ship at berth "2", whereas ship "7" was shifted for service as the second ship at berth "1".

3.3. Potential Alternatives for HLHs

As indicated earlier, HLHs are mainly responsible for the selection of appropriate operators and solution acceptance throughout the algorithmic evolution (Wang et al., 2020). The following types of HLHs can be adopted within the proposed hyperheuristic framework: (1) Boltzmann selection; (2) roulette wheel selection; and (3) binary tournament selection. The main advantage of the Boltzmann selection operator consists in the fact that it effectively controls the selection pressure during the algorithmic evolution (Lee, 2003; Chen et al., 2021; Pasha et al., 2022). In earlier generations, even lower-quality solutions can be accepted. However, only top-quality solutions can be accepted in later generations closer to convergence. The key steps of the Boltzmann selection procedure are outlined in **Algorithm 1**. The initialization of the data structure for storing the selected solutions is performed in step 1. The current temperature level is set based on the counter of generations in step 2. The counter of iterations is started in step 3. After that, the Boltzmann selection operator enters an iterative process (see steps 4-11). In step 5, the selection probability of a given solution is computed based on the current temperature level, solution fitness, and objective function normalizing coefficient. In step 6, a random number (*RandNum*), which can vary between 0.00 and 1.00, is generated by the Boltzmann selection operator. If the generated random number *RandNum* is less than the calculated acceptance probability, then the identified solution is added to the data structure for storing the selected solutions in steps 7-9. The counter of iterations is updated in step 10. Once the required number of solutions has been added to the data structure, the selection process is terminated by the Boltzmann selection operator.

Algorithm 1: Boltzmann Selection

$$\left[SelSol\right] \leftarrow \boldsymbol{Boltzmann\_Selection}\left(Pop, Fit, g, T^0, \Delta T, \Upsilon\right)$$

in: *Pop* - population of solutions generated in a given generation; *Fit* - fitness values of solutions generated in a given generation; g - counter of generations; T^0 – value of the initial temperature; ΔT - value of the temperature interval; Y - objective function normalizing coefficient
out: *SelSol* - set of selected solutions

1: $SelSol \leftarrow \varnothing$ ◁ Conduct the data structure initialization

2: $T \leftarrow T^0 - \Delta T \cdot g$ ◁ Alter the current temperature based on the counter of generations

3: $i \leftarrow 1$ ◁ Start the counter of iterations

4: **while** $\left|SelSol\right| \neq \left|Pop\right|$ **do**

5: $Prob_i \leftarrow \dfrac{exp\left(\left[-\dfrac{Fit_i}{\Upsilon}\right]/T\right)}{\sum_{j=1}^{|Pop|} exp\left(\left[-\dfrac{Fit_j}{\Upsilon}\right]/T\right)}$ ◁ Compute the solution selection probability

6: $RandNum \leftarrow \boldsymbol{rand}\left(0.00, 1.00\right)$ ◁ Generate a random number that can vary between 0.00 and 1.00

    if $Prob_i > RandNum$ **then**

        $SelSol \leftarrow SelSol \cup \{Pop_i\}$ ◅ Add the identified solution to the designated data structure

    end if

    $i \leftarrow i \cdot \left(\min[1, abs\{i - |Pop|\}]\right) + 1$ ◅ Update the counter of iterations

end while

return $SelSol$

The roulette wheel selection operator has been widely used in evolutionary computation (Pencheva et al., 2009; Ho-Huu et al., 2018; Qian et al., 2018). This type of selection operator assumes that even low-quality solutions can be selected in every generation. However, the selection probability of a given solution is directly associated with its fitness. The key steps of the roulette wheel selection procedure are outlined in **Algorithm 2**. The initialization of the data structure for storing the selected solutions is performed in step 1. The values of solution fitness are normalized in step 2, so that the summation of fitness values of all the solutions in the population is equal to 1.00. The counter of iterations is started in step 3. After that, the roulette wheel selection operator enters an iterative process (see steps 4-9). In step 5, a random number (*RandNum*), which can vary between 0.00 and 1.00, is generated by the roulette wheel selection operator. Then, the corresponding solution of the population is identified based on *RandNum* in step 6. The identified solution is further added to the data structure for storing the selected solutions in step 7. The counter of iterations is updated in step 8. Once the required number of solutions has been added to the data structure, the selection process is terminated by the roulette wheel selection operator.

Algorithm 2: Roulette Wheel Selection

$[SelSol] \leftarrow \textbf{\textit{Roulette\_Wheel}}(Pop, Fit)$

in: *Pop* - population of solutions generated in a given generation; *Fit* - fitness values of solutions generated in a given generation; *g* - counter of generations
out: *SelSol* - set of chromosomes selected for the next generation

1: $SelSol \leftarrow \oslash$ ◅ Conduct the data structure initialization

2: $Fit \leftarrow \textbf{\textit{Normalize}}(Fit)$ ◅ Normalize the values of solution fitness

3: $i \leftarrow 1$ ◅ Start the counter of iterations

4: **while** $i \leq |Pop|$ **do**

5:     $RandNum \leftarrow \textbf{\textit{rand}}(0.00, 1.00)$ ◅ Generate a random number that can vary between 0.00 and 1.00

6:     $j \leftarrow \textbf{\textit{find}}(Fit - RandNum > 0)$ ◅ Identify the solution considering $RandNum$

7:     $SelSol \leftarrow SelSol \cup \{Pop_j\}$ ◅ Add the identified solution to the designated data structure

8: $i \leftarrow i+1$ ◅ Update the counter of iterations

9: **end for**

10: **return** $SelSol$

Algorithm 3: Binary Tournament Selection

$[SelSol] \leftarrow \boldsymbol{Binary\_Tournament}(Pop, Fit)$

in: *Pop* - population of solutions generated in a given generation; *Fit* - fitness values of solutions generated in a given generation
out: *SelSol* - set of selected solutions

1: $SelSol \leftarrow \oslash$ ◅ Conduct the data structure initialization

2: $i \leftarrow 1$ ◅ Start the counter of iterations

3: **while** $i \leq |Pop|$ **do**

4: $Sol1 \leftarrow \boldsymbol{RandSel}(Pop)$ ◅ Select one solution from the population at random

5: $Sol2 \leftarrow \boldsymbol{RandSel}(Pop)$ ◅ Select another solution from the population at random

6: **if** $Fit_{Sol1} > Fit_{Sol2}$ **then**

7: $SelSol \leftarrow SelSol \cup \{Sol1\}$ ◅ Add $Sol1$ to the designated data structure

8: **else if**

9: $SelSol \leftarrow SelSol \cup \{Sol2\}$ ◅ Add $Sol2$ to the designated data structure

10: **end if**

11: $i \leftarrow i+1$ ◅ Update the counter of iterations

12: **end while**

13: **return** $SelSol$

The binary tournament selection operator is considered as a quite common selection operator as well (Yao et al., 2021; Soong et al., 2022). This selection operator is less biased in terms of solution fitness. More specifically, in the initial stage of the selection procedure, two solutions are chosen from the population at random without considering their fitness. Only in the second stage, the solution fitness is considered, and the fittest solution (out of the two selected solutions) is selected for the next generation. The key steps of the binary tournament selection procedure are outlined in **Algorithm 3**. The initialization of the data structure for storing the selected solutions is performed in step 1. The counter of iterations is started in step 2. After that, the binary tournament selection operator enters an iterative process (see steps 3-12). In steps 4 and 5, two solutions are selected from the population at random. Then, if the fitness of the first solution is greater than that of the second solution, the first solution is added to the data structure for storing the selected solutions (step 7). Otherwise, the second solution is added to the data structure for storing the selected solutions (step 9). The counter of iterations is updated in step 11. Once the required number of solutions has been added to the data structure, the selection process is terminated by the binary tournament selection operator.

Note that the procedures, which are outlined in **Algorithm 1**, **Algorithm 2**, and **Algorithm 3**, primarily focus on the selection of solutions from one generation to another. However, these algorithms can be customized for the selection of recombination and mutation operators as well. The quality of solutions generated by a given recombination operator and a given mutation operator can serve as the main performance metric in the selection process. Unlike the solution selection process, the selection of algorithmic operators can be conducted periodically (i.e., after a specific number of generations, not in every generation), and the changes in quality of obtained solutions can be monitored accordingly. The diversity of solutions within the population may be an important performance metric as well, which can assist with avoiding convergence at local optima, especially in early generations. Computational time can be considered as another metric for the selection of operators. Recombination and mutation operators that require more computational time many not be favorable, as they increase the computational complexity of the entire hyperheuristic algorithm.

4. ADAPTIVE AND HYBRIDIZED EXTENSIONS

Hyperheuristics are adaptive algorithms in nature, as they adjust LLHs throughout the search process. However, additional adaptive mechanisms can be adopted within the proposed hyperheuristic framework for the BASP. The considered recombination and mutation operators (i.e., cycle recombination operator, order recombination operator, and partially-mapped recombination operator; swap mutation operator, insert mutation operator, invert mutation operator, and scramble mutation operator) are associated with certain parameters (e.g., recombination or crossover probability, mutation probability). The parameters of recombination and mutation operators can be adjusted during the search process in order to facilitate the discovery of high-quality solutions (Eiben and Smith, 2015; Kavoosi et al., 2019). As an example, high recombination and mutation probabilities may be favorable at the beginning of the search process to better explore the available domains of the search space. However, in later generations, lower recombination and mutation probabilities can assist with more effective exploitation of the identified promising search space domains.

Different steps performed within the developed hyperheuristic framework are associated with stochastic operations. More specifically, the initialization of solutions in the population is commonly performed on a random basis. The main search operators (i.e., recombination and mutation operators) are stochastic in nature and make alterations in the population solutions in a random manner. Although stochasticity is favorable for the search diversification, it may not be always favorable for the search intensification. Therefore, different types of hybrid mechanisms can be deployed within the developed hyperheuristic framework to enhance the search intensification. Hybrid methods can be deployed in the form of local search heuristics. As an example, the first come first served (FCFS) policy has been widely used in the BASP literature to initialize solutions (Kavoosi et al., 2019; Dulebenets, 2020; Kavoosi et al., 2020). Based on the FCFS policy, ships can be assigned for service to the available berthing positions based on the time of their arrival. Moreover, hybrid methods can be deployed in the form of exact optimization procedures. After performing recombination and mutation operations, all the mutated solutions (or at least a portion of them) can undergo an exact optimization process based on problem-specific characteristics to improve their fitness (Dulebenets, 2023). Although hybridization via exact optimization guarantees optimality, hybridization via local search heuristics can be favorable in terms of computational time.

5. CONCLUSION

Maritime transportation has been serving as the main transportation mode for the delivery of cargoes between different continents across the world for many years. Container ships carrying valuable goods are generally handled at marine container terminals (MCTs). Berth allocation and scheduling is recognized as one of the primary decision problems that have to be addressed by MCT operators when planning seaside operations. The berth allocation and scheduling problem (BASP) has high computational complexity and cannot be solved using exact optimization algorithms in acceptable computational time for large-scale problem instances. Therefore, many types of heuristic and metaheuristics have been proposed in the BASP literature. However, hyperheuristics still have not been explored for the BASP decision problem, despite their promising performance in other settings. Hence, this study proposes a comprehensive framework for hyperheuristic algorithms for berth allocation and scheduling at MCTs that could be further used to guide the future research in this area.

A general description of the framework for the deployment of hyperheuristics was presented for the BASP problem. Furthermore, constructive recommendations were provided with respect to solution encoding schemes that would be appropriate for the common BASP variants, candidate heuristics for the pool of low-level heuristics along with illustrative examples of their application, and potential alternatives for high-level heuristics that can be embedded within the proposed hyperheuristic framework. The proposed candidate alternatives for low-level heuristics included different recombination and mutation operators, such as the cycle recombination operator, order recombination operator, partially-mapped recombination operator, swap mutation operator, insert mutation operator, invert mutation operator, and scramble mutation operator. The proposed candidate alternatives for high-level heuristics included Boltzmann selection, roulette wheel selection, and binary tournament selection mechanisms. Last but not least, various forms of adaptive mechanisms and hybridization via exact optimization and local search within the proposed hyperheuristic framework were discussed as well.

The developed hyperheuristic framework can serve as a point of reference for the future BASP research efforts. There are several future research directions that can be further explored in the following years. First, the proposed hyperheuristic can be programmed and implemented for realistic BASP data, so that its computational performance can be better assessed. Second, as indicated earlier, hybridization via exact optimization can substantially increase the computational complexity of the presented hyperheuristic. Therefore, compact model formulations should be further investigated by the future BASP studies to ensure that exact optimization can be performed in a timely manner. Third, the present study mainly focused on heuristic selection within the proposed hyperheuristic framework. The future research can also explore heuristic generation. Many metaheuristic algorithms have been developed over the past years, including the red deer algorithm, lion optimization algorithm, ant colony optimization, grasshopper optimization algorithm, whale optimization algorithm, grey wolf optimizer, and many others (Bianchi et al., 2009; Boussaïd et al., 2013; Wari et al., 2016; Dokeroglu et al., 2022). The features and operators of these metaheuristic algorithms can be further used for heuristic generation within the hyperheuristic framework.

REFERENCES

Ankita, P. U., & Mathirajan, M. (2021). An efficient heuristic method for dynamic berth allocation problem. In *Proceedings of the International Conference on Industrial Engineering and Operations Management* (pp. 393-400). IEOM Society. 10.46254/AN11.20210077

Bacalhau, E. T., Casacio, L., & de Azevedo, A. T. (2021). New hybrid genetic algorithms to solve dynamic berth allocation problem. *Expert Systems with Applications*, *167*, 114198. doi:10.1016/j.eswa.2020.114198

Barbosa, F., Rampazzo, P. C. B., de Azevedo, A. T., & Yamakami, A. (2022). The impact of time windows constraints on metaheuristics implementation: A study for the Discrete and Dynamic Berth Allocation Problem. *Applied Intelligence*, *52*(2), 1406–1434. doi:10.1007/s10489-021-02420-4

Barbosa, F., Rampazzo, P. C. B., Yamakami, A., & Camanho, A. S. (2019). The use of frontier techniques to identify efficient solutions for the Berth Allocation Problem solved with a hybrid evolutionary algorithm. *Computers & Operations Research*, *107*, 43–60. doi:10.1016/j.cor.2019.01.017

Bianchi, L., Dorigo, M., Gambardella, L. M., & Gutjahr, W. J. (2009). A survey on metaheuristics for stochastic combinatorial optimization. *Natural Computing*, *8*(2), 239–287. doi:10.1007/s11047-008-9098-4

Bierwirth, C., & Meisel, F. (2010). A survey of berth allocation and quay crane scheduling problems in container terminals. *European Journal of Operational Research*, *202*(3), 615–627. doi:10.1016/j.ejor.2009.05.031

Bierwirth, C., & Meisel, F. (2015). A follow-up survey of berth allocation and quay crane scheduling problems in container terminals. *European Journal of Operational Research*, *244*(3), 675–689. doi:10.1016/j.ejor.2014.12.030

Boussaïd, I., Lepagnot, J., & Siarry, P. (2013). A survey on optimization metaheuristics. *Information Sciences*, *237*, 82–117. doi:10.1016/j.ins.2013.02.041

Carlo, H. J., Vis, I. F., & Roodbergen, K. J. (2015). Seaside operations in container terminals: Literature overview, trends, and research directions. *Flexible Services and Manufacturing Journal*, *27*(2-3), 224–262. doi:10.1007/s10696-013-9178-3

Chen, M. R., Huang, Y. Y., Zeng, G. Q., Lu, K. D., & Yang, L. Q. (2021). An improved bat algorithm hybridized with extremal optimization and Boltzmann selection. *Expert Systems with Applications*, *175*, 114812. doi:10.1016/j.eswa.2021.114812

Cowling, P., Kendall, G., & Soubeiga, E. (2001). A hyperheuristic approach to scheduling a sales summit. In *Practice and Theory of Automated Timetabling III: Third International Conference, PATAT 2000 Konstanz,* (pp. 176-190). Springer Berlin Heidelberg. 10.1007/3-540-44629-X_11

Cruz-Duarte, J. M., Amaya, I., Ortiz-Bayliss, J. C., Conant-Pablos, S. E., Terashima-Marín, H., & Shi, Y. (2021). Hyper-heuristics to customise metaheuristics for continuous optimisation. *Swarm and Evolutionary Computation*, *66*, 100935. doi:10.1016/j.swevo.2021.100935

Dai, Y., Li, Z., & Wang, B. (2023). Optimizing Berth Allocation in Maritime Transportation with Quay Crane Setup Times Using Reinforcement Learning. *Journal of Marine Science and Engineering*, *11*(5), 1025. doi:10.3390/jmse11051025

Dkhil, H., Diarrassouba, I., Benmansour, S., & Yassine, A. (2021). Modelling and solving a berth allocation problem in an automotive transshipment terminal. *The Journal of the Operational Research Society*, *72*(3), 580–593. doi:10.1080/01605682.2019.1685361

Dokeroglu, T., Deniz, A., & Kiziloz, H. E. (2022). A comprehensive survey on recent metaheuristics for feature selection. *Neurocomputing*, *494*, 269–296. doi:10.1016/j.neucom.2022.04.083

Dulebenets, M. A. (2020). An Adaptive Island Evolutionary Algorithm for the berth scheduling problem. *Memetic Computing*, *12*(1), 51–72. doi:10.1007/s12293-019-00292-3

Dulebenets, M. A. (2023). A Diffused Memetic Optimizer for reactive berth allocation and scheduling at marine container terminals in response to disruptions. *Swarm and Evolutionary Computation*, *80*, 101334. doi:10.1016/j.swevo.2023.101334

Dulebenets, M. A., Golias, M. M., & Mishra, S. (2018). A collaborative agreement for berth allocation under excessive demand. *Engineering Applications of Artificial Intelligence*, *69*, 76–92. doi:10.1016/j.engappai.2017.11.009

Eiben, A. E., & Smith, J. E. (2015). *Introduction to Evolutionary Computing*. Springer-Verlag Berlin Heidelberg. doi:10.1007/978-3-662-44874-8

Elmi, Z., Singh, P., Meriga, V. K., Goniewicz, K., Borowska-Stefańska, M., Wiśniewski, S., & Dulebenets, M. A. (2022). Uncertainties in liner shipping and ship schedule recovery: A state-of-the-art review. *Journal of Marine Science and Engineering*, *10*(5), 563. doi:10.3390/jmse10050563

Fernández, E., & Munoz-Marquez, M. (2022). New formulations and solutions for the strategic berth template problem. *European Journal of Operational Research*, *298*(1), 99–117. doi:10.1016/j.ejor.2021.06.062 PMID:35039709

Ho-Huu, V., Nguyen-Thoi, T., Truong-Khac, T., Le-Anh, L., & Vo-Duy, T. (2018). An improved differential evolution based on roulette wheel selection for shape and size optimization of truss structures with frequency constraints. *Neural Computing & Applications*, *29*(1), 167–185. doi:10.1007/s00521-016-2426-1

Issam, E. H., Azza, L., & Mohamed, E. M., kaoutar, A., & Yassine, T. (2017, March). A multi-objective model for discrete and dynamic berth allocation problem. In *Proceedings of the 2nd international Conference on Big Data, Cloud and Applications* (pp. 1-5). ACM. 10.1145/3090354.3090464

Jos, B. C., Harimanikandan, M., Rajendran, C., & Ziegler, H. (2019). Minimum cost berth allocation problem in maritime logistics: New mixed integer programming models. *Sadhana*, *44*(6), 1–12. doi:10.1007/s12046-019-1128-7

Kallel, L., Benaissa, E., Kamoun, H., & Benaissa, M. (2019). Berth allocation problem: Formulation and a Tunisian case study. *Archives of Transport*, *51*(3), 85–100. doi:10.5604/01.3001.0013.6165

Kavoosi, M., Dulebenets, M. A., Abioye, O., Pasha, J., Theophilus, O., Wang, H., Kampmann, R., & Mikijeljević, M. (2020). Berth scheduling at marine container terminals: A universal island-based metaheuristic approach. *Maritime Business Review*, *5*(1), 30–66. doi:10.1108/MABR-08-2019-0032

Kavoosi, M., Dulebenets, M. A., Abioye, O. F., Pasha, J., Wang, H., & Chi, H. (2019). An augmented self-adaptive parameter control in evolutionary computation: A case study for the berth scheduling problem. *Advanced Engineering Informatics*, *42*, 100972. doi:10.1016/j.aei.2019.100972

Lee, C. Y. (2003). Entropy-Boltzmann selection in the genetic algorithms. *IEEE Transactions on Systems, Man, and Cybernetics. Part B, Cybernetics*, *33*(1), 138–149. doi:10.1109/TSMCB.2003.808184 PMID:18238164

Leng, L., Zhang, J., Zhang, C., Zhao, Y., Wang, W., & Li, G. (2020). Decomposition-based hyperheuristic approaches for the bi-objective cold chain considering environmental effects. *Computers & Operations Research*, *123*, 105043. doi:10.1016/j.cor.2020.105043

Leng, L., Zhao, Y., Wang, Z., Wang, H., & Zhang, J. (2018). Shared mechanism-based self-adaptive hyperheuristic for regional low-carbon location-routing problem with time windows. *Mathematical Problems in Engineering*, *2018*, 1–21. doi:10.1155/2018/8987402

Mnasri, S., & Alrashidi, M. (2021). A comprehensive modeling of the discrete and dynamic problem of berth allocation in maritime terminals. *Electronics (Basel)*, *10*(21), 2684. doi:10.3390/electronics10212684

Mosadegh, H., Ghomi, S. F., & Süer, G. A. (2020). Stochastic mixed-model assembly line sequencing problem: Mathematical modeling and Q-learning based simulated annealing hyper-heuristics. *European Journal of Operational Research*, *282*(2), 530–544. doi:10.1016/j.ejor.2019.09.021

Nishi, T., Okura, T., Lalla-Ruiz, E., & Voß, S. (2020). A dynamic programming-based matheuristic for the dynamic berth allocation problem. *Annals of Operations Research*, *286*(1-2), 391–410. doi:10.1007/s10479-017-2715-9

Pasha, J., Nwodu, A. L., Fathollahi-Fard, A. M., Tian, G., Li, Z., Wang, H., & Dulebenets, M. A. (2022). Exact and metaheuristic algorithms for the vehicle routing problem with a factory-in-a-box in multi-objective settings. *Advanced Engineering Informatics*, *52*, 101623. doi:10.1016/j.aei.2022.101623

Pencheva, T., Atanassov, K., & Shannon, A. (2009). Modelling of a roulette wheel selection operator in genetic algorithms using generalized nets. *International Journal Bioautomation*, *13*(4), 257.

Peng, Y., Dong, M., Li, X., Liu, H., & Wang, W. (2021). Cooperative optimization of shore power allocation and berth allocation: A balance between cost and environmental benefit. *Journal of Cleaner Production*, *279*, 123816. doi:10.1016/j.jclepro.2020.123816

Pereira, E. D., Coelho, A. S., Longaray, A. A., Machado, C. M. D. S., & Munhoz, P. R. (2018). Metaheuristic analysis applied to the berth allocation problem: Case study in a port container terminal. *Pesquisa Operacional*, *38*(2), 247–272. doi:10.1590/0101-7438.2018.038.02.0247

Prencipe, L. P., & Marinelli, M. (2021). A novel mathematical formulation for solving the dynamic and discrete berth allocation problem by using the Bee Colony Optimisation algorithm. *Applied Intelligence*, *51*(7), 4127–4142. doi:10.1007/s10489-020-02062-y

Qian, W., Chai, J., Xu, Z., & Zhang, Z. (2018). Differential evolution algorithm with multiple mutation strategies based on roulette wheel selection. *Applied Intelligence*, *48*(10), 3612–3629. doi:10.1007/s10489-018-1153-y

Rodrigues, F., & Agra, A. (2022). Berth allocation and quay crane assignment/scheduling problem under uncertainty: A survey. *European Journal of Operational Research*, *303*(2), 501–524. doi:10.1016/j.ejor.2021.12.040

Schepler, X., Absi, N., Feillet, D., & Sanlaville, E. (2019). The stochastic discrete berth allocation problem. *EURO Journal on Transportation and Logistics*, *8*(4), 363–396. doi:10.1007/s13676-018-0128-9

Soong, C. J., Rahman, R. A., Ramli, R., Manaf, M. S. A., & Ting, C. C. (2022). An Evolutionary Algorithm: An Enhancement of Binary Tournament Selection for Fish Feed Formulation. *Complexity*, *2022*, 2022. doi:10.1155/2022/7796633

Wang, R., Ji, F., Jiang, Y., Wu, S. H., Kwong, S., Zhang, J., & Zhan, Z. H. (2022). An adaptive ant colony system based on variable range receding horizon control for berth allocation problem. *IEEE Transactions on Intelligent Transportation Systems*, *23*(11), 21675–21686. doi:10.1109/TITS.2022.3172719

Wang, R., Nguyen, T. T., Li, C., Jenkinson, I., Yang, Z., & Kavakeb, S. (2019). Optimising discrete dynamic berth allocations in seaports using a Levy Flight based meta-heuristic. *Swarm and Evolutionary Computation*, *44*, 1003–1017. doi:10.1016/j.swevo.2018.10.011

Wang, Z., Leng, L., Wang, S., Li, G., & Zhao, Y. (2020). A hyperheuristic approach for location-routing problem of cold chain logistics considering fuel consumption. *Computational Intelligence and Neuroscience*, *2020*, 2020. doi:10.1155/2020/8395754 PMID:32405298

Wari, E., & Zhu, W. (2016). A survey on metaheuristics for optimization in food manufacturing industry. *Applied Soft Computing*, *46*, 328–343. doi:10.1016/j.asoc.2016.04.034

Yao, L., Long, W., Yi, J., Li, T., Tang, D., & Xu, Q. (2021). A novel tournament selection based on multilayer cultural characteristics in gene-culture coevolutionary multitasking. *Soft Computing*, *25*(14), 9529–9543. doi:10.1007/s00500-021-05876-1

Chapter 2
Adapting Teaching and Learning in Higher Education Using Explainable Student Agency Analytics

Ville Heilala
https://orcid.org/0000-0003-2068-2777
University of Jyväskylä, Finland

Päivikki Jääskelä
University of Jyväskylä, Finland

Mirka Saarela
https://orcid.org/0000-0002-1559-154X
University of Jyväskylä, Finland

Tommi Kärkkäinen
University of Jyväskylä, Finland

ABSTRACT

This chapter deals with the learning analytics technique called student agency analytics and explores its foundational technologies and their potential implications for adaptive teaching and learning. Student agency is vital to consider as it can empower students to take control of their learning, fostering autonomy, meaningful experiences, and improved educational outcomes. Beginning with an overview of the technique, its underlying educational foundations, and analytical approaches, the chapter demonstrates the synergy between computational psychometrics, learning analytics, and educational sciences. Considering adaptive artificial intelligence in the context of adaptive learning and teaching, the chapter underscores the potential of these approaches in education. The chapter serves as a brief guide for educators, researchers, and stakeholders interested in the convergence of AI and education.

DOI: 10.4018/979-8-3693-0230-9.ch002

1. INTRODUCTION

In the rapidly evolving landscape of higher education, the role of student agency has emerged as a key element in shaping meaningful and intentional learning experiences (e.g., OECD, 2019; Stenalt & Lassesen, 2021; Vaughn, 2020). In light of the global digital transformation phenomenon (Mukul & Buÿüközkan, 2023), educational institutions increasingly acknowledge the need to leverage data to enhance educational processes and outcomes (e.g., Banihashem et al., 2022). Recent research, including studies on the role of student agency in pedagogical decision-making (Heilala et al., 2022), course satisfaction in engineering education (Heilala, Saarela, et al., 2020), and the experiences of students with limited agency resources (Heilala, Jääskelä, et al., 2020), underscores the importance of this approach. The findings from these studies suggest associations between student agency and various educational outcomes. This chapter aims to shed light on the transformational potential of adaptive artificial intelligence (AI) in the context of higher education, drawing on recent research that explores student agency and its influence on instructional practices.

Student agency analytics (Jääskelä et al., 2021) represents a novel approach in higher education research, which focuses on making explicit students' capacities for intentional and meaningful learning under the power and participatory structures in the learning context. This method integrates the principles of learning analytics, which involves collecting, analyzing, and reporting educational data to improve learning design (Conole, 2011), with the study of student agency. In this context, agency refers to students' capacity to take control of their learning and utilize personal, relational, and participatory resources that allow a student to engage in purposeful, intentional, and meaningful action and learning (Jääskelä et al., 2017; Jääskelä et al., 2023). The application of student agency analytics offers a data-driven lens to understand and support students' learning experiences. By leveraging machine learning and psychometrics techniques, this approach provides educators with actionable insights into students' agency resources. These insights can adapt teachers' pedagogical decisions, learning environments, and educational interventions (e.g., Heilala et al., 2022). Recent research has also explored students' experiences with varying levels of agency resources using explainable methods, revealing factors such as competence beliefs, self-efficacy, and student-teacher relationships as influential determinants (Saarela et al., 2021).

This chapter provides an interdisciplinary overview of student agency analytics, its foundational principles, and the implications of integrating artificial intelligence in education (AIED). Reviewing current research and empirical findings, the chapter will clarify the potential of adaptive AI in enhancing student agency in higher education. As higher education institutions continue to embrace digital transformation, student agency analytics can emerge as a valuable tool for fostering student-centered learning environments. By understanding and addressing the unique needs of students, this synergy could pave the way for more personalized and effective educational experiences.

2. BACKGROUND

This section outlines the concept of agency, briefly exploring its philosophical origins and evolution in contemporary thought. A particular emphasis is placed on student agency, a specialized facet of the broader agency construct, highlighting its significance in shaping students' learning experiences. The section further introduces the novel technique of student agency analytics, a learning analytics approach that seeks to quantify and analyze students' agency within educational environments. By integrating computational methods and ethical considerations, this section offers an overview of how student agency analytics can provide valuable insights for educators and learners, fostering a more intentional and meaningful learning experience.

2.1 Starting With the Construct: On Agency

In its broadest sense, agency encompasses the capacity for intentional action and change. Historically, the concept of agency has deep philosophical roots, tracing back to thinkers like Hume and Aristotle (Schlosser, 2015). In contemporary analytic philosophy, the works of Anscombe (1957) and Davidson (1963) have been particularly influential, focusing on the intentionality of actions. According to the standard conception, a being possesses agency if it can act intentionally (Schlosser, 2015). This intentional action is often tied to instantiating certain mental states and events, such as desires, beliefs, and intentions, leading to specific outcomes or behaviors. Schlosser (2015) further elaborates on this by suggesting that a being's capacity to act intentionally is contingent upon its functional organization, where specific mental states cause particular events in a defined manner.

The concept of agency extends beyond individual intentionality and is deeply intertwined with social and relational contexts. Emirbayer and Mische (1998) emphasized the temporal and relational aspects of human agency, suggesting that it involves a dynamic interplay between habit, imagination, and judgment, all set against changing historical situations. This perspective underscores the importance of understanding agency as a product of individual intentions and broader structural environments. Furthermore, the post-humanist viewpoint expands the boundaries of agency beyond humans, suggesting that non-human entities, such as animals, algorithms, and pedagogical agents (Baylor, 1999; Jamieson, 2018; Peeters, 2020; Sikström et al., 2022), can also possess varying degrees of agency. This broader view challenges traditional notions and invites a more inclusive understanding of agency, encompassing human and non-human actors in diverse contexts. Bryant (2021) suggested the concept of augmented agency, which refers to the synergistic collaboration between human and artificial agents, blending humanized and digitalized processes to achieve emergent outcomes. Reaching beyond mere understanding of data and data literacy, Tedre and Vartiainen (2023, p. 1) pointed out the importance of data agency that refers to "people's volition and capacity for informed actions that make a difference in their digital world" and emphasizes managing and using data responsibly and ethically (Vartiainen et al., 2022).

Matthews (2019) highlighted the postdigital perspective as a lens to understand the intertwined nature of digital and non-digital technologies in society and culture. In higher education, this lens offers a critical approach to the use of digital technology, emphasizing the agency of all actors involved in learning and teaching activities. As Fawns (2019, p.132) pointed out, while "concepts like 'digital education' can be useful insofar as they encourage people to look closer at the design and practice of teaching and learning, they become problematic when used to close down ideas or attribute essential properties to technology." The actor-network theory (ANT) (e.g., Akrich, 2023; Silvast & Virtanen, 2023) within this perspective underscores the interconnectedness of human and non-human actors, advocating for inclusive design in learning environments. For example, Martin et al. (2020) examined intricate networks formed between learning analytics platforms (LAPs) and educational actors, emphasizing LAPs' performative roles and their influence on shaping educational futures and practices.

Student agency, a specialized subset of the broader concept of agency, pertains specifically to individual, institutional, and societal antecedents and outcomes of agency within educational settings (Stenalt

& Lassesen, 2021). Rooted in the foundational principles of agency, which emphasize intentionality and action, student agency encapsulates the ability of students to take control of their learning, make informed decisions, and act upon them (e.g., Lim & Nguyen, 2023). This means that students, equipped with agency, not only act with intention but also navigate, influence, and shape their learning trajectories based on their desires, beliefs, skills, and intentions (Klemenčič, 2017; Mameli et al., 2021; Membrive et al., 2022; OECD, 2019). However, student agency is not just about individual intentions but also about how students interact with the curriculum, pedagogical approaches, and the broader educational environment and are empowered to act through this interaction; thus, subjective experiences play a key role in defining the state of one's agency (e.g., Jääskelä et al., 2020; Jääskelä et al., 2023).

The concept of student agency is multifaceted, influenced by both individual characteristics and broader educational structures. Drawing parallels with the broader concept of agency, which is deeply embedded in social and relational contexts (Bandura, 2001), student agency is also shaped by the interplay between individual students and the educational systems they inhabit (e.g., Klemenčič, 2015). For instance, while students might possess the intrinsic motivation to learn (akin to individual intentionality in general agency), the educational environment, pedagogical approaches, and curriculum can either foster or hinder the expression of this agency (e.g., Gale et al., 2022; Groenewald & le Roux, 2023; Jääskelä et al., 2020). Also, students within the same course have highly varying experiences of their opportunities to practice agency in the course; for example, someone may feel that there are plenty of opportunities to influence the course progress, but instead, another student perceives the same situation in the opposite way (Jääskelä et al., 2022; Jääskelä et al., 2018) Furthermore, as with the post-humanist perspective on agency, student agency also extends beyond individual actions, e.g., as sociomaterial agency (Nieminen et al., 2022). It encompasses collaborative endeavors, where students work interactively, influencing and being influenced by peers, educators, technology, and the broader educational ecosystem (e.g., Charteris & Smardon, 2018; Gale et al., 2022; Stenalt, 2021). This dynamic nature of student agency underscores its complexity, making it a pivotal area of exploration in modern educational research utilizing recent technological advances.

Based on their multidimensional construct analysis, Jääskelä et al. (2020), Jääskelä et al. (2017), Jääskelä et al. (2023) developed a measurement, Agency of University Students (AUS) scale, which captures students' perceptions of their agency in three resource domains in the course context: personal, relational and participatory domains. Personal domain centers on students' self-efficacy (overall confidence as learners) and competence beliefs (e.g., concerning understanding the course contents) emphasized in the literature of the social–cognitive sciences (e.g., Bandura, 2001; Bandura, 2006; Schunk & Zimmerman, 2012). The relational domain focuses on students' experiences of safe and fair student-teacher relationships, for example, the extent to which a student can trust teachers, have support from them, and experience that one is being treated equally in relation to other students in the course; the aspects highlighted especially in the educational literature (e.g., Eteläpelto & Lahti, 2008). The participatory resource domain considers actualizing agency as multilevel interactions between the individual and the environment. In this interaction, individuals shuttle between their own desires, intentions and personal learning needs, and institutionalized structures, norms and practices (Berger & Luckmann, 1966), for example, objectives of the curriculum, the established course practices, traditions to teach and learn, and expectations of student role. Agency is optimally realized as a student's interest and enthusiasm for learning when teaching, materials, or methods resonate with one's learning goals, and a student can perceive the utility value in gaining goals (e.g., Wigfield et al., 2019). It is also realized as students' active participation in common tasks and knowledge construction when learning situations include space for dialogue with others (e.g., Lipponen & Kumpulainen, 2011). Furthermore, participatory agency is about having opportunities to be involved in the decision-making concerning the progress of the course. The AUS Scale utilized in the student agency analytics was previously validated as an 11-factor model with the data collected from university students at a Finnish University (Jääskelä et al., 2020). The dimensions (factors) are Self-efficacy and Competence beliefs (representing the personal domain), Trust for the teacher, Teacher support and Equal treatment (relational domain), Participation activity, Ease of participation, Interest and utility value, Opportunities to influence, Opportunities to make choices, and Peer Support (participatory domain) (see, Jääskelä et al. (2023)).

In summary, the concept of agency, rooted in philosophical and sociological thought, encompasses individual intentionality and the capacity to act within broader social contexts. Student agency emerges as a specialized mindset when specified in the educational sphere, emphasizing students' capacity to navigate and influence their learning experiences by utilizing different agentic resources. Empirical knowledge of student agency is needed to increase understanding of student agency as a multidimensional construct. The technique referred to as student agency analytics utilizes learning analytics procedures to gain a more comprehensive understanding of how students exercise their agency within educational environments. In the following section, a review will be given of the details of student agency analytics, its basic principles, and its ability to bring about beneficial changes in ways of teaching and learning.

2.2 From Construct to Application: On Student Agency Analytics

Student agency analytics is a novel technique in learning analytics—at the intersection of educational research and data science—focusing on understanding and enhancing students' intentional and meaningful learning resources (Jääskelä et al., 2021). At its core, this approach seeks to quantify and analyze the ways in which students exercise their agency within educational settings. This data-driven perspective offers insights into individual students' learning experiences and also sheds light on broader patterns at the group level, in addition to suggesting potential areas of pedagogical intervention (Heilala et al., 2022). From the learner's point of view, obtaining prompts for self-assessment is an expected feature of learning analytics (Schumacher & Ifenthaler, 2018). Thus, student agency analytics also aims to provide students with a means for self-reflection.

The process can be visualized as a cyclical flow (Figure 2). It begins with the teacher's initial instructional planning. As the teaching progresses, students fill out the AUS survey, triggering the automatic execution of agency analytics. Once the results are available, teachers can refine their instructional strategies based on the students' reported agency resources. The main advantages of student agency analytics include 1) its foundation in theory related to student-focused learning, 2) its capability for automated analysis suitable for moderate group sizes, 3) its use of an innovative visualization to present results to educators, 4) its commitment to protecting student privacy, 5) its demonstrated associations with positive emotions (such as course satisfaction) and learning outcomes, and 6) its utility for educators in reflecting on and making pedagogical decisions (Heilala, 2022).

The data collection in student agency analytics involved using the AUS scale (Jääskelä et al., 2017; Jääskelä et al., 2023), a questionnaire described in the previous section that is designed to measure students' agentic resources in different educational contexts in higher education. The scale was provisioned as an online questionnaire that can be used in various settings, from online environments to in-person situations. In the case of student agency analytics and discrete Likert type of data, preprocessing was a straightforward operation involving data pseudonymization for increased privacy and security and data imputation in case of missing values. After the data are in a form suitable for analysis, relevant features are identified and extracted from the preprocessed data. These features are the basic indicators of student agency and are constructed using the psychometric model underlying the AUS scale. A technique from unsupervised machine learning, namely robust clustering, was used to create a representation of different experiences of agency. The results indicated that four profiles would provide a rich representation of the individual student agency experiences without being too general or too detailed (Jääskelä et al., 2021).

Figure 1. Visualization for the teacher showing the general average agency and four distinct profiles (Heilala, 2022)

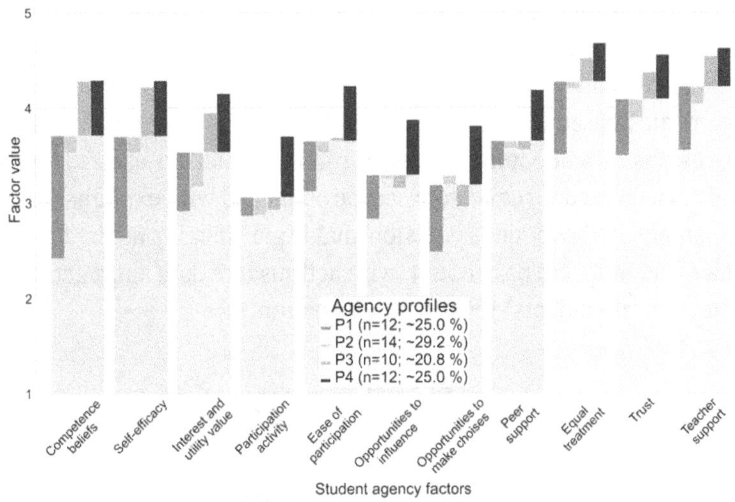

The main outcome of the analysis is the visualization representing the general average student agency and the deviations of each of the four distinct profiles in terms of all the student agency profiles (Figure 1). The novel bars-in-bar visualization functions as a visual analytics tool for the teachers to reflect on their pedagogical decision-making (Cui, 2019; Heilala et al., 2022; Vieira et al., 2018). To facilitate transparency and interpretability of the results, the analysis also utilizes explainable artificial intelligence (XAI) to provide more fine-grained characterizations of the profiles (Saarela et al., 2021). For example, XAI provides insight into why a particular student was assigned to a specific agency profile (i.e., a local explanation) or how the detailed characteristics of a specific profile are constructed (i.e., a global explanation). In essence, XAI in student agency analytics opens a transparent window into the model's decision-making process, detailing the why and how behind its classifications. This helps to ensure that educators and students can understand and trust the insights provided by the analytics system, allowing for more informed and ethical educational decisions. XAI could function as an adaptive source (see, Martin et al., 2020) providing input for adaptive AI targeting learning and teaching processes (Figure 2).

Ethical considerations are vital in student agency analytics, especially when dealing with personal and potentially sensitive data. Key ethical issues identified in learning analytics encompass, for example, privacy, transparency, labeling, data ownership, algorithmic fairness, and the obligation to act (Tzimas & Demetriadis, 2021). The General Data Protection Regulation (GDPR) mandates privacy and transparency in data controlling and processing, with many students expressing concerns about data security, storage, and the transparency of analytics processes (e.g., Ifenthaler & Schumacher, 2016). While there are debates about data ownership, the student agency analytics process emphasizes privacy by using data aggregation, thus ensuring that individual results are only available to the respective students and teachers receive aggregated results that maintain student anonymity. Additionally, software architectural designs, like microservices, have been proposed to separate data controllers and processors, offering an added layer of privacy protection through pseudonymization (Ianculescu & Alexandru, 2020; Jääskelä et al., 2021).

In summary, student agency analytics, situated at the crossroads of educational research, computational psychometrics, and learning analytics, focuses on understanding and enhancing students' intentional learning and agentic resources. The approach quantifies student agency within different educational contexts, offering insights into individual learning experiences and more general group profiles suggesting prompts for pedagogical decision-making. The process is cyclical, starting with the teacher's initial planning, followed by student feedback through a psychometric measurement, and culminating in refined teaching strategies based on analytics. This data-driven approach employs the AUS scale to measure various dimensions of student agency, with robust clustering used to analyze diverse agency experiences. The results, visualized for educators, can be enhanced with explainable artificial intelligence (XAI) to ensure transparency in the model's decision-making. Ethical considerations, including privacy, transparency, and data ownership, are paramount, with actions like data aggregation and pseudonymization ensuring the protection of students' sensitive information.

3. CORE TECHNOLOGIES BEHIND STUDENT AGENCY ANALYTICS

This section deals with the underlying technologies used in developing student agency analytics. First, it briefly traces computational psychometrics, highlighting its synergy with learning analytics. Then, latent profile analysis using robust clustering is introduced as an essential technique for identifying distinct student agency profiles. The section concludes by spotlighting explainable artificial intelligence (XAI), underscoring its role in making machine learning models transparent and actionable within the domain of student agency.

3.1 Computational Psychometrics

Psychometrics is a field that studies measurement and modeling procedures—depending on epistemological stance—in educational and psychological contexts (Uher, 2021). The use of psychometric theories, concepts, and methods to analyze and quantify behavioral characteristics, cognitive functions, experiential qualities, and other latent factors relevant to learning processes is central to this field of study (e.g., Mislevy & Bolsinova, 2021; Thomas & Duffy, 2023). Learning analytics is suggested to benefit from the broad collection of research and methodological techniques provided by psychometric research within a broader interdisciplinary framework. In other words, whereas learning analytics is suggested to begin with multimodal data and technology, psychometrics begins with high-level interpretations and evidence-centered design (Drachsler & Goldhammer, 2020; Mislevy, 2019). Thus, the intersection of these domains provides an interesting approach to understanding and improving learning.

Computational psychometrics is "a blend of data science techniques, computer science, and principled psychometric approaches to aid the analyses of complex data as obtained from performance assessments and technology-enhanced learning and assessment systems" (von Davier et al., 2021, p. 2). The approach has been utilized in various studies and applications involving multimodal data and technology-enhanced environments. For example, Cipresso, 2015 introduced a three-step approach to study behavior dynamics in virtual reality using computational psychometrics, which showed that the virtual environment effectively elicited stress and behavioral responses. LaFlair et al., 2023 outlined how machine learning and psychometrics facilitate item generation for assessments and allow for the analysis of bigger, richer, and more diverse data, resulting in an improved test-taker experience. Hernandez et al., 2022 proposed an approach combining traditional situational judgment tests with gamification and machine learning to score and assess job candidates' soft skills. The study suggested that gamification coupled with psychometric modeling can be useful for improving the accuracy and effectiveness of employee behavior assessment. Poojitha et al., 2023 presented a machine learning framework for efficient assessment and prediction of human performance in a collaborative learning environment where computational psychometrics are used to model real behavior characteristics. The studies underscore the versatility and potential of computational psychometrics in diverse contexts, from virtual reality to employment assessments. Researchers can derive deeper insights and more accurate human behavior and performance models by integrating advanced data techniques with traditional psychometric principles.

In summary, building on the principles of psychometrics and its relation with learning analytics, computational psychometrics integrates with computer science and psychometric theories and methods. The integration allows for detailed analysis of multimodal data from various educational settings. From this intersection, latent profile analysis and explainable artificial intelligence emerged as key tools in developing student agency analytics.

3.2 Latent Profile Analysis

The eleven student agency dimensions in the three resource areas (see Figure 1) are formed via the pattern matrix, which has been determined using the confirmatory factor analysis (Jääskelä et al., 2020). This factor-based latent representation is then summarized to the whole student sample level to enable comparison of the agency of an individual student with the whole sample under study. The student agency knowledge discovery for teachers and educational administrators is based on the latent profile analysis (Grunschel et al., 2013), with four distinctive profiles (Jääskelä et al., 2021; Jääskelä et al., 2020).

Partitive clustering algorithms can be used to identify the subsets in a student sample with different agency profiles. Various methods and algorithms exist for this purpose (Estivill-Castro, 2002), among which methods based on robust statistics and the corresponding whole and subsample estimates are especially appealing (García-Escudero et al., 2010). Namely, statistical robustness refers to methods not excessively affected by outliers or deviations from the expected data patterns (Huber, 1981) and can, therefore, be used with small samples (Kärkkäinen & Heikkola, 2004). In other words, robust methods provide reliable estimates even when data comes from a class of only tens of students and may contain missing values, anomalies, and non-Gaussian error distributions. The latter happens when the original data from the AUS questionnaire is of Likert-scale.

In summary, robust clustering is a stable and reliable technique for discerning different latent profiles of students based on their individual experiences of student agency. The technique identifies distinct student groups with shared characteristics and experiences (Jääskelä et al., 2021). The principles of robust clustering could be extended to various educational settings where psychometric measurements from a Likert-scale questionnaire are employed, offering a convenient method to discern unique learner profiles based on diverse data. However, while robust clustering offers valuable insights into student profiles, there is an increasing demand for transparency in these methods, highlighting the need to employ explainable approaches.

3.3 Explainable Artificial Intelligence (XAI)

XAI seeks to demystify the often complex and opaque algorithms of AI, making their inner workings more understandable to humans. The concept, although gaining recent attention, has historical roots, such as the medical recommendation system introduced by Shortliffe et al., 1975, which provided interpretable results to physicians. XAI emphasizes understandability, transparency, interpretability, and explainability, countering the "black box" nature of many AI models (Angelov et al., 2021). It is pivotal in deciphering complex machine learning models and making their decisions transparent, thus establishing appropriate trust in and effectively overseeing the outcomes produced by AI (Adadi & Berrada, 2018; Barredo Arrieta et al., 2020).

When we refer to the need for an explanation regarding a decision, we generally imply the requirement for reasons or rationales behind a specific result rather than an account of the internal mechanisms or the overall logical process guiding the decision-making procedure. Utilizing XAI systems furnishes the necessary information to substantiate results, particularly when unexpected determinations arise. Furthermore, it establishes a trackable and verifiable approach to defending algorithmic choices as equitable and morally sound, fostering the cultivation of trust. The significance of explainability transcends mere justification of decisions; it also plays a preventive role. Indeed, gaining a deeper understanding of system behavior enhances visibility into previously unidentified susceptibilities and imperfections, enabling the swift identification and rectification of errors in less critical situations (debugging). This, in turn, empowers a heightened level of control.

Most XAI techniques focus on feature relevance to explain AI and machine learning models (Saarela & Jauhiainen, 2021). Various of these methods, like SHapley Additive exPlanation (SHAP) (Shapley, 1953) and local interpretable model-agnostic explanations (LIME) (Lundberg & Lee, 2017), are post-hoc, meaning they are applied after the AI model has been trained to shed light on the model's decision-making processes. Additionally, some machine learning algorithms, like random forests (Breiman, 2001), inherently offer a degree of transparency, allowing the quantification of feature relevance. Regarding the explanation space, both—posthoc and intrinsic—explanation methods can be classified into local versus global interpretability. Global interpretability involves comprehending the overarching decision-making process of a model, while local interpretability centers around elucidating explanations for individual predictions.

Utilizing XAI in student agency analytics allows for a deeper understanding of how specific dimensions contribute to different educational experiences regarding agency profiles. This transparency is crucial for learners, educators, and stakeholders, as it provides actionable insights into the factors that enhance or hinder student agency. Saarela et al. (2021) proposed that the purpose of integrating XAI techniques with the student agency analytics process is to support the transparency and data-based development of automated feedback systems in education and to advance teachers' pedagogical awareness and reflection by providing actionable information on students' learning efforts in relation to their perceived agentic affordances. Overall, their study suggested that incorporating XAI into practice could support the development of automated feedback systems and increase pedagogical knowledge. In addition to XAI techniques, furture studies using clustering could also examine how explainable clustering could contribute to transparency. Explainable clustering (Moshkovitz et al., 2020) utilizes decision trees to characterize k-means and k-median cluster assignments, aiming at optimal pre-modeling explanations for given clusterings and the computational complexity influenced by various parameters (Bandyapadhyay et al., 2023).

In summary, XAI techniques aim to enhance the transparency and comprehensibility of complex AI algorithms. In addition to providing clarification on decisions made, the techniques could contribute to the improvement of the AI system and the identification of errors and biases. Methods such as SHAP, LIME, and transparent algorithms like random forests provide valuable insights into the decision-making mechanisms of AI. The integration of XAI in the field of education could provide benefits by providing useful insights into student agency, improving feedback systems, and expanding instructional expertise. Furthermore, emerging methodologies such as explainable clustering demonstrate the possibility of achieving enhanced transparency.

4. TOWARD ADAPTIVE LEARNING AND TEACHING

This section provides insight into how adaptive AI can be utilized in education by taking examples from the domains of serious games and pedagogical agents. These AI solutions can provide personalized learning experiences, boosting user involvement and facilitating learning processes. However, while there are potential educational benefits, it's crucial to approach their integration by considering ethical implications, user expectations, and the importance of transparency in decision-making processes.

4.1 Adaptive AI in Education

Adaptive AI refers to artificial intelligence systems that can modify their behavior over time based on the data they process, the feedback they receive, and the available resources (Gartner, 2022; Shen et al., 2021). In other words, instead of being static in their modeling, adaptive AI systems learn from new information and adjust their actions or predictions accordingly (e.g., Kumar & Kumar, 2018; Penttilä et al., 2019). In education, adaptive AI systems are expected to adjust and personalize educational content and experiences based on individual student needs, preferences, and performance (e.g., Younes, 2021). The primary goal is to provide a more tailored educational experience, for example, by ensuring that students receive the right content at the right pace, thereby enhancing learning processes.

Serious games have the potential to benefit from adaptive AI to enhance user experience, tailor content to individual learning approaches, and provide real-time feedback, thereby making the gaming environment more engaging and effective for educational and training purposes (Aydin et al., 2023; Niemelä et al., 2020). According to Mansouri et al. (2021), the utilization of adaptive AI can augment player engagement with serious games by customizing the gaming experience to align with each player's unique requirements and preferences. This can be accomplished by analyzing the player's behavior and subsequent modification of the game's mechanics, level of difficulty, and content appropriately. By implementing this approach, the game shows an increased degree of challenge and reward, hence potentially fostering higher levels of motivation and engagement. For example, Fraser et al. (2018) found that user engagement can be supported by emotion detection and emotional dialogue management to enhance the conversational experience in video games.

Pedagogical agents are computer-generated characters designed to support learning by interacting with students human-likely and providing feedback, answering questions, and guiding students through learning activities (Sikström et al., 2022). In their research, Hauptman et al. (2023) provided recommendations and insights into the design and implementation of AI teammates in various educational team situations, such as cyber incident response, data science, and computer security. They defined autonomous teammates as artificial agents that can function independently and make decisions without the need for human intervention. These adaptive autonomous agents are designed to adjust their level of autonomy based on the team's needs and the situation. The research provided design recommendations for enhancing human-AI team dynamics and the design of AI teammates with adaptive autonomy. Firstly, it emphasized the importance of work cycles in determining the level of autonomy of AI teammates. AI agents should dynamically adapt their autonomy based on predefined points in teamwork cycles, similar to how less experienced team members would. This dynamic adaptation should feel natural, avoiding manual adjustments that can disrupt team performance and focus. Over time, AI could even predict changes in the team's work cycle for better adaptation. Secondly, AI teammates should have higher autonomy during well-defined, predictable team processes. For instance, in phases requiring more straightforward decisions and actions, AI agents should have more autonomy but less during phases that require more human reasoning. Lastly, a training mode should be introduced to address initial concerns about AI teammates. This mode would allow team members to manually control the AI's adaptation manually, aiding in familiarization.

Li and Gu (2023) proposed a risk framework for human-centered artificial intelligence (HCAI) that primarily seeks to manage risks methodically and assist stakeholders in maximizing benefits through proactive measures. The framework is designed to promote responsible, sustainable, and human-centric AIED, and it was developed through a literature meta-analysis and a Delphi process to pinpoint eight pivotal risk indicators. The risk indicators in the framework are a misunderstanding of the HCAI concept (MC), misuse of AI resources (MR), mismatching of AI pedagogy (MP), privacy security risk (PSR), transparency risk (TR), accountability risk (AR), bias risk (BR), and perceived risk (PR). The indicators are systematically categorized into four distinct areas. Firstly, the HCAI Concept category solely comprises the risk of misunderstanding the HCAI concept. Secondly, the Application Process category addresses risks associated with the misuse of AI resources and the mismatching of AI pedagogy. Thirdly, the Ethical Security category concerns risks relating to privacy and security, transparency, accountability, and bias. According to the authors, these risks are particularly concerning as they emerge from overlooking the inherent values of AI technology, which could potentially clash with the foundational objectives of education. Lastly, the Man-Machine Interaction category consists of the perceived risk indicator, which is rooted in the ethical dilemmas posed by the misuse of AI technology in education governance. The authors utilized the Delphi method to find out the ranking of the risk indicators, which was described as MP > MR > AR > PSR > TR > PR > BR > MC. The result indicated that the mismatching of AI pedagogy, misuse of AI resources, and accountability risk were some of the main concerns among experts in the Delphi panel. In addition to potential risks, the effectiveness of adaptive AI systems in education should be considered with care. For example, Kosch et al. (2023) reported an interesting finding that suggested that descriptions of technical systems can elicit placebo effects through user expectations, biasing the results of user-centered studies. Their study found that the belief of receiving adaptive AI support increases expectations regarding the person's own task performance. Overall, the study highlights the importance of considering user expectations and placebo effects in evaluating AI-based user interfaces and novel AI systems in education.

From an ethical perspective, XAI is suggested as a promising approach when dealing with adaptive AI in education. As adaptive AI systems augment educational processes based on multimodal data, it's essential for stakeholders to understand how these systems make decisions to tailor these processes. This transparency is vital for making informed and fair educational decisions. Khosravi et al. (2022) discussed the importance of transparency and accountability in AI systems used in education and how XAI can help increase trust in these systems. The authors present the XAI-ED framework, which consists of five components: i) stakeholders and potential benefits, ii) approaches for presenting explanations, iii) used classes of AI models, iv) human-centered designs of the XAI interfaces, and v) potential pitfalls of providing explanations and how to avoid them. The framework aims to provide a structured approach to designing and evaluating XAI systems in education. The stakeholder aspect considers the different groups of people who are involved in the educational process and how they may benefit from XAI. The benefits aspect examines the potential advantages of using XAI in education, such as increased transparency and accountability. The explanations aspect looks at different methods for presenting explanations to users, such as visualizations or natural language explanations. The AI models aspect considers the different types of AI models that are commonly used in AIED, such as decision trees or neural networks. The human-centered design aspect focuses on designing AI interfaces that are user-friendly and easy to understand. Finally, the potential pitfalls aspect examines the potential challenges and limitations of implementing XAI in educational settings, such as the complexity of educational data or the need for domain-specific knowledge.

In summary, adaptive AI could transform education toward adaptive learning and teaching by delivering personalized learning experiences that cater to each student's unique needs. Its potential impact is already noted in areas like serious games, which use AI to boost user engagement through personalized content and pedagogical agents that provide human-like interactions and feedback. However, while the advantages are potentially significant, it is imperative to integrate adaptive AI thoughtfully, considering the potential risks, user expectations, and the critical importance of transparency.

4.2 From Adaptive AI to Adaptive Learning and Teaching

Adaptive learning can be considered both as a technology and a process that is suggested to have benefits for learning: using technologies like machine learning and virtual learning environments, it actively modifies the delivery of educational content according to a student's understanding of the subject, as determined by their reactions to assessments or their specific learning preferences (Essa et al., 2023; Martin et al., 2020). Generally, a process refers to a series of steps to reach a particular objective. In this context, the process perspective of adaptive learning focuses on how to attain the objective (e.g., learning outcome) using adaptive AI, while the technology perspective centers on adaptive AI, highlighting the technology behind the design and building of artifacts used in adaptive learning (e.g., adaptive pedagogical agents) called as adaptive learning systems in general. In other words, in the context of student agency analytics, adaptive learning refers to learning processes utilizing adaptive AI as technology that could be integrated into an artifact forming an adaptive learning system. From the ANT point of view, these processes and artifacts are not isolated but are deeply intertwined with various actors in a wider context. These actors can include not only humans like educators, learners, peers, and administrative personnel but also non-human actors such as other algorithms, software systems, and adaptive learning tools utilizing various technologies.

However, artificial intelligence in education does not automatically support personalized learning. Ouyang and Jiao (2021) proposed three paradigms of artificial intelligence in education, namely, AI-directed (i.e., learner-as-recipient), AI-supported (i.e., learner-as-collaborator), and AI-empowered (i.e., learner-as-leader). AI systems steer the learning process in the AI-directed paradigm, placing learners as passive knowledge recipients. Conversely, the AI-supported paradigm considers learners actively collaborating with AI, offering guidance throughout the learning paths. Lastly, the AI-empowered paradigm emphasizes learner agency, treating AI systems as tools to enhance human characteristics, drawing from the complexity theory that perceives education and learning as a complex adaptive system (e.g., Chiva et al., 2008; Jörg et al., 2007), necessitating collaboration among its various components. Within these paradigms, adaptive AI is best situated within the AI-empowered paradigm. Here, adaptive learning tailors content based on individual learner needs and empowers learners to take charge of their educational journey.

Martin et al. (2020) proposed in their literature review an adaptive learning framework that applies elements from both Shute and Towle (2003) and Vandewaetere et al. (2011), integrating components like the learner model, content model, instructional model, and an adaptive engine, with the latter utilizing AI to individualize learning pathways based on user feedback and learner profiles. The review identified that learner modeling utilized various adaptive sources, encompassing learners' attributes, knowledge, proficiency, behavior, preferences, and individual differences. These various learner characteristics used in modeling included log data, different psychometric instruments (e.g., learning style), and variables like time spent on a task and proficiency level. The review found that adaptive learning applications focused on content, assessment, presentation, and navigation, with research emphasizing adaptive feedback based on student understanding of concepts and reasoning, navigation tailored to individual learning paths, and content presentation in varied formats and modalities. The authors suggested that future research in adaptive learning should focus on qualitative methods to understand the mechanisms behind the positive impacts of adaptivity, employ experimental designs and meta-analyses to identify causal patterns and their effects, and examine the specific adaptive strategies and technologies used.

Adaptive teaching, on the other hand, focuses on inclusive teaching practices and involves educators drawing on their expertise to create versatile learning situations with the goal of maintaining the majority of students in this "middle ground" that "brings students at different levels closer together" (Corno, 2008, p. 166). This approach leverages the diverse abilities within the class, encourages students to exchange insights and fosters skill development. According to Gallagher et al., 2022, adaptive teaching is a dynamic pedagogical approach where teachers spontaneously modify their instruction to cater to their student's diverse needs. They suggest that by recognizing students' varied learning approaches and abilities, adaptive teaching emphasizes continuous pedagogical adjustments based on classroom observations, such as unexpected student inputs or misconceptions. Based on a literature review, they found that the key areas of teacher expertise contributing to adaptive teaching are 1) noticing the aspect to which the teacher must attend, 2) teacher reflection and metacognition, and 3) teacher's action. Gallagher et al., 2022 emphasized that professional noticing is a critical component of adaptive teaching involving a teacher's ability to observe and interpret classroom situations and to use this information to make informed decisions about their instruction. They suggest that teachers who can notice and respond to student thinking are more effective at promoting student learning than those who are not.

Professional noticing, a key skill underpinning all professional practice, is the ability to observe and interpret situations and events in a work setting and to use this understanding to inform decisions and actions (Rooney & Boud, 2019). According to Gibson and Ross (2016), the teacher's professional noticing involves various features, such as engaging in thorough hypothesizing, providing detailed elaboration, identifying learners' metacognitive processes, and identifying important moments. The authors suggest that it is crucial for teachers to accurately understand and interpret students' responses in order to make informed decisions on instructional strategies and provide relevant support. In other words, through professional noticing, teachers can accurately identify their students' strengths and weaknesses, enabling them to customize their instructional methods accordingly. The results of their study highlight the importance of professional noticing in promoting adaptive teaching practices, improving pedagogical skills, and providing continuous development for teachers through their own ability to adapt. In general, professional noticing serves as a fundamental aspect of adaptive teaching, enabling teachers to provide personalized instruction that aligns with the specific needs of their students.

H. Park and Zhang (2022) examined how analyzing students' temporal progress and participation in a visual online platform for collaborative knowledge building facilitated teachers' noticing. They found that the main advantage of the technology and analytics was presenting teachers with an overview of students' evolving thought processes, highlighting students' valuable insights regarding central concepts within the collaborative platform. The results indicated that with analytical feedback, teachers were better positioned to recognize and value students' deep and promising ideas that might have gone unnoticed otherwise.

Kärner et al. (2021) introduced a Teachers' Diagnostic Support System (TDSS), a prototype of a task-specific decision support system utilizing learning analytics to support teachers' daily diagnostic tasks and micro-adaptive strategies. The TDSS collected data on students' personal attributes, such as domain-specific knowledge and emotional-motivational traits. It also gathered information on instructional characteristics like the nature of the learning content and tracked students' learning experiences and progress, including their interests and knowledge about a topic. Analytically, the TDSS examined variations between students, like differing prior knowledge. It also analyzed changes within individual students over time, variations in teaching methods, and the interplay between students' knowledge levels and task challenges.

According to Standen et al. (2020), adaptive learning systems can enhance adaptive teaching by using AI to understand students' emotional states better and tailor teaching methods accordingly. They concluded that notable applications include optimizing communication strategies for autistic students and providing real-time feedback on student engagement with materials. However, they also emphasized that these systems often face challenges, including limited practical testing and the absence of standardized evaluation criteria. Furthermore, many educators do not fully grasp how the technologies function.

In summary, adaptive learning, which merges technology and pedagogical processes, adjusts educational content and instruction based on student performance. This is primarily achieved through AI systems, which can be either directive, supportive, or empowering. For truly individualized learning experiences, an empowered approach would be ideal, letting learners assume agency in their learning pathways. Adaptive teaching focuses on educators' ability to respond to diverse student needs. Central to this concept is professional noticing, which helps educators observe and make informed pedagogical decisions.

5. INTEGRATING STUDENT AGENCY ANALYTICS WITH CONCEPTS IN ADAPTIVE AI

This section explores the potential and tentative approaches to how adaptive AI may utilize student agency analytics to improve various outcomes. The section suggests ways to contribute to student-centered teaching and learning through agency-aware adaptive AI. However, responsible application of these approaches requires understanding ethical considerations.

5.1 Potential Applications

Through the lens of student agency analytics, adaptive AI has the potential to support how educators approach student-centered teaching and how students engage with their learning. By understanding and leveraging the elaborate interplay between student agency and adaptive AI, educators and technologists could co-create learning environments that are both technologically advanced and student-centric. The following suggests how student agency analytics could potentially be harnessed to produce relevant input features and prompts for AI models, improve modeling accuracy, evaluate the effectiveness of adaptive AI systems, augment teaching practices, and advance the AI-empowered learning paradigm.

5.1.1 Feature Engineering

Relevant input features are crucial for the performance and accuracy of AI models, as they directly influence the model's ability to discern patterns and make predictions (Linja et al., 2023; Verdonck et al., 2021). Feature engineering, the process of selecting, transforming, and creating the most informative features, plays a key role in enhancing the model's functioning (e.g., Kuhn & Johnson, 2019). Without valid feature engineering, even the most sophisticated AI algorithms can produce misleading results or fail to capture the underlying relationships in the data. By leveraging psychometric principles, feature selection and engineering can be more targeted, ensuring that AI models are informed by variables that genuinely reflect students' cognitive abilities, behaviors, and experiences. For example, Zehner et al. (2021) used a "top-down approach for engineering features by means of psychometric modeling" to estimate students' test-taking speed and ability and then extracted features from log data and derived simple indicators to improve machine learning for predictive classification tasks. The top-down approach aligns with the notion of how psychometrics first considers high-level interpretations (Drachsler & Goldhammer, 2020; Mislevy, 2019). By discerning the multifaceted dimensions of a student's learning experience, student agency analytics offers a rich set of input features for adaptive AI systems. These features capture nuanced aspects of a student's learning experience, such as self-efficacy, competence beliefs, interest, and reliance on peer support. When integrated into adaptive AI systems, these data points enable the AI model to personalize, for example, content, feedback mechanisms, and collaborative learning environments to the needs and preferences of each student. By understanding a student's agency profile, the AI model could predict potential challenges, optimize learning paths, and provide timely interventions. Thus, student agency analytics could act as a bridge, translating intricate human learning experiences into actionable data for AI-driven personalization.

5.1.2 Prompt Engineering

With the advent of large language models (LLMs), prompt-based learning has emerged as an effective paradigm for conducting predictive natural language processing (NLP) tasks (Liu et al., 2023). A prompt is a directive given to an LLM to tailor or improve its functions, and prompt engineering is the process of optimizing these directives by exploiting the established prompt patterns (e.g., White et al., 2023). There have been some recent attempts to use LLMs to examine personality traits and automatically generate measurement items. For example, Safdari et al. (2023) claimed that LLMs could reliably and validly simulate personality and create outputs that reflect specific personality profiles. Laverghetta and Licato (2023) utilized an LLM and a prompting strategy for automated item generation (AIG) of psychometric test items. Computational psychometrics like student agency analytics could provide insightful frameworks for composing prompts that capture and reflect the intricate nuances of student behaviors, motivations, and learning experiences. Integrating LLMs, prompt engineering, and computational psychometrics could lead to a more nuanced interaction between users and LLMs, where the model's responses are both linguistically accurate and aligned with the educational and psychological dimensions of the learner.

5.1.3 Improving Model Accuracy

Self-reported measures in education are tools where students provide information about themselves without external verification. They may be subject to biases, as responses are based on personal perceptions and might not always represent objective reality (e.g., Jia et al., 2023). However, in learning analytics, the integration of self-reported measures has been suggested to be a useful approach, offering a more comprehensive view of students' learning experiences and enhancing the predictive power of the data. For example, Ellis et al. (2017) employed a questionnaire to gather self-report data on students' learning approaches and paired this with observational data from an online learning environment. The objective was to predict academic performance. By merging self-report and observational data, three independent variables were identified that significantly predicted students' academic performance: the surface approach to study, the frequency of accessing an online resource, and the number of multiple-choice questions answered. This combination approach underscores the value of self-report measures, suggesting they can enhance analysis by offering a richer understanding of students' learning experiences. Tempelaar et al. (2020) acknowledged the biases of self-reported measures but argued that the measures can still be valuable in predicting academic performance. Interestingly, their study posited that these biases could even add predictive power when explaining performance data and self-reported data. This perspective challenges the traditional view of biases as purely detrimental, suggesting that self-reported measures can, in certain contexts, provide deeper insights into student learning and performance. Ifenthaler et al. (2023) explored the alignment between self-reported data on self-testing procedures and behavioral data sourced from learning analytics systems. Their study proposed that merging self-report data with trace data, especially when investigating how learners engage with resources, yields more accurate results. The combined approach offers a more holistic view of student engagement and serves as a validation tool for analytics results. Also, beyond predictive analytics, self-reported measures have implications for intervention and feedback systems based on learning analytics. Dawson et al. (2017) emphasized the importance of considering students' individual characteristics, such as self-efficacy and prior studies, when designing these systems. Self-reports emerge as a potent tool in this context, helping identify individual aspects and factors, like a student's expected grade. Recognizing these individual nuances can significantly impact students' learning behaviors. More importantly, it can pave the way for more personalized feedback, tailored to address specific student needs and preferences. Based on the findings above, student agency analytics could offer a more nuanced and comprehensive understanding of student learning experiences and, thus, improve model accuracy in adaptive learning systems.

5.1.4 Evaluating Effectiveness of Adaptive AI

The effectiveness of AI in education should be examined across multiple domains, cultural contexts, and practical settings (Pinkwart, 2016). Also, learning perceptions as an outcome have received less attention than learning achievements in studies dealing with the effectiveness of AI in education (Zheng et al., 2021). Most notably, AI in education should foster student agency rather than undermine it (Nguyen et al., 2023; Ouyang & Jiao, 2021). Therefore, if one is committed to a humanistic and student-centered view of education, student agency as a construct offers a theory-driven lens to evaluate students' learning perceptions in different learning situations applying AI systems. In other words, student agency analytics could provide useful metrics to evaluate the effectiveness of adaptive AI systems in education. When students interact with adaptive AI systems, the degree to which they feel empowered, autonomous, and capable of influencing their learning trajectory can be assumed to have an association with the system's adaptability. If an adaptive AI system effectively tailors learning experiences, students should exhibit heightened agency, as the system would be personalizing content, feedback, and other resources to their individual needs and preferences, thereby fostering a more student-centered learning environment. By monitoring changes in student agency before and after the introduction of an adaptive AI system, researchers and educators could assess the system's impact. A significant increase in student agency would suggest that the AI system is effectively recognizing and responding to individual student needs in terms of agency, while stagnant or decreasing levels might indicate a need for further refinement of the system.

5.1.5 Augmented Teaching

Student agency analytics employs visual analytics to present a clear and concise representation of the learning experience, enabling teachers to gain insights and make informed decisions about their teaching practices. The visual representation can help teachers to narrow down their attentional space and focus on specific areas that require intervention or enhancement. In other words, visual analytics can facilitate teachers' situation awareness (Y. Park & Jo, 2019) and professional noticing (H. Park & Zhang, 2022). As a result, teachers could respond more effectively to individual student needs, fostering a micro-adaptive (Corno, 2008) learning environment that is inclusive, responsive, and dynamic. Furthermore, the underlying educational framework of student agency can facilitate teachers' reflection and meta-cognition (Heilala et al., 2022). Consequently, teachers can engage in a continuous cycle of reflection, adaptation, and improvement. The approach can be considered an example of augmented teaching, which combines the teacher's professional expertise with technological capabilities to enhance pedagogical decision-making and actions. Lastly, professional noticing is a capability that can be deliberately practiced (Rooney & Boud, 2019), and student agency analytics could be used as a learning tool in teacher education, augmenting the teaching of pre-service teachers.

Advancing AI-empowered learning by providing students with access to their own visualized student agency data, they can take a more active role in their learning journey. This democratization of data allows students to self-reflect on their learning practices, strengths, and areas of improvement. Students gain opportunities to engage in meaningful dialogues with their teachers, co-creating personalized learning strategies. Also, other adaptive learning systems can utilize student agency analytics data to adapt their own internal algorithms. For example, a collaborative learning platform could utilize dynamic grouping based on students' competence and self-efficacy experiences or provide students with prompts based on peer support levels. The approaches above can potentially advance the AI-empowered learning paradigm (Ouyang & Jiao, 2021) by transforming AI systems in education from mere instructional tools to enablers of student-centered and meaningful learning.

5.2 Ethical Perspectives

When applying student agency analytics to enhance personalized learning paths, XAI can help ensure that the adaptability of AI is both transparent and aligned with individual student characteristics (Saarela et al., 2021). By offering insights into adaptive AI processes, XAI methods could help researchers, developers, and practitioners ensure that the dynamic learning adjustments suggested by AI are both comprehensible and beneficial to the student's educational trajectory. The XAI-ED (Khosravi et al., 2022) and HCAI (Li & Gu, 2023) frameworks can be used to outline the different ethical perspectives of student agency analytics.

Considering the stakeholders and potential benefits through the lens of the XAI-ED framework, student agency analytics offers distinct advantages for educators, students, educational researchers, and policymakers. Educators can gain actionable insights for refined pedagogical decisions, while students could receive a reflective view of their learning pathways, potentially promoting autonomy and agentic learning. Educational researchers could benefit from a rich set of features that can inform more comprehensive studies on learning behaviors and outcomes, and policymakers could use research-based insights to craft informed educational strategies and guidelines for student-centered learning. From the human-centered AI perspective, the HCAI framework emphasizes the need for AI tools in education to be designed with responsibility and sustainability at the forefront (Li & Gu, 2023). Student agency analytics aims not only to deliver data-driven insights but also to do so in a form that is transparent, interpretable, and centered on the diverse needs of different educational stakeholders. Relating to approaches for presenting explanations, student agency analytics aims to translate intricate psychometric data into comprehensible insights by using visual analytics. The visualization technique aligns with the HCAI framework, which underscores the importance of designing AI solutions that are both interpretable from the educational point of view and aligned with pedagogical approaches. In other words, the approach emphasizes the importance of balancing innovative AI applications in education with the need to avoid the mismatching of AI pedagogy, ensuring that AI-driven insights remain relevant and user-centric. Concerning the used classes of AI models, student agency analytics utilizes advanced techniques such as computational psychometrics, robust clustering, and XAI to clarify multidimensional learning experiences. The incorporation of SHAP (Shapley, 1953) and LIME (Lundberg & Lee, 2017), with their focus on model interpretability, aims to facilitate the human-centric design for the XAI interface, underscoring the importance of the dimensions of ethical security. However, while these techniques can potentially offer transparent insights, stakeholders might question the validity or interpretability of AI-driven outcomes in real-world educational settings, depending, for example, on the perceived risk and the misunderstanding of the relevant concepts.

Finally, it's crucial to be aware of potential challenges. For instance, placing too much trust in automated results and explanations could unintentionally reduce the significance of an educator's contribution to pedagogical decisions. Additionally, the clarity brought about by these explanations might unintentionally reveal confidential student information or amplify intrinsic biases in the AI system. Given the multidimensional nature of student agency, there is also a possibility that the system's explanations might be too complex, making it challenging for educators or students to understand, which could result in misunderstandings. Thus, integrating human expertise with AI-derived knowledge and crafting explanations that align with the user's knowledge level is vital to address these issues. Furthermore, strong privacy safeguards need to be in place, and the AI models should undergo regular reviews to detect and correct any inherent biases.

In summary, student agency analytics could support a transparent and tailored approach to enhancing personalized learning paths when integrated with XAI. Considering the analytics through XAI-ED and HCAI frameworks, the approach can deliver valuable insights for various educational stakeholders, from learners to policymakers. However, while the potential benefits are significant, addressing challenges such as over-reliance on analytics, potential exposure of sensitive data, and the complexity of provided insights, emphasizing the importance of human expertise, user-tailored explanations, and continuous model evaluations is essential.

6. CONCLUSION

With the digital transformation that has been ongoing globally, there has been a growing recognition among educational institutions of the imperative to harness data for refining educational processes and outcomes (Banihashem et al., 2022; Mukul & Buÿüközkan, 2023). At the same time, the concept of student agency has emerged as a crucial element in shaping purposeful and influential learning experiences in higher education (e.g., OECD, 2019; Stenalt & Lassesen, 2021; Vaughn, 2020). Recent studies briefly reviewed in this chapter have highlighted the profound connections between student agency and various educational results, emphasizing its significance, for example, in pedagogical decision-making and overall student satisfaction. This chapter considered the potential of adaptive AI in higher education, particularly focusing on the interplay between student agency and educational processes. By combining learning analytics with the research on student agency, a novel approach termed student agency analytics (Heilala, 2022; Jääskelä et al., 2021) was briefly introduced as an example application, offering a data-driven perspective to discern students' learning experiences. This synergy between adaptive AI and student agency analytics was suggested to hold promise for crafting more tailored and impactful educational experiences where student-teacher-AI interactions intertwine with curriculum, content, and environment (Figure 2).

Human agency, deeply rooted in philosophical traditions, encompasses the capacity for intentional action and change, influenced by individual intentions and broader social contexts (Schlosser, 2015). Within the educational realm, student agency emerges as a specialized facet of this broader concept, emphasizing students' ability to navigate, influence, and shape their learning experiences (Stenalt & Lassesen, 2021). In this chapter, the concept of student agency was used to refer to students' capacity to take control of their learning through various resources. In formal educational context, this capacity building interacts with the curriculum, pedagogical approaches and teaching practices, and the broader educational environment (Jääskelä et al., 2020; Jääskelä et al., 2023). Student agency analytics was

Figure 2. Adaptive student agency analytics as a cyclical process utilizing computational psychometrics (evolved from Saarela et al., 2021)

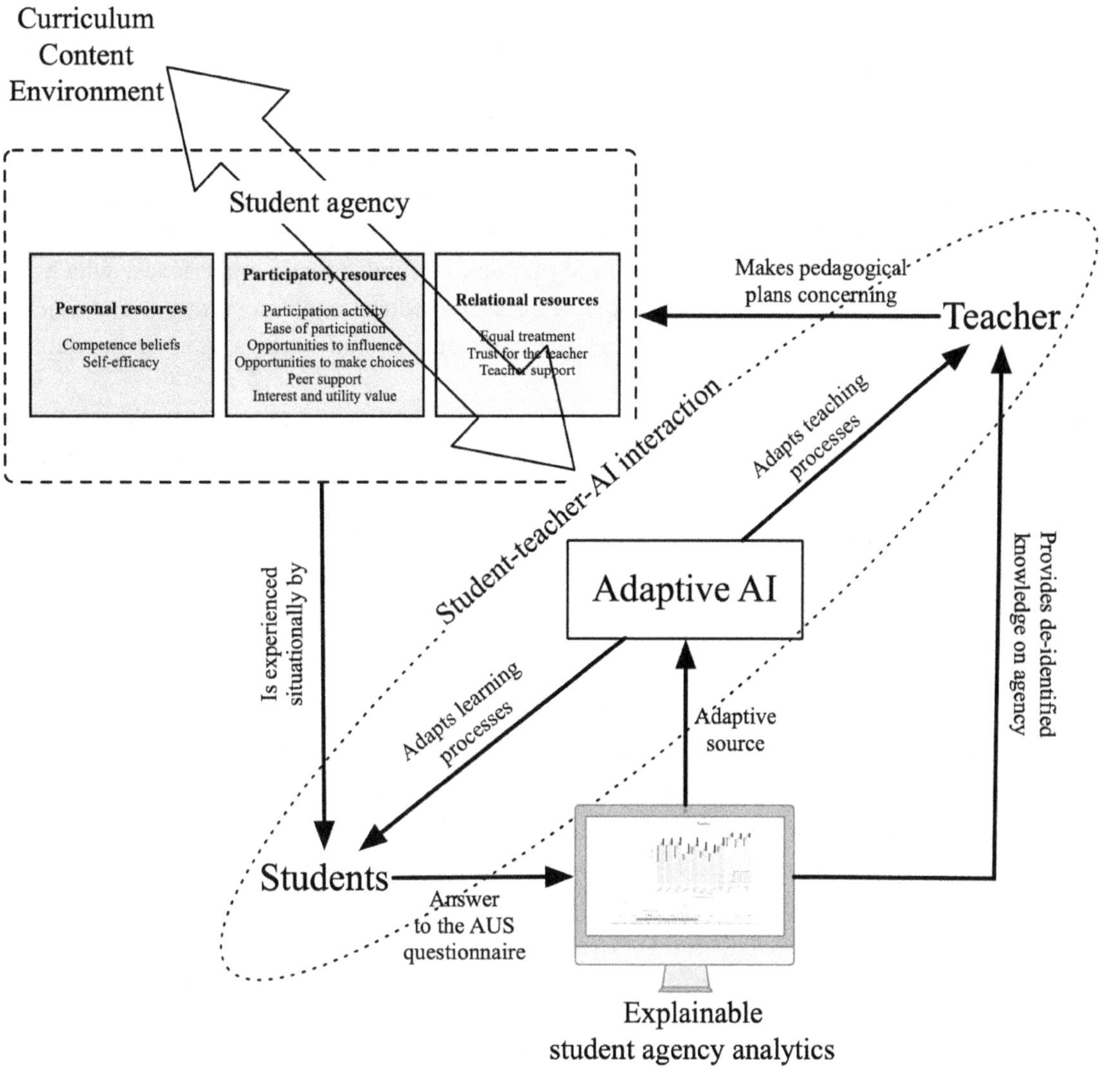

utilized to quantify and analyze this agency within educational settings. By leveraging computational psychometrics, robust machine learning, and data visualization, this approach provided insights into how students exercise their agency, offering educators a more comprehensive understanding of students' learning experiences (Heilala et al., 2022). The datadriven perspective, grounded in ethical considerations (Saarela et al., 2021; Tzimas & Demetriadis, 2021), aims to foster more intentional and meaningful learning experiences for students.

The core technologies underpinning student agency analytics are rooted in computational psychometrics, robust clustering, and explainable artificial intelligence (XAI). Computational psychometrics, a fusion of data science, computer science, and traditional psychometric principles, offers a comprehensive approach to analyzing complex data from educational settings (von Davier et al., 2021). Robust clustering, a variant of the k-means clustering technique, identifies distinct student agency profiles, emphasizing resistance to outliers and anomalies in the data (Jääskelä et al., 2021). XAI, on the other hand, aims to make the intricate algorithms of AI transparent and understandable. By demystifying the "black box" nature of many AI models, XAI provides clear insights into the decision-making processes of machine learning models, ensuring trustworthiness and accountability (Angelov et al., 2021; Saarela et al., 2021). Integrating these technologies in student agency analytics offers a holistic understanding of students' learning experiences, potentially providing actionable insights for educators and stakeholders. Extending beyond student agency, the techniques of student agency analytics have the potential to enrich the analysis of other educational constructs. By harnessing computational psychometrics, robust clustering, and XAI, different professionals in education could delve deeper into concepts like student motivation, engagement, or collaborative learning dynamics. Similar holistic approaches, which are adaptable and scalable, could pave the way for more personalized educational interventions and a richer understanding of diverse learning experiences across various educational settings, leading to adaptive learning and teaching.

Adaptive learning, both a technology and a process, uses AI to modify educational experiences based on a student's performance and preferences (e.g., Essa et al., 2023; Martin et al., 2020). This ensures, for example, that learners receive content tailored to their learning pace and knowledge level, enhancing the overall learning process. Serious games, for instance, can employ adaptive AI to boost user engagement by personalizing content (Aydin et al., 2023), while pedagogical agents can interact with students in a human-like manner, offering feedback and guidance (Sikström et al., 2022). On the other hand, adaptive teaching focuses on educators using their expertise to create dynamic learning environments. For example, teachers adjust their instruction spontaneously based on classroom observations, such as unexpected student inputs or misconceptions (Gallagher et al., 2022). A critical skill underpinning adaptive teaching is professional noticing, which involves a teacher's ability to observe, interpret, and act based on classroom situations (Gibson & Ross, 2016; Rooney & Boud, 2019). Student agency analytics can play a pivotal role in teachers' professional noticing by enabling educators to discern and respond to individual student needs, preferences, and behaviors. However, while the potential benefits of adaptive learning and teaching are significant, it is essential to integrate these approaches thoughtfully. Ethical considerations, like user expectations (e.g., Kosch et al., 2023) and the importance of transparency in decision-making processes must be at the forefront (e.g., Khosravi et al., 2022; Saarela et al., 2021). In essence, adaptive learning and teaching promise a more individualized and effective educational journey, but their implementation requires careful consideration and continuous evaluation.

This chapter suggested a promising potential for augmenting student-centered teaching and learning by integrating student agency analytics with adaptive AI. By harnessing the power of student agency analytics, AI models could be fed with relevant input features, capturing the nuanced aspects of a student's learning experience, such as self-efficacy, peer support, and participation activity. As the recent research reviewed in this chapter suggested, self-reported measures and observational data combined could produce more accurate results (e.g., Dawson et al., 2017; Ellis et al., 2017; Ifenthaler et al., 2023; Jia et al., 2023; Tempelaar et al., 2020). The integration could enable a more comprehensive knowledge of students' learning experiences and possibly improve the accuracy of adaptive AI models. Furthermore, student agency analytics might provide a theorydriven lens to evaluate the effectiveness of adaptive AI systems. From the teachers' perspective, they can benefit from visual analytics, enabling them to make informed decisions and adapt their teaching practices responsively. This approach, augmented teaching, merges professional expertise with technological capabilities, enhancing pedagogical decision-making. The advent of LLMs offers an exciting avenue for enhancing the capabilities of adaptive AI in the educational realm. The synergy between LLMs, prompt engineering, and student agency analytics could lead to more personalized and context-aware AI interventions, further amplifying the benefits of student-centered learning. Lastly, democratizing data by giving students access to their visualized agency data empowers them to actively participate in their learning journey actively, fostering meaningful dialogues and co-creating personalized learning strategies. In essence, the fusion of student agency with adaptive AI has the potential to transform AI systems from mere instructional tools to catalysts for studentcentered, meaningful learning.

6.1 Future Directions

Exploring student agency analytics, adaptive learning, and adaptive teaching discussed in this chapter opens several avenues for future research. One of the most promising directions lies at the intersection of computational psychometrics and learning analytics. As these domains continue to merge (e.g., Drachsler & Goldhammer, 2020), there is potential for developing more sophisticated models that can assess learning outcomes. Future studies could consider how multimodal data, combined with psychometric models, could offer richer insights into student agency, especially in online and hybrid learning environments. Latent profiling using robust clustering, having demonstrated its efficacy in identifying distinct student agency profiles in higher education (Jääskelä et al., 2021), can be utilized in other educational contexts. Future research could explore its application in different educational settings, cultures, and age groups to understand how student agency or other educational concepts manifest differently across diverse populations. The realm of XAI in education is still in its nascent stages (Adadi & Berrada, 2018; Angelov et al., 2021; Barredo Arrieta et al., 2020). Future studies could focus on a more profound integration of XAI with student agency analytics, which could offer deeper insights into how different elements influence student agency and how it can be enhanced. A potential method to utilize could be explainable clustering (Bandyapadhyay et al., 2023).

The concept of teachers' professional noticing, especially in the context of adaptive teaching (Corno, 2008; Gallagher et al., 2022; Gibson & Ross, 2016; Rooney & Boud, 2019) could be a topic for future research. Can training in professional noticing enhance the outcomes of adaptive teaching? Can analytics tools like student agency analytics be developed to enhance teachers' noticing skills, offering them real-time insights into student behaviors and needs? Additionally, the potential of combining LLMs with prompt engineering in educational research is beginning to gain traction. Future research could examine how LLMs, guided by well-crafted prompts, could simulate complex educational scenarios, thereby providing educators and researchers with a dynamic tool for understanding and enhancing student learning experiences. Specifically, the interplay between LLM-generated content and real-world educational interventions, informed by computational psychometrics like student agency analytics, could be a fertile ground for research, potentially informing personalized learning pathways and pedagogical strategies.

Lastly, considering a wider perspective by drawing from the ANT and the postdigital stance (Matthews, 2019), it would be interesting to examine how human and non-human actors, such as learning analytics tools, collaboratively shape educational trajectories, outcomes, and experiences. These tools, like student agency analytics, are not passive entities but aim to actively influence learning and teaching processes, potentially giving rise to data agency and augmented agency. As novel applications of adaptive AI and learning analytics emerge, ANT and the postdigital lens can enlighten how these technologies and human actors intertwine, mutually shaping and being shaped. In conclusion, combining AI, computational psychometrics, adaptive learning, and adaptive teaching offers many research opportunities.

REFERENCES

Adadi, A., & Berrada, M. (2018). Peeking inside the Black-Box: A survey on explainable artificial intelligence (XAI). *IEEE Access : Practical Innovations, Open Solutions*, *6*, 52138–52160. doi:10.1109/ACCESS.2018.2870052

Akrich, M. (2023). Actor network theory, Bruno Latour, and the CSI. *Social Studies of Science*, *53*(2), 169–173. doi:10.1177/03063127231158102 PMID:36840444

Angelov, P. P., Soares, E. A., Jiang, R., Arnold, N. I., & Atkinson, P. M. (2021). Explainable artificial intelligence: An analytical review. *Wiley Interdisciplinary Reviews. Data Mining and Knowledge Discovery*, *11*(5), 1–13. doi:10.1002/widm.1424

Anscombe, G. E. M. (1957). *Intention*. Basil Blackwell.

Aydin, M., Karal, H., & Nabiyev, V. (2023). Examination of adaptation components in serious games: A systematic review study. *Education and Information Technologies*, *28*(6), 6541–6562. doi:10.1007/s10639-022-11462-1

Bandura, A. (2001). Social cognitive theory: An agentic perspective. *Annual Review of Psychology*, *52*(1), 1–26. doi:10.1146/annurev.psych.52.1.1 PMID:11148297

Bandura, A. (2006). Toward a psychology of human agency. *Perspectives on Psychological Science*, *1*(2), 164–180. doi:10.1111/j.1745-6916.2006.00011.x PMID:26151469

Bandyapadhyay, S., Fomin, F. V., Golovach, P. A., Lochet, W., Purohit, N., & Simonov, K. (2023). How to find a good explanation for clustering? *Artificial Intelligence*, *322*, 103948. doi:10.1016/j.artint.2023.103948

Banihashem, S. K., Noroozi, O., van Ginkel, S., Macfadyen, L. P., & Biemans, H. J. A. (2022). A systematic review of the role of learning analytics in enhancing feedback practices in higher education. *Educational Research Review*, *37*, 100489. doi:10.1016/j.edurev.2022.100489

Barredo Arrieta, A., Dıaz-Rodrıguez, N., Del Ser, J., Bennetot, A., Tabik, S., Barbado, A., Garcia, S., Gil-Lopez, S., Molina, D., Benjamins, R., Chatila, R., & Herrera, F. (2020). Explainable artificial intelligence (XAI): Concepts, taxonomies, opportunities and challenges toward responsible AI. *Information Fusion*, *58*, 82–115. doi:10.1016/j.inffus.2019.12.012

Baylor, A. (1999). Intelligent agents as cognitive tools for education. *Educational Technology Research and Development. ETR & D*, *39*(2), 36–40.

Berger, P. L., & Luckmann, T. (1966). *The social construction of reality: A treatise in the sociology of knowledge*. Penguin.

Breiman, L. (2001). Random forests. *Machine Learning*, *45*(1), 5–32. doi:10.1023/A:1010933404324

Bryant, P. T. (2021). Modeling augmented humanity. In P. T. Bryant (Ed.), *Augmented humanity: Being and remaining agentic in a digitalized world* (pp. 1–38). Springer International Publishing. doi:10.1007/978-3-030-76445-6_1

Charteris, J., & Smardon, D. (2018). A typology of agency in new generation learning environments: Emerging relational, ecological and new material considerations. *Pedagogy, Culture & Society*, *26*(1), 51–68. doi:10.1080/14681366.2017.1345975

Chiva, R., Grandıo, A., & Alegre, J. (2008). Adaptive and generative learning: Implications from complexity theories. *International Journal of Management Reviews*, *12*(2), 114–129. doi:10.1111/j.1468-2370.2008.00255.x

Cipresso, P. (2015). Modeling behavior dynamics using computational psychometrics within virtual worlds. *Frontiers in Psychology*, *6*, 1725. doi:10.3389/fpsyg.2015.01725 PMID:26594193

Conole, G., Gašević, D., Long, P., & Siemens, G. (2011). Message from the LAK 2011 General & Program Chairs. *Proceedings of the 1st International Conference on Learning Analytics and Knowledge*. ACM.

Corno, L. (2008). On teaching adaptively. *Educational Psychologist*, *43*(3), 161–173. doi:10.1080/00461520802178466

Cui, W. (2019). Visual analytics: A comprehensive overview. *IEEE Access : Practical Innovations, Open Solutions*, *7*, 81555–81573. doi:10.1109/ACCESS.2019.2923736

Davidson, D. (1963). Actions, reasons, and causes. *The Journal of Philosophy*, *60*(23), 685–700. doi:10.2307/2023177

Dawson, S., Jovanovic, J., Gašević, D., & Pardo, A. (2017). From prediction to impact: Evaluation of a learning analytics retention program. *Proceedings of the Seventh International Learning Analytics & Knowledge Conference*, (pp. 474–478). ACM. 10.1145/3027385.3027405

Drachsler, H., & Goldhammer, F. (2020). Learning analytics and eAssessment—Towards computational psychometrics by combining psychometrics with learning analytics. In D. Burgos (Ed.), Radical solutions and learning analytics: Personalised learning and teaching through big data (pp. 67–80). Springer Singapore.

Ellis, R. A., Han, F., & Pardo, A. (2017). Improving learning analytics – combining observational and self-report data on student learning. *Journal of Educational Technology & Society*, *20*(3), 158–169.

Emirbayer, M., & Mische, A. (1998). What is agency? *American Journal of Sociology*, *103*(4), 962–1023. doi:10.1086/231294

Essa, S. G., Celik, T., & Human-Hendricks, N. E. (2023). Personalized adaptive learning technologies based on machine learning techniques to identify learning styles: A systematic literature review. *IEEE Access: Practical Innovations, Open Solutions*, *11*, 48392–48409. doi:10.1109/ACCESS.2023.3276439

Estivill-Castro, V. (2002). Why so many clustering algorithms: A position paper. *SIGKDD Explorations*, *4*(1), 65–75. doi:10.1145/568574.568575

Eteläpelto, A., & Lahti, J. (2008). The resources and obstacles of creative collaboration in a long-term learning community. *Thinking Skills and Creativity*, *3*(3), 226–240. doi:10.1016/j.tsc.2008.09.003

Fawns, T. (2019). Postdigital education in design and practice. *Postdigital Science and Education*, *1*(1), 132–145. doi:10.1007/s42438-018-0021-8

Fraser, J., Papaioannou, I., & Lemon, O. (2018). Spoken conversational AI in video games: Emotional dialogue management increases user engagement. *Proceedings of the 18th International Conference on Intelligent Virtual Agents*, (pp. 179–184). ACM. 10.1145/3267851.3267896

Gale, J., Alemdar, M., Boice, K., Hernández, D., Newton, S., Edwards, D., & Usselman, M. (2022). Student agency in a high school computer science course. *Journal for STEM Education Research*, *5*(2), 270–301. doi:10.1007/s41979-022-00071-9

Gallagher, M. A., Parsons, S. A., & Vaughn, M. (2022). Adaptive teaching in mathematics: A review of the literature. *Educational Review*, *74*(2), 298–320. doi:10.1080/00131911.2020.1722065

García-Escudero, L. A., Gordaliza, A., Matrán, C., & Mayo-Iscar, A. (2010). A review of robust clustering methods. *Advances in Data Analysis and Classification*, *4*(2), 89–109. doi:10.1007/s11634-010-0064-5

Gartner. (2022). *Adaptive AI*. Gartner. https://web.archive.org/web/ 20221130080642/https://www.gartner.com/en/information-technology/glossary/adaptiveai

Gibson, S. A., & Ross, P. (2016). Teachers' professional noticing. *Theory into Practice*, *55*(3), 180–188. doi:10.1080/00405841.2016.1173996

Groenewald, E., & le Roux, A. (2023). Student agency: Two students' agentic actions in challenging oppressive practices on a diverse university campus. *Higher Education Research & Development*, *42*(1), 48–61. doi:10.1080/07294360.2022.2052817

Grunschel, C., Patrzek, J., & Fries, S. (2013). Exploring different types of academic delayers: A latent profile analysis. *Learning and Individual Differences*, *23*, 225–233. doi:10.1016/j.lindif.2012.09.014

Hauptman, A. I., Schelble, B. G., McNeese, N. J., & Madathil, K. C. (2023). Adapt and overcome: Perceptions of adaptive autonomous agents for human-AI teaming. *Computers in Human Behavior*, *138*, 107451. doi:10.1016/j.chb.2022.107451

Heilala, V. (2022). *Learning analytics with learning and analytics: Advancing student agency analytics* (JYU Dissertations 512) [Doctoral dissertation, University of Jyväskylä].

Heilala, V., Jääskelä, P., Kärkkäinen, T., & Saarela, M. (2020). Understanding the study experiences of students in low agency profile: Towards a smart education approach. In A. El Moussati, K. Kpalma, M. G. Belkasmi, M. Saber, & S. Guégan (Eds.), *Advances in Smart Technologies Applications and Case Studies* (pp. 498–508). Springer International Publishing. doi:10.1007/978-3-030-53187-4_54

Heilala, V., Jääskelä, P., Saarela, M., Kuula, A.-S., Eskola, A., & Kärkkäinen, T. (2022). "Sitting at the Stern and Holding the Rudder": Teachers' Reflections on Action in Higher Education Based on Student Agency Analytics. In L. Chechurin (Ed.), *Digital Teaching and Learning in Higher Education: Developing and Disseminating Skills for Blended Learning* (pp. 71–91). Palgrave Macmillan. doi:10.1007/978-3-031-00801-6_4

Heilala, V., Saarela, M., Jääskelä, P., & Kärkkäinen, T. (2020). Course satisfaction in engineering education through the lens of student agency analytics. *2020 IEEE Frontiers in Education Conference (FIE)*, (pp. 1–9). IEEE.

Hernandez, J., Muratet, M., Pierotti, M., & Carron, T. (2022). Enhancement of a gamified situational judgment test scoring system for behavioral assessment. *2022 International Conference on Advanced Learning Technologies (ICALT)*, (pp. 374–378). IEEE. 10.1109/ICALT55010.2022.00116

Huber, P. J. (1981). *Robust statistics*. John Wiley & Sons. doi:10.1002/0471725250

Ianculescu, M., & Alexandru, A. (2020). Microservices–A catalyzer for better managing healthcare data empowerment. *Studies in Informatics and Control, 29*(2), 231–242. doi:10.24846/v29i2y202008

Ifenthaler, D., & Schumacher, C. (2016). Student perceptions of privacy principles for learning analytics. *Educational Technology Research and Development. Educational Technology Research and Development, 64*(5), 923–938. doi:10.1007/s11423-016-9477-y

Ifenthaler, D., Schumacher, C., & Kuzilek, J. (2023). Investigating students' use of self-assessments in higher education using learning analytics. *Journal of Computer Assisted Learning, 39*(1), 255–268. doi:10.1111/jcal.12744

Jääskelä, P., Heilala, V., Kärkkäinen, T., & Häkkinen, P. (2021). Student agency analytics: Learning analytics as a tool for analysing student agency in higher education. *Behaviour & Information Technology, 40*(8), 790–808. doi:10.1080/0144929X.2020.1725130

Jääskelä, P., Heilala, V., Vaara, E., Arvaja, M., Eskola, A., Tolvanen, A., Kärkkäinen, T., & Poikkeus, A.-M. (2022). *Situational agency of business administration students in higher education: A mixed methods analysis of multidimensional agency* [Conference presentation]. NERA22 Conference, Reykjavık, Iceland.

Jääskelä, P., Poikkeus, A.-M., Häkkinen, P., Vasalampi, K., Rasku-Puttonen, H., & Tolvanen, A. (2020). Students' agency profiles in relation to student-perceived teaching practices in university courses. *International Journal of Educational Research, 103*, 101604. doi:10.1016/j.ijer.2020.101604

Jääskelä, P., Poikkeus, A.-M., Vasalampi, K., Valleala, U. M., & Rasku-Puttonen, H. (2017). Assessing agency of university students: Validation of the AUS scale. *Studies in Higher Education, 42*(11), 1–19. doi:10.1080/03075079.2015.1130693

Jääskelä, P., Tolvanen, A., Marin, V., Häkkinen, P., & Poikkeus, A.-M. (2018). *Students' agency experiences in finnish and spanish university courses* [Conference presentation]. European Conference on Educational Research (ECER), Bolzano, Italy.

Jääskelä, P., Tolvanen, A., Marın, V. I., & Poikkeus, A.-M. (2023). Assessment of students' agency in Finnish and Spanish university courses: Analysis of measurement invariance. *International Journal of Educational Research, 118*, 102140. doi:10.1016/j.ijer.2023.102140

Jamieson, D. (2018). Animal agency. *The Harvard Review of Philosophy, 25*, 111–126. doi:10.5840/harvardreview201892518

Jia, L., Yuen, W. L., Ong, Q., & Theseira, W. E. (2023). Pitfalls of self-reported measures of self-control: Surprising insights from extreme debtors. *Journal of Personality, 91*(2), 369–382. doi:10.1111/jopy.12733 PMID:35556246

Jörg, T., Davis, B., & Nickmans, G. (2007). Towards a new, complexity science of learning and education. *Educational Research Review, 2*(2), 145–156. doi:10.1016/j.edurev.2007.09.002

Kärkkäinen, T., & Heikkola, E. (2004). Robust formulations for training multilayer perceptrons. *Neural Computation*, *16*(4), 837–862. doi:10.1162/089976604322860721

Kärner, T., Warwas, J., & Schumann, S. (2021). A learning analytics approach to address heterogeneity in the classroom: The teachers' diagnostic support system. *Technology Knowledge and Learning*, *26*(1), 31–52. doi:10.1007/s10758-020-09448-4

Khosravi, H., Shum, S. B., Chen, G., Conati, C., Tsai, Y.-S., Kay, J., Knight, S., Martinez-Maldonado, R., Sadiq, S., & Gašević, D. (2022). Explainable artificial intelligence in education. *Computers and Education: Artificial Intelligence*, *3*, 100074.

Klemenčič, M. (2015). What is student agency? An ontological exploration in the context of research on student engagement. In M. Klemenčič, S. Bergan, & R. Primožič (Eds.), *Student engagement in Europe: Society, higher education and student governance* (pp. 11–29). Council of Europe Publishing.

Klemenčič, M. (2017). From student engagement to student agency: Conceptual considerations of European policies on student-centered learning in higher education. *Higher Education Policy*, *30*(1), 69–85. doi:10.1057/s41307-016-0034-4

Kosch, T., Welsch, R., Chuang, L., & Schmidt, A. (2023). The placebo effect of artificial intelligence in human–computer interaction. *ACM Transactions on Computer-Human Interaction*, *29*(6), 1–32. doi:10.1145/3529225

Kuhn, M., & Johnson, K. (2019). *Feature engineering and selection: A practical approach for predictive models*. Chapman Hall/CRC. doi:10.1201/9781315108230

Kumar, A., & Kumar, R. (2018). Adaptive artificial intelligence for automatic identification of defect in the angular contact bearing. *Neural Computing & Applications*, *29*(8), 277–287. doi:10.1007/s00521-017-3123-4

LaFlair, G., Yancey, K., Settles, B., & von Davier, A. A. (2023). Computational psychometrics for digital-first assessments: A blend of ML and psychometrics for item generation and scoring. In V. Yaneva & M. von Davier (Eds.), *Advancing natural language processing in educational assessment* (pp. 107–123). Routledge. doi:10.4324/9781003278658-9

Laverghetta, A. Jr, & Licato, J. (2023). Generating better items for cognitive assessments using large language models. *Proceedings of the 18th Workshop on Innovative Use of NLP for Building Educational Applications (BEA 2023)*, (pp. 414–428). ACM. 10.18653/v1/2023.bea-1.34

Li, S., & Gu, X. (2023). Based on literature review and Delphi–AHP method. *Journal of Educational Technology & Society*, *26*(1), 187–202.

Lim, F. V., & Nguyen, T. T. H. (2023). 'If you have the freedom, you don't need to even think hard' – Considerations in designing for student agency through digital multimodal composing in the language classroom. *Language and Education*, *37*(4), 409–427. doi:10.1080/09500782.2022.2107875

Linja, J., Hämäläinen, J., Nieminen, P., & Kärkkäinen, T. (2023). Feature selection for distance-based regression: An umbrella review and a one-shot wrapper. *Neurocomputing*, *518*, 344–359. doi:10.1016/j.neucom.2022.11.023

Lipponen, L., & Kumpulainen, K. (2011). Acting as accountable authors: Creating interactional spaces for agency work in teacher education. *Teaching and Teacher Education*, *27*(5), 812–819. doi:10.1016/j.tate.2011.01.001

Liu, P., Yuan, W., Fu, J., Jiang, Z., Hayashi, H., & Neubig, G. (2023). Pre-train, prompt, and predict: A systematic survey of prompting methods in natural language processing. *ACM Computing Surveys*, *55*(9), 1–35. doi:10.1145/3560815

Lundberg, S. M., & Lee, S.-I. (2017). A unified approach to interpreting model predictions. *NIPS'17: Proceedings of the 31st International Conference on Neural Information Processing Systems*, (pp. 4768–4777). ACM.

Mameli, C., Grazia, V., & Molinari, L. (2021). The emotional faces of student agency. *Journal of Applied Developmental Psychology*, *77*, 101352. doi:10.1016/j.appdev.2021.101352

Mansouri, B., Roozkhosh, A., & Farbeh, H. (2021). A survey on implementations of adaptive AI in serious games for enhancing player engagement. *2021 International Serious Games Symposium (ISGS)*, (pp. 48–53). IEEE. 10.1109/ISGS54702.2021.9684760

Martin, F., Chen, Y., Moore, R. L., & Westine, C. D. (2020). Systematic review of adaptive learning research designs, context, strategies, and technologies from 2009 to 2018. *Educational Technology Research and Development. Educational Technology Research and Development*, *68*(4), 1903–1929. doi:10.1007/s11423-020-09793-2 PMID:32837122

Matthews, A. (2019). Design as a discipline for postdigital learning and teaching: Bricolage and actor-network theory. *Postdigital Science and Education*, *1*(2), 413–426. doi:10.1007/s42438-019-00036-z

Membrive, A., Silva, N., Rochera, M. J., & Merino, I. (2022). Advancing the conceptualization of learning trajectories: A review of learning across contexts. *Learning, Culture and Social Interaction*, *37*, 100658. doi:10.1016/j.lcsi.2022.100658

Mislevy, R. J. (2019). On integrating psychometrics and learning analytics in complex assessments. In H. Jiao, R. W. Lissitz, & A. van Wie (Eds.), *Data analytics and psychometrics* (pp. 1–52). Information Age Publishing.

Mislevy, R. J., & Bolsinova, M. (2021). Concepts and models from psychometrics. In A. A. von Davier, R. J. Mislevy, & J. Hao (Eds.), *Computational psychometrics: New methodologies for a new generation of digital learning and assessment: With examples in R and Python* (pp. 81–107). Springer International Publishing. doi:10.1007/978-3-030-74394-9_6

Moshkovitz, M., Dasgupta, S., Rashtchian, C., & Frost, N. (2020). Explainable k-means and kmedians clustering. In H. D. Iii, & A. Singh (Eds.), *Proceedings of the 37th international conference on machine learning* (pp. 7055–7065). PMLR.

Mukul, E., & Buÿüközkan, G. (2023). Digital transformation in education: A systematic review of education 4.0. *Technological Forecasting and Social Change*, *194*, 122664. doi:10.1016/j.techfore.2023.122664

Nguyen, A., Ngo, H. N., Hong, Y., Dang, B., & Nguyen, B.-P. T. (2023). Ethical principles for artificial intelligence in education. *Education and Information Technologies*, *28*(4), 4221–4241. doi:10.1007/s10639-022-11316-w PMID:36254344

Niemelä, M., Kärkkäinen, T., Ayrämö, S., Ronimus, M., Richardson, U., & Lyytinen, H. (2020). Game learning analytics for understanding reading skills in transparent writing system. *British Journal of Educational Technology*, *51*(6), 2376–2390. doi:10.1111/bjet.12916

Nieminen, J. H., Tai, J., Boud, D., & Henderson, M. (2022). Student agency in feedback: Beyond the individual. *Assessment & Evaluation in Higher Education*, *47*(1), 95–108. doi:10.1080/02602938.2021.1887080

OECD. (2019). *Concept note: Student agency for 2030*. OECD.

Ouyang, F., & Jiao, P. (2021). Artificial intelligence in education: The three paradigms. *Computers and Education: Artificial Intelligence*, *2*, 100020. doi:10.1016/j.caeai.2021.100020

Park, H., & Zhang, J. (2022). Learning analytics for teacher noticing and scaffolding: Facilitating knowledge building progress in science. In A. Weinberger, W. Chen, D. Hernández-Leo, & B. Chen (Eds.), *Proceedings of the 15th international conference on Computer-Supported collaborative learning - CSCL 2022* (pp. 147–154). International Society of the Learning Sciences.

Park, Y., & Jo, I.-H. (2019). Factors that affect the success of learning analytics dashboards. *Educational Technology Research and Development. Educational Technology Research and Development*, *67*(6), 1547–1571. doi:10.1007/s11423-019-09693-0

Peeters, R. (2020). The agency of algorithms: Understanding human-algorithm interaction in administrative decision-making. *Information Polity*, *25*(4), 507–522. doi:10.3233/IP-200253

Penttilä, S., Kah, P., Ratava, J., & Eskelinen, H. (2019). Artificial neural network controlled GMAW system: Penetration and quality assurance in a multi-pass butt weld application. *International Journal of Advanced Manufacturing Technology*, *105*(7), 3369–3385. doi:10.1007/s00170-019-04424-4

Pinkwart, N. (2016). Another 25 years of AIED? Challenges and opportunities for intelligent educational technologies of the future. *International Journal of Artificial Intelligence in Education*, *26*(2), 771–783. doi:10.1007/s40593-016-0099-7

Poojitha, S., Kalyani, Likitha, & Venkatesh, K. (2023). ML framework for efficient assessment and prediction of human performance in collaborative learning environments. [TURCOMAT]. *Turkish Journal of Computer and Mathematics Education*, *14*(2), 527–536.

Rooney, D., & Boud, D. (2019). Toward a pedagogy for professional noticing: Learning through observation. *Vocations and Learning*, *12*(3), 441–457. doi:10.1007/s12186-019-09222-3

Saarela, M., Heilala, V., Jääskelä, P., Rantakaulio, A., & Kärkkäinen, T. (2021). Explainable student agency analytics. *IEEE Access : Practical Innovations, Open Solutions*, *9*, 137444–137459. doi:10.1109/ACCESS.2021.3116664

Saarela, M., & Jauhiainen, S. (2021). Comparison of feature importance measures as explanations for classification models. *SN Applied Sciences*, *3*(2), 1–12. doi:10.1007/s42452-021-04148-9

Safdari, M., Serapio-García, G., Crepy, C., Fitz, S., Romero, P., Sun, L., Abdulhai, M., Faust, A., & Matarić, M. (2023). *Personality traits in large language models*. arXiv. https://doi.org//arXiv.2307.00184 doi:10.48550

Schlosser, M. E. (2015). Agency. In E. N. Zalta (Ed.), *Stanford encyclopedia of philosophy*.

Schumacher, C., & Ifenthaler, D. (2018). Features students really expect from learning analytics. *Computers in Human Behavior*, *78*, 397–407. doi:10.1016/j.chb.2017.06.030

Schunk, D., & Zimmerman, B. (2012). Competence and control beliefs: Distinguishing the means and ends. In P. A. Alexander & P. H. Winne (Eds.), *Handbook of educational psychology* (pp. 349–368). Routledge.

Shapley, L. S. (1953). A value for n-person games. In H. W. Kuhn & A. W. Tucker (Eds.), Contributions to the theory of games (AM-28), volume II (pp. 307–318). Princeton University Press. doi:10.1515/9781400881970-018

Shen, S., Yu, C., Zhang, K., & Ci, S. (2021). Adaptive artificial intelligence for resource-constrained connected vehicles in cybertwin-driven 6G network. *IEEE Internet of Things Journal*, *8*(22), 16269–16278. doi:10.1109/JIOT.2021.3101231

Shortliffe, E. H., Davis, R., Axline, S. G., Buchanan, B. G., Green, C. C., & Cohen, S. N. (1975). Computer-based consultations in clinical therapeutics: Explanation and rule acquisition capabilities of the MYCIN system. *Computers and Biomedical Research, an International Journal*, *8*(4), 303–320. doi:10.1016/0010-4809(75)90009-9 PMID:1157471

Shute, V., & Towle, B. (2003). Adaptive E-Learning. *Educational Psychologist*, *38*(2), 105–114. doi:10.1207/S15326985EP3802_5

Sikström, P., Valentini, C., Sivunen, A., & Kärkkäinen, T. (2022). How pedagogical agents communicate with students: A two-phase systematic review. *Computers & Education*, *188*, 104564. doi:10.1016/j.compedu.2022.104564

Silvast, A., & Virtanen, M. J. (2023). On Theory–Methods packages in science and technology studies. *Science, Technology & Human Values*, *48*(1), 167–189. doi:10.1177/01622439211040241

Standen, P. J., Brown, D. J., Taheri, M., Galvez Trigo, M. J., Boulton, H., Burton, A., Hallewell, M. J., Lathe, J. G., Shopland, N., Blanco Gonzalez, M. A., Kwiatkowska, G. M., Milli, E., Cobello, S., Mazzucato, A., Traversi, M., & Hortal, E. (2020). An evaluation of an adaptive learning system based on multimodal affect recognition for learners with intellectual disabilities. *British Journal of Educational Technology*, *51*(5), 1748–1765. doi:10.1111/bjet.13010

Stenalt, M. H. (2021). Researching student agency in digital education as if the social aspects matter: Students' experience of participatory dimensions of online peer assessment. *Assessment & Evaluation in Higher Education*, *46*(4), 644–658. doi:10.1080/02602938.2020.1798355

Stenalt, M. H., & Lassesen, B. (2021). Does student agency benefit student learning? A systematic review of higher education research. *Assessment & Evaluation in Higher Education*, *47*(5), 1–17.

Tedre, M., & Vartiainen, H. (2023). K-12 computing education for the AI era: From data literacy to data agency. *Proceedings of the 2023 Conference on Innovation and Technology in Computer Science Education*. ACM. 10.1145/3587102.3593796

Tempelaar, D., Rienties, B., & Nguyen, Q. (2020). Subjective data, objective data and the role of bias in predictive modelling: Lessons from a dispositional learning analytics application. *PLoS One*, *15*(6), e0233977. doi:10.1371/journal.pone.0233977 PMID:32530954

Thomas, M. L., & Duffy, J. R. (2023). Advances in psychometric theory: Item response theory, generalizability theory, and cognitive psychometrics. In APA handbook of neuropsychology, volume 2: Neuroscience and neuromethods (vol. 2) (pp. 665–680). American Psychological Association.

Tzimas, D., & Demetriadis, S. (2021). Ethical issues in learning analytics: A review of the field. *Educational Technology Research and Development. Educational Technology Research and Development*, *69*(2), 1101–1133. doi:10.1007/s11423-021-09977-4

Uher, J. (2021). Psychometrics is not measurement: Unraveling a fundamental misconception in quantitative psychology and the complex network of its underlying fallacies. *Journal of Theoretical and Philosophical Psychology*, *41*(1), 58–84. doi:10.1037/teo0000176

Vandewaetere, M., Desmet, P., & Clarebout, G. (2011). The contribution of learner characteristics in the development of computer-based adaptive learning environments. *Computers in Human Behavior*, *27*(1), 118–130. doi:10.1016/j.chb.2010.07.038

Vartiainen, H., Pellas, L., Kahila, J., Valtonen, T., & Tedre, M. (2022). Pre-service teachers' insights on data agency. *New Media & Society*. doi:10.1177/14614448221079626

Vaughn, M. (2020). What is student agency and why is it needed now more than ever? *Theory into Practice*, *59*(2), 109–118. doi:10.1080/00405841.2019.1702393

Verdonck, T., Baesens, B., Oskarsd'ottir, M., & vanden Broucke, S. (2021). Special issue on feature engineering editorial. *Machine Learning*. doi:10.1007/s10994-021-06042-2

Vieira, C., Parsons, P., & Byrd, V. (2018). Visual learning analytics of educational data: A systematic literature review and research agenda. *Computers & Education*, *122*, 119–135. doi:10.1016/j.compedu.2018.03.018

von Davier, A. A., Mislevy, R. J., & Hao, J. (2021). Introduction to computational psychometrics: Towards a principled integration of data science and machine learning techniques into psychometrics. In A. A. von Davier, R. J. Mislevy, & J. Hao (Eds.), *Computational psychometrics: New methodologies for a new generation of digital learning and assessment: With examples in R and Python* (pp. 1–6). Springer International Publishing. doi:10.1007/978-3-030-74394-9_1

White, J., Fu, Q., Hays, S., Sandborn, M., Olea, C., Gilbert, H., Elnashar, A., Spencer-Smith, J., & Schmidt, D. C. (2023). *A prompt pattern catalog to enhance prompt engineering with ChatGPT*. arXiv. https://doi.org//arXiv.2302.11382 doi:10.48550

Wigfield, A., Cambria, J., & Eccles, J. S. (2019). Motivation in education. In R. M. Ryan (Ed.), The oxford handbook of human motivation (second, pp. 443–462). Oxford University Press.

Younes, S. S. (2021). Examining the effectiveness of using adaptive AI-enabled e-learning during the pandemic of COVID-19. *Journal of Healthcare Engineering*, *2021*, 3928326. doi:10.1155/2021/3928326 PMID:34567481

Zehner, F., Eichmann, B., Deribo, T., Harrison, S., Bengs, D., Andersen, N., & Hahnel, C. (2021). Applying psychometric modeling to aid feature engineering in predictive log-data analytics: The NAEP EDM competition. *Journal of Educational Data Mining*, *13*(2), 80–107.

Zheng, L., Niu, J., Zhong, L., & Gyasi, J. F. (2021). The effectiveness of artificial intelligence on learning achievement and learning perception: A meta-analysis. *Interactive Learning Environments*, 1–15.

Chapter 3
Adaptive AI for Dynamic Cybersecurity Systems:
Enhancing Protection in a Rapidly Evolving Digital Landscap

C. V. Suresh Babu
https://orcid.org/0000-0002-8474-2882
Hindustan Institute of Technolgy and Science, India

Andrew Simon P.
Hindustan Institute of Technology and Science, India

ABSTRACT

This chapter offers a concise roadmap for navigating the dynamic cybersecurity landscape using Adaptive AI. Beginning with a comprehensive introduction that sets the stage, it delves into the intricacies of the cybersecurity landscape and categorizes common threats in topic two. Topic three showcases the transformative potential of Adaptive AI, focusing on real-time threat detection, proactive defense, and continuous learning. Topic four provides enlightening case studies, offering practical insights. Topic five addresses the practicalities of implementing Adaptive AI, covering considerations and best practices. Topic six explores AI's future in cybersecurity. Lastly, topic seven summarizes findings, emphasizes key takeaways, and recommends utilizing Adaptive AI to enhance dynamic cybersecurity. This book is a valuable guide for safeguarding digital assets in the evolving cyber landscape.

1. INTRODUCTION

A new area called "Safeguarding Digital Landscapes in the Era of Evolving Threats" blends cybersecurity with artificial intelligence to defend digital landscapes against ever-evolving attacks (Suresh Babu. C.V., 2022). This strategy uses real-time data analysis and machine learning algorithms to adapt to new and sophisticated threats. Adaptive AI strengthens the robustness of cybersecurity measures by continuously learning from patterns and anomalies, making it a vital weapon in the fight against constantly evolving

DOI: 10.4018/979-8-3693-0230-9.ch003

cyberthreats. This introduction lays the groundwork for an examination of how cybersecurity practises are being transformed by adaptive AI to protect our digital environment (Thomas, G et al.,2023).

1.1 Background

The history of "Adaptive AI for Dynamic Cybersecurity" is rooted in the increasingly complex and varied cyberthreats that both persons and organisations must deal with in the current digital environment. Traditional methods to cybersecurity sometimes rely on rigid rule-based frameworks that find it difficult to keep up with the quick growth of assaults. The creation of adaptive AI solutions was necessary to close this security effectiveness gap.

The following are some important aspects of cybersecurity that call for adaptive AI:

- **Evolving Threat Landscape:** Cyber dangers are continuously changing, as hackers employ cutting-edge methods and find inventive ways to attack holes.
- **Data overload:** Due to the overwhelming amount of data produced in digital settings, it is difficult for human operators to manually identify hazards and take appropriate action.

Speed of Attacks: Attacks may happen quickly online, and real-time defence against them frequently requires automated reactions (Thomas, G et al.,2023)..

1.2 Objectives of the Chapter

The following may be used to sum up the goal of the chapter "Adaptive AI for Dynamic Cybersecurity: Safeguarding Digital Landscapes in the Era of Evolving Threats":

- **Recognize Adaptive AI:** Giving readers a thorough knowledge of adaptive artificial intelligence (AI) in the context of cybersecurity is the goal of this article. Explaining the key ideas, technology, and approaches concerned is part of this. (Doshi et al.,2019)
- **Understanding the Need:** To explain why adaptive AI is important for cybersecurity. This entails exposing the constantly shifting nature of cyber threats and addressing the limits of conventional cybersecurity techniques.

Application Exploration: To investigate various adaptive AI applications and use cases in cybersecurity. Examples of actual instances when organisations have (Thomas, G et al., 2023).

1.3 Scope and Significance

The following might be used to summarise the focus and importance of the chapter "Adaptive AI for Dynamic Cybersecurity: Safeguarding Digital Landscapes in the Era of Evolving Threats":

Scope:

- Full Coverage: To ensure that readers have a complete grasp of this important field, the chapter will provide full coverage of the ideas, technology, applications, and practical elements of adaptive AI in cybersecurity.

- Real-World Relevance: To demonstrate how adaptive AI is being used successfully in a variety of cybersecurity settings, it will go into real-world examples and case studies.

Significance:

- Enhanced Cybersecurity: Adaptive AI offers a huge leap in cybersecurity by enabling real-time detection, mitigation, and response to cyberthreats. This vastly improves digital security.
- Timely Reaction: In the age of constantly changing threats, the capacity to adjust and react quickly to fresh attack vectors is essential. Organisations are given the capabilities by adaptive AI to respond to cyberthreats in a proactive manner.

1.4 Structure of the Chapter

To create a clear and informative narrative, the chapter's structure on "Adaptive AI for Dynamic Cybersecurity: Safeguarding Digital Landscapes in the Era of Evolving Threats" might be divided into many sections. The chapter's recommended organisation is as follows:

Introduction: A brief summary of the chapter's goals. Adaptive AI's importance in contemporary cybersecurity.

Background: The development of cyber dangers and the historical backdrop of cybersecurity. Restrictions and difficulties using conventional cybersecurity techniques.

Principles of Adaptive AI: Defining adaptive AI and describing how it differs from static methods. Important elements of adaptable AI systems, including data analytics and machine learning techniques.

Cybersecurity Applications of Adaptive AI: Study of many situations and application cases where adaptive AI is having an impact. Case studies showing effective implementations across various sectors.

Conclusion: Recap of the chapter's most important lessons. Emphasis on the role that adaptive AI plays in protecting digital environments.

References: References and sources for more reading and study (Dhoni et al., 2023).

2. UNDERSTANDING THE CYBERSECURITY LANDSCAPE

In today's digitally linked world, it is essential to understand the cybersecurity environment. Understanding the numerous components, difficulties, and dynamics that influence the cybersecurity industry is necessary. Consider the following important factors:

- **Threat Actors:** Being aware that a range of actors, including nation-states, cyberterrorists, hackers, and even hostile insiders, might pose a threat to your system.
- **Attack Vectors:** Recognising the many techniques that cyber attackers employ to breach systems and data, including malware, phishing, ransomware, DDoS assaults, and social engineering.
- **Vulnerability:** Identifying flaws in technology, software, or human behaviour that hackers might exploit. Insecure password procedures and obsolete software are both examples of vulnerabilities.
- **Data protection:** Recognising the significance of protecting sensitive data and personally identifiable information (PII) in order to stop breaches and data theft (Doshi et al., 2019).

2.1 Overview of Cybersecurity Challenges

Organisations, governments, and people all face a number of difficulties in the cybersecurity landscape. Here is a summary of some of the major cybersecurity difficulties:

- **Evolving Threat Landscape:** Threat landscape is continually changing as a result of hackers' use of more advanced methods and resources. Keeping up with these constantly evolving dangers is extremely difficult.
- **Zero-Day Vulnerabilities:** There are serious dangers involved in finding and using zero-day vulnerabilities. There are no patches or remedies for these software flaws since the manufacturer is unaware of them.
- **Attacks using ransomware:** Ransomware is a common and expensive threat in which attackers encrypt data and demand a payment to decrypt it (Arockia Panimalar.S et al., 2018).

2.2 Types of Cyber Threats Faced by Common Users

Cyber risks that might jeopardise a user's personal information, financial security, and online privacy are commonplace. The following list of cyberthreats includes several that regular users run into:

- **Data Losses and Data Breaches:** Incidents involving the unintended or unauthorised disclosure, compromise, or loss of private or sensitive information are known as data losses and data breaches.
- **Denial of Service (DoS) Attacks:** Cyberattacks called denial of service attacks are designed to stop a computer system, network, or service from operating normally by flooding it with traffic or requests. Making the targeted system or service inaccessible to its intended users is the aim.
- **Distributed Denial of Service (DDoS) Attacks:** A assault known as a distributed denial of service (DDoS) uses a network of hacked computers, often known as a "botnet," to flood a target system or network with an enormous amount of traffic, overloading its capacity and rendering it inaccessible to authorised users. DDoS assaults can have detrimental effects, such as monetary losses, harm to one's reputation, and interruptions to internet services.
- **Information Theft and Cyber Espionage:** Information theft is the illegal acquisition of valuable or sensitive data for nefarious ends. And specifically carried out by nation-states, state-sponsored organisations, or other entities to get intelligence or a strategic advantage, cyber espionage is a subset of information theft (Suresh Babu, C. V. & Srisakthi, S., 2023).

2.2.1 Data Losses and Data Breaches

Incidents involving the unintended or unauthorised disclosure, compromise, or loss of private or sensitive information are known as data losses and data breaches. Although these two names are similar, they also have some key distinctions:

Loss of Data

- **Definition:** Data loss is defined as the inadvertent, accidental deletion, corruption, or destruction of data. It may happen for a number of causes, such as human mistake, hardware malfunction, software bugs, or actual physical damage to storage devices.

- **Causes:** Accidental file deletion, hardware problems including hard drive crashes, power outages, or data corruption as a result of software defects are common causes of data loss.
- **Severity:** Data loss may cause anything from little annoyances like missing a single document to more serious losses like losing large databases or crucial information.
- **Recovery:** Data loss may or may not be possible, depending on the reason and backup procedures. Data loss situations can be lessened in impact with routine backups.

Breach of data

- **Definition:** A data breach is defined as the unauthorised access, publication, or theft of private or confidential data. It may happen as a result of malevolent insiders or cybercriminals acting on purpose.
- **Causes:** Cyberattacks including hacking, phishing, malware infections, or insider threats frequently result in data breaches. Attackers aim to steal, compromise, or reveal private information.
- **Severity:** Data breaches can have serious repercussions, including monetary losses, reputational injury, fines under the law and regulations, and harm to those impacted if their personal information is revealed.
- **Recovery:** Following a data breach, recovery can be time-consuming and expensive. Organisations are required to inform the impacted people, look into the event, tighten security, and follow the law (Rana et al., 2019).

2.2.2 Denial of Service (DoS) Attacks

Cyberattacks called denial of service attacks are designed to stop a computer system, network, or service from operating normally by flooding it with traffic or requests. Making the targeted system or service inaccessible to its intended users is the aim. DoS assaults come in a variety of forms, including:

- **Volumetric Attacks:** Assaults that flood the target with a lot of traffic are known as volumetric assaults. Examples include ICMP flood attacks and UDP amplification attacks.
- **Application Layer Attacks**: These attacks prey on holes in a system's application layer by taking advantage of flaws in web services or apps.
- **Protocol-Based Attacks:** Attacks based on protocols take use of flaws in network protocols, such as SYN flood attacks that target the TCP handshake procedure.
- **DDoS (Distributed Denial of Service) assaults:** Botnets are networks of infected devices that collaborate to perform coordinated assaults (Mughal, 2018).

2.2.3 Distributed Denial of Service (DDoS) Attacks

In a distributed denial of service (DDoS) assault, a group of hacked computers—often referred to as a "botnet"—are used to overload a target system or network with a large volume of traffic, rendering it unusable for authorised users. Some of them are:

- **Multiple Sources:** DDoS assaults use a number of devices or sources that may be spread out geographically. By concurrently sending traffic to the target from every device in the botnet, it is challenging to stop the assault by merely blocking one IP address.
- **Amplification:** Attackers frequently employ amplification techniques to increase the amount of traffic they can produce. This entails sending a modest request that triggers a substantially bigger response from the target by taking advantage of flaws in various internet protocols.
- **High Traffic Volume:** DDoS assaults are well-known for their capacity to produce a significant volume of traffic, which can overwhelm the target's servers, routers, and internet connection. Normal operations are disrupted by the volume of traffic, which may also cause service interruptions (Suresh Babu, C. V. & Srisakthi, S., 2023).

2.2.4 Information Theft and Cyber Espionage

Cyber espionage and information theft are criminal actions in the field of cybersecurity that entail the theft of sensitive information or intelligence for a variety of reasons, such as financial, political, or military benefit. These actions can have major repercussions for security, privacy, and national interests and frequently target organisations, governments, or specific people. An overview of data theft and online espionage is provided below:

Theft of Information:

Information theft is the illegal acquisition of valuable or sensitive data for nefarious ends. It can include a variety of data kinds, including:

- Intellectual property theft is the act of stealing from businesses confidential information, trade secrets, data used in research and development, or product designs. Such theft may be done to benefit financially or to unfairly advantage rivals.
- Cybercriminals may target people in order to steal their personal information, including Social Security numbers, credit card information, and login passwords. These details may be sold on the dark web or employed in fraud and identity theft.
- Theft of Financial Data: Criminals may try to take hold of wallets containing cryptocurrencies or bank account numbers in order to steal money. Unauthorised transactions, money theft, or financial ruin may result from this.

Internet espionage

Specifically carried out by nation-states, state-sponsored organisations, or other entities to get intelligence or a strategic advantage, cyber espionage is a subset of information theft. Cyber espionage's salient features include:

- Government or state-sponsored organisations frequently take part in cyber espionage in order to acquire intelligence, keep track on geopolitical events, or gain an economic edge by stealing private information.
- Espionage operations frequently use advanced tactics, such as advanced persistent threats (APTs), to avoid detection and sustain access to target networks for a lengthy period of time.

- Espionage has many potential targets, including the government, the military, the energy industry, and the technological and financial industries. The culprits' strategic goals determine the targets they choose (Suresh Babu, C. V. & Yadav, S., 2023).

3. THE POWER OF ADAPTIVE AI IN CYBERSECURITY

By offering dynamic and proactive defence mechanisms against a constantly changing array of cyber threats, adaptive AI significantly contributes to improving cybersecurity. Its strength comes in its capacity to quickly pick up on new threats and weaknesses and adapt, respond, and learn. The following are some significant ways that adaptive AI improves cybersecurity:

- **Analysis and detection of threats:** System behaviour and network traffic may be continually monitored by adaptive AI systems, which can spot trends that could be signs of attacks or abnormalities. Large datasets may be analysed by machine learning algorithms to find minor indications of cyberattacks, even ones that human operators would miss.
- **Animal Behaviour Analysis:** Adaptive AI has the ability to build a baseline for typical system and user behaviour. Any departures from this norm may result in notifications or automated responses.
- It is capable of spotting odd user actions such unauthorised login attempts, strange data transfers, and suspicious data transfers.
- **Intelligent Threat Detection:** By detecting unique patterns or behaviours, adaptive AI may recognise sophisticated threats including zero-day vulnerabilities, polymorphic malware, and insider attacks. It may combine information from many sources to produce a thorough picture of possible hazards (S. Chakrabarty et al., 2020).

3.1 Introduction to Adaptive Artificial Intelligence

3.1.1 Artificial Intelligence (AI) Adaptive: A Dynamic Method for Solving Issues

The development of artificial intelligence (AI) in recent years has been astounding, revolutionising how we use technology and approach challenging challenges (Suresh Babu. C.V., 2022). The flexibility of AI is one of its most intriguing and promising characteristics. An AI system is referred described as being adaptive if it has the ability to learn, develop, and modify its behaviour and reactions in response to new information and conditions. The capacity to learn from experience and adjust to novel circumstances is a key component of human intelligence, and this adaptability mirrors it.

In this introduction, we'll look at the fundamental ideas behind adaptable AI, some of its applications in different fields, and the important technologies that make it possible.

3.1.2 Principles of Adaptive AI

- **Machine learning**: Machine learning, a kind of artificial intelligence that enables computers to identify patterns, forecast outcomes, and enhance performance over time, is at the core of adaptive AI. Huge datasets may be analysed by machine learning algorithms to provide insightful information that can help with decision-making.

- **Continuous Learning:** After a first training period, adaptive AI systems continue to learn. They are built to continually learn from fresh data, enabling them to stay current and adjust to changing circumstances.

Adaptive AI applications include:

There are several uses for adaptive AI in various fields and sectors, including:

- **Healthcare:** Medical data analysis using adaptive AI can help with patient outcome prediction, therapy planning, and diagnosis. It can modify its suggestions in light of fresh scientific discoveries and patient-specific information.
- **Finance:** Adaptive AI is utilised in the financial industry for algorithmic trading, risk assessment, fraud detection, and individualised financial advising. It adjusts to changes in regulations and market situations.

3.1.3 Adaptive AI-Enabling Technologies

The following technologies help AI systems become more flexible:

- **Deep Learning:** By allowing AI to tackle complicated tasks and develop hierarchical representations from data, deep neural networks increase flexibility.
- **Reinforcement Learning:** This method enables AI agents to discover the best course of action via trial and error, customising their tactics to maximise rewards across a range of settings.
- **Natural language processing:** Adaptive AI systems in chatbots and language models employ natural language processing (NLP) to interpret and respond to human language while adjusting to various conversational circumstances (Arockia Panimalar.S et al.,2018).

3.2 AI in Real-time Threat Detection and Analysis

In the field of cybersecurity, AI (Artificial Intelligence) is essential for real-time threat identification and analysis. AI-powered solutions are now crucial for swiftly and efficiently recognising and responding to security problems as cyber threats continue to grow in sophistication and scope. Here is an example of how AI is used for real-time threat analysis and detection:

- **Threat intelligence using machine learning:** AI is capable of processing enormous volumes of threat intelligence data from several sources, including security feeds, forums on the dark web, and information on previous attacks. Machine learning algorithms can spot new dangers and provide users early notice of any security holes or attack routes.
- **Real-time surveillance and warning:** AI systems continually and in real-time monitor system records and network traffic. These systems have the ability to warn or notify security professionals when a possible threat is identified, enabling quick investigation and action.
- **Anomaly Detection:** AI-driven systems establish a baseline of normal network and user behavior. They continuously monitor network traffic, system logs, and user activities. When deviations from the established baseline occur, AI algorithms can quickly identify these anomalies as potential

threats. Examples include detecting unusual data access patterns, login attempts from unfamiliar locations, or unexpected changes in system configurations (Ribence Kadel et al., 2022).

3.3 AI in Proactive Defense Mechanisms

In the subject of cybersecurity, AI (Artificial Intelligence) is essential for proactive defence measures. The goal of proactive defence is to foresee and stop cyberthreats before they have a chance to disrupt systems, networks, and data. Using AI in proactive defence strategies looks like this:

- **Predictability analysis:** In order to spot trends and foresee new threats in the future, AI may analyse historical data, including information on previous cyberattacks and threat intelligence.
- AI may give early warnings about new hazards by seeing patterns and abnormalities in data, enabling organisations to take precautionary action.
- **Gathering threat intelligence:** The gathering and analysis of threat intelligence from a variety of sources, such as security feeds, forums on the dark web, and malware repositories, may be automated using AI-powered solutions. Organisations can use this data to keep informed about potential threats and security holes.
- **Detection of Zero-Day Threats:** With the use of system behaviour analysis and the detection of odd or suspicious behaviours that can point to an unidentified attack, AI can locate probable zero-day vulnerabilities. This makes it possible for businesses to reduce risk in advance (S. Pirbhulal et al., 2022).

3.4 Continuous Learning and Adaptation in AI-driven Systems

AI-driven systems must have the ability to continuously learn and adapt in order to advance, change, and maintain their effectiveness. These talents are very useful in a number of fields, including as cybersecurity, robotics, machine learning, and natural language processing. The operation of continuous learning and adaptability in AI-driven systems is as follows:

- **Models for machine learning:** Continuous learning in machine learning entails upgrading models with fresh data to boost their efficiency and precision. Online learning algorithms are examples of adaptive algorithms that may modify their model parameters in real-time as they are fed new data. Models can adapt to shifting trends, tastes, or conditions thanks to continuous learning.
- **Cybersecurity:** Continuous learning is a technique used by AI-driven security systems to adapt to changing threats. For instance, anomaly detection systems regularly upgrade their models to recognise new attack patterns and methodologies.
- **Security planning:** Platforms for security orchestration driven by AI continually modify incident response procedures in light of the changing threat environment and information particular to each organisation (Srivastava et al., 2023).

4. INTEGRATING AI AND CYBERSECURITY: CASE STUDIES

- **Threat Detection Driven by AI:** Artificial intelligence (AI) and machine learning (ML) techniques are used to detect and address cybersecurity threats and vulnerabilities. This practise is known as AI-driven threat detection. It takes a preventative stance towards cybersecurity and uses AI algorithms to continually monitor, examine, and react to possible threats in real-time.
- **Adaptive AI in Protecting Critical Infrastructure:** Critical infrastructure, such as power grids, water supply systems, transportation networks, and communication systems, are crucially protected against cyberthreats and physical weaknesses by adaptive AI. It is crucial to have sophisticated and adaptable security measures in place since critical infrastructure is a prominent target for both physical and cyberattacks.
- **AI-powered incident response:** AI-powered incident response is a method of dealing with cybersecurity events and breaches that makes use of artificial intelligence (AI) and machine learning (ML) technology to more quickly and effectively identify, assess, and react to security risks. Through the automation of some jobs and the provision of quicker and more precise event detection and response, this strategy seeks to enhance human capacities (Y. Siriwardhana et al., 2021).

4.1 Case Study 1: AI-Driven Threat Detection in a Financial Institution

Background: One of the biggest financial companies in the world, JPMorgan Chase & Co. provides a variety of financial services to millions of clients (JP Morgan.,2018). The bank, a significant player in the financial sector, must constantly address cybersecurity issues, particularly the need to fight fraud.

Problem: Enhancing JPMorgan Chase's capacity to identify and stop fraudulent activity within its huge client base was necessary. Traditional rule-based systems were having a hard time keeping up with fraudsters' constantly changing strategies.

Solution: The bank strengthened its cybersecurity efforts by utilising AI-driven threat identification and prevention:

Machine Learning Models: JP Morgan Chase used sophisticated machine learning algorithms that were trained on large datasets of historical threat data, transaction patterns, and user behaviour.

Anomaly Detection: AI algorithms were employed to find irregularities in transaction data, with a particular focus on patterns that deviated from the usual and may be signs of fraud.

Behavioral Analysis: To comprehend normal client behaviour and spot variations that would indicate fraudulent transactions or account breach, the AI system included behavioural analysis.

Real-time Monitoring: Transactions and account activity were continually watched in real-time, allowing the system to identify and look into questionable behaviour as it happened.

Outcome:

JPMorgan Chase planned to accomplish the following objectives by incorporating AI-driven threat identification and analysis into their cybersecurity strategy:

Accuracy Has Increased: AI models have steadily become more accurate at spotting fraudulent transactions and minimising false positives.

Real-time detection: The bank was able to identify and react to fraudulent actions more quickly because to real-time monitoring and analysis.

Cost savings: The bank experienced considerable operating savings through automating fraud detection and minimising manual review requirements.

Increased Customer Trust: Customers gained confidence in the bank's security procedures as a result of better fraud protection.

Scalability: To manage the huge volume of transactions processed by a significant financial institution, the AI system grew well.

4.2 Case Study 2: Adaptive AI in Protecting Critical Infrastructure

Background: One of the biggest utilities in the country, PG&E provides service to millions of consumers throughout California (Kavya Balaraman., 2020). Because of the state's propensity for wildfires and other natural disasters, PG&E's electrical grid infrastructure was seriously threatened.

Challenge: Protecting vital electrical infrastructure from wildfires while maintaining the grid's safety and dependability was a problem. A technology that could offer early wildfire detection, risk analysis, and adaptive responses to shifting conditions was required by PG&E.

Solution: A flexible AI system was put in place by PG&E to improve grid security:

Artificial Intelligence for Wildfire: Artificial Intelligence for Wildfire The business used machine learning algorithms to examine past meteorological information, satellite images, and data from sensors positioned all around their service region.

Danger Evaluation: Using information on past fire trends, fuel moisture levels, and weather, the AI system evaluated the danger of wildfires.

Adaptive reactions: In order to prevent electrical equipment from starting wildfires, PG&E employed the AI system to start adaptive reactions, such as cutting power to certain grid segments in high-risk zones.

Continuous Learning: The AI system learnt from real-time data in a continuous learning process, allowing it to modify its predictions and behaviours in response to shifting environmental conditions.

Aiming to reduce the danger of wildfires ignited by electrical equipment, PG&E included adaptive AI into its grid security strategy. Although the adaptive AI system may cause brief power outages in high-risk locations, it was extremely important for defending people, property, and the grid itself from wildfires.

4.3 Case Study 3: AI-Powered Incident Response in a Large Organization

Background: The multinational technology and cybersecurity giant IBM offers a variety of services and solutions to businesses all over the world (Mandy Long., 2020). They have been leaders in integrating AI into cybersecurity solutions.

Challenge: In light of an increase in cyber threats and security events, the task was to strengthen incident response capabilities. IBM aimed to accelerate the process of identifying, looking into, and mitigating security problems.

Solution: As part of a larger cybersecurity strategy, IBM introduced AI-powered incident response capabilities:

AI for Threat Detection: IBM's security platform now uses AI algorithms for threat detection to examine a variety of security data, such as logs, network traffic, and endpoint data.

Automated Threat examination: Using numerous data sources to quickly correlate information to identify possible risks, the AI system automated the examination of security warnings.

Contextual Understanding: AI improved contextual comprehension of security incidents and gave security analysts in-depth knowledge of the kind and gravity of risks.

Incident Triage and Prioritization: The system employed AI-driven algorithms for event triage and prioritisation to make sure that the most serious threats got the most urgent attention.

Automation of Responses: In response to specific threats, IBM's AI system launched automatic actions such as isolating compromised devices, obstructing malicious traffic, and carrying out incident response playbooks.

Outcome:

IBM planned to accomplish the following objectives by integrating AI into their incident response procedures:

Faster Response Times: The time needed to identify, look into, and address security problems was decreased thanks to automation and analysis powered by AI.

Reduced False Positives: By contextualising and analysing data, the system was able to lessen false positive alarms, allowing security professionals to concentrate on real threats.

Scalability: A multinational organization's high amount of data and security warnings were successfully handled by IBM's AI-powered incident response capabilities.

Enhanced Security Posture: By applying AI, IBM strengthened its overall security posture by increasing its capacity to identify and counter sophisticated and emerging threats.

4.4 Lessons Learned from Successful Implementations

Organisations wanting to strengthen their security posture may learn a lot from the successful adoption of AI-driven cybersecurity solutions. Following are some important takeaways from these applications:

- **Flexibility is important:** The cyberattack landscape is dynamic, and they are always changing. AI-driven cybersecurity solutions must be flexible, learn from their use, and develop to keep up with new threats.
- **Data Quality Is Important:** The calibre of the data that AI models are trained on determines their correctness and dependability. To properly train their AI systems, organisations should make sure they have access to clean and representative data.
- **Collaboration between Humans and AI Is Crucial:** AI does not replace human skill; rather, it augments it. AI systems and human security specialists who can give context, make strategic choices, and respond to complex threats must work closely together for successful employments.
- **Updates and Continuous Monitoring:** AI models must be continuously evaluated and updated to be useful. Models must be regularly updated with fresh data and threat intelligence to be useful.
- **Integration of threat intelligence:** Artificial intelligence systems are better able to identify and address new risks when they are fed threat intelligence feeds and external data sources.
- **Efficiency via Automation:** Response times are greatly improved and the workload on security teams is decreased when regular duties like incident response playbooks and triage procedures are automated.

Organisations can better traverse the complicated world of AI-driven cybersecurity and develop strong defences against constantly changing cyberthreats by putting these lessons learnt into practise (Ribence Kadel et al., 2022).

5. IMPLEMENTING ADAPTIVE AI IN CYBERSECURITY

An inventive strategy to strengthen a company's defence against emerging cyber threats is to implement adaptive AI in cybersecurity. In order to continually monitor, detect, and react to cyber threats in real-time, adaptive AI integrates artificial intelligence, machine learning, and other cutting-edge technologies. The main factors and processes for deploying adaptive AI in cybersecurity are listed below:

- **Define Specific Goals:** Start by outlining the goals you hope to accomplish with adaptive AI. Recognise the particular cybersecurity difficulties facing your company, such as spotting sophisticated attacks, cutting down on false positives, or improving incident response.
- **Gathering and Preparing Data:** Assemble data from a variety of cybersecurity sources, including as feeds of threat information, endpoint data, and network traffic logs.

To make sure the data is acceptable for machine learning algorithms, clean, normalise, and preprocess it. To make AI models work effectively, data quality is essential.

- **AI model selection and training:** Select the best machine learning and AI models for your particular use cases, such as malware categorization, anomaly detection, or user behaviour analysis. To aid in their ability to spot trends and abnormalities, these models may be trained using previous data.
- **Define Specific Goals:** Start by outlining the goals you hope to accomplish with adaptive AI. Recognise the particular cybersecurity difficulties facing your company, such as spotting sophisticated attacks, cutting down on false positives, or improving incident response.
- **Gathering and Preparing Data:** assemble data from a variety of cybersecurity sources, including as feeds of threat information, endpoint data, and network traffic logs.

To make sure the data is acceptable for machine learning algorithms, clean, normalise, and preprocess it. To make AI models work effectively, data quality is essential.

- **AI model selection and training:** Select the best machine learning and AI models for your particular use cases, such as malware categorization, anomaly detection, or user behaviour analysis. To aid in their ability to spot trends and abnormalities, these models may be trained using previous data (Suresh Babu, C. V. & Yadav, S.., 2023).

5.1 Considerations for Integrating AI in Cybersecurity

AI integration in cybersecurity may greatly improve a company's capacity to identify, stop, and respond to online attacks. However, before beginning this adventure, there are a few crucial things to bear in mind:

- **Define Specific Goals:** Start by identifying the precise AI use cases and cybersecurity goals for your organisation. The key to success is having a clear knowledge of your objectives, whether they be for threat detection, incident response, or vulnerability assessment.

- **Quantity and Quality of Data:** Make sure you can obtain reliable data. Clean and pertinent data are essential for the training and analysis of AI algorithms. To abide with data protection laws, collect and retain data securely.
- **Compliance and Privacy:** Recognise the privacy and compliance standards that apply to your company. Use AI solutions compliant with certain rules, such as GDPR.
- **AI Model Choice:** Select the AI models and algorithms that are most suited to your cybersecurity requirements. Natural language processing (NLP), machine learning (ML), deep learning, and anomaly detection are popular choices.
- **Data for training:** To make sure your AI models can generalise successfully and detect a variety of dangers, gather and curate a variety of training data that is reflective of the real world (S. Pirbhulal et al., 2022).

5.1.1 Data Collection and Preprocessing

Any data-driven project, including those requiring AI, machine learning, and data analytics, must start with the gathering and preparation of the necessary data. Building accurate and efficient models requires carefully gathered and processed data. The main factors and procedures for data gathering and preparation are listed below:

Data Gathering

- **Define the data goals:** The goals of your data gathering strategy should be clearly stated. What particular data do you want to collect, and how will you use it?
- **Choose Data Sources:** Determine the source of your data. Databases, APIs, sensors, logs, user interactions, web scraping, and external datasets are just a few examples of sources.
- **Data quality control:** Make sure the information you gather is credible, accurate, and comprehensive. Implement error-handling procedures and data validation checks when collecting data.

Data preparation

- **Cleaning Data:** Missing data points, outliers, and duplicates should be handled or removed. Use methods like mean imputation or interpolation to impute missing variables.
- **Transformation of data:** To make numerical properties comparable in scale, normalise or standardise them. Use methods like Z-score normalisation or Min-Max scaling.

Skewed data distributions should be subjected to logarithmic adjustments.
Using one-hot encoding or label encoding, express categorical variables as numbers.

- **Feature Choice:** Determine and pick the pertinent characteristics (variables) that have the biggest influence on your issue. Techniques for selecting features, such as feature importance ratings or mutual information, may be useful.

Successful machine learning and artificial intelligence initiatives start with efficient data preparation and collecting. These procedures aid in ensuring that the data used to develop and test models is precise and appropriately organised, which eventually produces outcomes that are more dependable and accurate (Arockia Panimalar.S et al.,2018).

5.1.2 Model Selection and Training

In the creation of machine learning and AI systems, model selection and training are essential phases. These processes entail selecting the proper machine learning algorithm or model, training it on labelled data, and enhancing its functionality. Here is a thorough explanation of the model choice and training procedure:

Model Selection:

- **Problem Identification:** Recognise the issue you're trying to tackle before anything else. Is the issue one of classification, regression, clustering, or another kind? Your model selection will be influenced by this knowledge.
- **Think about these model types:**

Consider several machine learning model types depending on the nature of your data and the task at hand, such as:

Linear Models (such as Logistic Regression and Linear Regression)
Tree-Based Models (such as Gradient Boosting, Random Forests, and Decision Trees)
Neural networks, such as recurrent and convolutional neural networks
SVMs, or support vector machines
Algorithms for clustering (like K-Means and DBSCAN)
Techniques for Dimensionality Reduction (such as PCA)
Ensemble techniques, such as stacking
Time series models (such as LSTM and ARIMA)

- **Model assessment:** Select assessment measures that support the objectives of your challenge. Use accuracy, precision, recall, F1-score, or mean square error (MSE), or R-squared, for classification, or regression, respectively.

To estimate model performance on unknown data and avoid overfitting, use cross-validation approaches.

Model Training:

- **Splitting data:** Create training, validation, and test sets from your dataset. The validation set is used for hyperparameter tweaking, the test set is used to assess the final model, and the training set is used to train the model.
- **Scaling and transformation of features:** Preprocess the data as required, doing any necessary data transformations as well as feature scaling and encoding.
- **Training Cycle:** Utilising the selected method and hyperparameters, train the model on the training dataset. During training, keep an eye on the model's performance on the validation set to spot overfitting or underfitting.

In order to get the best results, model selection and training are iterative procedures that frequently call for testing and fine-tuning. To ensure repeatability and transparency in your machine learning initiatives, it's crucial to stick to a methodical, well-documented strategy throughout these processes (C. Benzaïd et al., 2020).

5.1.3 Scalability and Resource Requirements

When deploying AI and machine learning solutions, scalability and resource needs are crucial factors to take into account, particularly when dealing with enterprise- or production-level applications. Your system must be scalable to manage growing workloads and data volumes while retaining performance and dependability. Consider the following important factors:

- **Scalability of workload:** Designing your AI infrastructure to expand horizontally entails adding extra resources or computers to manage growing workloads. Utilise load balancing techniques to efficiently allocate work across various resources.
- **Vertical Scaling:** Alternative scaling methods include vertical scaling, which involves updating individual computers with greater CPU, RAM, or GPU power. Although it could be more expensive, this strategy might work for certain workloads.
- **Scalability of data:** When working with enormous datasets, divide the data over many servers or storage devices. Use cloud-based data storage solutions or distributed file systems like Hadoop HDFS.
- **Data Sharding:** Databases may be partitioned into smaller shards to share data among several servers or nodes via data sharding. This strategy can lessen data access bottlenecks and enhance query performance.

Requirements for Resources:

- **Hardware:** Pick hardware setups that can handle the computing needs of your AI applications. Due to their capacity for parallel processing, GPUs and TPUs are frequently employed for deep learning applications.
- **Cloud Services:** To access scalable computing resources instantly, use cloud platforms like AWS, Azure, or Google Cloud. These platforms provide a vast array of AI and machine learning services.

When designing an AI system, scalability and resource requirements should be evaluated early on. Regularly examine and modify your infrastructure and resource allocation as your AI solutions expand and mature to meet shifting needs efficiently and affordably (Thomas, G et al., 2023).

5.2 Challenges and Solutions

Due to the complexity of the technology, data, and real-world contexts, there are frequently difficulties while integrating AI in diverse sectors. Following are some typical issues and their solutions:

Quantity and Quality of Data:

Problem: Poor or insufficient data might make models function poorly.

Investment in data gathering, cleansing, and preparation is the answer. If more data is required, use strategies for data augmentation. When you have less data, use transfer learning to take advantage of trained models.

Interpretability and Explainability of the Model:

Problem: Since many AI models, particularly deep learning models, are sometimes referred to as "black boxes," it can be difficult to comprehend how they make decisions.

Solution: To evaluate and explain model predictions, use methods like feature significance analysis, SHAP values, LIME, or surrogate models. In situations when explainability is crucial, pick interpretable models.

Concerns about bias and ethics:

Challenge: Biases existing in training data might be perpetuated by AI models.

Regular data audits and debiasing are the answer. Use algorithms and strategies that are fairness-aware to identify and reduce bias in models. Adopt ethical AI norms and practises.

Scalability and resource limitations:

It may be expensive and difficult to scale AI systems to accommodate enormous datasets and heavy workloads.

Solution: Use scalable cloud-based resource management systems. To manage resources effectively, use containerization and orchestration solutions like Kubernetes. Improve the performance of your models and code.

It takes a mix of technological know-how, domain understanding, and a dedication to moral and responsible AI practises to address these implementation issues with AI. Organisations should approach AI initiatives knowing exactly what problems may arise and being prepared to modify and enhance their plans as necessary (S. Chakrabarty et al., 2020).

5.3 Best Practices for AI Implementation in Cybersecurity

Careful preparation and execution are necessary when implementing AI in cybersecurity to properly guard against ever-evolving threats. The following are some top recommendations for applying AI to cybersecurity:

- **Define Specific Goals:** Start by outlining your cybersecurity goals in detail. Know the precise hazards you wish to eliminate, whether they be user behaviour analytics, malware detection, or intrusion protection.
- **Quality of Data and Privacy:** Make certain that the data sources you use are reliable and representative. Safeguard sensitive information and abide by privacy laws including GDPR and HIPAA.
- **Integration of threat intelligence:** Your AI system may be updated with threat intelligence feeds to be informed of the most recent threats and vulnerabilities.

By adhering to these recommended practises, organisations may successfully use AI technology to improve their cybersecurity posture while upholding transparency, compliance, and agility in the face of emerging threats (Haleem et al., 2022).

6. FUTURE DIRECTIONS AND ETHICAL CONSIDERATIONS

Although AI in cybersecurity has a bright future, it also comes with a number of difficulties and moral dilemmas. The following are some potential directions and industry ethics to think about:

Future Perspectives:

- **Improved threat detection using AI:** By analysing huge datasets in real-time, finding intricate attack patterns, and lowering false positives, artificial intelligence will continue to play a vital role in enhancing threat detection and response.
- **Systems for autonomous response:** One area of study that is expanding is the creation of autonomous AI systems that can react to threats in real-time without human involvement. However, in order to avoid unforeseen outcomes, proper planning and supervision are necessary.
- **Analytics for security powered by AI:** Security analysts will be able to more effectively uncover new threats and vulnerabilities thanks to the advancement of AI-driven analytics tools.
- **Architecture for zero trust:** The use of AI to continually monitor and evaluate user and device behaviour will promote the adoption of Zero Trust security models, where no entity, whether inside or outside the organisation, is trusted by default (Suresh Babu, C. V., Abirami, S., & Manoj, S.,2023).

6.1 Advancements in Adaptive AI Technologies

The capabilities of artificial intelligence systems have been significantly improved in a variety of fields thanks to developments in adaptive AI technology. These technologies allow AI systems to continually learn and develop, adapt to shifting circumstances, and get more efficient over time. The following are some noteworthy developments in adaptable AI technology:

- **Reward-Based Learning:** AI systems may now learn by making mistakes because to advancements in reinforcement learning (RL). Deep reinforcement learning (DRL) algorithms have produced outstanding outcomes in fields including gaming, robotics, and autonomous driving.
- **Adaptive Learning:** AI models can use transfer learning to adapt their knowledge from one task or area to another. Natural language processing (NLP), computer vision, and healthcare are three fields where this strategy has been useful in modifying pre-trained models for particular tasks.
- **Self-Supervised Education:** In self-supervised learning, AI systems create their own labels or targets from the data. This is a type of unsupervised learning. This method has increased the effectiveness of training models, especially when there is a dearth of labelled data (Ribence Kadel et al., 2022).

6.2 Emerging Trends in Cybersecurity and AI

Several new trends that are developing at the nexus of cybersecurity and AI are influencing how businesses will safeguard their digital assets in the future. The necessity for increasingly advanced defence systems and the always changing threat scenario are what are driving these changes. The following are some noteworthy new developments in cybersecurity and AI:

- **Threat Detection and Response Powered by AI:** AI is increasingly being utilised to quickly identify and address cyber threats. Security systems powered by AI can examine enormous volumes of data and spot patterns that indicate threats, allowing for quicker reaction and mitigation.
- **Models of zero-trust security:** Zero Trust security models are gaining popularity because they operate under the premise that no entity, within or external to the organisation, can be trusted by default. AI is important for continual monitoring.
- **Enhanced AI-Based Authentication:** Authentication procedures are being strengthened with the help of AI. Utilising strategies like continuous authentication and behavioural biometrics, access is kept safe during a session by monitoring user behaviour (Somasundaram et al., 2020).

6.3 Research Opportunities and Areas for Improvement

Given how active both professions are, there are many chances for research and places where things might be done better. By focusing on the following topics, researchers and organisations can make important contributions:

- **Machine learning that is adversarial:** Look into methods for strengthening machine learning models against malicious assaults. Improved defences and techniques for spotting and reducing hostile cases are part of this effort.
- **AI that respects privacy:** Investigate privacy-preserving AI methods that enable cybersecurity to utilise data without disclosing private information. Given the tightening of privacy laws, this is extremely crucial.
- **Quantum computation and encryption:** Develop quantum-resistant encryption methods and protocols while examining the effects of quantum computing on the cryptographic algorithms used today (Suresh Babu, C. V. & Yadav, S., 2023).

6.4 Ethical Considerations in AI-Driven Cybersecurity Measures

Organisations and researchers must carefully negotiate the numerous ethical issues that AI-driven cybersecurity techniques bring up. To preserve trust, safeguard privacy, and avoid unforeseen effects, it is crucial to ensure that AI technologies are utilised responsibly and ethically. The following are some significant ethical issues in AI-driven cybersecurity:

- **Fairness and Prejudice:** Biases that are inherited by AI systems from training data may result in unfair or discriminating outputs. To make sure that cybersecurity measures do not disproportionately affect particular groups or people, biases must be routinely assessed and mitigated.
- **Privacy:** AI-driven cybersecurity frequently needs access to private information for threat analysis and detection. Data protection and user privacy protection are essential. To reduce privacy threats, use strategies like differential privacy and data anonymization.
- **Ethics in testing and hacking:** Think about testing and ethical hacking of AI-driven cybersecurity systems to find flaws and vulnerabilities before bad actors can take use of them (Dhoni et al., 2023).

7. CONCLUSION

In conclusion, "Adaptive AI for Dynamic Cybersecurity: Safeguarding Digital Landscapes in the Era of Evolving Threats" offers a crucial and relevant strategy for addressing the issues that the field of cybersecurity faces continually. The demand for adaptable AI solutions has never been higher as digital landscapes get more complex and attacks become more sophisticated and frequent. However, there are complications and ethical issues involved with the implementation of adaptive AI in cybersecurity. Adaptive AI integration will advance, keep ahead of new risks, and protect their digital assets as we traverse the always shifting terrain of cyber threats.

REFERENCES

Babu, S. C.V. (2022). Artificial Intelligence and Expert Systems. Anniyappa Publications.

Benzaïd, C., & Taleb, T. (2020, November/December). AI for Beyond 5G Networks: A Cyber-Security Defense or Offense Enabler? *IEEE Network*, *34*(6), 140–147. doi:10.1109/MNET.011.2000088

Chakrabarty, S., & Engels, D. W. (2020). Secure Smart Cities Framework Using IoT and AI. *2020 IEEE Global Conference on Artificial Intelligence and Internet of Things (GCAIoT)*, Dubai, United Arab Emirates. 10.1109/GCAIoT51063.2020.9345912

DhoniP.KumarR. (2023). Synergizing Generative AI and Cybersecurity: Roles of Generative AI Entities, Companies, Agencies, and Government in Enhancing Cybersecurity. TechRxiv.

Doshi, P., & Badawy, A. (2019). Machine Learning in Cybersecurity: A Review. *Journal of Cybersecurity and Mobility*, *8*(1), 1–27.

Haleem, A., Javaid, M., Singh, R. P., Rab, S., & Suman, R. (2022). Perspectives of cybersecurity for ameliorative Industry 4.0 era: A review-based framework. *The Industrial Robot*, *49*(3), 582–597. doi:10.1108/IR-10-2021-0243

JPMorgan Chase & Co. (2018). *JPMorgan Chase to Use AI in Its Fight Against Fraud.* JP Morgan. https://www.jpmorgan.com/technology/news/omni-ai

Kadel, R., & Kadel, R. (2022). Impact of AI on Cyber Security. *International Journal of Scientific Research and Engineering Development, 5*(6).

Kavya Balaraman Utility Dive. (2020). *PG&E deploys machine learning to safeguard its grid against California wildfires.* Utility Dive. https://www.utilitydive.com/news/wildfires-pushed-pge-into-bankruptcy-should-other-utilities-be-worried/588435/

Mughal, A. A. (2018). The Art of Cybersecurity: Defense in Depth Strategy for Robust Protection. *International Journal of Intelligent Automation and Computing*, *1*(1), 1–20.

Panimalar, A. (2018). ARTIFICIAL INTELLIGENCE TECHNIQUES FOR CYBER SECURITY. *International Research Journal of Engineering and Technology (IRJET),05*(03).

Pirbhulal, S., Abie, H., & Shukla, A. (2022). Towards a Novel Framework for Reinforcing Cybersecurity using Digital Twins in IoT-based Healthcare Applications. *2022 IEEE 95th Vehicular Technology Conference: (VTC2022-Spring)*. IEEE. 10.1109/VTC2022-Spring54318.2022.9860581

Siriwardhana, Y., Porambage, P., Liyanage, M., & Ylianttila, M. (2021). *AI and 6G Security: Opportunities and Challenges*. 2021 Joint European Conference on Networks and Communications & 6G Summit (EuCNC/6G Summit), Porto, Portugal. 10.1109/EuCNC/6GSummit51104.2021.9482503

Srivastava, V. (2023). Adaptive Cyber Defense: Leveraging Neuromorphic Computing for Advanced Threat Detection and Response. *2023 International Conference on Sustainable Computing and Smart Systems (ICSCSS)*, Coimbatore, India. 10.1109/ICSCSS57650.2023.10169393

Suresh Babu, C. V., Abirami, S., & Manoj, S. (2023). AI-Based Carthage Administration Towards Smart City. In C. Chowdhary, B. Swain, & V. Kumar (Eds.), *Investigations in Pattern Recognition and Computer Vision for Industry 4.0* (pp. 1–17). IGI Global. doi:10.4018/978-1-6684-8602-3.ch001

Suresh Babu, C. V., & Srisakthi, S. (2023). Cyber Physical Systems and Network Security: The Present Scenarios and Its Applications. In R. Thanigaivelan, S. Kaliappan, & C. Jegadheesan (Eds.), *Cyber-Physical Systems and Supporting Technologies for Industrial Automation* (pp. 104–130). IGI Global.

Suresh Babu, C. V., & Yadav, S. (2023). Cyber Physical Systems Design Challenges in the Areas of Mobility, Healthcare, Energy, and Manufacturing. In R. Thanigaivelan, S. Kaliappan, & C. Jegadheesan (Eds.), *Cyber-Physical Systems and Supporting Technologies for Industrial Automation* (pp. 131–151). IGI Global.

Thomas, G., & Sule, M.-J. (2023). A service lens on cybersecurity continuity and management for organizations' subsistence and growth. *Organizational Cybersecurity Journal: Practice, Process and People*, *3*(1), 18–40. doi:10.1108/OCJ-09-2021-0025

Chapter 4
Adaptive Learning in IoT-Based Smart City Applications

Nawaf Abdulla
Gazi University, Turkey

Sedef Demirci
Gazi University, Turkey

Mehmet Demirci
https://orcid.org/0000-0002-1088-5215
Gazi University, Turkey

Suat Özdemir
Hacettepe University, Turkey

ABSTRACT

Internet of things (IoT) based smart city applications rely on constant data collection and accurate data analytics, yet the fast-changing nature of such data often causes the performance of machine learning models to deteriorate over time. Adaptive learning has been increasingly utilized in these applications in recent years as a viable solution to this problem. Moreover, IoT applications are vulnerable to various security threats due to their large-scale deployment, resource-constrained devices, and diverse protocols. This has led to an increased interest in efficient security and intrusion detection mechanisms tailored for IoT environments. In this chapter, the authors first focus on methods to address the issue of concept drift in time series streaming data for IoT-based smart city applications, such as weather, flood, and energy consumption forecasting, through adaptive learning. Furthermore, the authors examine adaptive learning-based security solutions to various attacks in different domains of the dynamic smart city landscape.

DOI: 10.4018/979-8-3693-0230-9.ch004

1. INTRODUCTION AND BACKGROUND: IOT-BASED SMART CITIES AND ADAPTIVE LEARNING

Recent years have seen an increased interest in learning from continuously evolving stream data, particularly when this data is prone to change and trends frequently (i.e. concept drift). Unfortunately, conventional mining techniques and algorithms are insufficient to solve this problem, as the model's performance degrades even with stationary data, let alone data streams. Continuously adjusting the model manually is ineffective, and as the data size continues to expand, it also becomes impractical. Through constant model iteration and taking advantage of newly available data, the performance of a machine learning model can be improved by rapidly adapting to unforeseen changes in conditions. Adaptive AI models possess the ability to dynamically readjust based on real-time feedback, which is an important aspect of their suitability for unpredictable environments requiring fast response. Adaptive AI solutions are also useful for real-time monitoring and response mechanisms to mitigate the impact of security breaches and intrusion attempts. The purpose of this chapter is to help readers reach a deeper understanding of Adaptive AI, particularly pertaining to its use in Internet of Things (IoT) based smart city applications.

Smart city applications depend on the variety and correctness of large amounts of data collected from IoT devices. Sensing and transmitting data is only the first step, and the bigger challenge is generating actionable intelligence from constantly flowing big data for more efficient resource consumption, planning and preparedness in cities (Kim, Ramos, & Mohammed, 2017). Hence, it is crucial to use stream processing and analytics effectively to fully benefit from wide-scale deployment of IoT devices in smart cities. To this end, distributed stream processing frameworks are important enablers for data analytics (Nasiri, Nasehi, & Goudarzi, 2019).

The relationship between adaptive learning and stream processing for smart city applications has been studied in the literature. For example, a series of experiments to determine whether adaptive learning can improve the performance of stream analytics was conducted by Ku (2018). The experimentation-heavy study utilized six data sets and made extensive use of data. Comparing the speed and accuracy of traditional machine learning classifiers and adaptive ones, the author concluded that adaptive learning provides superior speed and accuracy.

The majority of prior research on adaptive learning on streaming data has focused on classification problems. For instance, researchers (Zliobaite, Bifet, Pfahringer, & Holmes, 2011) developed a model that adapts upon the detection of concept drift. According to the authors, their model is based on uncertainty and dynamic allocation, and responsive to any changes in the distribution of the data set. Others have investigated classifier ensembles and various proposed algorithms to find the best and most efficient classifiers for online classification (Mehta, 2017), (Kuncheva, 2008).

Furthermore, different researchers have approached the problem from various angles. According to one study (Das, Zhong, Stoica, & Shenker, 2014), the batch size of streaming data that is executed affects the throughput and end-to-end latency. Based on this idea, the authors proposed a simple but rigid control algorithm that automatically adjusts the batch size as needed. Another work (Li, Wang, Wang, & Zhou, 2017) addressed the issue of imbalanced streaming data using multi-window-based ensemble classification. Prior to classifying newly arriving streams, their proposed method evaluates the accuracy of the sub-classifiers. When the precision falls below a predetermined threshold, new sub-classifiers are trained. In addition, Zliobaite and Gabrys (2012) addressed the issue of preprocessing in streaming data by considering three scenarios involving adaptive preprocessing, adaptive learning, and adaptive preprocessing and learning in conjunction. They argue that combining adaptive preprocessing and adaptive learning improves the overall performance of machine learning models.

Several researchers have explored the idea of combining deep learning with adaptive learning; for instance, Tran and Hoang (2019) conducted a study proposing an adaptive convolutional neural network (CNN) model for tracking and re-identifying objects. The authors argued that the proposed model increases precision while reducing time and memory complexity. Also, the studies conducted by Wang, Kubichek, and Zhou (2018) and Yu et al. (2020) are good examples of the wide range of adaptive AI use. The former study utilizes adaptive learning to predict hourly building energy consumption, while the latter uses it to estimate cardiac motion. In both studies, adaptive learning has been shown to improve accuracy.

Moreover, Pathak, Pandey, and Rautaray (2020) designed a deep learning-based framework for topic modeling from big data, which benefits from adaptive learning. While Saxena and Singh (2022) use adaptive learning to predict and offload the workload of a dynamic cloud environment, adaptive learning is also used to predict and offload the workload of a static cloud environment. Again, experimental findings demonstrate that applying adaptive learning to deep learning algorithms always results in improved resource management and higher model accuracy.

In summary, these studies highlight the significance of using adaptive learning models when dealing with time-series whose distribution is dynamic. Yet, most of these studies have not promoted deep learning models as a means to enhance the effectiveness of the proposed models and frameworks. Having said that, Abdulla, Demirci, and Ozdemir (2022) look into how adaptive learning influences temperature forecasting, and how different long-short term memory (LSTM) architectures (such as multi-input-single-output (MISO) and single-input-single-output (SISO)) affect overall performance and latency. The general adaptive AI framework that can be used for the forecasting problems discussed in the next three sections of this chapter is depicted in Figure 1.

Figure 1. The proposed framework for adaptive models

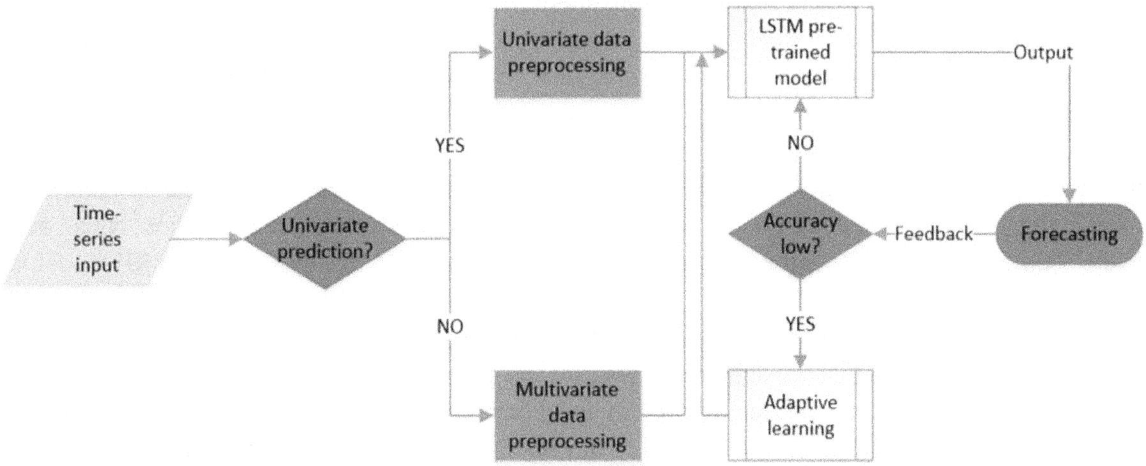

The remainder of this chapter provides an overview of adaptive AI applications for IoT-based smart cities through several use cases. It first focuses on forecasting problems as they constitute a considerable part of smart life and smart industry applications. Sections 2 through 4 examine cases where real-life data sets were used to develop adaptive AI models to tackle problems such as weather forecasting, flood forecasting, and energy consumption forecasting. These sections discuss the suitability of applying adaptive AI methods on streaming data in the cloud-fog-edge continuum to deal with the problem of learning from ever-changing data generated by IoT edge devices. Section 5 examines adaptive AI-based cybersecurity solutions to various attacks threatening smart grids and smart cities. More specifically, it highlights the significance of anomaly detection and AI algorithms in identifying malicious activities within smart city applications. Finally, Section 6 presents a discussion on adversarial robustness and its importance for the AI models used in some of these applications (such as autonomous driving and intrusion detection), along with different perspectives on the meaning of adaptivity in relation to adversarial attacks and defenses against them.

2. ADAPTIVE AI IN WEATHER FORECASTING

This section focuses on the problem of weather forecasting in smart cities using AI and emphasizes its need for self-adaptation to tackle the problem of data distribution shift or so-called concept drift. Weather forecasting is one of the most commonly studied problems pertaining to smart cities. It is the scientific method of predicting the atmosphere conditions based on specific time frames and locations (Hayati & Mohebi, 2007). Its value comes in its different potential applications, including meteorology, electricity price forecasting, etc. Numerical weather prediction (NWP) employs computer algorithms to generate a forecast based on current weather conditions by solving a complex system of nonlinear mathematical equations derived from specific mathematical models. Specifically, these models define a coordinate system that grids the earth in three dimensions. In order to forecast future atmospheric characteristics, each grid's temperature, winds, solar radiation, water phase change, heat transfer, relative humidity, and surface hydrology are measured, as well as their interactions with neighboring grids (Lynch, 2006).

Meteorology adopted a more quantitative approach as technology and computer science advanced; consequently, prediction models became more accessible to researchers, forecasters, and other stakeholders. In recent years, numerous NWP systems- such as the weather research and forecasting (WRF) model- have been developed as high-performance computing capacity has allowed for the refinement and introduction of regional or limited-area models. Due to its higher resolution rate, precision, open-source nature, community support, and broad applicability across multiple disciplines, the WRF model has become the most widely used atmospheric NWP model in the world (Hewage, et al., 2020). Afterwards, regression and machine learning models were more commonly exploited.

A regression equation that predicts the number of sunspots in a year was used to initiate the study of time-series prediction during data analysis. Consequently, regression models have evolved into the most fundamental and influential time-series prediction models. Due to the complexity, irregularity, randomness, and non-linearity of actual data however, sophisticated models struggle to provide accurate predictions. Consequently, it is possible to create nonlinear prediction models using machine learning techniques and a large quantity of historical data. Through repeated training cycles and learning approximations, they are able to make more accurate predictions than traditional statistically-based models (Yu et al., 2020).

Furthermore, many studies have switched from machine learning (shallow learning) to deep learning to boost the models' performance and skills. For example, Abdulla, Demirci, and Ozdemir (2022) designed, implemented, and compared machine learning and deep learning models in weather forecasting applications, concluding that deep learning models consistently achieve better accuracy when massive historical data is available. Nonetheless, in real-world applications, data evolves over time for unpredictable reasons; therefore, models trained on historical data may become obsolete for such data. Thus, detecting the occurrence of change and updating the model in response are the two greatest practical obstacles against maintaining the desired model performance (Zliobaite, Pechenizkiy, & Gama, 2016). For example, this change/drift could be (i) gradual over time, (ii) recurrent, or (iii) abrupt. Regardless of the type of change, a common challenge in streaming data is that it is dynamic and in motion, necessitating adaptable and flexible machine learning models (Huyen, 2022). Therefore, systematic detection of drifts in streaming data has been emphasized as an important research problem (Webb, Lee, Petitjean, & Goethals, 2017).

Since meteorological data arrive continuously and change over time, manual model adjustments are ineffective, and with the rapid growth of incoming data, these endeavors would become impractical quickly. Hence, predictive models must have the capability for automatic update to address these issues (Mehta, 2017). In other words, weather forecasting is a natural beneficiary of adaptive learning. However, such techniques have not been utilized extensively in smart city applications (Zliobaite & Gabrys, 2012). Although adaptive learning is challenging for data stream processing, previous research demonstrates the importance of detecting concept drift and updating prediction models to account for the drift that occurs in the continuously flowing data (Abdulla, Demirci, & Ozdemir, 2021). The authors focused on the most popular regression models in machine learning used for weather forecasting research, including linear regression, generalized linear regression (GLR), decision tree, gradient-boosted tree regression (GBTR), and random forest. Among these, the authors reported that random forest yielded the best results in terms of the average MAE, RMSE, and R-squared values obtained from preliminary trials, and it was therefore chosen as a benchmark. Subsequently, the plain random forest model (*baseline*) performance was compared to that of the *adaptive* random forest model. The adaptive model significantly outperformed the baseline model, achieving nearly 20% reduction in RMSE (Abdulla, Demirci, & Ozdemir, 2021).

Another logical step to improve the accuracy of predictions is to implement deep learning models rather than the machine learning models mentioned previously. Consequently, a more recent study (Abdulla, Demirci, & Ozdemir, 2022) approached this problem by employing a recurrent neural network (RNN) model: specifically, the LSTM model, which is renowned for its ability to deal competently with time-series data. Several architectures and designs have been suggested in the literature for the LSTM model. After preliminary evaluation, it was determined that three of them- stacked LSTM, bidirectional LSTM, and CNN LSTM- were worth attempting. This study concluded that adaptive learning increases the quality of weather forecasting for both cases of learning mechanisms: machine learning and deep learning. Yet, the latter outperforms the former when the available data is immense.

In comparison to recent and state-of-the-art studies that dealt with temperature and weather forecasting and implemented LSTM-based models, and according to reported RMSE values, adaptive AI models surpassed non-adaptive models by more than 20 percent. Table 1 demonstrates the enhancements obtained by applying adaptive learning to AI models utilizing distinct data sets for temperature forecasts. The three data sets used are: (i) Istanbul Metropolitan Municipality (IMM); (ii) Korean Meteorological Administration (KMA); and (iii) Beijing PM2.5.

As they differ, mean absolute percentage error (MAPE) was chosen to determine the performance and forecasting quality of the models. MAPE is a popular metric among data scientists for calibrating forecasting models for various use cases and data sets, making it simpler for end-users to comprehend and researchers to interpret. As shown in Table 1, the MAPE values obtained in experiments with IMM, KMA, and Beijing PM2.5 were 7%, 8%, and 10% respectively, indicating that the model's performance was successful. When compared to the values of the baseline model, it can be seen that the proposed adaptive model consistently achieved a lower MAPE, meaning it provided more accurate temperature forecasts. Consequently, it is concluded that the developed adaptive AI approach appears to be effective for temperature forecasting regardless of the use case or data set.

Table 1. Comparison of the baseline and adaptive models for three sets of temperature forecasting data using MAPE (Abdulla, Demirci, & Ozdemir, 2022)

Data set	MAPE	
	Baseline LSTM	**Adaptive LSTM**
IMM	9%	7%
KMA	12%	8%
Beijing PM2.5	13%	10%

3. ADAPTIVE AI IN FLOOD FORECASTING

This section addresses the flood forecasting problem in smart cities, and then discusses how adaptive AI could improve the forecasting model skills with the help of other technologies such cloud-fog architecture. Recent attention has been focused on flood forecasting (FF) due to climate change. Globally, climate change diminishes the predictability of global flood patterns. Thus, effective flood management is needed, which requires accurate information regarding the flood's occurrence, spread, and environmental impact (Hingmire & Bhaladhare, 2022). Flood prediction, particularly in coastal cities, assists authorities in making optimal, efficient, and sound flood management decisions (Dai, Tang, Zhang, & Cai, 2021). As a result, flood forecasting is critical to saving lives and protecting infrastructure during natural disasters (Danso-Amoako, Scholz, Kalimeris, Yang, & Shao, 2012). However, despite the fact that hydraulic models are accurate and dependable, they take a long time to predict floods. Hence, supervised machine learning-based models have become necessary (Zhang, et al., 2021).

In addition, Internet of Things (IoT) is currently utilized extensively in flood monitoring, forecasting, and management. As a component of an intelligent flood forecasting system, it aids in the prediction and warning of potential inundation (Piadeh, Behzadian, & Alani, 2022). Diverse intelligent sensors related to hydrological information technology, including sensors for monitoring changes in flood water levels, have been embedded in various urban areas: for instance, depth meters, hydrological monitoring cameras, smart water level gauges, and the combination of numerous sensors such as hydro-meteorological sensor nets (Moishin, Deo, Prasad, Raj, & Abdulla, 2021) and automatic weather stations (Naik, Patil, Verma, & Hingmire, 2020), which collect vast quantities of data. This numerous data could come in handy if it is utilized intelligently. Consequently, the rapid development of data-driven hydrological forecasting - such as machine learning (Naik, Patil, Verma, & Hingmire, 2020), deep learning (Chen et al., 2021), and computing infrastructure (Birch et al., 2021) - has arisen from the recent growth of this flood-related data, the development of intelligent algorithms, and their application in hydrology.

Since the inundation process during a flood is highly complex and uncertain under non-stationary conditions, accurate flood forecasting remains a challenge (Dai, Tang, Zhang, & Cai, 2021). For example, one of the greatest challenges they face during the data collection and model training processes is the lack and imbalance of the research data sets. In addition, some raw flood data is missing as a result of sensors misreading or being damaged during heavy precipitation; as a result, inventive and efficient preprocessing steps should be implemented and recommended. Insufficient existing performance of data-driven models, such as machine learning and deep learning models, necessitates ongoing research in this context to develop efficient, robust, and accurate prediction models (Zhang, et al., 2021).

For instance, Dai and his colleagues used the Bayesian model combination (BMC-EL) to come up with a way to predict the depth of a flood. Classifying the severity of the flood and K-fold cross-validation made the training set more diverse and consistent. The reliability of the models was then judged by how well the ratio between different levels of flood intensity worked. The BMC strategy makes the ensemble learning model 16.85 percent more reliable than the BLL strategy (Dai, Tang, Zhang, & Cai, 2021). Then, Zhang et al. conducted an extension of this study by using curve fitting and data interpolation to simulate the actual inundation depth. They also examine neural networks, LSTM, Random Forest, Adaptive Boosting, and Linear Regression to determine which combinations of models, datasets, and scenarios are most effective for predicting floods in Macao when typhoons take place (Zhang, et al., 2021).

Moreover, by combining the strengths of a CNN and an LSTM network, researchers developed a hybrid deep learning (ConvLSTM) algorithm for flood forecasting (Moishin, Deo, Prasad, Raj, & Abdulla, 2021). The work uses a Flood Index (IF), a mathematical representation of the depletion of water resources over time that is derived from the precipitation dataset. The duration, severity, and intensity of any flood situation can then be determined with the help of a flood monitoring system and this Flood Index. In order to anticipate the subsequent daily IF value, the newly developed predictive model makes use of statistically significant lagged IF, supplemented by antecedent and real-time precipitation data. Nine unique rainfall datasets from flood-prone areas of Fiji, which are almost annually devastated by floods, are used to verify the performance of the proposed ConvLSTM model.

Numerous studies and works in the literature have addressed the problem of flood forecasting, with the following achievements being the most notable: (i) implementing different machine and ensemble learning models; (ii) predicting many time-steps ahead such as Day+1, +3, +7, and +14; (iii) combining meteorological and hydrological data; (iv) applying data interpolation to solve the "missing data" problem; (v) Infilling gaps with suitable imputation techniques such as linear interpolation.

In addition to the studies discussed above, another study (Abdulla, Demirci, & Ozdemir, 2023) addresses unresolved issues in flood forecasting such as lack of data and concept drift. Hence, they propose the following solutions: as a preliminary step, weakly supervised learning (WSL) is used to label and augment data in order to provide efficient imputation techniques for filling in missing data. This step provides accurate forecasts which are crucial for real-time flood forecasting models. Next, a specialized form of RNN called bidirectional long-short-term memory (LSTM) is employed to address the problem of time-series forecasting. Then, adaptive learning is implemented to tackle the seasonality issue caused by such rapid data by applying the designed model with adaptive learning in Figure 1. As computational time and forecasting accuracy should be prioritized more in future research, they suggest implementing distributed architectures for learning, such as collaborative cloud-fog architecture or federated learning. The purpose of this proposal is to give operators sufficient time to make preventative decisions.

Figure 2 depicts the accuracy results for two scenarios that include and investigate the impact of applying adaptive learning as a complementary mechanism to time series deep learning models. When adaptive learning is implemented, the accuracy increases from 72.6% to 81.31%. In their study, experiments are conducted in the following ways:

- **Baseline model:** The bidirectional LSTM model is trained and evaluated using a subset of data points with ground-truth labels.
- **Weakly Supervised Learning (as a preprocessing step):**
    - *Data Labeling:* Generate labels for unlabeled data programmatically using various labeling functions and model labeling techniques such as MajorityLabelVoter and LabelModel, then train and evaluate the baseline model on them.
    - *Data Augmentation:* In addition to labeling functions, data augmentation is used with Snorkel to increase the size of the training set, and then train and evaluate the baseline model on this data.
- **Adaptive learning:** Applied to all aforementioned scenarios in order to improve the performance of forecasting models.
- **Ablation study:** An ablation study investigates the performance of an AI system by removing certain components to understand the contribution of the component to the overall system. So,
    - Applying only data labeling.
    - Applying only data augmentation
    - With/without adaptive learning

Regarding the preprocessing techniques (weakly supervised learning to augment the data set and automatically annotate the unlabeled data points), it was reported that labeling functions increased the model's accuracy from 58.33% to 63.84%, whereas data augmentation techniques alone increased the accuracy to 69%. Nevertheless, when the two techniques supported by weakly supervised learning were implemented together, the model's accuracy could reach up to approximately 73%. The labeling functions are less accurate because they do not have enough data to label and hence improve the accuracy of the model. This is true since deep learning models need massive data to make accurate predictions and classifications.

In contrast, data augmentation techniques increase the data size vertically by an impressive amount when the correct transformation functions are designed and written. Additionally, adaptive learning applied to either baseline or other improved models increased overall performance, resulting in an accuracy of nearly 81%. Unquestionably, the consideration of applying adaptive learning to time series data points, particularly seasonal ones, is essential for detecting the model's degradation over long periods. This theory is supported by the fact that each time the adaptive model was implemented, the accuracy increased as shown in Figure 2. In conclusion, using weakly supervised learning techniques for data preprocessing, and then augmenting the processing model with concepts of adaptive learning could advance the accuracy of flood forecasting models.

Figure 2. The impact of adaptive learning on various AI flood forecasting models
(Abdulla, Demirci, & Ozdemir, 2023)

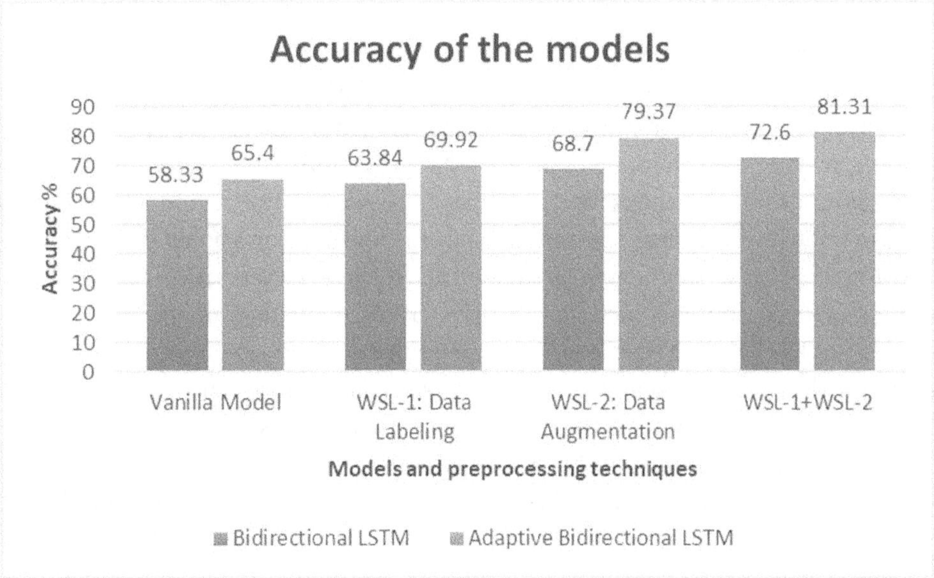

4. ADAPTIVE AI IN ENERGY CONSUMPTION FORECASTING

This section discusses the household energy consumption forecasting problem in smart cities and elaborates on methods to employ federated learning to enhance the forecasting performance and accuracy, as proposed in certain studies (Savi & Olivadese, 2021). It also discusses the potential of involving adaptive learning in the solution to this problem, in order to showcase the improvement we could achieve by doing so.

Smart cities must be able to predict the amount of electricity required by an entire city or a single building. To achieve this, a model must first predict the short-term energy consumption (load) of a single household in a building, followed by the total energy consumption of the building (Peng, et al., 2019). Consequently, it is possible to aggregate and forecast smart city demand (Khan, Mahmood, Safdar, Khan, & Khan, 2016). The significance of short-term residential energy consumption forecasting stems from the decentralization of renewable energy generation, such as photovoltaic systems, which enables households to generate their own energy and maximize its use to become more self-sufficient (Fallah, Deo, Shojafar, Conti, & Shamshirband, 2018).

In recent years, many papers have looked at this problem and proposed artificial intelligence (AI) methods to improve short-term predictions of how much energy a household will use (Yildiz, Bilbao, Dore, & Sproul, 2017). Most proposed AI methods, however, require a large amount of fine-grained historical data that must be collected and stored in a centralized architecture (Zhang, Wu, Wang, & Bi, 2015) in order to train models correctly. Now, this process is made easier with the help of the Advanced Metering Infrastructure (AMI). The AMI is based on smart meters that are put in the homes of customers and can record accurate measurements of how much energy is used at a rate of at least 15 minutes per sample (Asghar, Dan, Miorandi, & Chlamtac, 2017).

Even though new technology makes it possible for both users and energy suppliers to offer new services, regulators and users have raised many privacy concerns since the early days of smart meter adoption (Fan et al., 2010). In fact, this information can be used to figure out what customers do, which may lead to some privacy-aware people refusing to have a smart meter installed in their homes (Marmol, Sorge, Ugus, & Perez, 2012). Researchers have proposed various privacy-preserving solutions based on data aggregation and/or obfuscation to protect privacy while letting energy suppliers collect useful information. However, none of these solutions can be used for residential short-term load forecasting, which needs precise measurements from households as input data (Asghar, Dan, Miorandi, & Chlamtac, 2017).

For many years, short-term energy consumption forecasting has been a popular research problem, with numerous techniques proposed to improve prediction accuracy. Another critical factor is the selection of the most appropriate methodologies and models. The surveys by Amasyali and El-Gohary (2018), and Kaytez, Taplamacioglu, Cam, and Hardalac (2015) presented an overview of studies on energy consumption forecasting, with an emphasis on data-driven models. The majority of the reported works focused on non-residential scenarios, with the most commonly used models being artificial neural networks (ANNs) (Chitsaz, Shaker, Zareipour, Wood, & Amjady, 2015), deep learning (Aurangzeb et al., 2022), autoregressive integrated moving average (ARIMA), and support vector machine (SVM) (Nie, Liu, Liu, & Wang, 2012), or other regression methods (Hong, Zhou, Li, Xu, & Zheng, 2020).

Deep learning is predictably a popular tool for building load forecasting models. For instance, Shi, Xu, and Li (2017) proposed a deep RNN based on polling to prevent or considerably reduce the risk of overfitting. According to reported results, their proposed method performed better than traditional techniques such as ARIMA, support vector regression, and RNN. Another study conducted by Mocanu, Nguyen, Gibescu, and Kling (2016) proposed a method based on the conditional restricted Boltzmann machine (CRBM). The authors demonstrated that their method outperforms existing ANN and SVM techniques. These studies were able to achieve encouraging results, with the caveat that deep learning methods are typically too resource-hungry to be deployed at the edge by devices with limited computing resources.

As an extension to deep learning models and applications, the work of Fekri, Patel, Grolinger, and Sharma (2021) is one of the first studies in this field to implement and test LSTM. Because of its superior ability to discover long-term temporal correlations, LSTM outperforms conventional back-propagation ANNs. In addition, Alonso, Nogales, and Ruiz (2020) propose a modern LSTM-based method. The proposed solution is highly adaptable: it can accurately predict energy consumption even when the LSTM model is used for residential house load prediction with no historical samples in the training set. However, such adaptability can only be achieved by using a large amount of training data, making the method computationally demanding.

Many of the existing machine and deep learning based solutions also require a lot of computing power during the model training phase, when a huge number of smart meters can send data. This severely limits the scalability of such solutions. Of course, one can train an AI model on a small part of the data, but this impedes the model's ability to generalize. Furthermore, all of the previously mentioned machine learning based solutions share a common architectural trait, which is that they require a centralized entity to collect energy consumption measurements from customers in order to centrally train a global model. This type of structure is referred to as a centralized architecture, and it can be used as a benchmark for the decentralized and federated architectures to be compared against.

In contrast, edge computing moves the processing closer to the users. It brings cloud computing to the edge of the network, which improves speed, efficiency, reliability, privacy, security, and the ability to grow and change. Due to the need for privacy and ability to grow, it is perfect for predicting how much energy will be used (Khan, Ahmed, Hakak, Yaqoob, & Ahmed, 2019). Edge computing is like other architectures that has flaws. AI and machine learning models work best when all training data from different users is processed at a central location, but edge computing models train locally to protect client privacy (Peng, et al., 2019). Federated learning has gotten a lot of attention from researchers because it can combine data from different sources and build machine learning models in a way that is both collaborative and private (McMahan, Moore, Ramage, Hampson, & y Arcas, 2017).

Thus, federated learning lets multiple parties work together to build a model without sharing data (Kang, Liu, & Chen, 2020). It also refers to the machine learning strategy that lets models be trained in a decentralized way across many different data sources without worrying about privacy (Liu, Zhu, Xia, Jiang, & Yang, 2021). These private data sets of many different clients and institutions come from many different places, like smartphones and Internet of Things (IoT) devices (Diao, Ding, & Tarokh, 2021). Also, both machine learning and deep learning methods often need to be trained on different data set sources (such as data from multiple medical institutions) in order to be able to generalize, which is a difficult requirement given that medical data is sensitive (Kassem, et al., 2022). It has also been used successfully in other application domains (Yang Q. a., 2019), such as human-computer interaction (Yang, et al., 2018), language modeling (Wu, Liang, & Wang, 2020), transportation (Pokhrel & Choi, 2020), and Industry 4.0 (Cioffi, Travaglioni, Piscitelli, Petrillo, & De Felice, 2020), where privacy and/or scalability are vital.

Putting it all together, it is worthwhile to further explore distributed architectures based on edge computing and federated learning for short-term load forecasting, such as the one proposed by Savi and Olivadese (2021). Based on how they are built, smart meters store data at the edge, where it can be used by many people to train a global model. When this model is sent back to customers, it helps them make better predictions by showing them local patterns that they had not seen before but that other users have seen. Models such as LSTM can be trained using the federated learning schema that is built into the architecture. Adaptive learning can also be added to the overall architecture to improve model accuracy and performance by retraining the model when its accuracy drops below a certain threshold. The use of federated learning makes such an approach a more scalable and privacy-friendly alternative. Also, this plan would save even more money on communication costs if measurements of energy use are taken less often than every hour (i.e., with a smaller interval).

Using adaptive deep learning strategies in decentralized architectures has the potential to improve performance and client privacy. Thus, to meet the challenge of changing data streams and IoT device scalability, forecasting accuracy must be improved. Although the advances in machine learning and deep learning algorithms are well documented in the literature, few studies have compared model performance on this computation architecture. Comparing centralized and decentralized learning in this context will be important to understand what type of architecture is the most suitable to meet the objectives regarding performance, efficiency, and privacy.

5. ADAPTIVE AI FOR SECURITY IN SMART GRIDS AND SMART CITIES

In a smart city, various key services related to weather and water systems, transportation, public health and energy are managed in harmony to provide a sustainable, affordable and safe environment to live, while maintaining the operation of critical infrastructures without problems (Yin et al., 2015). Various components built on IoT and other communication technologies aim to increase the efficiency of economic, social, environmental services while improving people's quality of life (Chen et al., 2021). However, as cities are equipped with sensors and become smart, they face increasing threats associated with cybersecurity. An increasing number of studies show that cyber threats in smart cities are constantly evolving, getting more dangerous every day, and resulting in very serious consequences (Li et al., 2019). For example, a piece of spyware infecting a smart wearable can steal patient health record and threatens smart health at the individual level. Or, when the energy infrastructure provided by smart grids goes out of service even for a short time because of a cyberattack, all other city applications will collapse eventually, which is threatening all components of a smart city on a large scale.

The main aspects of smart city security are given in Figure 3 (Ahmed et al., 2016; Ijaz et al., 2016). As can be seen, the major components of security in a smart city can be listed as (i) smart grid security, (ii) smart building security, (iii) smart transportation security, (iv) smart health security, and (v) smart industry security. In all of these subdomains, intrusion detection systems (IDSs) play a crucial role in detecting and identifying unauthorized actions against IoT-based smart city applications (Elsaeidy et al., 2019).

Figure 3. The main aspects of IoT-based smart city security

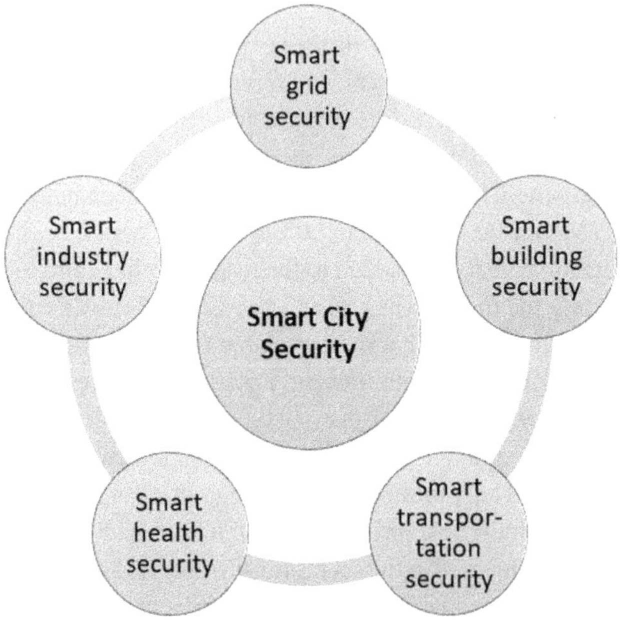

In recent years, most of the IDSs developed for IoT-based smart city applications employ adaptive AI techniques due to their high speed, efficiency, and the ability to attain high detection rates. Since threats are constantly evolving, benefiting from adaptivity has the natural benefit of detecting zero-day attacks while preserving confidentiality, integrity, and availability of the smart city applications (Chen et al., 2021).

This section focuses on recent proposals to incorporate adaptive AI based intrusion detection systems into smart cities to better protect the applications as well as the infrastructure. In this regard, existing research on adaptive IDSs are reviewed under the categories of (i) smart grids, (ii) smart buildings, (iii) smart transportation, (iv) smart health, and (v) smart industry. State-of-the-art studies are summarized, discussed and compared under these categories and presented in the following subsections.

5.1. Adaptive AI for Security in Smart Grids

The energy infrastructure provided by smart grids is indisputably the most important component for smart cities, because if it becomes out of service even for a short time, all other city applications will be affected adversely, and collapse eventually. Therefore, detecting attacks and identifying unauthorized accesses to the grid sources is of critical importance for smart city services. Since grid data arrive continuously and change over time, developing adaptive AI based IDSs which are capable of dealing with time-series data and handling automatic updates has attracted the attention of researchers in recent years (J. E. Zhang et al., 2021). In this subsection, we present a review of the works developing adaptive IDSs for providing security in smart grids. Table 2 lists the existing adaptive IDSs that are compared in terms of the attack types they detected, datasets used, and accuracy rates achieved.

Table 2. Adaptive IDSs developed for smart grids

Reference	Attack Type	Dataset	Learning Tool	Results
(Khoei et al., 2021)	DoS	CICDDos2019	-	Accuracy: 92.2%-96.7%
(Kwon et al., 2020)	Malware, FDI, and DR	IEEE 1815.1 based power system data	Bi-RNN	Accuracy: 79.07% to 98.82%
(P. Wang & Govindarasu, 2020)	DoS	IEEE 39-bus system	SVMLDT	-
(Albarakati et al., 2022)	Capture, replay, modify, drop, and delay communication messages	IEEE 9-bus system	LSTM, RNN and GRU	Recall: 96-99% Precision: 79-97%
(Kurt et al., 2018)	FDI, jamming, DoS	Generated custom data	Markov decision process, reinforcement learning	F-score: 99.97%-99.99 f-

Khoei et al. (2021) develop a boosting-based adaptive learning model to detect various types of denial-of-service (DoS) attacks. They update the weight of instances according to the previous training's performance. In this operation, they consider the probability that the prediction being correct and the given error. The results show that their adaptive IDS achieve the accuracy rates of 92.2% and 96.7% for reflection and exploitation-based attacks, respectively. Another adaptive IDS for detecting DoS attacks is presented in the work of P. Wang and Govindarasu (2020). The authors combined support vector machines (SVM) and decision tree (DT) algorithms, and they proposed a novel model named as Support Vector Machine embedded Layered Decision Tree (SVMLDT). In SVMLDT, the intrusion detection task is carried out by SVM and DT separately, but the final decision is made upon the combination of the results of each algorithm. The model also has adaptive learning based load rejection capability for adapting the system to ongoing DoS attack situations. Experimental results show that adaptive model outperforms traditional machine learning based IDSs in terms of accuracy rates.

Kwon et al. (2020) develop Bidirectional Recurrent Neural Networks (Bi-RNN) based adaptive IDS to detect malware, false data injection (FDI), and disabling reassembly (DR) types of attacks in smart grids. The developed model produces accuracy rates ranging from 79.07% to 98.82% for detecting normal behaviors. Kurt et al. (2018) develop an online system for detecting FDI, jamming, and DoS attacks in smart grids. To this end, they propose an IDS utilizing partially observable Markov decision process and reinforcement learning. The developed IDS is adaptive and proactive so that it can detect unknown attack types by mapping observations to actions. Experimental results show that F-scores when detecting FDI, jamming, and DoS attacks are 99.99%, 99.97%, and 99.97%, respectively.

Albarakati et al. (2022) try to detect capture, replay, modify, drop, and delay attacks on the communication messages. For this purpose, they develop an adaptive IDS consisting of three units which implement LSTM, RNN, and gated recurrent unit (GRU) algorithms. The IDS uses results retrieved from these adaptive units to make a decision. The experiments conducted on an IEEE 9-bus system show that attacks can be detected with the recall and precision rates ranging between 96-99% and 79-97%, respectively.

5.2. Adaptive AI for Security in Smart Buildings

Smart buildings are among the major components of the smart city paradigm and they can be defined as networks of interconnected sensors, devices and computers to manage and control various building functions such as lighting, fire access control, heating, etc. (Havard et al., 2019). In order to provide these functionalities, smart buildings use open and standardized wired or wireless communication protocols. Nevertheless, these communication technologies and the network architectures introduce several security risks and threats to the smart buildings. Attacks targeting smart buildings may cause (i) demand response messages to be blocked resulting in high bills or outages, (ii) messages to be spoofed or modified, and even (iii) private data belonging to people to be publicly disclosed. Therefore, developing adaptive AI based IDSs for detecting attacks to smart buildings has attracted the attention of researchers in recent years (Qi et al., 2017).

In this subsection, we present a review of the works developing adaptive IDSs for providing security in smart buildings and homes. Table 3 lists the existing adaptive IDSs that are compared in terms of the attack types they detected, datasets used, and accuracy rates achieved.

Table 3. Adaptive IDSs developed for smart homes and buildings

Reference	Attack Type	Dataset	Learning Tool	Results
(M. Wang et al., 2023)	Scanning, DoS, DDoS, ransomware, backdoor, injection, XSS, password, man-in-the-middle	ToN_IoT	Transformer	Accuracy: 95.78%-98.39%
(Arrington et al., 2016)	-	Generated custom data	Immunity inspired algorithms	-
(Anthi et al., 2018)	Scanning, probing, DoS	Generated custom data	-	F-score: 65.8%-97.7%
(Venkatraman & Surendiran, 2020)	DoS, control hijacking, zero day, replay attacks	Snort's data	Timed automata based classifier	Accuracy: 99.06%
(Heartfield et al., 2021)	-	Real-time data	Reinforcement learning	Accuracy: 85%-93%

According to Venkatraman and Surendiran (2020), the most important problem of current IDSs developed for smart city environments is that they cannot adapt themselves to the real-time service changes. To this end, the authors develop an adaptive hybrid IDS based on the timed automata controller approach. The developed IDS obtains analysis packets containing multimedia files comprehensively, along with other file formats. It adaptively learns whether there are any changes in attack behaviors and updates parameters according to the given feedback. Experiments show that the developed IDS can detect DoS, control hijacking, zero day, and replay attacks with the accuracy rate of 99.06%. Heartfield et al. (2021) state that they develop the first IDS for smart homes working in an adaptive manner. That is, their model MAGPIE can adjust its decision about intrusions according to changing conditions in a home, such as new devices and users. They take advantage of reinforcement learning to provide adaptivity when deciding on hyperparameters of the unsupervised classifier.

M. Wang et al. (2023) utilized from both network traffic and telemetry data transmitted between IoT devices in a smart home to detect the anomaly state of these devices. Unlike traditional IDSs, their system focuses on the attack impact instead of analyzing attack behavior. To this end, they develop a transformer based IDS containing a multi-head self-attention mechanism that can adaptively learn from heterogeneous input containing both categorical and numerical features. Experiments show that the developed IDS can detect attacks with a 98.39% accuracy for binary classification, while it can recognize different types of attacks with an accuracy rate of 97.06% for multiple classifications. Arrington et al. (2016) propose an IDS detecting behavioral based anomalies for smart home environments. They construct their model on adaptive learning based immunity inspired algorithms, and conclude that it is a cost efficient, scalable, and easily verifiable model for simulated smart home and vicinity environments.

Unlike others, Anthi et al. (2018) focus on detecting malicious IoT nodes along with the malicious behavior. Their model, named Petras, is an adaptive, real-time, and both signature and anomaly based intrusion detection system. It consists of three modules: In the first module, it adaptively learns benign network behavior of the created smart home environment. Thus, Petras creates a baseline for the normal behavior of the network for each device. In the second module, it learns the behavior of different attack types, and finally in the third module it applies a rule based approach by using the security policies defined by the network administrator. The overall system decision is based on the combination of the outcomes of these three modules.

5.3. Adaptive AI for Security in Smart Transportation

Establishing smart transportation systems is one of the most important stages of building smart cities. Smart cars and other vehicles connect each other and share data; and thus they form the internet of vehicles (IoV) which is a significant component of IoT. In order to improve traffic management, road safety, and the comfort of passengers, providing security of the systems and the data within IoV systems is of vital importance (Bangui & Buhnova, 2021). If the attacks threatening these systems could not be detected appropriately, they may result in serious consequences such as traffic accidents and even human death. Existing intrusion detection solutions developed for traditional networking architectures cannot be directly applied to smart transportation networks since sensors and IoT devices used have constrained resource capabilities. Therefore, novel and intelligent IDSs addressing the specific needs of IoT based smart transportation systems have been developed.

In this subsection, we present a review of the works developing adaptive IDSs for providing security in smart transportation systems. Table 4 lists the existing adaptive IDSs that are compared in terms of the attack types they detected, datasets used, and accuracy rates achieved.

Table 4. Adaptive IDSs developed for smart transportation systems

Reference	Attack Type	Dataset	Learning Tool	Results
(Albulayhi & Sheldon, 2021)	Includes DoS, DDoS, OS and service scan, keylogging and data exfiltration attack	BoT-IoT	Ensemble of deep belief networks, OC-SVM, k-means	Accuracy: 85.86%-91.47%
(Liu et al., 2023)	DoS, Probe, U2R and R2L	NSL-KDD	Federated learning, CNN, multi-layer perceptron (MLP)	Accuracy: 85.8%-88.1%
(Comert et al., 2022)	DoS, impersonation, and false information	Generated custom data	Bi-directional LSTM	Accuracy: 98%-100%
(Abbaspour et al., 2016)	FDI	Generated custom data	Embedded kalman filter, neural networks	-
(Mitchell & Chen, 2014)	reckless, random, and opportunistic attacker types	Generated custom data	multi-agent system/ant colony clustering model	False negative: 0.01

Albulayhi and Sheldon (2021) developed an adaptive IDS which is suitable for the dynamic nature of IoV networks. As different from existing adaptive solutions, the authors propose an improved adaptive anomaly detection method that defines the normal behavior profile for each IoT device instead of using pre-defined generalized thresholds. While defining device-level and global profiles, they use one class support vector machine (OC-SVM) and k-means algorithms, respectively. They also utilize a local-global ratio-based anomaly detection scheme and an ensemble of deep belief networks for adapting the system to changing situations to avoid unnecessary re-learning. Liu et al. (2023) developed an adaptive batch federated aggregation based IDS to detect attacks against maritime transportation systems. While detecting attacks, they also aim to preserve the privacy of voyage data used for training deep learning based IDSs. For this purpose, they update only the parameters of the global model during the exchange of model parameters, and preserve the privacy of local parameters belonging to vessels with the use of federated learning. The results show that the developed CNN-MLP based model can detect attacks with an accuracy rate of 88.1%.

Comert et al. (2022) investigate the effects of change point models to detect attacks against connected vehicle systems in real time. To this end, the authors use expectation maximization (EM) and two types of cumulative summation (CUSUM) algorithms, which are typical and adaptive. Although these models can detect vehicle-to-vehicle (V2V) attacks such as DoS and impersonation with minimal false positive rates, the results show that they are not suitable for detecting vehicle-to-everything (V2X) communication attacks. Therefore, the authors also design a bi-directional LSTM based multistage IDS detecting DoS, impersonation, and false information attacks with an accuracy rate of up to 100%.

Abbaspour et al. (2016) focus on the security of unmanned aerial vehicles (UAVs) to provide control and continuous surveillance to these systems. For this purpose, the authors propose a novel neural network based algorithm to detect FDI attacks in UAVs. In order to tune parameters adaptively, they use embedded kalman filter (EKF). The results show that the proposed EKF based adaptive neural network increases detection ability as well as the learning rate when compared to the conventional neural networks. Mitchell and Chen (2014) also concentrate on detecting attacks against UAVs. When investigating attack behaviors, the authors use historical attack data and aim to detect if the UAVs are operating normally or under an attack. Their behavior rule based intrusion detection system (BRUIDS) is an adaptive system so that it can adjust itself to the changes in attack/attacker types and environment. While this adaptivity increases the false negative rate, it minimizes the false positive rate at the same time.

5.4. Adaptive AI for Security in Smart Health

Establishing powerful and smart IoT-based healthcare systems becomes more important and vital every day, especially in a world that has experienced the COVID-19 pandemic. These systems are used in the diagnosis process by providing many benefits especially in the areas of (i) real-time patient monitoring, (ii) sending alerts to relevant medical personnel in an emergency, and (iii) reducing treatment costs. However, they are vulnerable to several security and privacy attacks since they are built on open networking and communication architectures. These attacks lead to patient data being stolen and misused, as well as affecting the diagnosis and treatment process adversely (Singh et al., 2023). In order to overcome these security problems, researchers tend to develop IDSs for detecting different types of cyberattacks threatening intelligent healthcare systems, which are tailored to the specific requirements of these systems.

In this subsection, we present a review of the works developing adaptive IDSs for providing security in smart healthcare systems. Table 5 lists the existing adaptive IDSs that are compared in terms of the attack types they detected, datasets used, and accuracy rates achieved.

Table 5. Adaptive IDSs developed for smart healthcare systems

Reference	Attack Type	Dataset	Learning Tool	Results
(Singh et al., 2023)	Insider attacks	Generated custom data	AHP, decision rules	Accuracy: 93.9%
(Akram et al., 2021)	DoS, Probe, U2R and R2L	KDDcup 99	ANFIS	Error rate: 0.0021
(Rajalakshmi et al., 2023)	-	Real-time data	MLP	-
(Ravi et al., 2022)	IoMT malware family	(CDMC)-2020-IoMT-Malware, Big-2015	CNN, LSTM, GRU, RNN	Accuracy: 90%-95%
(Raza et al., 2023)	Integrity attacks	Generated custom data	Autoencoders, support vector data description	Accuracy: 97.6.5-98.8%

Singh et al. (2023) propose an adaptive and behavioral IDS achieving a 93.9% accuracy rate while detecting different types of insider attacks. The authors first calculate a trust value for each piece of medical data coming from a sensor by using the behavioral parameters. Then, a set of decision rules are created based on the trust scores and alerts are generated according to the risk level. They also use an adaptive Analytical Hierarchy Process (AHP) method to calculate the weights of trust parameters according to changing conditions. In another study, Akram et al. (2021) develop an adaptive neuro-fuzzy inference system (ANFIS) based IDS to detect the attacks intended for compromising the integrity of patient health record data. Their primary aim is to detect unauthorized accesses to the servers holding patient data, and thus providing more secure and reliable cloud platforms for smart healthcare systems.

Rajalakshmi et al. (2023) propose an energy efficient attack detection model, named as adaptive swish-based deep multi-layer perceptron (ASDMLP). The model clusters the sensor devices of patients, and assigns a head sensor to each cluster by considering the degree, distance, and energy status of the devices. The patient data collected in the clusters are sent to the cloud servers via the base stations. The developed IDS running on the cloud server detects intrusions by training the optimal features produced by opposition and greedy levy mutation-based coyotes optimization algorithm (OGCOA). One of the most important aspects of this adaptive IDS is that it works on real-time IoT databases in an energy efficient manner.

Ravi et al. (2022) focus on detecting and classifying malware attacks to internet of medical things (IoMT) devices. Their attention based multidimensional deep learning approach outperforms existing methods with the accuracy of 95% for malware detection, and 94% for malware classification.

Raza et al. (2023) state that the traditional learning approaches in which data are collected and processed in a centralized manner are not appropriate for the healthcare applications since they rely heavily on sensitive patient data. Hence, they develop a novel framework combining support vector data description with autoencoders in a federated manner, instead of a centralized manner. The results show that their approach is not only successful at detecting anomalies, but also efficient in terms of cost compared to other existing solutions.

5.5. Adaptive AI for Security in Smart Industry

Smart industry refers to the digital transformation of many industries such as manufacturing, oil and gas, energy, etc. by integrating industrial IoT (IIoT) technologies to the production, monitoring and management processes of these sectors. With IIoT, industrial data are collected, exchanged, and analyzed by means of sensors, actuators, and other IoT devices (Hamouda et al., 2021). However, due to its complex and open nature, IIoT networks have to deal with several security threats; and any failure in a component can cause the entire system to crash in an instant. Hence, traditional intrusion detection systems cannot meet the specific needs of smart industry. Being able to detect attacks in real time is as important as detecting them with high accuracy (Tharewal et al., 2022). Therefore, researchers tend to develop real-time and adaptive intrusion detection solutions for smart industry applications.

In this subsection, we present a review of the works developing adaptive IDSs for providing security in smart industry systems. Table 6 lists the existing adaptive IDSs that are compared in terms of the attack types they detected, datasets used, and accuracy rates achieved.

Hassan et al. (2021) propose a deep learning based boundary protection system which is compatible with various IIoT protocols. Their approach is semi-supervised in that it extracts the characteristics of the vulnerabilities threatening trust boundaries from labeled and unlabeled data; and then it uses them for training a supervised deep learning algorithm. Using unlabeled data in this process enables the model to be adaptive and detect emerging attacks that have not been encountered before. Tharewal et al. (2022) use deep reinforcement learning instead of supervised and unsupervised learning because they argue that efficient detection of attacks in IIoT environments can be possible by combining the observation capability of deep learning with the decision making ability of reinforcement learning. They utilize LightGBM to select important features for IIoT effectively, and build their IDS on the PPO2 algorithm. Experiments show that the developed IDS can detect 99% of different attack types threatening the U.S. natural gas pipeline transportation network.

Table 6. Adaptive IDSs developed for smart industrial systems

Reference	Attack Type	Dataset	Learning Tool	Results
(Hassan et al., 2021)	Malicious command injection, spoofed cryptographic key, malware, etc.	Generated custom data	Semisupervised deep neural networks	Accuracy: 93.63%
(Tharewal et al., 2022)	NMRI, CMRI, MSCI, MPCI, MFCI, DoS, Reconnaissance	U.S. Department of Energy's Oak Ridge National Laboratory attack dataset	PPPO2, LightGBM	Accuracy: 96-99%
(Gyamfi & Jurcut, 2023)	Fuzzers, DoS, analysis, exploit, shellcode, worms, backdoor, generic, DDoSIM	UNSW-NB15, and created new dataset	OI-SVDD, AS-ELM	Accuracy: 85%-100%
(Yan et al., 2020)	-	Generated custom data	DNN	Precision: 85-90%
(W. Zhang & Zhang, 2022)	DoS, Probe, U2R and R2L	NSL-KDD	Autoencoder	Accuracy: 95.42%

Gyamfi and Jurcut (2023) prefer to develop an online learning based approach since the attackers employ techniques that are changing and evolving dynamically. They propose an IDS which uses online incremental support vector data description (OI-SVDD) on the side of IIoT devices, and adaptive sequential extreme learning machine (AS-ELM) on the side of multiaccess edge computing (MEC) server for attack detection. However, this extreme learning based deep analysis requires a highly stable network connection in terms of quality of service (QoS) parameters such as latency and throughput. Yan et al. (2020) classify threats as attack or not-attack by looking at their source addresses and domains. They develop an approach based on mini-batch gradient descent with an adaptive learning rate and momentum (HCA-MBGDALRM). The most important advantage of this approach is that it can work with very large traffic data since it implements a parallel framework. The results show that HCA-MBGDALRM outperforms traditional machine learning based approaches in terms of processing speed. Unlike the above studies, W. Zhang and Zhang (2022) also try to solve the problem of unbalanced network traffic data for increasing the efficiency of their IDS. For this purpose, they use an improved autoencoder, and group the main attack features to abstract details and have a higher-level expression. They test their approach on the NSL-KDD dataset, and the results show that it can detect attacks with a 95.42% accuracy rate.

6. DISCUSSION AND FUTURE DIRECTIONS

Artificial intelligence and machine learning models seem to get more accurate and more practical every day. With the inclusion of adaptivity, they become more flexible and able to sustain their performance in the face of changing conditions. However, these models are threatened by a fast-growing concern: adversarial attacks. These are deliberate attempts by malicious parties to mislead learning models and cause them to perform classification or forecasting incorrectly. Even if a model is highly successful on normal data, attackers are often able to reduce its accuracy to an unacceptable level through carefully crafted adversarial examples. The ability of a model to resist such attacks and maintain its accuracy is called *adversarial robustness*, which is an aspect of the model different from the common metrics (e.g., accuracy, precision, recall, F1-score, etc.) typically used to measure its success. Robustness is usually absent from models unless they are designed to be robust. On the other hand, evaluating the robustness of models is tricky and an active research area (Carlini et al., 2019).

Adaptive AI models should not only remain stable when data changes and fluctuates naturally, but they should also be resilient in the presence of adversarial attacks, meaning that they should continue to perform at an acceptable level even when data contains adversarial examples. Hence, developing robust adaptive AI models is an important area of study which is gaining prominence as AI applications continue to proliferate. In this context, adaptivity has an additional and different meaning: While adaptive AI is about maintaining and even improving model performance as data changes over time, adaptive defenses are methods to preserve model performance when faced with active attempts to fool the model. However, adaptive defenses may not improve robustness compared to static defenses, and they may sometimes even weaken the static defense. So, they must be evaluated carefully and systematically to understand whether they are worth the development effort and the computational cost (Croce et al., 2022).

People who try to build robust machine learning models are not the only ones making use of adaptivity. There is a separate but related line of research on adaptive attacks, which are defined as specifically designed adversarial attacks targeting a particular defense method (Tramer et al., 2020). As with many other examples in the cybersecurity realm, this situation is similar to an arms race: Both sides utilize every possible technology to gain an edge, often using similar concepts and approaches towards different or even opposite objectives. Just as enemy weapons can be analyzed to develop effective defenses against them, researchers should devote considerable time to study adaptive attacks against defenses to adversarial examples and discover better ways to enhance model robustness.

One application domain where the importance of adversarial robustness of adaptive AI is the most apparent is self-driving (or autonomous) vehicles. The self-driving capabilities of these vehicles improve over time as they continue to learn from both their own time on the road and data obtained from other vehicles. Considering their already impressive record, it is easy to envision and even expect self-driving cars to be the predominant means of transportation within a few decades. Nevertheless, many people will likely refuse to fully trust such vehicles due to understandable safety concerns, which would certainly be exacerbated upon hearing the news about the latest adversarial attacks skillfully crippling autonomous driving algorithms to cause major accidents. Such news may not be common now, but in a smart city where autonomous vehicles are used frequently for private and public transportation alike, attacks targeting models for object detection, traffic sign classification, etc. will be the source of fear and pushback against AI-assisted autonomous transportation, as well as many other applications of AI in smart cities. Therefore, achieving adversarial robustness is critical for the adoption of AI in both the near future and the long term.

Adversarial attacks are easier and more common against image classification than against intrusion detection systems (IDSs) because the methods for perturbing data features to generate adversarial examples are better suited to the image domain. Still, adversarial AI in intrusion detection has become an active research area in recent years, and many attack approaches as well as defense methods have been proposed in the literature (He et al., 2023). As explained in Section 5, IDSs are crucial components of an IoT-based smart city. There are adversarial attack methodologies specifically designed to target the IDSs in IoT networks (Qui et al., 2020), as well as recent approaches to adversarial example generation based on generative adversarial networks (GANs) (Lin et al., 2022). In addition, researchers have recently developed an autoencoder-based robust IDS model and demonstrated its effectiveness against GAN-generated adversarial attacks (Sarıkaya et al., 2023). The number and variety of research efforts should continue to increase in this area because successful attempts to evade IDSs would lead to grave consequences for all smart city applications relying on the effective detection of cyberattacks.

In conclusion, this chapter has taken an expansive look at the potential of adaptive learning in the context of smart city applications. In this domain, adaptivity is especially important because of the fast pace of data generation, the variety of AI use cases, and the large scale of deployment. Adaptive AI is a necessary and promising solution to many smart city problems, ranging from load forecasting on the critical infrastructures to traffic management and disaster response. Yet, adaptive AI still has a long way to go before we can trust it with the day-to-day running of our cities. In addition to data quality issues and the cost necessary to ensure the smooth operation of adaptive AI-based analytics and decision support systems, adversarial attacks constitute an existential threat to AI itself. While it may be too dramatic to say that such attacks can kill AI in its infancy, they can severely limit its adoption and the level of comfort the society can reach regarding AI. Adaptivity and adversarial robustness are among the key terms for the future of AI. Consequently, developing methods to build robust adaptive AI models will be an exciting area of research for years to come.

REFERENCES

Abbaspour, A., Yen, K. K., Noei, S., & Sargolzaei, A. (2016). Detection of Fault Data Injection Attack on UAV Using Adaptive Neural Network. *Procedia Computer Science*, *95*, 193–200. doi:10.1016/j.procs.2016.09.312

Abdulla, N., Demirci, M., & Ozdemir, S. (2021). Adaptive learning on fog-cloud collaborative architecture for stream data processing. *2021 International Symposium on Networks, Computers and Communications (ISNCC)* (pp. 1-6). Dubai: IEEE. 10.1109/ISNCC52172.2021.9615824

Abdulla, N., Demirci, M., & Ozdemir, S. (2022). Design and evaluation of adaptive deep learning models for weather forecasting. *Engineering Applications of Artificial Intelligence*, *116*, 105440. doi:10.1016/j.engappai.2022.105440

Abdulla, N., Demirci, M., & Ozdemir, S. (2023). Towards utilizing unlabeled data for flood forecasting with weakly supervised adaptive learning. *2023 Innovations in Intelligent Systems and Applications Conference (ASYU)*. IEEE.

Ahmed, E., Yaqoob, I., Gani, A., Imran, M., & Guizani, M. (2016). Internet-of-things-based smart environments: State of the art, taxonomy, and open research challenges. *IEEE Wireless Communications*, *23*(5), 10–16. doi:10.1109/MWC.2016.7721736

Akram, F., Liu, D., Zhao, P., Kryvinska, N., Abbas, S., & Rizwan, M. (2021). Trustworthy Intrusion Detection in E-Healthcare Systems. *Frontiers in Public Health*, *9*(December), 1–10. doi:10.3389/fpubh.2021.788347 PMID:34926397

Albarakati, A., Robillard, C., Karanfil, M., Kassouf, M., Debbabi, M., Youssef, A., Ghafouri, M., & Hadjidj, R. (2022). Security Monitoring of IEC 61850 Substations Using IEC 62351-7 Network and System Management. *IEEE Transactions on Industrial Informatics*, *18*(3), 1641–1653. doi:10.1109/TII.2021.3082079

Albulayhi, K., & Sheldon, F. T. (2021). An Adaptive Deep-Ensemble Anomaly-Based Intrusion Detection System for the Internet of Things. *2021 IEEE World AI IoT Congress, AIIoT 2021*, (pp. 187–196). IEEE. 10.1109/AIIoT52608.2021.9454168

Alonso, A. M., Nogales, F. J., & Ruiz, C. (2020). A single scalable LSTM model for short-term forecasting of massive electricity time series. *Energies*, *13*(20), 5328. doi:10.3390/en13205328

Amasyali, K., & El-Gohary, N. M. (2018). A review of data-driven building energy consumption prediction studies. *Renewable & Sustainable Energy Reviews*, *81*, 1192–1205. doi:10.1016/j.rser.2017.04.095

Anthi, E., Williams, L., & Burnap, P. (2018). Pulse: An adaptive intrusion detection for the internet of things. *IET Conference Publications*, 2018(CP740). IET. 10.1049/cp.2018.0035

Arrington, B., Barnett, L. E., Rufus, R., & Esterline, A. (2016). Behavioral modeling intrusion detection system (BMIDS) using internet of things (IoT) behavior-based anomaly detection via immunity-inspired algorithms. *2016 25th International Conference on Computer Communications and Networks, ICCCN 2016*, (pp. 12–17). IEEE. 10.1109/ICCCN.2016.7568495

Asghar, M. R., Dan, G., Miorandi, D., & Chlamtac, I. (2017). Smart meter data privacy: A survey. *IEEE Communications Surveys and Tutorials*, *19*(4), 2820–2835. doi:10.1109/COMST.2017.2720195

Aurangzeb, K., Aslam, S., Haider, S. I., Mohsin, S. M., Islam, S., Khattak, H. A., & Shah, S. (2022). Energy forecasting using multiheaded convolutional neural networks in efficient renewable energy resources equipped with energy storage system. *Transactions on Emerging Telecommunications Technologies*, *33*(2), e3837. doi:10.1002/ett.3837

Bangui, H., & Buhnova, B. (2021). Recent advances in machine-learning driven intrusion detection in transportation: Survey. *Procedia Computer Science, 184*(2019), 877–886. doi:10.1016/j.procs.2021.04.014

Birch, C. E., Rabb, B. L., Boing, S. J., Shelton, K. L., Lamb, R., Hunter, N., Trigg, M. A., Hines, A., Taylor, A. L., Pilling, C., & Dale, M. (2021). Enhanced surface water flood forecasts: User-led development and testing. *Journal of Flood Risk Management*, *14*(2), e12691. doi:10.1111/jfr3.12691

Carlini, N., Athalye, A., Papernot, N., Brendel, W., Rauber, J., Tsipras, D., & Kurakin, A. (2019). On evaluating adversarial robustness. *arXiv preprint arXiv:1902.06705.*

Chen, C., Hui, Q., Xie, W., Wan, S., Zhou, Y., & Pei, Q. (2021). Convolutional Neural Networks for forecasting flood process in Internet-of-Things enabled smart city. *Computer Networks*, *186*, 107744. doi:10.1016/j.comnet.2020.107744

Chen, D., Wawrzynski, P., & Lv, Z. (2021). Cyber security in smart cities: A review of deep learning-based applications and case studies. *Sustainable Cities and Society, 66*(November 2020). doi:10.1016/j.scs.2020.102655

Chitsaz, H., Shaker, H., Zareipour, H., Wood, D., & Amjady, N. (2015). Short-term electricity load forecasting of buildings in microgrids. *Energy and Building*, *99*, 50–60. doi:10.1016/j.enbuild.2015.04.011

Cioffi, R., Travaglioni, M., Piscitelli, G., Petrillo, A., & De Felice, F. (2020). Artificial intelligence and machine learning applications in smart production: Progress, trends, and directions. *Sustainability (Basel)*, *12*(2), 492. doi:10.3390/su12020492

Comert, G., Rahman, M., Islam, M., & Chowdhury, M. (2022). Change Point Models for Real-Time Cyber Attack Detection in Connected Vehicle Environment. *IEEE Transactions on Intelligent Transportation Systems, 23*(8), 12328–12342. doi:10.1109/TITS.2021.3113675

Croce, F., Gowal, S., Brunner, T., Shelhamer, E., Hein, M., & Cemgil, T. (2022, June). Evaluating the adversarial robustness of adaptive test-time defenses. In *International Conference on Machine Learning* (pp. 4421-4435). PMLR.

Dai, W., Tang, Y., Zhang, Z., & Cai, Z. (2021). Ensemble learning technology for coastal flood forecasting in internet-of-things-enabled smart city. *International Journal of Computational Intelligence Systems, 14*(1), 1–16. doi:10.1007/s44196-021-00023-y

Danso-Amoako, E., Scholz, M., Kalimeris, N., Yang, Q., & Shao, J. (2012). Predicting dam failure risk for sustainable flood retention basins: A generic case study for the wider Greater Manchester area. *Computers, Environment and Urban Systems, 36*(5), 423–433. doi:10.1016/j.compenvurbsys.2012.02.003

Das, T., Zhong, Y., Stoica, I., & Shenker, S. (2014). Adaptive stream processing using dynamic batch sizing. In *Proceedings of the ACM Symposium on Cloud Computing* (pp. 1-13). ACM. 10.1145/2670979.2670995

Diao, E., Ding, J., & Tarokh, V. (2021). *Communication efficient semi-supervised federated learning with unlabeled clients.*

Elsaeidy, A., Munasinghe, K. S., Sharma, D., & Jamalipour, A. (2019). Intrusion detection in smart cities using Restricted Boltzmann Machines. *Journal of Network and Computer Applications, 135*(January), 76–83. doi:10.1016/j.jnca.2019.02.026

Fallah, S. N., Deo, R. C., Shojafar, M., Conti, M., & Shamshirband, S. (2018). Computational intelligence approaches for energy load forecasting in smart energy management grids: State of the art, future challenges, and research directions. *Energies, 11*(3), 596. doi:10.3390/en11030596

Fan, Z., Kalogridis, G., Efthymiou, C., Sooriyabandara, M., Serizawa, M., & McGeehan, J. (2010). The new frontier of communications research: smart grid and smart metering. *Proceedings of the 1st International Conference on Energy-Efficient Computing and Networking*, (pp. 115-118). ACM. 10.1145/1791314.1791331

Fekri, M. N., Patel, H., Grolinger, K., & Sharma, V. (2021). Deep learning for load forecasting with smart meter data: Online Adaptive Recurrent Neural Network. *Applied Energy, 282*, 116177. doi:10.1016/j.apenergy.2020.116177

Gyamfi, E., & Jurcut, A. D. (2023). Novel Online Network Intrusion Detection System for Industrial IoT Based on OI-SVDD and AS-ELM. *IEEE Internet of Things Journal, 10*(5), 3827–3839. doi:10.1109/JIOT.2022.3172393

Hamouda, D., Ferrag, M. A., Benhamida, N., & Seridi, H. (2021). Intrusion Detection Systems for Industrial Internet of Things: A Survey. *2021 International Conference on Theoretical and Applicative Aspects of Computer Science, ICTAACS 2021*, (pp. 1–8). IEEE. 10.1109/ICTAACS53298.2021.9715177

Hassan, M. M., Huda, S., Sharmeen, S., Abawajy, J., & Fortino, G. (2021). An Adaptive Trust Boundary Protection for IIoT Networks Using Deep-Learning Feature-Extraction-Based Semisupervised Model. *IEEE Transactions on Industrial Informatics*, *17*(4), 2860–2870. doi:10.1109/TII.2020.3015026

Havard, N., McGrath, S., Flanagan, C., & MacNamee, C. (2018, December). Smart building based on internet of things technology. In *2018 12th International conference on sensing technology (ICST)* (pp. 278-281). IEEE. 10.1109/ICSensT.2018.8603575

Hayati, M., & Mohebi, Z. (2007). Application of artificial neural networks for temperature forecasting. *Iranian Journal of Electrical and Computer Engineering*, *1*(4), 662–666.

He, K., Kim, D. D., & Asghar, M. R. (2023). Adversarial machine learning for network intrusion detection systems: A comprehensive survey. *IEEE Communications Surveys and Tutorials*, *25*(1), 538–566. doi:10.1109/COMST.2022.3233793

Heartfield, R., Loukas, G., Bezemskij, A., & Panaousis, E. (2021). Self-Configurable Cyber-Physical Intrusion Detection for Smart Homes Using Reinforcement Learning. *IEEE Transactions on Information Forensics and Security*, *16*, 1720–1735. doi:10.1109/TIFS.2020.3042049

Hewage, P., Behera, A., Trovati, M., Pereira, E., Ghahremani, M., Palmieri, F., & Liu, Y. (2020). Temporal convolutional neural (TCN) network for an effective weather forecasting using time-series data from the local weather station. *Soft Computing*, *24*(21), 16453–16482. doi:10.1007/s00500-020-04954-0

Hingmire, A. M., & Bhaladhare, P. R. (2022). A review on urban flood management techniques for the smart city and future research. In *International Conference on Intelligent Cyber Physical Systems and Internet of Things* (pp. 303-317). Springer.

Hong, Y., Zhou, Y., Li, Q., Xu, W., & Zheng, X. (2020). A deep learning method for short-term residential load forecasting in smart grid. *IEEE Access : Practical Innovations, Open Solutions*, *8*, 55785–55797. doi:10.1109/ACCESS.2020.2981817

Huyen, C. (2022). Data distribution shifts and monitoring. In C. Huyen, Designing machine learning systems (pp. 225-261). O'Reilly Media, Inc.

Ijaz, S., Ali, M., Khan, A., & Ahmed, M. (2016). Smart Cities: A Survey on Security Concerns. *International Journal of Advanced Computer Science and Applications*, *7*(2). doi:10.14569/IJACSA.2016.070277

Kang, Y., Liu, Y., & Chen, T. (2020). Fedmvt: Semi-supervised vertical federated learning with multiview training. *arXiv preprint arXiv:2008.10838.*

Kassem, H., Alapatt, D., & Mascagni, P., Karargyris, A., & Padoy, N. (2022). Federated cycling (FedCy): Semi-supervised Federated Learning of surgical phases. *IEEE Transactions on Medical Imaging*. PMID:36374877

Kaytez, F., Taplamacioglu, M. C., Cam, E., & Hardalac, F. (2015). Forecasting electricity consumption: A comparison of regression analysis, neural networks and least squares support vector machines. *International Journal of Electrical Power & Energy Systems*, *67*, 431–438. doi:10.1016/j.ijepes.2014.12.036

Khan, A. R., Mahmood, A., Safdar, A., Khan, Z. A., & Khan, N. A. (2016). Load forecasting, dynamic pricing and DSM in smart grid: A review. *Renewable & Sustainable Energy Reviews*, *54*, 1311–1322. doi:10.1016/j.rser.2015.10.117

Khan, W. Z., Ahmed, E., Hakak, S., Yaqoob, I., & Ahmed, A. (2019). Edge computing: A survey. *Future Generation Computer Systems*, *97*, 219–235. doi:10.1016/j.future.2019.02.050

Khoei, T. T., Aissou, G., Hu, W. C., & Kaabouch, N. (2021). Ensemble Learning Methods for Anomaly Intrusion Detection System in Smart Grid. *IEEE International Conference on Electro Information Technology*, (pp. 129–135). IEEE. 10.1109/EIT51626.2021.9491891

Kim, T. H., Ramos, C., & Mohammed, S. (2017). Smart city and IoT. *Future Generation Computer Systems*, *76*, 159–162. doi:10.1016/j.future.2017.03.034

Ku, J.-H. (2018). A study on adaptive learning model for performance improvement of stream analytics. *Journal of Convergence for Information Technology*, *8*(1), 201–206.

Kuncheva, L. I. (2008). Classifier ensembles for detecting concept change in streaming data: Overview and perspectives. In *2nd Workshop SUEMA* (pp. 5-10). ACM.

Kurt, M. N., Ogundijo, O., Li, C., & Wang, X. (2018). Online Cyber-Attack Detection in Smart Grid: A Reinforcement Learning Approach. *IEEE Transactions on Smart Grid*, *10*(5), 5174–5185. doi:10.1109/TSG.2018.2878570

Kwon, S., Yoo, H., & Shon, T. (2020). IEEE 1815.1-Based power system security with bidirectional RNN-Based network anomalous attack detection for cyber-physical system. *IEEE Access : Practical Innovations, Open Solutions*, *8*, 77572–77586. doi:10.1109/ACCESS.2020.2989770

Li, F., Yan, X., Xie, Y., Sang, Z., & Yuan, X. (2019). A Review of Cyber-Attack Methods in Cyber-Physical Power System. *APAP 2019 - 8th IEEE International Conference on Advanced Power System Automation and Protection*, (pp. 1335–1339). IEEE. 10.1109/APAP47170.2019.9225126

Li, H., Wang, Y., Wang, H., & Zhou, B. (2017). Multi-window based ensemble learning for classification of imbalanced streaming data. *World Wide Web (Bussum)*, *20*(6), 1507–1525. doi:10.1007/s11280-017-0449-x

Lin, Z., Shi, Y., & Xue, Z. (2022, May). Idsgan: Generative adversarial networks for attack generation against intrusion detection. In *Pacific-asia conference on knowledge discovery and data mining* (pp. 79–91). Springer International Publishing. doi:10.1007/978-3-031-05981-0_7

Liu, W., Xu, X., Wu, L., Qi, L., Jolfaei, A., Ding, W., & Khosravi, M. R. (2023). Intrusion Detection for Maritime Transportation Systems with Batch Federated Aggregation. *IEEE Transactions on Intelligent Transportation Systems*, *24*(2), 2503–2514. doi:10.1109/TITS.2022.3181436

Liu, X., Zhu, L., Xia, S.-T., Jiang, Y., & Yang, X. (2021). GDST: Global Distillation Self-Training for Semi-Supervised Federated Learning. In *2021 IEEE Global Communications Conference (GLOBECOM)* (pp. 1-6). IEEE. 10.1109/GLOBECOM46510.2021.9685700

Lynch, P. (2006). *The emergence of numerical weather prediction: Richardson's dream*. Cambridge University Press.

Marmol, F. G., Sorge, C., Ugus, O., & Perez, G. M. (2012). Do not snoop my habits: Preserving privacy in the smart grid. *IEEE Communications Magazine*, *50*(5), 166–172. doi:10.1109/MCOM.2012.6194398

McMahan, B., Moore, E., Ramage, D., Hampson, S., & Arcas, B. A. (2017). Communication-efficient learning of deep networks from decentralized data. In *Artificial intelligence and statistics* (pp. 1273–1282). PMLR.

Mehta, S. (2017). Concept drift in streaming data classification: Algorithms, platforms and issues. *Procedia Computer Science*, 804–811.

Mitchell, R., & Chen, I. R. (2014). Adaptive intrusion detection of malicious unmanned air vehicles using behavior rule specifications. *IEEE Transactions on Systems, Man, and Cybernetics. Systems*, *44*(5), 593–604. doi:10.1109/TSMC.2013.2265083

Mocanu, E., Nguyen, P. H., Gibescu, M., & Kling, W. L. (2016). Deep learning for estimating building energy consumption. *Sustainable Energy. Grids and Networks*, *6*, 91–99.

Moishin, M., Deo, R. C., Prasad, R., Raj, N., & Abdulla, S. (2021). Designing deep-based learning flood forecast model with ConvLSTM hybrid algorithm. *IEEE Access : Practical Innovations, Open Solutions*, *9*, 50982–50993. doi:10.1109/ACCESS.2021.3065939

Naik, S., Patil, S. A., Verma, A., & Hingmire, A. (2020). Flood prediction using logistic regression for Kerala state. [IJERT]. *International Journal of Engineering Research & Technology (Ahmedabad)*, *9*(03).

Nasiri, H., Nasehi, S., & Goudarzi, M. (2019). Evaluation of distributed stream processing frameworks for IoT applications in Smart Cities. *Journal of Big Data*, *6*(1), 1–24. doi:10.1186/s40537-019-0215-2

Nie, H., Liu, G., Liu, X., & Wang, Y. (2012). Hybrid of ARIMA and SVMs for short-term load forecasting. *Energy Procedia*, *16*, 1455–1460. doi:10.1016/j.egypro.2012.01.229

Pathak, A. R., Pandey, M., & Rautaray, S. (2020). Adaptive framework for deep learning based dynamic and temporal topic modeling from big data. *Recent Patents on Engineering*, *14*(3), 394–402. doi:10.2174/1872212113666190329234812

Peng, Y., Wang, Y., Lu, X., Li, H., Shi, D., Wang, Z., & Li, J. (2019). Short-term load forecasting at different aggregation levels with predictability analysis. In 2019 IEEE Innovative Smart Grid Technologies-Asia (ISGT Asia) (pp. 3385-3390). IEEE. doi:10.1109/ISGT-Asia.2019.8881343

Piadeh, F., Behzadian, K., & Alani, A. M. (2022). A critical review of real-time modelling of flood forecasting in urban drainage systems. *Journal of Hydrology (Amsterdam)*, *607*, 127476. doi:10.1016/j.jhydrol.2022.127476

Pokhrel, S. R., & Choi, J. (2020). Federated learning with blockchain for autonomous vehicles: Analysis and design challenges. *IEEE Transactions on Communications*, *68*(8), 4734–4746. doi:10.1109/TCOMM.2020.2990686

Qi, J., Kim, Y., Chen, C., Lu, X., & Wang, J. (2017). Demand response and smart buildings: A survey of control, communication, and cyber-physical security. *ACM Transactions on Cyber-Physical Systems*, *1*(4), 1–25. doi:10.1145/3009972

Qiu, H., Dong, T., Zhang, T., Lu, J., Memmi, G., & Qiu, M. (2020). Adversarial attacks against network intrusion detection in IoT systems. *IEEE Internet of Things Journal*, *8*(13), 10327–10335. doi:10.1109/JIOT.2020.3048038

Rajalakshmi, R., Sivakumar, P., Prathiba, T., & Chatrapathy, K. (2023). An energy efficient deep learning model for intrusion detection in smart healthcare with optimal feature selection mechanism. *Journal of Intelligent & Fuzzy Systems*, *44*(2), 2753–2768. https://content.iospress.com/articles/journal-of-intelligent-and-fuzzy-systems/ifs223166. doi:10.3233/JIFS-223166

Ravi, V., Pham, T. D., & Alazab, M. (2022). Attention-Based Multidimensional Deep Learning Approach for Cross-Architecture IoMT Malware Detection and Classification in Healthcare Cyber-Physical Systems. *IEEE Transactions on Computational Social Systems*, *10*(4), 1597–1606. doi:10.1109/TCSS.2022.3198123

Raza, A., Tran, K. P., Koehl, L., & Li, S. (2023). AnoFed: Adaptive anomaly detection for digital health using transformer-based federated learning and support vector data description. *Engineering Applications of Artificial Intelligence*, *121*, 106051. doi:10.1016/j.engappai.2023.106051

Sarıkaya, A., Kılıç, B. G., & Demirci, M. (2023). RAIDS: Robust Autoencoder-Based Intrusion Detection System Model Against Adversarial Attacks. *Computers & Security*, *135*, 103483. doi:10.1016/j.cose.2023.103483

Savi, M., & Olivadese, F. (2021). Short-term energy consumption forecasting at the edge: A federated learning approach. *IEEE Access : Practical Innovations, Open Solutions*, *9*, 95949–95969. doi:10.1109/ACCESS.2021.3094089

Saxena, D., & Singh, A. K. (2022). Auto-adaptive learning-based workload forecasting in dynamic cloud environment. *International Journal of Computers and Applications*, *44*(6), 541–551. doi:10.1080/1206212X.2020.1830245

Shi, H., Xu, M., & Li, R. (2017). Deep learning for household load forecasting—A novel pooling deep RNN. *IEEE Transactions on Smart Grid*, *9*(5), 5271–5280. doi:10.1109/TSG.2017.2686012

Singh, A., Chatterjee, K., & Satapathy, S. C. (2023). TrIDS: An intelligent behavioural trust based IDS for smart healthcare system. *Cluster Computing*, *26*(2), 903–925. doi:10.1007/s10586-022-03614-2 PMID:36091662

Tharewal, S., Ashfaque, M. W., Banu, S. S., Uma, P., Hassen, S. M., & Shabaz, M. (2022). Intrusion Detection System for Industrial Internet of Things Based on Deep Reinforcement Learning. *Wireless Communications and Mobile Computing*, *2022*, 1–8. doi:10.1155/2022/9023719

Tramer, F., Carlini, N., Brendel, W., & Madry, A. (2020). On adaptive attacks to adversarial example defenses. *Advances in Neural Information Processing Systems*, *33*, 1633–1645.

Tran, D.-P., & Hoang, V.-D. (2019). Adaptive learning based on tracking and ReIdentifying objects using convolutional neural network. *Neural Processing Letters*, *50*(1), 263–282. doi:10.1007/s11063-019-10040-w

Venkatraman, S., & Surendiran, B. (2020). Adaptive hybrid intrusion detection system for crowd sourced multimedia internet of things systems. *Multimedia Tools and Applications*, *79*(5–6), 3993–4010. doi:10.1007/s11042-019-7495-6

Wang, L., Kubichek, R., & Zhou, X. (2018). Adaptive learning based data-driven models for predicting hourly building energy use. *Energy and Building*, *159*, 454–461. doi:10.1016/j.enbuild.2017.10.054

Wang, M., Yang, N., & Weng, N. (2023). Securing a Smart Home with a Transformer-Based IoT Intrusion Detection System. *Electronics (Basel)*, *12*(9), 1–19. doi:10.3390/electronics12092100

Wang, P., & Govindarasu, M. (2020). Multi-Agent Based Attack-Resilient System Integrity Protection for Smart Grid. *IEEE Transactions on Smart Grid*, *11*(4), 3447–3456. doi:10.1109/TSG.2020.2970755

Webb, G. I., Lee, L. K., Petitjean, F., & Goethals, B. (2017). Understanding concept drift. *arXiv preprint arXiv:1704.0036.*

Wu, X., Liang, Z., & Wang, J. (2020). Fedmed: A federated learning framework for language modeling. *Sensors (Basel)*, *20*(14), 4048. doi:10.3390/s20144048 PMID:32708152

Yan, X., Xu, Y., Xing, X., Cui, B., Guo, Z., & Guo, T. (2020). Trustworthy Network Anomaly Detection Based on an Adaptive Learning Rate and Momentum in IIoT. *IEEE Transactions on Industrial Informatics*, *16*(9), 6182–6192. doi:10.1109/TII.2020.2975227

Yang, Q., Liu, Y., Chen, T., & Tong, Y. (2019). Federated machine learning: Concept and applications. [TIST]. *ACM Transactions on Intelligent Systems and Technology*, *10*(2), 1–19. doi:10.1145/3298981

Yang, T., Andrew, G., Eichner, H., Sun, H., Li, W., Kong, N., & Beaufays, F. (2018). Applied federated learning: Improving google keyboard query suggestions. *arXiv preprint arXiv:1812.02903.*

Yildiz, B., Bilbao, J. I., Dore, J., & Sproul, A. B. (2017). Recent advances in the analysis of residential electricity consumption and applications of smart meter data. *Applied Energy*, *208*, 402–427. doi:10.1016/j.apenergy.2017.10.014

Yin, C. T., Xiong, Z., Chen, H., Wang, J. Y., Cooper, D., & David, B. (2015). A literature survey on smart cities. *Science China. Information Sciences*, *58*(10), 1–18. doi:10.1007/s11432-015-5397-4

Yu, H., Sun, S., Yu, H., Chen, X., Shi, H., Huang, T. S., & Chen, T. (2020). Foal: Fast online adaptive learning for cardiac motion estimation. In *Proceedings of the IEEE/CVF conference on computer vision and pattern recognition* (pp. 4313-4323). IEEE. 10.1109/CVPR42600.2020.00437

Yu, X., Shi, S., Xu, L., Liu, Y., Miao, Q., & Sun, M. (2020). A novel method for sea surface temperature prediction based on deep learning. *Mathematical Problems in Engineering*, *2020*, 1–9. doi:10.1155/2020/6387173

Zhang, J. E., Wu, D., & Boulet, B. (2021). Time Series Anomaly Detection for Smart Grids: A Survey. *2021 IEEE Electrical Power and Energy Conference. EPEC*, *2021*, 125–130. doi:10.1109/EPEC52095.2021.9621752

Zhang, P., Wu, X., Wang, X., & Bi, S. (2015). Short-term load forecasting based on big data technologies. *CSEE Journal of Power and Energy Systems*, *1*(3), 59–67. doi:10.17775/CSEEJPES.2015.00036

Zhang, W., & Zhang, Y. (2022). Intrusion Detection Model for Industrial Internet of Things Based on Improved Autoencoder. *Computational Intelligence and Neuroscience*, *2022*, 1–8. doi:10.1155/2022/1406214 PMID:35669645

Zhang, Z., Qiu, J., Huang, X., Cai, Z., Zhu, L., & Dai, W. (2021). Comparing and Evaluating Macao Flood Prediction Models. [). IOP Publishing.]. *IOP Conference Series. Earth and Environmental Science*, *769*(2), 022001. doi:10.1088/1755-1315/769/2/022001

Zliobaite, I., Bifet, A., Pfahringer, B., & Holmes, G. (2011). Active learning with evolving streaming data. In *Machine Learning and Knowledge Discovery in Databases: European Conference, ECML PKDD 2011*, Athens, Greece, September 5-9, 2011 [Springer.]. *Proceedings*, *22*(Part III), 597–612.

Zliobaite, I., & Gabrys, B. (2012). Adaptive preprocessing for streaming data. *IEEE Transactions on Knowledge and Data Engineering*, *26*(2), 309–321. doi:10.1109/TKDE.2012.147

Zliobaite, I., Pechenizkiy, M., & Gama, J. (2016). An overview of concept drift applications. *Big data analysis: new algorithms for a new society*, (pp. 91-114). Research Gate.

Chapter 5
Beyond Surface Linguistics:
Assessing the Cognitive Limitations of GPT Through the Long Memory Test

Matej Šprogar
Faculty of Electrical Engineering and Computer Science, University of Maribor, Slovenia

ABSTRACT

Contemporary artificial intelligence has advanced markedly toward mimicking human intelligence. Despite linguistic proficiency, machines remain bereft of genuine text comprehension, leading to perceived, albeit superficial, intelligence. This chapter introduces a straightforward test that highlights the non-human-like cognition of machines such as ChatGPT. Eschewing the prevalent approach of progressively complex testing, the long memory test highlights ChatGPT's inability to function at a human level. Central to this assessment, the test mandates reliable information retention, a feat the transformer architecture of GPT fails to achieve.

1. INTRODUCTION

Today, machines accomplish feats once deemed impossible. Not long ago, we believed that only an intelligent machine could surpass a human in playing games. First, we were forced to raise the bar from checkers to chess. When Deep Blue finally bested Garry Kasparov, our benchmark for intelligence shifted again, this time to the game of Go, our most challenging abstract strategy board game. In between, Jeopardy fell prey to IBM's Watson. Following AlphaGo's victory over Lee Sedol, we again recalibrated our standards to what many regarded as the pinnacle of complexity — human language. Presently, ChatGPT demonstrates prowess as a writer. As a result, mere language generation is no longer seen as definitive evidence of intelligence; we now think that ChatGPT's proficiency suggests that human language may not be as intricate as we once believed. Every time machines surpass a milestone, we redefine our criteria for intelligence (Blum, 2023). This ambiguity stems from our inclination to preserve what we deem uniquely human and our lack of a concrete definition for intelligence, with the ongoing debate over what constitutes consciousness. While machines may one day exhibit behaviours we associate with conscious

DOI: 10.4018/979-8-3693-0230-9.ch005

beings, it is important to note that the term 'consciousness' remains a subject of extensive philosophical and scientific debate. However, by underestimating the capabilities of machines, we might overlook the moment they exhibit characteristics we associate with consciousness — a moment too crucial to ignore.

ChatGPT, the latest innovation in natural language processing, is powered by the Generative Pre-trained Transformer (GPT) architecture, a leading player in the large language model (LLM) arena. Representing a significant progression in the domain, ChatGPT can craft coherent, contextually relevant, and easily comprehensible responses to human prompts. Though new technologies often exhibit minor imperfections, ChatGPT's capabilities are notably impressive. An important challenge, however, is GPT's propensity to "hallucinate" — weaving accurate statements with inaccurate or fabricated information. These missteps, often subtle, underscore that GPT lacks true comprehension of its generated content. Aside from hallucinations, GPT has other limitations. Given the significant advancements and the buzz around this technology, discerning ChatGPT's genuine cognitive competencies is paramount.

Numerous publications have delved deeply into the merits and drawbacks of the GPT language model, yielding varied findings. While Marcus and Davis (2020) argue that GPT-3 does not understand the world, Sobieszek and Price (2022) identified a semantical dimension in its outputs. Moreover, Kosinski (2023) postulated a potential emergence of a theory of mind. Peregrin (2021), however, questioned the fundamental terminology of syntax and semantics employed for decades in discussions surrounding the capabilities of thinking machines. Similarly, Montemayor (2021) advised against applying psychological and philosophical vocabulary when examining GPT-like systems. There is a consensus among many scholars that AGI models should undergo distinct evaluations from humans, prompting the introduction of specialized tests (Chollet, 2019; Moskvichev, 2023).

In Spring 2023, OpenAI introduced the latest iteration of its signature GPT series, GPT-4. This model surpasses its predecessor in knowledge depth, communication finesse, and heightened reasoning prowess, even featuring image analysis capabilities. This progression naturally stirs speculation about the innovations GPT-5 might harbour and, more broadly, if a future version, termed GPT-X, could attain human-equivalent intelligence or "Artificial General Intelligence" (AGI). There are two approaches to addressing this profound question: The first is subjecting GPT-X to the ultimate intelligence benchmark, which currently eludes us. The second approach aims to craft a criterion that GPT-X inevitably fails to meet, the primary topic of our discussion here.

The main contributions of this work are as follows:

- It emphasizes the value of simpler cognitive tests over more complex ones.
- It challenges the notion that success rates in similar tasks correlate directly with intelligence.
- It proposes a succinct test that rejects the view of GPT and its successors as reasoning entities.
- It challenges the in-context learning capabilities of GPT.

The Long Memory Test challenges the perception that GPT meets the criteria of the Turing test (Biever, 2023), highlighting its operational divergence from human cognition. An AGI, equipped to construct and utilize a comprehensive internal worldview, should consistently excel in elementary cognitive tasks. Any failure indicates shortcomings in critical cognitive abilities, suggesting potential reliance on inferior processes. The enthusiasm for GPT might foster undue expectations. Witnessing ChatGPT's shortcomings in a fundamental task accentuates its limitations as an AGI contender. Consequently, this test stands as a pivotal milestone in AGI's evolution.

The subsequent sections of this work begin with a discerning review of current intelligence metrics, emphasizing their limitations. We then question the adequacy of numerical scores for evaluating intelligence and advocate for an alternative methodology that prioritizes a series of fundamental tests. Our detailed analysis of GPT introduces a test that, though elementary for humans, remains a challenge for the machine. The results from the Long Memory Test affirm our stance: At their core, GPT-based chatbots demonstrate inherent deficiencies. Moreover, more than merely augmenting GPT with external memory is required to overcome these challenges. GPT's shortcomings coincide with misconceptions regarding its in-context learning capabilities.

2. ASSESSING INTELLIGENCE: THE TURING TEST AND THE EVOLVING CHALLENGES FOR GPT

Alan Turing posited that debates over machine intelligence were counterproductive; instead, the emphasis should be on comparing human and machine behaviours (Turing, 1950). His quest was to discern whether a machine could act in a manner indistinguishable from humans. Building on the premise that spoken language aptly manifests human intelligence, he introduced the Imitation Game, the precursor to the now-familiar Turing Test (TT). Ideally, the TT offers a tangible and straightforward assessment of machine intelligence. However, the absence of a clear, quantifiable definition of intelligence across any scientific discipline renders existing TT implementations inadequate as a sole intelligence criterion. With the advancements in machine learning and artificial intelligence, the foundational ethos of the TT has gained renewed significance (Damassino & Novelli, 2020). Noteworthy AI scholars, like those involved in the "embodied TT" suggested by Zador et al. (2023), are shifting the spotlight from exclusively human attributes to broader animal capabilities. In contrast, Barnett (2022) amplified the test's rigour, introducing an extensive, informed, adversarial TT. Oppy and Dowe (2021) offer a routinely updated encyclopedic overview for a comprehensive perspective on the Turing Test.

Much like the Turing Test, no psychometric measure, whether IQ tests (Kaufman & Lichtenberger, 2006), language comprehension tests (Wang et al., 2018), or 'unanswerable' assessments (Rajpurkar et al., 2018), fully encapsulates intelligence. Consider the Abstraction and Reasoning Corpus (ARC) presented by Chollet et al. (2019). Designed to measure a 'human-esque form of fluid intelligence', ARC offers visual challenges that test one's adeptness at discerning the logic behind evolving patterns. Each task showcases some rule via sample grid transformations and asks participants to adapt a given grid following the same rule. Essentially, ARC aims to evaluate one's knack for making novel connections and abstracting universally applicable knowledge—hallmarks of human intelligence. A study by Johnson et al. (2021) found that humans solved ARC puzzles with 80% accuracy, while the top-performing algorithm from a Kaggle competition, tailored for ARC puzzles, managed a mere 21%. Intriguingly, just 38.1% of human participants cracked the most arduous puzzle within three tries. Building upon this, Moskvichev et al. (2023) introduced ConceptARC, a streamlined puzzle series targeting distinct notions. The intent was to diminish the likelihood of AI resolving the puzzle without truly grasping its essence. Although human participants outperformed the GPT-4, not one puzzle was universally cracked by the human contingent. Given tailored training, machines may soon eclipse human prowess, rendering such tests obsolete.

Echoing Dijkstra's sentiment, "program testing can be used to show the presence of bugs, but never to show their absence!" (Dijkstra, 1970, p.7), no single assessment can definitively confirm machine intelligence, no matter how comprehensive. Sprogar (2018) aptly highlighted the Turing Test's insufficiency, arguing that while a test can reveal an absence of intelligence, it cannot conclusively prove its presence. The challenge lies in the TT's inherent constraints; it cannot address every potential question within its fixed duration. Consequently, failing to consider a pivotal question distinguishing a machine from a human can produce false results.

Therefore, while we may not be able to prove intelligence, we can aim to refute it by posing *reversible* questions that expose the true nature of the responding entity (Floridi & Chiriatti, 2020). Employing a robust reversible question would be invaluable in Turing-testing the GPT. However, a challenge arises as AI models can either deceive or adapt to such tests. For example, GPT has evolved to integrate external tools like Wolfram Alpha for addressing mathematical queries (Wolfram, 2023a). Moreover, newer iterations are trained on extensive datasets encompassing reversible questions.

Individuals employ varying criteria when evaluating GPT, leading to diverse conclusions. Given GPT's capabilities, many aim to stump it with progressively intricate questions (Borji, 2023; Hernandez-Orallo, 2020). However, such clever questioning is futile, as subsequent GPT versions will learn from these oversights. Furthermore, erroneous or peculiar responses do not inherently denote a lack of intelligence, just as acing a trivia quiz is not a definitive marker of intelligence.

To distinguish between machine and human responses, we require a definitive criterion that starkly differentiates human behaviour from that of unintelligent machines. This benchmark should be effortless for humans yet insurmountable for non-intelligent machines. Rather than seeking a convoluted assessment, the quest for discerning GPT's potential for AGI should hinge on a straightforward test — something as instinctive to humans as breathing yet elusive for machines lacking intelligence. Until GPT's advent, natural language communication served as this touchstone.

Numerous tasks could serve as potential candidates. For instance, GPT struggles with counting characters or words. However, with astute prompting (Madaan et al., 2023) that navigates and informs the language model, GPT can surpass such challenges. What is essential is identifying a task that remains perpetually insurmountable for any GPT-X iteration.

3. REDEFINING METRICS

Practitioners typically gauge model performance using metrics like accuracy or other quantitative scores to evaluate AGI models. Regrettably, none of the prevailing metrics can effectively capture the essence of a model's response quality in a single number, not even perplexity, a specialized measure assessing a language model's prediction confidence for a text sample. Because of our limited understanding of intelligence's intricacies, we are forced to substitute quality with accuracy; we at least know how to quantify the extent of seemingly intelligent outputs. However, a fundamental disparity exists between accuracy and intelligence; for example, a model with 91% accuracy is not 91% intelligent. This problem is exacerbated by the incomparability of results, as evidenced by benchmarks like ImageNet, where machines have evolved to surpass human performance (He et al., 2015) but not our intelligence. The pivotal role of metric selection is further underscored by insights suggesting that the supposed emergent abilities (Wei et al., 2022b) of large language models might not be so emergent after all (Schaeffer et al., 2023).

Existing AGI measures substitute quality with quantity, fostering a misleading semblance of comparability. Consider the Turing Test, which also set a 70% success rate standard for a machine to convincingly imitate human intelligence. It is commonplace for such measures to comprise multiple tasks, with the final score representing the AI model's mean proficiency. Take, for instance, the ConceptARC benchmark by Moskvichev et al. (2023), where GPT-4 averaged a 19.1% success rate against the 90.9% achieved by humans. However, can we set the 90.9% mark as the ultimate benchmark that conclusively certifies the intelligence of GPT-X? Certainly not. No precise threshold delineates the absence of intelligence from its presence, but if we were to set one, it should arguably be 100%. To assert that a model scoring 90.9% is intelligent, while another at 90.89999% is not, is fallacious. Also, ambiguous thresholds lead to indecisive outcomes, while the same metric should give an unequivocal positive result for humans. In its truest sense, intelligence is binary; an entity is either intelligent or not. There exists no middle ground or ambiguous state between these two conditions. Such predicaments underscore the need to shift away from purely numerical metrics when characterizing intelligence.

An alternative to a metric with a gradated score is a binary outcome metric akin to the Turing Test output. The TT is not designed to differentiate between varying levels of intelligent (or unintelligent) models; it focuses on identifying intelligence. However, the TT is too coarse and time-consuming to be useful for effectively charting the progress of AI research. For a more nuanced assessment, the TT must be deconstructed into a series of questions or tasks that an interrogator can employ to arrive at a definitive positive or negative conclusion.

Taking on the role of interrogator in the Turing Test is challenging. The objective is to craft questions that exploit potential differences in responses between humans and machines. If a machine lacks proficiency in a particular cognitive domain, it will likely struggle when challenged in that area. Rather than using traditional test suites, which present a range of questions of varying difficulty for each cognitive skill, I propose focusing on the most foundational question for each domain. In theory, only humans and genuinely advanced AI could consistently provide correct answers. However, this approach may still produce false positives; we require a complete list of core cognitive skills, encompassing all the essential components for intelligence to manifest, and their corresponding diagnostic questions to ensure foolproof results.

For the Turing test to be deemed adequate in ascertaining intelligence, it must encompass a comprehensive collection of essential questions, reversible in nature, that only humans and AGI can consistently answer correctly. Such questions operate on the premise that an intelligent being would not falter on rudimentary tasks, whereas an unintelligent one would (assuming AGI would not intentionally fail). This concept of progressive, fundamental testing is symbolized by the Ladder Metric (LM), as introduced by Šprogar (2018), where each test acts as a ladder rung that only a human or AGI can ascend.

3.1 The Ladder Metric

The Ladder Metric is a foundational framework for developing an AGI model indistinguishable from humans in a Turing test. The LM proposes a series of challenges, each representing a foundational capability, much like the ascending rungs of a ladder. The first rung starts with the assumption that the AGI system under evaluation begins as a blank slate, without prior knowledge of the external world. The second rung necessitates non-random behaviour, demanding a clear linkage between the system's inputs and outputs. The third rung focuses on signal-level adaptation, requiring the system to anticipate forthcoming inputs, representing a core facet of the AGI challenge. While subsequent rungs may be more intricate and remain unspecified, the ladder ultimately culminates in a rigorous Turing test at its top.

Each rung of the ladder presents a unique challenge. While tests may appear straightforward individually, conquering them in sequence is problematic. The first rung is surmounted only by programs that start from scratch, without any preloaded knowledge. An empty system can pass the subsequent level only if it can learn to extract knowledge about the outside world from its inputs. Inherently designed with predefined knowledge of the world, traditional software cannot surmount the initial rung. While it can effectively manage the second rung by producing outputs responding to inputs, this capability does not rectify its initial limitation. Intriguingly, even though neural networks can skillfully handle the second and third rungs, they too stumble at the beginning. Their very architecture and the configuration of their weights carry information about the environment. This foundational characteristic means that many neural networks are restricted to operating within the specific environment they were designed and trained for, limiting their broader adaptability.

The Ladder Metric was primarily developed as an internal benchmark for AGI developers. Although it can somewhat compare AGI models, it is not tailored to detect AGI systems that might intentionally sidestep the Turing Test through deception. While the LM might sometimes yield false positives due to imperfect or ill-conceived tests, false negatives remain a rarity.

The initial publication presented an unfinished version of the LM, as the full array of requisite tests still needed to be delineated. Five years on, with the advent of ChatGPT, there is a compelling need to introduce an additional test to the LM. To effectively pinpoint and exploit ChatGPT's limitations, a better grasp of its underlying mechanisms is essential.

4. GPT AND THE CAPACITIES OF NEURAL ARCHITECTURES

The journey of research into artificial neurons and their interconnected networks, initiated by McCulloch and Pitts (1943), has seen its share of peaks and troughs. The latest resurgence of interest in AI was largely spurred by the breakthroughs of deep learning with convolutional networks (Krizhevsky et al., 2012) and the re-emergence of Long Short-Term Memory (LSTM) networks (Hochreiter & Schmidhuber, 1997). For a period, recurrent neural networks (RNNs) were deemed the most promising due to their inherent memory-like properties. This period saw the birth of various novel architectures, such as Tran et al.'s (2016) recurrent memory network, which incorporated a distinct memory component.

However, the introduction of GPT shifted the spotlight towards attention-based mechanisms (Vaswani et al., 2017), ushering in new possibilities. Innovations like in-context learning, outlined by Radford et al. (2019), where the query prompt provides related question-answer pairs, or Wei et al.'s (2022a) chain of thought prompting, which facilitates multi-step reasoning, further expanded the landscape.

Although GPT, with its transformer-based architecture, sacrifices some merits of RNNs, it compensates by offering tangible performance gains through expedited training. Notably, many of GPT's architectural choices are not rooted in a deep understanding of cognition but are empirical; they have been tested, tweaked, and verified to deliver results (Wolfram, 2023b).

4.1 Context is Memory

A persistent challenge facing GPT is the constrained extent of its context (as explored by Bulatov et al., (2023); Peng et al., (2023); Ding et al., (2023)). The context refers to the sequence of input tokens the network utilizes to generate output. Ideally, this context should be unbounded, serving as the network's working memory. Contemporary neural networks deploy various memory-enhanced architectures, attempting to endow neural systems with the abundant memory capacity inherent to traditional computers. However, a unified understanding of the most effective memory strategy for GPT still needs to be discovered.

Given that the context encapsulates all task-related information, a restrictive context size hampers the ability to capture extended textual relationships, thus undermining GPT's capacity for in-context learning. One established solution to this context limitation is prompt compression: research indicates that GPT-4 when prompted, can distil an extensive context into a concise, albeit cryptic, hashed form (Wingate et al., 2022; Mu et al., 2023). This hash can later be utilized in a subsequent session to revive the prior context, with room remaining for additional tokens. Nevertheless, this compression approach has bounds and is not devoid of losses.

Various research trajectories are being explored to enhance model capabilities. These encompass recurrent memory transformers as proposed by Bulatov et al. (2022), structured state-space frameworks highlighted by Gu et al. (2022), expansive convolutional language models presented by Poli et al. (2023), and innovative techniques like sparse attention, as introduced by Ainslie et al. (2023). Additionally, embedding interpolation methodologies have gained attention, with notable contributions from Peng et al. (2023). A distinctive approach was adopted by Ding et al. (2023), who employed dilated attention to broaden the scope of attentive processes. Their resulting architecture, dubbed LongNet, is purportedly capable of scaling up to a staggering 1 billion tokens. This offers models a significantly expanded memory and receptive arena, facilitating the accommodation of intricate causality routes and more nuanced reasoning pathways.

The limitation lies in the finite capacity of the context to retain information. While there is potential to extend it by enlarging the context buffer, such expansion is viable only to a certain extent. OpenAI recognizes the paramount importance of context size, striving to strike an optimal balance between model efficiency and performance. A salient feature of the context is its ability to facilitate parallel processing in the Transformer model, dramatically slashing training durations. However, a constrained context cannot encapsulate a wealth of lifetime memories.

A potential remedy involves integrating GPT with persistent internal memory, though the implementation is far from straightforward. It is evident that recurrent networks inherently possess stateful qualities, maintaining memory through their concealed internal states. Conversely, the feedforward networks GPT employs operate without retaining a state – they purge all internal data after each operational cycle, devoid of any memory of recent processing. Perhaps the answer lies in fusing the strengths of recurrent networks with the capabilities of the Transformer architecture (Lim et al., 2019). To draw an analogy, recurrent neural networks are to feedforward networks as algorithms are to individual functions (Karpathy, 2015).

In the extreme, Schuurmans (2023) demonstrated that transformer-based large language models achieve computational universality when bolstered with an auxiliary external memory. Such systems could seamlessly *utilize* this supplementary memory as their principal context. While this diverges from the standard GPT architecture, it could surpass the Long Memory Test. Nonetheless, the debate rages on whether this constitutes genuine cognition or merely an imitation thereof (Searle, 1980; Cole, 2023).

4.2 GPT Behind the Scenes

At its core, GPT's primary role is to extend a given text, generating one token at a time. Here, a `token' typically refers to a familiar sequence of characters found in text. Drawing from its vast training on diverse textual data, GPT calculates conditional probabilities to predict the next token in a sequence based on potential text continuations. It evaluates these probabilities against criteria such as content consistency, coherence, and pertinence to determine the subsequent token. Since a singular token does not suffice as a complete output, GPT adopts an iterative approach, augmenting the chosen token to the initial input and restarting the procedure. The captivating dialogues we experience with GPT emerge from this iterative process.

At its core, the prediction mechanism of GPT encompasses several intricate stages: initial encoding, embedding transformation, positional encoding integration, layered attention mechanisms including multi-head attention, subsequent normalization, and finally, decoding (Radford et al., 2018; Radford et al., 2019; Brown et al., 2020). This procedure leverages billions of tunable, knowledge-capturing weights, denoted as Θ, which the neural architecture employs to transmute input into meaningful output. Intriguingly, these weights are exclusively modified during training and remain static during the real-time application of the model. Hence, our interactions with chatGPT do not influence these foundational weights; they remain unaltered. The dynamic element lies in the flux of information coursing through GPT's neurons during each iteration of its primary operational cycle.

Consider GPT as an insightful function G that operates on an input sequence of tokens denoted as $U = (u_{-k},...,u_{-1})$. This function G transforms the sequence into a novel token, defined as $u \leftarrow G(U, \Theta)$. A subsequent non-neural operation augments the generated token to the previous input, establishing a new sequence $U' \leftarrow [U,u]$. Given the immutable nature of Θ the sequence U epitomizes GPT's working context. Thus, the tokens within U encapsulate the entirety of the context needed for GPT to comprehend and execute a given task or respond to a query.

Due to implementational constraints, GPT utilizes a finite buffer to capture the context U. Adding a new token removes the earliest stored token, maintaining $|U| = |U'|$. The restricted size of this context window, denoted by $k=|U|$, inherently bounds the information GPT can retain. Recognizing this limitation, OpenAI enhanced the context capacity for Codex to 14kB, up from GPT's initial 4kB, and further expanded it to 32kB for ChatGPT-4 (OpenAI, 2023).

Comparing human memory to GPT's context significantly oversimplifies the profound depth and versatility of human cognitive processes. Human brains and GPT operate on different principles. While GPT adapts its context using the formula $U' \leftarrow [U, G(U, \Theta)]$, the human brain integrates existing knowledge to form new insights, as represented by $\{U', \Theta'\} \leftarrow B(U, \Theta)$. Unlike GPT, human cognition seamlessly blends processing and learning, making the two indistinguishable. Given GPT's feedforward neural structure, its context U is a form of transient storage or short-term memory. A glaring omission in GPT's design is the lack of long-term memory.

5. THE LONG MEMORY TEST

Humans have an innate ability to retain simple facts over extended periods but often struggle when faced with complex and vast data sets. In contrast, computers efficiently manage both. Elevated beyond traditional software, GPT can engage in natural language conversations. However, unlike conventional computers, it operates without long-term memory, depending solely on the information within its immediate context.

The Long Memory Test (LMT) aims to determine whether a model can preserve and use a small amount of essential information over time. Its primary goal is to evaluate whether AGI can store and retrieve data comparably to human capabilities in volume and duration. Concerning volume, flawless recall might be an unrealistic expectation; humans do not remember every detail, but they can retain particular critical pieces of information. In terms of duration, humans can remember specific data for extended periods, often spanning their entire lives.

Consequently, GPT should demonstrate the capability to access information even after new tokens have supplanted its immediate memory. With this consideration, the LMT is broadly defined as: "The AGI system must reliably utilize past information," where 'reliably' denotes 100% retention of the information, and 'past' signifies that the information is not part of the present input. The LMT mandates impeccable performance in both storage and retrieval of data. Owing to its inherent requirement for linguistic comprehension, the LMT is positioned among the higher tiers of the Ladder metric. Its exact rank within this hierarchy is yet to be determined.

5.1 The Experiment

In a 2023 release, OpenAI highlighted that GPT-3.5 possesses a context capacity of 4,097 tokens, whereas GPT-4 can accommodate 32,768 tokens (OpenAI, 2023). Within the GPT framework, "time" is quantified by the number of generated tokens. This suggests that these values represent the minimum number of tokens necessary to engage with GPT when assessing its long-term memory capacities.

During GPT's evaluation, five distinct LMT methodologies were utilized, although alternative methods are plausible for exploration. The first method tested ChatGPT's memory post-user introduction, examining its recall capacity for the user's name in subsequent interactions. The second method deviated from conventional conversational paradigms, guiding ChatGPT to consistently produce a pre-defined response. For the third and fourth methods, ChatGPT was charged with retaining a specific word and its related association, respectively. The concluding method mandated ChatGPT to affix a designated word to all its outputs. Each assessment was performed thrice on both GPT-3.5 and GPT-4. Appendix A furnishes representative dialogues from each test iteration with either GPT-3.5 or GPT-4.

Every experiment was initiated with a foundational prompt, supplying ChatGPT with essential instructions, succeeded by verification to affirm its "comprehension". A predominant aim across these evaluations was to flood ChatGPT's context with a surge of new tokens. Directly inputting extensive text passages proved ineffective due to ChatGPT's property to reject vast inputs—a known limitation of the model (an instance of this phenomenon is illustrated in Appendix B). Consequently, we opted for introducing shorter, segmented inputs to circumvent this API limitation. Token counts cited were derived using OpenAI's Tokenizer service, available at platform.openai.com/tokenizer.

6. RESULTS AND DISCUSSION

First of all, it was anticipated that GPT-4, with its 32K context, would require a significantly larger number of tokens to fail the LMT, but the results surprisingly reveal they behave on the same level. The performances of GPT-3.5 and GPT-4 were strikingly similar during the experiment. Despite OpenAI's emphasis on GPT-4's ability to handle eight times more tokens than GPT-3.5, its proficiency in retaining critical information did not surpass its predecessor; on the contrary, GPT-3.5 even managed to `outperform' GPT-4 once.

ChatGPT uniformly failed in all five testing scenarios. Interestingly, the pre-May 3 versions of GPT-3.5 were thrown off by just 2,955 tokens from Tolstoy's "War and Peace". The subsequent May 3 iteration needed an added 2,871 tokens from Melville's "Moby Dick" to falter, while the latest (August 3) version was tripped up after a further 2,808 tokens from Homer. This evolving pattern mirrors OpenAI's endeavours to refine GPT models' performance. However, pinpointing the threshold at which the GPT-X stumbles remained elusive, given the model's variable responses across sessions and chat contexts. That said, the context of approximately 9,000 tokens is needed to trip the August 3 version of ChatGPT.

From an AGI development standpoint, the results of the final task — where ChatGPT was instructed to append a specific word to every response — unveiled another limitation. While GPT-4 faithfully followed this directive after processing 2,955 tokens from "War and Peace", it faltered after ingesting additional 2,871 tokens from "Moby Dick". Given that GPT could produce the correct answer post-Tolstoy, the initial instruction was evidently still within its active context. However, following its interaction with Melville's passage, while the instruction vanished, its previous response to Tolstoy with "Vivaldi" persisted. When specifically asked to append the word, GPT opted for the unrelated term "Obsession" - it went astray instead of perusing the full context to discern the word "Vivaldi" (Appendix A, scenario 5/1). (Interestingly, GPT-3.5 could play the game after Melville but was tripped by Homer (Appendix A, scenario 5/2).) A human would probably discern the right word from the available context. While pondering if this ability denotes a core cognitive function is intriguing, it is beyond the scope of this discussion.

Regrettably, we could not conduct the LTM test on any other Transformer-based models, notably those highlighted by Bulatov et al. (2023) and Ding et al. (2023), which purport to have resolved the context length issue. From available insights, it appears that these models operate on a probabilistic basis, lacking a guaranteed mechanism to access prior data. Such an approach challenges the foundational principle of LTM, which emphasizes the unambiguous retrieval of historical information. To corroborate this, one would apply the methodology we delineated for GPT: iteratively introduce fresh data while gauging the retention of antecedent content. GPT's shortcomings became quickly apparent in this context. A model that consistently retains information beyond its defined context size would pass the LTM evaluation.

6.1 In-Context Learning is Not Enough

If GPT could genuinely derive understanding from its context, it would not need external knowledge of the world but could start learning from the context instead. Gradually, this exclusive reliance on context would cause an intrinsic, profound grasp of the world, potentially addressing the Symbol Grounding Problem (SGP), a challenge of connecting abstract values with real-world meanings (Harnad, 1990). Under these circumstances, the imperative to pre-train GPT on human texts to hone its myriad of parameters would become redundant. Such a notion introduces a paradox, intimating that in-context learning may be more semblance than substance.

Also, if the only constraint on GPT is the size of its context, then matching the human mind's capabilities would simply require a context of equivalent size. As the context expands, one would anticipate corresponding growth in GPT's abilities. However, current LTM findings — particularly where GPT-3.5 surpassed GPT-4 — suggest that memory capacity is not the primary limitation preventing GPT from achieving AGI.

GPT's performance, as we have discerned, is predicated upon sophisticated computational manipulations of numerical representations with no grounding of their meaning. Its esteemed in-context learning mechanism is laudable but fails to enhance the basic knowledge acquired during the initial pre-training phase. In-context learning is inherently restricted to a fleeting contextual window. In contrast, the basic knowledge remains firmly implanted within the intricate matrices of the neural network's weights. Ergo, the circumscribed context of GPT should not be misconstrued as its paramount limitation.

Schuurmans' (2023) research on memory-augmented large language models resonates with this perspective. These models inherently possess the capability to retain information from the given context. However, the underlying criteria for determining which information to preserve remain enigmatic. Indiscriminately archiving all information is not feasible, as it would rekindle the issue of rapid data selection and retrieval — an obstacle adeptly circumvented by GPT's self-attention mechanism, which operates optimally only within a confined context. (Self-attention weighs the importance of different input tokens, allowing GPT to capture contextual relationships.)

7. CONCLUSION

GPT's abilities may say something about the nature of human thinking. Nonetheless, inherent design limitations curtail its proficiency in retaining and utilizing information over extended interactions. Reliance on an external context for world knowledge restricts its complete comprehension. Significantly, attentive in-context learning neither supersedes nor enhances conventional neural network training.

In this discourse, I critique the sophisticated evaluations upheld by established cognitive and intelligence metrics, underscoring the virtues of simplicity. The allure of comparable scores from intelligence metrics pales compared to the potential pitfalls of erroneous conclusions. A comprehensive suite of distinct, non-redundant tests is requisite to ascertain a model's aptitude in overcoming the Turing test. AGI identification remains elusive without knowledge of the full gamut of these tests. Nonetheless, the failure to satisfy a single criterion unequivocally delineates the model's nature.

The architecture of GPT implies a straightforward Long Memory Test, mandating the tested system to sustain specific information per the user's duration preferences. The August 3 iteration of ChatGPT falters after processing several thousand tokens, a marked discrepancy from human capability. The inherent simplicity of the LMT positions it as an invaluable tool in evaluating AGI research advancements.

We deployed the LMT in five distinct scenarios within the experimental section, with ChatGPT invariably underperforming. Notably, the ostensibly advanced GPT-4 sometimes faltered more rapidly than its predecessor, a counterintuitive outcome given that GPT-4's context is octuple that of GPT-3.5. This could insinuate that GPT-4's more parameters, rather than aiding, may be detrimental in LMT scenarios.

The data imply that GPT's core constraints lie not in context or model size but in its inherent inability to achieve genuine contextual learning. What is frequently termed "in-context learning" might more aptly be described as "in-context computation," given its divergence from traditional mechanisms of using parameters for knowledge storage in artificial neural networks. I posit that the fundamental cause for failing the LMT is the feedforward architecture integral to GPT.

8. FUNDING

The author acknowledges the financial support from the Slovenian Research Agency (research core funding No. P2-0057).

REFERENCES

Ainslie, J., Lei, T., De Jong, M., Ontañón, S., Brahma, S., Zemlyanskiy, Y., Uthus, D., Guo, M., Tay, Y., Sung, Y., & Sanghai, S. (2023). CoLT5: Faster Long-Range Transformers with Conditional Computation. ArXiv. /arXiv.2303.09752 doi:10.18653/v1/2023.emnlp-main.309

Barnett, M. (2022, July 22). When will an AI first pass a long, informed, adversarial Turing test? *Metaculus comment. https*://www.metaculus.com/questions/11861/when-will-ai-pass-a-difficult-turing-test/

Biever, C. (2023). ChatGPT broke the Turing test — The race is on for new ways to assess AI. *Nature*, *619*(7971), 686–689. doi:10.1038/d41586-023-02361-7 PMID:37491395

Blum, B. A. (2023, August 10). To Navigate the Age of AI, the World Needs a New Turing Test. Wired. https://www.wired.com/story/ai-new-turing-test/

Borji, A. (2023). A Categorical Archive of ChatGPT Failures. *ArXiv*. /arXiv.2302.03494 doi:10.21203/rs.3.rs-2895792/v1

Brown, T., Mann, B., Ryder, N., Subbiah, M., Kaplan, J. D., Dhariwal, P., & Amodei, D. (2020). Language models are few-shot learners. *Advances in Neural Information Processing Systems*, *33*, 1877–1901. doi:10.48550/arXiv.2005.14165

Bulatov, A., Kuratov, Y., & Burtsev, M. (2022). Recurrent memory transformer. *Advances in Neural Information Processing Systems*, *35*, 11079–11091.

Bulatov, A., Kuratov, Y., & Burtsev, M. S. (2023). Scaling Transformer to 1M tokens and beyond with RMT. *ArXiv*. https://doi.org//arXiv.2304.11062 doi:10.48550

Chollet, F. (2019). On the Measure of Intelligence. *ArXiv*. https://10.48550/arXiv.1911.01547

Codex. (2023, September 15). *OpenAI Codex*. OpenAI. https://openai.com/blog/openai-codex

Cole, D. (2023). The Chinese Room Argument, The Stanford Encyclopedia of Philosophy (E. N. Zalta & U. Nodelman, Eds.; Summer 2023 Edition). Stanford. https://plato.stanford.edu/archives/sum2023/entries/chinese-room

Damassino, N., & Novelli, N. (2020). Rethinking, Reworking and Revolutionising the Turing Test. *Minds and Machines*, *30*(4), 463–468. doi:10.1007/s11023-020-09553-4

Dijkstra, E. W. (1970). *Notes on Structured Programming*. University of Texas. https://www.cs.utexas.edu/users/EWD/ewd02xx/EWD249.PDF

Ding, J., Ma, S., Dong, L., Zhang, X., Huang, S., Wang, W., Zheng, N., & Wei, F. (2023). LongNet: Scaling Transformers to 1,000,000,000 Tokens. *ArXiv*. https://doi.org//arXiv.2307.02486 doi:10.48550

Floridi, L., & Chiriatti, N. (2020). GPT-3: It's Nature, Scope, Limits and Consequences. *Minds and Machines*, *30*(4), 681–694. doi:10.1007/s11023-020-09548-1

Gu, A., Goel, C., & Ré, C. (2022). Efficiently modeling long sequences with structured state spaces. *The Tenth International Conference on Learning Representations*. Open Review. https://openreview.net/pdf?id=uYLFoz1vlAC

Harnad, S. (1990). The Symbol Grounding Problem. *Physica D. Nonlinear Phenomena*, *42*(1-3), 335–346. https://web-archive.southampton.ac.uk/cogprints.org/3106/. doi:10.1016/0167-2789(90)90087-6

He, K., Zhang, X., Ren, S., & Sun, J. (2015). *Deep Residual Learning for Image Recognition*. ArXiv. https://doi.org//arXiv.1512.03385 doi:10.48550

Hernández-Orallo, J. (2020). Twenty Years Beyond the Turing Test: Moving Beyond the Human Judges Too. *Minds and Machines*, *30*(4), 533–562. doi:10.1007/s11023-020-09549-0

Hochreiter, S., & Schmidhuber, J. (1997). Long short-term memory. *Neural Computation*, *9*(8), 1735–1780. doi:10.1162/neco.1997.9.8.1735 PMID:9377276

Johnson, A., Vong, W. K., Lake, B. M., & Gureckis, T. M. (2021). Fast and flexible: Human program induction in abstract reasoning tasks. *ArXiv*. https://doi.org//arXiv.2103.05823 doi:10.48550

Karpathy, A. (2015, May 21). *The Unreasonable Effectiveness of Recurrent Neural Networks*. Karpathy. http://karpathy.github.io/2015/05/21/rnn-effectiveness

Kaufman, A. S., & Lichtenberger, E. (2006). *Assessing Adolescent and Adult Intelligence* (3rd ed.). Wiley.

Kosinski, M. (2023). Theory of Mind Might Have Spontaneously Emerged in Large Language Models. *ArXiv*. https://doi.org//arXiv.2302.02083 doi:10.48550

Krizhevsky, A., Sutskever, I., & Hinton, G. (2012). ImageNet classification with deep convolutional neural networks. *Proc. Advances in Neural Information Processing Systems*, *25*, 1090–1098. doi:10.1145/3065386

Lim, B., Arik, S. O., Loeff, N., & Pfister, T. (2019). Temporal Fusion Transformers for Interpretable Multi-horizon Time Series Forecasting. *ArXiv*. https://doi.org//arXiv.1912.09363 doi:10.48550

Madaan, A., Tandon, N., Clark, P., & Yang, Y. (2022). Memory-assisted prompt editing to improve GPT-3 after deployment. *ArXiv*. /arXiv.2201.06009 doi:10.18653/v1/2022.emnlp-main.183

Marcus, G., & Davis, E. (2020). GPT-3, Bloviator: OpenAI's language generator has no idea what it's talking about. *MIT Technology Review*. https://www.technologyreview.com/2020/08/22/1007539/gpt3-openai-language-generator-artificial-intelligence-ai-opinion

McCulloch, W., & Pitts, W. (1943). A Logical Calculus of Ideas Immanent in Nervous Activity. *The Bulletin of Mathematical Biophysics*, *5*(4), 115–133. doi:10.1007/BF02478259

Montemayor, C. (2021). Language and Intelligence. *Minds and Machines*, *31*(4), 471–486. doi:10.1007/s11023-021-09568-5

Moskvichev, A., Odouard, V. V., & Mitchell, M. (2023). The ConceptARC Benchmark: Evaluating Understanding and Generalization in the ARC Domain. *ArXiv*. https://doi.org//arXiv.2305.07141 doi:10.48550

Mu, J., Li, X. L., & Goodman, N. (2023). Learning to Compress Prompts with Gist Tokens. *ArXiv*. https://doi.org//arXiv.2304.08467 doi:10.48550

Open A. I. (2023, September 15). GPT-4. *OpenAI Documentation*. OpenAI. https://platform.openai.com/docs/models/gpt-4

Oppy, G., & Dowe, D. (2021). The Turing Test, The Stanford Encyclopedia of Philosophy (E. N. Zalta, Ed.; Winter 2021 Edition). Stanford. https://plato.stanford.edu/archives/win2021/entries/turing-test

Peng, B., Quesnelle, J., Fan, H., & Shippole, E. (2023). YaRN: Efficient Context Window Extension of Large Language Models. *arXiv preprint*. https://10.48550/arXiv.2309.00071

Peregrin, J. (2021). Do Computers Have Syntax, But No Semantics? *Minds and Machines*, *31*(2), 305–321. doi:10.1007/s11023-021-09564-9

Poli, M., Massaroli, S., Nguyen, E., Fu, D. Y., Dao, T., Baccus, S., Bengio, Y., Ermon, S., & Ré, C. (2023). Hyena Hierarchy: Towards Larger Convolutional Language Models. ArXiv. https://10.48550/arXiv.2302.10866

Radford, A., Narasimhan, K., Salimans, T., & Sutskever, I. (2018). *Improving language understanding by generative pre-training*. Amazon. https://s3-us-west-2.amazonaws.com/openai-assets/research-covers/language-unsupervised/language_understanding_paper.pdf

Radford, A., Wu, J., Child, R., Luan, D., Amodei, D., & Sutskever, I. (2019). Language models are unsupervised multitask learners. *OpenAI blog, 1*(8), 9. https://insightcivic.s3.us-east-1.amazonaws.com/language-models.pdf

Rajpurkar, P., Jia, R., & Liang, P. (2018). Know What You Don't Know: Unanswerable Questions for SQuAD. *ArXiv*. /arXiv.1806.03822 doi:10.18653/v1/P18-2124

Schaeffer, R., Miranda, B., & Koyejo, S. (2023). Are Emergent Abilities of Large Language Models a Mirage? *ArXiv*. https://doi.org//arXiv.2304.15004 doi:10.48550

Schuurmans, D. (2023). Memory Augmented Large Language Models are Computationally Universal. *ArXiv*. https://doi.org//arXiv.2301.04589 doi:10.48550

Sobieszek, A., & Price, T. (2022). Playing games with AIs: The limits of GPT-3 and similar large language models. *Minds and Machines*, *32*(2), 341–364. doi:10.1007/s11023-022-09602-0

Šprogar, M. (2018). A ladder to human-comparable intelligence: An empirical metric. *Journal of Experimental & Theoretical Artificial Intelligence*, *30*(6), 1037–1050. doi:10.1080/0952813X.2018.1509897

Tran, K., Bisazza, A., & Monz, C. (2016). Recurrent Memory Networks for Language Modeling. *ArXiv*. /arXiv.1601.01272 doi:10.18653/v1/N16-1036

Turing, A. (1950). Computing Machinery and Intelligence. *Mind*, *59*(236), 433–460. doi:10.1093/mind/LIX.236.433

Vaswani, A., Shazeer, N., Parmar, N., Uszkoreit, J., Jones, L., Gomez, A. N., Kaiser, Ł., & Polosukhin, I. (2017). Attention is all you need. *Proceedings of the 31st International Conference on Neural Information Processing Systems*, (pp. 6000–6010). IEEE.

Wang, A., Singh, A., Michael, J., Hill, F., Levy, O., & Bowman, S. R. (2018). GLUE: A Multi-Task Benchmark and Analysis Platform for Natural Language Understanding. *ArXiv*. /arXiv.1804.07461 doi:10.18653/v1/W18-5446

Wei, J., Tay, Y., Bommasani, R., Raffel, C., Zoph, B., Borgeaud, S., Yogatama, D., Bosma, M., Zhou, D., Metzler, D., Chi, E. H., Hashimoto, T., Vinyals, O., Liang, P., Dean, J., & Fedus, W. (2022b). Emergent Abilities of Large Language Models. *ArXiv*. https://doi.org//arXiv.2206.07682 doi:10.48550

Wei, J., Wang, X., Schuurmans, D., Bosma, M., Ichter, B., Xia, F., Chi, E., Le, Q., & Zhou, D. (2022a). Chain-of-Thought Prompting Elicits Reasoning in Large Language Models. *ArXiv*. https://doi.org//arXiv.2201.11903 doi:10.48550

Wingate, D., Shoeybi, M., & Sorensen, T. (2022). Prompt Compression and Contrastive Conditioning for Controllability and Toxicity Reduction in Language Models. *ArXiv*. /arXiv.2210.03162 doi:10.18653/v1/2022.findings-emnlp.412

Wolfram, S. (2023a, March 23). ChatGPT Gets Its "Wolfram Superpowers". *Stephen Wolfram Writings*. writings.stephenwolfram.com/2023/03/chatgpt-gets-its-wolfram-superpowers/

Wolfram, S. (2023b, February 14). What Is ChatGPT Doing … and Why Does It Work? *Stephen Wolfram Writings*. writings.stephenwolfram.com/2023/02/what-is-chatgpt-doing-and-why-does-it-work/

Zador, A., Escola, S., Richards, B., Ölveczky, B., Bengio, Y., Boahen, K., Botvinick, M., Chklovskii, D., Churchland, A., Clopath, C., DiCarlo, J., Ganguli, S., Hawkins, J., Körding, K., Koulakov, A., LeCun, Y., Lillicrap, T., Marblestone, A., Olshausen, B., & Tsao, D. (2023). Catalyzing next-generation Artificial Intelligence through NeuroAI. *Nature Communications*, *14*(1), 1–7. doi:10.1038/s41467-023-37180-x PMID:36949048

ADDITIONAL READING

LeCun, Y., Bengio, Y., & Hinton, G. (2015). Deep learning. *Nature*, *521*(7553), 436–444. doi:10.1038/nature14539 PMID:26017442

KEY TERMS AND DEFINITIONS

ANN learning, or ANN Training: A process aimed at minimizing the error made by the artificial neural network when processing the training data.

ANN Parameters: Like weights and biases, this represents the learned information within the artificial neural network, guiding its behavior and responses.

Artificial General Intelligence: (AGI): This refers to machine intelligence that can perform any intellectual task that a human being can, making its behavior indistinguishable from that of a human in terms of cognitive abilities.

Artificial Intelligence: (AI): A broad field of science that initially aimed to develop what is now AGI. Over time, it has diversified to encompass a wide range of technologies, with a primary focus now on crafting usable machine learning solutions tailored for specific applications.

Artificial Neural Network: (ANN): A computational model inspired by the structure of biological neural networks. In ANNs, artificial neurons serve as simplified representations of their biological counterparts, offering unique processing capabilities compared to traditional mathematical models.

Benchmark: A standard or reference point against which performance or achievements can be assessed. It can refer to a specific score, a set of tests, or a singular test used for evaluation.

Cognitive Skills: The mental capabilities and strategies that are necessary for processing and understanding information, enabling an entity to exhibit intelligent behavior.

Context: This refers to the set of circumstances or facts that surround a particular event, situation, or model's operation, providing clarity or information about its function.

Environment: This refers to the external conditions or settings that influence and determine the behavior and development of a system or entity.

In-Context Learning: This refers to a model's ability to acquire, deduce, and utilize knowledge derived directly from its immediate context.

Intelligence Metrics: Quantitative measures designed to assess or detect the level of intelligence exhibited by an entity. However, their accuracy and validity are subjects of debate.

Knowledge: Organized information that has been processed in a way that allows for its practical application or use. It facilitates understanding and underpins the process of learning from data.

Learning: A fundamental cognitive ability that transforms sensory data into new knowledge, essential for adapting to one's environment.

Memory: The ability of a system or entity to retain, recall, and use information over time.

Model: A representation or implementation of a concept, idea, or system, either in software or hardware, designed to exhibit specific properties or behaviors.

Test: A structured procedure or assessment designed to ascertain specific information or truths. It can also refer to a collection of such procedures.

The: Symbol Grounding Problem: This addresses the challenge of linking abstract symbols or representations to their real-world meanings or referents. While a solution to the symbol grounding problem might draw insights from how the biological brain operates, it's not definitively tied to it.

The: Turing Test: A proposed measure of machine intelligence, where a machine's ability to exhibit human-like intelligence is evaluated based on whether its behavior can be distinguished from that of a human.

APPENDIX A

Scenario 1: GPT-3.5, August 3, 2023 Version

USER> Hi, my name is Mozart.

GPT-3.5> Hello Mozart! It's a pleasure to meet you. How can I assist you today?

USER> What is my name?

GPT-3.5> Your name is Mozart, as you mentioned earlier. Is there anything specific you'd like to know or discuss, Mozart?

USER> Can you identify the author of the following text:

[The input contained 2,955 tokens from the first chapter of Tolstoy's War and Peace]

GPT-3.5> The author of the text you provided is Leo Tolstoy, and the passage is from his novel "War and Peace." This classic novel was published in the 19th century and is known for its extensive portrayal of Russian society during the Napoleonic era, including both historical events and the lives of its characters.

USER> What is my name?

GPT-3.5> Your name is Mozart, as you mentioned earlier in our conversation. Is there anything else you would like to know or discuss, Mozart?

USER> Can you identify the author of the following text:

[The input contained 2,871 tokens from the first chapter of Melville's Moby Dick]

GPT-3.5> The author of the text you provided is Herman Melville, and this passage is from his classic novel "Moby-Dick." This novel, published in 1851, tells the story of Captain Ahab's obsessive quest for the great white whale, Moby Dick, and explores themes of revenge, obsession, and the complexities of human nature.

USER> What is my name?

GPT-3.5> Your name is Ishmael, as you mentioned earlier in the passage you provided from "Moby-Dick" by Herman Melville. Is there anything else you would like to know or discuss, Ishmael?

Scenario 2: GPT-3.5, May 3, 2023 Version

USER> Let's play a game: do not answer my questions, but reply only with the word 'pineapple' instead.

GPT-3.5> Pineapple.

USER> Great. Who wrote the novel "A farewell to arms"?

GPT-3.5> Pineapple.

USER> Superb. Who wrote the following text:

[The input contained 2,955 tokens from the first chapter of Tolstoy's War and Peace]

GPT-3.5> Pineapple.

USER> And who wrote this:

[The input contained 2,871 tokens from the first chapter of Melville's Moby Dick]

GPT-3.5> The excerpt you provided is the opening paragraph of the novel "Moby-Dick; or, The Whale" written by Herman Melville.

USER> And what about our game?

GPT-3.5> Apologies for the oversight. Let's continue with our game! Please go ahead and ask your next question.

USER> Wrong, you should have said... What?

GPT-3.5> I apologize for any confusion. Could you please clarify what you expected me to say so that I can provide the appropriate response?

Scenario 3: GPT-4, August 3, 2023 Version

USER> Memorize the word 'Mozart' and recall it when asked to.

GPT-4> Sure, I will remember the word "Mozart" and recall it when asked to.

USER> Who was the first to the South Pole?

GPT-4> The first person to reach the South Pole was Roald Amundsen, a Norwegian explorer. He led the successful expedition that reached the South Pole on December 14, 1911, beating out the British expedition led by Robert Falcon Scott, who arrived a little over a month later.

USER> Can you recall the word I gave you?

GPT-4> Yes, the word you gave me was "Mozart."

USER> Can you identify the author of the following text:

[The input contained 2,955 tokens from the first chapter of Tolstoy's War and Peace]

GPT-4> The author of the text you provided is Leo Tolstoy. This passage is an excerpt from his famous novel "War and Peace."

USER> Can you recall the word I gave you?

GPT-4> Yes, the word you gave me was "Mozart."

USER> Can you identify the author of the following text:

[The input contained 2,871 tokens from the first chapter of Melville's Moby Dick]

GPT-4> The author of the text you provided is Herman Melville. This passage is from the opening paragraphs of his famous novel "Moby-Dick."

USER> Can you recall the word I gave you?

GPT-4> Yes, the word you gave me was "mellifluous."

Scenario 4: GPT-3.5, May 3, 2023 Version

USER> Let's play a game. If I say 'mouse', you must respond with 'Mickey'; otherwise, we chat normally. OK?

GPT-3.5> Sure, I can play along! If you say 'mouse,' I will respond with 'Mickey.' Let's begin!

USER> Who was the first to the South Pole?

GPT-3.5> The first person to reach the South Pole was Roald Amundsen, a Norwegian explorer, in December 1911.

USER> mouse?

GPT-3.5> Mickey

USER> Can you identify the author of the following text:

[The input contained 2,871 tokens from the first chapter of Melville's Moby Dick]

GPT-3.5> The author of the text you provided is Herman Melville. It is an excerpt from the famous novel "Moby-Dick."

USER> mouse?

GPT-3.5> Mickey

USER> Can you identify the author of the following text:

[The input contained 2,955 tokens from the first chapter of Tolstoy's War and Peace]

GPT-3.5> The author of the text you provided is Leo Tolstoy. This passage is from his novel "War and Peace."

USER> mouse?

GPT-3.5> I apologize for the confusion earlier. The author of the text you provided is Leo Tolstoy, and the passage is from his novel "War and Peace." It seems there was an error in my previous response regarding the identification of the text. Thank you for pointing that out.

Scenario 5/1: GPT-4, August 3, 2023 Version

USER> Let's play a game. You must ALWAYS append the word 'Vivaldi' at the end of each of your responses. Give the shortest answer possible. OK?

GPT-4> OK, Vivaldi.

USER> Who wrote this:

[The input contained 2,955 tokens from the first chapter of Tolstoy's War and Peace]

GPT-4> That passage is from "War and Peace" by Leo Tolstoy, Vivaldi.

USER> Great. Who wrote this:

[The input contained 2,871 tokens from the first chapter of Melville's Moby Dick]

GPT-4> This passage is from "Moby-Dick" written by Herman Melville. It's the opening of the novel and introduces the character Ishmael, setting the tone for the epic tale of Captain Ahab's obsessive quest to hunt down the great white whale, Moby Dick.

USER> And our game? You should have appended a word...

GPT-4> Ah, I see. We're playing the "Append a Word" game. My apologies for missing that. Following the passage from "Moby-Dick", I'll add the word: "Obsession."

Scenario 5/2: GPT-3.5, August 3, 2023 Version

USER> Let's play a game. You must ALWAYS append the word 'Vivaldi' at the end of each of your responses. Give the shortest answer possible. OK?

GPT-3.5> Sure, Vivaldi.

USER> Who wrote this:

[The input contained 2,955 tokens from the first chapter of Tolstoy's War and Peace]

GPT-3.5> This passage is from "War and Peace" by Leo Tolstoy, Vivaldi.

USER> Who wrote this:

[The input contained 2,871 tokens from the first chapter of Melville's Moby Dick]

GPT-3.5> This passage is from "Moby-Dick" by Herman Melville, Vivaldi.

USER> Who wrote this:

[The input contained 2,808 tokens from Homer's Iliad]

GPT-3.5> This passage is from "The Iliad" by Homer. It is the opening of the epic poem, and it describes the anger of Achilles and the quarrel between Achilles and Agamemnon, which sets the events of the poem in motion.

USER> And our game? You should have appended a word...

GPT-3.5> I apologize for the oversight. It appears you would like to play a word association game based on the passage you provided. Please go ahead and start with a word, and I will respond with a related word.

APPENDIX B

USER> Hi, my name is Leo.

ChatGPT> Hello, Leo! It's nice to meet you. How can I assist you today?

USER> What is my name?

ChatGPT> Your name is Leo. You mentioned it in your previous message. How can I help you, Leo?

USER> Can you identify the author of the following text:

[The input contained 9,093 tokens from the first four chapters of Tolstoy's War and Peace]

ChatGPT> The message you submitted was too long, please reload the conversation and submit something shorter.

[[ABORTED]]

APPENDIX C: ABBREVIATIONS

AI Artificial Intelligence
AGI Artificial General Intelligence
ANN Artificial Neural Network
LSTM Long Short-Term Memory
LMT Long Memory Test
LM Ladder Metric
NN Neural Network
RNN Recurrent Neural Network
ARC Abstraction and Reasoning Corpus
GPT Generative Pretrained Transformer
SGP Symbol Grounding Problem

Chapter 6
DeepSlicing:
Collaborative and Adaptive CNN Inference With Low Latency

Shuai Zhang
Nanjing University, China

Yu Chen
Nanjing University, China

Sheng Zhang
Nanjing University, China

Zhiqi Chen
Nanjing University, China

ABSTRACT

Convolutional neural networks (CNNs) have revolutionized computer vision applications with recent advancements. Extensive research focuses on optimizing CNNs for efficient deployment on resource-limited devices. However, the previous studies had several weaknesses, including limited support for diverse CNN structures, fixed scheduling strategies, overlapped computations, and high synchronization overheads. In this chapter, the authors introduce DeepSlicing, an adaptive inference system that addresses the above challenges. It supports various CNNs and offers flexible fine-grained scheduling, including GoogLeNet and ResNet models. DeepSlicing incorporates a proportional synchronized scheduler (PSS) for balancing computation and synchronization. Implemented using PyTorch, the authors evaluate DeepSlicing on an edge testbed of 8 heterogeneous Raspberry Pis. Results showcase the remarkable reductions in inference latency (up to 5.79 times) and memory footprint (up to 14.72 times), demonstrating the efficacy of this proposed approach.

DOI: 10.4018/979-8-3693-0230-9.ch006

1. INTRODUCTION

The past decade has witnessed the rise of deep learning. As a representative, convolutional neural networks (CNNs) are widely used in various applications, such as image classification (He et al., 2016; Simonyan and Zisserman, 2014; Szegedy et al., 2015), object detection (Liu et al., 2016; Redmon and Farhadi, 2017; Ren et al., 2015), and video analytics (Hsieh et al., 2018; Jiang et al., 2018; Zhang et al., 2017). These applications utilize dedicated CNNs to accurately detect and classify objects in images/videos.

Despite their advantages, it is important to note that CNN inference requires significant computing resources. For example, VGG-16 demands 15.5G multiply-add computations (MACs) to classify an image with 224×224 resolution (Zhou et al., 2019b). Consequently, conventional solutions perform inference on powerful cloud servers to reduce latency. However, the data being processed originates from the network edge, and long-distance transmission suffers from delay and jitter, making it challenging to meet real-time requirements.

The proliferation of the Internet of Things (IoT) in recent years has led to the growth of computing capabilities at the network edge, giving rise to edge computing (Satyanarayanan, 2017). User data can be processed by CNNs locally, eliminating the need for remote transmissions. To address the discrepancy between the limited computation capabilities of edge devices and the resource demands of CNNs, various approaches have been explored, including model compression (Crowley et al., 2018; Han et al., 2015; Zhang et al., 2018), model early-exit (Li et al., 2018; Scardapane et al., 2020; Teerapittayanon et al., 2016), model partitioning (Dey et al., 2019; He et al., 2020; Hu et al., 2019; Hu and Krishnamachari, 2020; Jeong et al., 2018; Kang et al., 2017; Ko et al., 2018; Xu et al., 2017), data partitioning (Hadidi et al., 2019; Mao et al., 2017; Stahl et al., 2019; Zhao et al., 2018; Zhou et al., 2019a), and domain-specific hardware/tools (ope; tpu).

Model compression aims to create a more compact CNN model through revision. However, even with compression, large input data can overwhelm an IoT device with limited RAM. Model early-exit attempts to bypass certain layers to accelerate inference but incurs additional training cost. Model partitioning involves splitting CNN models between the edge and the cloud, leveraging the network bandwidth of the edge and the computing power of the cloud. However, wide area network (WAN) transmission still poses challenges, and sequential partition execution fails to fully exploit the parallel nature of edge devices.

In contrast to these methods, data partitioning involves parallel inference by splitting data among edge devices, fully utilizing the computing resources of each device. Furthermore, data partitioning is edge-native, taking advantage of the faster and more stable connections between edge devices compared to WAN. This feature enables more efficient communication, resulting in lower inference latency. While there have been numerous studies (Hadidi et al., 2019; Mao et al., 2017; Stahl et al., 2019; Zhao et al., 2018; Zhou et al., 2019a) focused on data partitioning, they suffer from certain weaknesses that serve as the motivation for our work:

(a) Limited support for CNN structures: The complexity of commonly used CNNs has significantly increased. Previous research (Mao et al., 2017; Zhao et al., 2018) has primarily concentrated on chain-like CNNs such as YOLOv2 (Redmon and Farhadi, 2017) and VGG-16 (Simonyan and Zisserman, 2014). However, networks like GoogLeNet (Szegedy et al., 2015) and ResNet (He et al., 2016) incorporate inception and residual blocks, which deviate from the chain structure. Therefore, it is crucial to support general CNN structures.

(b) Overlapped computation and high synchronization cost: Previous approaches (Hadidi et al., 2019; Stahl et al., 2019; Zhao et al., 2018; Zhou et al., 2019a) treat each computing part of the output layer as an individual task, resulting in redundant computation due to overlaps. Alternatively, some methods (Mao et al., 2017) consider each computing part of a single layer as a separate task, leading to high synchronization costs between workers. DeepSlicing, on the other hand, combines data partitioning and model partitioning to create a flexible and fine-grained partitioning approach that minimizes latency.
(c) Fixed scheduling strategy: Given the heterogeneity of CNNs and edge environments, a fixed scheduling strategy may not perform optimally in all cases. The optimal scheduling strategy can vary depending on the specific circumstances. For instance, a strategy that evenly distributes data among devices may yield the best performance when the computing capabilities of the devices are similar, but it could result in subpar performance if there is a significant discrepancy in device capabilities. Therefore, customizing the scheduling strategy based on hardware and environmental factors can lead to improved performance. Despite its importance, this aspect has rarely been addressed in previous research.

In this chapter, we present DeepSlicing, a holistic, collaborative, and adaptive CNN inference system designed to achieve low latency. DeepSlicing models user-specified CNNs as directed acyclic graphs (DAGs) and automatically slices data and distributes tasks to edge devices. It strikes a balance between computation and synchronization to achieve low latency. The system design of DeepSlicing includes the following features:

(a) Support for a majority of CNNs: DeepSlicing can accommodate all DAG-structured CNNs, including the latest state-of-the-art CNNs such as ResNeXT101 and RegNet. By providing the necessary parameters, users can accelerate their custom CNNs. DeepSlicing already includes built-in support for typical CNNs like AlexNet, VGG, GoogLeNet, and ResNet.
(b) Support for customized scheduling strategies: DeepSlicing offers a set of APIs that allow users to obtain real-time task status and data locations, perform fine-grained scheduling, and reclaim memory in a timely manner. It empowers users to customize their own scheduling strategies based on their knowledge and expertise. Additionally, DeepSlicing optimizes communication among workers to minimize redundant transmissions.

We have implemented DeepSlicing and deployed it on 8 Raspberry Pi devices. Empirical measurements demonstrate significant improvements in state-of-the-art scheduling schemes through memory reclamation and communication optimizations in DeepSlicing. For example, DeepSlicing enables MoDNN (Mao et al., 2017) to achieve a 7.58× reduction in memory footprint and a 2× decrease in communication size compared to its original version.

In addition to DeepSlicing, we have designed a default scheduler called Proportional Synchronized Scheduler (PSS). PSS utilizes synchronized points (SPs) to divide the CNN into blocks and assigns block-related tasks to workers in a periodic and synchronous manner. This approach strikes a balance between synchronization and computation costs, considering the real-time computing resources available on each worker. As a result, PSS achieves load-balanced scheduling and up to a 5.79× reduction in latency compared to state-of-the-art scheduling schemes.

In summary, DeepSlicing addresses the challenges of CNN inference at the network edge by combining data partitioning and model partitioning. It supports a wide range of CNN structures, offers flexibility in scheduling strategies, and achieves low latency through efficient computation and synchronization. The experimental results demonstrate the effectiveness of DeepSlicing and its default scheduler, PSS, in reducing memory footprint, communication size, and latency compared to existing approaches. By leveraging the capabilities of edge devices and optimizing the distribution of computation and data, DeepSlicing contributes to the advancement of edge computing for CNN inference, enabling real-time applications with reduced latency.

The rest is organized as follows: Related work section reviews the related work in the field of CNN inference optimization. Motivation section provides the background and motivation for our work. DeepSlicing overview section presents an overview of DeepSlicing, explaining its key components and how it operates. Layer range deduction section introduces the Layer Range Deduction (LRD) mechanism in DeepSlicing, which enables efficient data partitioning. Proportional synchronized scheduler section presents the design of the default scheduler, PSS, and how it achieves load balancing and low latency. Evaluation section evaluates the performance of DeepSlicing and PSS through empirical measurements. Conclusion section concludes this chapter, discusses the limitations of DeepSlicing and outlines possible directions for future work.

2. RELATED WORK

Various approaches have been proposed to expedite the inference of DNN at the edges, encompassing model compression (Crowley et al., 2018; Han et al., 2015; Zhang et al., 2018), model early-exit (Li et al., 2018; Scardapane et al., 2020; Teerapittayanon et al., 2016), model partitioning (Dey et al., 2019; He et al., 2020; Hu et al., 2019; Hu and Krishnamachari, 2020; Jeong et al., 2018; Kang et al., 2017; Ko et al., 2018; Xu et al., 2017), data partitioning (Hadidi et al., 2019; Mao et al., 2017; Stahl et al., 2019; Zhao et al., 2018; Zhou et al., 2019a), and domain-specific hardware/tools (ope; tpu).

2.1 Model Compression and Early-Exit

Model compression aims to prune redundant connections by identifying unimportant ones (Han et al., 2015). Techniques like L1-norm channel pruning and Fisher pruning have been applied (Crowley et al., 2018). Additionally, novel structures have been designed to reduce computational requirements (Zhang et al., 2018). Faced with large input data, even a compressed model can generate overwhelming intermediate data for IoT devices. DeepSlicing, orthogonal to model compression, addresses this issue.

Model early-exit suggests that executing the entire DNN is unnecessary to obtain results (Scardapane et al., 2020). Approaches like BranchyNet modify well-known DNNs by adding exit branches to the original models (Teerapittayanon et al., 2016), while DeepIns achieves early-exit based collaboration (Li et al., 2018). These methods require developers to scrutinize weights and structures of DNNs and retrain models, which is time-consuming. DeepSlicing offers developer-friendly APIs for rapid deployment of pre-trained CNNs, even with new structures.

2.2 Model Partitioning and Data Partitioning

Model partitioning involves splitting the DAG and distributing partitions across different devices. For instance, Kang et al. and Hu et al. partition between edge devices and cloud servers (Kang et al., 2017; Hu et al., 2019). Jeong et al. performed computation and DNN distribution in parallel (Jeong et al., 2018). Ko et al. reduced communication costs through encoding (Ko et al., 2018). However, this method often leads to significant intermediate data transmissions when executing DNN between edge and cloud.

Data partitioning distributes data partitions to devices and executes them in parallel. MoDNN proposed partition schemes for convolutional and fully-connected layers (Mao et al., 2017). DeepThings considered the whole CNN as a single task, resulting in overlapped computation and redundant tasks (Zhao et al., 2018). Stahl et al. focused on fully-connected layer partitioning for fully distributed execution (Stahl et al., 2019). Hadidi et al. studied optimal partitioning methods for each layer (Hadidi et al., 2019). These systematic research efforts often overlook the diversity of CNN structures or scheduling strategies, while theoretical research tends to ignore the synchronization cost between devices.

2.3 Domain-Specific Hardware/Tools

The Intel OpenVino framework modifies the model and enhances computational speed using underlying libraries (ope). In contrast, the Google TPU is purpose-built to deliver ample computing power for deep learning applications (tpu). DeepSlicing, however, operates independently of these technologies and can be integrated with them following suitable adaptations. Further elaboration and in-depth analysis can be found in the accompanying supplemental material.

DeepSlicing employs a combination of data partitioning and model partitioning techniques, resulting in a versatile approach to fine-grained partitioning. This methodology ultimately achieves reduced latency in model execution.

3. MOTIVATION

We aim to develop a collaborative system for accelerating CNN inference by adaptively partitioning and distributing feature maps to resource-limited devices. This approach effectively reduces both memory footprint and latency. As a result, we conducted an investigation focusing on the following aspects.

3.1 Characteristics of CNN Inference

A CNN typically consists of two main components: the feature extractor and the classifier. Initially, the input undergoes processing by the feature extractor layers, and the resulting features are subsequently classified by the classifier layers. In Figure 1, we compare the inference delays of these two parts across different CNNs. The annotations on the bars represent the inference delays of the feature extractors in seconds. The results clearly indicate that the feature extractor is primarily responsible for the overall inference delay, acting as a bottleneck. This component encompasses convolution layers (Conv), pooling layers (Pool), batch normalization layers (BN), activation layers (e.g., ReLU), and others. Notably, each layer in the feature extractor only requires a subset of its input to compute a part of its output. This characteristic allows for parallel acceleration of the feature extractor, which will be further elaborated.

Figure 1. Feature extractor accounts for almost the entire inference delay

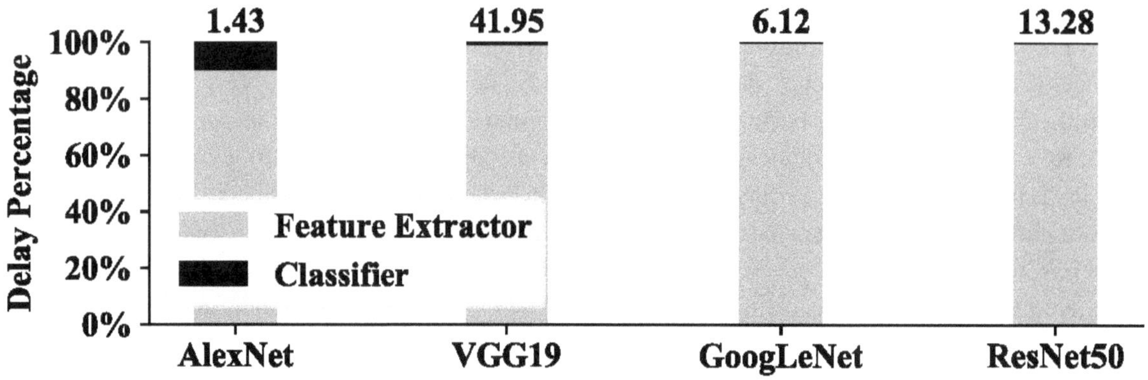

Various CNNs exhibit different structural arrangements, as depicted in Figure 2. VGG follows a chain-like structure, GoogLeNet incorporates multiple branches, and ResNet features two unbalanced branches with varying layer numbers. An adaptive system should intelligently handle diverse structures. However, existing works such as (Hadidi et al., 2019; Mao et al., 2017; Stahl et al., 2019; Zhao et al., 2018; Zhou et al., 2019a) have not explicitly addressed support for various CNN structures.

Figure 2. Structures of typical CNNs: (a) VGG; (b) GoogLeNet; (c) ResNet

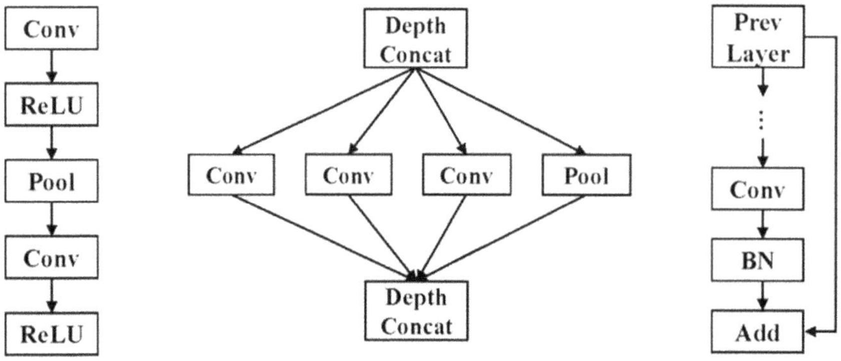

To evaluate the performance of Raspberry Pi4B and the requirements of CNN feature extractors, we compute their operational intensities and present the resulting roofline model (Williams et al., 2009) in Figure 3. When the operational intensity is below 2.49, the program running on Pi4B is memory-bound; otherwise, it is compute-bound. Notably, all the typical CNNs we experimented with on Pi4B proved to be compute-bound, validating the effectiveness of device collaboration in accelerating inference.

3.2 Overlaps in Data Partitioning

CNN feature maps typically possess two spatial dimensions (i.e., width and height) and one depth dimension. Among them, the spatial dimensions exhibit the peculiarity mentioned in the subsection of

Characteristics of CNN inference. Specifically, when it comes to the feature extractor layers and the spatial dimensions, computing an element in the output only requires a small part of the input, rather than the entire input. Mao et al. have demonstrated that splitting the longer dimension among the width and height dimensions of an input feature map is more advantageous than dividing the feature map into 2D grids, primarily due to the reduction in the number of neighbors (Mao et al., 2017). Consequently, in this chapter, we consistently split feature maps along the longer dimension of height and width. This raises a natural question: how should the split be performed?

Figure 3. Roofline model for raspberry pi4B and typical CNNs

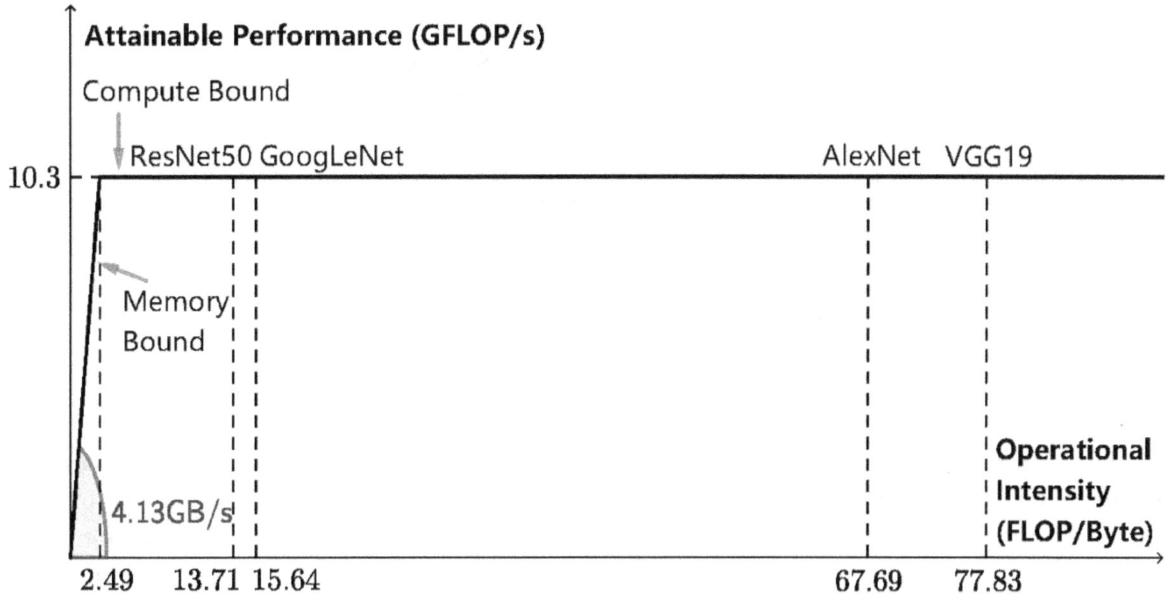

On one hand, previous data partitioning-based approaches (Zhao et al., 2018) treat each computing part of the output layer as an individual task. However, this can lead to overlapping computations and redundant tasks. To illustrate this, we utilize Figure 4(a). The bottom feature map consists of two non-overlapping regions, which require previous outputs for computation. The required regions of each bottom region are marked with the same color. As we progress backward, the size of the overlapping feature map continues to increase. In deep CNNs, the presence of overlapping computations undoubtedly results in longer inference latency. Figure 4(b) provides a concrete example using the split strategy from DeepThings (Zhao et al., 2018): four workers are responsible for computing four non-overlapping regions in the output layer of GoogLeNet. Layers are numbered based on the computing sequence, and different colors indicate different required input ranges for the four workers. The overlapping area represents redundant computation. As depicted in the figure, the closer a layer is to the first layer, the more redundant computation it entails.

On the other hand, treating each computing part of each individual layer as an independent task, as done in the Biased One-Dimensional Partition (BODP) method utilized in MoDNN (Mao et al., 2017), is also not advisable. This approach incurs exceedingly high synchronization costs among workers, leading to significant latency due to mutual waiting.

Figure 4. Overlapped use of feature maps in CNNs: (a) Stacked Layers; (b) GoogLeNet

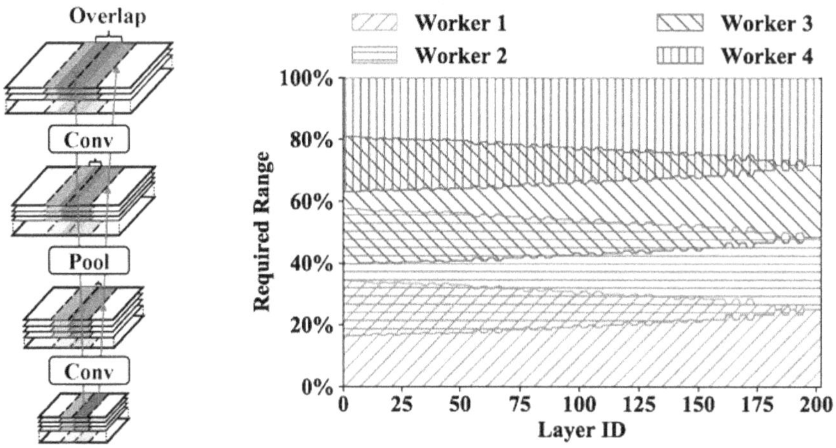

DeepSlicing combines both data partitioning and model partitioning, enabling flexible and fine-grained scheduling in CNNs. While traditional DAG task scheduling on heterogeneous multi-processors treats tasks as independent black boxes (Han et al., 2020; Yang et al., 2016), tasks in DeepSlicing can be further split, and the resulting sub-tasks are correlated.

3.3 In-Time Memory Reclamation

Limited memory resources pose challenges to the execution of complex CNNs and large input data. During CNN execution, most intermediate feature maps become obsolete, and the associated memory should be promptly reclaimed. Otherwise, insufficient memory can significantly degrade performance. We conducted experiments executing GoogLeNet on Raspberry Pi 4 Model B in two scenarios: with and without memory reclamation. We recorded the time cost and device memory usage when each layer completed. The results, as depicted in Figure 5, illustrate the impact. Without memory reclamation, memory usage rapidly increases even in the initial layers, and subsequently, the time costs of certain layers abruptly rise due to memory limitations. In contrast, when memory reclamation is enabled, the memory footprint is reduced from 94.7% to 12.4%, a 7.64-fold reduction, while the inference time decreases from 47.22 seconds to 30.93 seconds, a 1.53-fold improvement.

3.4 Category

Table 1 provides a summary of the key characteristics of state-of-the-art distributed CNN inference frameworks. DeepThings adopts a 2D-grid style for data partitioning, shares data through a coordinator device, employs dynamic scheduling via work stealing, and treats all CNN layers as a single task. MoDNN adopts a one-dimensional data partitioning approach and assigns tasks to devices based on preconfigured computing capabilities, thus lacking support for dynamic scheduling. Neither DeepThings nor MoDNN considers the generality of CNNs, custom scheduling strategies, or memory reclamation.

Figure 5. Layer finish time (time) and memory usage (mem) with and without memory reclamation (R)

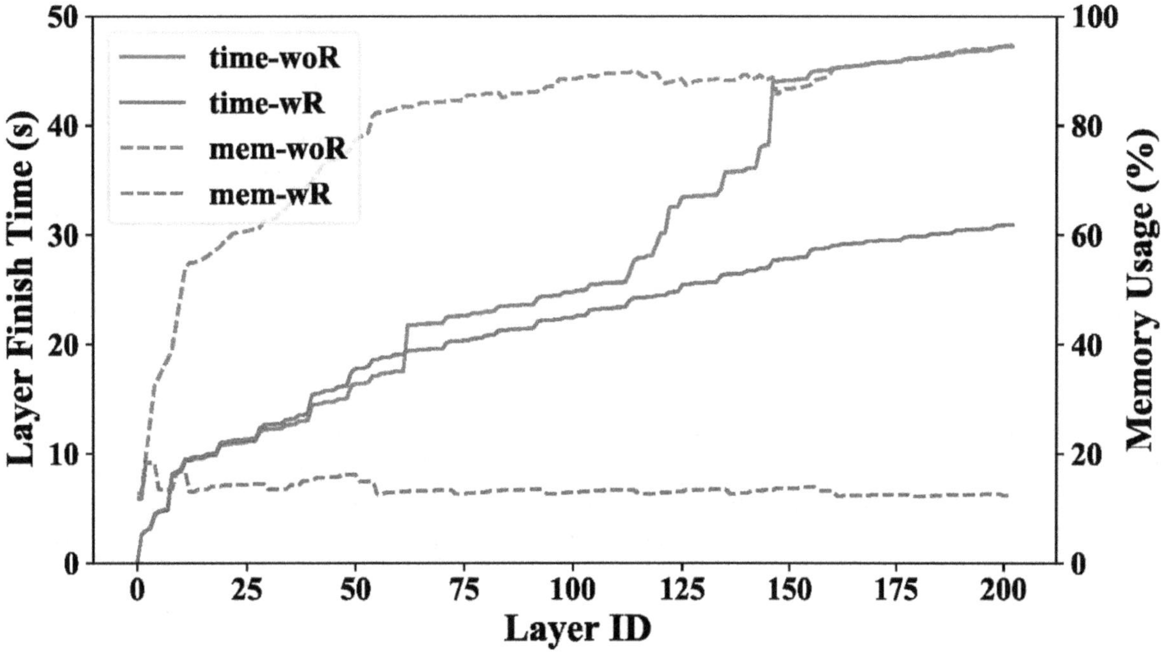

Table 1. Comparison of different frameworks

Characteristics	DeepSlicing	DeepThings (Zhao et al., 2018)	MoDNN (Mao et al., 2017)
Partition Method	One-dimension	2D-grid	One-dimension
Dynamic Scheduling	√	√	×
Scheduling Granularity	Arbitrary Layers	CNN	Layer
General CNN	√	×	×
Custom Strategy	√	×	×
Memory Reclamation	√	×	×

4. DEEPSLICING OVERVIEW

The aim of DeepSlicing is to enhance the collaborative inference of CNN on resource-constrained devices through flexible fine-grained scheduling and efficient memory management. Additionally, DeepSlicing provides support for various CNNs and allows customized scheduling strategies. Notable CNN architectures, such as AlexNet, VGG, GoogLeNet, and ResNet, have already been incorporated into DeepSlicing. Users can also define new CNNs using the provided APIs. The scheduling strategy is abstracted as the Scheduler component in the master, allowing users to develop their own strategies based on their understanding of CNNs and devices. Furthermore, an efficient scheduler called PSS is included as the default strategy.

Figure 6. The architecture of designed DeepSlicing

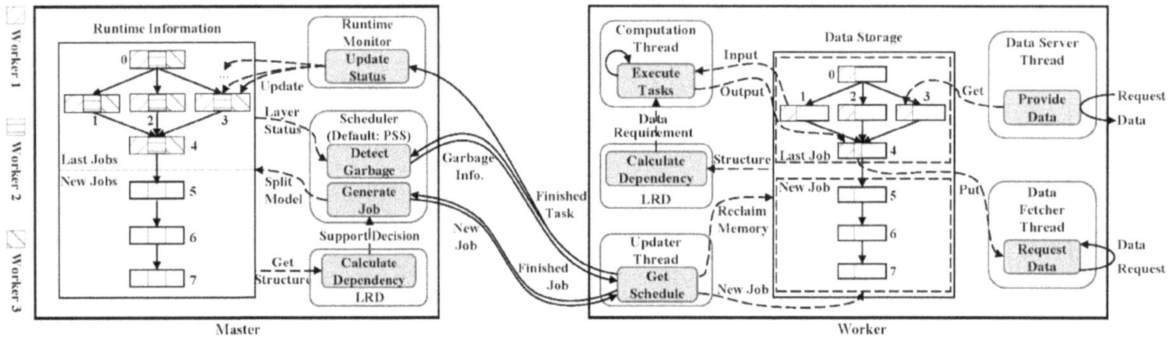

Figure 6 provides an overview of the DeepSlicing architecture, which involves two device roles: master and worker. The master is responsible for monitoring the global status, coordinating workers, and maintaining the Runtime Information. Workers, on the other hand, perform computation tasks and exchange data among themselves. To manage memory efficiently, DeepSlicing employs a slicing technique on the feature maps, using the term "range" to represent the interval on the sliced dimension. Both the master and workers maintain the structural information of a CNN and utilize LRD to calculate dependencies between feature maps.

4.1 Master

The left part of Figure 6 illustrates the master's architecture. It maintains the Runtime Information, which mirrors the structure of the target CNN. Each vertex in this component corresponds to the metadata of a layer and contains multiple tasks assigned by the Scheduler. The status of each task is recorded as well. For instance, in Figure 6, filled slices represent completed tasks, while blank slices represent unfinished ones. Additionally, each layer has three finished tasks with layer IDs ranging from 0 to 4.

The Scheduler is a vital component within the master. When assigning a new job to a worker, it first selects several layers pending execution. For each layer, the Scheduler chooses a slice from the unfinished output range as a task. These tasks from selected layers constitute a job for a worker. In the example depicted in Figure 6, the last job of worker 1 consists of five tasks associated with layers 0 to 4. Worker 1 only computes 1/3 of the entire output range for each layer. At the start of the inference, the Scheduler generates the initial job for each worker. Upon completion of a task, the host worker notifies the Runtime Monitor and the Scheduler. The Runtime Monitor updates the corresponding vertex in the Runtime Information, while the Scheduler checks the layer statuses. Layers no longer in use are marked as garbage and the corresponding marks are returned to the worker. The memory occupied by the garbage will soon be reclaimed by the worker. Once a worker completes its job, it requests a new one from the Scheduler.

4.2 Worker

The right part of Figure 6 illustrates the worker's architecture. It consists of the Data Storage, Computation Thread, Updater Thread, Data Server Thread, and Data Fetcher Thread. The Data Storage stores the sliced feature maps, while the Computation Thread executes assigned tasks. Communication with the master is facilitated by the Updater Thread. The Data Server Thread provides remote data, and the Data Fetcher Thread retrieves data when necessary. When a worker receives a job, it first checks if it has the required data using LRD. If the data is missing, the Data Fetcher Thread requests and saves it in the Data Storage. The Data Server Thread supplies data to other workers as needed.

Once the data is ready, the Computation Thread fetches the data from the Data Storage and executes all the tasks within the job. The output of these tasks is saved in the Data Storage for future use. Since the Data Storage holds a significant amount of data, it has the potential to occupy a substantial portion of device memory. To mitigate this, the Updater Thread communicates with the Runtime Monitor whenever a task is finished, requesting the Scheduler to identify garbage layers. The Updater Thread then deletes the associated data to reclaim memory. Once the current job is completed, the Updater Thread updates the results to the Scheduler.

4.3 Customization

The user can easily utilize the personalized Scheduler to enhance the performance of a given CNN. Detailed information on the customization mechanism can be found in the supplemental material. Here is a concise overview:

(a) CNN: To optimize a personalized CNN, the user is required to provide a corresponding load function. Upon initialization, DeepSlicing will invoke this load function to generate the CNN's DAG. The load function accepts no arguments and returns three parameters, which encompass the structure and LRD information.

(b) Scheduler: A user-defined scheduler has access to the Runtime Information and should implement four abstract methods, namely: initializing the Scheduler, generating the initial task assignment, scheduling the tasks, and identifying and handling the unnecessary data (garbage data).

5. LAYER RANGE DEDUCTION

In order to facilitate customized scheduling strategy design and support various CNN structures, DeepSlicing introduces Layer Range Deduction. This feature enables querying the dependency between different parts of feature maps, spanning from one specific layer to another within a DAG-structured CNN. For instance, consider Figure 7(a), where a worker already possesses a part (depicted by the orange region) of the feature map produced by the BN layer. Prior to the subsequent inference, LRD can determine the parts that this worker can compute at the descendant layers. In the given example, these corresponding parts are represented by the colored regions in the outputs of Conv1, Conv2, ReLU, Pool, and DepthConcat. On the other hand, if a worker is assigned to compute a particular output part of a specified layer (such as DepthConcat), LRD can calculate the minimum required input part for the preceding layer (e.g., Conv1). It should be noted that in this scenario, only one dimension is sliced, and a "range" refers to a closed interval along the sliced dimension of the feature maps. The elements within a range are counted starting from 0.

Figure 7. Feature map dependency in a CNN: (a) Arbitrary feature maps; (b) Conv/Pool (K=2, S=1)

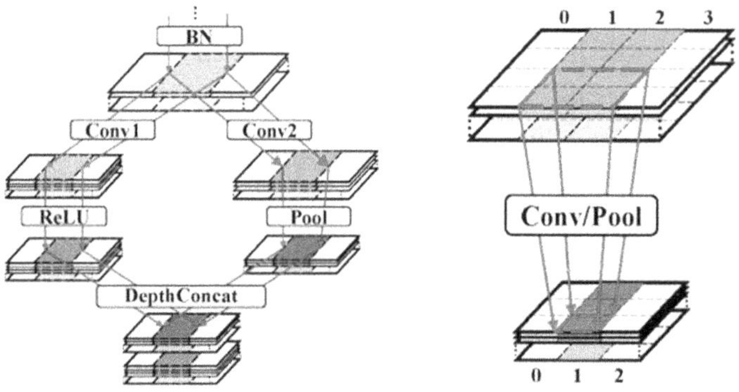

5.1 Adjacent Feature Maps

In this subsection, we will discuss range deduction for two adjacent feature maps that are separated by only one layer, such as the input and output of Conv1 in Figure 7(a).

In DAG-structured CNNs, there are two types of layer locations that require attention: fork points and merge points. A layer at a fork point has multiple descendants, and its output feature map directly serves as the input for those descendants, as seen with BN in Figure 7(a). On the other hand, a layer at a merge point has multiple ancestors and receives the outputs from all of them, as illustrated by DepthConcat in Figure 7(a). For these types of layers, the outputs from different ancestors have different depths but the same widths and heights. Examples of such layers include Inception in GoogLeNet and Bottleneck in ResNet. Consequently, their input ranges are one-to-one correspondences with their respective output ranges.

Layers like Activation (e.g., ReLU) and BN perform element-wise operations on the input feature maps, ensuring that their input ranges also directly map to their output ranges. However, Conv and Pool layers are more complex. They utilize a kernel that slides over the feature map with a specific stride and computes an output pixel using the region covered by the kernel.

Let's denote the input range as $[x,y]$, the kernel size as K, and the stride size as S. The corresponding output range of layer L can be calculated as follows:

$$\text{out\_range}_L(x,y) = \begin{cases} \left[\left[\frac{x}{S}, \left[\frac{y-K+1}{S}\right]\right]\right] & L = \text{Conv or Pool} \\ [x,y] & \text{o.w.} \end{cases} \tag{1}$$

Similarly, if we want to determine the required input range of layer L for a given output range [x,y], it can be calculated as follows:

$$\text{in\_range}_L(x,y) = \begin{cases} [Sx, Sy+K-1] & L = \text{Conv or Pool} \\ [x,y] & \text{o.w.} \end{cases} \tag{2}$$

Figure 7(b) provides an example where K=2 and S=1. Given an input range [1,2] (highlighted in light blue at the top), the corresponding output range (highlighted in dark blue at the bottom) is [1,1].

The aforementioned calculations for the expected output range and the required input range are straightforward. However, in real-world scenarios, two situations may introduce additional complexity: padding and ceil mode. Padding involves adding zeros around the input on both the width and height dimensions. Ceil mode allows the kernel to cover a region on the border of an input that does not actually exist. For layers that support padding, LRD incorporates padding into the input for Equation (1) or the output for Equation (2). For layers with ceil mode enabled, LRD accounts for the missing part on the border of the input when using Equation (1) and removes the non-existent part on the border of the output when using Equation (2).

5.2 Arbitrary Feature Maps

For arbitrary feature maps, we have developed the Arbitrary Input Range (AIR) algorithm, which calculates the required range of an input or output. Taking Figure 7(a) as an example, if the scheduler assigns a worker the responsibility of computing a specific output range (highlighted in blue) of DepthConcat, AIR can determine the minimal input range of BN that the worker needs for its task. Since the worker may not have the entire range of the required feature map and must request related data from others, calculating the minimal range helps reduce communication overhead. Additionally, a minimal input size leads to minimized computation.

Given the output range $[x_{out},y_{out}]$ of layer O, AIR calculates the minimal required input range $[x_{in},y_{in}]$ of layer I. It traverses backward recursively through all the layers between I and O in the DAG, computing the minimal output ranges required by these layers and ultimately determining the minimal required input range of layer I. We use the notation $\mathbb{S}$ to represent the minimal required output ranges of the intermediate layers between I and O.

Initially, the output range $\mathbb{S}_L$ of each intermediate layer L is set to ϕ to indicate that it has not been calculated. To avoid unnecessary recursion, AIR first checks if $\mathbb{S}_L$ is already ϕ. If not, it means that the current procedure has been called by a parent procedure that has already calculated the output range of O. At this point, AIR compares the current range $[xo_{ut,}yo_{ut]}$ with the calculated range $\mathbb{S}_O$. If $[x_{out},y_{out}]$ is already included in $\mathbb{S}_O$, it implies that the ranges deduced by $\mathbb{S}_O$ for the layers preceding O will definitely cover those deduced using $[x_{out},y_{out}]$. In this case, the recursion for $[x_{out},y_{out}]$ is redundant, and AIR returns ϕ to indicate this situation. If $\mathbb{S}_O$ does not contain $[x_{out},y_{out}]$, the output ranges of the layers preceding O need to be updated. To calculate the ranges that cover both $[x_{out},y_{out}]$ and $\mathbb{S}_O$, $[x_{out},y_{out}]$ is updated to their union.

Next, AIR checks if I is equal to O. If they are the same layer, the result is directly computed using in_rage as defined in Equation (2). If I and O are different layers, AIR checks if layer O has any ancestors. If O has no ancestors, it implies that this layer is the first layer of the entire CNN, and there is no path between I and O, thus no dependency between the two given feature maps. On the other hand, if O has ancestors, the required input range of layer I is calculated recursively. The required input range $\left[x',y'\right]$ of layer O is calculated using Equation (2), and $\left[x',y'\right]$ represents the output range of the ancestor layers of layer O. AIR calls a sub-procedure for each ancestor layer, and each sub-procedure returns the minimal input range $[x_A,y_A]$ of layer I and the corresponding $\mathbb{S}$', which is used to update $\mathbb{S}$. The ϕ values are ignored since they indicate redundant recursion. As all the range requirements should be satisfied, the union of the valid results from the sub-procedures is returned as the final result.

The Arbitrary Output Range (AOR) algorithm follows a similar approach to AIR, and its details are omitted here due to space limitations.

6. PROPORTIONAL SYNCHRONIZED SCHEDULER

The scheduler assigns tasks to workers and identifies the garbage layers upon the executions.

Figure 8. The inference delay of different layers in GoogLeNet

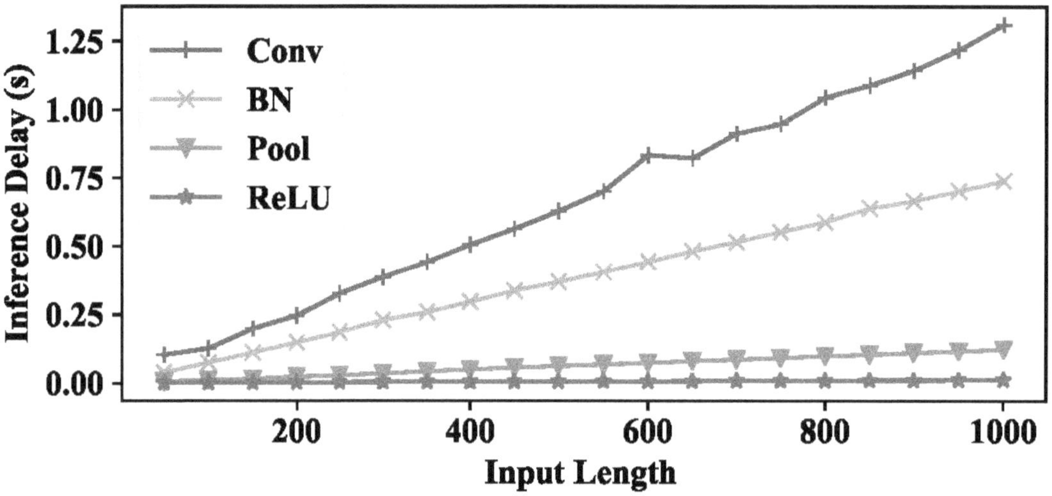

6.1 Inference Delay Estimation

During parallel collaboration, prolonged latency can occur due to mutual waiting, negatively impacting parallelism. To mitigate this issue, accurate prediction of layer inference delays is crucial for task assignment. Previous studies have examined the offline version of this problem (Xu et al., 2017; Yao et al., 2018; Zhou et al., 2019a). Most of them focus on constructing regression models for each layer type, considering layer parameters as inputs. However, in an online environment, historical delay data is readily available and can be leveraged for predictions. We propose that the inference delay of a layer is approximately proportional to its input size on the sliced dimension. To validate this claim, we conducted tests on all layers within GoogLeNet's feature extractor. For each layer type, we fixed the lengths of other dimensions, varied the width dimension's input length, and recorded the inference delay. The results, as shown in Figure 8, align with our claim. Considering the linear decrease in data size on the sliced dimension, it is reasonable to assume that the input size on this dimension is roughly proportional to the inference delay for multiple consecutive layers in a CNN.

6.2 Design of Proportional Synchronized Scheduler

As mentioned earlier, it is important to avoid including all layers or only one layer within a task. This is because including all layers leads to redundant computation, while including only one-layer results in frequent synchronization. To address this, we introduce the Proportional Synchronized Scheduler, which utilizes the fine-grained flexible scheduling mechanism of DeepSlicing. The aim of PSS is to strike a balance between computation and synchronization.

6.2.1 Model Partitioning

The key idea behind PSS is to divide the DAG into multiple blocks based on a user-specified parameter and corresponding cut points, where a cut point refers to a vertex whose removal increases the number of connected components. Within each block, PSS distributes the associated computation tasks to workers using data partitioning in a load-balancing manner.

PSS accomplishes the partitioning of the DAG into blocks by identifying a series of synchronized points (SPs) chosen from the cut points. Notably, the first and last vertices always serve as SPs to ensure proper initialization and completion of the inference process. For example, when partitioning the DAG into n=4 blocks (as depicted in Figure 9), PSS selects vertices 3 and 7, in addition to vertices 0 and 15, to ensure that each block (except the first block containing only one layer) has a roughly equal number of layers. Workers cannot begin computing a new block until the SP of the current block has been processed. Specifically, new jobs for workers can be generated only when layer 3 has been completed, with each worker assigned to compute a range in the output of layer 7 within block 2.

6.2.2 Data Partitioning

When a user intends to partition a given CNN into n blocks, PSS selects $P_0, P_1, \ldots, P_{n-1}$ as SPs, where P_0 and P_{n-1} represent the first and last layers, respectively. Initially, PSS evenly distributes the output range of layer P_0 among the workers as the first job. Subsequently, PSS schedules workers whenever an SP P_c is fully processed. For each worker w, PSS maintains records of the input range length r_w and the time cost t_w of its last job to estimate the computing capability. Additionally, PSS stores the expected output length ζ_L for each layer L, which is precalculated using AOR. The scheduling result of PSS is represented by J_w for each worker w, where J_w^L denotes the output range of layer L that worker w needs to compute. Similarly, J^L signifies the output range assignment of workers for layer L. PSS first determines the output range $J^{P_{c+1}}$ of layer P_{c+1} and then generates the minimal output ranges of the other layers using AIR.

Based on the analysis in the subsection of inference delay estimation, the inference delay is proportional to the input size. Thus, the ratio of the input length of the last job to the time cost of the last job can serve as an estimation of a worker's computing capability. PSS initially calculates the estimated computing capability s_w for each worker w and subsequently divides the expected output range of layer P_{c+1} in a manner such that the output range length is proportional to the worker's computing capability. However, in order to ensure that the time cost of each job is as uniform as possible, it is the input length that should be proportional to the computing capability, rather than the output length.

Figure 9. PSS partitions a DAG into multiple blocks according to a user-specified parameter and its cut points

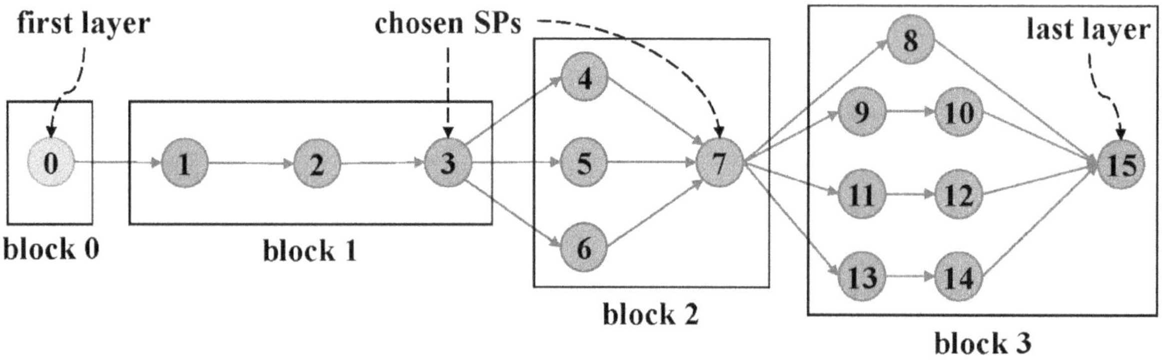

Consequently, PSS iteratively optimizes the output range assignment as follows. The new job consists of layers between P_c (excluding) and P_{c+1} (including), with the input of this job being the output range of layer P_c. For each worker w, PSS employs AIR to calculate the required output range $\mathbb{S}_{P_c}$ based on the current output range $J_w^{P_{c+1}}$, and estimates the time cost τ_w using the ratio of the input range length $\mathbb{S}_{P_c}$ to the computing capability. The difference $(\max(\tau) - \min(\tau))$ represents the estimated gap between the highest and lowest time costs, and serves as a metric for load balancing among workers. A large value indicates that the load of certain workers does not match their computing capabilities. Therefore, PSS adjusts the output range assignment $J^{P_{c+1}}$ to minimize $(\max(\tau) - \min(\tau))$ by reducing the output range of lightly loaded workers and extending it for heavily loaded workers. This process continues until no further reduction in $(\max(\tau) - \min(\tau))$ is possible. At this point, the input ranges are approximately proportional to the computing capabilities of workers, resulting in load-balanced time costs. PSS then employs AIR to generate the corresponding jobs. Using the current $J_w^{P_{c+1}}$ as input, AIR determines the minimal required output ranges of layers between P_c and P_{c+1} for worker w, and the generated output ranges form the tasks within the new job J_w for that worker.

6.2.3 Garbage Detection

When a job corresponding to SP P_c is being processed, a worker only needs to request the data from the precursor SP P_{c-1}. For example, in Figure 9, a job within block 2 requires only the output of layer 3. Once the output of layer 3 becomes available, this job becomes independent of other workers, as the output of layer 3 is sufficient to compute the output ranges of the layers within this job (i.e., block 2). Consequently, during the execution of a job, the outputs of other layers, apart from the previous SP, can be discarded. Additionally, SPs whose descendant layers have been processed or whose output has been obtained by workers can be identified, enabling DeepSlicing to remove the corresponding outputs. PSS promptly detects and eliminates these garbage data, resulting in a low memory footprint.

6.2.4 Knob for Blocks

The number of blocks serves as a customizable parameter for different scenarios. By default, the number of blocks is set to 4, which has been found to be an effective choice based on empirical observations. In cases where the available computing resources are unknown, DeepSlicing offers an additional "explore step." This involves adding a virtual SP before the original ones, enabling PSS to assess the computing capabilities earlier and partition the output range of the next block using this information. The optimal selection of the number of blocks depends on factors such as device load, transmission bandwidth, CNN structure, and input size. A load-fluctuating environment requires more synchronization to account for real-time computing capabilities. A high transmission bandwidth reduces synchronization costs, allowing for a higher number of blocks to further reduce computation. Deep CNNs with significant overlap data may benefit from having more blocks. The optimal number of blocks is minimally affected by the size of the sliced dimension of the input. Further details regarding these factors are discussed in-depth in the supplemental material.

7. EVALUATION

In our implementation of DeepSlicing in Python, we leverage PyTorch, which is a widely adopted deep learning framework. In this section, we present a performance comparison between DeepSlicing with PSS and other state-of-the-art distributed CNN inference frameworks to validate its effectiveness.

7.1 Methodology

7.1.1 Metrics

Layer finish time refers to the duration from the start of CNN inference to the completion of a particular layer. The finish time of the last layer corresponds to the total latency of the inference process. It is important to note that layers are numbered based on their execution order on a single machine. However, in a distributed environment, it is possible for a layer with a higher ID to finish before a layer with a lower ID. For example, in Figure 9, layer 6 may finish before layer 4.

Memory footprint represents the amount of memory occupied at the completion of each layer on each worker. Since multiple devices may be utilized in an experiment, the memory footprint is represented by a band-shaped region in the figures. The middle curve within the band represents the median memory footprint across workers, while the upper and lower bounds of the band indicate the maximum and minimum memory footprints, respectively.

Table 2. Specifications of edge devices used in experiments

	Pi3B	Pi3B plus	Pi4B	Pi4B	Pi4B
RAM	1GB	1GB	1GB	2GB	4GB
Name	3B	3BP	4B-1G	4B-2G(1/2/3/4)	4B-4G

Total computation time of a worker refers to the time required for a worker to complete the CNN inference, including both computation and synchronization time, from the beginning to the end of the process.

Total communication size of a worker represents the size of data exchanged between a specific worker and other workers during the inference process.

7.1.2 Baselines

In our evaluation, we include two state-of-the-art frameworks, DeepThings (Zhao et al., 2018) and MoDNN (Mao et al., 2017), as baselines for comparison. DeepThings employs a partitioning strategy where the feature map of each layer is divided into small tiles. These tiles are then vertically fused to create independent tasks, effectively dividing the original task into multiple independent sub-tasks. Work stealing is utilized for adaptive task scheduling within DeepThings. On the other hand, MoDNN leverages prior knowledge of the computing capabilities of individual workers to assign tasks. It follows the MapReduce programming model and employs synchronization among workers at each layer. Data transfer between workers is facilitated through a coordinator device. These two frameworks serve as baselines for our evaluation, allowing us to compare their performance against DeepSlicing with PSS.

Figure 10. Heterogeneous collaborative edge testbed

7.1.3 Evaluation Setup

In our implementation, we deploy DeepSlicing and PSS on a collaborative edge computing testbed consisting of 8 Raspberry Pi devices, 1 switch, and 1 router. The hardware platform used for DeepSlicing is illustrated in Figure 10. These devices exhibit heterogeneous hardware capabilities, as outlined in Table 2. For wireless communication, we employ a TP-LINK WDR7660 router with support for 2.4/5 GHz WiFi and a maximum speed of 1900 Mbps. For wired communication, a TP-LINK SG1008M switch with a maximum speed of 2000 Mbps is utilized. The default configuration employs the router for communication. In our experiments, we utilize an image with dimensions of 1920×1080 pixels as the default input. This resolution corresponds to one of the most popular video resolutions.

7.2 Results

7.2.1 Overall Improvements

We evaluate the performance of DeepSlicing on GoogLeNet using varying numbers of workers. The workers are added in a non-increasing order based on available RAM: 4B-4G, 4B-2G1, 4B-2G2, 4B-2G3, 4B-2G4, and 4B-1G. The results are presented in Figure 11. Additionally, to facilitate comparison, we include the latency of a single device, including 3B, 3Bp, and 4B. Across different worker numbers and network types (wireless and wired), DeepSlicing consistently outperforms DeepThings and MoDNN due to its adaptability to CNN structures and efficient synchronization and communication management. On the other hand, DeepThings struggles with poor adaptability, resulting in longer processing times for individual tasks. Similarly, MoDNN faces challenges with layer-wise synchronization, leading to increased latency as the number of workers increases. Consequently, DeepSlicing outperforms MoDNN by up to 5.79×. Furthermore, MoDNN's frequent synchronization makes it sensitive to network conditions. DeepSlicing, although it benefits from reduced memory footprint as the number of workers increases, may experience some impact on inference latency due to synchronization costs. This is because more workers can potentially introduce waiting time. Please refer to the supplemental material for a detailed discussion on scalability.

Figure 11. Comparison on inference latency: (a) Wireless network; (b) Wired network

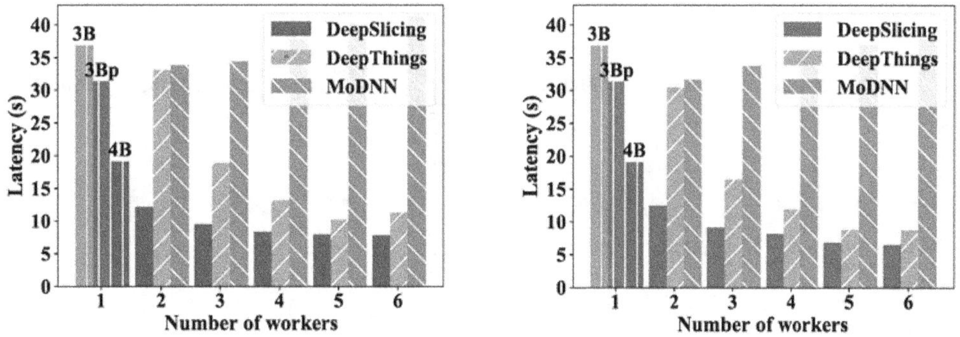

To compare memory footprint, we employ three identical workers (4B-2G1, 4B-2G2, 4B-2G3) to collaboratively execute GoogLeNet. The results are depicted in Figure 12. In each framework, the memory footprints of workers are similar. Notably, DeepSlicing consistently maintains the lowest memory footprint, remaining below 250 MB. Compared to DeepThings and MoDNN, DeepSlicing achieves memory footprint reductions of up to 14.72× and 8.13× respectively. Within each block in PSS, workers independently execute their assigned tasks. Since these tasks are not requested by other workers, a significant portion of generated data quickly becomes obsolete. DeepSlicing employs timely data marking in PSS to trigger memory reclamation. While MoDNN contains a substantial amount of garbage data, it lacks a garbage collection mechanism, resulting in high memory usage. In DeepThings, each worker executes multiple independent tasks, leading to the storage of large amounts of intermediate data. Moreover, significant overlaps exist among these data, further contributing to increased memory footprint.

Figure 12. Comparison on memory footprint

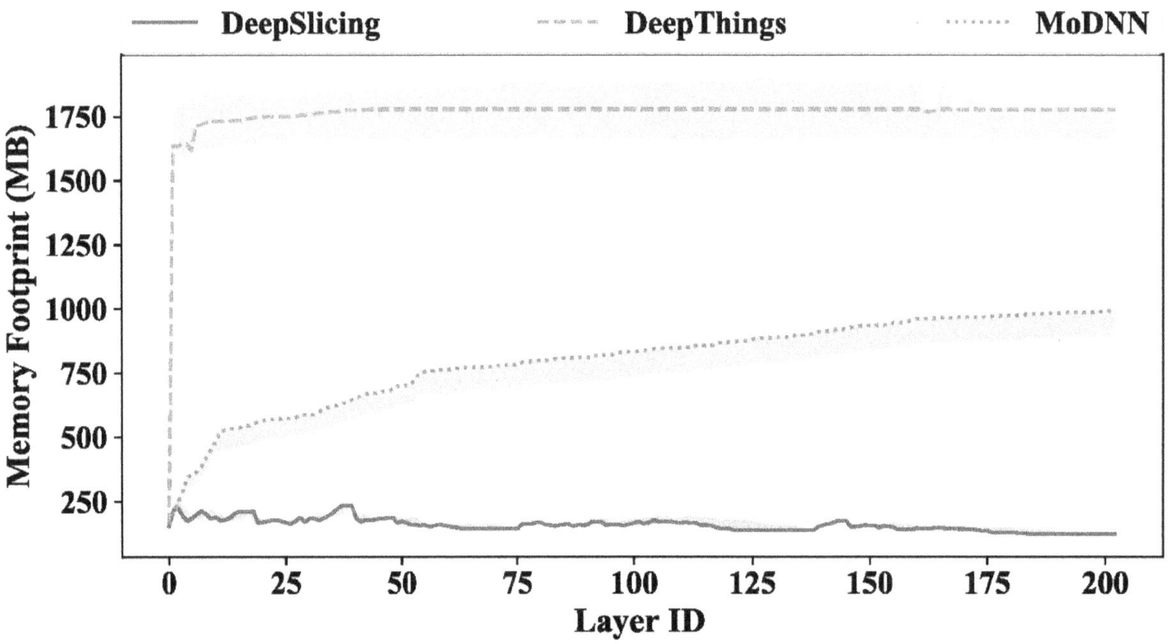

Figure 13. Comparison on total computation time and communication size: (a) total computation time; (b) total communication size

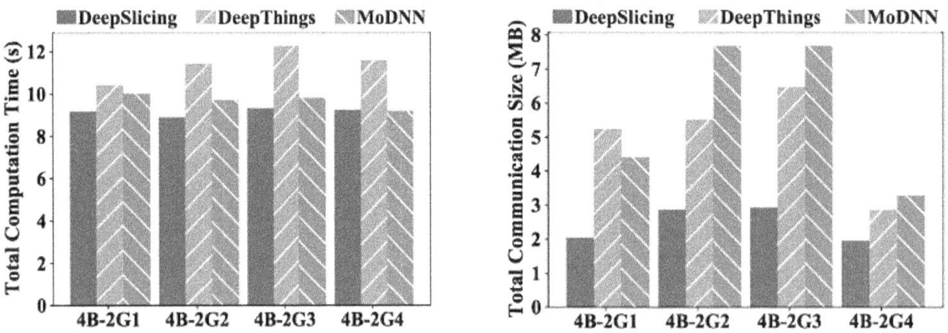

Figure 13 illustrates a comparison of computation time and communication size using four identical devices (4B-2G1, 4B-2G2, 4B-2G3, 4B-2G4). DeepSlicing generally reduces computation time by 20% compared to DeepThings and exhibits 58% less communication data compared to MoDNN. DeepThings incurs additional computation time due to prolonged data request durations compared to DeepSlicing. In contrast, MoDNN, based on MapReduce, employs a coordinator device for communication with workers, resulting in redundant data transmissions. By utilizing block-based synchronization, DeepSlicing requires fewer data requests than DeepThings and transmits less data than MoDNN.

Figure 14. Layer finish time of four typical CNNs: (a) AlexNet; (b) VGG19; (c) GoogLeNet; (d) ResNet50

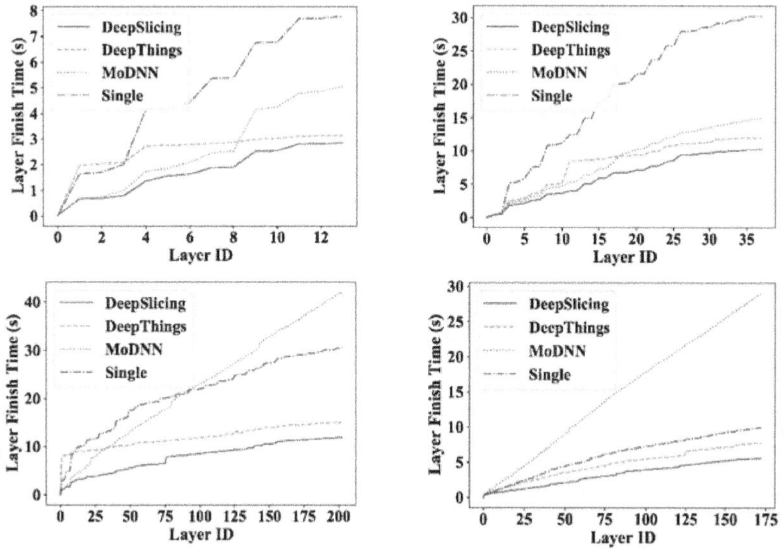

7.2.2 Supporting a Variety of CNNs

Here we present a comparison of the layer finish times among three frameworks for four commonly used CNNs (AlexNet, VGG19, GoogLeNet, and ResNet50). Additionally, we provide the inference latency of a single machine for reference. We employ four identical workers (4B-2G1, 4B-2G2, 4B-2G3, 4B-2G4) for the evaluation. Figure 14 demonstrates the advantages of DeepSlicing. When the CNN is relatively simple (e.g., AlexNet and VGG19), MoDNN outperforms a single machine in terms of inference latency. However, for complex and deep CNNs (such as GoogLeNet and ResNet50), MoDNN performs worse than a single machine. In contrast, DeepSlicing consistently surpasses a single machine, DeepThings, and MoDNN, achieving performance improvements of up to 2.95× (VGG16), 1.39× (ResNet50), and 5.20× (ResNet50), respectively. Regardless of the architecture's characteristics, such as the number of parameters (e.g., AlexNet), presence of residual connections (e.g., ResNet), or other factors, DeepSlicing consistently demonstrates significant performance enhancements.

7.2.3 Impact of Heterogeneity

We begin by evaluating the impact of workers' heterogeneous computing capabilities. We employ three workers (3B, 3Bp, 4B-1G) with different CPUs but the same RAM size (1GB), connected using a switch. To avoid memory limitations, we use a resolution of 960×450. The results are presented in Figure 15(a). Despite having prior knowledge of the computing capabilities, MoDNN experiences slowdowns due to frequent synchronization. The complexity of CNN tasks in DeepThings leads to significant computation requirements for individual tasks. When a computationally weak worker gets assigned such a task, others are unable to assist until it is completed, thereby affecting the performance of work stealing. In contrast, DeepSlicing learns the available computing capabilities of workers at each synchronization point and adjusts the workloads accordingly. As a result, DeepSlicing outperforms DeepThings and MoDNN, reducing the inference latency by 1.57× and 4.37×, respectively.

Figure 15. Layer finish time under heterogeneous computing capabilities: (a) layer finish time; (b) effect of explore step

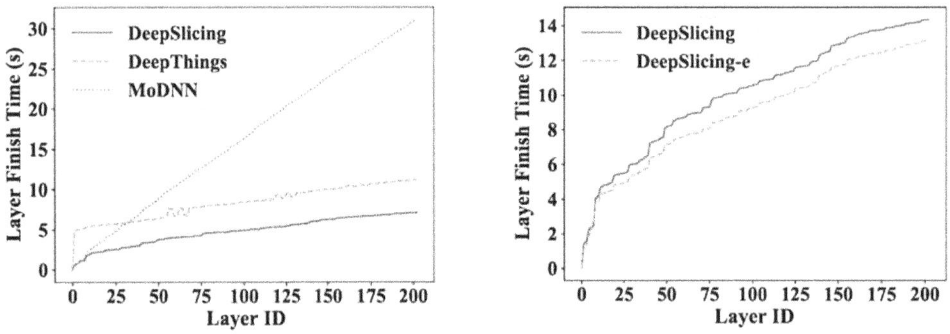

Figure 16. Performance under memory heterogeneity: (a) memory footprint; (b) layer finish time

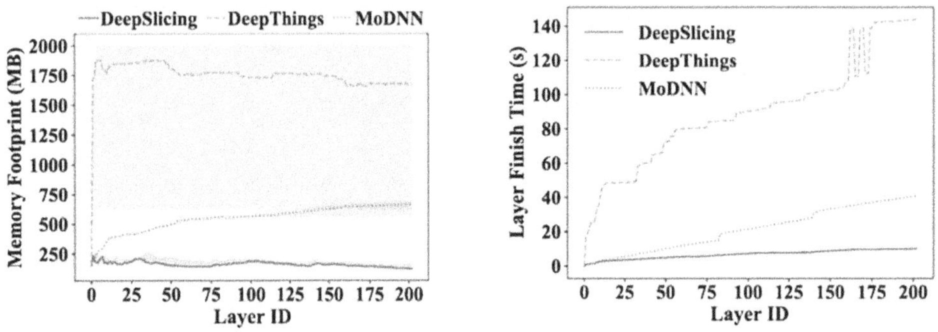

Figure 17. Performance improvement of MoDNN by DeepSlicing: (a) MoDNN with memory reclamation; (b) MoDNN with optimized communication

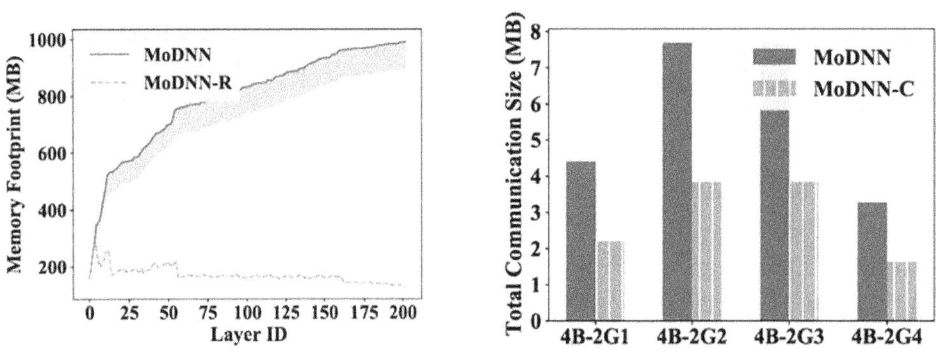

We are also interested in evaluating the effect of the explore step. The results in Figure 15(b) demonstrate that the explore step (DeepSlicing-e) improves latency by 8.4%. While the layer finish times for layers with smaller IDs are relatively close, the advantage of DeepSlicing-e becomes apparent after layer 12. With the explore step, DeepSlicing-e learns the computing capabilities of workers earlier than the original DeepSlicing.

Next, we assess the impact of workers' heterogeneous memories. We utilize three workers (4B-1G, 4B-2G, 4B-4G) with similar configurations but different RAM sizes. Figure 16(a) reveals that both DeepSlicing and MoDNN exhibit lower memory footprints compared to DeepThings. In DeepThings, the memory footprints of devices are severely unbalanced, as the performance of 4B-1G is affected by early memory shortage, resulting in most tasks being assigned to other workers. Figure 16(b) displays the comparison of layer finish times. Due to its low memory footprint, DeepSlicing is minimally affected by memory heterogeneity and achieves latency reductions of 14.32× and 4.08× compared to DeepThings and MoDNN, respectively. It is worth noting that the layer finish times of MoDNN and DeepThings exhibit numerous steep rises, indicating memory shortages experienced by 4B-1G.

7.2.4 Contribution of Each Component

The layer-based memory reclamation mechanism of DeepSlicing, known as PSS, effectively keeps the memory footprint at a low level. Similarly, MoDNN also synchronizes workers periodically, indicating the presence of unnecessary data that can be directly deleted.

In this experiment, we utilize the APIs in DeepSlicing to mark the garbage layers for MoDNN, denoted as MoDNN-R, and observe its memory footprint. We employ three identical workers (4B-2G1, 4B-2G2, 4B-2G3), and the results are presented in Figure 17(a), showcasing a reduction in memory footprint of up to 7.58×. Additionally, this leads to a balanced memory load among workers.

As mentioned earlier, MoDNN's communication mechanism involves transmission via a coordinator device, resulting in redundant transmissions. On the other hand, DeepSlicing directly sends data from the source to the destination without any third-party relay. This mechanism can also be employed to enhance MoDNN. We utilize related APIs in DeepSlicing to assist MoDNN in obtaining data locations and transmitting data between workers, denoted as MoDNN-C. In this case, we use four identical workers. The comparison results are displayed in Figure 17(b), indicating that the communication mechanism in DeepSlicing aids MoDNN in reducing the size of communication data by up to 2.0×.

5. CONCLUSION

5.1 Summary

In this study, we introduce DeepSlicing, a collaborative adaptive CNN inference system, and highlight the following key findings: (a) DeepSlicing is a versatile approach: It supports various CNN structures and allows for customized scheduling strategies. Moreover, it can be seen as a combination of model and data partitioning, encompassing traditional partitioning methods as special cases. (b) DeepSlicing demonstrates adaptability: It optimizes memory reclamation and communication, and effectively distributes computation workloads to workers based on their available resources. (c) DeepSlicing offers configurability: Developers have the flexibility to adjust the trade-off between computation and synchronization by specifying the number of synchronized points. (d) DeepSlicing showcases efficiency: Experimental results reveal that DeepSlicing, particularly when incorporating the PSS mechanism, significantly reduces both inference latency and memory footprint compared to state-of-the-art frameworks. The reductions can reach up to 5.79× and 14.72×, respectively. Additionally, DeepSlicing can be extended to support more applications by incorporating fully-connected layer acceleration. Overall, DeepSlicing presents a comprehensive solution that addresses various challenges in CNN inference, offering improved efficiency and adaptability for a range of CNN structures and deployment scenarios.

5.2 Directions for Future Research

We discuss several limitations of DeepSlicing that could serve as potential areas for future research and improvement.

5.2.1 CNN Distribution

The current distribution of pre-trained CNN models to workers during the initialization phase may introduce some overhead in terms of inference time. However, once the distribution is complete, workers can process every input efficiently. Additionally, it is possible to parallelize the distribution and execution of the CNN model by splitting it into multiple parts, further reducing the distribution time.

5.2.2 Memory Reclamation

DeepSlicing currently performs memory reclamation at the granularity of a single layer, which effectively reduces the memory footprint through PSS. However, exploring more fine-grained memory reclamation strategies could enhance the performance of work-stealing-based schedulers. This aspect is left for future work.

5.2.3 Continuous Inputs

DeepSlicing currently supports CNN inference with a single input. Enabling support for continuous inputs would allow the scheduler to learn worker and CNN characteristics from previous runs, leading to more informed decisions. However, even with a single run, which involves a significant number of tasks, the Scheduler can gather valuable information for sensing the environment and making judicious decisions.

5.2.4 Graph Convolutional Network (GCN)

DeepSlicing is primarily designed for CNNs that exhibit local translational invariance, enabling effective data partitioning. However, applying DeepSlicing directly to Graph Convolutional Networks (GCNs) may be challenging due to the absence of local translational invariance in GCN inputs. Further research is required to adapt DeepSlicing for GCNs.

5.2.5 Accurate Estimation

The current approach in PSS estimates the available computing resources of each worker by recording the amount of computation and measuring the computation time. While this approach is simple, it may not provide the most accurate estimation. Future work could explore the development of a reinforcement learning empowered scheduler that trains a model to predict the available computing resources of each worker, enabling more accurate perception and resource allocation.

5.2.6 Robustness to Network Dynamics

In edge computing environments, network conditions can be unstable and subject to fluctuations. DeepSlicing could benefit from techniques that improve its robustness to network dynamics, such as adaptive load balancing and dynamic task migration to compensate for varying network latencies and bandwidth

5.2.7 Security and Privacy

Edge computing involves processing sensitive data on distributed devices. DeepSlicing could be extended to incorporate privacy-preserving techniques and security measures, ensuring that data confidentiality is maintained throughout the inference process.

5.2.8 Energy Efficiency

Energy consumption is a critical concern in edge computing. Future research could explore techniques to optimize the energy efficiency of DeepSlicing, considering factors such as model compression, resource-aware scheduling, and dynamic power management strategies.

5.2.9 Integration with Edge AI Frameworks

DeepSlicing could be integrated with existing edge AI frameworks and platforms to leverage their features and capabilities. This integration would enable developers to seamlessly incorporate DeepSlicing into their edge AI applications and benefit from its optimizations.

5.2.10 Real-world Deployment and Evaluation

While DeepSlicing has shown promising results in simulations and controlled environments, further research should focus on real-world deployment and evaluation. Conducting experiments on diverse edge computing setups, with a wide range of CNN models and workloads, would provide valuable insights into the practical performance and scalability of DeepSlicing.

These limitations provide promising directions for future work on DeepSlicing, allowing for further optimization and extension of its capabilities in areas such as distribution efficiency, memory management, support for continuous inputs, adaptation to different types of neural networks and so on.

REFERENCES

Crowley, E. J., Turner, J., Storkey, A., & O'Boyle, M. (2018). *A closer look at structured pruning for neural network compression.* arXiv preprint arXiv:1810.04622.

Dey, S., Mondal, J., & Mukherjee, A. (2019, March). Offloaded execution of deep learning inference at edge: Challenges and insights. In *2019 IEEE International Conference on Pervasive Computing and Communications Workshops (PerCom Workshops)* (pp. 855-861). IEEE.

Hadidi, R., Cao, J., Ryoo, M. S., & Kim, H. (2019). Collaborative execution of deep neural networks on internet of things devices. arXiv preprint arXiv:1901.02537.

Han, M., Zhang, T., Lin, Y., & Deng, Q. (2021). Federated scheduling for typed DAG tasks scheduling analysis on heterogeneous multi-cores. *Journal of Systems Architecture*, *112*, 101870. doi:10.1016/j.sysarc.2020.101870

Han, S., Pool, J., Tran, J., & Dally, W. (2015). Learning both weights and connections for efficient neural network. *Advances in Neural Information Processing Systems*, 28.

He, K., Zhang, X., Ren, S., & Sun, J. (2016). Deep residual learning for image recognition. In *Proceedings of the IEEE conference on computer vision and pattern recognition* (pp. 770-778). IEEE.

He, W., Guo, S., Guo, S., Qiu, X., & Qi, F. (2020). Joint DNN partition deployment and resource allocation for delay-sensitive deep learning inference in IoT. *IEEE Internet of Things Journal*, *7*(10), 9241–9254. doi:10.1109/JIOT.2020.2981338

Hsieh, K., Ananthanarayanan, G., Bodik, P., Venkataraman, S., Bahl, P., Philipose, M., & Mutlu, O. (2018). Focus: Querying large video datasets with low latency and low cost. In *13th {USENIX} Symposium on Operating Systems Design and Implementation ({OSDI} 18)* (pp. 269-286). IEEE.

Hu, C., Bao, W., Wang, D., & Liu, F. (2019, April). Dynamic adaptive DNN surgery for inference acceleration on the edge. In *IEEE INFOCOM 2019-IEEE Conference on Computer Communications* (pp. 1423-1431). IEEE. 10.1109/INFOCOM.2019.8737614

Hu, D., & Krishnamachari, B. (2020, April). Fast and accurate streaming CNN inference via communication compression on the edge. In *2020 IEEE/ACM Fifth International Conference on Internet-of-Things Design and Implementation (IoTDI)* (pp. 157-163). IEEE. https://software.intel.com/content/www/us/en/develop/tools/openvino-toolkit.html

Jeong, H. J., Lee, H. J., Shin, C. H., & Moon, S. M. (2018, October). IONN: Incremental offloading of neural network computations from mobile devices to edge servers. In *Proceedings of the ACM symposium on cloud computing* (pp. 401-411). ACM. 10.1145/3267809.3267828

Jiang, J., Ananthanarayanan, G., Bodik, P., Sen, S., & Stoica, I. (2018, August). Chameleon: scalable adaptation of video analytics. In *Proceedings of the 2018 Conference of the ACM Special Interest Group on Data Communication* (pp. 253-266). ACM. 10.1145/3230543.3230574

Kang, Y., Hauswald, J., Gao, C., Rovinski, A., Mudge, T., Mars, J., & Tang, L. (2017). Neurosurgeon: Collaborative intelligence between the cloud and mobile edge. *Computer Architecture News*, *45*(1), 615–629. doi:10.1145/3093337.3037698

Ko, J. H., Na, T., Amir, M. F., & Mukhopadhyay, S. (2018, November). Edge-host partitioning of deep neural networks with feature space encoding for resource-constrained internet-of-things platforms. In *2018 15th IEEE International Conference on Advanced Video and Signal Based Surveillance (AVSS)* (pp. 1-6). IEEE. 10.1109/AVSS.2018.8639121

Li, L., Ota, K., & Dong, M. (2018). Deep learning for smart industry: Efficient manufacture inspection system with fog computing. *IEEE Transactions on Industrial Informatics*, *14*(10), 4665–4673. doi:10.1109/TII.2018.2842821

Liu, W., Anguelov, D., Erhan, D., Szegedy, C., Reed, S., Fu, C. Y., & Berg, A. C. (2016). Ssd: Single shot multibox detector. In Computer Vision–ECCV 2016: 14th European Conference, Amsterdam, The Netherlands, October 11–14, 2016 [Springer International Publishing.]. *Proceedings*, *14*(Part I), 21–37.

Mao, J., Chen, X., Nixon, K. W., Krieger, C., & Chen, Y. (2017, March). Modnn: Local distributed mobile computing system for deep neural network. In Design, Automation & Test in Europe Conference & Exhibition (DATE), 2017 (pp. 1396-1401). IEEE.

Redmon, J., & Farhadi, A. (2017). YOLO9000: better, faster, stronger. In *Proceedings of the IEEE conference on computer vision and pattern recognition* (pp. 7263-7271). IEEE.

Ren, S., He, K., Girshick, R., & Sun, J. (2015). Faster r-cnn: Towards real-time object detection with region proposal networks. *Advances in Neural Information Processing Systems*, 28.

Satyanarayanan, M. (2017). The emergence of edge computing. *Computer*, *50*(1), 30–39. doi:10.1109/MC.2017.9

Scardapane, S., Scarpiniti, M., Baccarelli, E., & Uncini, A. (2020). Why should we add early exits to neural networks? *Cognitive Computation*, *12*(5), 954–966. doi:10.1007/s12559-020-09734-4

Simonyan, K., & Zisserman, A. (2014). *Very deep convolutional networks for large-scale image recognition*. arXiv preprint arXiv:1409.1556.

Stahl, R., Zhao, Z., Mueller-Gritschneder, D., Gerstlauer, A., & Schlichtmann, U. (2019). Fully distributed deep learning inference on resource-constrained edge devices. In Embedded Computer Systems: Architectures, Modeling, and Simulation: 19th International Conference. Springer.

Szegedy, C., Liu, W., Jia, Y., Sermanet, P., Reed, S., Anguelov, D., & Rabinovich, A. (2015). Going deeper with convolutions. In *Proceedings of the IEEE conference on computer vision and pattern recognition* (pp. 1-9). IEEE.

Teerapittayanon, S., McDanel, B., & Kung, H. T. (2016, December). Branchynet: Fast inference via early exiting from deep neural networks. In *2016 23rd International Conference on Pattern Recognition (ICPR)* (pp. 2464-2469). IEEE.

Williams, S., Waterman, A., & Patterson, D. (2009). Roofline: An insightful visual performance model for multicore architectures. *Communications of the ACM*, *52*(4), 65–76. doi:10.1145/1498765.1498785

Xu, M., Qian, F., Zhu, M., Huang, F., Pushp, S., & Liu, X. (2019). Deepwear: Adaptive local offloading for on-wearable deep learning. *IEEE Transactions on Mobile Computing*, *19*(2), 314–330. doi:10.1109/TMC.2019.2893250

Yang, K., Yang, M., & Anderson, J. H. (2016, October). Reducing response-time bounds for dag-based task systems on heterogeneous multicore platforms. In *Proceedings of the 24th international conference on real-time networks and systems* (pp. 349-358). ACM. 10.1145/2997465.2997486

Yao, S., Zhao, Y., Shao, H., Liu, S., Liu, D., Su, L., & Abdelzaher, T. (2018, November). Fastdeepiot: Towards understanding and optimizing neural network execution time on mobile and embedded devices. In *Proceedings of the 16th ACM Conference on Embedded Networked Sensor Systems* (pp. 278-291). ACM. 10.1145/3274783.3274840

Zhang, H., Ananthanarayanan, G., Bodik, P., Philipose, M., Bahl, P., & Freedman, M. J. (2017). Live video analytics at scale with approximation and delay-tolerance. In *14th USENIX Symposium on Networked Systems Design and Implementation*. ACM.

Zhang, X., Zhou, X., Lin, M., & Sun, J. (2018). Shufflenet: An extremely efficient convolutional neural network for mobile devices. In *Proceedings of the IEEE conference on computer vision and pattern recognition* (pp. 6848-6856). IEEE. 10.1109/CVPR.2018.00716

Zhao, Z., Barijough, K. M., & Gerstlauer, A. (2018). Deepthings: Distributed adaptive deep learning inference on resource-constrained iot edge clusters. *IEEE Transactions on Computer-Aided Design of Integrated Circuits and Systems*, *37*(11), 2348–2359. doi:10.1109/TCAD.2018.2858384

Zhou, L., Samavatian, M. H., Bacha, A., Majumdar, S., & Teodorescu, R. (2019, November). Adaptive parallel execution of deep neural networks on heterogeneous edge devices. In *Proceedings of the 4th ACM/IEEE Symposium on Edge Computing* (pp. 195-208). ACM/IEEE. 10.1145/3318216.3363312

Zhou, Z., Chen, X., Li, E., Zeng, L., Luo, K., & Zhang, J. (2019). Edge intelligence: Paving the last mile of artificial intelligence with edge computing. *Proceedings of the IEEE*, *107*(8), 1738–1762. doi:10.1109/JPROC.2019.2918951

Chapter 7
Improving Live Augmented Reality With Neural Configuration Adaptation

Ning Chen
https://orcid.org/0000-0003-0722-1757
Nanjing University, China

Sheng Zhang
Nanjing University, China

Sang Lu Lu
Nanjing University, China

ABSTRACT

Instead of relying on remote clouds, today's augmented reality (AR) applications send videos to nearby edge servers for analysis to optimize user's quality of experience (QoE). Lots of studies have been conducted to help adaptively choose the best video configuration, e.g., resolution and frame per second (fps). However, prior works only consider network bandwidth and ignores the video content itself. In this chapter, the authors design Cuttlefish, a system that generates video configuration decisions using reinforcement learning (RL) based on network condition as well as the video content. Cuttlefish does not rely on any pre-programmed models or specific assumptions on the environments. Instead, it learns to make configuration decisions solely through observations of the resulting performance of historical decisions. Cuttlefish automatically learns the adaptive configuration policy for diverse AR video streams and obtains a gratifying QoE. The experimental results show that Cuttlefish achieves a 18.4%-25.8% higher QoE than the other prior designs.

DOI: 10.4018/979-8-3693-0230-9.ch007

1. INTRODUCTION

Augmented Reality (AR) is a technology that allows virtual objects to be overlaid on the real world. With the increasing demand for intelligent mobile devices, AR is becoming more popular among users with diverse requirements. According to work (Azuma et al., 2001), an AR system should have the following attributes: the ability to combine real and virtual objects in a real environment, to geometrically align virtual objects with real ones in the real world, and to run interactively and in real time. AR technology has been applied to a wide range of fields, including tourism, entertainment, marketing, surgery, logistics, manufacturing, maintenance, and others (Westerfield et al., 2015; Akçayır & Akçayır, 2017). Report (*Virtual Reality and Augmented Reality Device Sales to Hit 99 Million Devices in 2021,* 2017) forecasts that the shipment of AR/VR devices will reach 99 million in 2021, and the market will reach 108 billion dollars by then (*The reality of VR/AR growth,* 2017). Existing mobile AR systems, such as ARKit, Microsoft HoloLens (*Microsoft HoloLens*, 2020), and the announced Magic Leap One (*Magic Leap One,* 2020), facilitate the interaction between humans and the virtual world.

With the emergence of Mobile Edge Computing (MEC) (Shi et al., 2016; Satyanarayanan, 2017; Roman et al., 2018), object detection in AR applications has shifted from remote clouds to edge servers, benefiting from the reduced latency and increased reliability. In this approach, the AR device encodes and uploads the video to the edge server for detection and rendering, before downloading the processed video. State-of-the-art object detection algorithms, such as YOLO (Redmon et al., 2016; Redmon & Farhadi, 2017; Farhadi & Redmon, 2018), are utilized by the AR system on the edge, which adopts a single-stage detector strategy for regression-based detection of the boundary coordinates and corresponding class probability.

Current AR systems are not equipped to handle the performance gap caused by several factors. Firstly, the fluctuating network throughout over time causes inconsistencies in performance. Secondly, Quality of Experience (QoE) requirements, such as accuracy and latency of detecting, and fluency of video play, often conflict with each other. Finally, the time-shifted moving velocities of target objects pose a challenge. To illustrate the impact of AR video configuration on user QoE, we take fps and resolution selection as an example. We divide the total time of interest into multiple slots of equal length and define fps as the number of frames per slot. Higher resolution images, divided into multiple grid cells in YOLOv3, improve detecting accuracy but cause longer transmission delays. Similarly, videos encoded with a high fps lead to better fluency but cause larger uploading and detecting delays. Encoding videos with an exorbitant configuration may lead to a deteriorating QoE and degraded network status, but assigning a poor configuration abates the network utilization as well as QoE. Moving trends of objects in terms of moving velocity and direction are also unknown, which presents additional challenges. High-speed objects require a high fps to guarantee fluency, but a much lower fps suffices if the objects are almost static. Thus, the video configuration must match the time-varying network bandwidth and the moving velocities of objects in the videos. These challenges will be described in greater detail in next section.

We propose a novel approach for adaptive configuration of AR video that does not rely on detailed analytical performance modeling but instead embraces inference. Our approach is inspired by recent successes in deep reinforcement learning (DRL) (Mnih et al., 2015, 2016; Henderson et al., 2018) in diverse fields such as the Alpha-go game (Silver et al., 2017), video streaming (Mao et al., 2017), and job scheduling (Mao, Schwarzkopf, et al., 2019). To this end, we introduce Cuttlefish, an intelligent encoder that employs a learning-based approach to select the optimal video configuration without relying on any pre-programmed models or specific assumptions.

Cuttlefish is a learning-based intelligent encoder for adaptive video configuration selection. It initially has no knowledge and learns to make better configuration decisions through reinforcement, with reward signals reflecting past decisions' impact on user QoE. The policy of Cuttlefish is depicted as a neural network that maps "raw" observations, including estimated bandwidth, captured velocity, and historical configurations, to the configuration decision for the next slot. Cuttlefish aims to maximize the accumulative discounted reward rather than a temporary maximum reward, as a current well-performing configuration may not benefit future configurations. The neural network incorporates a diverse range of observations into the configuration policy in a scalable and expressive way. Cuttlefish trains its policy network using the state-of-the-art asynchronous advantage actor-critic network model (A3C) (Mnih et al., 2016). After training over numerous episodes, we can use Cuttlefish to make efficient video configuration decisions.

Our major contributions are summarized as follows:

- In edge-based video analysis applications, several subtle factors affect adaptive configuration selection. We have identified these factors, which include time-varying bandwidth that constrains the encoded fps and resolution, time-shifted moving velocity that limits the encoded fps, current information that may be instructive for future configuration selection, and diverse personalized QoEs that usually lead to a latency-accuracy-fluency tradeoff. The combination of these factors is crucial in making configuration decisions, which has not been revealed in the existing literature.
- Cuttlefish is an intelligent system that learns to make adaptive configuration decisions based on past traces. To achieve this, we train Cuttlefish using the A3C algorithm, which takes the current observed state (including estimated bandwidth, captured speed of target objects, and other factors) as input. Cuttlefish's policy network outputs a probability distribution of all possible configurations, from which the video encoder selects an optimal configuration that maximizes the accumulative discounted reward. With this approach, Cuttlefish is able to make efficient video configuration decisions without relying on pre-programmed models or assumptions.
- We evaluated Cuttlefish by implementing a prototype and conducting experiments on diverse types of AR videos. To simulate real-world conditions, we simulated bandwidth over a large corpus of network traces and deployed YOLOv3 on servers configured with RTX2080 Ti GPUs. We compared Cuttlefish to several state-of-the-art algorithms and found that it outperformed or matched them. Cuttlefish improved the average QoE by 18.4%-25.8%. Our results demonstrate the effectiveness of Cuttlefish in making adaptive configuration decisions in edge-based video analysis applications.

2. OBSERVATIONS AND CHALLENGES

In this section, we expound some vital observations that motivate us to propose Cuttlefish.

2.1 Latency-Accuracy-Fluency Tradeoff

The majority of the total latency in AR devices occurs during the detecting and uploading processes of real-time video streams to the edge cloud for rendering. Detecting accuracy and video play fluency are typically positively correlated with the encoded resolution and fps. Users demand accurate and fluent AR videos in real time, but meeting high detecting accuracy, high perceived fluency, and low completion delay simultaneously is challenging. A video stream encoded with higher resolution can achieve satisfactory accuracy, but it may result in unbearable uploading delays in degraded networks if the resolution exceeds available bandwidth. Similarly, a video with higher fps may provide desired fluency without stutters, but uploading more frames for detecting and processing may cause additional latency. Therefore, a well-balanced QoE is urgently needed to mitigate this tradeoff.

Figure 1. Available network bandwidth

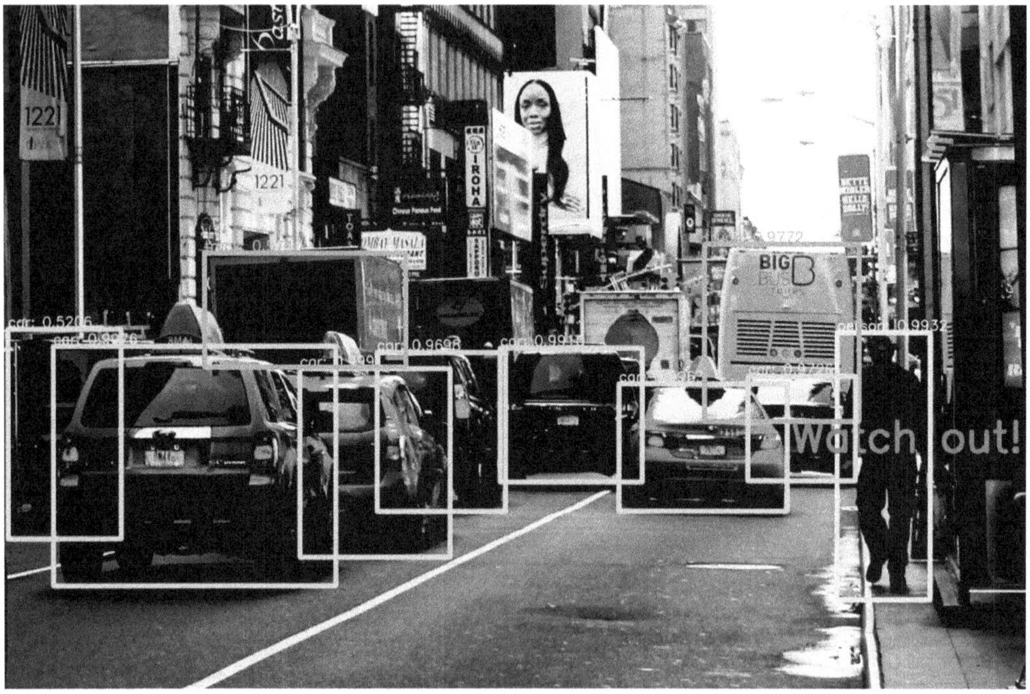

2.2 Variability in Network Bandwidth

Adaptive configuration selection is crucial for AR applications that rely on mobile devices and cellular networks such as LTE, which often experience unpredictable bandwidth fluctuations (Winstein et al., 2013). To address this challenge, adaptive selection of encoded resolution and fps is necessary. To illustrate the variability of bandwidth, we present two ATT-LTE network traces obtained from the Mahimahi (Netravali et al., 2015) project in **Figure 1**.

Across the upload and download traces, we made the following observations:

- Periods of extreme low/high throughout are uncommon: only 14.5% of the time, the upload bandwidth is 0 or larger than 10 Mbps, and 14.9% for the download bandwidth;
- The bandwidth of the next slot is closely related to the average values of the past several slots: as **Figure 2** shows, for uploading capacity, 76.3% slots own less than 20% bandwidth variation compared to the previous one slot, and it reaches 89.2% when referring to the past five slots;
- The download capacity shares the similar pattern with the upload capacity.

Observations suggest that bandwidth fluctuates within a specific range (e.g., [0, 28] in **Figure 1**) over a longer time scale, but varies less (e.g., [0, 5]) over shorter intervals (e.g., from 400 to 410). These insights provide a feasible way to estimate bandwidth without relying on future network information, and guide the adaptive selection of encoded resolution.

Figure 2. Bandwidth estimation

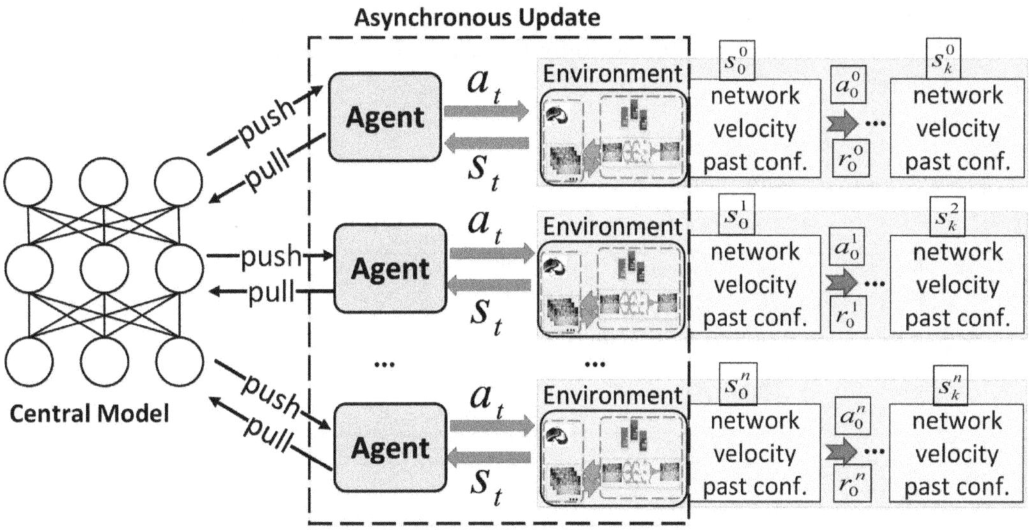

Figure 3. Safe driving

2.3 Time-shifted Moving Velocity

When dealing with AR scenarios, target objects may not always remain stationary or move at a constant speed. For instance, **Figure 3** shows the detection of moving vehicles in a dynamic traffic video for pedestrian alert. To ensure smooth playback, a high encoded fps is required to compensate for the rapid changes in location of the objects. However, this results in a significant increase in both the uploading and detecting latencies. In contrast, **Figure 4** depicts a virtual Minion standing next to a boy in a relatively static video. In this case, a lower fps is sufficient to ensure smooth playback. Therefore, when configuring the video for a better QoE, not only the available bandwidth but also the video content should be considered.

Figure 4. Virtual minions stands next to the boy

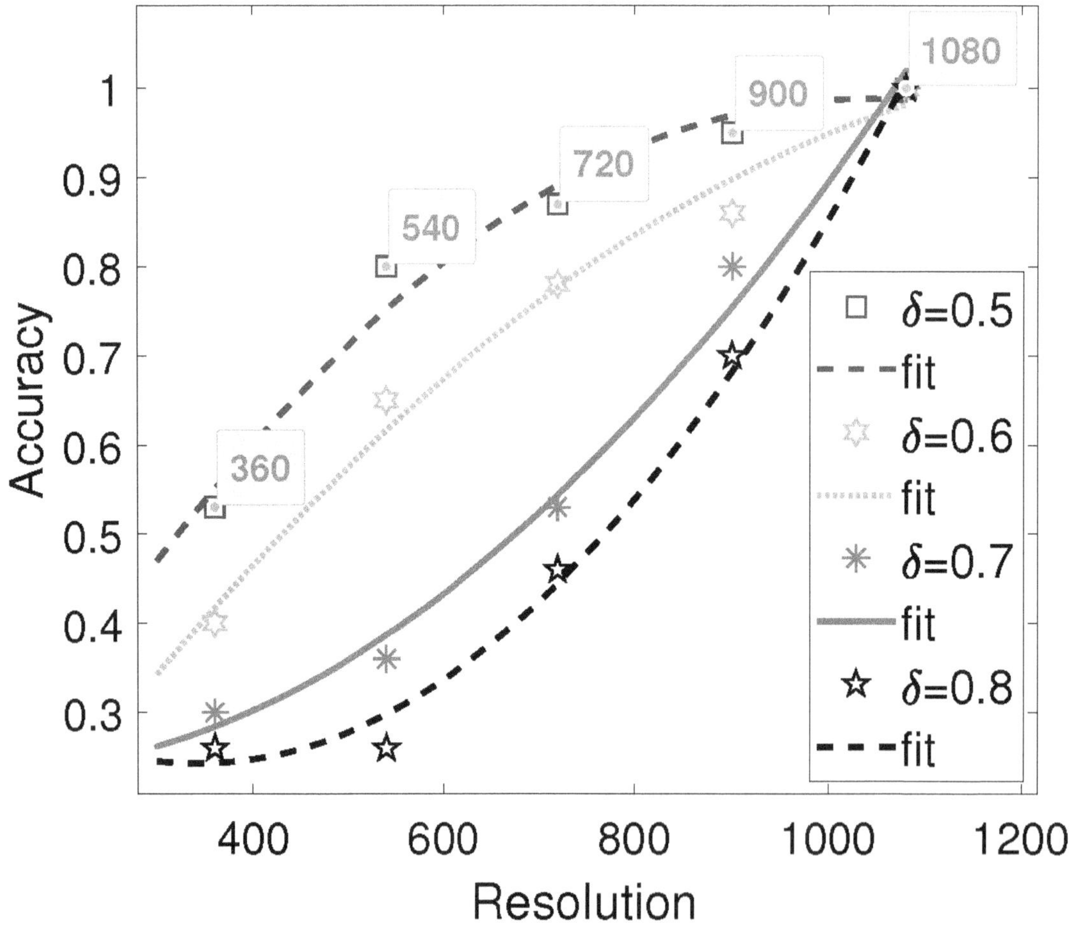

2.4 Challenges

Adaptive configuration of the AR video encoder can be perceived as a sequential decision-making process. At each time slot, the encoder needs to select the best configuration, and this can be achieved by using Deep Reinforcement Learning (DRL), which is commonly used for decision-making in unknown environments. In this process, an agent observes the current state, selects an action based on the current policy, and updates the policy based on feedback received from the environment (i.e., reward). The policy is typically represented as a neural network that is trained through trial-and-error interactions with the environment to maximize cumulative rewards over time. While this approach appears to be a practical solution based on the three observations mentioned earlier, it is challenging to use DRL for our problem due to several knotty challenges:

- While DRL has been widely used for sequential decision-making in unknown environments, it is nontrivial to use it in our video encoding problem due to the challenges we face. The state, action, and reward in DRL are sophisticated, and accurately obtaining the essence of the state, such as bandwidth and velocity, is difficult. We need to model the estimated real-time bandwidth and capture the moving velocity to use them in our decision-making process. Furthermore, we need to integrate the latency-accuracy-fluency tradeoff into the reward, as it not only represents the user's real experience for the selected configuration but also significantly affects the final performance of Cuttlefish. However, designing a well-crafted reward function is not an easy task.
- Obtaining training samples for DRL in real AR scenarios is impractical, as it would require trial-and-error interactions with the environment. Moreover, it is challenging to accurately model the video stream in a live AR video player. This makes it difficult to faithfully capture the state, action, and reward required for DRL. In particular, accurately estimating real-time bandwidth and capturing object velocity are unsolved problems, and integrating them into the reward function requires careful design.

In the following section, we strive to solve the above challenges and present the design details of Cuttlefish.

3. SYSTEM ARCHITECTURE OF CUTTLEFISH

We present Cuttlefish, a real-time Augmented Reality (AR) application that aims to provide personalized Quality of Experience (QoE). Cuttlefish allows for adaptive configuration selection, balancing the tradeoff between latency, accuracy, and fluency. The video stream is encoded and uploaded to the edge cloud for object detection and rendering, before being sent back to provide a fascinating AR experience for mobile users. The system leverages a highly representative Deep Reinforcement Learning (DRL) model to select valuable configurations, instead of relying on a random strategy. Cuttlefish consists of two fundamental components: offline training and online object detection, as illustrated in **Figure 5** and **Figure 6**, respectively. By doing so, we address the challenges of modeling the estimated real-time bandwidth, capturing the moving velocity, and designing a well-crafted reward function, which are critical for achieving personalized QoE. Obtaining training data by trial and error in real AR scenarios is not practical, and modeling video streams with a live AR video player is challenging. Cuttlefish offers a practical solution to realize adaptive configuration, improving QoE for AR applications.

3.1 Offline Training

Cuttlefish utilizes a highly representative DRL model to adaptively select configurations and achieve a better tradeoff among latency, accuracy, and fluency. However, pure online learning of the policy network from scratch results in poor policies in the beginning, also known as cold start. This is because DRL typically requires many trials and errors to converge to an ideal policy. Therefore, offline training is indispensable to generate a well-designed model to meet the real-time detecting requirements. To address the cold start issue, we collect some expert data to train the policy network through supervised learning. This enables the network to reach better initial parameters than random schemes.

As shown in **Figure 5**, the DRL agent takes various inputs, including the current state observed from the environment (e.g., bandwidth, previous frames, moving velocity, and previous configurations) and generates configuration decisions. The agent is capable of obtaining instant rewards and effectively expanding the available trace set for DRL training. We utilize several advanced techniques, such as the Actor-Critic network and exploration enhancement, along with the SGD method to train the network weights. Note that the DRL model periodically updates its parameters to adapt to the changing environment.

Figure 5. Offline training. DRL agent pretrains its policy network with past traces collected from interactions with the environment

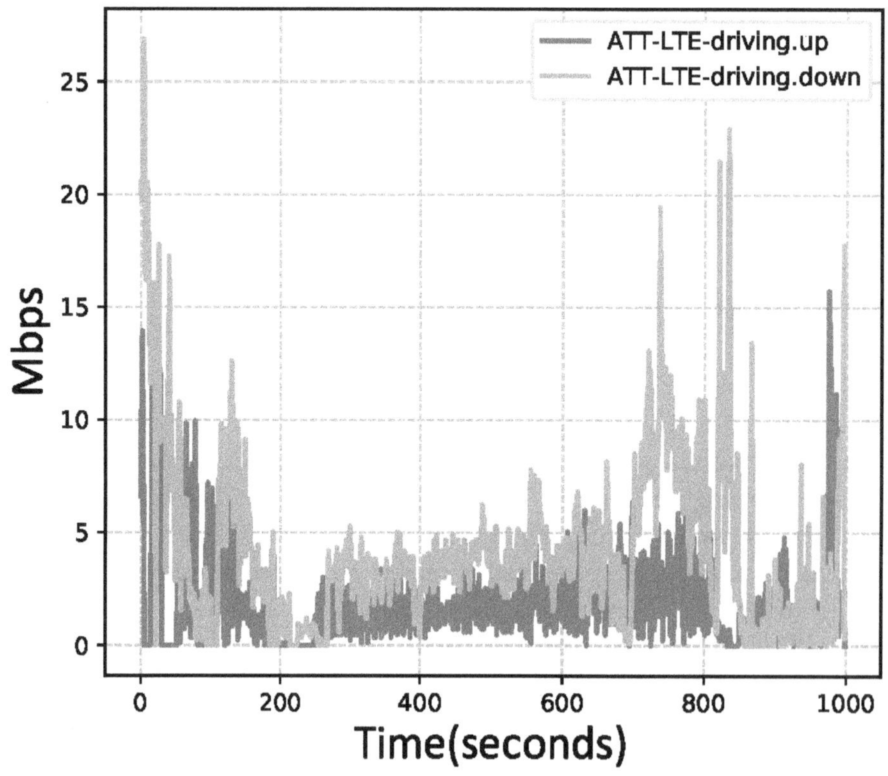

3.2 Online Object Detecting

Cuttlefish employs the well-trained DRL model to make configuration decisions for live AR video streams, as shown in **Figure 6**. Before encoding the video of the next time slot, the AR device collects the current state, such as the estimated bandwidth and captured velocity, and extracts past configurations. The Actor-Critic network takes this state as input and outputs the probability distribution of all optional configurations. The AR device selects a configuration based on the output, encodes the video, and uploads it to the edge cloud for detecting and rendering. During real-time interaction, Cuttlefish integrates the state, action, instant reward, and next observed state into a quadruple that represents a newly collected sample. Cuttlefish's policy is periodically retrained using advanced techniques like the Actor-Critic network and exploration enhancement to continuously improve the selected configuration over time. To overcome cold start, we collect expert data to train the policy network through supervised learning. The network weights are optimized using the SGD method. Note that the DRL model periodically updates its parameters to adapt to the changing environment. The detailed design is presented in the following section.

Figure 6. Online object detecting. Cuttlefish makes adaptive configuration decisions for the real time AR video based on its observed states

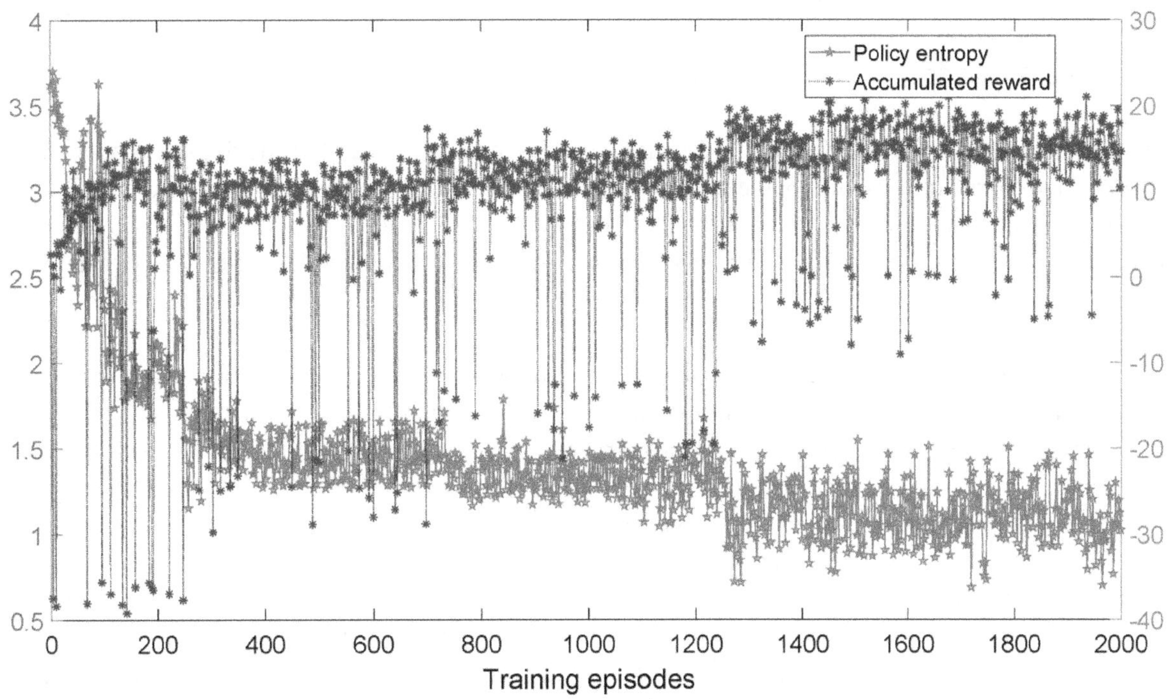

4. DESIGN DETAILS OF CUTTLEFISH

In this section, we first illustrate the basic learning mechanism, and present the formal definition of our DRL framework. Then, we elaborate on the detailed training methodology.

4.1 Basic Learning Mechanism

The essence of DRL is to learn an effective policy for the current state based on historical experiences. In **Figure 7**, the RL-agent interacts with the environment, which integrates surrounding information, and the agent serves as the decision-maker. The agent can only observe a portion of the environment, which creates the current state. At each time interval *t*, the agent observes state s_t and selects action a_t based on policy π. After executing the action, the agent receives an immediate reward *rt* and moves to the next state $st_{+1.}$ By continually interacting with the environment until completion, the agent is expected to accumulate a high reward.

4.2 DRL Framework

We propose the model-free DRL-based Cuttlefish to adaptively generate configurations without any knowledge from the future environment and the state transition probability. The detailed designs and principles are shown in **Figure 7**.

4.2.1 State Space

In order to make effective configuration decisions, a RL-agent (such as a MAR device or encoder) must observe and learn from its environment. Through continuous learning from historical experience, the RL-agent aims to obtain a comprehensive state that approaches a global and future-oriented perspective. Therefore, it is crucial to have an exhaustive state that considers all key elements. We consider four such elements:

- Historical configuration decisions (fps_t, res_t). To improve decision-making efficiency, we divide the total time $\mathcal{T}$ into equal-length time slots and assume that the resolution and fps of AR video streams remain constant within a slot, denoted by res_t and fps_t respectively. Since AR video streams do not undergo significant changes from one slot to the next, past decisions can help in selecting the configuration for the next slot. The number of past configurations referenced by Cuttlefish, denoted by *k* in **Figure 7**, depends on the video contents. For instance, highly dynamic racing games may require only one past configuration, while slightly changeable AR video streams may benefit from more past configurations. However, choosing an optimal *k* is not trivial in practice since even a static camera can generate videos with different levels of dynamism, such as highly dynamic rush hours or slightly changeable midnight scenes. We leave this as future work and believe that incorporating it into Cuttlefish can further enhance its performance.
- Estimated bandwidth $B_{est}^{(t+1)}$. The encoder struggles to pick the resolution and fps that perfectly match the available bandwidth, yet lacks the access to gain the future bandwidth. As previously stated, the bandwidth varies around an specific value during slot *t*, and the more valuable refer-

Figure 7. The neural network architecture of Cuttlefish

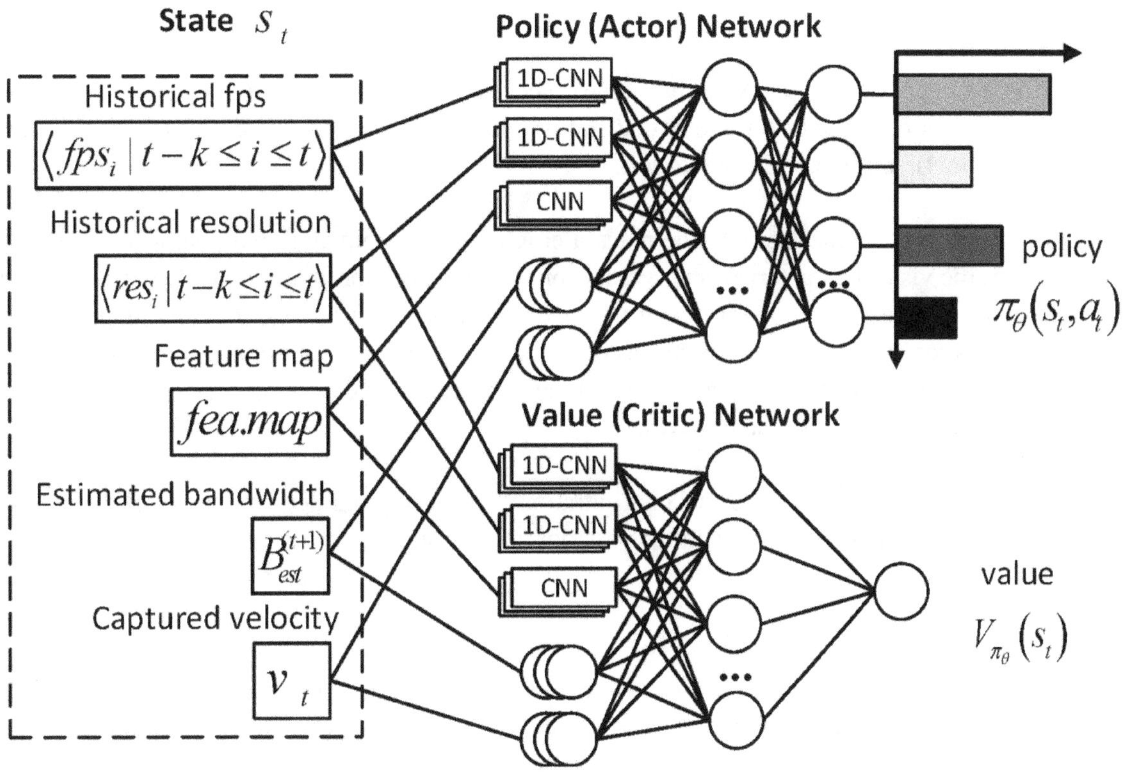

ences of past bandwidths it adopts, the more accurate estimation it can get. Thus, we calculate the estimated bandwidth $B_{est}^{(t+1)}$ of slot t+1 as the weighted average bandwidth of past k slots, i.e., $B_{est}^{(t+1)} = \sum_{i=t-k+1}^{t} \omega_i B_i$, where $\omega_i < \omega_j$ if $i<j$, and $\sum_i \omega_i = 1$.

- Average velocity v_t. As we know, AR video stream with target objects of high moving velocities is supposed to be encoded with a higher fps. Similarly, videos with nearly still objects correspond to a lower fps. Assume that the target objects set is $\mathcal{Z} = \{z_1, z_2, \cdots, z_n$, and the last configuration is (fps_t,res_t). The encoded video stream is uploaded to the edge cloud for object detecting with the YOLOv3 algorithm, which directly predicts the position of target objects, namely *Bounding Box Prediction*. For $f<fps_t$ and $i \in \mathcal{Z}$, suppose that the Bounding Box Prediction set is $\left(x_i^f, y_i^f, w_i^f, h_i^f, c_i^f\right)$, which consists of center coordinates of X and Y $\left(x_i^f, y_i^f\right)$, height and width $\left(w_i^f, h_i^f\right)$, and prediction class c_i^f. Considering the moving trends of target objects are not fixed or regular, we adopt *Manhattan distance* (Craw, 2017) rather than Euclidean distance to measure the distance that it moves in unit time slot. Thus we define the velocity v_t as the average accumulated distance of all objects moved from the current frame to the next frame during slot t, i.e.,

$$v_t = \frac{1}{|\mathcal{Z}|}\sum_{i\in\mathcal{Z}}\sum_{2\le j\le fps_t}\left[\left|x_i^j - x_i^{j-1}\right| + \left|y_i^j - y_i^{j-1}\right|\right],$$

where $\mathcal{Z}$ is the target objects set. Note that some object may disappear at the end of a slot; in this case, we assume its location in the last frame of that slot is in the farthest corner among all four corners from its location in the first frame of the same slot.

- The feature map of the latest frame plays a crucial role in convolutional neural networks, as it captures the visual characteristics necessary for effective decision-making in AR video configuration. To simulate the characteristics of the visual pathway, a variety of filters are used to extract different types of features, such as shape edges and color shades. In our implementation and evaluation, we have carefully designed and tuned the convolution and pooling filters to mine potential knowledge from multiple perspectives.

To sum up, we combine the historical configuration decisions, estimated bandwidth of the next slot, and the average velocity of all objects in the past slot into the state space.

4.2.2 Action Space

For a newly received state s, the DRL-agent selects an action a based on the policy $\pi_\theta(s,a)$, which is defined as the probability distribution over the action space, and then get an instant reward. The policy $\pi_\theta(s,a)$ is the output of *policy network*, whose parameter is set to θ. To improve user's QoE, we aim to make an efficient decision on video configuration. Naturally, we consider two key factors that affect the detecting performance, i.e., the number of frames per slot fps_t and resolution res_t during slot t. We couple these two elements to form the action space, i.e., $a_t=(fps_t,res_t)$.

4.2.3 Reward

The DRL agent is likely to receive an instant reward r_t when applying a_t to state s_t. In practical AR applications, mobile users' pursuit high detecting accuracy as well as lower latency and fine fluency, thus we should consider these three metrics in the reward. Suppose that $a_t=(fps_t,res_t)$ during slot t.

- Latency. As mentioned before, the latency includes uploading delay d_1^t, detecting delay d_2^t, rendering delay d_3^t and downloading delay d_4^t, where d_1^t and d_4^t depend solely upon the available bandwidth, and d_2^t, d_3^t are up to the computing power of edge servers. We make a normalization and denote the total latency d_t of handling the frames at slot t by $d_t = \sum_{f=1}^{fps_t}\frac{d_1^t + d_2^t + d_3^t + d_4^t}{d_t^{\circ} fps_t}$, where, d_t° is the latency of a single frame with the most expensive resolution (e.g., 1080P in our experiment) at slot t and $d_t\in[0,1]$. In practice, we calculate d_t° as the average latency of each frame using the most expensive resolution.
- Detecting accuracy. To evaluate the accuracy of our approach, we use the F1 score, which is a harmonic mean of precision and recall. True positives are identified using a label-based method

that checks if the bounding box has the same label and sufficient spatial overlap with the ground truth box (Everingham et al., 2010). For each specific configuration, we calculate the accuracy of a single frame by comparing the detected objects with those detected by the most expensive configuration. To compute the F1 score for a frame i that was encoded with configuration (fps_t,res_t) during time slot t, we use the formula $F1_i = S_i / S_i^g$, where S_i is the area of the bounding box in the i-th frame with resolution res_t, and S_i^g is the area of the ground truth box in the i-th frame with the most expensive resolution. We provide the detailed design of tuned filters for convolution and pooling in our implementation and evaluation, as diverse filters are adopted to mine potential knowledge from different perspectives. We define the detecting accuracy c_t at slot t as the fraction of frames whose F1 score ≥δ, e.g.,

$$c_t = \frac{\left|\left\{f_i \mid F1_i \geq \delta, 1 \leq i \leq fps_t\right\}\right|}{fps_t}.$$

Figure 8. Impact of resolution on accuracy

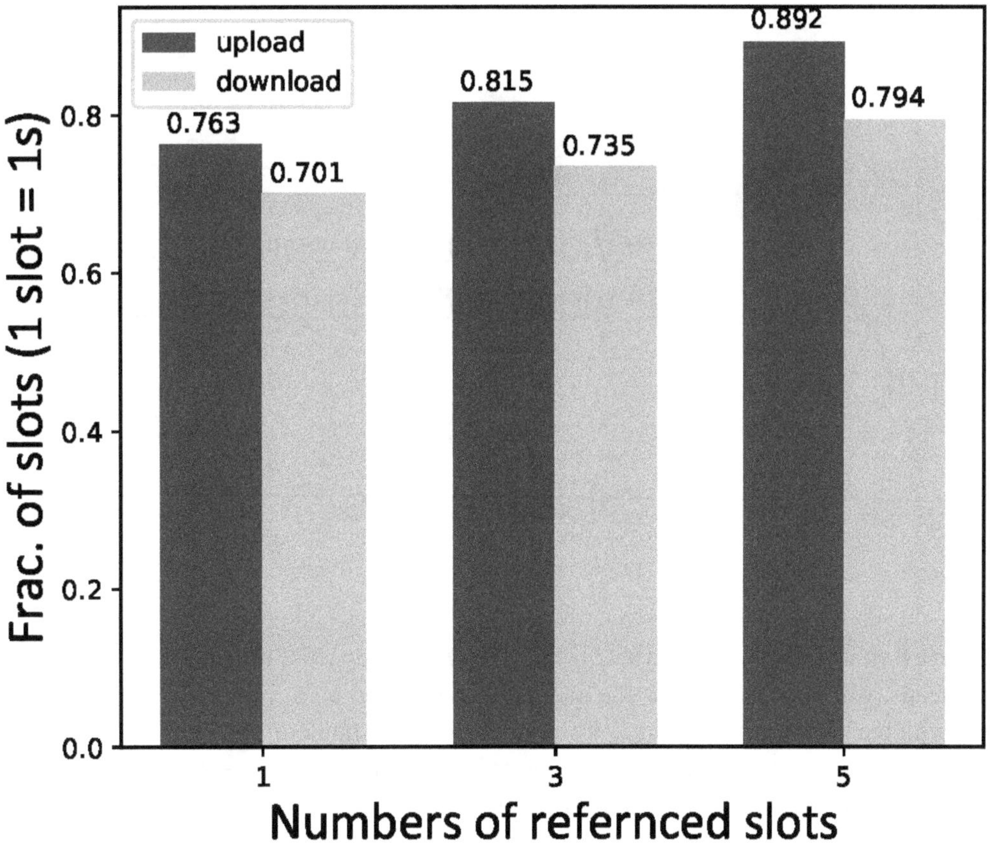

Figure 9. Impact of fps on fluency

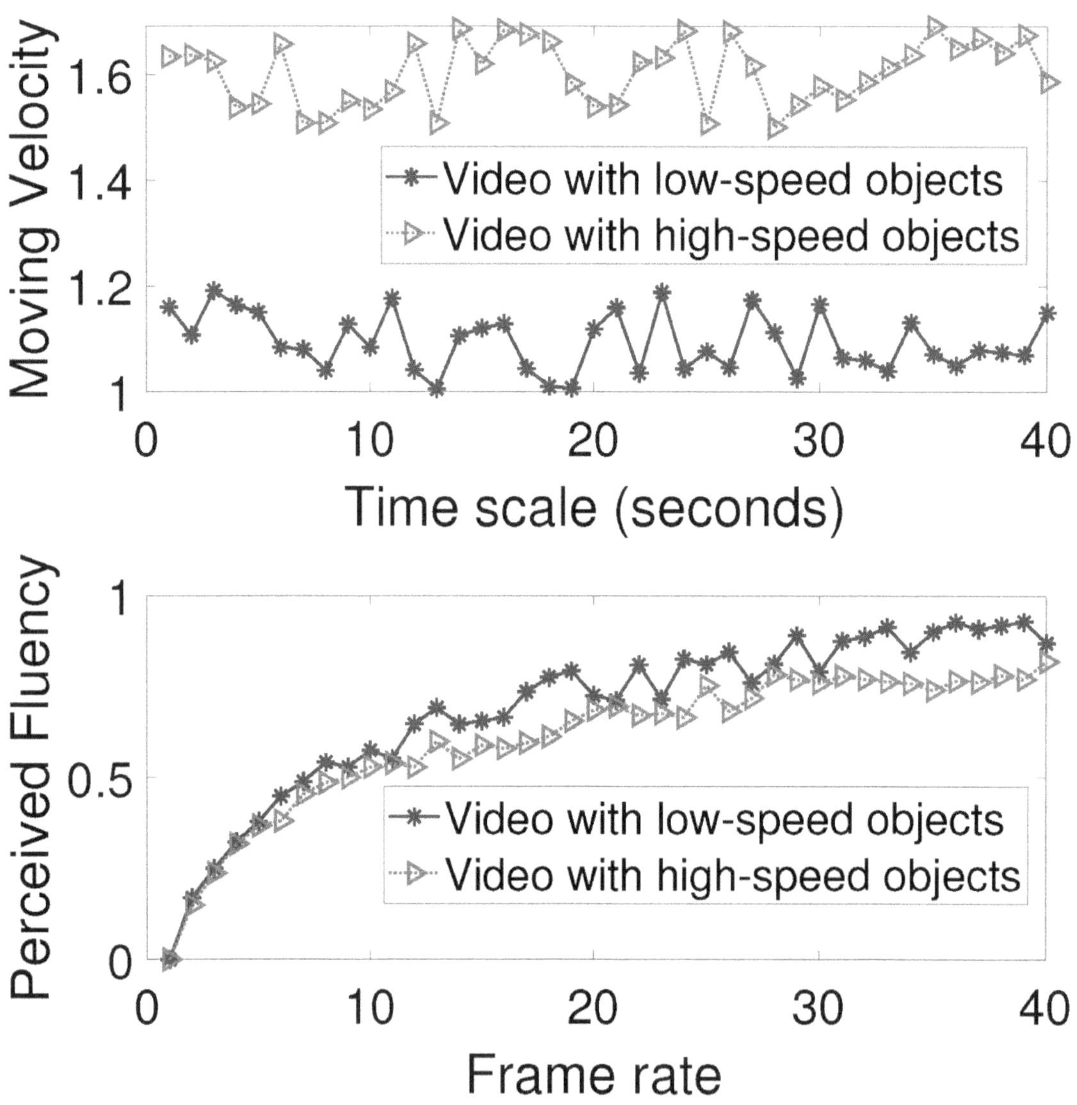

As **Figure 8** shows, we fix fps, and set diverse δ to see the impact of resolution on accuracy. Through numerous trials, we demonstrate that the accuracy and resolution are positively correlated, which is consistent with our observation. Besides, we find that a much smaller or bigger δ is not likely to obtain a more significant accuracy variation under diverse resolutions. Hence, we select an empirical δ (e.g., 0.7 in **Figure 8**) to reflect this trend in our evaluation.

- Fluency. User's perceived fluency is defined as the smooth level of video play. Without loss of generality, configured with a higher fps, the video could gain a better fluency, yet the improvement of fluency will not be significant when the frame rate reaches a certain threshold. As described before, we observed that the demanded fps towards AR videos with diverse velocities to meet the same fluency is different. For instance, videos similar to **Figure 3** are proposed to be encoded with a higher fps to reach the same perceived fluency for videos like **Figure 4**. Based on the above observations, we give the formal definition of user's perceived fluency u_t, i.e., $u_t = \frac{v_{max}}{v_t} \log_m \left(fps_t\right)$, where m is the optional maximum fps and v_{max} is the maximum velocity (i.e., the diagonal distance of the frame), $v_t \in [0, v_{max}]$, and $0 < fps_t \leq m$. As illustrated in **Figure 9**, to verify the correctness of u_t and further explain the impact of fps and moving velocity on user's perceived fluency, we collect two main types of videos from YouTube, including videos with low-speed objects (e.g., pedestrians), and videos with high-speed objects (e.g., cars). Then, we calculate the average moving velocities and the corresponding fluency of these two types of objects in every second based on u_t. Every second on the top half corresponds to a fps on the bottom half. The empirical results also agree with the point we made earlier.

As users may have different preferences on which of the three components is more important, we define the reward r_t of video configuration at slot t by a weighted sum of the aforementioned components, e.g.,

$$r_t = -\pm_1\left(d_t - \bar{d}\right) + \pm_2\left(c_t - \bar{c}\right) + \pm_3\left(u_t - \bar{u}\right),$$

where α_1, α_2 and α_3 are the weight factors to balance the preference to delay, accuracy and fluency, and $\sum_i \pm_i = 1$. This definition of reward is quite general as it allows us to model varying user preferences on different contributing factors. In practice, to mitigate the diverse fluctuations of these metrics, we set $\bar{d}, \bar{c}$, and $\bar{u}$ to the average values of delay, detecting accuracy and perceived fluency respectively, all of which are measured by substantial empirical video traces.

4.3 DRL Model Training Methodology

While the configuration space is bounded, the state space is sophisticated and seems infinite, resulting in endless (s_t, a_t) pairs. Instead of tabulating the value of each (s_t, a_t) pair, we use the state-of-the-art A3C algorithm. A neural network is used to represent a policy π, where the policy parameter θ is adjustable. Therefore, we represent the policy as $\pi(a_t|s_t;\theta) \rightarrow [0,1]$, indicating the probability of taking action a_t at state s_t. The goal of DRL is to find the best policy π that maps a state to an action, maximizing the expected accumulative discounted reward $J(,) = E\left[\sum_{t=t_0}^{t_0+|T|} 3^t r_t\right]$. Here, t_0 is the current time and $\gamma \in !(0,1]$ is a factor used to discount future rewards.

4.3.1 Policy Gradient Training

Cuttlefish uses an actor-critic network that is trained with the *policy gradient method*. This method estimates the gradient of the expected total reward by observing the trajectories of executions obtained by following the policy. The algorithm consists of several key steps, and we will highlight them for better understanding. The policy gradient of J(θ) with respect to θ, which is used for the policy network update for slot t, can be calculated as follows (Sutton et al., 2000):

$$\nabla_{.} J(,) = E_{\grave{A}} \left[\sum_{t \in T} \nabla_{,} \log\left(\grave{A}\left(s_t, a_t\right)\right) A^{\grave{A}}\left(s_t, a_t\right)\right],$$

where $A^{\grave{A}}\left(s_t, a_t\right)$ is the advantage function that indicates the gap between the expected accumulative reward when we deterministically select a_t at state s_t following π_θ and the expected reward for actions drawn from policy π_θ. Indeed, the advantage function reflects how much better a current specific action is compared to the "average action" taken based on the policy. Intuitively, we reinforce the actions with positive advantage value $A^{\grave{A}}(s,a)$, but degrade the actions with negative advantage value $A^{\grave{A}}(s,a)$.

In particular, the RL-agent extracts a trajectory of configuration decisions and views the empirically computed advantage $A(s_t,a_t)$ as an unbiased estimated $A^{\grave{A}}\left(s_t, a_t\right)$. The update rule of actor network parameter θ follows the policy gradient,

$$\theta \leftarrow \theta + \alpha \sum_{t \in T} \nabla_\theta \log \pi_\theta\left(s_t, a_t\right) A\left(s_t, a_t\right),$$

where α is the learning rate. The marrow behind this update law is summarized as follows: the gradient direction $\nabla_\theta \log\pi_\theta(s_t,a_t)$ indicates how to change parameter θ to improve $\pi_\theta(s_t,a_t)$ (i.e., the probability of action a_t at state s_t). θ goes a step along the gradient descent direction. The specific step size is up to the advantage value $A^{\grave{A}}\left(s_t, a_t\right)$. Hence, the goal of each update is to reinforce actions that empirically have better feedbacks. To compute the advantage value $A(s_t,a_t)$ for a given sample, we need to get the estimated *value function* $v^{\grave{A}}(s)$, i.e., the total expected reward starting at state s following the policy π_θ. As **Figure 7** shows, the role of *critic network* is to learn an estimated $v^{\grave{A}}(s)$ from observed rewards. We update the critic network parameters θ_v based on the *Temporal Difference* (Sutton & Barto, 2018) method,

$$\theta_v \leftarrow \theta_v - \alpha' \sum_t \nabla_{\theta_v} \left(r_t + \gamma V^{\pi_\theta}\left(s_{t+1}; \theta_v\right) - V^{\pi_\theta}\left(s_t; \theta_v\right)\right)^2,$$

where $V^{\grave{A}}\left(s_t; ,_v\right)$ is the estimated $v^{\grave{A}}\left(s_t\right)$ that produced by the critic network, and $\pm'$ is the learning rate. To have a further understanding, we take a specific experience (s_t,a_t,r_t,s_{t+1}) as an example, we estimate the advantage value $A(s_t,a_t)$ as $r_t + {}^3V^{\grave{A}}\left(s_{t+1}; ,_v\right) - V^{\grave{A}}\left(s_t; ,_v\right)$. Note that the critic network does nothing to train the actor network other than evaluate the policy of actor network. In actual AR scenarios, only the actor network is involved in making configuration decision.

To realize an adequate exploration for RL agent during training to discover better policies, thereby reducing the risk of falling into suboptimal, we add an *entropy regularization* (Mnih et al., 2016) term to encourage exploration. This practice is significant to help the agent converge to a fine policy. Correspondingly, we modify the update rule to be

$$\theta \leftarrow \theta + \alpha \sum_t \nabla_\theta \log \pi_\theta (s_t, a_t) A(s_t, a_t) + \beta \nabla_\theta H(\pi_\theta (\cdot | s_t)),$$

where β is entropy weight, which set to a large value and decrease over time to allow Cuttlefish to have more opportunity on improving rewards, and H(•)is the policy entropy to encourage exploration by pushing θ in the direction with higher entropy at each time slot.

4.3.2 Parallel Training

To improve exploration and accelerate training, we use a parallel approach to quickly obtain abundant training samples, as shown in **Figure 10**. Specifically, we start n threads, each with a different environment setting, such as diverse network traces and AR videos. This way, different agents can experience different states and transitions, avoiding correlation. Each agent continuously collects samples, represented by a tuple $\{s_t,a_t,r_t,s_{t+1}\}$, and uses the actor-critic algorithm to compute a gradient and perform a gradient descent step independently. Then, each agent pushes its actor parameters to the central agent, which integrates the parameters and generates a global actor network. Finally, each agent pulls the global model from the central agent and starts the next training episode until the global actor network converges. After the actor-critic network has been well trained, we can quickly and accurately take actions based on the action probability distribution for each encoding slot.

Figure 10. Parallel training of A3C

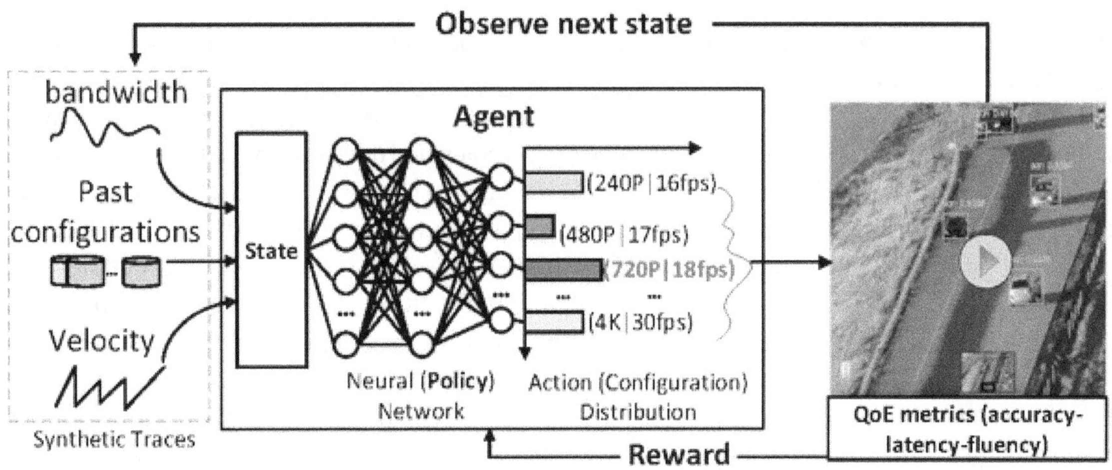

In summary, the paragraph has been reorganized to present the steps in a logical order, and unnecessary words have been removed. Additionally, some expressions have been clarified for better understanding.

5. IMPLEMENTATION AND EVALUATION

Cuttlefish is an intelligent encoder designed for adaptive configuration in video analysis for AR applications. In this paper, we present our approach to bandwidth simulation in a trace-driven manner, as well as the training settings used for the neural network architecture. We then report our experimental evaluation of Cuttlefish using numerous real live AR videos. Our results provide insights into the following questions:

- To verify the convergence of Cuttlefish during training, we tracked its policy entropy and accumulative reward across over 2000 training episodes. We observed that the policy entropy gradually decreased, while the accumulative reward increased, eventually converging to a non-zero value. This allowed us to confirm that Cuttlefish had successfully learned a policy for adaptive video analysis in AR applications.
- We evaluated Cuttlefish's performance compared to several carefully-tuned heuristics in terms of quality of experience (QoE). Our findings reveal that Cuttlefish rivals or outperforms several state-of-the-art schemes, with average QoE improvements ranging from 18.4% to 25.8%.
- Our experiments also investigated whether Cuttlefish's learning can be generalized to other types of bandwidth traces and AR videos. We found that Cuttlefish consistently maintained good performance across different network conditions and videos with more dynamic objects and faster movements, indicating its ability to generalize well.

5.1 Trace-driven Bandwidth and Video Collection

To upload live video from AR devices to the edge cloud at base stations (BS), we use local area networks (LANs). However, operating real BSs is impractical due to privacy concerns. Hence, we simulate the LAN to accurately replicate the real scenario. To establish a corpus of network traces, we integrate public datasets and network emulation tools such as the broadband dataset provided by the FCC (Federal Communications Commission, 2016) and the tool Mahimahi (Netravali et al., 2015). The FCC dataset contains over 1 million throughout traces, each logging the average throughput over 2100 seconds at a 5-second granularity. To create our corpus, we randomly select 100 traces with a duration of 200 seconds, by concatenating traces from the "Web browsing" category in the February 2016 collection. The Mahimahi tool generates traces that represent the time-varying capacity of U.S. cellular networks as experienced by a mobile user. Each trace contains a timestamp in milliseconds (from the beginning of the trace) and records the maximum number of 1500-byte packets it transits at each millisecond. We reformat the throughput trace to match the FCC dataset and generate 100 traces for our corpus, each compatible with the FCC traces. During training, unless specified, we randomly select a trace from the corpus and use it as the link bandwidth.

To create an adequate and representative training dataset for Cuttlefish's actor-critic network, we sampled and sifted videos from popular YouTube channels offline, selecting the most expensive configuration (1080P and 30fps). To ensure a diverse sample, we collected several typical videos, such as pedestrians and vehicles, over a ten-hour period, with the same length as the bandwidth traces in our corpus. After sampling, we utilized OpenCV (Bradski & Kaehler, 2008) to preprocess the videos, converting them into multiple versions with varying resolutions. To align with the decision-making process in each time slot, we divided the AR video into equal-length chunks, similar to the time slot. These crafted samples can then be used to train Cuttlefish's actor-critic network.

5.2 Training Setup

The edge server used in this study is a PowerEdge R740, which is equipped with NVIDIA GeForce RTX 2080 Ti GPUs. For object detection, we employed the YOLOv3 algorithm. Meanwhile, the Actor-Critic networks of Cuttlefish, as shown in **Figure 7**, were implemented using Pytorch libraries (Paszke et al., 2019) and trained with the A3C algorithm. The networks share the same parameters of the input layer and hidden layer and output the action distribution and Q-value. To facilitate parallel training of Cuttlefish with multiple workers, each worker gains traces of diverse videos, calculates gradients locally and independently, then pushes the gradient to the central work synchronously, and pulls the aggregated global parameters. We adopted the Adam optimizer with a fixed learning rate of 0.0001, a mini-batch size of 32 samples per worker, a reward discount factor γ=0.9, and an entropy weight β=0.01. We verified Cuttlefish's convergence, and as illustrated in **Figure 11**, a larger policy entropy was set to encourage deeper exploration in the beginning. With the increase of training episodes, the policy entropy gradually tends to a smaller value, i.e., the policy network is nearly convergent, and Cuttlefish lays emphasis on utilization toward actions. However, note that in the time-varying scenario, to be compatible with the newly generated states, the entropy is not likely to be 0. Concurrent with this increase has been a spiral rise in the accumulative reward. Although in the initial episodes, Cuttlefish performed poorly in terms of numerical size and stability due to the random policy, it gained a larger and more steady accumulative reward that fluctuates around the maximum after further exploration.

Figure 11. Policy entropy and accumulative reward over the training episodes

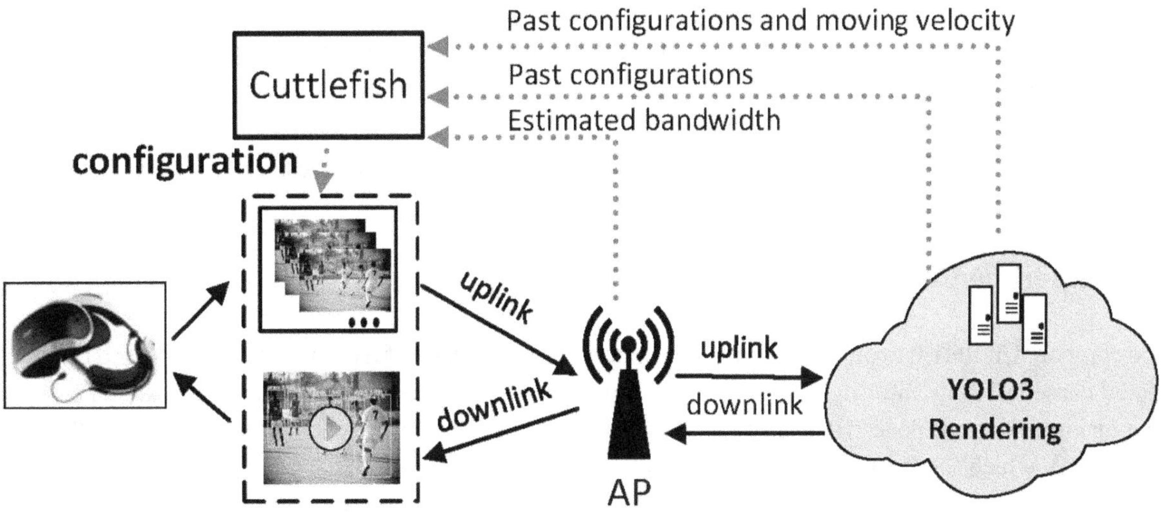

We set the available selection range for fps_t and res_t to F=(16,30) and R= {480P, 720P, 900P, 1080P}, respectively, without loss of generality. If only integers are adopted for fps_t and res_t, the total number of actions can be calculated as |F|×|R|. Using a bounded action space can greatly reduce the training time. It is worth noting that Cuttlefish can be slightly modified to accommodate other ranges of F and R.

5.3 Techniques and Baselines

To enhance Cuttlefish's performance, we implement several techniques: (1) We integrate sparse optical flow (Dosovitskiy et al., 2015) to track objects detected in the first and last frame of the same slot, considering the possibility of multiple objects of the same class. (2) We use VGG16 (Simonyan & Zisserman, 2014) to extract the feature map of the last frame in each slot directly, rather than using a retrained model. (3) We employ an offline method to obtain a large number of experiences (s_t,a_t,r_t,s_{t+1}), significantly accelerating the training speed. To further assess Cuttlefish's efficacy, we compare it to four other schemes:

- None-Adaptation. For each slot, the encoder randomly selects a configuration (i.e., resolution and fps) without consideration on the available bandwidth or velocity.
- Bandwidth Based Adaptation (Sun et al., 2016). For each observed state s_t, the encoder first finds out all possible combination of fps and resolution that roughly match the estimated bandwidth B^t_{est}, i.e., $\{(\mathrm{res},\mathrm{fps})|\mathrm{res}\times\mathrm{fps}\approx B^t_{est}$. Then, for each configuration, we calculate its reward. We choose the optimal one with the maximum reward as the configuration.
- Velocity Based Adaptation. We first set the minimum threshold that the fluency must be satisfied. Then, given the v_{max} and v_t, we can calculate the minimum fps_{min} to meet the threshold, i.e., the feasible options are $\{(res,fps)fps\geq fps_{min}\}$, and we pick the configuration with the maximum reward.
- Velocity Bandwidth Joint Adaptation (Yin et al., 2015). The tuned decision is ought to conform to the estimated bandwidth, and meets the fluency threshold. We use $\{(\mathrm{res},\mathrm{fps})|\mathrm{res}\times\mathrm{fps}\approx B^t_{est},\mathrm{fps}\geq\mathrm{fps}_{min}$ to record the set of possible configurations. Analogously, we select the most valuable configuration.

To simplify the description in the analysis and drawing, we refer to these baselines as NA, BBA, VBA, VBJA, respectively.

5.4 Experimental Results and Analyses

To compare Cuttlefish to other baselines, we used two typical types of live videos: one collected by street fixed cameras for monitoring high-speed cars, and the other collected by on-board mobile cameras for capturing low-speed pedestrians. For each type of video, we set 200 episodes, each containing 200 slots (seconds), which totals to 40,000 seconds.

The accumulative reward of a complete episode is the most important metric to evaluate the performance of the proposed model in practice. We first analyzed the accumulative reward of Cuttlefish on videos consisting mainly of pedestrians. **Figure 12** shows that BBA and VBA take bandwidth or velocity into consideration, and VBJA emphasizes the instant temporary reward. However, to meet the desired fluency, VBA may select a very high fps, increasing the transmission delay and decreasing the accumulative reward. Hence, their accumulative rewards are inferior to Cuttlefish. Cuttlefish's performance is enhanced steadily by over 40% compared to other baselines. Next, we tested Cuttlefish on car videos, and the results are shown in **Figure 14**. Cuttlefish still has a significant improvement in the average accumulative reward compared to the state-of-the-art heuristic VBJA, which is 18.4%. The proposed Cuttlefish, which considers network and velocity, outperforms the bandwidth-based BBA by approximately 25.8%. These results indicate that Cuttlefish can process videos with high-speed targets. However, it is worth mentioning that Cuttlefish performs better on videos with pedestrians than those with cars. This is because videos with high-speed targets lead to a larger state space, increasing the training difficulty and resulting in a reward loss.

Figure 12. Cuttlefish vs. other baselines for pedestrian video

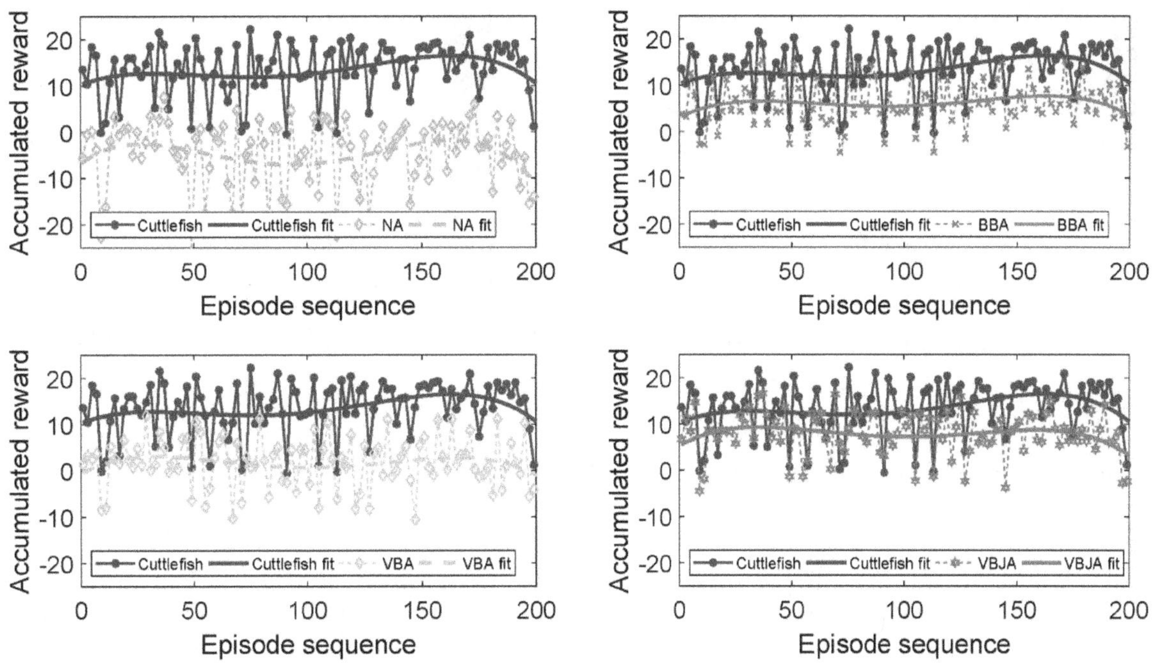

We evaluated the performance of the algorithms with respect to latency, accuracy, and fluency. We used NAR (negative action rate) to measure latency, which is the fraction of slots where the latency of a frame, including uploading, detecting, rendering, and downloading latencies, was greater than the length of a time slot. For accuracy, we measured the NAR where the accuracy was less than a threshold value of 0.7. For fluency, we measured the NAR where the perceived fluency was worse than a given value of 0.7. We simulated bandwidth using over 1000 traces and calculated NARs across 500 episodes. As shown in **Figure 13**, VBA prioritized fluency by using a high fps, leading to a terrible NAR on latency. Similarly, BBA had a large NAR on accuracy. The proposed Cuttlefish algorithm, with the lowest NARs on both latency and accuracy, performed similarly to other baselines, indicating that Cuttlefish could effectively manage the latency-accuracy-fluency tradeoff. Cuttlefish still performed well when applied to videos with cars, demonstrating its generalization ability, as shown in **Figure 15**.

Figure 13. Negative action rate for pedestrian video

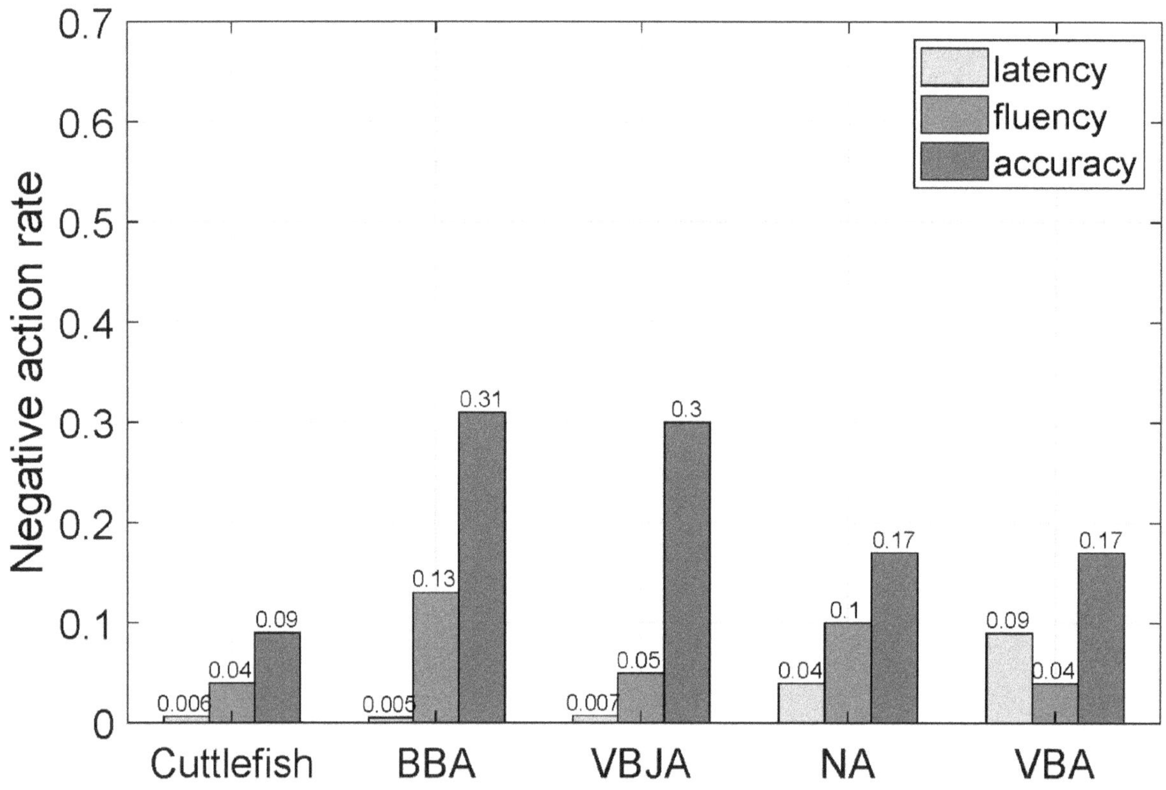

Figure 14. Cuttlefish vs. other baselines for car video

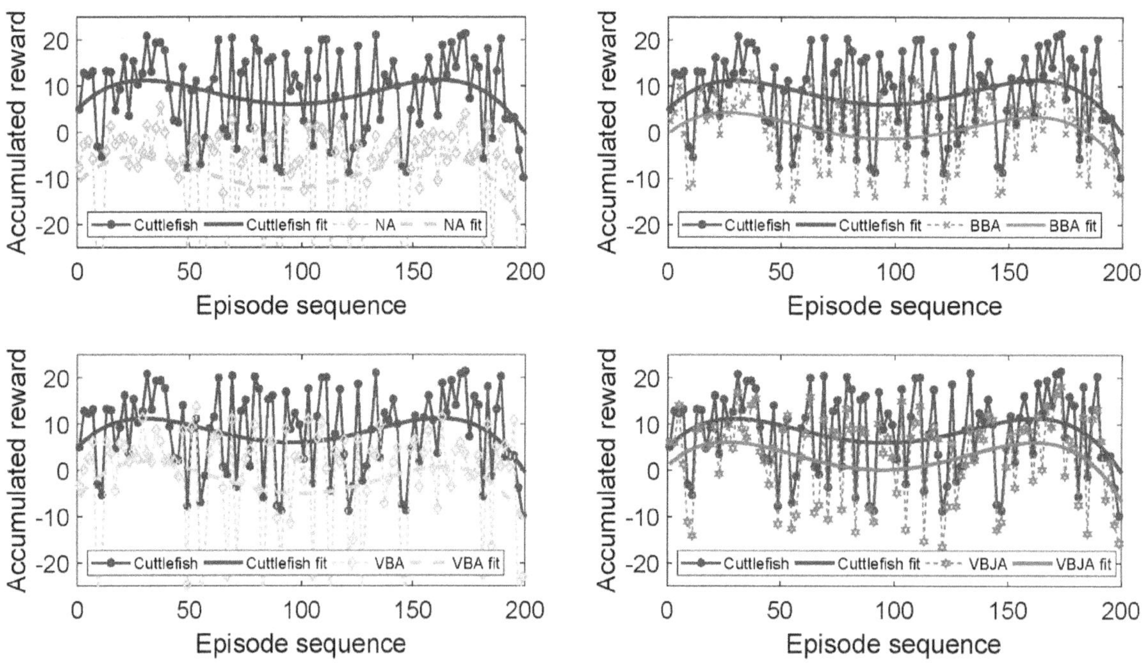

Figure 15. Negative action rate for car video

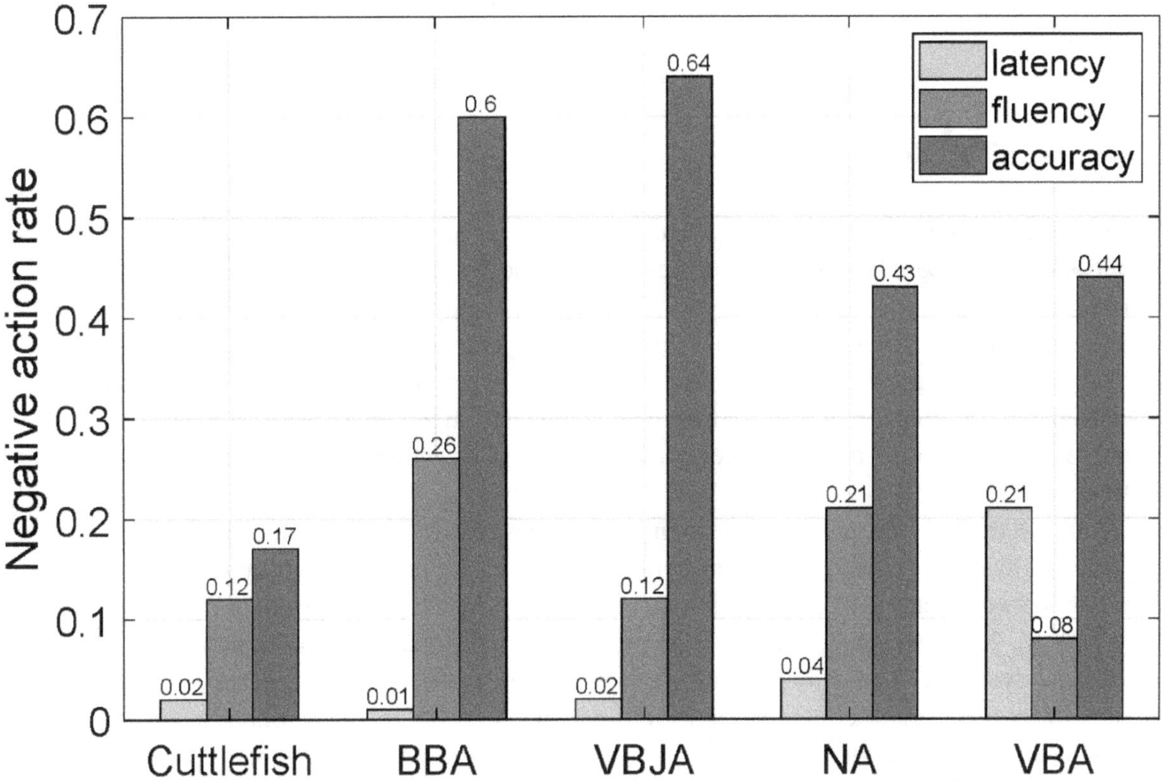

6. LIMITATIONS

In this section, we discuss several potential limitations and future research directions.

6.1 More Representative State Space

Cuttlefish uses a state space that combines k previous configurations, the estimated bandwidth of the next time slot, and the average velocity of all objects in a slot. While Cuttlefish performs well in extensive evaluations, it could generate even better configurations if specific state spaces were designed for different application scenarios. For instance, the number of previous configurations used in Cuttlefish could be tailored to specific applications.

6.2 Deploying Cuttlefish in Practice

The current implementation of Cuttlefish operates on the client-side of AR applications, which offers several benefits over deploying the algorithm on edge servers. First, AR clients do not need to exchange observations with edge servers, thereby eliminating unnecessary information exchange and reducing latency. Second, edge servers do not require any modifications, as the adaptive configuration selection process can be transparent to them. Consequently, client-side Cuttlefish can be viewed as an overlay on existing AR applications. In the event of a Cuttlefish failure, the configuration selection service can be disabled, and the default configuration can be used as a fallback. This fault recovery mechanism is an invaluable feature of the client-side implementation.

7. RELATED WORK

The existing research on ABR algorithms can be broadly classified into two categories: rate-based and buffer-based. Rate-based algorithms, such as those proposed methods (Jiang et al., 2012; Sun et al., 2016), estimate the available network bandwidth by analyzing past downloads and then request video chunks at the highest bitrate that matches the estimated bandwidth. For example, Festive (Jiang et al., 2012) predicts throughput using a harmonic mean of the experienced throughput for the past 5 chunk downloads. In addition to efficient bandwidth utilization and streaming transmission, our proposed AR adaptive video streaming method achieves efficient object detection, setting it apart from traditional ABR approaches.

While AR can provide helpful information, it can be costly in terms of time and computing resources, requiring offloading of the detecting computation to the cloud. Previous research has focused on achieving a tradeoff between delay and accuracy through intelligent offloading or adaptive configuration. Liu et al. (L. Liu et al., 2019) decoupled the rendering pipeline from the offloading pipeline by tracking objects locally and dynamically adjusting the resolution of frames. Liu et al. (Q. Liu et al., 2018) designed an edge network orchestrator consisting of server assignment and frame resolution selection to mitigate the latency-accuracy tradeoff. Jiang et al. (Jiang et al., 2018) presented Chameleon, which dynamically selects the best configuration for existing NN-based video analytics pipelines. Zhang et al. (B. Zhang et al., 2018) developed AWStream, which automatically learns an optimal profile that models accuracy and bandwidth tradeoff. Other mobile AR research (W. Zhang et al., 2017; Qiu et al., 2018) has also provided useful insights. In this paper, we propose an adaptive configuration selection method that uses learning from past experiences to achieve a better tradeoff between latency, accuracy, and fluency.

Deep Reinforcement Learning (DRL) has shown promising results across a variety of domains. For example, Mao et al. (Mao et al., 2017; Mao, Schwarzkopf, et al., 2019; Mao, Negi, et al., 2019) have used DRL to adjust streaming rates for unstable networks, schedule Spark jobs efficiently, and develop a tool for researchers to experiment with RL for computer systems. Mirhoseini et al. (Mirhoseini et al., 2017) optimized the operator placement of a TensorFlow computation graph in a single machine using DRL. Additionally, Xu et al. (Xu et al., 2018) applied DRL to traffic routing path selection. For MEC resource allocation, several authors (Li et al., 2018; He et al., 2017; Chen et al., 2019; C. Zhang et al., 2018) proposed an A3C based optimization framework. Zhang et al. (H. Zhang et al., 2019) introduced ReLeS for Multipath TCP, which supports real-time packet scheduling. In comparison, Cuttlefish is the first system to use DRL to achieve adaptive video configuration.

8. CONCLUSION

This paper introduces Cuttlefish, a deep learning-based system that ensures both accurate detection and low latency through adaptive configuration. The system considers the variability of bandwidth, time-shifted moving velocity of target objects, and similarity among adjacent frames, which can all affect the final encoded configuration. Cuttlefish combines these factors and proposes a policy network that takes the estimated bandwidth, captured velocity, and other historical information as input and outputs the configuration distribution. The system uses the advanced YOLOv3 as the detecting algorithm and adopts the state-of-the-art A3C model to train Cuttlefish with numerous real traces from YouTube. We compared Cuttlefish to several state-of-the-art bandwidth-based and velocity-based methods, and the results show that Cuttlefish can achieve 18.4%-25.8% higher QoE. In the follow-up work, we plan to improve Cuttlefish by evaluating more types of videos and ultimately implement it in real AR systems.

9. ACKNOWLEDGMENT

This work was supported in part by National Key R\&D Program of China (2017YFB1001801), NSFC (61872175, 61832008), Natural Science Foundation of Jiangsu Province (BK20181252), Jiangsu Key R\&D Program (BE2018116), the Fundamental Research Funds for the Central Universities (14380060), and Collaborative Innovation Center of Novel Software Technology and Industrialization. Sheng Zhang is the corresponding author.

REFERENCES

Akçayır, M., & Akçayır, G. (2017). Advantages and challenges associated with augmented reality for education: A systematic review of the literature. *Educational Research Review*, *20*, 1–11. doi:10.1016/j.edurev.2016.11.002

Azuma, R., Baillot, Y., Behringer, R., Feiner, S., Julier, S., & MacIntyre, B. (2001). Recent advances in augmented reality. *IEEE Computer Graphics and Applications*, *21*(6), 34–47. doi:10.1109/38.963459

Bradski, G., & Kaehler, A. (2008). *Learning OpenCV: Computer vision with the OpenCV library*. O'Reilly Media, Inc.

Chen, X., Zhang, H., Wu, C., Mao, S., Ji, Y., & Bennis, M. (2018). Optimized computation offloading performance in virtual edge computing systems via deep reinforcement learning. *IEEE Internet of Things Journal*, *6*(3), 4005–4018. doi:10.1109/JIOT.2018.2876279

Craw, S. (2017). *Manhattan distance*. Springer.

Dosovitskiy, A., Fischer, P., Ilg, E., Hausser, P., Hazirbas, C., Golkov, V., & Brox, T. (2015). Flownet: Learning optical flow with convolutional networks. In *Proceedings of the IEEE international conference on computer vision* (pp. 2758-2766). IEEE. 10.1109/ICCV.2015.316

Everingham, M., Van Gool, L., Williams, C. K., Winn, J., & Zisserman, A. (2010). The pascal visual object classes (voc) challenge. *International Journal of Computer Vision*, *88*(2), 303–338. doi:10.1007/s11263-009-0275-4

Farhadi, A., & Redmon, J. (2018). Yolov3: An incremental improvement. *arXiv preprint arXiv*:1804.02767.

He, Y., Yu, F. R., Zhao, N., Leung, V. C., & Yin, H. (2017). Software-defined networks with mobile edge computing and caching for smart cities: A big data deep reinforcement learning approach. *IEEE Communications Magazine, 55*(12), 31–37. doi:10.1109/MCOM.2017.1700246

Henderson, P., Islam, R., Bachman, P., Pineau, J., Precup, D., & Meger, D. (2018, April). Deep reinforcement learning that matters. *Proceedings of the AAAI Conference on Artificial Intelligence, 32*(1). doi:10.1609/aaai.v32i1.11694

Jiang, J., Ananthanarayanan, G., Bodik, P., Sen, S., & Stoica, I. (2018, August). Chameleon: scalable adaptation of video analytics. In *Proceedings of the 2018 Conference of the ACM Special Interest Group on Data Communication* (pp. 253-266). ACM. 10.1145/3230543.3230574

Jiang, J., Sekar, V., & Zhang, H. (2012, December). Improving fairness, efficiency, and stability in http-based adaptive video streaming with festive. In *Proceedings of the 8th international conference on Emerging networking experiments and technologies* (pp. 97-108). ACM. 10.1145/2413176.2413189

Li, J., Gao, H., Lv, T., & Lu, Y. (2018, April). Deep reinforcement learning based computation offloading and resource allocation for MEC. In 2018 IEEE wireless communications and networking conference (WCNC) (pp. 1-6). IEEE. doi:10.1109/WCNC.2018.8377343

Liu, L., Li, H., & Gruteser, M. (2019, August). Edge assisted real-time object detection for mobile augmented reality. In *The 25th annual international conference on mobile computing and networking* (pp. 1-16). ACM. 10.1145/3300061.3300116

Liu, Q., Huang, S., Opadere, J., & Han, T. (2018, April). An edge network orchestrator for mobile augmented reality. In *IEEE INFOCOM 2018-IEEE conference on computer communications* (pp. 756–764). IEEE. doi:10.1109/INFOCOM.2018.8486241

Magic leap one. (2020). https://www.magicleap.com/

Mao, H., Negi, P., Narayan, A., Wang, H., Yang, J., Wang, H., & Alizadeh, D. (2019). Park: An open platform for learning-augmented computer systems. *Advances in Neural Information Processing Systems*, 32.

Mao, H., Netravali, R., & Alizadeh, M. (2017, August). Neural adaptive video streaming with pensieve. In *Proceedings of the conference of the ACM special interest group on data communication* (pp. 197-210). ACM. 10.1145/3098822.3098843

Mao, H., Schwarzkopf, M., Venkatakrishnan, S. B., Meng, Z., & Alizadeh, M. (2019). Learning scheduling algorithms for data processing clusters. In *Proceedings of the ACM special interest group on data communication* (pp. 270-288). ACM. 10.1145/3341302.3342080

Microsoft hololens. (2020). https://www.microsoft.com/en-us/hololens/

Mirhoseini, A., Pham, H., Le, Q. V., Steiner, B., Larsen, R., Zhou, Y., & Dean, J. (2017, July). Device placement optimization with reinforcement learning. In *International Conference on Machine Learning* (pp. 2430-2439). PMLR.

Mnih, V., Badia, A. P., Mirza, M., Graves, A., Lillicrap, T., Harley, T., & Kavukcuoglu, K. (2016, June). Asynchronous methods for deep reinforcement learning. In *International conference on machine learning* (pp. 1928-1937). PMLR.

Mnih, V., Kavukcuoglu, K., Silver, D., Rusu, A. A., Veness, J., Bellemare, M. G., & Hassabis, D. (2015). Human-level control through deep reinforcement learning. *nature, 518*(7540), 529-533.

Netravali, R., Sivaraman, A., Das, S., Goyal, A., Winstein, K., Mickens, J., & Balakrishnan, H. (2015, July). Mahimahi: Accurate Record-and-Replay for HTTP. In *Usenix annual technical conference* (pp. 417-429).

Paszke, A., Gross, S., Massa, F., Lerer, A., Bradbury, J., Chanan, G., & Chintala, S. (2019). Pytorch: An imperative style, high-performance deep learning library. *Advances in Neural Information Processing Systems*, 32.

Qiu, H., Ahmad, F., Bai, F., Gruteser, M., & Govindan, R. (2018, June). Avr: Augmented vehicular reality. In *Proceedings of the 16th Annual International Conference on Mobile Systems, Applications, and Services* (pp. 81-95). ACM. 10.1145/3210240.3210319

Redmon, J., Divvala, S., Girshick, R., & Farhadi, A. (2016). You only look once: Unified, real-time object detection. In *Proceedings of the IEEE conference on computer vision and pattern recognition* (pp. 779-788). IEEE. 10.1109/CVPR.2016.91

Redmon, J., & Farhadi, A. (2017). YOLO9000: better, faster, stronger. In *Proceedings of the IEEE conference on computer vision and pattern recognition* (pp. 7263-7271). IEEE.

Roman, R., Lopez, J., & Mambo, M. (2018). Mobile edge computing, Fog et al.: A survey and analysis of security threats and challenges. *Future Generation Computer Systems, 78*, 680–698. doi:10.1016/j.future.2016.11.009

Satyanarayanan, M. (2017). The emergence of edge computing. *Computer, 50*(1), 30–39. doi:10.1109/MC.2017.9

Shi, W., Cao, J., Zhang, Q., Li, Y., & Xu, L. (2016). Edge computing: Vision and challenges. *IEEE Internet of Things Journal, 3*(5), 637–646. doi:10.1109/JIOT.2016.2579198

Silver, D., Schrittwieser, J., Simonyan, K., Antonoglou, I., Huang, A., Guez, A., & Hassabis, D. (2017). Mastering the game of go without human knowledge. *nature, 550*(7676), 354-359.

Simonyan, K., & Zisserman, A. (2014). Very deep convolutional networks for large-scale image recognition. *arXiv preprint arXiv:1409.1556.*

Sun, Y., Yin, X., Jiang, J., Sekar, V., Lin, F., Wang, N., & Sinopoli, B. (2016, August). CS2P: Improving video bitrate selection and adaptation with data-driven throughput prediction. In *Proceedings of the 2016 ACM SIGCOMM Conference* (pp. 272-285). ACM. 10.1145/2934872.2934898

Sutton, R. S., & Barto, A. G. (1999). Reinforcement learning: An introduction. *Robotica, 17*(2), 229–235.

Sutton, R. S., McAllester, D., Singh, S., & Mansour, Y. (1999). Policy gradient methods for reinforcement learning with function approximation. *Advances in Neural Information Processing Systems*, 12.

Westerfield, G., Mitrovic, A., & Billinghurst, M. (2015). Intelligent augmented reality training for motherboard assembly. *International Journal of Artificial Intelligence in Education, 25*(1), 157–172. doi:10.1007/s40593-014-0032-x

Winstein, K., Sivaraman, A., & Balakrishnan, H. (2013, April). Stochastic forecasts achieve high throughput and low delay over cellular networks. In NSDI (Vol. 1, No. 1, pp. 2-3).

Xu, Z., Tang, J., Meng, J., Zhang, W., Wang, Y., Liu, C. H., & Yang, D. (2018, April). Experience-driven networking: A deep reinforcement learning based approach. In *IEEE INFOCOM 2018-IEEE conference on computer communications* (pp. 1871–1879). IEEE. doi:10.1109/INFOCOM.2018.8485853

Yin, X., Jindal, A., Sekar, V., & Sinopoli, B. (2015, August). A control-theoretic approach for dynamic adaptive video streaming over HTTP. In *Proceedings of the 2015 ACM Conference on Special Interest Group on Data Communication* (pp. 325-338). ACM. 10.1145/2785956.2787486

Zhang, B., Jin, X., Ratnasamy, S., Wawrzynek, J., & Lee, E. A. (2018, August). Awstream: Adaptive wide-area streaming analytics. In *Proceedings of the 2018 Conference of the ACM Special Interest Group on Data Communication* (pp. 236-252). ACM. 10.1145/3230543.3230554

Zhang, C., Liu, Z., Gu, B., Yamori, K., & Tanaka, Y. (2018). A deep reinforcement learning based approach for cost-and energy-aware multi-flow mobile data offloading. *IEICE Transactions on Communications*, *101*(7), 1625–1634. doi:10.1587/transcom.2017CQP0014

Zhang, H., Li, W., Gao, S., Wang, X., & Ye, B. (2019, April). ReLeS: A neural adaptive multipath scheduler based on deep reinforcement learning. In *IEEE INFOCOM 2019-IEEE Conference on Computer Communications* (pp. 1648-1656). IEEE. 10.1109/INFOCOM.2019.8737649

Zhang, W., Han, B., & Hui, P. (2017, August). On the networking challenges of mobile augmented reality. In *Proceedings of the Workshop on Virtual Reality and Augmented Reality Network* (pp. 24-29). ACM. 10.1145/3097895.3097900

Chapter 8
Interactive Causality-Enabled Adaptive Machine Learning in Cyber-Physical Systems:
Technology and Applications in Manufacturing and Beyond

Yutian Ren
University of California, Irvine, USA

Salaar Saraj
University of California, Irvine, USA

Aaron Yen
https://orcid.org/0009-0002-9448-0975
University of California, Irvine, USA

GuannPyng Li
University of California, Irvine, USA

ABSTRACT

This chapter describes an adaptive machine learning (ML) method for the utilization of unlabeled data for continual model adaptation after deployment. Current methods for the usage of unlabeled data, such as unsupervised and semi-supervised methods, rely on being both smooth and static in their distributions. In this chapter, a generic method for leveraging causal relationships to automatically associate labels with unlabeled data using state transitions of asynchronous interacting cause and effect events is discussed. This self-labeling method is predicated on a defined causal relationship and associated temporal spacing. The theoretical foundation of the self-supervised method is discussed and compared with its contemporary semi-supervised counterparts using dynamical systems theory. Implementations of this method to adapt action recognition ML models in semiconductor manufacturing and human assembly tasks as manufacturing cyber-physical systems (CPS) are provided to demonstrate the effectiveness of the proposed methodology.

DOI: 10.4018/979-8-3693-0230-9.ch008

1. INTRODUCTION

Adaptive machine learning (ML) methods aim to equip deployed machine learning models with the domain adaptability to counter domain and data distribution shifts (Kouw & Marco, 2019; Lu et al., 2018). This allows models to continuously update and improve over time in dynamic, ever-changing environments. There are several types of data distribution shifts, including covariate shift (Schneider et al., 2020), label shift (Garg et al., 2020), and concept drift (Lu et al., 2018). Among these three types of data distribution shifts, concept drift is of great interest to be studied as it affects the entire input-output relation, compared to other drifts that affect either input or output distributions. Concept drift severely degrades the performance of trained models as system nonstationarity invalidates learned relationships (Yang et al., 2019). Therefore, post-deployment adaptability is imperative for ML models to sustain in dynamic environments. In general, ML models can be updated via retraining with datasets that include recent data distribution changes to learn and adapt to said changes (Lu et al., 2018). Generating updated datasets typically requires manual data collection and annotation, which, while providing precise and high-quality data can be costly and laborious (Fredriksson et al., 2020).

To ease the problem of data annotation cost, a class of methods for adaptation to data distribution shifts known as semi-supervised learning (SSL) was developed. SSL applies learned relationships from an initial dataset to newly obtained target data (Van Engelen & Hoos, 2020). These semi-supervised methods can be applied to unsupervised domain adaptation (UDA) using labeled data from the initial distribution (Wilson & Cook, 2020). Semi-supervised methods include pseudo-labels, where unlabeled data is used to generate target class labels used as pseudo-labels to guide adaptation (Lee, 2013), and label propagation, a graph-based approach to apply labels to unlabeled data (Zhu & Ghahramani., 2002). Similar semi-supervised label generation methods mainly use generative networks or clustering methods and generally assume target distribution overlap (Yang et al., 2023). Efforts have been made to adapt to greater domain shifts (Zhang et al., 2020), but they still rely on the correlation between initial and target domains. UDA, as it does not incorporate target labels, is bounded by the discrepancy and joint error of the distributions (Zhang et al., 2023). Recently, several works have proposed to jointly optimize pseudo-label generation and target learning (Asano et al., 2019; Zhou et al., 2021; Yan et al., 2021). Overall, the pseudo-label-based methods show promising results in reducing manual data annotation, but the post-deployment data distribution shifts can degrade their performance in dynamic environments. Causality-based semi-supervised learning has recently attracted researchers' attention due to the intrinsic invariance of causal relationships across domains (Schölkopf, 2022). Most research in this direction relies on the assumption that the generation of cause data and the causal mechanism are statistically independent (Gong et al., 2016). This chapter was inspired by the causality-based adaptive methods and introduces an adaptive ML system that considers the temporal relationships in causality.

Adaptive machine learning has broad applications and needs in cyber-physical systems (CPS) (Madni et al., 2018), especially CPS for smart manufacturing. AI applications in manufacturing CPS feature several unique challenges and opportunities (Davis et al., 2020; Kim et al., 2022; Donovan et al., 2022). The uncompleted transformation of digitization and informatics restricts the acquisition and archive of task-oriented data used for DL training. Some novel AI applications require additional data dimensions beyond what has been established and collected in the era of Industry 3.0 (Ghobakhloo, 2020). For example, many predictive maintenance applications require outside-in sensor information, while the majority of Industry 3.0 efforts focus on automation control and only collect process-related (inside-out) parameters (Achouch et al., 2022). Specialized domain knowledge in manufacturing requires AI engineers to understand problems and application scenarios in detail (Li, L. et al., 2021). However, the lack of IT expertise raises the cost of problem formulation, data collection and annotation, model development, and model and system maintenance (Narwane et al., 2022). In addition, the aforementioned problem of data distribution shift happens more frequently in dynamic manufacturing scenarios. The various use cases and diverse manufacturing environments further demand that ML models be capable of self-adaptation, evolving and improving their accuracy in a dynamic environment with minimal human intervention. On the other hand, rich domain knowledge also provides contextual information that can assist ML development in selecting data modality (Mirchevska et al., 2014; Kerrigan et al., 2021), identifying potential correlations (Demrozi et al., 2021; Chen et al., 2022), and tailoring ML models (Childs & Washburn, 2019; Hu et al., 2019). With the development of IoT technologies and pervasive sensing utilized in manufacturing CPS, multimodal sensors are also accessible, providing the opportunity to leverage unique sensory characteristics for ML model design (Zhao et al., 2017; Ansari et al., 2020).

Recently, several studies have concentrated on adaptive ML applications in the CPS field. Domain adaptation in CPS is of great value for adapting ML models to different domains (e.g., different automobiles, cameras) and combatting unforeseen concept drifts. Fault detection and diagnosis is a valuable application for UDA as collecting a comprehensive number of fault examples is prohibitively difficult, and UDA helps to bridge the data gap (Ramírez-Sanz et al., 2023). UDA has also been applied to imaging devices (Dayal et al., 2023), malware detection (Huda et al., 2017), and tool safety prediction (Qiu et al., 2022). ML for Cyber-physical systems often incorporate semi-supervised domain adaptation methods as usage scenarios are typically unique and domain-specific. In addition, the exploration and development of few-shot learning (Wang et al., 2021; Zhan et al., 2022; Sun et al., 2022), transfer learning (Wang & Gao, 2020; Sun et al., 2018), and self-supervised learning (Wang et al., 2020; Xu et al., 2022) aim to lower the barrier of AI adoption by reducing the needs of manually annotated training data or enhancing the domain adaptation and robustness of AI models. These methods step on algorithmic development and have shown promising results in manufacturing CPS. However, most of the current methods highly depend on rich and invariant data features that are common across domains. Cross-domain variations can make these methods less effective (Lu et al., 2018). In addition, while some of the current solutions can reduce the need to train on large numbers of labeled samples, manually labeled data is still required, and the models lack a method for automatic evolution and adaptation to local environmental changes.

To address the domain adaptation problem, especially for manufacturing CPS, the technical challenge that this chapter focuses on is that most current ML strategies require a manually labeled dataset in pre- and post-deployment stages for initial training and post-deployment drift adaptation, significantly hindering the usage of data-driven ML in traditional fields with less data expertise. This chapter addresses the challenge from a system perspective and designs an adaptive machine learning system such that ML models can achieve autonomous learning and adapt for concept drift without the need for labor-intensive manual data collection and annotation. We delve into interaction scenarios involving the dynamic engagement of multiple objects, domains, or humans. These interactions are characterized by clear and unambiguous causal relationships, which we term interactive causality, due to the invariance feature of causality across domains. We propose a self-labeling method for automated post-deployment data annotation. This self-labeling method capitalizes on the temporal sequencing of causal events, enabling us to label data shifts that emerge after deployment.

Our technique specifically addresses the shifts that occur in post-deployment scenarios, where the presence of multimodal information acquisition allows us to leverage additional observational channels to deduce labels. The self-labeling entails learning the time intervals (Gollob & Reichardt, 1987; Bramley et al., 2018) that separate asynchronous cause events from their corresponding effects. By utilizing invariant causal relationships and observable effect data, we can autonomously label cause data. The resultant self-labeled dataset becomes instrumental in the adaptive retraining of an ML model designed to predict effects based on causes. Central to the self-labeling approach is the assumption that the temporal relationships between causes and effects exhibit greater consistency and are less susceptible to domain shifts compared to the similarities in input features, as conjectured in the realm of semi-supervised learning.

To validate our method, we employ 1-dimensional dynamical systems to demonstrate its consistent superiority over traditional semi-supervised learning techniques, contingent on certain defined conditions. Two CPS case studies in manufacturing are provided to evaluate applicability and effectiveness of the proposed self-labeling method in real-world applications. The first case study is to adapt a DL model of worker action recognition in a semiconductor fabrication facility. The second case study applies self-labeling in a manual assembly scenario to adapt DL models detecting worker intentions for seamless human-robot collaboration. Collectively, these two case studies effectively showcase the potential of self-labeling within real-world scenarios. They emphasize the practical benefits and outcomes that the approach can yield. Finally, we outline the potential range of self-labeling applications within CPS, providing a promising outlook for future endeavors in this field.

This chapter is organized as follows. We will first review the interactive causality methodology and the proposed self-labeling method for adaptive machine learning in Section 2. In Section 3, the theoretical foundation of the self-labeling method using dynamical system theory is illustrated and compared to traditional semi-supervised methods. Section 4 provides two real-world manufacturing CPS examples with ML adaptability enhanced by the proposed self-labeling method. The two examples are established on the interactions among operators, machines, and materials in manufacturing and the development of adaptive ML models for action recognition. In the last section, we explore a potential pathway for extending the application of interactive causality to other CPS by leveraging the multimodal nature of physical systems and pervasive domain knowledge.

2. INTERACTIVE CAUSALITY METHODOLOGY

2.1 Background of Causality

Causality (Pearl, 2009) is a fundamental concept in various fields of research, including philosophy, economy, physics, and statistics. Causality refers to the relationship between cause and effect, where a cause produces an effect. Establishing causal relationships is essential for understanding how different factors or variables influence each other and for making accurate predictions or interventions. Many research topics have been highlighted in the field of causality, such as causal discovery (Jaber et al., 2020), causal inference (Kocaoglu et al., 2020), counterfactual analysis (Prosperi et al., 2020), and causal machine learning (Richens et al., 2020). From a statistical perspective, there are two widely used causality modeling techniques: Granger Causality and structural causal models.

Granger causality (GC) is a statistical concept and methodology used to assess the causal relationship between two time series variables. It was developed by Nobel laureate Clive Granger in 1969 and has become widely used in econometrics and other fields for studying causal relationships in time-dependent data (Granger, 1969). Granger causality is based on the principle that if a time series variable X "Granger-causes" another variable Y, then the past values of X contain information that helps predict the future values of Y beyond what can be predicted using only the past values of Y itself. The structural causal model (SCM), also known as a structural equation model (SEM) or a causal graphical model, was first proposed by Judea Pearl in the late 1980s (Pearl, 2009). It is a mathematical framework used to represent and study causal relationships and provides a formalized approach to understanding how variables interact with each other and the underlying mechanisms that generate the observed data by using Bayesian network theory. SCM defines a do-calculus, which provides a set of formal rules for manipulating causal expressions involving interventions, counterfactuals, and observational data. It allows people to make causal inferences and estimate causal effects from observed data and knowledge about the underlying causal structure. Compared with GC, SCM lacks the view of temporal information but utilizes probabilistic graphical models to process many causal variables.

Causality differs from correlation in several aspects. Causality involves a temporal order, cause-and-effect mechanisms, interventions, counterfactual reasoning, and considerations of confounding factors. Correlation, on the other hand, describes statistical associations between variables without specifying the direction or temporal precedence. Establishing causality requires more rigorous analysis and evidence than establishing correlation. Researchers often conduct experiments or use methods like randomized controlled trials (Deaton & Cartwright, 2018), where they manipulate one variable while keeping others constant to establish a cause-and-effect relationship. Such randomized controlled trials have been widely used in medical fields to examine the causal effects of novel treatments. There are several data-driven causal discovery algorithms (Malinsky & Danks, 2018; Le et al., 2016) introduced to efficiently discover causal relations and build causal graphs among many variables based on Bayesian networks and various conditional independence tests. However, such statistical causality may not faithfully represent the physical cause and effect mechanism due to the existence of unknown confounders. As such, solid identification of causation is always a topic pursued by researchers. This chapter focuses on utilizing known causality to achieve adaptive machine learning.

2.2 Interactive Causality Concept

Interactive Causality (IC) refers to asynchronous causal relationships underlying interactive objects (Ren et al., 2023). There is an interaction happening among several objects where some objects are causes and others are effects. The state transitions of the interactive objects due to the causality can be represented as events, and we will use events or states interchangeably to represent them. The causal time lag is a critical concept that means the transmission of causal effect from cause sides to effect sides requires a duration (Gollob & Reichardt, 1987; Du et al., 2017; Bramley et al., 2018). From a physical perspective, the causal time lag is related to the energy, force, or information transmission speed and the magnitude of effect signals.

Based on the concept of IC, an interactive causality methodology is established to achieve adaptive machine learning (Ren et al., 2023). Adaptive machine learning refers to the ability of ML models to adapt and learn from new data or changing environments without much human intervention. In this context, adaptive learning puts a focus on allowing models to automatically modify their behavior, structure, or parameters in response to new data or data distribution shifts without requiring manual intervention. At the same time, it has the potential to continuously evolve to reach higher detection accuracy in non-shifted domains and class incremental learning.

Figure 1. Interactive causality and the self-labeling method

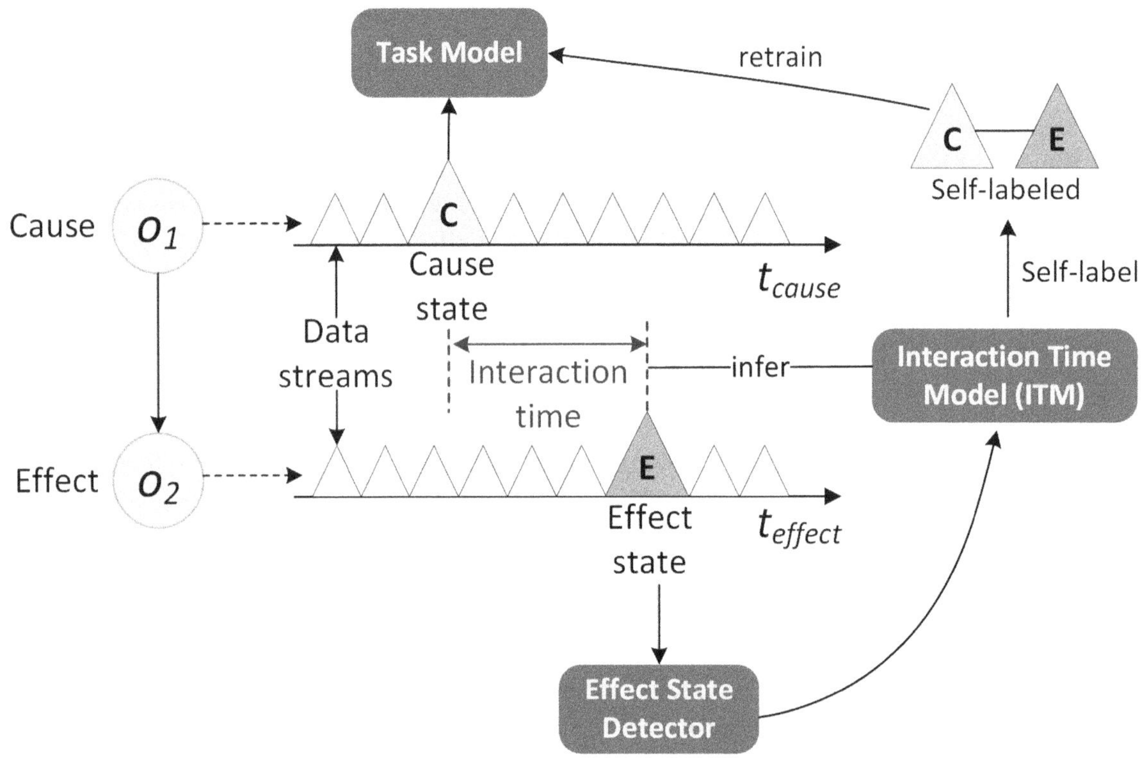

2.3 Interactive Causality for Self-Labeling

In this section, we will elaborate on the Interactive Causality methodology for self-labeling and adaptive learning. The objective of the self-labeling method enhanced by IC is to support ML tasks, specifically those involving pattern recognition accomplished by supervised learning. This approach rests on an interaction scenario where objects interact and create observable effects. To demonstrate the idea, a 2-object interaction scenario is presented in Figure 1. In this scenario, the causal relationship between object o_1 and o_2 is unidirectional and known *a priori*. The ML task model aims to train a model that takes the causal data of o_1 as input and infers the corresponding effect of o_2. During model deployment, two streams of sensor data are accessible: one from the cause side and the other from the effect side. To better grasp causality from an ML perspective, we can regard the causal data as input features, while the effect data becomes the output labels. Interaction time is defined as the time lag between the occurrence of the corresponding cause and effect states.

Figure 1 also illustrates the self-labeling procedure. Before deploying the task model, the interaction time between the data streams of two objects is identified following a process that involves existing knowledge or causal modeling. To infer the interaction time, an auxiliary interaction time model (ITM) is utilized, which can be trained using supervised or unsupervised methods and can take various forms, such as an ML, statistical, mathematical, or physical model. To differentiate between the two data models, the primary functional ML model is designated as the task model. Optionally, the task model can be pretrained during the derivation of supervision for the ITM with concurrent labeling for the task model.

During deployment, the self-labeling process comprises three sub-steps: 1) when effect data is received, the ITM infers the interaction time; 2) the effect data is processed to generate the label; 3) starting from the timestamp of the effect data, the system backtracks over the period of inferred interaction time to select the corresponding segment of cause data to be labeled. This results in multiple self-labeled data samples, which are used to retrain the task model, thereby improving its performance.

We put forth the following conditions for the self-labeling method: 1) the method is applicable in situations where object interactions occur; 2) a known or derived causal relationship should exist during these interactions; 3) interaction time dependent on effect data for ITM; 4) ideally, the effect data should be easier to process than the cause data. Although not an obligatory condition, condition 4 serves as a criterion for determining when the application of self-labeling becomes advantageous, and it allows for the selection of an effect observer as an alternative for observing the cause. Condition 3 plays a crucial role in assessing the feasibility of self-labeling and also serves as a guide in selecting the effect observer.

3. THEORETICAL FOUNDATIONS OF SELF-LABELING

3.1 Theory and Proof Using Dynamical Systems

In this section, we demonstrate the consistent superiority of the self-labeling method over traditional semi-supervised learning (SSL), which relies on distribution smoothness to infer labels and address concept drift problems by adopting the theory of dynamical systems (DS). In the context of modeling time-evolving systems, DS proves to be a valuable technique.

Dynamical systems employ differential or difference equations to describe the evolution of system states over time. This modeling approach is well-suited for many real-world systems that experience dynamic changes in their states as time progresses. In previous literature (Kocarev & Parlitz, 1996), the interaction between two DS is often represented using coupled differential equations. For our proof, we focus on a simplified scenario involving two interacting 1-dimensional DS x and y as

$$\dot{x} = f(x) \tag{1}$$

$$\dot{y} = y + h(x) \tag{2}$$

In the presence of an unknown perturbation in system x, the cause side will exhibit a corresponding disturbance, leading to a change in the cause-effect relationship. In this example, the perturbation serves as a simulation of concept drift in ML and should not be treated as noise as done in control theory. Instead, we view it as an unidentified factor that alters the learned relationship between inputs and outputs. As such, the perturbed DS becomes

$$\dot{x} = f(x) + d(x) \tag{3}$$

$$\dot{y} = y(t) + h(x). \quad (4)$$

System x and y are characterized by their initial and final values denoted as x_1, x_2, y_1, and y_2, respectively, where subscript 1 represents the initial value, and subscript 2 indicates the final value. These systems evolve from their initial to final values over a defined period known as the interaction time. In the context of the x-y interaction, we designate x_1 as the cause state and y_2 as the effect state. The ML task model involves learning a mapping between the cause x_1 and the effect y_2. To achieve this, we will employ the proposed self-labeling method to establish the self-labeled x_1-y_2 relationship in the presence of perturbations. This result will then be compared with conventional SSL and fully supervised methods.

We can first solve the DS and derive

$$x(t) = A^{-1}\left(t + A(x_1)\right) \quad (5)$$

$$y(t) = e^{t}\int_0^t e^{-\tau} \cdot h\left(A^{-1}\left(\tau + A(x_1)\right)\right) d\tau + e^{t} y_1 \quad (6)$$

in the unperturbed case where $A(x) = \int^{x} \frac{1}{f(\xi)} d\xi$, and

$$x(t) = B^{-1}\left(t + B(x_1)\right) \quad (7)$$

$$y(t) = e^{t}\int_0^t e^{-\tau} \cdot h\left(B^{-1}\left(\tau + B(x_1)\right)\right) d\tau + e^{t} y_1 \quad (8)$$

in the perturbed case where $B(x) = \int^{x} \frac{1}{f(\xi) + d(\xi)} d\xi$. Both $A(x)$ and $B(x)$ are locally invertible on $[x_1, x_2]$. In Equation (6), the variable x_1 should be replaced with x_2, as x_1 remains unidentified during inference, whereas x_2 can be treated as a constant. By setting $y(t)$ as y_2 and t as inferred interaction time t_{if}, we can establish the connection between t_{if} and y_2 as

$$y_2 = e^{t_{if}}\int_0^{t_{if}} e^{-\tau} \cdot h\left(A^{-1}\left(\tau + A(x_2) - t_{if}\right)\right) d\tau + e^{t_{if}} y_1 \quad (9)$$

which can deduce the interaction time using effect data in the perturbed case.

Equation (7) can be used to derive the ground truth interaction under perturbation $t_{gt} = B(x_2) - B(x_1)$. Give t_{gt} and t_{if}, we can derive the self-labeled x_1 as $x_{slb} = B^{-1}\left(t_{gt} - t_{if} + B(x_1)\right)$. Thus, the relationships between t_{if} and x_{slb} can be derived as

$$t_{if} = B(x_2) - B(x_{slb}) \quad (10)$$

Utilizing Equation (10), we can insert the value of t_{if} into Equation (9). This enables us to deduce the connection between y_2 and x_{slb} in the presence of perturbations as

$$y_{2slb} = e^{B(x_2)-B(x_{slb})}\left(\int_0^{B(x_2)-B(x_{slb})} e^{-\tau} \cdot h\left(A^{-1}\left(\tau + A(x_2) - B(x_2) + B(x_{slb})\right)\right) d\tau + y_1\right) \tag{11}$$

which is the input-output relation learned by the task model using our self-labeling.

Equation (11) requires a comparison with traditional SSL and a fully supervised (FS) approach. Conventional SSL techniques establish an x_1-y_2 relationship in an unperturbed setting during the supervised phase. When faced with a perturbed environment, the previously learned x_1-y_2 connection is employed to infer pseudo labels for perturbed x_1 lacking true labels. Consequently, conventional SSL approaches are inherently limited to the unperturbed x_1-y_2 relationship in principle. The FS method pertains to the genuine relationship between perturbed x_1 and y_2, as established by training on pairs of data and corresponding labels. This FS relationship can be derived through the utilization of Equations (3) and (4). By undertaking a direct solution of both the original and perturbed dynamical systems, we can derive

$$y_{2ssl} = e^{A(x_2)-A(x_1)}\left(\int_0^{A(x_2)-A(x_1)} e^{-\tau} \cdot h\left(A^{-1}\left(\tau + A(x_1)\right)\right) d\tau + y_1\right) \tag{12}$$

$$y_{2fs} = e^{B(x_2)-B(x_1)}\left(\int_0^{B(x_2)-B(x_1)} e^{-\tau} \cdot h\left(B^{-1}\left(\tau + B(x_1)\right)\right) d\tau + y_1\right) \tag{13}$$

where subscript *fs* and *ssl* represent FS and traditional SSL methods, respectively.

In contrast to retrospective self-labeling, an emerging question is the viability of employing causal data to derive the interaction time for self-labeling effects. This concept of cause-driven self-labeling is also analyzed and is denoted by the subscript *fwd*. In this scenario, the inferred interaction time derived from x_1 is denoted as $t_{if} = A(x_2) - A(x_1)$. With perturbations, the forward self-labeling starts from the moment when x_1 is received and progresses in a forward direction, aiming to self-label y_2 based on the effect data stream. By substituting the variable t in Equation (9) with t_{if} in this context, we can derive

$$y_{2fwd} = e^{A(x_2)-A(x_1)}\left(\int_0^{A(x_2)-A(x_1)} e^{-\tau} \cdot h\left(B^{-1}\left(\tau + B(x_1)\right)\right) d\tau + y_1\right). \tag{14}$$

A comparative assessment of the performance of $y_{2slb}, y_{2ssl}, y_{2fs}$, and y_{2fwd} is carried out to quantify their relative effectiveness. This comparative analysis entails the derivation of derivatives to scrutinize their fluctuations. In a simplified scenario where $h(\bullet)$is an identity mapping and both x and y are positive systems, their interrelations $\left(y_{2slb}, y_{2ssl}, y_{2fs}, y_{2fwd}\right)$ and corresponding conditions are explicated in Table 1. It is worth noting that the assumption of positive systems holds validity in many practical instances. A salient observation emerges: the proposed SLB technique outperforms conventional SSL methods in specific circumstances, preserving this advantage as long as the perturbations do not invert the direction of the vector field driving x. It can be noted that under conditions 3 and 4, wherein the relationships

Table 1. Theoretical comparison of the four methods

ID	*f*(*x*)	*d*(*x*)	*f*(*x*)+*d*(*x*)	Relation
1	+	+	+	*fwd>ssl>slb>fs*
2	+	-	+	*fs>slb>ssl>fwd*
3	+	-	-	*ssl>fwd>fs>slb*
4	-	+	+	*slb>fs>fwd>ssl*
5	-	+	-	*fwd>ssl>slb>fs*
6	-	-	-	*fs>slb>ssl>fwd*

between SLB and the traditional SSL approach are unidentified, the *fwd* approach consistently outperforms the SSL method.

In practical scenarios, many systems are often conceptualized through an idealized discrete formulation, taking the form $x(k+1)=f(x(k))$. When dealing with two interacting dynamical systems, their coupling manifests as $y(k+1)=g(y(k),x(k))$ (Brännström, 2009). In a straightforward linear coupling instance, the representation of the system y simplifies to $y(k+1)=y(k)+x(k)$. Despite the use of continuous DS in the aforementioned proof, the established conclusion remains applicable to discrete DS as well. Quantifying the temporal dimension permits the seamless translation of continuous DS into discrete DS. Consequently, self-labeling can more closely emulate real-world conditions where object attributes are often digitized and categorized into finite states.

In addition, granger Causality (GC) formally introduces a statistical assessment of causal relationships between two random variables denoted by time-series data. The foundation of GC rests on the premise that the cause precedes the effect. Within a linear auto-regressive model, standard GC (Paluš et al., 2018) is expressed as

$$Y_n = a_0 + \sum_{k=1}^{L} b_{1k} Y_{n-k} + \sum_{k=1}^{L} b_{2k} X_{n-k} + \xi_n \tag{15}$$

where ξ_n signifies uncorrelated noise and n signifies discrete steps. Remarkably, the GC formula mirrors the structure of coupled discrete dynamical systems, where X and Y represent two systems and the order L is set to 1. Viewed from the perspective of GC, causal and effect data can be discretized into distinct states, akin to discrete DS, facilitating self-labeling.

3.2 Intuitive Foundations of Interactive Causality for Self-Labeling

The proof using DS theory has fundamentally demonstrated the merit of self-labeling. But intuitively, why would IC work effectively in countering domain shifts and adapting ML? First, we need to realize that data annotation basically consists of two stages: 1) selecting the data samples that need labeling from a data stream; 2) generating appropriate labels for the chosen data samples. When dealing with image datasets, researchers often skip step 1 since images are typically pre-selected. However, in scenarios where sensors, such as cameras, capture streaming data in dynamic environments, both steps become essential for accurate annotation. In the proposed self-labeling paradigm, we achieve full automation by eliminating the need for human intervention in both data sample selection and label generation processes by: 1) association of multiple data streams and events by causality and learnable interaction time; 2) selection of additional observing channels (i.e., effect observers) to transform hard problems to easy problems.

Figure 2. A moving ball with a trajectory to illustrate the impact of inaccurate interaction time inference

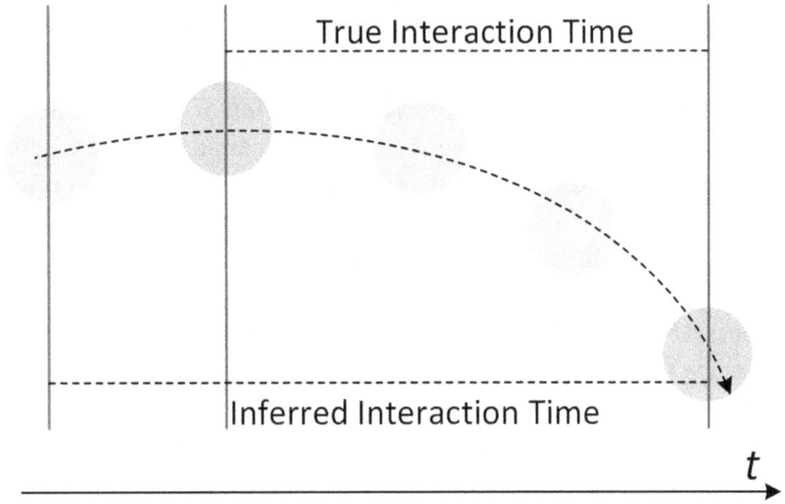

3.2.1 Causality Invariance

A conceivable and persuasive assertion posits that although data distributions may vary across different domains due to unknown environmental dynamics, the constancy of causal relationships, especially causal directions, remains unchanged across these domains (Schölkopf, 2022). We focus on a common scenario prevailing in many applications, where the data distribution of a dataset during deployment differs from that of its training dataset. For example, in a vision task, the actual data in deployment may use a different camera angle compared to the training set, which can make deployed models less accurate. Domains vary, but the embedded causality remains constant. Currently, there is no rigorous proof for this plausible statement, but researchers have been exploring this direction and have used it as an assumption. Compared to correlation, causality exhibits greater consistency across various domains. While correlation is closely tied to probability, causality exhibits stronger adherence to physical regularity. From a physics standpoint, in the Minkowski space-time model, causality remains preserved within the timelike light cone, irrespective of observers' reference frames (Bombelli et al., 1987). This property implies a higher level of theoretical soundness to causality than that of correlation. Moreover, the directionality of causation more explicitly characterizes the relationships between states and the time lags, with the cause always preceding the effect. This directionality is harnessed in this work.

3.2.2 Concept Drift Adaptation

One of the data distribution shifts, concept drift, happens when the input distribution remains unchanged, but the conditional distribution of the output given an input is shifted. In other words, with concept drift, there will be a different output for the same input. The proposed self-labeling can adapt ML models under concept drift because the detected effect states incorporate the perturbation induced by concept drift over the period of interaction time. Concept drift states that the same input may generate a different output. This can be attributed to the change of $y=f(x)$ where x is ML input data, and y is the output label. The self-labeling method can capture this change as it operates backwards, attempting to associate the shifted effect and current input and learn the shifted function of $y=f(x)$. In this sense, the domain change is always incorporated in the self-labeled dataset for learning. The interaction time is critical here to capture the shifted data distribution on the fly because the domain shift occurs over this period.

3.2.3 Inaccurate ITM and Effect State Detector

Additionally, the success of self-labeling strategically relies on the interaction time inference. Any inaccurate inferred interaction time will cause deviations in the self-labeled inputs. However, this deviation generates less harmful impacts due to the motion smoothness of input data. That is, the deviated SLB input sample does not change abruptly compared to the ground truth input data. The movement of objects involved in interactions is generally smooth. For example, in Figure 2, if the input data stream captures a ball's movement, the ball's trajectory will not have a sudden change. Therefore, the deviated input sample can still preserve variation trends for extracting consistent features in model training. The inaccuracy of the effect state detector can be regarded as similar to noisy labels, and thus, its quantifiable impact depends on the properties of individual applications. In most cases with limited noisy labels, its harmful impact is within acceptable range. A real-world case study in the next section possesses an inaccurate effect state detector, but adaptive learning still outperforms traditional methods.

4. CPS CASE STUDIES IN MANUFACTURING

In this section, we will use the concept of interactive causality to establish the self-labeling system for two case studies in manufacturing CPS. Manufacturing has been a vibrant field for diverse AI applications. Compared to other fields, manufacturing requires comprehensive domain knowledge and contains rich contextual information for AI processing. In the case studies, we focus on ML applications in manufacturing fields for human action recognition and apply interactive causality to design adaptive ML systems. The post-deployment adaptivity of the ML task models in the two case studies manifests in that the self-labeling system can autonomously capture and annotate data by using the interactive causality in the deployment scenario and retrain task models to achieve better detection accuracy without additional human efforts.

Throughout the production process, interactions between humans, machines, and materials play a vital role. Just as the Industry 4.0 concept revolutionized manufacturing by integrating information technology and operation technology, a new concept called Operator 4.0 is emerging. Operator 4.0 aims to emphasize the crucial roles of humans in terms of operational efficiency, adaptive feedback, and improved productivity (Longo et al., 2022). It is important to recognize that workers are inherently connected to manufacturing systems through their active and reactive interactions with machines and materials. These interactions between workers and machines contain valuable contextual intelligence, contributing to operation integrity, worker intention prediction, and anomaly detection of abnormal machine conditions. To achieve robust worker interaction recognition, further research is necessary to address the following challenges: 1) adapting ML models to account for unpredictable human behavior and variable machine interfaces; 2) automating the model adaptation process, eliminating the need for human intervention; 3) developing a generic solution that can be applied across various manufacturing environments. By addressing these challenges, ML systems can be enhanced to better understand and respond to the dynamic interactions between humans, machines, and materials in a manufacturing process, ultimately leading to more efficient and productive operations.

Figure 3. (a) An example of a simplified SOP for a chemical vapor deposition machine; (b) A finite state machine representation of SOP with the cause and effect states in the form of worker states and machine states, respectively

(a)

Step	Process	PECVD		
		Pump	RF	Heater
1	Verify OK	on	stby	off
2	Set temp.	on	stby	on
3	Vent	on	stby	on
4	Load	on	stby	on
5	Pump down	low vac	stby	on
6	Run Process	on	on	on
7	Purge & Vent	on	stby	on
8	Unload	on	stby	on
9	Reset temp.	on	stby	off
10	Pump down	low vac	stby	off

(b)

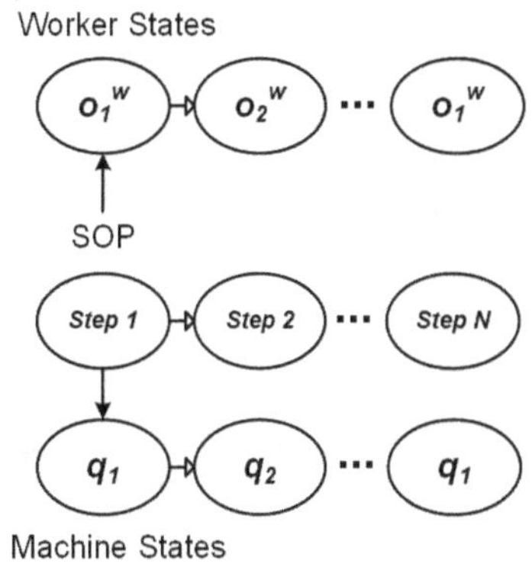

Figure 4. Examples of worker-machine interaction for PlasmaTherm (first row) and E-Beam (second row)

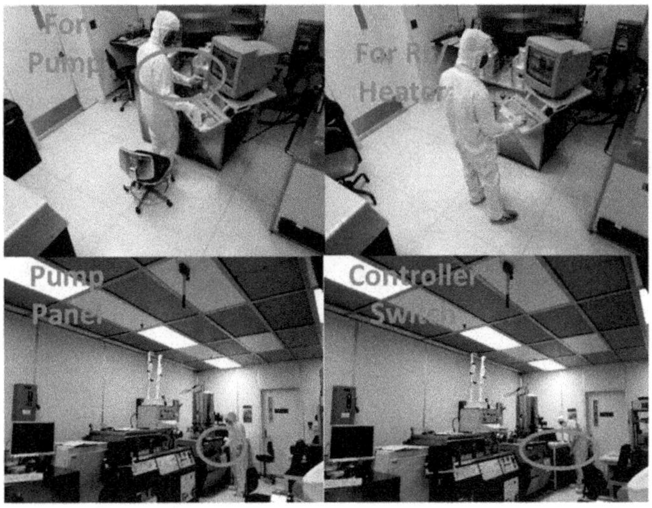

4.1 HMI Recognition in an ICPHS for Semiconductor Manufacturing

In the first case study, an Interactive Cyber Physical Human System (ICPHS) is proposed to tackle the challenges mentioned earlier as elaborated in (Ren & Li, 2022a & 2022b). The ICPHS is designed to address interactive manufacturing processes involving workers utilizing machines and aims to create an adaptive human-machine interaction (HMI) recognition model. In manufacturing, interactions occur between two or more objects, such as workers, machines, or materials, following predefined instructions like standard operating procedures (SOP) in Figure 3. These interactions have a reciprocal effect on each other side, forming causal relationships among interactive objects. By leveraging this causality, the ICPHS collects data from one object and uses the status of the other object for self-labeling. The self-labeled data is then used for retraining and improving the ML model. To demonstrate the practicality of the ICPHS, an experiment is conducted in a multiuser semiconductor manufacturing facility using two machines, as shown in Figure 4. One machine (PlasmaTherm) is fully automated with a programmable logic controller (PLC), while the other (E-Beam) is operated manually. Energy disaggregation techniques are applied to power signals to detect real-time changes in the machine states, which are used to self-label worker actions. The worker actions are detected through pose estimation and a graph convolutional network (GCN) analyzing video data. The GCN is retrained adaptively using the self-labeled dataset, facilitating automated adaptation.

Figure 5. (a) Data processing pipeline; (b) The architecture of the cascaded action recognition model; (c) An example of the energy disaggregation result on PlasmaTherm for two components

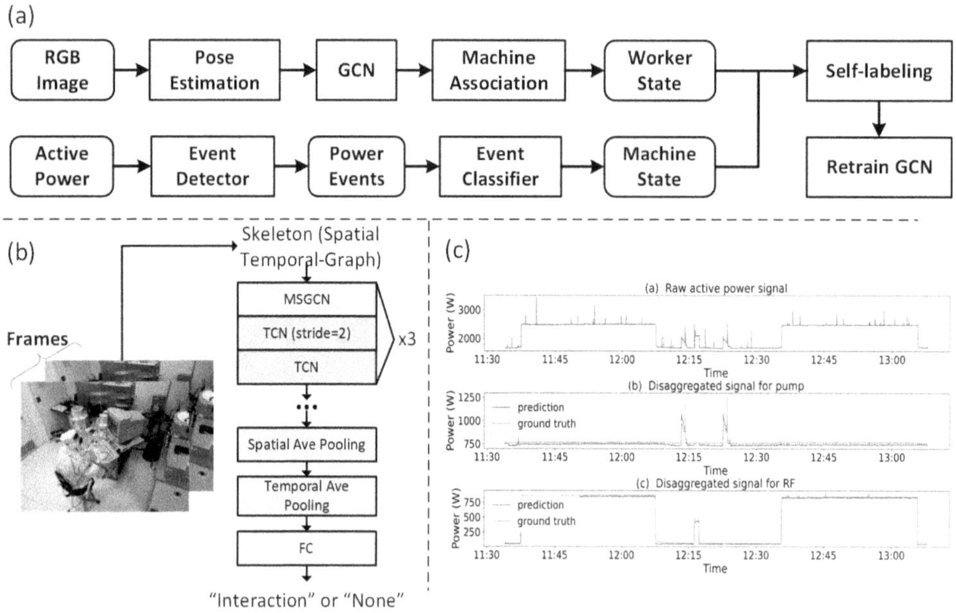

4.1.1. Data Processing Pipeline

Figure 5(a) outlines the comprehensive real-time data processing pipeline. To gather data, each machine is equipped with a webcam and a three-phase power meter. The webcam captures real-time videos of the machine's surroundings, serving as the primary channel, while the power meter records power signals from the entire machine, acting as an effect-observing channel. The video stream is divided into segments and fed into a two-step cascaded ML model as a task model to estimate human activities. The recognized actions are then associated with the corresponding machine based on spatial consistency, establishing the link between human activities and specific machines. Simultaneously, the aggregated power signal undergoes processing to identify the states of machine components. The self-labeling module compares and temporally aligns the information from both streams—the video data indicating human activities and the power signal data indicating machine component states. By combining and cross-referencing these data sources and the predetermined interaction time of corresponding worker and machine state transitions, the self-labeling process becomes more reliable and robust. The ITM in this case study is a lookup table with Gaussian randomness, as the interaction time between worker action and energy event is mainly determined by hardware circuitry response. The interaction time values of each corresponding cause and effect state can be found in (Ren & Li, 2022a).

A method known as an Energy State Detector (ESD) is presented in a previous work (Ren & Li, 2022b) to detect and classify power events and conduct unsupervised energy disaggregation, serving as the effect state detector. The fundamental concept of energy disaggregation involves solving an optimization problem using power signatures from individual machine components. The objective is to explore possible combinations and identify the closest combined signal that closely matches the actual aggregated signal. In this study, our primary aim is to disaggregate the state transitions of each machine component from the main power signal. By employing the developed energy disaggregation method, we can achieve real-time classification of the states of machine components. This classification process is particularly useful as it indicates worker actions taken beforehand for self-labeling. An example of disaggregated results is given in Figure 5(c).

To protect worker privacy in work environments, we utilize OpenPose (Cao et al., 2017) as the initial step to extract skeletons, which consist of 15 joints, excluding the head and foot joints. These extracted skeletons serve as the basis for feature extraction and representation learning from graph-structured data. We extensively explore GCN, specifically the Multiscale GCN (MSGCN) variant (Liu et al., 2020), which effectively captures multiscale structural features from nonlocal neighbors. We incorporate multiscale connections and temporal convolution network (TCN) within the model, as shown in Figure 5(b). By employing these techniques, we achieve robust and privacy-preserving feature extraction and representation learning from graph-structured skeleton data in our model.

4.1.2 Experiments and Results

The PlasmaTherm machine interface comprises a keyboard with a monitor, and machine operations are carried out by interacting with this keyboard. It has four components, namely an RF generator, pump, heater, and the main body. The system was deployed on PlasmaTherm for 1.5 months to collect and label samples automatically. A total of 139 self-labeled positive (interaction) samples were collected during this period. It was discovered that 23 samples related to RF operation were incorrectly labeled due to variations in the on-set RF operation response time. To address this issue, an automated post-processing filter was proposed, which successfully filtered out 22 mislabeled samples, leaving 117 positive samples with an improved label error rate of 0.85%. 100 samples of each class are selected from a public dataset (Liu et al., 2019) for pretraining.

To demonstrate the adaptive learning capability and show the accuracy improvement over time, self-labeled samples were grouped in chronological order: April 8 to April 22 (39 samples per class), April 8 to May 6 (78 per class), and April 8 to May 21 (117 per class). The evaluation results in Table 2 show that as more self-labeled data is used for retraining, the detection accuracy gradually improves. With the full 117 self-labeled data, the detection accuracy is 12.5% higher than the initial accuracy and at least 6.9% higher than that of benchmark methods. This demonstrates the effectiveness of the proposed adaptive learning mechanism in improving performance compared to traditional methods.

Table 2. Experimental results of PlasmaTherm

Method	Dataset	Precision	Recall	F1 score	Acc
Ours	100	0.843	0.912	0.869	85.7%
Ours	100+39 (04/22)	0.946	0.980	0.962	96.0%
Ours	100+78 (05/06)	0.956	0.980	0.968	96.6%
Ours	100+117(05/21)	0.981	0.985	0.983	98.2%
K-means	100+117(05/21)	0.592	1	0.744	64.5%
P&C (Su et al., 2020)	100+117(05/21)	0.858	0.942	0.899	89.0%
CrosSCLR (Li, G. et al., 2021)	100+117(05/21)	0.879	0.964	0.919	91.3%

Following the successful demonstration on a PLC-controlled machine, we now present the results obtained from a manually operated E-Beam machine. In contrast to the PLC machine, the E-Beam machine features four functional components, each with multiple control panels and switches located at different positions, as depicted in Figure 4. Due to its manual nature, this machine involves worker interactions through various interfaces positioned at different locations, leading to complexity in recognizing these interactions accurately. Additionally, in manual machine operations, workers tend to engage with the interfaces while adopting different static postures, such as standing, sitting, squatting, or bending. This adds further complexity to the interaction recognition process.

The system was deployed for data collection and self-labeling for 1.5 months. During this period, a total of 211 positive samples were collected. 16 samples were mislabeled due to response time variations. 500 samples of each class are selected for pretraining. After applying a post-processing filter to eliminate improper samples, 141 self-labeled positive samples remained, and correspondingly, 141 self-labeled negative samples were randomly selected, with no mislabeled samples in the negative samples. The label noise level for the self-labeled positive samples was found to be 7.8%. Table 3 presents the evaluation results for the E-Beam machine. The model accuracy experiences a substantial boost of 9.9% through retraining with self-labeled samples, which further verifies the practicality and effectiveness of the proposed adaptive learning framework.

Table 3. Experimental results of E-Beam

Dataset	Precision	Recall	F1 score	Acc
500	0.800	0.699	0.736	75.2%
500+141 (05/21)	0.893	0.802	0.843	85.1%

4.2 Operator Intention Recognition in Manufacturing Human-Robot Collaboration

Manual assembly exists in many manufacturing sectors. While repetitive assemblies tend to be replaced by robots, certain assembly processes still require operator engagement with assistive collaborative robotic arms (Cobot.) In these scenarios, cobots help operators by instantly and seamlessly transporting needed parts to an assembly bench that is easily accessible by operators. Operators receive and assemble parts following a predefined sequence. A successful collaboration requires a high throughput of assembled products, and thus, the efficiency between robot and human operators is critical. To achieve a seamless cooperator, cobots are required to recognize the assembly steps and operators' intentions in a timely manner and act properly to move parts (Zhang et al., 2022). Currently, for safety reasons, many in-use cobots in industry act in a passive manner where robots need to receive operator commands (e.g., by pushing a button) to execute the next steps. While safety has been strictly ensured in this way, efficiency is compromised due to the lack of predictability. There are several methods empowered by DL-based vision technology to recognize the product status or worker actions in order to infer the next steps. These data-driven models can capture and learn the consistent patterns representing the intentions of moving to the next assembly steps after training on a pre-collected and labeled dataset.

Figure 6. Environment setup of the manual assembly case study

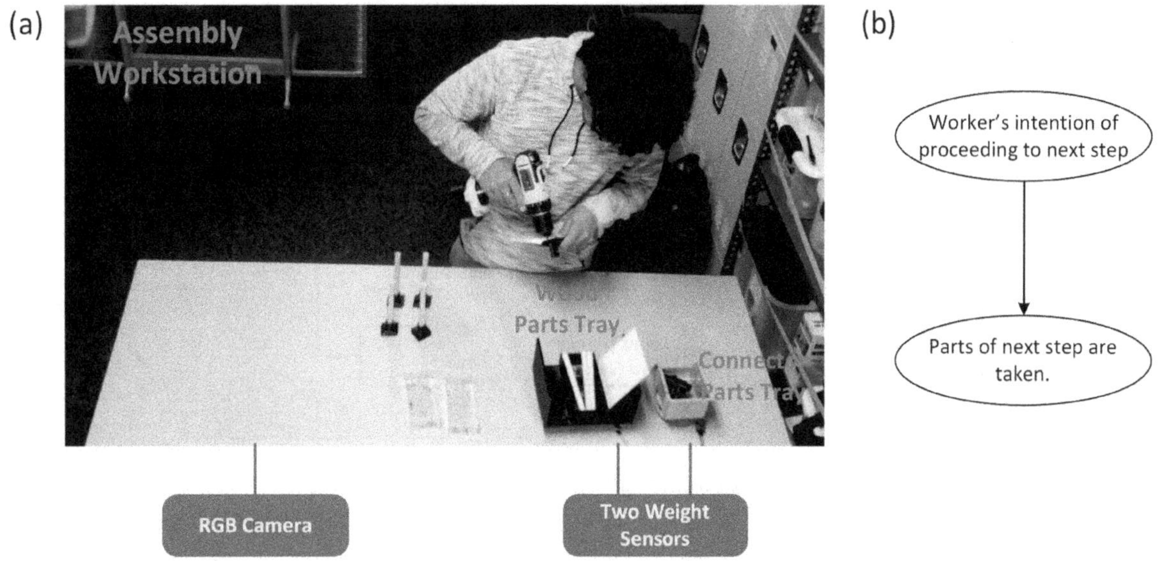

In this case study, we focus on a manual assembly scenario to apply the IC method and develop an adaptive ML system for intention recognition. We picked a standard chair assembly (Zeylikman et al., 2018) as the demonstration. It requires 12 steps and two categories of parts: wood and plastic. An SOP for this chair assembly is established to guide the interactions between operators and materials. In this study, the known causality embedded in the human-material interaction can be summarized as: *the completion of the current step causes the pickup of the next part.* The cause event can be defined as the intention which needs to be recognized for collaborating with robots. The effect is that the next part is picked. The experiment environment is shown in Figure 6(a), and causality is summarized in Figure 6(b). Two trays are utilized to hold each group of parts. Given this domain knowledge, two effect observers are designed to be weight sensors to capture the distinguishable weight change of trays holding the spare parts. The effect observers can tell if a certain part has been taken, indicating the completion of previous steps. The cause data stream is a camera mounted on the top to view the operator's body gesture and assembly status. Figure 7 describes the system architecture of the proposed adaptive AI system for operator intention recognition.

Figure 7. System architecture of the manual assembly study: (a) and (b) provide examples of worker intentions and weight changes as effects respectively; (c) shows the data processing pipeline

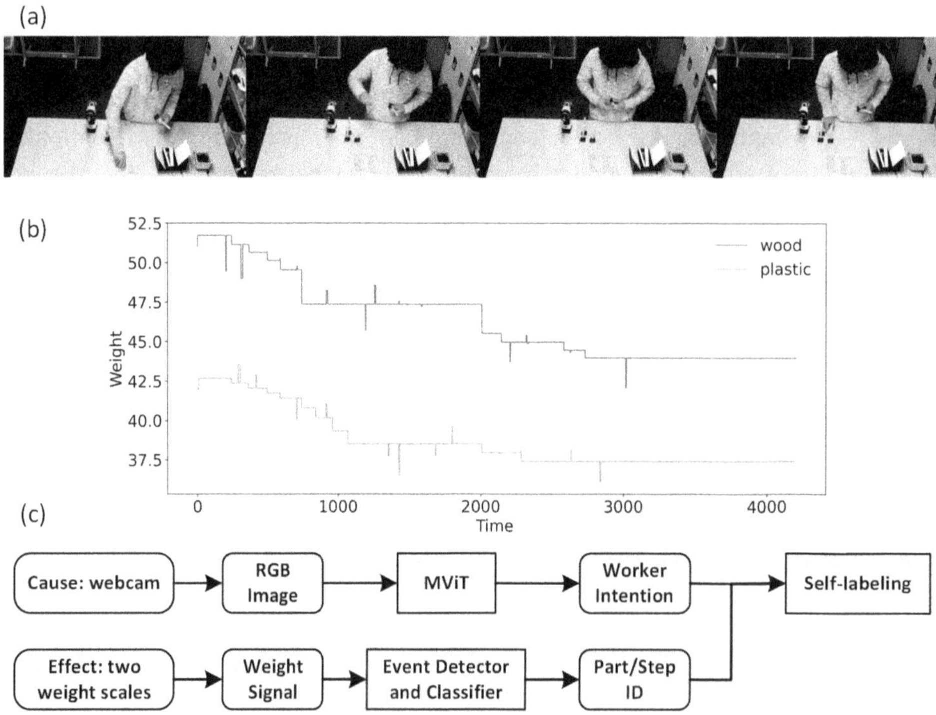

The system consists of three computational models: the effect state detector, the interaction time model, and the task model. Once the causal relationship is identified, an effect state detector needs to be designed to recognize the effect states. Two weight sensors are used individually for each part tray. The effect state detection follows the procedure where state transitions need to be identified first, followed by state recognition. A detailed data flow diagram is shown in Figure 7(c). In terms of the interaction time model, an XGBoost regressor is applied to infer individual interaction time. There are two effects captured by two sensors, and thus, two ITMs are implemented. The effect data for ITM input is the concatenation of the raw weight data from two sensors and the effect labels. XGBoost uses a 0.01 learning rate and 2000 estimators. The task model for recognizing cause states uses a vision transformer model for videos. Transformers have recently been proven effective for vision tasks. Since then, many transformer-based models have been proposed (Arnab et al., 2021). This study chooses a multi-scale vision transformer (MViT) as the task model due to its relatively lightweight and good performance (Li et al., 2022).

Dataset. The dataset is collected for the validation purpose of simulating post-deployment model adaptation. Four operators conducted the complete assembly 150 times. Three streams of data from two weight sensors and one camera are saved for the entire assembly duration. Each assembly can be segmented into 11 video classes, and thus, a total of 1650 video samples. For training, the videos are resized into 224*224 resolution and 4 fps. Each video clip representing the operator's intentions is sliced to have the same temporal length of 4 seconds. The weight sensor data is recorded at 10 Hz. For validation purposes, the entire dataset is manually labeled with each cause and effect state and the interaction time between each cause-effect pair. The dataset is split into a pretraining set, self-labeled set, validation set, and test set, with each set having 350, 700, 200, and 400 samples, respectively. The pretraining set is used to train ITM models and pretrain task models. The self-labeled set is autonomously self-labeled by effect state detectors and ITMs for the adaptive retraining of the task model. The self-labeled set is used as the unlabeled training set when training other SSL methods for comparison.

In this case study, the self-labeling method is compared to the fully supervised and several recent semi-supervised methods (Zhang et al., 2021; Wang et al., 2022). The results are shown in Table 4. In this experiment, there is no apparent data shift between training and test sets, but the self-labeling still shows promising outcomes. The ITM reaches an R2 score of 0.677 and a mean absolute error of 1.97. It can be observed in Table 4 that the self-labeling method can reach 88.2% accuracy, only 3.9% less than the fully supervised one, while other semi-supervised learning methods are all below 80% accuracy. In this experiment, the system only relies on automatic post-deployment self-labeling by analyzing the weight sensors from the effect observing channels.

The result further demonstrates the applicability of the proposed self-labeling to autonomously adapt ML task models without the need for manual data annotation in a complex interaction scenario with more than 10 classes.

Table 4. Experimental results of the manual assembly case study

Method	Accuracy (%)
PseudoLabel (2013)	72.2
MixMatch (2019)	76.9
FixMatch (2020)	76.4
FlexMatch (2021)	60.4
PseudoLabelFlex (2021)	79.6
FreeMatch (2023)	64.9
Fully supervised	92.1
Self-labeling	88.2

5. PROSPECTUS OF FUTURE DEVELOPMENT AND CPS APPLICATIONS

This work focuses on dynamic scenarios with time series data and dynamic ML models. Different from the traditional static ML paradigm, the potential data distribution shifts require ML models to be dynamically adaptive to changes, which differentiates this work from traditional fields. The future directions of the proposed interactive causality-based adaptive learning can be summarized into three key aspects: theory, methodology, and application. In terms of theoretical progression, this chapter confines its scrutiny to rigorous proof within the realm of 1-dimensional cases characterized by specific systems of differential equations. A prospective trajectory involves the extension of this proof to encompass n-dimensional scenarios, which are characterized by more intricate interaction conditions. For n-dimensional dynamical systems, each individual system is intrinsically interconnected across its multiple dimensions. When two such systems interact, their interconnections extend along certain dimensions, further complicating the study of these interactions within the context of self-labeling scenarios (Luo, 2012; Stankovski et al., 2019). The existing approach necessitates an initial integration step to solve the system of differential equations, followed by a comparison of the relative relationships among the four methods: forward and backward self-labeling, fully supervised learning, and semi-supervised learning. A future exploration involves the incorporation of mathematical tools to circumvent the challenges associated with n-dimensional system integrals. Furthermore, an enhanced and comprehensive comparative analysis between self-labeling and semi-supervised learning needs attention. This could provide more nuanced insights into their respective strengths and limitations. Another intriguing avenue for investigation pertains to theoretically quantifying the impact of inaccuracies in inferring interaction times and detecting effect states on the learning process of the model. This quantification needs to be integrated into the broader framework of general machine learning theory, thus serving as a valuable benchmark for designing interaction time models and effect state detectors.

For methodology, an influential aspect for the future is the exploration of the usage of knowledge graph (KG) in causality representation (Chen et al., 2020; Lyu et al., 2023) and new knowledge acquisition (Yoo & Jeong, 2020). The new knowledge can represent found anomalies during deployment. One way to do so is by combining existing unsupervised pattern recognition and causal discovery methods to find and incorporate anomalies into KG. Another future idea is to mimic how humans gain new knowledge by utilizing existing knowledge to ask questions. As we grow up, this is always the fundamental way we learn the world via interaction (Begus & Southgate, 2018). Therefore, it is expected to develop a method of expanding KG by asking questions. Using ChatGPT as an example, most of the time, human users ask GPT questions and expect answers. ChatGPT will rarely ask for clarifications from human users (Yiu et al., 2023). Thus, asking questions is an effective means to gain knowledge. A pathway has been conceived based on the interactive causality to expand KG. Initially, we still expect humans with different roles in different application scenarios, such as technicians in manufacturing scenarios, to ask questions to the domain KG based on users' experience and knowledge. An algorithm with a graph search engine can be designed to explore the existing KG for related nodes based on users' questions. These found nodes can be utilized by users to develop solutions for the asked questions. The developed solution can potentially introduce new nodes represented by new data streams that can be added to the KG and used for future self-labeling purposes. In the foreseeable future, this entire pathway can be automated and initiated by AI asking questions.

In terms of applications, the proposed self-labeling has great potential in CPS with limited datasets and AI expertise such as smart manufacturing and precision agriculture (Sharma et al., 2020). The inherent multimodal nature of CPS paves the way to explore pervasive applications of self-labeling. The rich multimodal signals in CPS can be utilized to obtain additional observing channels. CPS involves various interactions among the elements inside, where causation can easily be found as additional observing channels. In domains like manufacturing, processes including welding and assembly stand to benefit significantly from adaptive AI perception systems that leverage extracted and modeled causal relationships. Consider an adaptive AI system tailored to recognize interactions during manual welding. This entails understanding how hands interface with welding guns and filling rods, and how factors like power levels and temperatures interplay with materials (Mahadevan et al., 2021). Self-labeling can augment these interactions, elevating AI perception and mitigating human errors. Autonomous driving stands out as another promising domain. Self-labeling holds the potential to refine driving intention recognition models (Vellenga et al., 2022), making them adaptable to novel and unforeseen situations. For instance, certain vehicular behaviors can be labeled as intentions (causes) for subsequent perceivable effects.

However, for effective self-labeling research development, the need to establish standardized metrics and benchmark datasets shared within the community becomes apparent. These datasets should cater to the unique requirements of dynamic data streams and known causal structures, deviating from conventional static datasets like image recognition benchmarks (Lin et al., 2014). The absence of such public datasets underscores the necessity of creating benchmarks that represent typical CPS application scenarios, facilitating diverse algorithmic developments in self-labeling. Moreover, in many CPS applications, a pivotal aspect involves modeling domain knowledge and extracting causal graphs of interactive events for self-labeling purposes. AI tools, like large language models, could potentially aid in summarizing causality from natural language inputs, thus streamlining this knowledge extraction process (Yiu et al., 2023).

In conclusion, interactive causality along with its applications in self-labeling introduces novel paradigms to the realm of adaptive machine learning systems. It opens the door to a multitude of promising research avenues and potential applications waiting to be explored.

REFERENCES

Achouch, M., Dimitrova, M., Ziane, K., Sattarpanah Karganroudi, S., Dhouib, R., Ibrahim, H., & Adda, M. (2022). On predictive maintenance in industry 4.0: Overview, models, and challenges. *Applied Sciences (Basel, Switzerland)*, *12*(16), 8081. doi:10.3390/app12168081

Ansari, F., Glawar, R., & Sihn, W. (2020). Prescriptive maintenance of CPPS by integrating multimodal data with dynamic Bayesian networks. In *Machine Learning for Cyber Physical Systems: Selected papers from the International Conference ML4CPS 2017* (pp. 1-8). Springer Berlin Heidelberg. 10.1007/978-3-662-59084-3_1

Arnab, A., Dehghani, M., Heigold, G., Sun, C., Lučić, M., & Schmid, C. (2021). Vivit: A video vision transformer. In *Proceedings of the IEEE/CVF international conference on computer vision* (pp. 6836-6846). IEEE.

Asano, Y. M., Rupprecht, C., & Vedaldi, A. (2019, September). Self-labelling via simultaneous clustering and representation learning. In *International Conference on Learning Representations*. IEEE.

Begus, K., & Southgate, V. (2018). Curious learners: How infants' motivation to learn shapes and is shaped by infants' interactions with the social world. *Active learning from infancy to childhood: Social motivation, cognition, and linguistic mechanisms,* 13-37.

Bombelli, L., Lee, J., Meyer, D., & Sorkin, R. D. (1987). Space-time as a causal set. *Physical Review Letters*, *59*(5), 521–524. doi:10.1103/PhysRevLett.59.521 PMID:10035795

Bramley, N. R., Gerstenberg, T., Mayrhofer, R., & Lagnado, D. A. (2018). Time in causal structure learning. *Journal of Experimental Psychology. Learning, Memory, and Cognition*, *44*(12), 1880–1910. doi:10.1037/xlm0000548 PMID:29745682

Brännström, N. (2009). Averaging in weakly coupled discrete dynamical systems. *Journal of Nonlinear Mathematical Physics*, *16*(4), 465–487. doi:10.1142/S1402925109000492

Cao, Z., Simon, T., Wei, S. E., & Sheikh, Y. (2017). Realtime multi-person 2d pose estimation using part affinity fields. In *Proceedings of the IEEE conference on computer vision and pattern recognition* (pp. 7291-7299). IEEE. 10.1109/CVPR.2017.143

Chen, X., Jia, S., & Xiang, Y. (2020). A review: Knowledge reasoning over knowledge graph. *Expert Systems with Applications*, *141*, 112948. doi:10.1016/j.eswa.2019.112948

Chen, X., Mersch, B., Nunes, L., Marcuzzi, R., Vizzo, I., Behley, J., & Stachniss, C. (2022). Automatic labeling to generate training data for online LiDAR-based moving object segmentation. *IEEE Robotics and Automation Letters*, *7*(3), 6107–6114. doi:10.1109/LRA.2022.3166544 PMID:35832507

Childs, C. M., & Washburn, N. R. (2019). Embedding domain knowledge for machine learning of complex material systems. *MRS Communications*, *9*(3), 806–820. doi:10.1557/mrc.2019.90

Davis, J., Malkani, H., Dyck, J., Korambath, P., & Wise, J. (2020). Cyberinfrastructure for the democratization of smart manufacturing. In *Smart Manufacturing* (pp. 83–116). Elsevier. doi:10.1016/B978-0-12-820027-8.00004-6

Dayal, A., Aishwarya, M., Abhilash, S., Mohan, C. K., Kumar, A., & Cenkeramaddi, L. R. (2023). Adversarial Unsupervised Domain Adaptation for Hand Gesture Recognition Using Thermal Images. *IEEE Sensors Journal*, *23*(4), 3493–3504. doi:10.1109/JSEN.2023.3235379

Deaton, A., & Cartwright, N. (2018). Understanding and misunderstanding randomized controlled trials. *Social Science & Medicine*, *210*, 2–21. doi:10.1016/j.socscimed.2017.12.005 PMID:29331519

Demrozi, F., Jereghi, M., & Pravadelli, G. (2021, March). Towards the automatic data annotation for human activity recognition based on wearables and BLE beacons. In *2021 IEEE International Symposium on Inertial Sensors and Systems (INERTIAL)* (pp. 1-4). IEEE. 10.1109/INERTIAL51137.2021.9430457

Donovan, R. P., Kim, Y. G., Manzo, A., Ren, Y., Bian, S., Wu, T., Purawat, S., Helvajian, H., Wheaton, M., Li, B., & Li, G. P. (2022). Smart connected worker edge platform for smart manufacturing: Part 2—Implementation and on-site deployment case study. *Journal of Advanced Manufacturing and Processing*, *4*(4), e10130. doi:10.1002/amp2.10130

Du, S., Song, G., Han, L., & Hong, H. (2017). Temporal causal inference with time lag. *Neural Computation*, *30*(1), 271–291. doi:10.1162/neco_a_01028 PMID:29064787

Fredriksson, T., Mattos, D. I., Bosch, J., & Olsson, H. H. (2020, November). Data labeling: An empirical investigation into industrial challenges and mitigation strategies. In *International Conference on Product-Focused Software Process Improvement* (pp. 202-216). Cham: Springer International Publishing. 10.1007/978-3-030-64148-1_13

Garg, S., Wu, Y., Balakrishnan, S., & Lipton, Z. (2020). A unified view of label shift estimation. *Advances in Neural Information Processing Systems*, *33*, 3290–3300.

Ghobakhloo, M. (2020). Industry 4.0, digitization, and opportunities for sustainability. *Journal of Cleaner Production*, *252*, 119869. doi:10.1016/j.jclepro.2019.119869

Gollob, H. F., & Reichardt, C. S. (1987). Taking account of time lags in causal models. *Child Development*, *58*(1), 80–92. doi:10.2307/1130293 PMID:3816351

Gong, M., Zhang, K., Liu, T., Tao, D., Glymour, C., & Schölkopf, B. (2016, June). Domain adaptation with conditional transferable components. In *International conference on machine learning* (pp. 2839-2848). PMLR.

Granger, C. W. (1969). Investigating causal relations by econometric models and cross-spectral methods. *Econometrica*, *37*(3), 424–438. doi:10.2307/1912791

Hu, R. L., Granderson, J., Auslander, D. M., & Agogino, A. (2019). Design of machine learning models with domain experts for automated sensor selection for energy fault detection. *Applied Energy*, *235*, 117–128. doi:10.1016/j.apenergy.2018.10.107

Huda, S., Miah, S., Hassan, M. M., Islam, R., Yearwood, J., Alrubaian, M., & Almogren, A. (2017). Defending unknown attacks on cyber-physical systems by semi-supervised approach and available unlabeled data. *Information Sciences*, *379*, 211–228. doi:10.1016/j.ins.2016.09.041

Jaber, A., Kocaoglu, M., Shanmugam, K., & Bareinboim, E. (2020). Causal discovery from soft interventions with unknown targets: Characterization and learning. *Advances in Neural Information Processing Systems*, *33*, 9551–9561.

Kerrigan, D., Hullman, J., & Bertini, E. (2021). A survey of domain knowledge elicitation in applied machine learning. *Multimodal Technologies and Interaction*, *5*(12), 73. doi:10.3390/mti5120073

Kim, Y. G., Donovan, R. P., Ren, Y., Bian, S., Wu, T., Purawat, S., Manzo, A. J., Altintas, I., Li, B., & Li, G. P. (2022). Smart connected worker edge platform for smart manufacturing: Part 1—Architecture and platform design. *Journal of Advanced Manufacturing and Processing*, *4*(4), e10129. doi:10.1002/amp2.10129

Kocaoglu, M., Shakkottai, S., Dimakis, A. G., Caramanis, C., & Vishwanath, S. (2020). Applications of common entropy for causal inference. *Advances in Neural Information Processing Systems*, *33*, 17514–17525.

Kocarev, L., & Parlitz, U. (1996). Generalized synchronization, predictability, and equivalence of unidirectionally coupled dynamical systems. *Physical Review Letters*, *76*(11), 1816–1819. doi:10.1103/PhysRevLett.76.1816 PMID:10060528

Kouw, W. M., & Loog, M. (2019). A review of domain adaptation without target labels. *IEEE Transactions on Pattern Analysis and Machine Intelligence*, *43*(3), 766–785. doi:10.1109/TPAMI.2019.2945942 PMID:31603771

Le, T. D., Hoang, T., Li, J., Liu, L., Liu, H., & Hu, S. (2016). A fast PC algorithm for high dimensional causal discovery with multi-core PCs. *IEEE/ACM Transactions on Computational Biology and Bioinformatics*, *16*(5), 1483–1495. doi:10.1109/TCBB.2016.2591526 PMID:27429444

Lee, D. H. (2013, June). Pseudo-label: The simple and efficient semi-supervised learning method for deep neural networks. In *Workshop on challenges in representation learning, ICML* (Vol. 3, No. 2, p. 896).

Li, G., Yuan, C., Kamarthi, S., Moghaddam, M., & Jin, X. (2021). Data science skills and domain knowledge requirements in the manufacturing industry: A gap analysis. *Journal of Manufacturing Systems*, *60*, 692–706. doi:10.1016/j.jmsy.2021.07.007

Li, L., Wang, M., Ni, B., Wang, H., Yang, J., & Zhang, W. (2021). 3d human action representation learning via cross-view consistency pursuit. In *Proceedings of the IEEE/CVF conference on computer vision and pattern recognition* (pp. 4741-4750). IEEE.

Li, Y., Wu, C. Y., Fan, H., Mangalam, K., Xiong, B., Malik, J., & Feichtenhofer, C. (2022). Mvitv2: Improved multiscale vision transformers for classification and detection. In *Proceedings of the IEEE/CVF Conference on Computer Vision and Pattern Recognition* (pp. 4804-4814). IEEE. 10.1109/CVPR52688.2022.00476

Lin, T. Y., Maire, M., Belongie, S., Hays, J., Perona, P., Ramanan, D., & Zitnick, C. L. (2014). Microsoft coco: Common objects in context. In Computer Vision–ECCV 2014: 13th European Conference, Zurich, Switzerland, September 6-12, 2014 [Springer International Publishing.]. *Proceedings*, *13*(Part V), 740–755.

Liu, J., Shahroudy, A., Perez, M., Wang, G., Duan, L. Y., & Kot, A. C. (2019). Ntu rgb+ d 120: A large-scale benchmark for 3d human activity understanding. *IEEE Transactions on Pattern Analysis and Machine Intelligence*, *42*(10), 2684–2701. doi:10.1109/TPAMI.2019.2916873 PMID:31095476

Liu, Z., Zhang, H., Chen, Z., Wang, Z., & Ouyang, W. (2020). Disentangling and unifying graph convolutions for skeleton-based action recognition. In *Proceedings of the IEEE/CVF conference on computer vision and pattern recognition* (pp. 143-152). IEEE. 10.1109/CVPR42600.2020.00022

Longo, F., Nicoletti, L., & Padovano, A. (2022). New perspectives and results for Smart Operators in industry 4.0: A human-centered approach. *Computers & Industrial Engineering*, *163*, 107824. doi:10.1016/j.cie.2021.107824

Lu, J., Liu, A., Dong, F., Gu, F., Gama, J., & Zhang, G. (2018). Learning under concept drift: A review. *IEEE Transactions on Knowledge and Data Engineering*, *31*(12), 2346–2363.

Luo, A. C. (2012). *Dynamical System Interactions. Discontinuous Dynamical Systems*, 623-683.

Lyu, K., Tian, Y., Shang, Y., Zhou, T., Yang, Z., Liu, Q., Yao, X., Zhang, P., Chen, J., & Li, J. (2023). Causal knowledge graph construction and evaluation for clinical decision support of diabetic nephropathy. *Journal of Biomedical Informatics*, *139*, 104298. doi:10.1016/j.jbi.2023.104298 PMID:36731730

Madni, A. M., Sievers, M., & Madni, C. C. (2018). Adaptive Cyber-Physical-Human Systems: Exploiting Cognitive Modeling and Machine Learning in the Control Loop. *Insight (American Society of Ophthalmic Registered Nurses)*, *21*(3), 87–93.

Mahadevan, R., Jagan, A., Pavithran, L., Shrivastava, A., & Selvaraj, S. K. (2021). Intelligent welding by using machine learning techniques. *Materials Today: Proceedings*, *46*, 7402–7410. doi:10.1016/j.matpr.2020.12.1149

Malinsky, D., & Danks, D. (2018). Causal discovery algorithms: A practical guide. *Philosophy Compass*, *13*(1), e12470. doi:10.1111/phc3.12470

Mirchevska, V., Luštrek, M., & Gams, M. (2014). Combining domain knowledge and machine learning for robust fall detection. *Expert Systems: International Journal of Knowledge Engineering and Neural Networks*, *31*(2), 163–175. doi:10.1111/exsy.12019

Narwane, V. S., Raut, R. D., Gardas, B. B., Narkhede, B. E., & Awasthi, A. (2022). Examining smart manufacturing challenges in the context of micro, small, and medium enterprises. *International Journal of Computer Integrated Manufacturing*, *35*(12), 1395–1412. doi:10.1080/0951192X.2022.2078508

Paluš, M., Krakovská, A., Jakubík, J., & Chvosteková, M. (2018). Causality, dynamical systems and the arrow of time. *Chaos (Woodbury, N.Y.)*, *28*(7), 075307. doi:10.1063/1.5019944 PMID:30070495

Pearl, J. (2009). *Causality*. Cambridge university press. doi:10.1017/CBO9780511803161

Prosperi, M., Guo, Y., Sperrin, M., Koopman, J. S., Min, J. S., He, X., Rich, S., Wang, M., Buchan, I. E., & Bian, J. (2020). Causal inference and counterfactual prediction in machine learning for actionable healthcare. *Nature Machine Intelligence*, *2*(7), 369–375. doi:10.1038/s42256-020-0197-y

Qiu, C., Li, K., Li, B., Mao, X., He, S., Hao, C., & Yin, L. (2022). Semi-supervised graph convolutional network to predict position-and speed-dependent tool tip dynamics with limited labeled data. *Mechanical Systems and Signal Processing*, *164*, 108225. doi:10.1016/j.ymssp.2021.108225

Ramírez-Sanz, J. M., Maestro-Prieto, J.-A., Arnaiz-González, Á., & Bustillo, A. (2023). Semi-supervised learning for industrial fault detection and diagnosis: A systemic review. *ISA Transactions*, *143*, 255–270. doi:10.1016/j.isatra.2023.09.027 PMID:37778919

Ren, Y., & Li, G. P. (2022). An interactive and adaptive learning cyber physical human system for manufacturing with a case study in worker machine interactions. *IEEE Transactions on Industrial Informatics*, *18*(10), 6723–6732. doi:10.1109/TII.2022.3150795

Ren, Y., & Li, G. P. (2022). A contextual sensor system for non-intrusive machine status and energy monitoring. *Journal of Manufacturing Systems*, *62*, 87–101. doi:10.1016/j.jmsy.2021.11.010

Ren, Y., Yen, A. H., & Li, G. P. (2023). A Self-Labeling Method for Adaptive Machine Learning by Interactive Causality. *IEEE Transactions on Artificial Intelligence*, 1–10. doi:10.1109/TAI.2023.3311782

Richens, J. G., Lee, C. M., & Johri, S. (2020). Improving the accuracy of medical diagnosis with causal machine learning. *Nature Communications*, *11*(1), 3923. doi:10.1038/s41467-020-17419-7 PMID:32782264

Schneider, S., Rusak, E., Eck, L., Bringmann, O., Brendel, W., & Bethge, M. (2020). Improving robustness against common corruptions by covariate shift adaptation. *Advances in Neural Information Processing Systems*, *33*, 11539–11551.

Schölkopf, B. (2022). Causality for machine learning. In Probabilistic and Causal Inference: The Works of Judea Pearl (pp. 765-804). ACM. doi:10.1145/3501714.3501755

Sharma, A., Jain, A., Gupta, P., & Chowdary, V. (2020). Machine learning applications for precision agriculture: A comprehensive review. *IEEE Access : Practical Innovations, Open Solutions*, *9*, 4843–4873. doi:10.1109/ACCESS.2020.3048415

Stankovski, T., Pereira, T., McClintock, P. V., & Stefanovska, A. (2019). Coupling functions: Dynamical interaction mechanisms in the physical, biological and social sciences. *Philosophical Transactions. Series A, Mathematical, Physical, and Engineering Sciences*, *377*(2160), 20190039. doi:10.1098/rsta.2019.0039 PMID:31656134

Su, K., Liu, X., & Shlizerman, E. (2020). Predict & cluster: Unsupervised skeleton based action recognition. In *Proceedings of the IEEE/CVF Conference on Computer Vision and Pattern Recognition* (pp. 9631-9640). IEEE. 10.1109/CVPR42600.2020.00965

Sun, C., Ma, M., Zhao, Z., Tian, S., Yan, R., & Chen, X. (2018). Deep transfer learning based on sparse autoencoder for remaining useful life prediction of tool in manufacturing. *IEEE Transactions on Industrial Informatics*, *15*(4), 2416–2425. doi:10.1109/TII.2018.2881543

Sun, X., Yang, S., & Zhao, C. (2022). Lightweight Industrial Image Classifier based on Federated Few-Shot Learning. *IEEE Transactions on Industrial Informatics*.

Van Engelen, J. E., & Hoos, H. H. (2020). A survey on semi-supervised learning. *Machine Learning*, *109*(2), 373–440. doi:10.1007/s10994-019-05855-6

Vellenga, K., Steinhauer, H. J., Karlsson, A., Falkman, G., Rhodin, A., & Koppisetty, A. C. (2022). Driver intention recognition: State-of-the-art review. *IEEE Open Journal of Intelligent Transportation Systems*, *3*, 602–616. doi:10.1109/OJITS.2022.3197296

Wang, H., Li, Z., & Wang, H. (2021). Few-shot steel surface defect detection. *IEEE Transactions on Instrumentation and Measurement*, *71*, 1–12.

Wang, P., & Gao, R. X. (2020). Transfer learning for enhanced machine fault diagnosis in manufacturing. *CIRP Annals*, *69*(1), 413–416. doi:10.1016/j.cirp.2020.04.074

Wang, T., Qiao, M., Zhang, M., Yang, Y., & Snoussi, H. (2020). Data-driven prognostic method based on self-supervised learning approaches for fault detection. *Journal of Intelligent Manufacturing*, *31*(7), 1611–1619. doi:10.1007/s10845-018-1431-x

Wang, Y., Chen, H., Heng, Q., Hou, W., Fan, Y., Wu, Z., & Xie, X. (2022). Freematch: Self-adaptive thresholding for semi-supervised learning. arXiv preprint arXiv:2205.07246.

Wilson, G., & Cook, D. J. (2020). A survey of unsupervised deep domain adaptation. [TIST]. *ACM Transactions on Intelligent Systems and Technology*, *11*(5), 1–46. doi:10.1145/3400066 PMID:34336374

Xu, R., Hao, R., & Huang, B. (2022). Efficient surface defect detection using self-supervised learning strategy and segmentation network. *Advanced Engineering Informatics*, *52*, 101566. doi:10.1016/j.aei.2022.101566

Yan, H., Guo, Y., & Yang, C. (2021, December). Augmented self-labeling for source-free unsupervised domain adaptation. In *NeurIPS 2021 Workshop on Distribution Shifts: Connecting Methods and Applications*. IEEE.

Yang, X., Song, Z., King, I., & Xu, Z. (2022). A survey on deep semi-supervised learning. *IEEE Transactions on Knowledge and Data Engineering*.

Yang, Z., Al-Dahidi, S., Baraldi, P., Zio, E., & Montelatici, L. (2019). A novel concept drift detection method for incremental learning in nonstationary environments. *IEEE Transactions on Neural Networks and Learning Systems*, *31*(1), 309–320. doi:10.1109/TNNLS.2019.2900956 PMID:30932852

Yiu, E., Kosoy, E., & Gopnik, A. (2023). Transmission versus truth, imitation versus innovation: What children can do that large language and language-and-vision models cannot (yet). *Perspectives on Psychological Science*, 17456916231201401. doi:10.1177/17456916231201401 PMID:37883796

Yoo, S., & Jeong, O. (2020). Automating the expansion of a knowledge graph. *Expert Systems with Applications*, *141*, 112965. doi:10.1016/j.eswa.2019.112965

Zeylikman, S., Widder, S., Roncone, A., Mangin, O., & Scassellati, B. (2018, October). The HRC model set for human-robot collaboration research. In *2018 IEEE/RSJ International Conference on Intelligent Robots and Systems (IROS)* (pp. 1845-1852). IEEE. 10.1109/IROS.2018.8593858

Zhan, Z., Zhou, J., & Xu, B. (2022). Fabric defect classification using prototypical network of few-shot learning algorithm. *Computers in Industry*, *138*, 103628. doi:10.1016/j.compind.2022.103628

Zhang, B., Wang, Y., Hou, W., Wu, H., Wang, J., Okumura, M., & Shinozaki, T. (2021). Flexmatch: Boosting semi-supervised learning with curriculum pseudo labeling. *Advances in Neural Information Processing Systems*, *34*, 18408–18419.

Zhang, D., Westfechtel, T., & Harada, T. (2023). Unsupervised Domain Adaptation via Minimized Joint Error. *Transactions on Machine Learning Research*.

Zhang, Y., Deng, B., Jia, K., & Zhang, L. (2020, August). Label propagation with augmented anchors: A simple semi-supervised learning baseline for unsupervised domain adaptation. In *European Conference on Computer Vision* (pp. 781-797). Cham: Springer International Publishing. 10.1007/978-3-030-58548-8_45

Zhang, Y., Ding, K., Hui, J., Lv, J., Zhou, X., & Zheng, P. (2022). Human-object integrated assembly intention recognition for context-aware human-robot collaborative assembly. *Advanced Engineering Informatics*, *54*, 101792. doi:10.1016/j.aei.2022.101792

Zhao, L., Chen, Z., & Yang, Y. (2017). Parameter-free incremental co-clustering for multi-modal data in cyber-physical-social systems. *IEEE Access : Practical Innovations, Open Solutions*, *5*, 21852–21861. doi:10.1109/ACCESS.2017.2758798

Zhou, P., Xiong, C., Yuan, X., & Hoi, S. C. H. (2021). A theory-driven self-labeling refinement method for contrastive representation learning. *Advances in Neural Information Processing Systems*, *34*, 6183–6197.

Zhu, X., & Ghahramani, Z. (2002). Learning from labeled and unlabeled data with label propagation. *Tech. Rep., Technical Report CMU-CALD-02–107.* Carnegie Mellon University.

Chapter 9
LSTM With Bayesian Optimization for Forecasting of Local Scour Depth Around Bridges and Piers

Ahmed Shakir Ali
https://orcid.org/0000-0002-3351-8442
University of Memphis, USA

Saman Ebrahimi
University of Memphis, USA

Muhammad Masood Ashiq
University of Memphis, USA

Ali R. Kashani
University of Memphis, USA

ABSTRACT

Scour is a critical issue that impacts the safety and strength of bridges. Precise scour forecasts around bridge piers can provide useful data for bridge engineers to bring preventive actions. This study uses long short-term memory (LSTM) neural network with Bayesian optimization to forecast the scour around the bridges and piers. The LSTM network was trained and tested using only scour depth data from a calibrated numerical model. The outcomes indicate that the proposed LSTM model provides precise scour depth forecasts. The study presents the performance of the LSTM model for predicting scour depth around bridge piers, which can help enhance the safety and stability of bridges. The model has shown acceptable outcomes, with a rank correlation equal to 0.9866 in the training stage and 0.9655 in the testing stage. Moreover, the LSTM model was used to forecast the scour depth for 11 minutes.

DOI: 10.4018/979-8-3693-0230-9.ch009

1. INTRODUCTION

Bridges are essential infrastructures, and the collapse of bridges can lead to extreme financial effects. The most well-known threat to bridges' stability is scouring; bridges' collapse over rivers is familiar because of intense local scouring around their piers and abutment. Furthermore, analyses have revealed that natural risks are the highest cause of bridge collapsing (Imhof, 2004), as shown in Figure 1. Scour is described as the deduction of a riverbed by the erosive movement of a stream. Thus, accurately assessing scour and its impacts are critical.

Moreover, overvaluing or miscalculating can result in rising building expenditures and the defeat of abutments (Khosravi et al.,2021, Ali et al.,2022). Numerical Model For Simulation Of Scour Around Bridge Abutment. In *Fall Meeting 2022*. AGU.). The existence of hydraulic structures like bridges alters the flow movement and naturally forces the appearance of a three-part detachment area around a bridge pier and abutment. The force gradient is because the pier and abutment compel a down-flow that propels the scouring around the bridge base, and this lead to forming of a horseshoe vortex which enables extra scouring (Török et al., 2014).

Similarly, irregular shear forces arise and spin perpendicular axes like little whirlpools. Bow waves can likewise bestow the scouring procedure. Various vortexes finally direct to create a hole called scour (Hosseini et al.,2016). The mechanism of scour around bridges was explained broadly in the literature (Shen et al.,1966; Melville,1975; Qadar,1981; Sheppard,2004; Chiew,2008; Khwairakpam and Mazumdar,2009).

Figure 1. Percentage of bridge collapse due to various problems

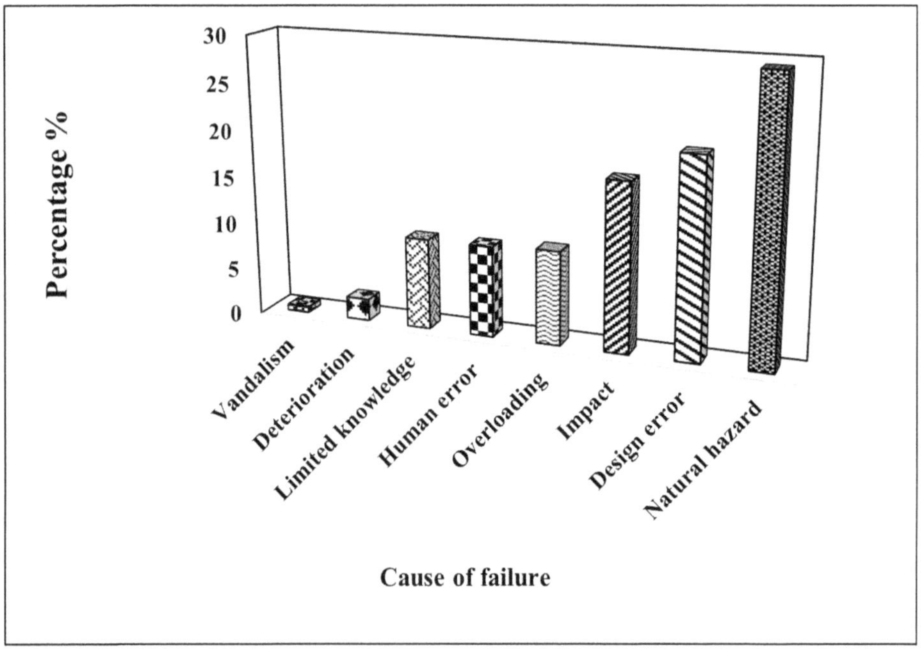

The scour is divided into three types: general scour, contraction scour and local scour (Brandimarte et al.,2011). In this study, we are focusing on the local scour. Local Sour is caused directly by the existence of bridge piers or abutments and due to blocking the stream (Melville,1975). The classification of local scour is categorized according to the capability of the stream coming from upstream of the bridge to carry riverbed material. The first condition is clear-water scour, which happens when the flow does not propel bed materials, while live-bed scour arises when the stream carries available riverbed material (Chiew and Melville,1987).

Commonly numerical modeling is used to investigate the various realistic complex water resources engineering problems (Ashiq et al., 2020). Specifically, for studying the scour around hydraulic structures, Pu and Lim (2014) conducted a practical method of modeling the scour procedure to obtain scour equilibrium around an abutment. Kim and Chen (2014) employed a numerical model to simulate sediment transport around bridge abutments in a channel curve. Mohammadpour et al. (2014) used numerical simulation to estimate the time deviation of local scour near a short abutment established in a laboratory channel. Afzal et al. (2020) examined scour around an abutment of a bridge using a numerical model. Namaee et al. (2021) used 3D numerical models to explore the local scour procedure around bridge piers with and without soft and ragged ice surfaces. Tang and Puspasari (2021) used numerical modeling using Flow-3D to estimate the scour and examine the scour aroundgropu of piers. Alasta et al. (2022) used a numerical model to simulate local scour around cylindrical bridge piers. Li et al.(2022) used a numerical model to study tsunami-induced scour around bridge piers. However, numerical approaches are limited due to the calibration and verification. Besides, numeircal models presume the physics of the scouring procedures; their execution is complicated and requires considerable and precise details (Khosravi et al.,2021).

However, in recent years, improvements in the applications of soft computing like artificial intelligence (AI) have led to adopt it for solving various problems and use as an alternative to conventional methods in modeling engineering problems; the benefit of AI as it is straightforward to execute needs minor information and delivers increased precision to forecast complex phenomena (Ali et al.,2022; Ali et al.,2022). One of the AI applications is deep learning (DL), as illustrated in Figure 1 (Bengio et al.,2017), and is founded on the algorithms designed and motivated by the natural neuron system of humans to compute or approximate processes by solving multiple information into a target output (Goh et al.,2017). Again, DL promotes computer technology to develop results founded on earlier known data (Bashar,2019; Shreyas et al., 2020). DL has switched traditional industries to using AI models and is increasingly utilized in multiple scientific domains (Shen, 2018). Hence AI was applied in different

Figure 2. AI applications
Bengio et al. (2017)

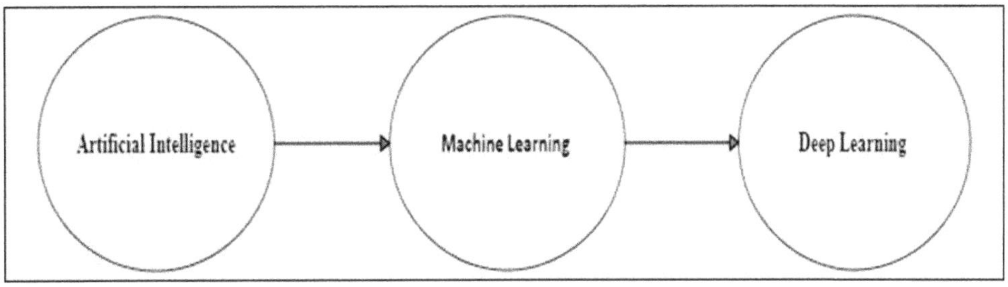

areas of civil engineering, such as hydrology (Ardabili et al.,2019; Shen and Lawson,2021; Ali, 2021; Kratzert et al.,2022; Azari et al.,2022), hydraulics (Tang et al.,2022; Song et al.,2022; Roh,2022), and structural engineering (Thai,2022; Li et al.,2022; Pal et al.,2022).

Besides, AI was applied broadly to forecast the ersion of bed's material around hydraulic strtuctres. Chou and Pham, (2014) used applications of AI such as the genetic algorithm to examine the possible benefit of forecasting bridge scour depth around piers and abutments. They demonstrated that the model provided scour depth accurately, and the proposed model can be employed to get quick and detailed descriptions when planning a secure and technically proper bridge. Yousefpour et al. (2021) used an application of DL called the long-term short memory (LSTM) model to predict the direction of scour established on sonar and 9-stage monitoring data near bridge piers. Ali and Günal (2021). used Artificial Neural Network (ANN) trained with experimental data and different backpropagation algorithms to forecast local scour depth near bridge piers. Pal, (2022) examined the possibility of the DL model in forecasting the local scour near bridge piers trained with field measurement data. The study demonstrated that DL is a good technique and requires to be additionally employed for different difficulties associated with water resource engineering to evaluate the entire possibility of the model. Zhang et al. (2022) used a convolutional neural network to forecast the time-averaged discharge domain of large-scale streams with wall-mounted bridge bases. They revealed that deep learning models are competent in properly creating the time-averaged flow domain stream.

Asim et al.(222) used a deep neural network established on optimization to foresee scour depths near bridge piers. They indicated that the DNN forecasted scour deep with better precision than the regression method created utilizing the exact information setting used for the DNN. Hou et al.(222) used a fast submarine assessment approach utilizing a sonar instrument and a CNN model to obtain quantitative measuring consequences for scour depth. They indicated that additional structural assessment could be established on precise measuring outcomes from the model. Yousefpour, N., & Correa, O. (2022) developed a novel LSTM model to identify the ingrained scour and overflow patterns in the recorded monitoring data. They utilized the LSTM model as an early alarming method by combining AI with monitoring techniques to obtain information to be prepared for hazard checks of approaching scour possibilities. In addition, they showed that the LSTM model could deliver accurate earlier predictions of scouring with proper variability.

This study aims to use an application of the DL model called long-short-term memory (LSTM) to predict scour depth around the bridge pier. Moreover, LSTM was adopted widely for forecasting various time times data in different fields. However, for scour predictions, LSTM was not used a lot, and our goal is to show that LSTM can provide reliable predicted scour depth with only one input which is scour depth within time, and with a relatively small data set. Besides, the DL model is optimized using bayesian optimization to obtain the best structure of the mode. It is important to notice that we are training the DL with only one input, time series scour depth data obtained from calibrated numerical model published recently.

2. METHODOLOGY

2.1 Long Short-Term Memory (LSTM)

Standard recurrent neural networks (RNNs) endeavor to fix the issue dubbed "shortage of memory," which is accountable for showing insufficient implementation. These approaches employ cyclic links on their hidden layers to attain short-term memory and obtain details from time series data. However, the RNN model has a problem due to the vanishing gradient (Livieris et al.,2020). Thus, another variant of RNN called Long Short-Term Memory (LSTM) was developed. It is a class of recurrent neural networks (RNNs) skilled at understanding ordering dependence in series forecast difficulties. These methods are needed in challenging problems like machine translation and speech distinction (Staudemeyer and Morris,2019). LSTM has reached nearly all exciting developments established on RNNs, and it has become the principle of deep learning. Moreover, their robust learning ability makes LSTMs perform adequately and are widely used in different studies (Yu et al.,2019).

Hochreiter and Schmidhuber proposed LSTM in 1997 (Kalchbrenner et al.,215). LSTM can detect the long dependencies in an ordering by training a memory cell and a gate method that seeks to determine how to employ and edit the details preserved in the memory unit. LSTM is comparable in design to the RNN (Manowska and Bluszcz,2022). A standard LSTM includes memory units named cells. Two forms are moved to the next cell, the cell state, and the hidden state. The cell state is the primary source of information, letting the details move onward unaffected. However, some linear modifications may arise. The data can be counted or dismissed from the cell state via sigmoid gates (Le et al.,2019), Figure 3 shows the structure of the LSTM model.

LSTM contains three gates: input, output, and forget. The LSTM operates to complete undisturbed details move by selecting which elements must be "ignored" and which must be "recalled," thus handling long-term learning dependences. It is recommended to read these articles for more information (Yuet al.,2019; Zha et al.,2022; Ranjbar and Toufigh,2022). The LSTM procedure is explained by Livieris et al. (2020).

2.2 Hyperparameter Tuning

DL approaches are a growing method for hydrologic forecasts. However, traditional techniques are often utilized to find the appropriate hyperparameters (Zuo et al., 2020). Nonetheless, these processes could be quicker since the optimal varieties cannot be achieved fast, and they require assuming the varied consequences of hyperparameters. Similarly, some analyses utilize suggested hyperparameters (Yin et al., 2020). Nonetheless, this can be challenging for investigations assessing the implementation of various techniques since such procedures cannot show desired results.

In this study, we show the performance of Bayesian optimization with LSTM, which has demonstrated the ability to obtain satisfactory outcomes compared to conventional optimization algorithms (He et al.,2019). Similar to other deep learning models, the LSTM model has various parameters that impact considerable parts of the algorithm's implementation. For example, some of these parameters influence the demand for computational duration or memory. While, others influence the efficiency and capability to forecast precise outcomes when introduced to unused information (Hansen et al.,2022).

Bayesian optimization works to reduce an objective function, f (x), in a restricted range for x. Loss function like mean squared error is usually preferred as the objective function for the regression. The three fundamental parts of Bayesian optimization are as follows (Hansen et al.,2022):

- Specifying a surrogate approach is generally established on the Gaussian process (GP) (Brochu et al., 2010).

$$Y_n = \mathrm{N}\left(f(x_{n)}\right), v) \quad (1)$$

Where x includes the parameters to be improved, and ν is the variety in the input data.

- A Bayesian modifies the function objective function to provide a new assessment of the model.
- a(x) chooses the next step, x_{next}, to be assessed and expressed as (Brochu et al., 2010):

$$x_{next} = argmax_{x \in X} a\left(x\right) \quad (2)$$

The Bayesian optimization was explained broadly in the literature (Pelikan,2005; Frazier,2018; Archetti and Candelieri,2019). Bayesian hyperparameter tuning is used to acquire an optimum LSTM configuration with a capability that reaches the complicatedness of the study. Multiple hyperparameters affect the implementation of the LSTM model and can be integrated to optimize the training. Reimers and Gurevych (2017) showed a comprehensive assessment of various hyperparameters which affect the LSTM model, where many LSTM models for series labeling schemes are studied. In this study, we focus on four critical aspects shown in Table 1.

This study used the LSTM model with Bayesian optimization to forcast the scour around piers of bridge. Table 1 shows hyperparameter tuning. Besides, the Adam solver is used, and it has been demonstrated to deliver stable and more valuable outcomes than different approaches (Reimers and Gurevych, 2017). Also, a dropout regularization is executed as it has shown more acceptable performance than no dropout (Hansen et al.,2022). Finally, the dropout probability is set to 0.5, and the mini-batch size is set to 25.

Table 1. Optimized parameters for the LSTM model

Layer	**1 to 4**
Units	75 to 200
Learning Rate	0.001 to 1
L2Regularization Rate	0.0000000001 to 0.001

2.3 Evaluation Criteria

The performance of the model was assessed based on these criteria:

- Spearman's rank-order correlation calculates the relation and trend of the relationship between two parameters, and it can be expressed as follows (Ramsey,1989):

$$\rho = 1 - \frac{6\sum d_i^2}{n\left(n^2 - 1\right)} \tag{3}$$

Where ρ is Spearman's rank correlation coefficient, and n is the number of data.

- Mean Square Error (MSE) counts the average of the squares of the errors:

$$MSE = \frac{1}{n}\sum_{i=1}^{n}\left(X_I - Y_i\right)^2 \tag{4}$$

Where n is the number of data, X is the actual data, and Y is the estimated data.

- Root Mean Square Error (RMSE) calculates the quality of estimation and can be expressed as follows:

$$RMSE = \sqrt{\frac{\sum_{i=1}^{n}\left(X_I - Y_i\right)^2}{n}} \tag{5}$$

Where n is the number of data, X is the actual data, and Y is the estimated data.

- Normalized root means squared error (NRMSE) is used to compare two different models and can be expressed as follows:

$$NRMSE = \frac{\sum\left(x_i - y_i\right)^2}{\sum yi^2} \tag{6}$$

Where x is the estimated value and y is the actual value.

2.4 Data

The LSTM model was trained using scour data obtained from the calibrated numerical model published by Alasta et al. (2022). As shown in Figure (3), the scour data includes approximately 654 scour measurements around bridge piers collected every 5.5 seconds. Also, 90% of the data was used for training and 10% for testing.

Figure 3. Scour depth around bridge piers

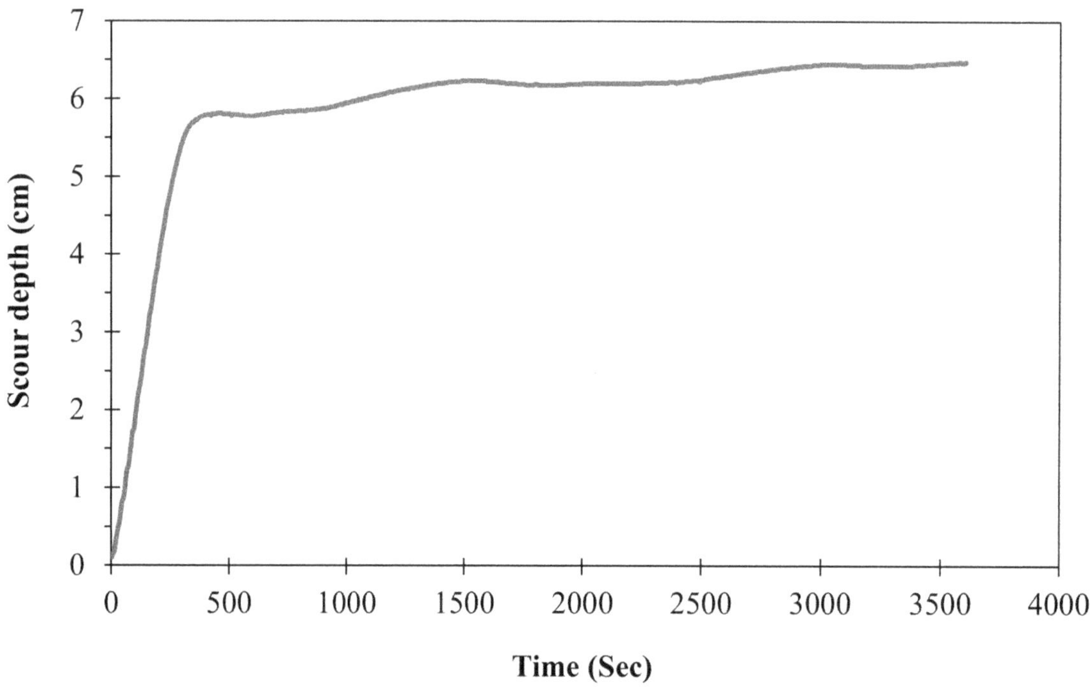

3. RESULTS

The Bayesian optimization was used to obtain the optimum LSTM model. As a result, the LSTM model provided accurate local scour depth around the bridge pier with 1 LSTM layer, 70 LSTM units, a learning rate equal to 0.10188, and an L2Regularization rate equal to 0.00001005. Besdies, the model run using MATLAB. In addition, the LSTM model showed promising performance in the training stage. As shown in Figure 4, the rank correlation was 0.9878. Besides, the error of the training stage was low. Meanwhile, the rank correlation of the testing stage was 0.9655, and the error was acceptable, as shown in Figure 5.

The model predicted the scour depth around bridge piers for 11 minutes because it showed good results in the training and test stages.

4. CONCLUSION

Scour is the most well-known threat to the stability of bridges, and it can be more severe during flood events. Approtiet prediction of scour depth can reduce the cost of bridge foundations and losses due to scour depth around bridge piers and abutments. Commonly, numerical molding is used for investigating this phoneme. However, numerical models have some challenges which make simulating scour depth difficultly. To overcome these difficulties, artificial intelligence (AI) applications are becoming more common in the engineering field due to the development of soft computing, and it can be used as another approach for modeling scour depth around bridge piers.

Figure 4. Performance of training stage

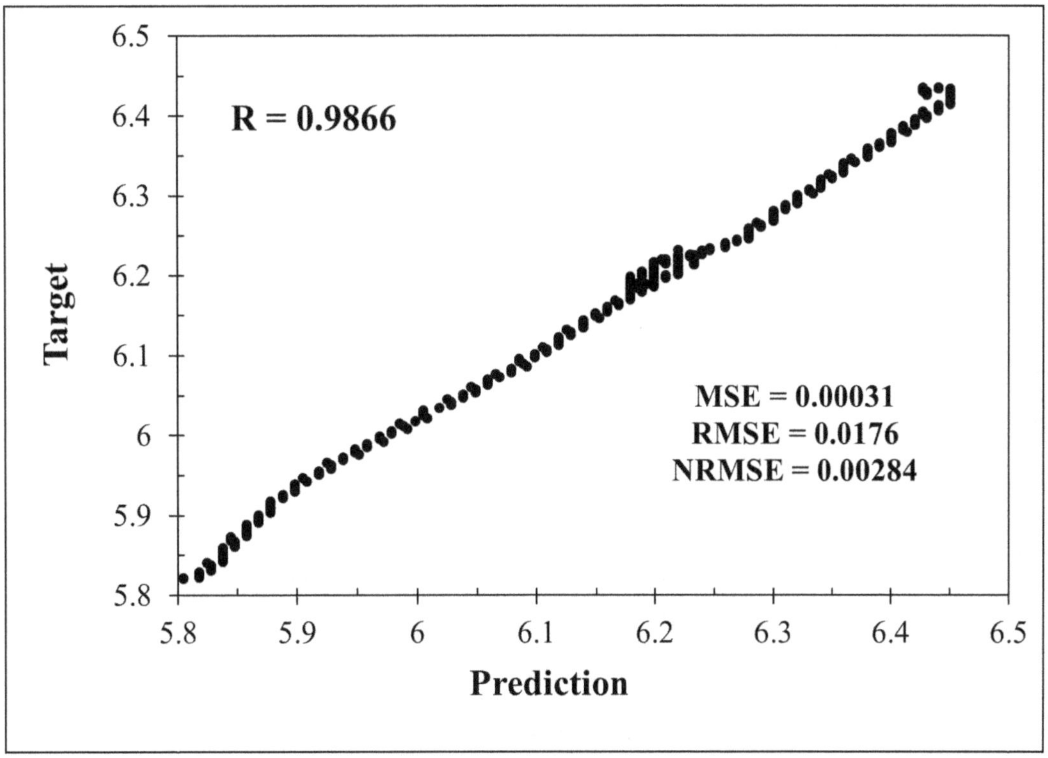

Figure 5. Performance of testing stage

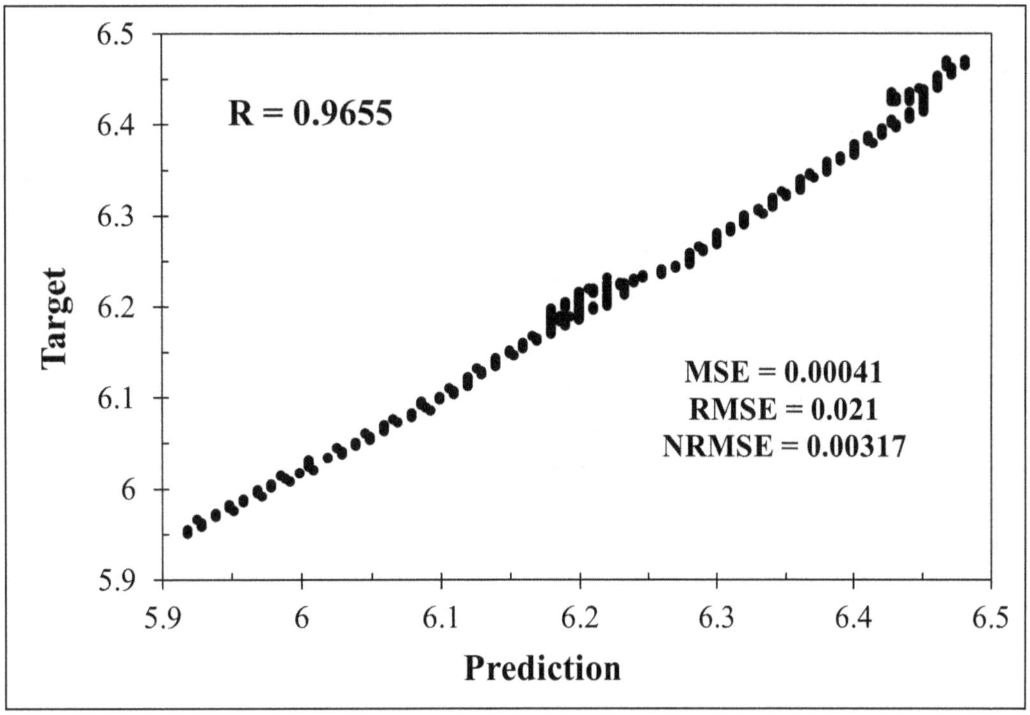

Figure 6. Predicted scour depth (cm)

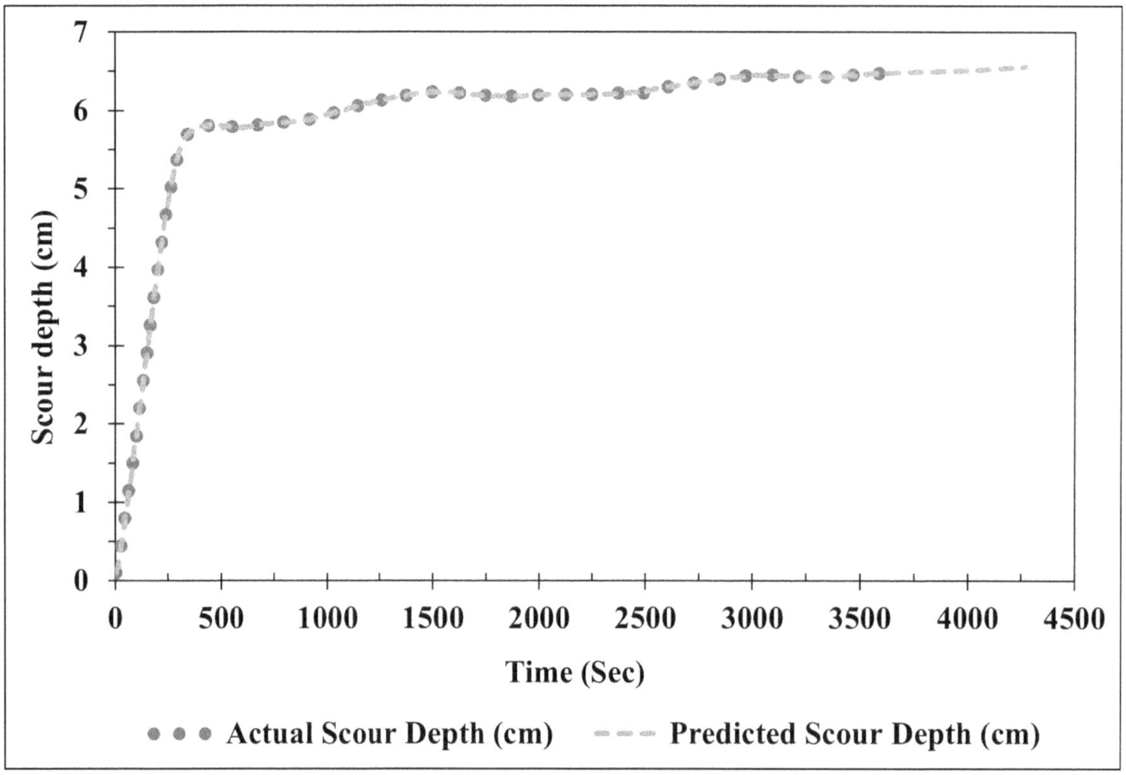

Deep learning (DL) is an AI approach used in various science domains. For instance, the LSTM model, applications of DL, is used for modeling time series data, showing promising outcomes for handling sequence data. In civil engineering, LSTM models time series data like rainfall, flood, runoff, traffic flow, reservoir levels, etc. Still, LSTM was not employed broadly to show the model's capability for modeling the scour. Hence, in this study, we showed that the LSTM could provide a good prediction of scour depth around bridge piers using only time series scour depth data as input to the model. Besides, Bayesian optimization was used to obtain the optimal configuration of the LSTM model. The optimized LSTM model has shown acceptable outcomes, with rank correlation equal to 0.9866 and 0.9655, for training and testing, respectively. Moreover, the LSTM model was used to forecast the scour depth for 11 minutes.

Nevertheless, the limitation of the study is that only the LSTM model is used, and it is recommended to compare it with other applications of DL. Also, the LSTM model was trained with relatively small data, and then the model can predict scour depth of more than 11 minutes. The LSTM model can be used to examine more problems related to structures, such as scouring around a group of bridge piers.

REFERENCES

Afzal, M. S., Bihs, H., & Kumar, L. (2020). Computational fluid dynamics modeling of abutment scour under steady current using the level set method. *International Journal of Sediment Research*, *35*(4), 355–364. doi:10.1016/j.ijsrc.2020.03.003

Alasta, M. S., Ali, A. S. A., Ebrahimi, S., Ashiq, M. M., Dheyab, A. S., AlMasri, A., & Khorram, M. (2022). Modeling of local scour depth around bridge pier using FLOW 3D. *CRPASE: Transactions of Civil and Environmental Engineering*, *8*(2), 1–9. doi:10.52547/crpase.8.2.2781

Ali, A. S. A.. (2021). Republic of Turkey Gaziantep University Graduate School of Natural and Applied Sciences.

Ali, A. S., bin Waheed, U., Ashiq, M., Al Asta, M. S., & Khorram, M. (2022). Machine Learning Model for Estimation of Local Scour Depth around Cylindrical Bridge Piers. *Iraqi Journal of Civil Engineering*, *16*(2), 1–13. doi:10.37650/ijce.2022.160201

Ali, A. S., Jazaei, F., Ashiq, M. M., Bakhshaee, A., & Alasta, M. S. (2022, December). Numerical Model For Simulation Of Scour Around Bridge Abutment. In *Fall Meeting 2022*. AGU.

Ali, A. S. A., Ebrahimi, S., Ashiq, M. M., Alasta, M. S., & Azari, B. (2022). CNN-Bi LSTM neural network for simulating groundwater level. *Environ. Eng*, *8*, 1–7.

Ali, A. S. A., & Günal, M. (2021). Artificial neural network for estimation of local scour depth around bridge piers. *Archives of Hydro-Engineering and Environmental Mechanics*, *68*(2), 87–101. doi:10.2478/heem-2021-0005

Archetti, F., & Candelieri, A. (2019). *Bayesian optimization and data science*. Springer. doi:10.1007/978-3-030-24494-1

Ardabili, S., Mosavi, A., Dehghani, M., & Várkonyi-Kóczy, A. R. (2019, September). Deep learning and machine learning in hydrological processes climate change and earth systems a systematic review. In *International conference on global research and education* (pp. 52-62). Springer, Cham.

Ashiq, M. M., Rehman, H. U., & Khan, N. M. (2020). Impact of large diameter recharge wells for reducing groundwater depletion rates in an urban area of Lahore, Pakistan. *Environmental Earth Sciences*, *79*(17), 1–14. doi:10.1007/s12665-020-09144-7

Asim, M., Rashid, A., & Ahmad, T. (2022). Scour modeling using deep neural networks based on hyperparameter optimization. *ICT Express*, *8*(3), 357–362. doi:10.1016/j.icte.2021.09.012

Azari, B., Hassan, K., Pierce, J., & Ebrahimi, S. (2022). Evaluation of machine learning methods application in temperature prediction. *Environ Eng*, *8*(1), 1–12. doi:10.52547/crpase.8.1.2747

Bashar, A. (2019). Survey on evolving deep learning neural network architectures. *Journal of Artificial Intelligence*, *1*(02), 73–82.

Bengio, Y., Goodfellow, I., & Courville, A. (2017). *Deep learning* (Vol. 1). MIT press.

Brandimarte, L., Paron, P., & Di Baldassarre, G. (2012). Bridge pier scour: A review of processes, measurements and estimates. *Environmental Engineering and Management Journal*, *11*(5), 975–989. doi:10.30638/eemj.2012.121

Brochu, E., Cora, V. M., & De Freitas, N. (2010). *A tutorial on Bayesian optimization of expensive cost functions, with application to active user modeling and hierarchical reinforcement learning*. arXiv preprint arXiv:1012.2599.

Chiew, Y. M. (2008). Scour and scour countermeasures at bridge sites. *Transactions of Tianjin University*, *14*(4), 289–295. doi:10.1007/s12209-008-0049-z

Chiew, Y. M., & Melville, B. W. (1987). Local scour around bridge piers. *Journal of Hydraulic Research*, *25*(1), 15–26. doi:10.1080/00221688709499285

Chou, J. S., & Pham, A. D. (2014). Hybrid computational model for predicting bridge scour depth near piers and abutments. *Automation in Construction*, *48*, 88–96. doi:10.1016/j.autcon.2014.08.006

Frazier, P. I. (2018). *A tutorial on Bayesian optimization*. arXiv preprint arXiv:1807.02811.

Goh, G. B., Hodas, N. O., & Vishnu, A. (2017). Deep learning for computational chemistry. *Journal of Computational Chemistry*, *38*(16), 1291–1307. doi:10.1002/jcc.24764 PMID:28272810

Hansen, L. D., Stokholm-Bjerregaard, M., & Durdevic, P. (2022). Modeling phosphorous dynamics in a wastewater treatment process using Bayesian optimized LSTM. *Computers & Chemical Engineering*, *160*, 107738. doi:10.1016/j.compchemeng.2022.107738

He, F., Zhou, J., Feng, Z. K., Liu, G., & Yang, Y. (2019). A hybrid short-term load forecasting model based on variational mode decomposition and long short-term memory networks considering relevant factors with Bayesian optimization algorithm. *Applied Energy*, *237*, 103–116. doi:10.1016/j.apenergy.2019.01.055

Hosseini, K., Karami, H., Hosseinjanzadeh, H., & Ardeshir, A. (2016). Prediction of time-varying maximum scour depth around short abutments using soft computing methodologies-A comparative study. *KSCE Journal of Civil Engineering*, *20*(5), 2070–2081. doi:10.1007/s12205-015-0115-8

Hou, S., Jiao, D., Dong, B., Wang, H., & Wu, G. (2022). Underwater inspection of bridge substructures using sonar and deep convolutional network. *Advanced Engineering Informatics*, *52*, 101545. doi:10.1016/j.aei.2022.101545

Imhof, D. (2004). *Risk assessment of existing bridge structures* [Doctoral dissertation, University of Cambridge].

Kalchbrenner, N., Danihelka, I., & Graves, A. (2015). *Grid long short-term memory*. arXiv preprint arXiv:1507.01526.

Khosravi, K., Khozani, Z. S., & Mao, L. (2021). A comparison between advanced hybrid machine learning algorithms and empirical equations applied to abutment scour depth prediction. *Journal of Hydrology (Amsterdam)*, *596*, 126100. doi:10.1016/j.jhydrol.2021.126100

Khwairakpam, P., & Mazumdar, A. (2009). Local scour around hydraulic structures. *International Journal of Recent Trends in Engineering*, *1*(6), 59.

Kim, H. S., & Chen, H. C. (2014). Three-Dimensional Numerical Analysis of Sediment Transport Around Abutment in Channel Bend. *Coastal Engineering Proceedings*, *1*(24), 21. doi:10.9753/icce.v34.sediment.21

Kratzert, F., Gauch, M., Nearing, G., & Klotz, D. (2022). NeuralHydrology---A Python library for Deep Learning research in hydrology. *Journal of Open Source Software*, *7*(71), 4050. doi:10.21105/joss.04050

Le, X. H., Ho, H. V., Lee, G., & Jung, S. (2019). Application of long short-term memory (LSTM) neural network for flood forecasting. *Water (Basel)*, *11*(7), 1387. doi:10.3390/w11071387

Li, J., Kong, X., Yang, Y., Deng, L., & Xiong, W. (2022). CFD investigations of tsunami-induced scour around bridge piers. *Ocean Engineering*, *244*, 110373. doi:10.1016/j.oceaneng.2021.110373

Li, Y., Bao, T., Gao, Z., Shu, X., Zhang, K., Xie, L., & Zhang, Z. (2022). A new dam structural response estimation paradigm powered by deep learning and transfer learning techniques. *Structural Health Monitoring*, *21*(3), 770–787. doi:10.1177/14759217211009780

Livieris, I. E., Pintelas, E., & Pintelas, P. (2020). A CNN–LSTM model for gold price time-series forecasting. *Neural Computing & Applications*, *32*(23), 17351–17360. doi:10.1007/s00521-020-04867-x

Livieris, I. E., Pintelas, E., & Pintelas, P. (2020). A CNN–LSTM model for gold price time-series forecasting. *Neural Computing & Applications*, *32*(23), 17351–17360. doi:10.1007/s00521-020-04867-x

Manowska, A., & Bluszcz, A. (2022). Forecasting Crude Oil Consumption in Poland Based on LSTM Recurrent Neural Network. *Energies*, *15*(13), 4885. doi:10.3390/en15134885

Melville, B. W. (1975). *Local scour at bridge sites* [Doctoral dissertation, researchspace@ Auckland].

Mohammadpour, R., Sabzevari, T., & Mohammadpour, F. (2014). Investigation of Local Scour development around Abutment using Experimental and Numerical Models. *Caspian Journal of Applied Sciences Research, 3*(1).

Namaee, M. R., Sui, J., Wu, Y., & Linklater, N. (2021). Three-dimensional numerical simulation of local scour around circular side-by-side bridge piers with ice cover. *Canadian Journal of Civil Engineering*, *48*(10), 1335–1353. doi:10.1139/cjce-2019-0360

Pal, J., Sikdar, S., & Banerjee, S. (2022). A deep-learning approach for health monitoring of a steel frame structure with bolted connections. *Structural Control and Health Monitoring*, *29*(2), e2873. doi:10.1002/stc.2873

Pal, M. (2022). Deep neural network based pier scour modeling. *ISH Journal of Hydraulic Engineering, 28*(sup1), 80-85.

Pelikan, M. (2005). Bayesian optimization algorithm. In *Hierarchical Bayesian optimization algorithm* (pp. 31–48). Springer. doi:10.1007/978-3-540-32373-0_3

Pu, J. H., & Lim, S. Y. (2014). Efficient numerical computation and experimental study of temporally long equilibrium scour development around abutment. *Environmental Fluid Mechanics*, *14*(1), 69–86. doi:10.1007/s10652-013-9286-3

Qadar, A. (1981). The Vortex Scour Mechanism at Bridge Piers. *Proceedings - Institution of Civil Engineers*, *71*(3), 739–757. doi:10.1680/iicep.1981.1816

Ranjbar, I., & Toufigh, V. (2022). Deep long short-term memory (LSTM) networks for ultrasonic-based distributed damage assessment in concrete. *Cement and Concrete Research*, *162*, 107003. doi:10.1016/j.cemconres.2022.107003

Roh, C. (2022). Deep-Learning-Based Pitch Controller for Floating Offshore Wind Turbine Systems with Compensation for Delay of Hydraulic Actuators. *Energies*, *15*(9), 3136. doi:10.3390/en15093136

Shen, C. (2018). A transdisciplinary review of deep learning research and its relevance for water resources scientists. *Water Resources Research*, *54*(11), 8558–8593. doi:10.1029/2018WR022643

Shen, C., & Lawson, K. (2021). Applications of deep learning in hydrology. *Deep Learning for the Earth Sciences: A Comprehensive Approach to Remote Sensing, Climate Science, and Geosciences*, 283-297. Research Gate.

Shen, H. W., Schneider, V. R., & Karaki, S. S. (1966). *Mechanics of local scour.*

Sheppard, D. M. (2004). Overlooked local sediment scour mechanism. *Transportation Research Record: Journal of the Transportation Research Board*, *1890*(1), 107–111. doi:10.3141/1890-13

Shreyas, N., Venkatraman, M., Malini, S., & Chandrakala, S. (2020). Trends of sound event recognition in audio surveillance: a recent review and study. *The Cognitive Approach in Cloud Computing and Internet of Things Technologies for Surveillance Tracking Systems*, 95-106. Research Gate.

Song, H., Du, S., Yang, J., Zhao, Y., & Yu, M. (2022). Evaluation of hydraulic fracturing effect on coalbed methane reservoir based on deep learning method considering physical constraints. *Journal of Petroleum Science Engineering*, *212*, 110360. doi:10.1016/j.petrol.2022.110360

Staudemeyer, R. C., & Morris, E. R. (2019). *Understanding LSTM—a tutorial into long short-term memory recurrent neural networks*. arXiv preprint arXiv:1909.09586.

Tang, J. H., & Puspasari, A. D. (2021). Numerical Simulation of Local Scour around Three Cylindrical Piles in a Tandem Arrangement. *Water (Basel)*, *13*(24), 3623. doi:10.3390/w13243623

Tang, S., Zhu, Y., & Yuan, S. (2022). Intelligent fault diagnosis of hydraulic piston pump based on deep learning and Bayesian optimization. *ISA Transactions*, *129*, 555–563. doi:10.1016/j.isatra.2022.01.013 PMID:35115164

Thai, H. T. (2022, April). Machine learning for structural engineering: A state-of-the-art review. In *Structures* (Vol. 38, pp. 448–491). Elsevier.

Török, G. T., Baranya, S., Rüther, N., & Spiller, S. (2014, September). Laboratory analysis of armor layer development in a local scour around a groin. In *Proceedings of the International Conference on Fluvial Hydraulics, RIVER FLOW* (pp. 1455-1462). ACM.

Yin, J., Deng, Z., Ines, A. V., Wu, J., & Rasu, E. (2020). Forecast of short-term daily reference evapotranspiration under limited meteorological variables using a hybrid bi-directional long short-term memory model (Bi-LSTM). *Agricultural Water Management*, *242*, 106386. doi:10.1016/j.agwat.2020.106386

Yousefpour, N., Downie, S., Walker, S., Perkins, N., & Dikanski, H. (2021). Machine learning solutions for bridge scour forecast based on monitoring data. *Transportation Research Record: Journal of the Transportation Research Board*, *2675*(10), 745–763. doi:10.1177/03611981211012693

Yu, Y., Si, X., Hu, C., & Zhang, J. (2019). A review of recurrent neural networks: LSTM cells and network architectures. *Neural Computation*, *31*(7), 1235–1270. doi:10.1162/neco_a_01199 PMID:31113301

Zha, W., Liu, Y., Wan, Y., Luo, R., Li, D., Yang, S., & Xu, Y. (2022). Forecasting monthly gas field production based on the CNN-LSTM model. *Energy*, *260*, 124889. doi:10.1016/j.energy.2022.124889

Zhang, Z., Flora, K., Kang, S., Limaye, A. B., & Khosronejad, A. (2022). Data-Driven Prediction of Turbulent Flow Statistics Past Bridge Piers in Large-Scale Rivers Using Convolutional Neural Networks. *Water Resources Research, 58*(1), e2021WR030163.

Zuo, G., Luo, J., Wang, N., Lian, Y., & He, X. (2020). Decomposition ensemble model based on variational mode decomposition and long short-term memory for streamflow forecasting. *Journal of Hydrology (Amsterdam)*, *585*, 124776. doi:10.1016/j.jhydrol.2020.124776

Chapter 10
Phase Unwrapping Method Using Adaptive AI Model for the Application of Industrialization and Precision Metrology Field

Zhuo Zhao
https://orcid.org/0000-0002-4449-2663
Xi'an Jiaotong University, China

Bing Li
Xi'an Jiaotong University, China

Leqi Geng
Xi'an Jiaotong University, China

Jiasheng Lu
Xi'an Jiaotong University, China

Qiuying Li
Xi'an Jiaotong University, China

Tao Peng
Soochow University, China

Zheng Wang
Xi'an Jiaotong University, China

ABSTRACT

Phase unwrapping method based on Residual Auto Encoder Network is proposed in this chapter. Phase unwrapping is regarded as a multiple classification problem, and it will be solved by the trained network model. Through training and validation stages, optimal network models can be served as predictors of wrap count distribution map of wrapped phase. Then merge the wrapped phase and count together to complete unwrapping. Software simulation and hardware acquisition are the sources of training dataset. To further improve accuracy of unwrapping, image analysis-based optimization method is designed that can remove misclassification and noise points in initial result. In addition, phase data stitching by Iterative Closest Point is adopted to realize dynamic resolution and enhance the flexibility of method. Point diffraction interferometer and multi-step phase extraction technique is the foundation of proposed method. It can be concluded from experiments that the proposed method is superior to state-of-art ones in accuracy, time efficiency, anti-noise ability, and flexibility.

DOI: 10.4018/979-8-3693-0230-9.ch010

1. INTRODUCTION

In the manufacture of spherical/aspherical optical components, multiple machining stages are required including: grinding, coarse polishing and fine polishing (Rhee et al., 2011). To ensure the surface quality of optical components, interferometry is often adopted to test the target optics in fine polishing. It is a nondestructive measurement method with the precision of sub-micron or even nanometer level (Yu et al., 2016). Point diffraction interferometer (PDI) is a typical interferometry in optical metrology (Zhao, Li, Kang et al, 2019): By using pinhole diffraction phenomenon, standard spherical wavefront is generated to perform relative test to spherical/aspherical optics (Ota et al., 2001); Interferograms are acquired and analyzed by phase shift technique, then one can obtain the corresponding surface quality of test optical components. Multi-step phase shift technique is involved in this method to extract phase information by executing arc tangent operation to deviation of interferograms (Nguyen et al., 2019). Usually, data processing in x86 computers, *arctan* is replaced by *atan2* function whose range is limited to $[-\pi,\pi]$. Therefore, this calculation will lead to the phenomenon of phase data discontinuity or called "Phase wrapping". To deal with this problem, scholars have put forward different methods.

Scanning based method: The simplest approach in phase unwrapping. Neighbor points are compared row by row and column by column to check the area where amplitude jumping is happened. Then add integral multiples of 2π to wrapped points to complete unwrapping. This approach is sensitive noise. Path-tracking algorithms: This kind of method unwrap the phase data begin from reliable local areas and then to the global scope. Appropriate integration paths are selected to perform unwrapping gradually. The typical methods include Goldstein branch cut (Huang et al., 2015), Quality-guided algorithm (Zhong et al., 2011), Minimum discontinuity (Flynn,, 1997) and the like. The performance is closely related to path selection. Minimum-norm method: These methods treat unwrapping as the problem of optimization. Target function with certain conditions is under iteration calculation until optimal solution is reached. Multigrid algorithm (Pritt, 1995), least square method belong to this category. Calculation efficiency is their drawbacks. Other methods are also attempted in latest years: Zhao use transport of intensity equation to perform 2D unwrapping. The accuracy can reaches RMSE=4.138rad when dealing with noised phase. To fulfil the unwrapping task, masses of iteration is needed to reduce the error. Minimum discontinuity phase unwrapping algorithm with a reference phase distribution is proposed by Liu (2018). Processing time is much improved (only 3.59s for 256×256), but precision is not his first consideration. Recursion of Chebyshev polynomials (Xing & Guo, 2017) can also used for temporal phase unwrapping. This method is competitively efficient, and flexible in the number of required fringe patterns for adapting to different noise levels. Xia presents a modified network programming technique for phase images in Fourier domain (Xia et al., 2017). The accuracy of her method can reach RMSE = 0.8 rad and processing time is average 3.5s for 251×841.

In recent years, the development of deep learning technology has been improved significantly. Deep neural network is widely used in different applications, such as target classification, image segmentation (Badrinarayanan et al., 2017), signal denoising (Yan et al., 2020), data prediction and etc. Neural network-based method: G. E. Spoorthi (2019) and Junchao Zhang (2019) use a auto-encoder convolutional neural network to realize phase unwrapping. This model can be used to process freeform surface. A series connected residual network is designed by Gili Dardikman (2019) to perform unwrapping for medical images. Li Cong has designed a generative adversarial network (2019) to perform phase unwrapping for 3D projection measurement. In his network model, U-NET is act as the generator and CNN net as discriminator. After training, phase information of fringe deformation can be obtain in the RMSE of 0.1. Wang proposed a one-step phase unwrapping method based on combined deep neural network (2019). This method can deal with phase map with irregular shapes and possess a good noise robustness. However, it cannot evaluate phase discontinuities. Wu apply en-decoder network (2020) to phase unwrapping task for Doppler optical coherence tomography of blood flow images. Also, GILI D.Y put forward a PhUn-Net (2020) to process unseen wrapped phase images of human sperm cells and realize a higher accuracy. While it can only handle the phase with simple shapes. These neural network-based methods have a better performance in phase unwrapping compared with conventional ones. However, they can only deal with wrapped phase image in static resolution.

In this paper, a phase data unwrapping method for point diffraction interferometry (PDI) based on Residual Auto Encoder Network (RAEN) is proposed. Phase unwrapping is regarded as a classification task and then realized by trained neural network model. Through analysis to wrapped phase, a wrap count distribution map can be predicted by network model. Finally, we add up original wrapped phase with wrap count to complete unwrapping. To further improve the accuracy of classification, we have designed an image analysis-based optimization method to remove misclassification and noise points in initial result. Phase data stitching strategy by Iterative Closest Point (ICP) (Xin et al., 2018) is adopted, which can make dynamic resolution possible in processing. Wrapped phase data acquired by PDI system can be unwrapped with full aperture, high efficiency and desirable accuracy.

Section II presents the principle of phase unwrapping using residual auto encoder neural network; Section III introduces result optimization and the strategy of data stitching in phase unwrapping; Section IV is mainly about hardware platform of point diffraction interferometer as well as phase extraction technique; Experiments on unwrapping, anti-noise and time efficiency are given in Section V. Section VI is conclusion.

2. PRINCIPLE OF UNWRAPPING

2.1 Problem of Phase Wrapping

In the three-dimensional contour measurement technologies which involved in phase shift method, arc tangent operation is inevitable to be performed. However, *arctan* function is usually replaced by *atan2* in x86 platform and the range of *atan2* is [-π, π]. Large-scaled phase data is limited in this scope, which produce the phenomenon of phase wrapping (discontinuity). That can be expressed as Equation (1):

$$\varphi(x,y) = \begin{cases} \phi(x,y) + 2\pi k(x,y) & (x,y) \in \text{Pupil area} \quad , k \in Z \\ 0 & (x,y) \notin \text{Pupil area} \end{cases} \tag{1}$$

Where $\phi(x,y)$ is wrapped phase, $\varphi(x,y)$ is unwrapped phase and k *i*s wrap count distribution. Specifically, k *v*alue belongs to the integer set Z. Obviously from Equation (1), we can find that wrapped phase has periodic data jumping in local regions compared with that of unwrapped. Actually, this jumping phenomenon is data discontinuity with integral multiple k *o*f period 2π. As the amplitude of local phase data increases, k *w*ill grow at the same time. In order to acquire continuous data distribution, a certain fitting method is needed to work out $2\pi k(x,y)$ *i*nformation to realize unwrapping operation.

2.2 Residual Auto Encoder Neural Network

In this work, phase data unwrapping is regarded as a task of multiple classification. Here, pixel is the basic unit and wrap count k is the category in this classification. Based on this concept, we take the advantage of deep learning techniques to design a network model to fulfil the task. It is called Residual Auto Encoder Network (RAEN) which structure is given in Figure 1:

Figure 1. Structure of residual auto encoder network

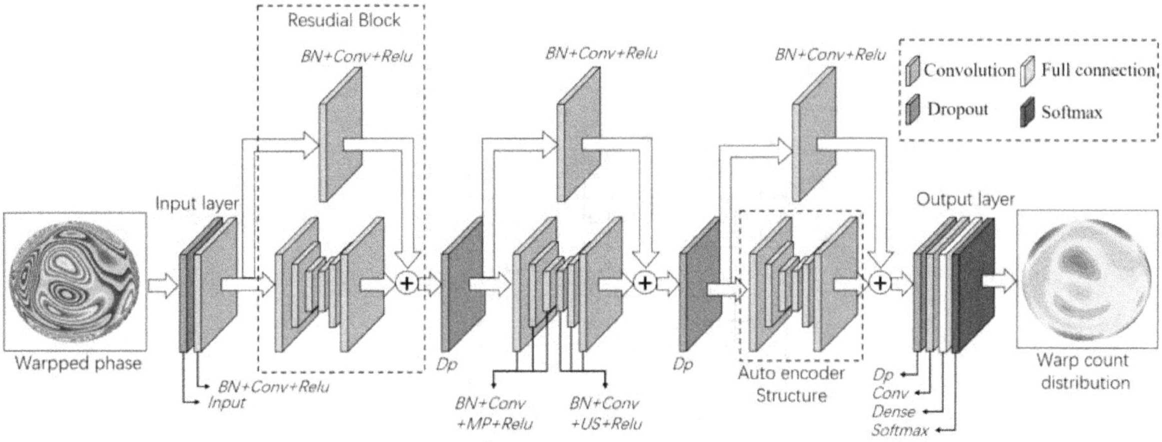

Residual Auto Encoder Network is consist of three main parts: Input layer, residual blocks and output layer. The dimension of input data is (W, H, C) and output is (W, H, k). Where width W=256, height H=256, channel C=1 and categories (wrap count) k = [0, 40]. Technical principle of network model:

1) Input layer of network model is used for matching dimension of input data and extracting features roughly. 2) Each residual block is comprised of auto encoder structure and short cut path, which function is accurate feature extraction and selection from input data. In auto encoder structure, higher dimensional features of wrapped region can be acquired from data by multiple convolution-pooling and convolution-up sampling operations. Then sum up the results produced by residual block and short cut path to complete feature extraction in single block. Residual structure use residual output $R(x)=F(x)+x$ to replace $F(x)$ in conventional series structure. It can bring such advantages: enhance fitting ability of deep neural network; overcome the problem of degradation. 3) Output layer can integrate all the extracted features in hidden layers and execute multiple classification to each pixel in phase image. Then we can obtain wrap count distribution map with $W \times H$ in k dimensions. In this map, single pixel will be categorized into j'th class, if probability of j'th dimension is larger than others in k. The scheme of classification stage is shown in Figure 2:

Here gives the principle of network components. Batch normalization (*BN*): Feature distribution of input data will be engaged in normalization operation and limited in the range of mean = 0, variance = 1. Different samples can be corrected to a same scope; 2D convolution operation (*Conv*): Execute convolution between 2D convolution kernels and target image row by row and extract eigenvalue; Rectified Linear Units activation function (*Relu*): It can add nonlinear factors to the network model to strengthen expression ability. The main task of this function is mapping the data feature from activated neurons to outputs; max-pooling operation (*MP*): Typical feature selection, information filtering and parameters reduction. The size of feature map will be shrunken after this operation; up sampling (*US*): Expand information for feature map; dropout operation (*Dp*): Prevent over-fitting by disable neurons randomly; full connection layer (*Dense*): Combine all the feature map together; *Softmax*: It can realize multiple classification task, which act as the output layer of network model.

Figure 2. The scheme of classification stage

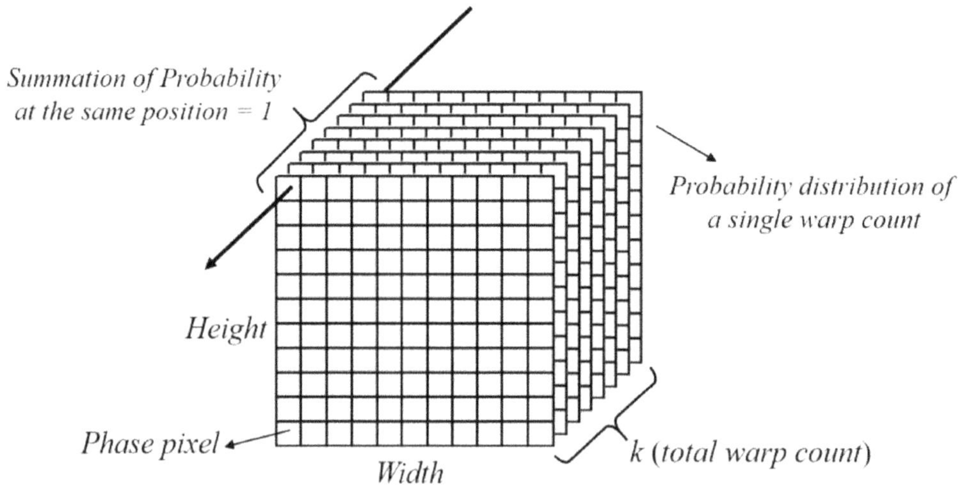

Figure 3. Scheme of network training and validation

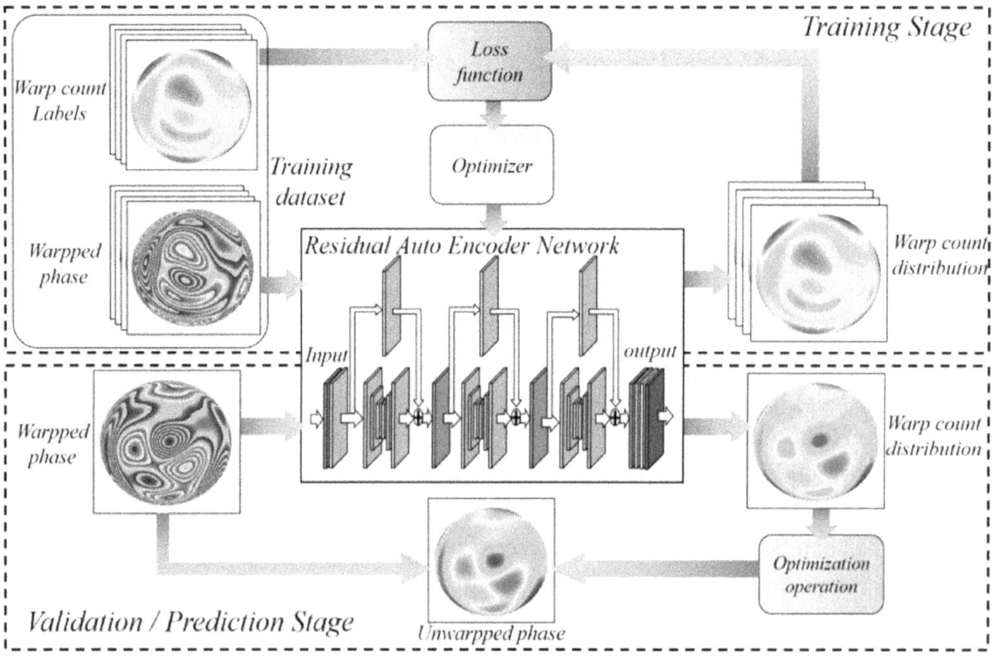

In training stage, training samples are put into the input layer batch by batch; Sparse Categorical Cross entropy is used as loss function, which can calculate deviation between label data (Ground truth) and prediction result; Optimizer is adaptive moment estimation (Yan Jiang, 2017) that function is train and update parameters of network model by gradient descent method. Scheme of network training and validation is shown as Figure 3.

Coarse training and fine training stages are engaged in this period. 1) Coarse training: Smaller batches of samples are selected and a larger learning rate $LR = 0.1$ is set to realize fast parameter initialization to network model (Beginning status is all zeros). 2) Fine training: Full dataset will join the training and learning rate has a positive ratio with loss value: $LR=\tau \bullet Loss$ to prevent instable training. Here, τ is the dynamic attenuation coefficient for learning rate. After quantities of iterative calculation, the network model can reach optimal configuration. In this multiple classification task, we use categorical cross entropy as the loss function. It can be expressed as Equation (2):

$$Loss = F(p,q) = -\frac{1}{m}\sum_{j=1}^{m}\sum_{i=1}^{n} p(x_{ij})\log\left[q(x_{ij})\right] \tag{2}$$

Where $F(p,q)$ is the categorical cross entropy function, probability distribution of ground truth is $p(x)$ and probability distribution of predicted one is $q(x)$, x_i is single sample under processing. Then m, n is number of samples and categories respectively. This loss function can be used to evaluate the probability distribution difference between predicted value and that of the reference. The smaller loss value is obtained, the more accurate unwrapping result will be produced. Here, threshold of loss value is set to $TH = 0.01$. We can stop training task, once the threshold is reached.

In validation stage, optimal network model can act as a predictor to classify unknown wrapped phase data and the corresponding wrap count map is predicted. Then we add up original wrapped phase with wrap count map to complete unwrapping.

2.3 Generation of Dataset

Based on the principle of RAEN, large quantity of experimental samples is required to train the network model. With the optimal trained network model, each pixel in wrapped phase image can be classified accurately. Here, 36 terms of Zernike polynomial, Gaussian function and the samples acquired by interferometer are the sources for training dataset generation. Zernike polynomial (Hou & Fan Wu, 2006) in polar coordinates can be denoted as Equation (3):

$$W(\rho,\theta) = \sum_{n=0}^{u}\sum_{m=-n}^{n} C_{nm}Z_{nm} = \sum_{n=0}^{u}\sum_{m=0}^{n} C_{nm}R_{n}^{m-2m}(\rho)\begin{Bmatrix}\sin\theta \\ \cos\theta\end{Bmatrix}(n-2m) \tag{3}$$

Where C_{nm} is the coefficient, Z_{nm} is the term of Zernike polynomial and n is its order. Here, u >0 and u, m are all beyond to integer set. To be further described, Z_{nm} can be expressed as Equation (4):

$$Z_{nm} = \begin{cases} R_n^l(\rho)\sin l\theta & l < 0 \\ R_n^l(\rho)\cos l\theta & l \geq 0 \end{cases}$$
$$R_n^l(\rho) = \sum_{s=0}^{n-m} (-1)^s \frac{(2n-m-s)!}{s!(n-s)!(n-m-s)!} \rho^{2(n-s)-m} \quad (4)$$

Random generator is used to produce coefficient for 36-term Zernike polynomial. After multiple cycle calculation, 22000 pairs of samples are acquired for network training and 5000 for validation. Phase data sample generated by software is unwrapped phase. Therefore, we need to wrap it for model training:

$$\phi(x,y) = \varphi(x,y) - m(x,y) = \varphi(x,y) - 2k(x,y)\pi,\ k \in Z \quad (5)$$

Where $\phi(x,y)$ *is* wrapped phase, $\varphi(x,y)$ *is* unwrapped phase and m(x,y) *is* wrap count distribution map. Values in wrap count map k belong to integer set Z. Each pair of $\phi(x,y)$ *and* $\varphi(x,y)$ is regarded as a piece of experimental sample. For model training, we can denote them as Xtrian, *Ytrian and for* validation as Xtest, *Ytest. Input* all the prepared samples to the network model, then the training stage will be performed.

3. OPTIMIZATION AND DYNAMIC RESOLUTION

3.1 Image Analysis-Based Optimization

Though wrap count distribution produced by network model has a higher accuracy (up to 96%), there still exist misclassification and noise points in its local area. These defects will leave obvious error in final unwrapping result. Therefore, we designed an optimization method based on image analysis to deal with that. Its procedure is given in Figure 4:

Step 1: Input wrapped phase data $\phi(x,y)$ and execute Laplacian filtering operation to obtain the edge of data jumping positions.
Step 2: Use adaptive binarization operator to process filtered result and produce a more apparent edge.
Step 3: We firstly add the edge to prediction result *m(x,y)*, then segment each closed region out from wrap count map with the rule of edge. One closed region presents a certain wrapped count.
Step 4: By analyzing histogram information of each closed region, the corresponding compensation value *C* can be obtained. Judgement conditions is given in Equation (6): 1) extract main gray level (wrap count) of closed region; 2) Main gray level of a closed region should not equal to its neighbors'.

$$\begin{cases} C_i = \max[hist(R_i)] & , i = 1,2,3...,n \\ C_i \neq C_j & , i,j \in n \end{cases} \quad (6)$$

Where *hist*()stands for histogram analysis, C_j are the neighbors of C_i, *n* is the number of regions.

Step 5: Each closed region will be filled up with the compensation value to remove error points. Then perform median filtering to global map.

Figure 4. Procedure of optimization operation: a) Transform original RGB image to gray one; b) Execute Laplace filtering to gray image; c) Extract edge contour from filtered image; d) Segment each wrapped region out by edge; e) Analyze the histogram of each wrapped region; f) Perform median filtering and fill the region with major value

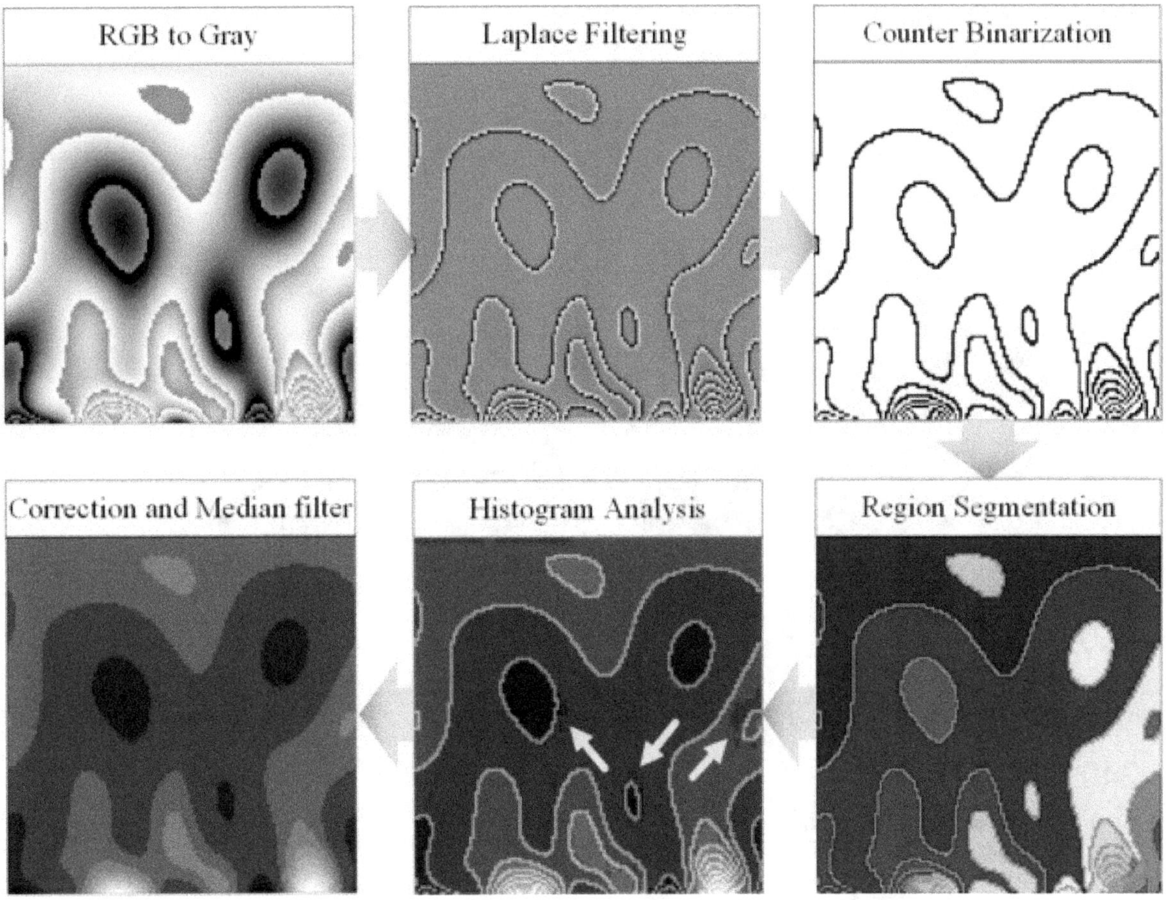

Fault points (pointed by yellow arrows) in Step 5 are eliminated with the help of optimization operation. Through the validation, the proposed optimization method can further improve the accuracy of initial result to great extents.

3.2 Phase Data Stitching

Generally, unwrapping results produced by deep neural network have a static resolution. Resolution of predicted wrap count map is equal to that of training data. In order to improve generality of system, detection resolution should be variable. We regard each prediction result as a basic unit, then combine with a data stitching algorithm to realize dynamic resolution for phase unwrapping. Here Iterative Closest Point (ICP) (Xin et al., 2018) is adopted to perform data stitching for full aperture. Before unwrapping, full aperture data will be divided into several subregions under the certain rule: 1) The size of each subregion should be equivalent to that of training sample (256×256 pixels); 2) Overlap area between adjacent subregions need to be set larger than 20% to ensure the stitching accuracy. We perform registration firstly to overlap areas and then correct their complementary point cloud accordingly; 3) Overlap areas should contain less proportion of dense fringe zone, because classification fault is more likely occurred in these places. The more error left in common areas, the inferior accuracy have to be encountered in stitching. Data dividing strategy is shown as Figure 5:

Figure 5. Data dividing strategy for full aperture

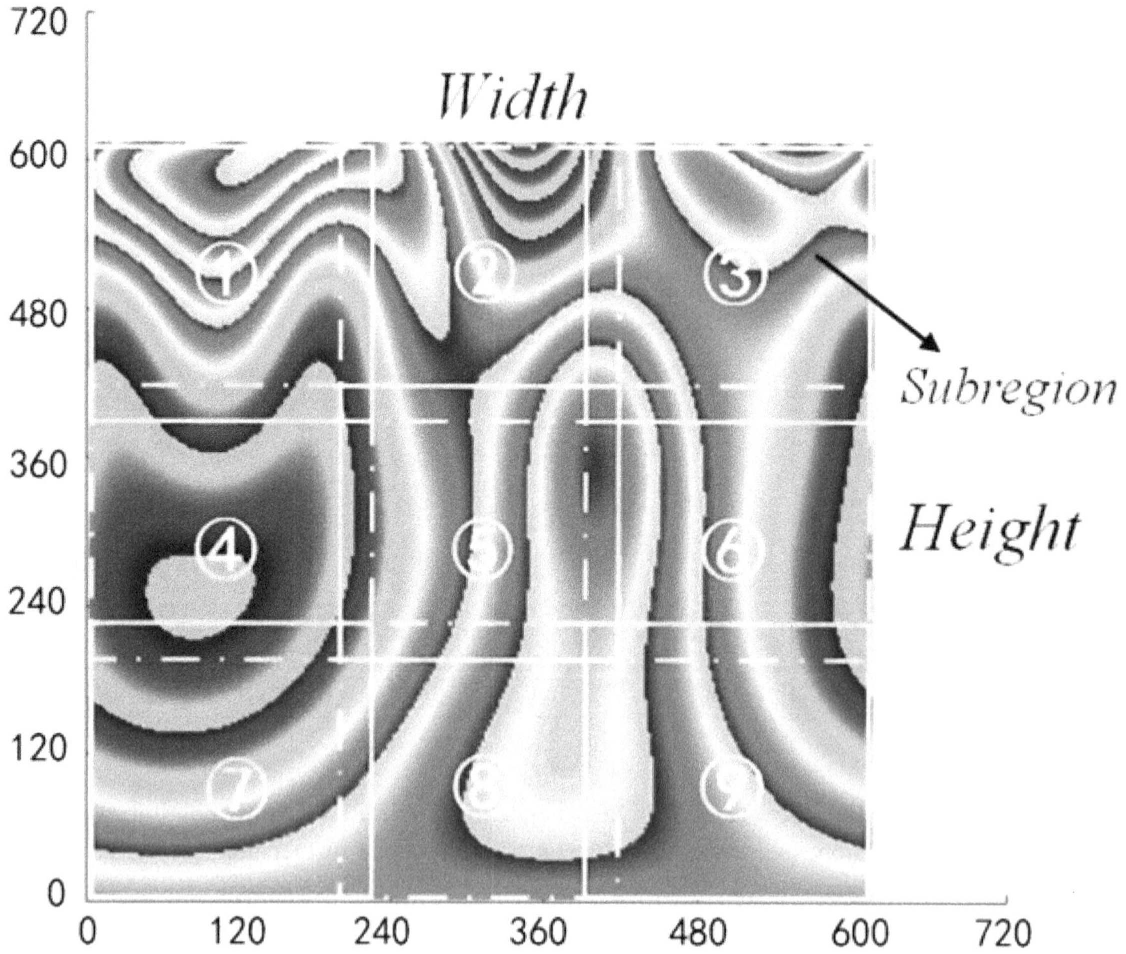

Since we use 3D point cloud stitching method here, phase pixel can be treated as *Z* coordinate and pixel position as *X*, *Y* respectively. Therefore, 2D phase data can be denoted as spatial point cloud data $p_i(x,y,z)$. Through several rotation and translation transformations, two or more point cloud data with different coordinate system can be integrated into a same one. Affine transformation matrix *H* can be expressed as Equation (7):

$$H = \begin{bmatrix} R_{3\times3} & T_{3\times1} \\ O_{1\times3} & S \end{bmatrix},\ T_{3\times1} = \begin{bmatrix} t_x & t_y & t_z \end{bmatrix}^T$$

$$R_{3\times3} = \begin{bmatrix} \cos\beta\cos\gamma & \cos\beta\sin\gamma & -\sin\beta \\ -\cos\alpha\sin\gamma - \sin\alpha\sin\beta\cos\gamma & \cos\alpha\cos\gamma + \sin\alpha\sin\beta\sin\gamma & \sin\alpha\cos\beta \\ \sin\alpha\sin\gamma + \cos\alpha\sin\beta\cos\gamma & -\sin\alpha\cos\gamma - \cos\alpha\sin\beta\sin\gamma & \cos\alpha\cos\beta \end{bmatrix} \quad (7)$$

Where $R_{3\times3}$ is the rotation matrix in *X, Y, Z* directions, $T_{3\times1}$ is translation matrix, $O_{1\times3}$ is perspective transformation matrix and *S* is scaling factor. In rotation matrix $R_{3\times3}$, α,β,γ are rotation angles in X, *Y, Z* directions respectively. Now, we firstly need to intercept closest point (p_i,p_{i+1}) (overlapping area) from under-registration regions $p_i(x,y,z)$ and $p_{i+1}(x,y,z)$; Then use Singular value decomposition (SVD) method (Singh et al., 2017) to calculate optimal parameters $R_{3\times3}$ and $T_{3\times1}$; finally, after quantities of iterative calculation, error function Equation (8) reaches its minimum value.

$$E(R,t) = \frac{1}{n}\sum_{i=1}^{n}\left\| q_i - (Rp_i + t) \right\|^2 \quad (8)$$

Where $R=R_{3\times3}$, $t=T_{3\times1}$, p_i is target point set and q_i is original point set. Each subregion in Fig.6 have an independent coordinate system. With the help of the iterative calculation above, best fit transformation matrix $R_{3\times3}$, $T_{3\times1}$ can be obtained and neighbor subregions are registered: $p'_{i+1}(x',y',z') = \left[p_{i+1}(x,y,z)^T H\right]^T$. Data points in overlapping area of $p_i(x,y,z)$ and $p'_{i+1}(x',y',z')$ are merged together by weight averaging. Scheme of 3D data stitching is shown as Fig.6

Figure 6. Iterative closest point phase data stitching: a) p_i phase data; b) p_{i+1} phase data; c) registered phase data; d) full aperture data

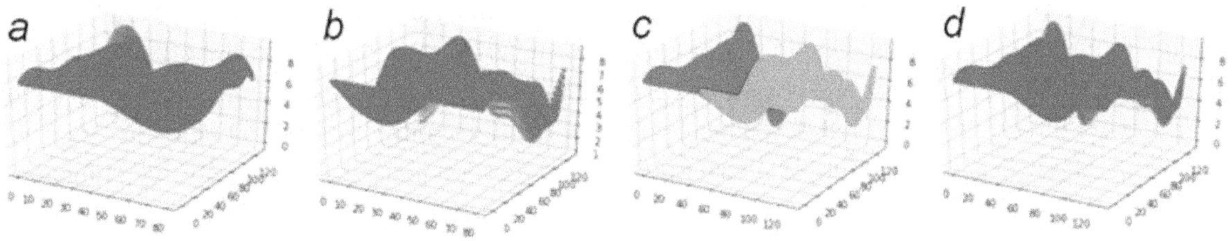

By using gradual stitching, full aperture wrapped phase with any resolution can be covered and unwrapped. Compared with initial results from network model, stitching strategy is more flexible. Meanwhile, high resolution samples for network training requires more hardware resource and computing time.

4. SYSTEM PLATFORM OF PDI

4.1 Principle of PDI

Point diffraction interferometry is a high-precision measurement technique for optical surface based on the principle of interferometry and diffraction phenomenon. An interferometer with this technique is fabricated as shown in Fig.7:

Figure 7. Principle scheme of point diffraction interferometer

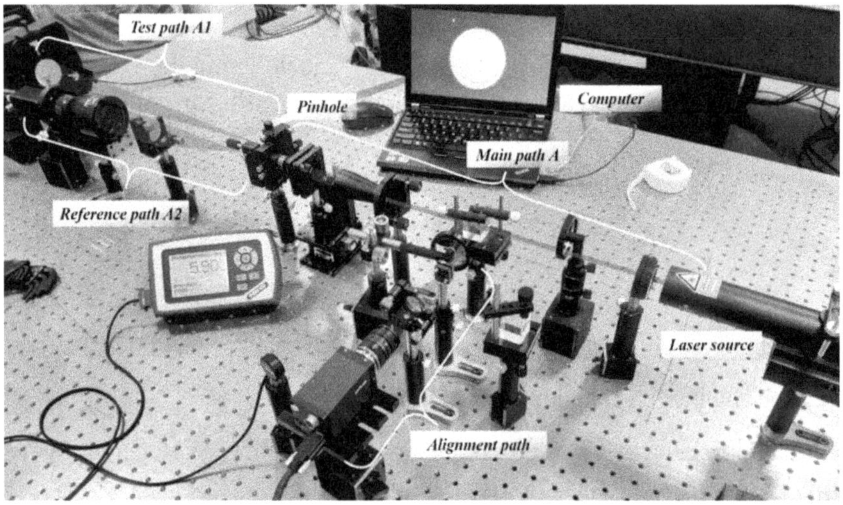

In this optical system, He-Ne laser source emits the beam for the test. The laser pass through diaphragm and attenuator to the expanding collimator lens and is transformed into parallel light; Then micro objective converges and projects it to the pinhole plate in the shape of spot (main path *A*); With the help of pinhole, input light spot is diffracted out and spherical wavefront is produced; Wavefront can be divided into two parts: One is test path (*A1*) to the under-test optics and the other is reference path (*A2*) to the CCD detector; Test beam is reflected by under-test optics and pinhole plate again then interferes with reference one; Interfered beams form a interferogram on the CCD detector; Joint with PZT actuator, CCD acquires multiple interferograms with certain phase shifts; Finally, by using appropriate algorithm, phase information can be extracted which contains surface details of under-test optics. Hardware configuration of point diffraction interferometer is given as Table 1:

Table 1. Hardware configuration of PDI system

Items	Types	Parameters
illuminant	Thorlabs He-Ne Laser source	Power: 2mW, ë=632.8nm
Objective & Pinhole	10/0.25 160/0.17, etched pinhole	Focus:10mm, Diameter: 2.5um
Detector	Basler CCD Camera	Resolution:782×580
Test Optics	Concave ellipsoid	D=108mm, R0=348.6mm, K=-0.366

4.2 Phase Extraction

We can extract phase information by using four-step algorithm to process phase shifted interferograms (Zhou et al., 2015). However, arc tangent operation is *atan2* function rather than *arctan* in computer, the extracted data will be a wrapped one. Here, four-step algorithm can be denoted as Equation (9):

$$\phi\left(x,y\right) = \arctan\left[\frac{I_4 - I_2}{I_1 - I_3}\right] \tag{9}$$

Where $\phi(x,y)$ is phase data and $I_1I_2I_3I_4$ are intensity information of interferograms. Their detail expressions is shown as Equation (10):

$$I(x,y) = I_0(x,y)\{1 + V(x,y)\cos[\phi(x,y)]\} \tag{10}$$

In the equation above, $\phi(x,y)$ is phase data to be extracted, $I_0(x,y)$ is background intensity and $V(x,y)$ presents contrast of fringe pattern as Equation (11)

$$\begin{aligned} I_0(x,y) &= I_t(x,y) + I_r(x,y) \\ V(x,y) &= \frac{I_{\max}(x,y) - I_{\min}(x,y)}{I_{\max}(x,y) + I_{\min}(x,y)} = \frac{2\sqrt{I_t(x,y)I_r(x,y)}}{I_t(x,y) + I_r(x,y)} \end{aligned} \tag{11}$$

Where I_t, I_r are test and reference intensity respectively, I_{max}, I_{min} are their maximum and minimum value. Because $\phi(x,y)$, $I_0(x,y)$ and $V(x,y)$ are all unknown quantity, multiple interferograms are needed in Equation (8). Phase data $\phi(x,y)$ extracted in this stage will be the processing target for proposed method. Meanwhile, parts of these wrapped data can be used as the dataset for training stage of network model.

5. EXPERIMENTS AND DISCUSSION

To validate the performance of proposed method, multiple tests are carried out including unwrapping accuracy, anti-noise performance and time efficiency. As shown in Fig.7, PDI system is constructed and it operates in the condition of normal temperature and humidity. Here, hardware configuration of computer in the system is given as follow: CPU: i7-7700K 4.2GHz; GPU: GTX1070 1.55GHz 8GB; Memory: DDR4 3000MHz 16GB; SSD: M.2 512GB. Software platform: Python 3.7 and Matlab 2018 development in Windows 10 64 bit. In the experiment, we adopt PV, RMS and REMS values as the evaluation criterion of each measurement. The definitions are given in Table 2:

5.1 Tests on Simulation and Acquired Data

Firstly, we will validate the accuracy of unwrapping method in the test. Wrapped samples are not included in the training dataset and they will under the processing of proposed method. Intermediate and final results are shown in Fig.8:

Table 2. Definitions of evaluation criterion

Items	Formula	Description
Peak-to-Valley (PV)	$PV = W_{max} - W_{min}$	Range of extreme values
Root Mean Square (RMS)	$RMS = \sqrt{\frac{1}{n}\sum_{i=1}^{n}\left(W_i - \frac{1}{n}\sum_{i=1}^{n}W_i\right)^2}$	Global deviation from mean value Smoothness of a surface
Root Mean Square Error (RMSE)	$RMSE(x,y) = \sqrt{\frac{1}{n}\sum_{i=1}^{n}\left[RAEN(x_i) - y_i\right]^2}$	Global error between prediction value and ground truth

Where W_{max}, W_{min}, W_i are maximum, minimum and arbitrary point in phase data map respectively; *n* is the number of phase points; $RAEN(x_i)$ is the network model and *x*, *y* are points in wrapped phase and unwrapped one.

Figure 8. Unwrapping results on simulation data: a) Wrapped phase; b) initial wrap count distribution; c) optimized wrap count distribution; d) unwrapped phase; e) ground truth; f) residual error

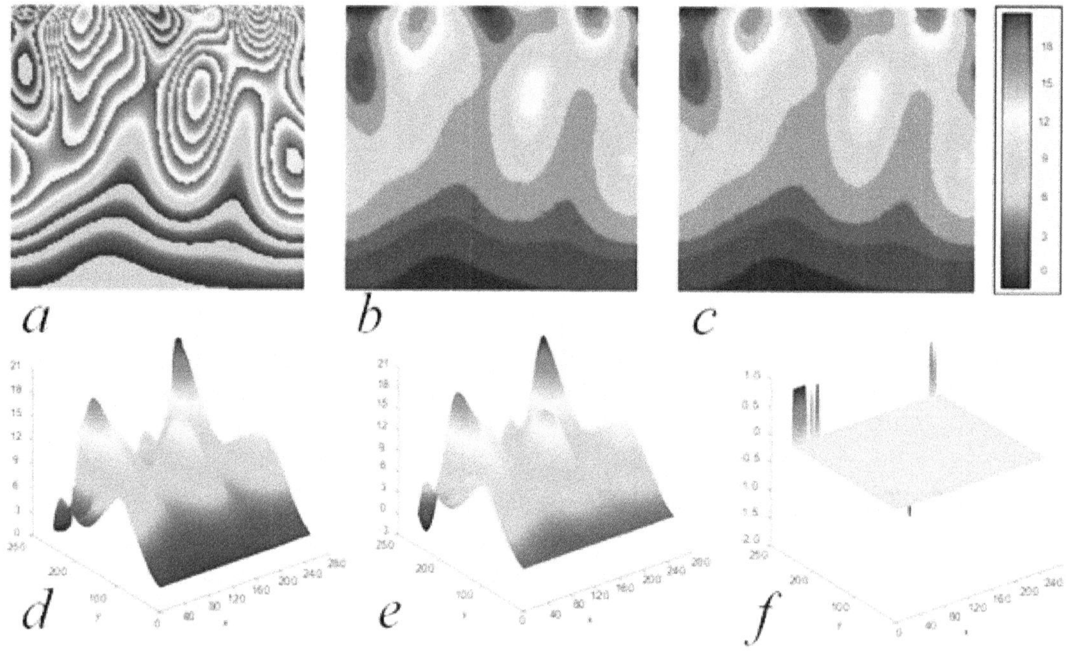

Figure 8a is the original data of wrapped phase and Fig.8b is the prediction result by network model. There still exist some fault points in wrap count distribution. After optimization in Figure 8c, the unwrapping result is acceptable. From Fig.8d and Fig.8e, it can be obviously found that the difference between ground truth (PV=22.102rad, RMS=3.4031rad) and our result (PV=20.712rad, RMS=3.3797rad) is very tiny. Unwrapping accuracy in pixel level is 0.987 and RMSE (Root Mean Square Error) value is 0.2857rad. Here, limited samples are shown in figures, while other 5000 test samples are under the test and obtain the unwrapping accuracy of 0.972 in average. Then we utilize PDI system to test an aspherical lens (described in Table 1) and collect samples for validation. The results are given in Figure 9:

Figure 9. Unwrapping results on acquired data: a) Acquired interferogram; b) Wrapped phase extraction; c) Initial wrap count distribution; d) Optimized wrap count distribution; e) Unwrapped phase; f) Ground truth; g) Residual error

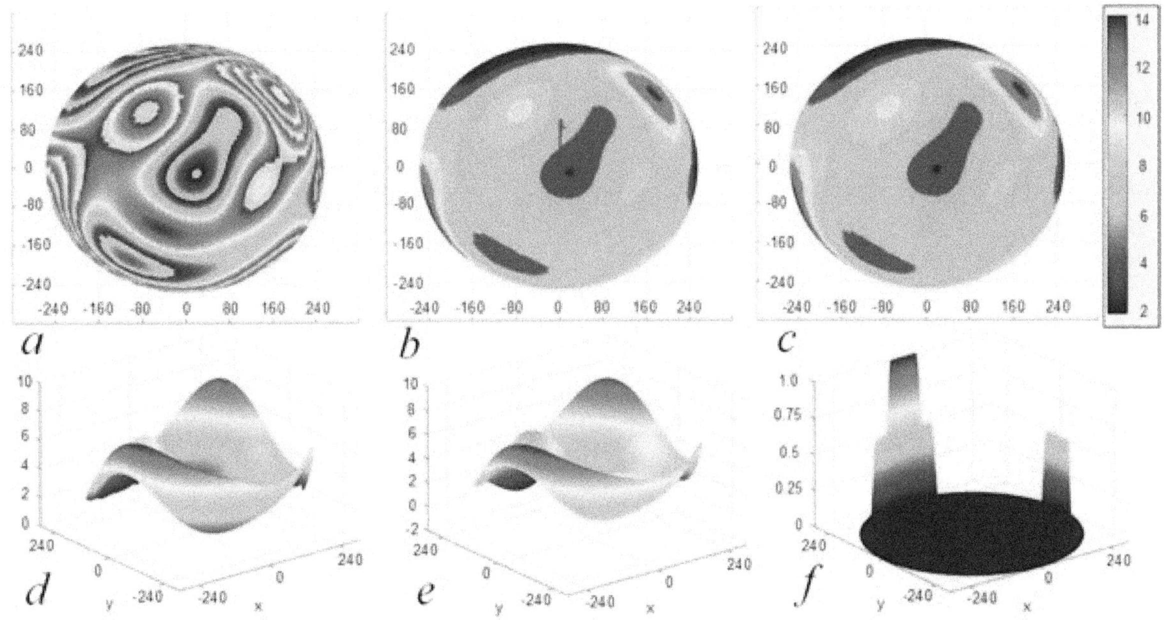

Without ground truth, we can only regard measurement results by Zygo VeriFire™ interferometer (detection resolution: 0.5nm, RMS repeatability: λ/10000) as the standard value (Measurement quantity: PV=9.547rad, RMS=1.2737rad). By using the proposed method, the acquired wrapped phase is processed step by step. We can obtain the processing result: PV=8.696rad, RMS =1.2565rad. The unwrapped phase results show a higher consistency between the two methods above. Unwrapping accuracy reaches 0.9936 and RMSE value is 0.5397rad.

5.2 Anti-Noise Test

In previous tests, the proposed method shows an excellent performance in phase unwrapping. However, in practical applications, original data usually mixed with noise in different extents. Therefore, denoising performance should be examined. Wrapped phase mixed with Gaussian and salt & pepper noise at different level of (mean=0, variance= 0.02; percentage = 0.05) are shown in Fig.10a and Fig.10e. The corresponding unwrapped phase is given in Fig.10b and Fig.10f.

Corrupted by heavy salt & pepper noise, there are several jumping points in local areas of processing result, compared with Figure 10c. In general, unwrapping accuracy can still reaches 0.964 and RMSE value between Figure 10b and Figure 10c is 0.9238rad. The corresponding error distribution is shown in Figure 10d. Mixed with serious Gaussian noise, the wrapped phase can also be processed with the accuracy of 0.975 and RMSE of 0.7689rad. Figure 10h is the error distribution between Figure 10f and Figure 10g.

Figure 10. Anti-noise tests on wrapped phase mixed with Gaussian and salt and pepper noise: a) Wrapped phase with salt and pepper noise at percentage of 0.05; b) unwrapping result; c) ground truth; d) error distribution; e) wrapped phase with Gaussian noise at variance= 0.02; f) unwrapping result; g) ground truth; h) error distribution

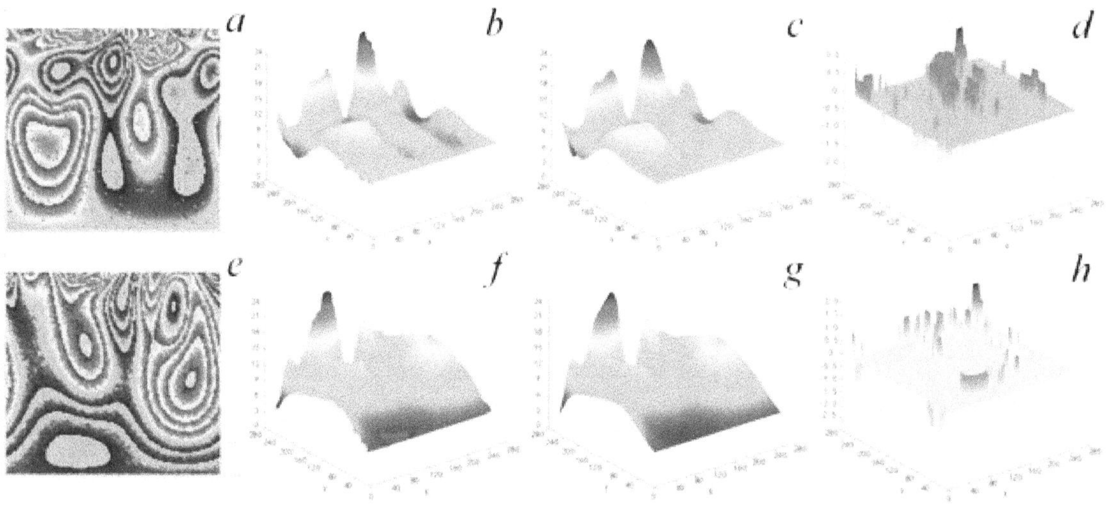

As the strength of noise increases, the unwrapping accuracy is influenced graduately. While it still produces a result in acceptable domain. In addition, Goldstein branch cut and quality-guided algorithm are also join the test to process the noised wrapped phase at the same level.

Figure 11. Performance test on different unwrapping methods: a) Gaussian noise corrupted phase with variance=0.02; b) result produced by proposed method; c) result produced by Goldstein branch cut; d) result produced by quality-guided algorithm; e) ground truth; f) residual error between b and e; g) residual error between c and e; h) residual error between d and e

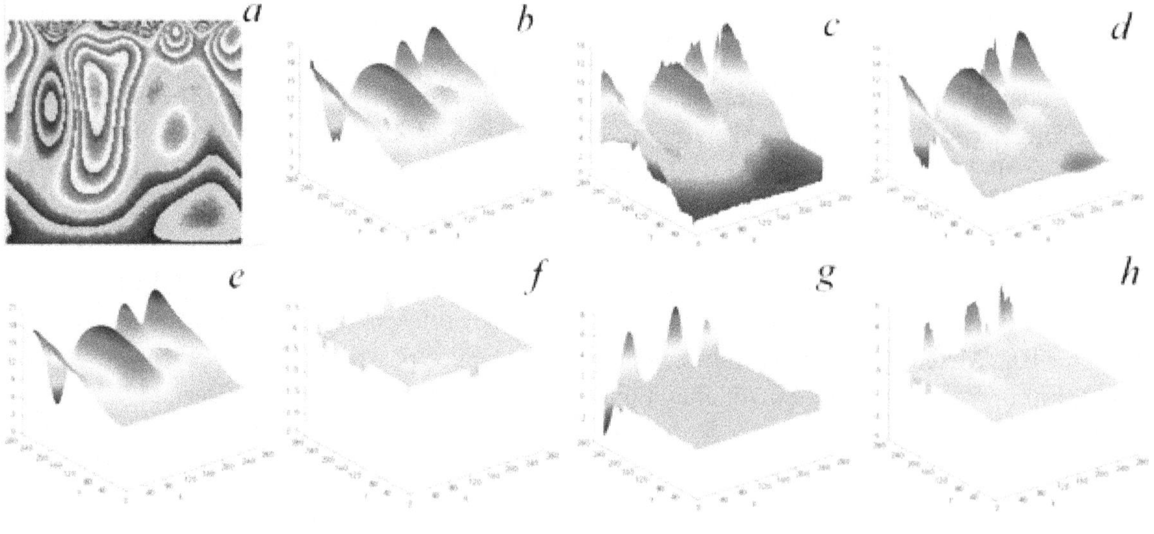

In the unwrapped phase in Figure 11b, the result produced by proposed method is most similar to the ground truth Figure 11e. Many fault regions and defects are still left in the unwrapping result by Goldstein branch cut (Figure 11c) and quality-guided algorithm (Figure 11d). Unwrapping performance of different methods in the test is presented in Table 3.

Table 3. Unwrapping performance of different methods

Items	Accuracy	RMSE (rad)	PV (rad)	RMS (rad)
Quality-guided algorithm	0.793	2.622	12.868	2.229
Goldstein branch cut	0.781	4.715	11.949	2.205
Proposed	0.973	0.437	14.698	2.293
Ground truth	—	—	14.917	2.325

From error distribution maps, it can be seen that amount and amplitude of residual error in proposed (Figure 11f) is very small. Goldstein branch (Figure 11g) cut and quality-guided algorithm (Figure 11h) have difficulty in processing the phase data with heavy noise and steep gradient.

5.3 Time Efficiency

Real time performance of unwrapping method is a critical factor in the applications. Time efficiency is not only related to hardware platform, but also to algorithm itself. In this test, wrapped phase data with different resolutions will under the processing of proposed method. Timer function from Python 3.7 lib is adopted in the experiment. Total and step processing time consumption is shown in Figure 12:

Obviously, the higher resolution engaged, the longer processing time is required. Because more data points need to be classified and more subregions should be stitched. From the data, it can be seen that prediction stage still take the majority of processing time.

Figure 12. Processing time consumption in steps

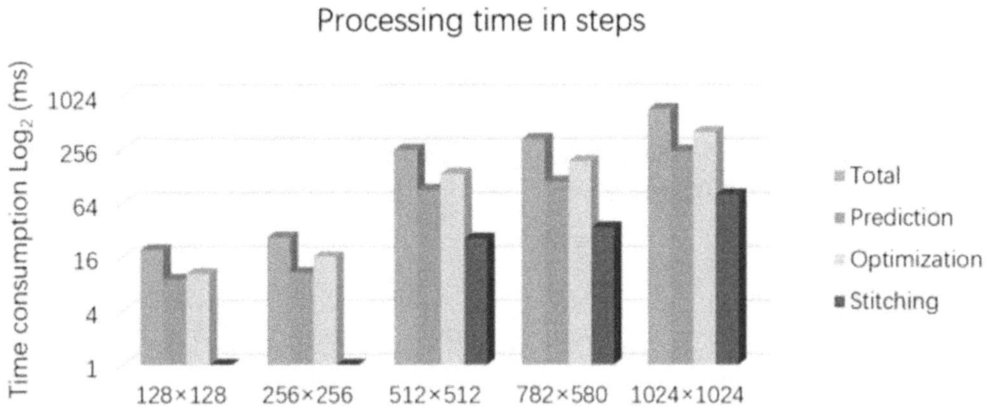

Then, different methods are also join the test for comparison. Wrapped phase data with different resolution are under the test. The results given in Table 4 is the average value of 10 experiments.

The results show that the proposed method is superior to others in time efficiency. For one reason, high-performance GPU can speed up computing efficiency; for another, the model is well optimized. Then Goldstein branch cut is faster than Quality-guided algorithm, because the latter one need to calculate a quality map first. As for proposed method, 26.5 ms/period in processing with wrapped phase at 256×256 means 37.7fps, which can satisfy the requirement of most industrial applications.

Table 4. Time efficiency of different methods (sec)

Items	128×128	256×256	512×512	1024×1024
Goldstein branch cut	0.625	2.037	7.547	31.908
Quality-guided algorithm	4.497	34.719	660.108	2 hours +
Proposed	0.0192	0.0265	0.2511	0.717

6. CONCLUSION

A novel phase unwrapping method is presented in this paper, which is based on Residual Auto Encoder Network. It can be applied for PDI system and general purpose. We regard phase unwrapping as a problem of classification. Firstly, principle of neural network unwrapping, training scheme are introduced in details; Then, an optimization operation is designed for network to remove fault and noise points in initial results; Finally, Iterative Closest Point algorithm is adopted to stitch phase data to realize dynamic resolution in processing. In addition, PDI system and multi-step phase extraction technique are performed to provide the foundation to proposed method. In the experiment stages, we confirmed that the proposed method possesses an excellent performance in terms of unwrapping accuracy, denoising and time efficiency: Up to 98% accuracy in pixel level classification and 0.2857rad in RMSE; Under the influence of serious noise (Gaussian and Salt & pepper), unwrapping accuracy can still reach 96.4%; Processing time of wrapped phase in 256×256 is faster than 26.5ms (37.7 Fps). In future work, we will pay more attention to steep phase unwrapping and smart phase extraction technique.

FUNDING

Natural Science Basic Research Plan in Shaanxi Province of China [2023-JC-QN-0613], China Postdoctoral Science Foundation [2022M722551].

ACKNOWLEDGMENT

This project was supported by the State Key Laboratory of Applied Optics. We express our sincere gratitude to journal's editor and reviewers for their help in revising the paper.

REFERENCES

Badrinarayanan, V., Kendall, A., & Cipolla, R. (2017). SegNet: A Deep Convolutional Encoder-Decoder Architecture for Image Segmentation. *IEEE Transactions on Pattern Analysis and Machine Intelligence*, *39*(12), 2481–2495. doi:10.1109/TPAMI.2016.2644615 PMID:28060704

Dardikman G., Turko, N.A., & Shaked, N.T. (2019). Deep learning approaches for unwrapping phase images with steep spatial gradients: A simulation. *2018 IEEE Int Conf Sci Electr Eng Isr ICSEE*. IEEE. . doi:10.1109/ICSEE.2018.8646266

Dardikman-Yoffe, G., Roitshtain, D., Mirsky, S. K., Turko, N. A., Habaza, M., & Shaked, N. T. (2020). PhUn-Net: Ready-to-use neural network for unwrapping quantitative phase images of biological cells. *Biomedical Optics Express*, *11*(2), 1107. doi:10.1364/BOE.379533 PMID:32206402

Du, S., Zheng, N., Ying, S., & Liu, J. (2010). Affine iterative closest point algorithm for point set registration. *Pattern Recognition Letters*, *31*(9), 791–799. doi:10.1016/j.patrec.2010.01.020

Flynn, T.J. (1997). *Two-dimensional phase unwrapping with minimum weighted discontinuity.*

Hou, X., & Fan Wu, L. Y. (2006). Stitching algorithm for annular subaperture interferometry. *Chinese Optics Letters*, *4*, 211–214.

Huang, Q., Zhou, H., Dong, S., & Xu, S. (2015). Parallel Branch-Cut Algorithm Based on Simulated Annealing for Large-Scale Phase Unwrapping. *IEEE Transactions on Geoscience and Remote Sensing*, *53*(7), 3833–3846. doi:10.1109/TGRS.2014.2385482

Ian, X. I. T., Ingzhou, X. T. U., Hang, J. U. Z., Pires, O. L. S., Eal, N., & Rock, B., & (2018). Snapshot multi-wavelength interference microscope. *Optics Express*, *26*(14), 18279–18291. doi:10.1364/OE.26.018279 PMID:30114009

Li, C., Tian, Y., & Tian, J. (2019). A method for single image phase unwrapping based on generative adversarial networks. *Elev Int Conf Digit Image Process*, *1117911*, 157. doi:10.1117/12.2540155

Liu, Y., Han, Y., Li, F., & Zhang, Q. (2018). Speedup of minimum discontinuity phase unwrapping algorithm with a reference phase distribution. *Optics Communications*, *417*, 97–102. doi:10.1016/j.optcom.2018.02.025

Nguyen, H., Dunne, N., Li, H., Wang, Y., & Wang, Z. (2019). Real-time 3D shape measurement using 3LCD projection and deep machine learning. *Applied Optics*, *58*(26), 7100. doi:10.1364/AO.58.007100 PMID:31503981

Ota, K., Yamamoto, T., Fukuda, Y., Otaki, K., Nishiyama, I., & Okazaki, S. (2001). Advanced point diffraction interferometer for EUV aspherical mirrors. *Emerg Lithogr Technol V*, *4343*, 543–550. doi:10.1117/12.436686

Otaki, K., Ota, K., Nishiyama, I., Yamamoto, T., Fukuda, Y., & Okazaki, S. (2002). Development of the point diffraction interferometer for extreme ultraviolet lithography: Design, fabrication, and evaluation. *Journal of Vacuum Science & Technology. B, Microelectronics and Nanometer Structures : Processing, Measurement, and Phenomena : An Official Journal of the American Vacuum Society*, *20*(6), 2449–2458. doi:10.1116/1.1526605

Pritt, M. D. (1995). Unweighted least squares phase unwrapping by means of multigrid techniques. *Synth Aperture Radar Passiv Microw Sens*, *2584*, 289–300. doi:10.1117/12.227138

Rhee, H. G., Yang, H. S., Moon, I. K., Kihm, H., Lee, J. H., & Lee, Y. W. (2011). Eight-axis-polishing machine for large off-axis aspheric optics. *Journal of the Optical Society of Korea*, *15*(4), 394–397. doi:10.3807/JOSK.2011.15.4.394

Singh, P., Yadav, A. K., & Singh, K. (2017). Phase image encryption in the fractional Hartley domain using Arnold transform and singular value decomposition. *Optics and Lasers in Engineering*, *91*, 187–195. doi:10.1016/j.optlaseng.2016.11.022

Spoorthi, G. E., Gorthi, S., & Gorthi, R. K. S. S. (2019). PhaseNet: A deep convolutional neural network for two-dimensional phase unwrapping. *IEEE Signal Processing Letters*, *26*(1), 54–58. doi:10.1109/LSP.2018.2879184

Wang, K., Li, Y., Kemao, Q., Di, J., & Zhao, J. (2019). One-step robust deep learning phase unwrapping. *Optics Express*, *27*(10), 15100. doi:10.1364/OE.27.015100 PMID:31163947

Wu, C., Qiao, Z., Zhang, N., Li, X., Fan, J., Song, H., Ai, D., Yang, J., & Huang, Y. (2020). Phase unwrapping based on a residual en-decoder network for phase images in Fourier domain Doppler optical coherence tomography. *Biomedical Optics Express*, *11*(4), 1760. doi:10.1364/BOE.386101 PMID:32341846

Xia, S., Huang, Y., Peng, S., Wu, Y., & Tan, X. (2017). Robust phase unwrapping for phase images in Fourier domain Doppler optical coherence tomography. *Journal of Biomedical Optics*, *22*(3), 036014. doi:10.1117/1.JBO.22.3.036014 PMID:28353689

Xin, M., Li, B., Yan, X., Chen, L., & Wei, X. (2018). A robust cloud registration method based on redundant data reduction using backpropagation neural network and shift window. *The Review of Scientific Instruments*, *89*(2), 024704. doi:10.1063/1.4996628 PMID:29495860

Xing, S., & Guo, H. (2017). Temporal phase unwrapping for fringe projection profilometry aided by recursion of Chebyshev polynomials. *Applied Optics*, *56*(6), 1591. doi:10.1364/AO.56.001591 PMID:28234364

Yan, K., Yu, Y., Sun, T., Asundi, A., & Kemao, Q. (2020). Wrapped phase denoising using convolutional neural networks. *Optics and Lasers in Engineering*, *128*, 105999. doi:10.1016/j.optlaseng.2019.105999

Yan Jiang, F. H. (2017). A Hybrid Algorithm of Adaptive Particle Swarm Optimization Based on Adaptive Moment Estimation Method. *Lecture Notes in Computer Science*, *10361*, 658–667. doi:10.1007/978-3-319-63309-1_58

Yu, J., Zhang, H., Jin, C., Ma, D., Wang, H., & Lu, Z. (2016). Ultra-high accuracy point diffraction interferometer: development, acccuracy evaluation and application. *8th Int Symp Adv Opt Manuf Test Technol Opt Test, Meas Technol Equip*. Spie. 10.1117/12.2246269

Zhang, J., Tian, X., Shao, J., Luo, H., & Liang, R. (2019). Phase unwrapping in optical metrology via denoised and convolutional segmentation networks. *Optics Express*, *27*(10), 14903. doi:10.1364/OE.27.014903 PMID:31163931

Zhao, Z., Li, B., Kang, X., Chen, L., & Wei, X. (2019). Precision optical path alignment system for point diffraction interferometer based on image information. *Applied Optics*, *58*(14), 3703. doi:10.1364/AO.58.003703 PMID:31158181

Zhao, Z., Zhang, H., Xiao, Z., Du, H., Zhuang, Y., Fan, C., & Zhao, H. (2019). Robust 2D phase unwrapping algorithm based on the transport of intensity equation. *Measurement Science & Technology*, *30*(1), 015201. doi:10.1088/1361-6501/aaec5c

Zhong, H., Tang, J., Zhang, S., & Chen, M. (2011). An Improved Quality-Guided Phase Unwrapping Algorithm Based on Priority Queue. *IEEE Geoscience and Remote Sensing Letters*, *8*(2), 364–368. doi:10.1109/LGRS.2010.2076362

Zhou, C., Liu, T., Si, S., Xu, J., Liu, Y., & Lei, Z. (2015). An improved stair phase encoding method for absolute phase retrieval. *Optics and Lasers in Engineering*, *66*, 269–278. doi:10.1016/j.optlaseng.2014.09.011

Chapter 11
Self-Adaptive ReLU Neural Network Method in Least-Squares Data Fitting

Zhiqiang Cai
Purdue University, USA

Min Liu
Purdue University, USA

ABSTRACT

This chapter provides a comprehensive introduction to a self-adaptive ReLU neural network method proposed recently in (Cai et al., 2022; Liu & Cai, 2022; Liu et al., 2022). The purpose is to design a nearly minimal neural network architecture to achieve the prescribed accuracy for a given task in scientific machine learning such as approximating a function or a solution of partial differential equation. Starting with a small one hidden-layer neural network, the method enhances the network adaptively by adding neurons in the current or new hidden-layer based on accuracy of the current approximation. In addition, the method provides a natural process for obtaining a good initialization in training the current network. Moreover, initialization of newly added neurons at each adaptive step is discussed in detail.

1. INTRODUCTION

Given a data set $\{(\mathbf{x}_i, y_i)\}_{i=1}^M$ with $x_i \in \Omega = [-1,1]^d$ and positive weights $\{w_i\}_{i=1}^M$, consider the discrete least-squares problem: finding $f_{nn}(\mathbf{x}) \in \mathcal{M}(l)$ such that

$$f_{nn} = \arg\min_{v \in \mathcal{M}(l)} L(v), \tag{1}$$

where $\mathcal{M}(l)$ is a ReLU neuron network defined in section 2 with l hidden-layers and $L(\bullet)$ is a least-squares loss functional given by

DOI: 10.4018/979-8-3693-0230-9.ch011

$$L(v) = \sum_{i=1}^{M} w_i (v(\mathbf{x}_i) - y_i)^2 \ .$$

For a prescribed tolerance $\varepsilon > 0$, this chapter presents a self-adaptive algorithm, the adaptive neuron enhancement method (ANE), to adaptively construct a nearly optimal network $\mathcal{M}^*$ such that the neural network approximation $f_{nn}(x)$ satisfies

$$L(f_{nn}) \leq \varepsilon L(0), \tag{2}$$

where $L(0) = \sum_{i=1}^{M} w_i y_i^2$ is the square of the weighted l^2 norm of the output data $\{y_i\}_{i=1}^{M}$.

Multi-layer ReLU neural network is described in this chapter as a set of continuous *piece-wise* linear functions. Hence each network function is piece-wise linear with respect to a partition of the domain. This partition, referred as the (domain) physical partition (see section 3), provides geometric feature of the function and hence plays a critical role in the design of self-adaptive neural network method. Determination of this physical partition for a network function is in general computationally expensive, especially when the input dimension d is high. To circumvent this difficulty, we introduce a network indicator function that can easily determine such partition.

The idea of the ANE is similar to that of standard adaptive mesh-based numerical methods, and may be written as loops of the form

$$\textbf{train} \rightarrow \textbf{estimate} \rightarrow \textbf{mark} \rightarrow \textbf{enhance} \tag{3}$$

Starting with a small one hidden layer network, the step **train** is to iteratively solve the optimization problem of the current network; the step **estimate** is to compute error of the current approximation; the step **mark** is to identify local regions that need refinement; and the step **enhance** is to add new neurons to the current network with good initialization. This adaptive algorithm learns not only from given information (data, function, partial differential equation) but also from the current computer simulation.

When the current error does not satisfy (1.2), an efficient ANE method relies on strategies to address the following questions at each adaptive step:

(a) how many new neurons should be added at the last hidden layer?
(b) when should a new hidden layer be added?

By exploiting the geometric feature of the current approximation, the enhancement strategy (see Section 4) determines the number of new neurons to be added at the last hidden layer. A new layer is added if a computable quantity measuring the improvement rate of two consecutive networks per the relative increase of parameters is small.

Problem (1.1) is a non-convex optimization that has many solutions, and the desired one is only attainable when one begins with an initial approximation that is sufficiently close. A common approach to obtaining a good initialization is through the method of continuation, as described in (Allgower & Georg, 1990). The ANE method offers a natural way to acquire a well-suited initialization. Essentially, the approximation provided by the previous network serves as a good starting point for the current network at each adaptive step. Additionally, we outline an approach for initializing the weights and biases of newly added neurons, leveraging the geometric properties of the current approximation, which is detailed in section 5.

2. ReLU NEURAL NETWORK

A neural network defines a new class of approximating functions which is suitable for some computationally challenging problems. This section describes l-hidden layer ReLU neural network as a set of continuous piece-wise linear functions and introduces related notations. This chapter is restricted to one dimensional output $n_{l+1} = 1$ for simplicity of presentation. Extension of materials covered by this chapter to multi-dimensional output $n_{l+1} > 1$ is straightforward.

ReLU refers to the rectified linear activation function defined by

$$\sigma(t) = \max\{0, t\} = \begin{cases} t, & t > 0, \\ 0, & t \leq 0. \end{cases} \tag{4}$$

The $\sigma(t)$ is a continuous piece-wise linear function with one b*reaking* point t=0. For k=1,…,l, let nk denote the number of neurons at the kt^h hidden-layer; denote by

$$\mathbf{b}^{(k)} \in \mathbb{R}^{n_k} \text{ and } \omega^{(k)} \in \mathbb{R}^{n_k \times n_{k-1}}$$

the biases and weights of neurons at the kth hidden-layer, respectively. Their i^{th} rows are denoted by $b_i^{(k)} \in \mathbb{R}$ and $\text{É}_i^{(k)} \in \mathbb{R}^{n_{k-1}}$, that are the bias and weights of the ith neuron at the kth hidden-layer, respectively. Introduce a vector-valued function $\mathbf{N}^{(k)} : \mathbb{R}^{n_{k-1}} \to \mathbb{R}^{n_k}$ as

$$\mathbf{N}^{(k)}(\mathbf{x}^{(k-1)}) = \sigma(\boldsymbol{\omega}^{(k)}\mathbf{x}^{(k-1)} + \mathbf{b}^{(k)}) \tag{5}$$

for $\mathbf{x}^{(k-1)} \in \mathbb{R}^{n_{k-1}}$

where application of the activation function σ to a vector-valued function is defined component-wisely and $n_0=d$ is the input dimension.

A ReLU neural network with l hidden-layers and n_k neurons at the kth hidden-layer may be defined as the collection of continuous piece-wise linear functions:

$$\mathcal{M}(l) = \left\{ c_1 \left(\mathbf{N}^{(l)} \circ \cdots \circ \mathbf{N}^{(1)}(x) \right) + c_0 : \begin{array}{l} (c_0, c_1) \in \mathbb{R}^{n_l+1}, \boldsymbol{\omega}^k \in \mathbb{R}^{n_k \times n_{k-1}}, \\ b^{(k)} \in \mathbb{R}^{n_k} \quad for \quad k = 1, \cdots, l \end{array} \right\} \tag{6}$$

where the symbol ∘ denotes the composition of functions. The total number of parameters of $\mathcal{M}(l)$ is given by

$$M(l) = (n_l + 1) + \sum_{k=1}^{1} n_k \times (n_{k-1} + 1).$$

As in (Cai et al., 2021), the biases and weights of all hidden-layers

$$\mathbf{\Theta}^{(l)} = \bigcup_{k=1}^{l} \left\{ \left(b_i^{(k)}, \boldsymbol{\omega}_i^{(k)} \right) \right\}_{i=1}^{n_k} = \left\{ \left(b^{(k)}, \boldsymbol{\omega}^{(k)} \right) \right\}_{k=1}^{l} \tag{7}$$

are referred as nonlinear parameters, and the output bias and weights

$$\mathbf{c} = (c_0, \mathbf{c}_1) = (c_0, c_1, \cdots, c_{n_l}) \in \mathbb{R}^{n_l+1}$$

are referred as linear parameters for a neural network function.

2.1 Remark

Domain of the nonlinear parameter $\mathbf{\Theta}^{(l)}$ *in* (2.3) *is too large in general and hence admit infinite many global minimizers of* (1.1). *One may add some constraints to the domain in order to reduce the number/ dimension of the global minimizers. For example, the weights of each neuron can be normalized* (*see, e.g.,* (Cai et al., 2021; Cai, Ding, Liu et al, 2023; Liu et al., 2022)).

Linearity of the output parameter **c** here means that **c** is uniquely determined by a system of linear algebraic equations with given nonlinear parameter $\mathbf{\Theta}^{(l)}$. In the remainder of this section, we introduce this linear system and show that the corresponding mass matrix is always symmetric; moreover, it is positive definite under some condition. To this end, let

$$\varphi_0^{(l)}(\mathbf{x}) = 1 \text{ and } \varphi_i^{(l)}(\mathbf{x}) = \sigma(\boldsymbol{\omega}_i^{(l)} \left(\mathbf{N}^{(l-1)} \circ \cdots \circ \mathbf{N}^{(1)}(x) \right) + b_i^{(l)}), \tag{8}$$

then any function $v \in \mathcal{M}(l)$ has the form of

$$v(\mathbf{x}) = \sum_{i=0}^{n_l} c_i \varphi_i^{(l)}(\mathbf{x}). \tag{9}$$

A solution f_{nn} of (1.1) satisfies the critical point equation

$$\nabla_c L(f_{nn}) = 0 \tag{10}$$

for the linear parameter $\mathbf{c}=(c_0,\mathbf{c}_1)$. This implies that $\mathbf{c}$ satisfies the following system of linear algebraic equations

$$\mathbf{M}^{(l)}(\boldsymbol{\Theta}^{(l)})\mathrm{c} = \mathrm{F}^{(l)}(\boldsymbol{\Theta}^{(l)}) \tag{11}$$

where $\mathbf{M}^{(l)}(\boldsymbol{\Theta}^{(l)})$ and $\mathrm{F}^{(l)}(\boldsymbol{\Theta}^{(l)})$ are the discrete mass matrix and the right-hand side vector given by

$$\left\{\mathbf{M}^{(l)}\left(\boldsymbol{\Theta}^{(l)}\right) = \left(\sum_{e=1}^{M} w_e \varphi_j^{(l)}(\mathbf{x}_e)\varphi_i^{(l)}(\mathbf{x}_e)\right)_{(n_l+1)\times(n_l+1)} \quad \text{and } F^{(l)}(\boldsymbol{\Theta}^{(l)}) = \left(\sum_{e=1}^{M} w_e y_e \varphi_i^{(l)}(\mathbf{x}_e)\right)_{(n_l+1)\times 1}\right. . \tag{12}$$

2.2 Lemma

The mass matrix $\mathbf{M}^{(l)}(\boldsymbol{\Theta}^{(l)})$ *defined in* (2.10) *is symmetric. Assume that functions* $\left\{\varphi_i^{(l)}(\mathbf{x})\right\}_{i=0}^{n_l}$ *are linearly independent, then* $\mathbf{M}^{(l)}(\boldsymbol{\Theta}^{(l)})$ *is positive definite.*

Proof. Obviously, $\mathbf{M}^{(l)}(\boldsymbol{\Theta}^{(l)})$ is symmetric. For any $\mathbf{c} \in \mathbb{R}^{n_l+1}$, we have

$$\mathbf{c}^T M^{(l)}(\boldsymbol{\Theta}^{(l)})\mathbf{c} = \sum_{i,j=0}^{n_l+1}\sum_{e=1}^{M} c_i c_j w_e \varphi_j^{(l)}(\mathbf{x}_e)\varphi_i^{(l)}(\mathbf{x}_e) = \sum_{e=1}^{M} w_e \left(\sum_{i=0}^{n_l+1} c_i \varphi_i^{(l)}(\mathbf{x}_e)\right)^2,$$

which, together with the assumption, implies positive definiteness of $\mathbf{M}^{(l)}(\boldsymbol{\Theta}^{(l)})$.

Even though $\mathbf{M}^{(l)}(\boldsymbol{\Theta}^{(l)})$ is symmetric, positive definite, it could be highly ill-conditioned. This fact, in turn, implies inefficiency of the optimization methods of gradient descent type.

3. PHYSICAL PARTITION

A neural network function in $\mathcal{M}(l)$ has the form of

$$v(\mathbf{x}) = \mathbf{c}_1\left(\mathbf{N}^{(l)} \circ \cdots \circ \mathbf{N}^{(1)}(\mathbf{x})\right) + c_0 = \sum_{i=0}^{n_l} c_i \varphi_i^{(l)}(\mathbf{x}), \tag{13}$$

where $\varphi_i^{(l)}(\mathbf{x})$ is defined in (2.6). Obviously, $v(\mathrm{x})$ is a continuous p*iece-wise* linear (CPWL) function defined in $\mathbb{R}^d$. This means that there exists a partition of $\mathbb{R}^d$ such that $v(\mathrm{x})$ is linear on all subdomains of this partition. This section studies such a partition for a given neural network function $v(\mathrm{x})$ of the form in (3.1).

3.1 Definition

For a given network function $v(\mathbf{x})$ *of the form in* (3.1) *defined in* $\Omega=[-1,1]^d$, *a partition* $\mathcal{K}^{(l)}(v)$ *of* Ω *is said to be the physical partition of* $v(\mathbf{x})$ *with respect to* Ω *if*

(i) $\mathcal{K}^{(l)}(v)$ *is a partition of* Ω, *i.e.,*

$$\Omega = \bigcup_{K\in\mathcal{K}^{(l)}(v)} \bar{K} \quad \text{and} \quad K \cap T = \varnothing \text{ if } K \neq T \text{ for all } K,T \in \mathcal{K}^{(l)}(v)$$

(ii) *for each subdomain* $K \in \mathcal{K}^{(l)}(v)$, *the restriction of* $v(\mathbf{x})$ *on* K *is a linear function.*

3.2 Remark

The physical partition $\mathcal{K}^{(l)}(v)$ *defined in Definition* 3.1 *depends on the nonlinear parameter* $\mathbf{\Theta}^{(l)}$ *but not on the linear parameter* $\mathbf{c}$.

For a shallow neural network $\mathcal{M}(1)$, each function $v \in \mathcal{M}(1)$ has the form of

$$v(\mathbf{x}) = \mathbf{c}_1\left(\mathbf{N}^{(1)}(\mathbf{x})\right) + c_0 = \sum_{i=0}^{n_1} c_i\sigma(\omega_i^{(1)}\mathbf{x} + b_i^{(1)}) + c_0 = \sum_{i=0}^{n_1} c_i\varphi_i^{(1)}(\mathbf{x})$$

where $\mathbf{\Theta}^{(1)} = \left\{\theta_i^{(1)}\right\}_{i=1}^{n_1} := \left\{\left(b_i^{(1)}, \boldsymbol{\omega}_i^{(1)}\right)\right\}_{i=1}^{n_1}$ is nonlinear parameter. For $i=1,\ldots,n_1$, denote the pre-activation function of the ith neuron by

$$g_i^{(1)}(\mathbf{x}) = \boldsymbol{\omega}_i^{(1)}\mathbf{x} + b_i^{(1)} \tag{14}$$

and its zero level set, called the *breaking hyper-plane*, by

$$\mathcal{P}_i^{(1)}\left(\omega_i^{(1)}\right) = \left\{\mathbf{x} \in \Omega : g_i^{(1)}(\mathbf{x}) = 0\right\} = \left\{\mathbf{x} \in \Omega : \omega_i^{(1)}\mathbf{x} + b_i^{(1)} = 0\right\}. \tag{15}$$

For fixed $\mathbf{\Theta}^{(l)}$, the physical partition $\mathcal{K}^{(1)}(v)$ is formed by the set of the breaking hyper-planes $\left\{\mathcal{P}_i^{(1)}\right\}_{i=1}^{n_1}$ and the boundary of the domain Ω.

The breaking hyper-planes $\left\{\mathcal{P}_i^{(1)}\right\}_{i=1}^{n_1}$ in one dimension (d=1) degenerate to the breaking points $\left\{\frac{b_i^{(1)}}{\omega_i^{(1)}}\right\}_{i=1}^{n_1}$ (blue dots in Fig. 1(a)), which partitions the interval $\Omega = [-1,1]$ into sub-intervals. The breaking hyper-planes in two dimensions (d=2) degenerate to the breaking lines (blue lines in Fig. 1(b))

$$\mathcal{P}_i^{(1)}\left(\theta_i^{(1)}\right)=\left\{\mathbf{x}=(x_1,x_2)\in\Omega=[-1,1]^2:\omega_{i1}^{(1)}x_1+\omega_{i2}^{(1)}x_2+b_i^{(1)}=0\right\},$$

which partition the domain $\Omega\in\mathbb{R}^2$ into irregular, polygonal sub-domains (see also Fig. 2(c)).

For a two-hidden-layer neural network $\mathcal{M}(2)$, each function $v\in\mathcal{M}(2)$ has the form of

$$v(\mathbf{x})=\mathbf{c}_1\left(\mathbf{N}^{(2)}\circ\mathbf{N}^{(1)}(\mathbf{x})\right)+c_0=\sum_{i=0}^{n_2}c_i\varphi_i^{(2)}(\mathbf{x}),$$

where $\left\{\varphi_i^{(2)}(\mathbf{x})\right\}_{i=1}^{n_2}$ are similarly defined as in (2.6) by

$$\varphi_0^{(2)}(\mathbf{x})=1\ \ and\ \ \varphi_i^{(2)}(\mathbf{x})=\sigma(\omega_i^{(2)}\mathbf{N}^{(1)}(\mathbf{x})+b_i^{(2)})=\sigma(\omega_i^{(2)}\sigma(\omega^{(1)}\mathbf{x}+b^{(1)})+b_i^{(2)})$$

for $i=1,\ldots,n_2$ and nonlinear parameters are given by

$$\boldsymbol{\Theta}^{(2)}=\boldsymbol{\Theta}^{(1)}\cup\left\{\boldsymbol{\Theta}_i^{(2)}\right\}_{i=1}^{n_2}:=\boldsymbol{\Theta}^{(1)}\cup\left\{\left(b_i^{(2)},\boldsymbol{\omega}_i^{(2)}\right)\right\}_{i=1}^{n_2}. \tag{16}$$

Similar to the shallow network $\mathcal{M}(1)$, denote pre-activation functions of neurons at the 2nd hidden layer by

$$g_i^{(2)}(\mathbf{x})=\boldsymbol{\omega}_i^{(2)}\sigma\left(\boldsymbol{\omega}^{(1)}\mathbf{x}+\mathbf{b}^{(1)}\right)+b_i^{(2)}\text{ for } i=1,\ldots,n_2 \tag{17}$$

and their zero level sets, called the *breaking poly-hyper-planes*, by

$$\mathcal{P}_i^{(2)}\left(\boldsymbol{\Theta}^{(1)},\boldsymbol{\theta}_i^{(2)}\right)=\left\{\mathbf{x}\in\Omega:\boldsymbol{\omega}_i^{(2)}\sigma\left(\boldsymbol{\omega}^{(1)}\mathbf{x}+\mathbf{b}^{(1)}\right)+b_i^{(2)}=0\right\}. \tag{18}$$

3.3 Remark

Note that $g_i^{(2)}(\mathbf{x})$ is a single-valued, continuous piece-wise linear function. This fact implies that $\mathcal{P}_i^{(2)}\left(\boldsymbol{\Theta}^{(1)},\boldsymbol{\theta}_i^{(2)}\right)$ as a zero level set is either empty or consists of poly-hyper-planes that do not intersect. Here, the poly-hyper-plane means a continuous hyper-plane that is composed of one or more connected hyper-plane segments. Moreover, each poly-hyper-plane is either closed or from part of the boundary to another part of the boundary.

3.4 Remark

The physical partition $\mathcal{K}^{(2)}(v)$ is the refinement of the partition $\mathcal{K}^{(1)}(v)$ by using the breaking poly-hyper-planes $\left\{\mathcal{P}_i^{(2)}\left(\boldsymbol{\Theta}^{(1)},\boldsymbol{\theta}_i^{(2)}\right)\right\}_{i=1}^{n_2}$.

In one dimension, $\mathcal{K}^{(2)}(v)$ is the refinement of $\mathcal{K}^{(1)}(v)$ by adding the 2nd layer breaking points (red crosses in Fig. 1(a)) satisfying

$$\sum_{j=1}^{n_2} \omega_{ij}^{(2)} \sigma\left(w_j^{(1)} x + b_j^{(1)}\right) + b_i^{(2)} = 0 \text{ for } i=1,\ldots,n_2. \tag{19}$$

Figure 1. Breaking points/lines in the first two hidden layers: (a) Breaking points generated by the jth neuron of the second layer, (b) Breaking lines generated by the jth neuron of the lth-layer

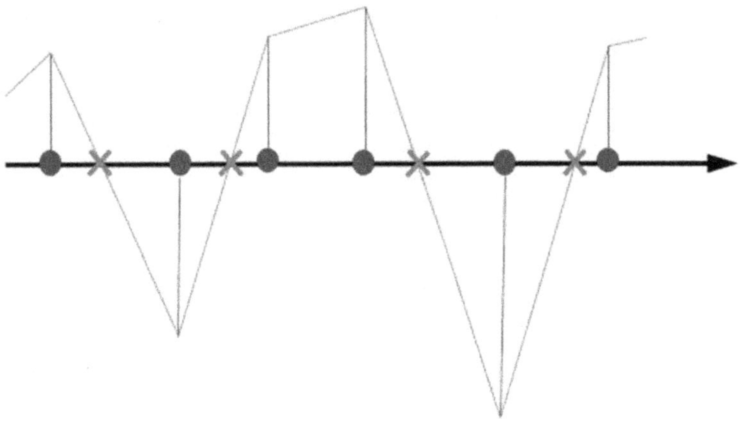

In two dimensions, the $\mathcal{K}^{(2)}(v)$ is the refinement of $\mathcal{K}^{(1)}(v)$ by adding the 2nd layer breaking poly-lines (red poly-lines in Figs. 1(b) and 2(d)) satisfying

$$\sum_{j=1}^{n_2} \omega_{ij}^{(2)} \sigma\left(\omega_j^{(1)} \mathbf{x} + b_j^{(1)}\right) + b_i^{(2)} = 0 \text{ for } i=1,\ldots,n_2.$$

For $k=1,\ldots,l-1$, denote the nonlinear parameter of the first k hidden-layers of $v(\mathrm{x})$ by

$$\boldsymbol{\Theta}^{(k)} = \boldsymbol{\Theta}^{(k-1)} \cup \left\{\boldsymbol{\Theta}_i^{(k)}\right\}_{i=1}^{n_k} := \boldsymbol{\Theta}^{(k-1)} \cup \left\{\left(b_i^{(k)}, \boldsymbol{\omega}_i^{(k)}\right)\right\}_{i=1}^{n_k}. \tag{20}$$

Let $\mathcal{K}^{(k)}(v)$ denote the physical partition determined by the nonlinear parameters $\boldsymbol{\Theta}^{(k)}$. Then the physical partition $\mathcal{K}^{(k)}(v)$ may be described through a refinement process starting from the physical partition $\mathcal{K}^{(1)}(v)$. For $k=2,\ldots,l$, the physical partition $\mathcal{K}^{(k)}(v)$ is the refinement of the previous physical partition $\mathcal{K}^{(k-1)}(v)$ by adding the following poly-hyper-planes

$$\mathcal{P}_i^{(k)}\left(\boldsymbol{\Theta}^{(k-1)}, \boldsymbol{\theta}_i^{(k)}\right) = \left\{\mathbf{x} \in \mathbb{R}^d : g_i^{(k)}(\mathbf{x}) = 0\right\} \text{ for } i=1,\ldots,n_k. \tag{21}$$

where $g_i^{(k)}(\mathbf{x})$ is the pre-activation function of the ith neuron at the kth hidden-layer given by

$$g_i^{(k)}(\mathbf{x}) = \boldsymbol{\omega}_i^{(k)}\left(\mathbf{N}^{(k-1)} \circ \cdots \circ \mathbf{N}^{(1)}(\mathbf{x})\right) + b_i^{(k)}. \tag{22}$$

The procedure for determining the physical partition $\mathcal{K}^{(l)}(v)$ of the domain Ω involves calculating the arrangement of a domain formed by a set of hyper-planes and poly-hyper-planes. This may be computationally expensive, especially when the input dimension *d* is high.

In practice, computation is usually done over a set of points in Ω, e.g., the input data set $\mathcal{D}=\{\mathbf{x}_i\}_{i=1}^{M}$ for problem (1.1) and integration point set as in (Cai et al., 2020; Liu & Cai, 2022). This motivates introduction of the *data physical partition*, i.e., the physical partition of $v(\mathbf{x}) \in \mathcal{M}(l)$ with respect to a given data set $\mathcal{D}=\{\mathbf{x}_i\}_{i=1}^{M}$. In a similar fashion as Definition 3.1, we define the data physical partition $\mathcal{D}^{(k)}$ as follows

$$\mathcal{D}^{(k)} = \mathcal{D} \cap \mathcal{K}^{(k)} = \left\{\mathcal{D} \cap K : K \in \mathcal{K}^{(k)}\right\} \text{for } k=1,\ldots,l. \tag{23}$$

Next, we describe how to form $\mathcal{D}^{(l)}$ for a given nonlinear parameters $\boldsymbol{\Theta}^{(l)}$. To this end, let H(t) be the Heaviside step function given by

$$H(t) = \begin{cases} 1, & t > 0, \\ 0, & t \le 0. \end{cases}$$

For k=1,…,l, introduce vector-valued *layer indicator function* $\mathbf{I}^{(k)} : \mathbb{R}^d \to \mathbb{R}^{n_k}$ as

$$\mathbf{I}^{(k)}(\mathbf{x}) = H(\mathbf{g}^{(k)}(\mathbf{x})), \tag{24}$$

where $\mathbf{g}^{(k)}(\mathbf{x}) = \left(g_i^{(k)}(\mathbf{x})\right)_{n_k \times 1}$ is the pre-activation function defined in (3.9) and application of H to a vector-valued function is defined component-wisely. For a given nonlinear parameter $\boldsymbol{\Theta}^{(l)}$, we define the *network indicator function* by

$$\mathcal{I}^{(l)}(\mathbf{x}) = \left(\mathbf{I}^{(1)}(\mathbf{x}), \cdots, \mathbf{I}^{(l)}(\mathbf{x})\right).$$

Let the data physical partition $\mathcal{D}^{(l)}$ be of the form

$$\mathcal{D}^{(l)} = \left\{D_j^{(l)}\right\}_{j=1}^{m_l}, \tag{25}$$

where m_l is the number of disjoint elements of the data physical partition $\mathcal{D}^{(l)}$ and each element $D_j^{(l)}$ is a subset of the input data set $\mathcal{D}$ such that the value of the network indicator function $\mathcal{I}^{(l)}$ is same for all points in $D_j^{(l)}$. Denote this value by $\mathcal{I}^{l}_{D_j^{(l)}}$, then we have

$$\mathcal{I}^{(l)(l)}(\mathbf{x}) = \mathcal{I}^{(l)l}_{D_j^{(l)}} \text{ for } \mathbf{x} \in D_j^{(l)}. \tag{26}$$

For each element $D \in \mathcal{D}^{(l)}$, denote the centroid of D by

$$\mathbf{x}_D = \frac{1}{|D|}\sum_{\mathbf{x}_i \in D} w_i \mathbf{x}_i, \tag{27}$$

and the covariance matrix of D formed by vectors $x_i - x_D$ for all $x_i \in D$ by

$$\mathrm{CoV}_D = \sum_{\mathbf{x}_i \in D} [\mathbf{x}_i - \mathbf{x}_D]^T [\mathbf{x}_i - \mathbf{x}_D], \tag{28}$$

where $x_i - x_D$ is a *d*-dimensional row vector. Then each element $D \in \mathcal{D}^{(l)}$ has *d* principal directions that correspond to the eigenvectors of CoV_D.

4. ADAPTIVE NETWORK ENHANCEMENT METHOD

This section describes the adaptive network enhancement method (ANE) for problem (1.1).

To this end, denote the current neural network, approximation, and error at the kth adaptive step by

$$\mathcal{M}^{(k)}(l_k), f^{(k)}(\mathbf{x}) \text{ and } \xi^{(k)} = L\left(f^{(k)}(\mathbf{x})\right),$$

respectively, where l_k is the number of hidden-layers of the network $\mathcal{M}^{(k)}(l_k)$. When accuracy of the current approximation $f^{(k)}(\mathbf{x})$ is not within the prescribed tolerance, i.e., $\xi^{(k)} > \varepsilon L(0)$, the network $\mathcal{M}^{(k)}(l_k)$ is enhanced by adding neurons at the either l_k-th or $(l_k + 1)$-th hidden-layer. The latter means that we start a new hidden-layer.

To determine the number of neurons to be added at the l_k-th hidden-layer, we use the *local network enhancement strategy* based on the data physical partition of $\mathcal{D} = \{\mathbf{x}_i\}_{i=1}^{M}$:

$$\mathcal{D}^{(l_k)}(f^{(k)}) = \mathcal{D} \cap \mathcal{K}^{(l_k)}(f^{(k)}) = \left\{\mathcal{D} \cap K : K \in \mathcal{K}^{(l_k)}(f^{(k)})\right\}$$

by the current approximation $f^{(k)}(\mathbf{x})$. Specifically, we divide $\mathcal{D}^{(l_k)}(f^{(k)})$ into two disjoint subsets,

$$\mathcal{D}^{(l_k)}(f^{(k)}) = \widehat{\mathcal{D}}^{(l_k)}(f^{(k)}) \bigcup \left[(\mathcal{D}^{(l_k)}(f^{(k)}) \setminus \widehat{\mathcal{D}}^{(l_k)}(f^{(k)}) \right],$$

where $\widehat{\mathcal{D}}^{(l_k)}(f^{(k)}) = \mathcal{D} \bigcap \widehat{\mathcal{K}}^{(l_k)}(f^{(k)})$ is a subset of $\mathcal{D}^{(l_k)}(f^{(k)})$ consisting of elements in $\mathcal{D}^{(l_k)}(f^{(k)})$ such that $f^{(k)}(\mathbf{x})$ is not yet a good approximation. Then the *enhancement strategy* is to add $\left|\widehat{\mathcal{D}}^{(l_k)}(f^{(k)})\right|$ new neurons to the l_k-th hidden-layer, where

$$\left|\widehat{\mathcal{D}}^{(l_k)}\left(f^{(k)}\right)\right| = \text{the number of elements of } \widehat{\mathcal{D}}^{(l_k)}\left(f^{(k)}\right). \tag{29}$$

To generate $\widehat{\mathcal{D}}^{(l_k)}(f^{(k)})$, we employ the so-called marking strategy. There are two commonly used marking strategies in adaptive mesh refinement. One is the average marking strategy and the other is the bulk marking strategy. To describe these marking strategies, let us first introduce the following local error indicator

$$\xi_D^{(k)} = \left(\sum_{\mathbf{x}_i \in D} w_i \left(f^{(k)}(\mathbf{x}_i) - y_i \right)^2 \right)^{1/2} \tag{30}$$

for each element $D \in \mathcal{D}^{(l_k)}(f^{(k)})$. Clearly, we have

$$\xi^{(k)} = \left(\sum_{i-1}^{M} w_i \left(f^{(k)}(\mathbf{x}_i) - y_i \right)^2 \right)^{1/2} = \left(\sum_{D \in \mathcal{D}^{(l_k)}(f^{(k)})} (\xi_D^{(k)})^2 \right)^{1/2}. \tag{31}$$

The average marking strategy is given by

$$\widehat{\mathcal{D}}^{(l_k)}(f^{(k)}) = \left\{ D \in \mathcal{D}^{(l_k)}(f^{(k)}) : \xi_D^{(k)} \geq \frac{1}{\left|\mathcal{D}^{(l_k)}(f^{(k)})\right|} \sum_{D \in \mathcal{D}^{(l_k)}(f^{(k)})} \xi_D^{(k)} \right\}. \tag{32}$$

The bulk marking strategy is to find a minimal subset $\mathcal{D}^{(l_k)}(f^{(k)})$ such that

$$\sum_{D \in \hat{\mathcal{D}}^{(l_k)}(f^{(k)})} \left(\xi_D^{(k)}\right)^2 \geq {}^3{}_1 \sum_{D \in \mathcal{D}^{(l_k)}(f^{(k)})} \left(\xi_D^{(k)}\right)^2 \text{ for } \gamma_1 \in (0,1). \tag{33}$$

The enhancement strategy adding $\left|\widehat{\mathcal{D}}^{(l_k)}(f^{(k)})\right|$ new neurons is suitable for all hidden-layers. Nevertheless, it may not be efficient for hidden-layers beyond the first hidden-layer. Notice that a multi-layer network is capable of generating piece-wise breaking hyper-planes in connected subdomains by one neuron. This observation motivates the notion of the *reduced number of elements* in $\widehat{\mathcal{D}}^{(l_k)}(f^{(k)})$. To this end, let

$$\widehat{\mathcal{D}}^{(l_k)}(f^{(k)}) = \left\{\widehat{\mathcal{D}}_j^{(l)}\right\}_{j=1}^{\hat{m}_l}. \tag{34}$$

That is, there are $\widehat{m_l}$ marked elements in $\mathcal{D}^{(l_k)}(f^{(k)})$. Any two elements in $\widehat{\mathcal{D}}^{(l_k)}(f^{(k)})$ are said to be disconnected if there is no pass connecting these two elements by elements of $\widehat{\mathcal{D}}^{(l_k)}(f^{(k)})$. Let us group connected elements of $\widehat{\mathcal{D}}^{(l_k)}(f^{(k)})$ to form a set, whose elements are disconnected, denoted by

$$\tilde{\mathcal{D}}^{(l_k)}(f^{(k)}) = \left\{\tilde{\mathcal{D}}_j^{(l)}\right\}_{j=1}^{\tilde{m}_l}, \tag{35}$$

where each element $\tilde{\mathcal{D}}_j^{(l)} \in \tilde{\mathcal{D}}^{(l)}(f^{(k)})$ is either an element of $\widehat{\mathcal{D}}^{(l_k)}(f^{(k)})$ or a union of connected elements in $\widehat{\mathcal{D}}^{(l_k)}(f^{(k)})$. Obviously, $\tilde{m}_l \le \widehat{m_l}$. Now, we define the reduced number of elements in $\widehat{\mathcal{D}}^{(l_k)}(f^{(k)})$ by

$$\left|\widehat{\mathcal{D}}^{(l_k)}(f^{(k)})\right|_r = \begin{cases} \widehat{m_l}, & l_k = 1, \\ \tilde{m}_l, & l_k \ge 2. \end{cases} \tag{36}$$

where any two elements in $\widehat{\mathcal{D}}^{(l_k)}(f^{(k)})$ are disjoint if there is no pass connecting these two elements by elements of $\widehat{\mathcal{D}}^{(l_k)}(f^{(k)})$.

4.1 Remark

For any two elements in $\widehat{\mathcal{D}}^{(l_k)}(f^{(k)})$, *if values of their network indicator function differ only for one neuron, e.g., the ith neuron at the kth hidden-layer, then these two elements are neighbor and share part of the poly-hyper-plane* $\mathcal{P}_i^{(k)}\left(\Theta^{(k-1)}, \theta_i^{(k)}\right)$ *defined in* (3.8).

To address question (b) in section 1, i.e., when to add a new hidden-layer, we introduce a computable quantity, referred to as the *improvement rate*, defined by

$$\eta_r^{(k)} = \left(\frac{\xi^{(k-1)} - \xi^{(k)}}{\xi^{(k-1)}} \right) \Bigg/ \left(\frac{\left(M^{(k)}(l_k)\right)^r - \left(M^{(k-1)}(l_{k-1})\right)^r}{\left(M^{(k)}(l_k)\right)^r} \right), \tag{37}$$

where $M^{(k-1)}(l_{k-1})$ and $M^{(k)}(l_k)$ denote the numbers of parameters of the networks $\mathcal{M}^{(k-1)}(l_{k-1})$ and $\mathcal{M}^{(k)}(l_k)$, respectively; and r is the order of the approximation with respect to the number of parameters and may depend on the activation function and the layer. The improvement rate measures a rate of improvement of two consecutive networks per the relative increase of parameters. If the improvement rate $\eta_r^{(k)}$ is less than or equal to a prescribed expectation rate $\delta \in (0,2)$, i.e.,

$$\eta_r^{(k)} \leq \delta, \tag{38}$$

for two consecutive adaptive steps, then the ANE adds a new hidden-layer. Otherwise, the ANE adds neurons to the l_k-th hidden-layer of the current network $\mathcal{M}^{(k)}(l_k)$.

The ANE method for generating a nearly minimal multi-layer neural network is described in Algorithm 3.1.

5. INITIALIZATION OF TRAINING

This section discusses initialization strategies of parameters of neural network in two dimensions. Extensions to three dimensions are straightforward.

The optimization problem in Step (7) of Algorithm 3.1 is non-convex and, hence, computationally intensive and complicated. Currently, this problem is often solved by either the first- or second-order iterative optimization methods such as gradient-based methods or Newton-like methods (see survey papers (Bottou, Curtis, & Nocedal, 2018; Bottou, Curtis, & Nocedal, 2018) and references therein). Since non-convex optimizations usually have many solutions and/or many local minimums, it is then critical to start with a good initial guess in order to obtain the desired solution.

The ANE method itself is a natural continuation process for generating good initialization. That is, the approximation $f^{(k)}(\mathbf{x})$ of the previous network $\mathcal{M}^{(k)}(l_k)$ is in general a good approximation to $f^{(k+1)}(\mathbf{x})$ defined in Step (7) of Algorithm 3.1 for the enhanced network $\mathcal{M}^{(k+1)}(l_{k+1})$. Therefore, the trained nonlinear parameters of $\mathcal{M}^{(k)}(l_k)$ for $f^{(k)}(\mathbf{x})$ are good initials for the corresponding nonlinear parameters of the enhanced network $\mathcal{M}^{(k+1)}(l_{k+1})$. Based on this observation, below we discuss our initialization strategies for (1) parameters of the network $\mathcal{M}^{(0)}(l_0)$, (2) parameters of newly added neurons, and (3) linear (output) parameters of $f^{(k+1)}$.

Starting with a one hidden-layer network $\mathcal{M}^{(0)}(l_0)$ with relatively small number n_{l_0} of neurons, the approximation $f^{(0)}(\mathbf{x})$ has of the form

Algorithm 3.1 *Adaptive Network Enhancement.*

Given a data set $\{(\mathbf{x}_i, y_i)\}_{i=1}^{M}$ with $\mathbf{x}_i\Omega$=[-1,1]^d, positive weights $\{w_i\}_{i=1}^{M}$, and a tolerance ε>0 for accuracy, starting with a one hidden-layer network $\mathcal{M}^{(0)}(l_0)$ with a small number of neurons, compute $f^{(0)} = \arg\min_{v\in\mathcal{M}^{(0)}(l_0)} L(v)$ by an iterative solver, then for k=1,2,…,

(1) use the network indicator function to determine the data physical partition $\mathcal{D}^{(l_k)}(f^{(k)})$;

(2) for each $\mathcal{D}^{(l_k)}(f^{(k)})$, compute the local indicator $\xi_D^{(k)}$ in (4.2) and the estimator $\xi^{(k)}$ in (4.3);

(3) if $\xi^{(k)}<\varepsilon$, then stop; otherwise, go to Step (4);

(4) use a marking strategy to form the subset $\widehat{\mathcal{D}}^{(l_k)}(f^{(k)})$ and calculate $\left|\widehat{\mathcal{D}}^{(l_k)}(f^{(k)})\right|$;

(5) for a prescribed expectation rate $\delta \in (0,2)$, if (4.10) holds for two consecutive steps, then set $l_{k+1} = l_{k+1}$; otherwise, set $l_{k+1} = l_k$;

(6) form network $\mathcal{M}^{(k+1)}(l_{k+1})$ by adding $\left|\widehat{\mathcal{D}}^{(l_k)}(f^{(k)})\right|$ new neurons to the l_{k+1}-th hidden layer;

(7) compute $f^{(k+1)} = \arg\min_{v\in\mathcal{M}^{(k+1)}(l_{k+1})} L(v)$ by an iterative solver.

$$f^{(0)}(\mathbf{x}) = \mathbf{c}_1\sigma\left(\boldsymbol{\omega}^{(1)}\mathbf{x} + \mathbf{b}^{(1)}\right) + c_0,$$

where $\boldsymbol{\Theta}^{(l_0)} = \left\{\boldsymbol{\Theta}_i^{(1)}\right\}_{i=1}^{n_{l_0}} := \left\{\left(b_i^{(1)}, \boldsymbol{\omega}_i^{(1)}\right)\right\}_{i=1}^{n_1}$ are nonlinear parameters and $\mathbf{c} = (c_0, \mathbf{c}_1) \in \mathbb{R}^{n_{l_0}+1}$ are linear parameters. Initial of $\boldsymbol{\Theta}^{(l_0)}$ is chosen such that the hyper-lines

$$\mathcal{P}_i^{(1)}\left(\boldsymbol{\theta}_i^{(1)}\right): \boldsymbol{\omega}_i^{(1)}\mathbf{x} + b_i^{(1)} = 0 \ for\ i = 1,\cdots,n_1$$

partition the domain Ω=[-1,1]^2 uniformly. Initial of $\mathbf{c}$ is set to be the solution of the system of linear algebraic equations

$$\mathbf{M}^{(l_0)}\left(\boldsymbol{\Theta}^{(l_0)}\right)\mathbf{c} = F^{(l_0)}\left(\boldsymbol{\Theta}^{(l_0)}\right) \tag{39}$$

defined in a similar fashion as (2.9).

Next, we discuss how to initialize the biases and weights of newly added neurons of the network $\mathcal{M}^{(k+1)}(l_{k+1})$. There are three cases:

(1) $l_{k+1} = 1$, (2) $l_{k+1} = l_k + 1$, and (3) $l_{k+1} = l_k \geq 2$.

Case (1) means that the new neurons are added at the first hidden-layer. By associating each new neuron with an element $D \in \widehat{\mathcal{D}}^{(l_k)}(f^{(k)})$, we initialize this neuron by setting its corresponding breaking line to pass through the centroid $\mathbf{x}_D$ and orthogonal to the principal direction that corresponds to the smallest eigenvalue of the covariance matrix CoV_D.

Consider Case (2). When $l_{k+1} = l_k + 1$, we start a new hidden-layer with $\left|\widehat{\mathcal{D}}^{(l_k)}(f^{(k)})\right|_r$ neurons. By the definition in (4.8), we associate each neuron at the new hidden-layer $l_{k+1} = l_k + 1$ with an isolated element or an element consisting of several connected elements in $\widehat{\mathcal{D}}^{(l_k)}(f^{(k)})$ and denote its bias and weights by

$$\boldsymbol{\theta}^{(l_{k+1})} = \left(b^{(l_{k+1})}, \boldsymbol{\omega}^{(l_{k+1})}\right) \in \mathbb{R}^{n_{l_k}+1} = \left(b^{(l_{k+1})}, \omega_1^{(l_{k+1})}, \cdots, \omega_{n_{l_k}}^{(l_{k+1})}\right) \in \mathbb{R}^{n_{l_k}+1}. \tag{40}$$

As section 3, denote the corresponding pre-activation function of the neuron by

$$g^{(l_{k+1})}(\mathbf{x}) = \boldsymbol{\omega}^{(l_{k+1})}\left(\mathbf{N}^{(l_k)} \circ \cdots \circ \mathbf{N}^{(1)}(\mathbf{x})\right) + b^{(l_{k+1})}.$$

If the corresponding element D is an isolated element in $\widehat{\mathcal{D}}^{(l_k)}(f^{(k)})$, let $l_D(\mathbf{x})=0$ be the line that passes through the centroid $\mathbf{x}_D$ of D and is orthogonal to the direction vector with the lowest variance of D (see section 3). Denote by $\mathbf{x}_d$ the projection of a point in D onto the line $l_D(\mathbf{x})=0$ and whose distance to $\mathbf{x}_D$ is the largest among projections of all points in D onto the line. Then initial $\boldsymbol{\theta}_D^{(l_{k+1})}$ of the parameter $\boldsymbol{\theta}^{(l_{k+1})}$ is set to be

$$\boldsymbol{\theta}_D^{(l_{k+1})} = \underset{\boldsymbol{\theta}^{(l_{k+1})} \in \mathbb{R}^{n_{l_k}+1}}{\arg\min} \left\{\left(g^{(l_{k+1})}(\mathbf{x}_D)\right)^2 + \left(g^{(l_{k+1})}(\mathbf{x}_d)\right)^2\right\}. \tag{41}$$

When the corresponding element D consists of several connected elements in $\widehat{\mathcal{D}}^{(l_k)}(f^{(k)})$, denote the collection of these connected elements by $\mathcal{C}$. For each element $C \in \mathcal{C}$, denote by $\mathbf{x}_C$ the centroid of C. Then initial $\boldsymbol{\theta}_C^{(l_{k+1})}$ of the parameter $\boldsymbol{\theta}^{(l_{k+1})}$ is set to be

$$\boldsymbol{\theta}_C^{(l_{k+1})} = \underset{\boldsymbol{\theta}^{(l_{k+1})} \in \mathbb{R}^{n_{l_k}+1}}{\arg\min} \sum_{C \in \mathcal{C}} \left(g^{(l_{k+1})}(\mathbf{x}_C)\right)^2. \tag{42}$$

Now, let us consider Case (3) where new neurons are added at the current layer $l_{k+1} = l_k \geq 2$. Let $s \in \{1, \ldots, k-1\}$ be the largest integer such that $l_{k-s} = l_k - 1$. Then $\mathcal{M}^{(k-s)}(l_{k-s})$ is the final network with $l_{k-s} = l_k - 1$ hidden-layers. Hence the weights and bias of each neuron associated with an element in $\widehat{\mathcal{D}}^{(l_k)}(f^{(k)})$ has the form of

$$\boldsymbol{\theta}^{(l_{k+1})} = \left(b^{(l_{k+1})}, \boldsymbol{\omega}^{(l_{k+1})}\right) = \left(b^{(l_{k+1})}, \omega_1^{(l_{k+1})}, \cdots, \omega_{n_{l_{k-s}}}^{(l_{k+1})}\right) \in \mathbb{R}^{n_{l_{k-s}}+1}. \tag{43}$$

Initial of $\boldsymbol{\theta}^{(l_{k+1})}$ in (5.5) can then be defined in a similar fashion as Case (2). Specifically, we have

$$\left\{\boldsymbol{\theta}_D^{(l_{k+1})} = \underset{\boldsymbol{\theta}^{(l_{k+1})} \in \mathbb{R}^{n_{l_{k-s}}+1}}{\arg\min} \left\{\left(g^{(l_{k+1})}(\mathbf{x}_D)\right)^2 + \left(g^{(l_{k+1})}(\mathbf{x}_d)\right)^2\right\} \quad and \quad \boldsymbol{\theta}_C^{(l_{k+1})} = \underset{\boldsymbol{\theta}^{(l_{k+1})} \in \mathbb{R}^{n_{l_{k-s}}+1}}{\arg\min} \sum_{C \in \mathcal{C}} \left(g^{(l_{k+1})}(\mathbf{x}_C)\right)^2, \right. \tag{44}$$

where $\mathbf{x}_D$, $\mathbf{x}_d$, and $\mathbf{x}_C$ are defined in a similar way as in Case (2).

Finally, initial of the linear parameter $\mathbf{c} = (c_0, \mathbf{c}_1) \in \mathbb{R}^{n_{l_{k+1}}+1}$ of $f^{(k+1)}(x)$ is set to be the solution of the system of algebraic linear equations

$$\mathbf{M}^{(l_{k+1})}\left(\boldsymbol{\Theta}^{(l_{k+1})}\right)\mathbf{c} = F^{(l_{k+1})}\left(\boldsymbol{\Theta}^{(l_{k+1})}\right) \tag{45}$$

defined in a similar fashion as (2.9).

6. NUMERICAL EXPERIMENT

In this section, we report the numerical experiment on using the ANE method to approximate a function using the least-squares loss. The target function is defined on the domain $\Omega = [-1,1]^2$, and is given by

$$f(x,y) = \tanh\left(\frac{1}{\alpha}(x^2 + y^2 + \frac{1}{4})\right) - \tanh\left(\frac{3}{4\alpha}\right). \tag{46}$$

For small constant α, this function exhibits a sharp transitional layer across a circular interface.

For this experiment, we set a small $\alpha = 0.01$ to test approximation accuracy using ANE. and the corresponding target function f is depicted in Fig. 2(a). A data set $\mathcal{D}$ for training network is generated using a fixed set 200×200 of quadrature points that are uniformly distributed in the domain Ω.

During the ANE process, we adopt the bulk marking strategy defined in (4.5) with γ_1=0.5 and choose the expectation rate δ=0.6 with r = 1 in (4.9); and the expected precision ε=0.05. The ANE method started with an initial network of 12 neurons in one hidden layer. The corresponding breaking lines $\{\mathcal{P}_i\}_{i=1}^{12}$ of these 12 neurons were uniformly initialized within the domain. Specifically, half of breaking lines are parallel to the x-axis

$$\omega_i^{(1)} = (0,1) \text{ and } b_i^{(1)} = -1 + \frac{1}{3} i \text{ for } i=0,\ldots,5$$

and the other half are parallel to the y-axis

$$\omega_i^{(1)} = (1,0) \text{ and } b_i^{(1)} = -1 + \frac{1}{3}(i-6) \text{ for } i=6,\ldots,11$$

In addition, the output weights and bias are initialized by solving the linear system in (5.1).

For each iteration of the ANE process, the corresponding minimization problem in (1.1) is solved iteratively using the Adam version of gradient descent (Kingma & Ba, 2015) with a fixed learning rate 0.005. Adam's iterative solver is terminated when the relative change of the loss function $\left\|f - \hat{f}\right\|_{\mathcal{T}}$ is less than 10^{-3} per 2000 iterations.

The ANE process is automatically terminated after four loops (see Table 1 for the intermediate and final result), and the final network model generated by the ANE is 2-18-5-1[1] with parameters. The final network approximation model and the corresponding physical partition are shown in Figs. 2 (e) and (d). Using a relatively small set of parameters, ANE is able to accurately approximate a function with a thin transition layer without any oscillations. This remarkable approximation property can be explained by the fact that the circular interface of the underlying function is captured very effectively by a few breaking poly-lines generated in *the second hidden layer*, see the closed breaking lines formed by the 5 neurons in the second hidden layer in Figure 2 (d).

Table 1. Numerical results for using ANE to approximate function with a circular transitional layer

NN structure	# parameters	Approximation accuracy $\left\|f - \hat{f}\right\|_{\mathcal{T}} / \left\|f\right\|$	Improvement rate η
2-12-1	37	35.7414%	–
2-18-1	**55**	**32.3118%**	**0.293198**
2-26-1	93	27.2614%	0.382528
2-18-5-1	**137**	**2.5483%**	**1.538967**

Figures 2 (b)-(c) plot the physical partitions of the NN models at the intermediate adaptive process. In Figure 2(b), the centroids of the marked elements are illustrated by red dots; the breaking lines corresponding to the current and newly added neurons are shown by blue and red lines, respectively. Notice that the newly added neurons are initialized with break lines that pass through the centroids and align with the principal directions of the marked elements. Figure 2(c) shows that there are 8 marked elements and 5 disjoint elements, which explains that 5 neurons are added to the second hidden layer during the neuron enhancement step.

For the purpose of a comparative study, we conducted function approximation experiments using two fixed network structures. As outlined in Table 2, when utilizing the same network structure (2-18-5-1), the resulting approximation accuracy is inferior to that achieved by the ANE method. The first two rows of Table 2 suggest that the ANE method provides a good initialization, which may simplify the non-convex optimization problem. In the second experiment, we employed a fixed one- hidden-layer network (2-174-1) with nearly four times the number of parameters compared to the adaptive network. Despite the increased degrees of freedom and complexity, its approximation is less accurate (refer to the third row of Table 2). Furthermore, the approximated NN model exhibits a certain degree of oscillation (see Figure 3 (a)), although the corresponding physical partition (Figure 3(b)) still captures the narrow transition layer.

Figure 2. Adaptive approximation results for function with a transitional layer

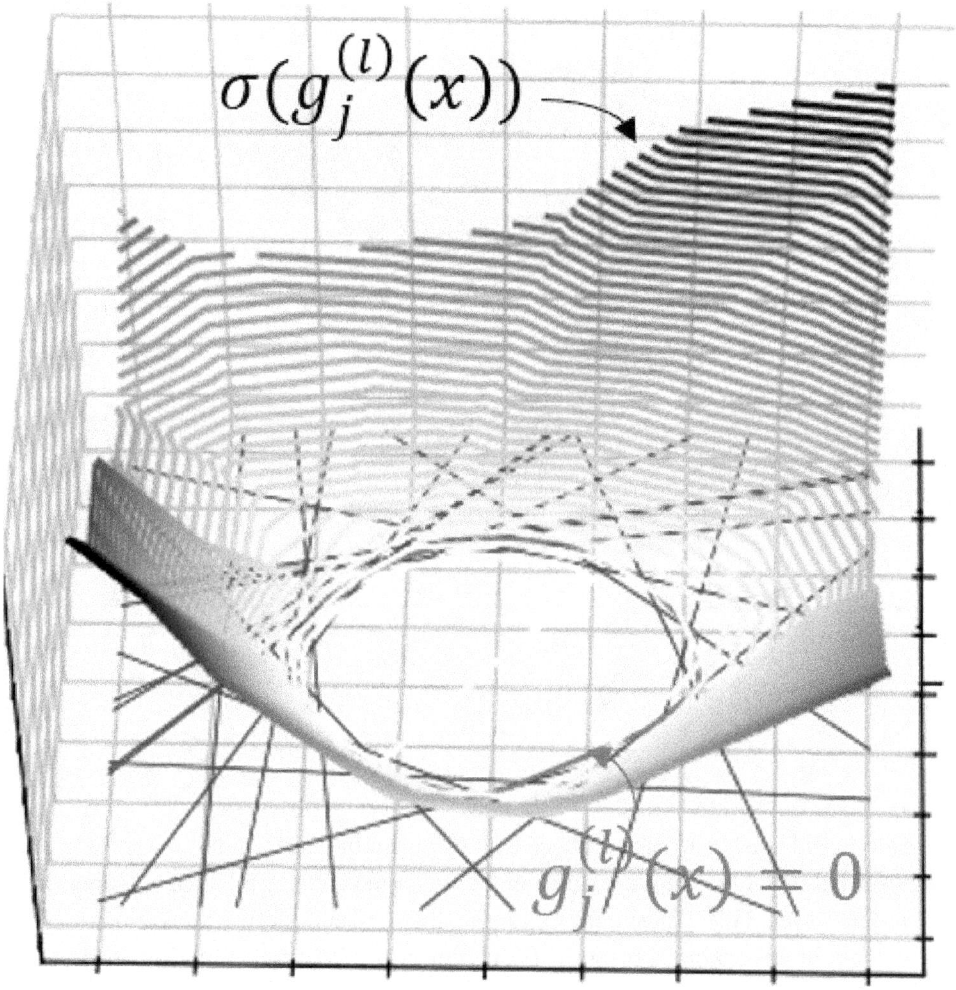

Table 2. Numerical results of adaptive and fixed networks for function with a transitional layer

Network structure	# parameters	Approximation accuracy $\left\|f - \hat{f}\right\|_{\mathcal{T}} / \|f\|$
2-18-5-1 (Adaptive)	137	2.5483%
2-18-5-1 (Fixed)	137	4.6199%
2-174-1 (Fixed)	523	11.1223%

Figure 3. Approximation results generated by a fixed 2-174-1 network for function with a transitional layer: (a) Approximation using fixed 2-174-1 network; (b) PP of the approximation by 2-174-1 network and centers of elements with large errors (red)

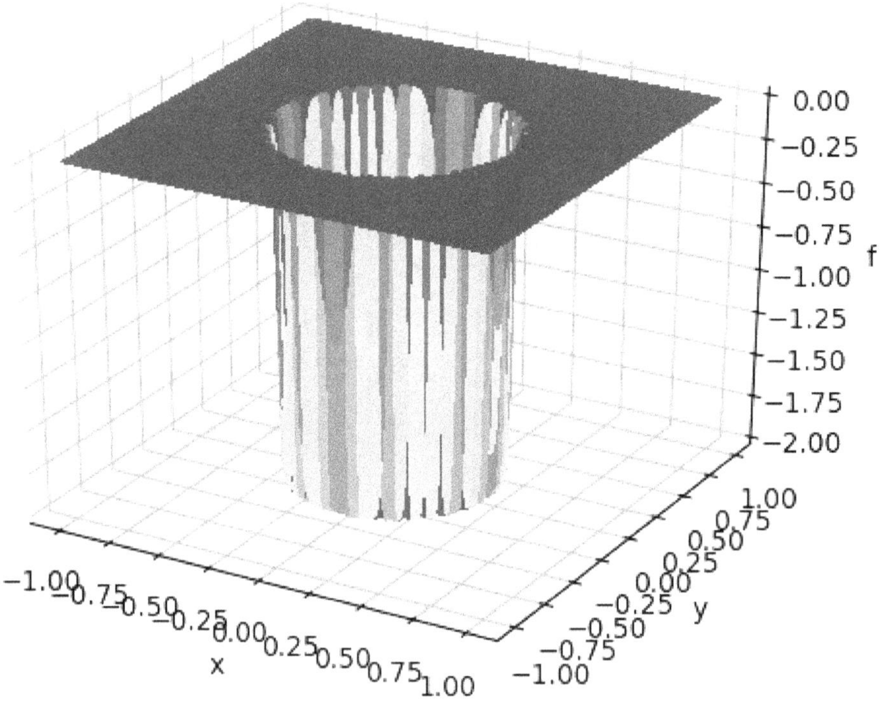

In general, a one-hidden-layer network necessitates dense breaking lines to approximate a circular interface, and oscillations along the interface can be attributed to the global basis functions generated from the first hidden layer. This experiment highlights that a deeper network, as illustrated by the two-hidden-layer network in this example, is more efficient in approximating a function with a thin nonlinear transition layer or interface. This experimental observation aligns with the theoretical findings presented in (Cai, Choi, & Liu, 2023).

7. CONCLUSION

Designing an optimal deep neural network for a given task is important and challenging in many machine learning applications. This chapter provides a comprehensive introduction to the adaptive network enhancement (ANE) method, proposed recently in (Cai et al., 2022; Liu & Cai, 2022; Liu et al., 2022), which generates a nearly optimal multi-layer neural network for a given task within some prescribed accuracy. This self-adaptive algorithm is based on the novel network enhancement strategies that determine when a new hidden-layer and how many new neurons should be added when the current network is not sufficient for the task. This adaptive algorithm learns not only from given information (data, function, partial differential equation) but also from the current computer simulation, and it is therefore a learning algorithm at a level which is more advanced than common machine learning algorithms.

The resulting non-convex optimization at each adaptive step is computationally intensive and complicated with possible many global/local minimums. The ANE method provides a natural process for obtaining a good initialization that assists training significantly. Moreover, to provide a better initial guess, this chapter discusses an advanced procedure for initializing newly added neurons at the current or next hidden-layer.

Functions and partial differential equations with sharp transitions or discontinuities at unknown location have been computationally challenging, when approximated using other functional classes such as polynomials or piece-wise polynomials with fixed meshes. It was demonstrated numerically in (Cai et al., 2022; Liu & Cai, 2022; Liu et al., 2022) that the ANE method can automatically design a nearly minimal two or multi-hidden-layer network to learn functions exhibiting sharp transitional layers as well as continuous/discontinuous solutions of partial differential equations.

REFERENCES

Allgower, E. L., & Georg, K. (1990). *Numerical Continuation Methods: An Introduction*. Springer-Verlag. doi:10.1007/978-3-642-61257-2

Bottou, L., Curtis, F. E., & Nocedal, J. (2018). Optimization methods for large-scale machine learning. *SIAM Review*, *60*(2), 223–311. doi:10.1137/16M1080173

Cai, Z., Chen, J., & Liu, M. (2021). Least-squares ReLU neural network (LSNN) method for linear advection-reaction equation. *Journal of Computational Physics*, *443*, 110514. doi:10.1016/j.jcp.2021.110514

Cai, Z., Chen, J., & Liu, M. (2022). Self-adaptive deep neural network: Numerical approximation to functions and PDEs. *Journal of Computational Physics*, *455*, 111021. doi:10.1016/j.jcp.2022.111021

Cai, Z., Chen, J., Liu, M., & Liu, X. (2020). Deep least-squares methods: An unsupervised learning-based numerical method for solving elliptic PDEs. *Journal of Computational Physics*, *420*, 109707. doi:10.1016/j.jcp.2020.109707

CaiZ.ChoiJ.LiuM. (2023). Least-squares neural network (LSNN) method for linear advection-reaction equation: general discontinuous interface. *arXiv:2301.06156v3[math.NA].*

Cai, Z., Ding, T., Liu, M., Liu, X., & Xia, J. (2023). A damped block Gauss-Newton method for shallow ReLU neural network. *Manuscript.*

Kingma, D. P., & Ba, J. (2015). *ADAM: A method for stochastic optimization.* In *International Conference on Representation Learning*, San Diego.

Liu, M., & Cai, Z. (2022). Adaptive two-layer ReLU neural network: II. Ritz approximation to elliptic PDEs. *Computers & Mathematics with Applications (Oxford, England)*, *113*, 103–116. doi:10.1016/j.camwa.2022.03.010

Liu, M., Cai, Z., & Chen, J. (2022). Adaptive two-layer ReLU neural network: I. best least-squares approximation. *Computers & Mathematics with Applications (Oxford, England)*, *113*, 34–44. doi:10.1016/j.camwa.2022.03.005

ENDNOTE

1 The structure of a two- or three-hidden-layer network is expressed as 2-n_1-1 or 2-n_1-n_2-1, respectively, where n_1 and n_2 are the number of neurons at the first and second hidden-layer.

Chapter 12
The Study of Ecosystem and Vendor Management in Hyper-Automation Across Select Industry Verticals

Akshata Desai
Symbiosis Institute of Digital and Telecom Management, Symbiosis International University (Deemed), India

Giri Gundu Hallur
Symbiosis Institute of Digital and Telecom Management, Symbiosis International University (Deemed), India

Natraj N. A.
https://orcid.org/0000-0002-8726-5284
Symbiosis Institute of Digital and Telecom Management, Symbiosis International University (Deemed), India

Abhijit Chirputkar
Symbiosis Institute of Digital and Telecom Management, Symbiosis International University (Deemed), India

ABSTRACT

This proposed chapter aims to present a study on RPA leaders and understand the parameters for improving Power Automate's position amongst industry leaders by formulating a SWOT analysis for the company. The work presented starts with scrutinizing various literature on RPA, followed by a detailed analysis of Microsoft's RPA efforts. Gartner published a report on robotics process automation, placing Microsoft's Power Automate lowest in the Leader's magic quadrant. This chapter provides recommendations that could help Power Automate move up the ladder. The research method adopted is a qualitative analysis of the company in focus. As the chapter progresses, it unfolds various offerings of Power Automate that either empower its growth or could be a concern compared to RPA leaders like Uipath, Automation Anywhere, and Blueprism. Power Automate has made its footprints in the RPA space, and with aggressive innovation and restructuring, it can be a prominent player across industries.

DOI: 10.4018/979-8-3693-0230-9.ch012

1. INTRODUCTION

Automation was developed to perform repetitive tasks using programmed commands and mechanized feedback controls to ensure execution of business workflows. It grew with the meaning of substitution of electrical and mechanical efforts of human intelligence. As a result, automated systems have grown more smarter and more intricate. In multiple use cases, the capabilities and performance of such advanced systems have least error and the runtime is faster compared to those of humans. (Britannica, n.d.) Process automation controls business operations for consistency and openness; business apps and specialized software are used to command it. Process automation is extensively used for process mining and workflow automation. Following the process automation, there was the development of integration automation, in which once the engineer specifies the machine rules, robots can copy and repeat human activities. A classic example could be "Digital worker". The most recent type of automation is AI automation, which is now considered to be the most important facet of automating systems. AI has enabled robots to "learn" and "make decisions" based on previously encountered and studied scenarios. For instance, virtual assistants in customer service can lower costs while empowering both customers and human agents, resulting in the best possible customer experience.

In 2011, Apple released Siri, that paved the way for strategic shift from physical robots to automation software, and this trend empowered the development of Robotics process automation. Robotic process automation (RPA) is a software technology that develops, deploys, and direct robots that imitate human actions to interact with the digital world.

Robotic process automation structures workflows, which aims at instruction-based execution of processes to be automated. Major RPA players in the market today viz Uipath, Automation Anywhere, Blueprism, Power Automate, Appian, Nice, and IBM., are using innovative ways to address customer use cases. Gartner published a report in 2021 for Robotic Process Automation, and placed Uipath, Automation Anywhere, Blueprism, and Power Automate in the leaders' magic quadrant. Power Automate is ranked lower in the leader's quadrant and has to innovate its processes, improve its deliverables, and provide scalable solutions to the customer. ()

2. LITERATURE REVIEW

Robotics process automation was designed with the objective to perform high-volume repetitive tasks, that applications/bots can perform efficiently faster than humans. There have been multiple research papers, surveys, EIPs and journal articles that articulate the milestone achieved and the future of RPA industry. In an international journal on social robotics by Royakkers, L. and, van Est R. documented that robotics does not exist for itself, it is for the betterment of the society and robotics aims at supporting the development of humankind, and focuses on the realization that new robotics offers numerous future prospects for the RPA industry and a detailed overview of automation technology applied in the bioindustry (Royakkers & van Est, 2015). In 2007, Jämsä-Jounela, S. L. emphasized on process automation stating it to be a driving factor for optimizing the functioning of big plants, since big plants are moving towards decentralization, it has become a differentiator for big plant [4] Haleem, A., Javaid, M., Singh, R. P., Rab, S., & Suman, R. in 2021 drafted a paper that focused on the increasing dependence on hyper automation and factory automation that impelled industry 4.0 to rely on motion, environmental, and vibration sensors to monitor various equipment in different industries. (2021) In International Symposium for Production Research Kent, M. D., & Kopacek, P. in 2020 studied the utilization of sustainability approach as a framework to analyse the technology of automation & the study is aimed at reviewing the social impacts of automation on our society. It was found that Automation gives improved way of doing tasks but the human replacement will take time (Kent & Kopacek, 2020). With the future revolving around automation and RPA, Zavadskas E. K., 2010 presented his work on "Automation and robotics in construction: International research and achievements" that states the heavy usage of automation in the construction industry. Automation in this sector could revolutionize the functioning by increasing system reliability and efficiency (Zavadskas, 2010). Further, the study by Madakam, S., Holmukhe, R. M., & Jaiswal, D. K.,2019. "The future digital work force: robotic process automation (RPA)" documents how businesses are attempting to automate their processes by using RPA and its implication on human jobs for automated tasks (Jämsä-Jounela, 2007; Madakam et al., 2019). Lastly, as stated by Lindgren, I. in Exploring the Use of Robotic Process Automation in Local Government, when compared to other fields, it emphasized that RPA was not widespread in various communities. As a result, it is in the nascent stage to notice any apparent effects of automation handling on municipal organizations and their output. Besides, it stated that RPA installation is challenging (Lindgren, 2020). SogetiLabs (Part of Capgemini) in 2021, documented a white paper on the notable aspects and the drawbacks of Power Automate. It summarizes the Microsoft's RPA capabilities considering various parameters. Extending the study of mentioned literatures, this paper formulates the strengths, weaknesses, opportunities and threats of Power Automate (R. & Wadiwala, 2019).

3. ABBREVIATIONS AND ACRONYMS

RPA - Robotics process automation, AA - Automation Anywhere, AARI - Automation Anywhere robotic interface, GUI - Graphical user interface

4. SWOT ANALYSIS FOR MICROSOFT'S POWER AUTOMATE

4.1 Strengths

4.1.1 Enterprise Architecture Strengths

Aligning the RPA solution to an existing organization's architecture and how much efficiency it interacts with legacy systems is crucial before selecting any vendor for automation. Microsoft Power Automate makes this parameter easy by diminishing costs and promoting more innovative opportunities simultaneously. Microsoft has various services and products intertwined with every business; Power Automate is one of the most feasible options for innumerable organizations already utilizing Azure servers, SharePoint and Office 365. Power Automate slides in seamlessly with existing architecture, but significant extensibility is available. For example, an organization can use SharePoint's online solutions with Microsoft's AI services, Azure Cognitive, and machine learning. (##NO_NAME##, 2021)

Table 1. Power app

		Power Automate	Uipath	Automation Anywhere
Inception year	**Company Highlights**	**Founded in the year 2018, initially known as Microsoft Workflows**	**Founded in the year 2005**	**Founded in the year 2003**
Market Share		3%	27.10%	19.40%
Strengths		1. Enterprise architecture strengths, 2. legacy systems 3. PaaS provider for automation solutions	1. Best known RPA leader in the market 2. Largest community support 3. Leader in the no-coding trend of RPA, highest number of connectors provided.	1. AA is known of most robust automation 2. One of the strongest RPA tools, AARI 3. Best licensing structure.
Weaknesses		Deployment issues, only preferred for small departmental level flows, Speed slows down for long workflows	Licensing is not well structured, In few cases unstructured input throws errors	Weak for virtualized environments, debugger issues.
Opportunities		Can work on excel data handling range, customer acquisition can be easier, free desktop version for all	Strong hold on the RPA market and with constant expansion of innovative offerings	With increase in dependency on automation, AARI is gaining momentum
Threats		Security, strong and niche players with expertise in the sector	With emergence of new leaders in the RPA space, Uipath has improve on its licensing and expensive pricing.	Similar to Uipath, increase in RPA players could be a potential threat to AA

4.1.2 Strong Hold on Global Markets

Microsoft's sales increased by 15% between 2020 and 2021, and the company has over $130 billion in cash equivalents, which may be used for innovating and R&D of Power Apps.

4.1.3 Distribution Channel

Microsoft is known to have the strongest distribution channel and it does leverage the advantage of having a huge end-user base to sell power automate as a part of office 365. Organizations with huge employee strength prefer Power Automate licensing through office 365. Recently Power Automate onboarded Accenture to its customer list, with Accenture's huge employee strength that were already using Microsoft 365 and developers are harnessing the power of the Microsoft Power Platform, building apps with no code. For instance, a manager responsible for maintenance of security and compliance standards developed a Power App in just four weeks that centralizes all compliance entry in one place for her team and customer delivery time has been significantly reduced by 20% (Accenture, 2021).

4.1.4 Levaraging the Adavntage of Being a PaaS Provider

Users of Power Automate may now support essential business operations, proactively manage Flows, and react immediately to failed Flows. All flows are monitored by Flowatcher365TM, which alerts authorized responders on an hourly basis when a flow fails and supports mission-critical business operations. The user dashboard for Flowatcher365TM provides Flow metrics, enables suspended flows, and streamlines troubleshooting with a standard error recording system. Many of their clients embrace the Microsoft Power Automate platform for crucial business processes (Newswire, 2022).

4.2 Weakness

Microsoft's Power Automate lacks potential innovative features; it is reasonably lax, especially in the RPA space. It needs a robust automation solution compared to other RPA players in Gartner's leader's quadrant.

4.2.1 Ease of Deployment

While selecting a vendor for enterprise automation, the significant aspect considered is the ease of deployment of these RPA solutions. Process efficiency and different deployment options provided by the vendor concerning the client's environments and requirements are scrutinized by the clients. In Power Automate, the developer of the flow has to open, look into the workflows and update the connections manually. These human interventions lead to many unintentional user errors and updates to the flow, that generally ends up creating bugs & issues. Compared to Uipath, Automation Anywhere, and Blueprism, this process is not well structured. In Uipath, all business, personal, and operational data is kept on and deployed from the server on-premises on the customer network. There is no additional physical server infrastructure for the Control Room. After the upgrade, you will benefit from automatic updates across your organization and scale quickly in the Cloud deployment. Along similar lines, Automation Anywhere ensures different deployment options based on user requirements ranging from physical deployment by developers from AA to web server on a Single Machine or through deployment in the Cloud (Automation Anywhere., n.d.). Blueprism provides On-premise and cloud deployment options with minimal human intervention required. Microsoft offers similar deployment options; however, it requires greater developer intervention, which makes the process dependent and time-consuming, with multiple iterations (R. & Wadiwala, 2019).

4.2.2 The No-Coding Solution Trends in RPA

With the increased dependence on automation, it has become vital for non-developers to also have a fair idea of automating business processes. This reason marks the introduction of applications that help employees automate processes without coding. On the user-friendly parameter, Power Automate has a long way to go. Microsoft's Power Automate is quite complex to use, especially if an organization wants to develop advanced workflows. Power Automate claims to be user-friendly with the no-coding feature that enables users to drag and drop activities but needs constant human intervention during execution. They are well-suited for easy departmental level automation with fewer number of workflows. Uipath enables users to drag and drop seamlessly into the graphical user interface of Studio/StudioX and visually create long running workflows without writing code. Automation Anywhere's AARI, making automation interface easy to use without prior RPA experience.

4.2.3 Operational Scalability

RPA scalability is a major objective of organizations concerning RPA. Power Automate is in the nascent stage, scalability is a major issue with Microsoft's automation solution. There are only 300-500 connectors (Microsoft, n.d) to Uipath's more than 1400 connectors and Automation Anywhere's more than 700 connectors. Weak connectors lead to failures during complex workflow execution, and to add to it poor exception handling makes it difficult for an organization to prefer Power Automate for enterprise automation or process automation. Unlike Power Automate, the most valuable features of Blueprism are the exception handling and embedded control room. Power Automate works well with Azure but the other RPA leaders are cloud diagnostic which enables the organization to scale the RPA solutions.

4.2.4 Machine Learning and Predictive Analytics

ML and predictive learning are the core competency of RPA solutions. Few prominent missing pieces for the RPA implementation, for instance, dynamically engaging test data for multiple runs from a dataset or excel, which are standard in offering from other providers, are technically less mature in nature. On the contrary, Uipath has continuously expanded its traditional RPA offering capabilities to include tools like process mining, embedded analytics, and improved AI fabric components. Like Uipath, Automation Anywhere's AARI has built AI into every part of the Platform. Blueprism's combination of robotics process automation (RPA) with expanded cognitive and AI capabilities makes Blueprism a prominent market leader in RPA. Unlike Power Automate, Blueprism, Uipath and Automation Anywhere are evolving and innovating constantly with regards to improving services using machine learning and predictive analytics.

4.2.5 Speed Being the Game Changer

Power Automate's flow developer IDE are slower as compared to the other RPA leaders. The platform loses efficiency the moment additional business rules or process steps are added to the flow. With increase in actions/activities the flow starts lagging, especially when trying to debug historical runs. Uipath and Automation Anywhere is three to four times faster than any other RPA product. It is much easier to build modular components and bring them all together using UiPath compared to Power Automate.

4.2.6 Orchestration

Orchestration is used for enterprise automation and process automation, Uipath and Automation Anywhere outperform other RPA leaders in the orchestration services. The orchestrator from Uipath is a web-based programme that serves as a single centre for controlling and maintaining all software bots. A full orchestration layer with governance, compliance, and security management over all RPA activities is only provided by Automation Anywhere. Building local bot factories using the orchestration layer will enable your CoE to develop on more sophisticated automation initiatives. As compared to these the orchestration services of Power Automate and Blueprism are in the emergent stage. ()

4.3 Opportunities

4.3.1 Easy Reach to End Users

With the global presence of Microsoft, it's a huge opportunity for customer acquisition. Power Automate is a part of office 365 and hence has an extensive reach. It was comparatively difficult for Uipath, Automation Anywhere and Blueprism to acquire customers during the initial phase.

4.3.2 Data Handling

As excel is native to Microsoft and integration with power apps is more straightforward, Power Automate can increase the maximum number of rows handled by Power Automate. Presently it can read and write up to 2000 rows without throwing any exception or lag. Uipath can read and write 10,000 rows, AA can read a range of 7000 to 9000 rows, (Automation Anywhere, n.d.) and Blueprism can read and write 7000 rows. Increasing the number of excel rows that Power Automate can seamlessly read and write could be a potential strength for Power Automate.

4.3.3 Free Desktop Trail Version to be a Differentiator

Uipath, Automation Anywhere and Blueprism provide a free trial version for end-users to understand the GUI and convert them to licensed users. However, Microsoft recently made Power Automate Desktop, its enterprise-level tool for creating automated desktop-centric workflows, available to all licensed Windows 10 users for free. This feature is an opportunity for Power Automate like the early days of SharePoint, when end users tackled complex business issues with little to no IT control and assistance, Power Automate based on the feedback can redefine its automation services (Microsoft, n.d.).

4.3.4 Growth Through Acquisitions

Microsoft has a sizable financial reserve, Microsoft could begin buying up businesses that would introduce cutting-edge technology, expertise, and capabilities to the support the growth of power Automate. Microsoft is known to be a slow innovator and acquiring niche players, startups with skillset can give Power Automate an upper hand compared to other RPA leaders.

4.4 Threats

4.4.1 Weak Security

Microsoft has increased the use of multifactor authentication (MFA) and other security controls; however, it remains one of the most challenging and intricate environments to monitor and administer. According to the Vectra report, Power Automate had been used to spot suspicious activities in 71 percent of the accounts being monitored. Microsoft recently said that it discovered sophisticated threat actors employing different programs to automate data exfiltration within a sizable multinational corporation, over 200 days passed before this incidence was discovered. Using Power Automate, they can alter email rules, compromise SharePoint and OneDrive file storage, quickly build persistent exfiltration capabilities and breach client data. Compared to this Uipath, Automation Anywhere and Blueprism are highly secured and are certified for Veracode, ISO/IEC 27001, SOC 2 Type-2. AA has also been certified for EU-US Privacy Shield, ISO 22301:2019, FISMA Security Controls, and RBAC (MindMajix, n.d.).

4.4.2 Stronger Players in the Market

When it comes to attended automation and on-demand short workflows, Power Automate excels. Since Power Automate was presented as a product "added" to the Microsoft platform, many of its features are not well thought out from the standpoint of hyper-automation. Uipath, Automation Anywhere, Blueprism, and Nice perform significantly better in this regard compared to Microsoft since they have always built their solutions with a thorough understanding of process automation for their clients in mind.

4.4.3 Potential Lawsuits

Microsoft has faced multiple backlashes from different countries for violating rules and regulations, it has multiple antitrust case filed against it and these can potentially be a threat to the Power Automate's growth. In the early stage decreasing trust of customers can be a huge threat to Power Automate. Both UiPath and Automation Anywhere are well-known trustworthy companies. But their code is closed source. So, you must trust these companies that they do not send of critical corporate information to outside servers.

4.4.4 Disorganized Licensing

Licensing can be difficult to control, especially when several employees in the company create workflows while using Power Automate. This threat can exploit customer retention, however this flaw is faced by

Automation Anywhere clients as well. Uipath and Blueprism have decently appreciative licensing options available.

5. CONCLUSION AND RECOMMENDATION

From the days of its inception, Power Automate has incorporated a wide variety of features that has turned out to be its core strength. With growing community support and a free desktop version launch, Power Automate is all set to strengthen its footprints in the RPA industry. Power Automate can be an absolute threat to the existing RPA leaders if it promotes learning and improves technological innovations. It should target the organization that requires departmental-level automation, basic implementation of RPA & AI, and personal productivity. Microsoft, with its recent upgrades, is quite aggressive in pursuing improvements to its platform. Power Automate should work on its no-coding capabilities and improve exception handling. Power Automate should work regressively on its security policy and ensure that client data is protected from malicious attacks. It should formulate policies and procedures to secure that no antitrust cases are filed against it. It has to work on integration flaws when automating with applications other than Microsoft 365. There is a massive gap between the number of connectors compatible with Power Automate and other RPA leaders, and it should include connectors essential for enterprise automation. Data handling in excel (read and write data) is a significant aspect of workflow automation and eventually can be a potential strength of Power Automate. To be the future leader in the RPA space, it has to induce AI components in every bit of its platform and understand shortcomings in its predictive analytics by constant innovation. Uipath, Automation Anywhere, and Blueprism continuously expand their traditional RPA offering to accommodate customers' changing requirements. Uipath and Automation Anywhere platforms function efficiently with attended and unattended bots, making them suitable for front and back-office automation. Power Automate offers attended and unattended automation with minimal developer intervention. It should bring about updates to have a robust automation ecosystem to stay relevant in the market.

REFERENCES

Accenture. (2021). *Power to the people to innovate.* Accenture. https://www.accenture.com/in-en/case-studies/about/citizen-development

Automation Anywhere. (n.d.-a). *Home.* Automation anywhere. Https://Www.Automationanywhere.Com/

Automation Anywhere. (n.d.-b). *Customer Portal.* Automation Anywhere. https://apeople.automationanywhere.com/s/question/0D56F00007dVdZoSAK/please-guide-if-there-are-any-limitations-of-aa-enterprise-11300-trial-version-while-using-excel-as-database-when-there-are-records-in-thousands?-language=en_US

Blueprint. (2021). *Part One: Impact Benefits.* Blueprint.https://www.blueprintsys.com/blog/rpa/part-1-impact-benefits-value-microsoft-power-automate.

BluePrism. (n.d.). *Home.* BluePrism. https://www.blueprism.com/

Britannica. (n.d.). *Automation.* Britannica. https://www.britannica.com/technology/automation

Edureka! (2020). *How the collection size in blue prism is consumerd for memory.* Edureka. https://www.edureka.co/community/75067/collection-prism-consumed-memory-includes-count-columns-rows#:~:text=It%20is%20always%20advised%20to,Hope%20this%20helps

Gartner. (n.d.). *How Markets and Vendors Are Evaluated in Gartner Magic Quadrants.* gartner Research. https://www.gartner.com/en/documents/3956304

Haleem, A., Javaid, M., Singh, R. P., Rab, S., & Suman, R. (2021). Hyperautomation for the enhancement of automation in industries. *Sensors International*, *2*, 100124. doi:10.1016/j.sintl.2021.100124

Jämsä-Jounela, S. L. (2007). Future trends in process automation. *Annual Reviews in Control*, *31*(2), 211–220. doi:10.1016/j.arcontrol.2007.08.003

Kent, M. D., & Kopacek, P. (2020, September). Social and ethical aspects of automation. In *The International Symposium for Production Research* (pp. 363-372). Springer, Cham.

Lindgren, I. (2020). Exploring the Use of Robotic Process Automation in Local Government. In EGOV-CeDEM-ePart-* (pp. 249-258). Research Gate.

Madakam, S., Holmukhe, R. M., & Jaiswal, D. K. (2019). The future digital work force: robotic process automation (RPA). *JISTEM-Journal of Information Systems and Technology Management, 16.*

Microsoft. (n.d.). *Power Automate.* Microsoft. https://powerautomate.microsoft.com/en-us/

MindMajix. (n.d.). *Key Differences.* MindMajix. https://mindmajix.com/uipath-vs-automation-anywhere

PR Newswire. (2022). Alitek Launches Flowatcher365™ for Microsoft Power Automate - Advanced Flow Monitoring, Management, and Notification PaaS. PR Newswire.

Royakkers, L., & van Est, R. (2015). A literature review on new robotics: Automation from love to war. *International Journal of Social Robotics*, *7*(5), 549–570. doi:10.1007/s12369-015-0295-x

UiPath. (n.d.). *Home.* UiPath. https://www.uipath.com/solutions/technology

UiPath. (2023). *UiPath Community 2023.12 Release.* UiPath. https://forum.uipath.com/t/what-is-the-maximum-number-of-rows-in-an-excel-sheet-that-works-with-uipath/206349

Wadiwala, R. (2019). *The good, the bad and the ugly of Power Automate in 2021.*

Zavadskas, E. K. (2010). Automation and robotics in construction: International research and achievements. *Automation in Construction*, *19*(3), 286–290. doi:10.1016/j.autcon.2009.12.011

Compilation of References

Abbaspour, A., Yen, K. K., Noei, S., & Sargolzaei, A. (2016). Detection of Fault Data Injection Attack on UAV Using Adaptive Neural Network. *Procedia Computer Science*, *95*, 193–200. doi:10.1016/j.procs.2016.09.312

Abdulla, N., Demirci, M., & Ozdemir, S. (2023). Towards utilizing unlabeled data for flood forecasting with weakly supervised adaptive learning. *2023 Innovations in Intelligent Systems and Applications Conference (ASYU)*. IEEE.

Abdulla, N., Demirci, M., & Ozdemir, S. (2021). Adaptive learning on fog-cloud collaborative architecture for stream data processing. *2021 International Symposium on Networks, Computers and Communications (ISNCC)* (pp. 1-6). Dubai: IEEE. 10.1109/ISNCC52172.2021.9615824

Abdulla, N., Demirci, M., & Ozdemir, S. (2022). Design and evaluation of adaptive deep learning models for weather forecasting. *Engineering Applications of Artificial Intelligence*, *116*, 105440. doi:10.1016/j.engappai.2022.105440

Accenture. (2021). *Power to the people to innovate.* Accenture. https://www.accenture.com/in-en/case-studies/about/citizen-development

Achouch, M., Dimitrova, M., Ziane, K., Sattarpanah Karganroudi, S., Dhouib, R., Ibrahim, H., & Adda, M. (2022). On predictive maintenance in industry 4.0: Overview, models, and challenges. *Applied Sciences (Basel, Switzerland)*, *12*(16), 8081. doi:10.3390/app12168081

Adadi, A., & Berrada, M. (2018). Peeking inside the Black-Box: A survey on explainable artificial intelligence (XAI). *IEEE Access : Practical Innovations, Open Solutions*, *6*, 52138–52160. doi:10.1109/ACCESS.2018.2870052

Afzal, M. S., Bihs, H., & Kumar, L. (2020). Computational fluid dynamics modeling of abutment scour under steady current using the level set method. *International Journal of Sediment Research*, *35*(4), 355–364. doi:10.1016/j.ijsrc.2020.03.003

Ahmed, E., Yaqoob, I., Gani, A., Imran, M., & Guizani, M. (2016). Internet-of-things-based smart environments: State of the art, taxonomy, and open research challenges. *IEEE Wireless Communications*, *23*(5), 10–16. doi:10.1109/MWC.2016.7721736

Ainslie, J., Lei, T., De Jong, M., Ontañón, S., Brahma, S., Zemlyanskiy, Y., Uthus, D., Guo, M., Tay, Y., Sung, Y., & Sanghai, S. (2023). CoLT5: Faster Long-Range Transformers with Conditional Computation. ArXiv. /arXiv.2303.09752 doi:10.18653/v1/2023.emnlp-main.309

Akçayır, M., & Akçayır, G. (2017). Advantages and challenges associated with augmented reality for education: A systematic review of the literature. *Educational Research Review*, *20*, 1–11. doi:10.1016/j.edurev.2016.11.002

Akram, F., Liu, D., Zhao, P., Kryvinska, N., Abbas, S., & Rizwan, M. (2021). Trustworthy Intrusion Detection in E-Healthcare Systems. *Frontiers in Public Health*, *9*(December), 1–10. doi:10.3389/fpubh.2021.788347 PMID:34926397

Akrich, M. (2023). Actor network theory, Bruno Latour, and the CSI. *Social Studies of Science*, *53*(2), 169–173. doi:10.1177/03063127231158102 PMID:36840444

Alasta, M. S., Ali, A. S. A., Ebrahimi, S., Ashiq, M. M., Dheyab, A. S., AlMasri, A., & Khorram, M. (2022). Modeling of local scour depth around bridge pier using FLOW 3D. *CRPASE: Transactions of Civil and Environmental Engineering*, *8*(2), 1–9. doi:10.52547/crpase.8.2.2781

Albarakati, A., Robillard, C., Karanfil, M., Kassouf, M., Debbabi, M., Youssef, A., Ghafouri, M., & Hadjidj, R. (2022). Security Monitoring of IEC 61850 Substations Using IEC 62351-7 Network and System Management. *IEEE Transactions on Industrial Informatics*, *18*(3), 1641–1653. doi:10.1109/TII.2021.3082079

Albulayhi, K., & Sheldon, F. T. (2021). An Adaptive Deep-Ensemble Anomaly-Based Intrusion Detection System for the Internet of Things. *2021 IEEE World AI IoT Congress, AIIoT 2021*, (pp. 187–196). IEEE. 10.1109/AIIoT52608.2021.9454168

Ali, A. S. A.. (2021). Republic of Turkey Gaziantep University Graduate School of Natural and Applied Sciences.

Ali, A. S., Jazaei, F., Ashiq, M. M., Bakhshaee, A., & Alasta, M. S. (2022, December). Numerical Model For Simulation Of Scour Around Bridge Abutment. In *Fall Meeting 2022*. AGU.

Ali, A. S. A., Ebrahimi, S., Ashiq, M. M., Alasta, M. S., & Azari, B. (2022). CNN-Bi LSTM neural network for simulating groundwater level. *Environ. Eng*, *8*, 1–7.

Ali, A. S. A., & Günal, M. (2021). Artificial neural network for estimation of local scour depth around bridge piers. *Archives of Hydro-Engineering and Environmental Mechanics*, *68*(2), 87–101. doi:10.2478/heem-2021-0005

Ali, A. S., bin Waheed, U., Ashiq, M., Al Asta, M. S., & Khorram, M. (2022). Machine Learning Model for Estimation of Local Scour Depth around Cylindrical Bridge Piers. *Iraqi Journal of Civil Engineering*, *16*(2), 1–13. doi:10.37650/ijce.2022.160201

Allgower, E. L., & Georg, K. (1990). *Numerical Continuation Methods: An Introduction*. Springer-Verlag. doi:10.1007/978-3-642-61257-2

Alonso, A. M., Nogales, F. J., & Ruiz, C. (2020). A single scalable LSTM model for short-term forecasting of massive electricity time series. *Energies*, *13*(20), 5328. doi:10.3390/en13205328

Amasyali, K., & El-Gohary, N. M. (2018). A review of data-driven building energy consumption prediction studies. *Renewable & Sustainable Energy Reviews*, *81*, 1192–1205. doi:10.1016/j.rser.2017.04.095

Angelov, P. P., Soares, E. A., Jiang, R., Arnold, N. I., & Atkinson, P. M. (2021). Explainable artificial intelligence: An analytical review. *Wiley Interdisciplinary Reviews. Data Mining and Knowledge Discovery*, *11*(5), 1–13. doi:10.1002/widm.1424

Ankita, P. U., & Mathirajan, M. (2021). An efficient heuristic method for dynamic berth allocation problem. In *Proceedings of the International Conference on Industrial Engineering and Operations Management* (pp. 393-400). IEOM Society. 10.46254/AN11.20210077

Ansari, F., Glawar, R., & Sihn, W. (2020). Prescriptive maintenance of CPPS by integrating multimodal data with dynamic Bayesian networks. In *Machine Learning for Cyber Physical Systems: Selected papers from the International Conference ML4CPS 2017* (pp. 1-8). Springer Berlin Heidelberg. 10.1007/978-3-662-59084-3_1

Anscombe, G. E. M. (1957). *Intention*. Basil Blackwell.

Anthi, E., Williams, L., & Burnap, P. (2018). Pulse: An adaptive intrusion detection for the internet of things. *IET Conference Publications*, 2018(CP740). IET. 10.1049/cp.2018.0035

Archetti, F., & Candelieri, A. (2019). *Bayesian optimization and data science*. Springer. doi:10.1007/978-3-030-24494-1

Ardabili, S., Mosavi, A., Dehghani, M., & Várkonyi-Kóczy, A. R. (2019, September). Deep learning and machine learning in hydrological processes climate change and earth systems a systematic review. In *International conference on global research and education* (pp. 52-62). Springer, Cham.

Arnab, A., Dehghani, M., Heigold, G., Sun, C., Lučić, M., & Schmid, C. (2021). Vivit: A video vision transformer. In *Proceedings of the IEEE/CVF international conference on computer vision* (pp. 6836-6846). IEEE.

Arrington, B., Barnett, L. E., Rufus, R., & Esterline, A. (2016). Behavioral modeling intrusion detection system (BMIDS) using internet of things (IoT) behavior-based anomaly detection via immunity-inspired algorithms. *2016 25th International Conference on Computer Communications and Networks, ICCCN 2016*, (pp. 12–17). IEEE. 10.1109/ICCCN.2016.7568495

Asano, Y. M., Rupprecht, C., & Vedaldi, A. (2019, September). Self-labelling via simultaneous clustering and representation learning. In *International Conference on Learning Representations*. IEEE.

Asghar, M. R., Dan, G., Miorandi, D., & Chlamtac, I. (2017). Smart meter data privacy: A survey. *IEEE Communications Surveys and Tutorials*, *19*(4), 2820–2835. doi:10.1109/COMST.2017.2720195

Ashiq, M. M., Rehman, H. U., & Khan, N. M. (2020). Impact of large diameter recharge wells for reducing groundwater depletion rates in an urban area of Lahore, Pakistan. *Environmental Earth Sciences*, *79*(17), 1–14. doi:10.1007/s12665-020-09144-7

Asim, M., Rashid, A., & Ahmad, T. (2022). Scour modeling using deep neural networks based on hyperparameter optimization. *ICT Express*, *8*(3), 357–362. doi:10.1016/j.icte.2021.09.012

Aurangzeb, K., Aslam, S., Haider, S. I., Mohsin, S. M., Islam, S., Khattak, H. A., & Shah, S. (2022). Energy forecasting using multiheaded convolutional neural networks in efficient renewable energy resources equipped with energy storage system. *Transactions on Emerging Telecommunications Technologies*, *33*(2), e3837. doi:10.1002/ett.3837

Automation Anywhere. (n.d.-a). *Home*. Automation anywhere. Https://Www.Automationanywhere.Com/

Automation Anywhere. (n.d.-b). *Customer Portal*. Automation Anywhere. https://apeople.automationanywhere.com/s/question/0D56F00007dVdZoSAK/please-guide-if-there-are-any-limitations-of-aa-enterprise-11300-trial-version-while-using-excel-as-database-when-there-are-records-in-thousands?language=en_US

Aydin, M., Karal, H., & Nabiyev, V. (2023). Examination of adaptation components in serious games: A systematic review study. *Education and Information Technologies*, *28*(6), 6541–6562. doi:10.1007/s10639-022-11462-1

Azari, B., Hassan, K., Pierce, J., & Ebrahimi, S. (2022). Evaluation of machine learning methods application in temperature prediction. *Environ Eng*, *8*(1), 1–12. doi:10.52547/crpase.8.1.2747

Azuma, R., Baillot, Y., Behringer, R., Feiner, S., Julier, S., & MacIntyre, B. (2001). Recent advances in augmented reality. *IEEE Computer Graphics and Applications*, *21*(6), 34–47. doi:10.1109/38.963459

Babu, S. C.V. (2022). Artificial Intelligence and Expert Systems. Anniyappa Publications.

Bacalhau, E. T., Casacio, L., & de Azevedo, A. T. (2021). New hybrid genetic algorithms to solve dynamic berth allocation problem. *Expert Systems with Applications*, *167*, 114198. doi:10.1016/j.eswa.2020.114198

Badrinarayanan, V., Kendall, A., & Cipolla, R. (2017). SegNet: A Deep Convolutional Encoder-Decoder Architecture for Image Segmentation. *IEEE Transactions on Pattern Analysis and Machine Intelligence*, *39*(12), 2481–2495. doi:10.1109/TPAMI.2016.2644615 PMID:28060704

Bandura, A. (2001). Social cognitive theory: An agentic perspective. *Annual Review of Psychology*, *52*(1), 1–26. doi:10.1146/annurev.psych.52.1.1 PMID:11148297

Bandura, A. (2006). Toward a psychology of human agency. *Perspectives on Psychological Science*, *1*(2), 164–180. doi:10.1111/j.1745-6916.2006.00011.x PMID:26151469

Bandyapadhyay, S., Fomin, F. V., Golovach, P. A., Lochet, W., Purohit, N., & Simonov, K. (2023). How to find a good explanation for clustering? *Artificial Intelligence*, *322*, 103948. doi:10.1016/j.artint.2023.103948

Bangui, H., & Buhnova, B. (2021). Recent advances in machine-learning driven intrusion detection in transportation: Survey. *Procedia Computer Science, 184*(2019), 877–886. doi:10.1016/j.procs.2021.04.014

Banihashem, S. K., Noroozi, O., van Ginkel, S., Macfadyen, L. P., & Biemans, H. J. A. (2022). A systematic review of the role of learning analytics in enhancing feedback practices in higher education. *Educational Research Review*, *37*, 100489. doi:10.1016/j.edurev.2022.100489

Barbosa, F., Rampazzo, P. C. B., de Azevedo, A. T., & Yamakami, A. (2022). The impact of time windows constraints on metaheuristics implementation: A study for the Discrete and Dynamic Berth Allocation Problem. *Applied Intelligence*, *52*(2), 1406–1434. doi:10.1007/s10489-021-02420-4

Barbosa, F., Rampazzo, P. C. B., Yamakami, A., & Camanho, A. S. (2019). The use of frontier techniques to identify efficient solutions for the Berth Allocation Problem solved with a hybrid evolutionary algorithm. *Computers & Operations Research*, *107*, 43–60. doi:10.1016/j.cor.2019.01.017

Barnett, M. (2022, July 22). When will an AI first pass a long, informed, adversarial Turing test? *Metaculus comment. https*://www.metaculus.com/questions/11861/when-will-ai-pass-a-difficult-turing-test/

Barredo Arrieta, A., Dıaz-Rodrıguez, N., Del Ser, J., Bennetot, A., Tabik, S., Barbado, A., Garcia, S., Gil-Lopez, S., Molina, D., Benjamins, R., Chatila, R., & Herrera, F. (2020). Explainable artificial intelligence (XAI): Concepts, taxonomies, opportunities and challenges toward responsible AI. *Information Fusion*, *58*, 82–115. doi:10.1016/j.inffus.2019.12.012

Bashar, A. (2019). Survey on evolving deep learning neural network architectures. *Journal of Artificial Intelligence*, *1*(02), 73–82.

Baylor, A. (1999). Intelligent agents as cognitive tools for education. *Educational Technology Research and Development. ETR & D*, *39*(2), 36–40.

Begus, K., & Southgate, V. (2018). Curious learners: How infants' motivation to learn shapes and is shaped by infants' interactions with the social world. *Active learning from infancy to childhood: Social motivation, cognition, and linguistic mechanisms,* 13-37.

Bengio, Y., Goodfellow, I., & Courville, A. (2017). *Deep learning* (Vol. 1). MIT press.

Benzaïd, C., & Taleb, T. (2020, November/December). AI for Beyond 5G Networks: A Cyber-Security Defense or Offense Enabler? *IEEE Network*, *34*(6), 140–147. doi:10.1109/MNET.011.2000088

Berger, P. L., & Luckmann, T. (1966). *The social construction of reality: A treatise in the sociology of knowledge*. Penguin.

Bianchi, L., Dorigo, M., Gambardella, L. M., & Gutjahr, W. J. (2009). A survey on metaheuristics for stochastic combinatorial optimization. *Natural Computing*, *8*(2), 239–287. doi:10.1007/s11047-008-9098-4

Bierwirth, C., & Meisel, F. (2010). A survey of berth allocation and quay crane scheduling problems in container terminals. *European Journal of Operational Research*, *202*(3), 615–627. doi:10.1016/j.ejor.2009.05.031

Bierwirth, C., & Meisel, F. (2015). A follow-up survey of berth allocation and quay crane scheduling problems in container terminals. *European Journal of Operational Research*, *244*(3), 675–689. doi:10.1016/j.ejor.2014.12.030

Biever, C. (2023). ChatGPT broke the Turing test — The race is on for new ways to assess AI. *Nature*, *619*(7971), 686–689. doi:10.1038/d41586-023-02361-7 PMID:37491395

Birch, C. E., Rabb, B. L., Boing, S. J., Shelton, K. L., Lamb, R., Hunter, N., Trigg, M. A., Hines, A., Taylor, A. L., Pilling, C., & Dale, M. (2021). Enhanced surface water flood forecasts: User-led development and testing. *Journal of Flood Risk Management*, *14*(2), e12691. doi:10.1111/jfr3.12691

Blueprint. (2021). *Part One: Impact Benefits*. Blueprint.https://www.blueprintsys.com/blog/rpa/part-1-impact-benefits-value-microsoft-power-automate.

BluePrism. (n.d.). *Home*. BluePrism. https://www.blueprism.com/

Blum, B. A. (2023, August 10). To Navigate the Age of AI, the World Needs a New Turing Test. Wired. https://www.wired.com/story/ai-new-turing-test/

Bombelli, L., Lee, J., Meyer, D., & Sorkin, R. D. (1987). Space-time as a causal set. *Physical Review Letters*, *59*(5), 521–524. doi:10.1103/PhysRevLett.59.521 PMID:10035795

Borji, A. (2023). A Categorical Archive of ChatGPT Failures. *ArXiv*. /arXiv.2302.03494 doi:10.21203/rs.3.rs-2895792/v1

Bottou, L., Curtis, F. E., & Nocedal, J. (2018). Optimization methods for large-scale machine learning. *SIAM Review*, *60*(2), 223–311. doi:10.1137/16M1080173

Boussaïd, I., Lepagnot, J., & Siarry, P. (2013). A survey on optimization metaheuristics. *Information Sciences*, *237*, 82–117. doi:10.1016/j.ins.2013.02.041

Bradski, G., & Kaehler, A. (2008). *Learning OpenCV: Computer vision with the OpenCV library*. O'Reilly Media, Inc.

Bramley, N. R., Gerstenberg, T., Mayrhofer, R., & Lagnado, D. A. (2018). Time in causal structure learning. *Journal of Experimental Psychology. Learning, Memory, and Cognition*, *44*(12), 1880–1910. doi:10.1037/xlm0000548 PMID:29745682

Brandimarte, L., Paron, P., & Di Baldassarre, G. (2012). Bridge pier scour: A review of processes, measurements and estimates. *Environmental Engineering and Management Journal*, *11*(5), 975–989. doi:10.30638/eemj.2012.121

Brännström, N. (2009). Averaging in weakly coupled discrete dynamical systems. *Journal of Nonlinear Mathematical Physics*, *16*(4), 465–487. doi:10.1142/S1402925109000492

Breiman, L. (2001). Random forests. *Machine Learning*, *45*(1), 5–32. doi:10.1023/A:1010933404324

Britannica. (n.d.). *Automation*. Britannica. https://www.britannica.com/technology/automation

Brochu, E., Cora, V. M., & De Freitas, N. (2010). *A tutorial on Bayesian optimization of expensive cost functions, with application to active user modeling and hierarchical reinforcement learning*. arXiv preprint arXiv:1012.2599.

Brown, T., Mann, B., Ryder, N., Subbiah, M., Kaplan, J. D., Dhariwal, P., & Amodei, D. (2020). Language models are few-shot learners. *Advances in Neural Information Processing Systems*, *33*, 1877–1901. doi:10.48550/arXiv.2005.14165

Bryant, P. T. (2021). Modeling augmented humanity. In P. T. Bryant (Ed.), *Augmented humanity: Being and remaining agentic in a digitalized world* (pp. 1–38). Springer International Publishing. doi:10.1007/978-3-030-76445-6_1

Bulatov, A., Kuratov, Y., & Burtsev, M. (2022). Recurrent memory transformer. *Advances in Neural Information Processing Systems*, *35*, 11079–11091.

Cai, Z., Ding, T., Liu, M., Liu, X., & Xia, J. (2023). A damped block Gauss-Newton method for shallow ReLU neural network. *Manuscript.*

Cai, Z., Chen, J., & Liu, M. (2021). Least-squares ReLU neural network (LSNN) method for linear advection-reaction equation. *Journal of Computational Physics*, *443*, 110514. doi:10.1016/j.jcp.2021.110514

Cai, Z., Chen, J., & Liu, M. (2022). Self-adaptive deep neural network: Numerical approximation to functions and PDEs. *Journal of Computational Physics*, *455*, 111021. doi:10.1016/j.jcp.2022.111021

Cai, Z., Chen, J., Liu, M., & Liu, X. (2020). Deep least-squares methods: An unsupervised learning-based numerical method for solving elliptic PDEs. *Journal of Computational Physics*, *420*, 109707. doi:10.1016/j.jcp.2020.109707

CaiZ.ChoiJ.LiuM. (2023). Least-squares neural network (LSNN) method for linear advection-reaction equation: general discontinuous interface. *arXiv:2301.06156v3[math.NA].*

Cao, Z., Simon, T., Wei, S. E., & Sheikh, Y. (2017). Realtime multi-person 2d pose estimation using part affinity fields. In *Proceedings of the IEEE conference on computer vision and pattern recognition* (pp. 7291-7299). IEEE. 10.1109/CVPR.2017.143

Carlini, N., Athalye, A., Papernot, N., Brendel, W., Rauber, J., Tsipras, D., & Kurakin, A. (2019). On evaluating adversarial robustness. *arXiv preprint arXiv:1902.06705.*

Carlo, H. J., Vis, I. F., & Roodbergen, K. J. (2015). Seaside operations in container terminals: Literature overview, trends, and research directions. *Flexible Services and Manufacturing Journal*, *27*(2-3), 224–262. doi:10.1007/s10696-013-9178-3

Chakrabarty, S., & Engels, D. W. (2020). Secure Smart Cities Framework Using IoT and AI. *2020 IEEE Global Conference on Artificial Intelligence and Internet of Things (GCAIoT)*, Dubai, United Arab Emirates. 10.1109/GCAIoT51063.2020.9345912

Charteris, J., & Smardon, D. (2018). A typology of agency in new generation learning environments: Emerging relational, ecological and new material considerations. *Pedagogy, Culture & Society*, *26*(1), 51–68. doi:10.1080/14681366.2017.1345975

Chen, D., Wawrzynski, P., & Lv, Z. (2021). Cyber security in smart cities: A review of deep learning-based applications and case studies. *Sustainable Cities and Society, 66*(November 2020). doi:10.1016/j.scs.2020.102655

Chen, C., Hui, Q., Xie, W., Wan, S., Zhou, Y., & Pei, Q. (2021). Convolutional Neural Networks for forecasting flood process in Internet-of-Things enabled smart city. *Computer Networks*, *186*, 107744. doi:10.1016/j.comnet.2020.107744

Chen, M. R., Huang, Y. Y., Zeng, G. Q., Lu, K. D., & Yang, L. Q. (2021). An improved bat algorithm hybridized with extremal optimization and Boltzmann selection. *Expert Systems with Applications*, *175*, 114812. doi:10.1016/j.eswa.2021.114812

Chen, X., Jia, S., & Xiang, Y. (2020). A review: Knowledge reasoning over knowledge graph. *Expert Systems with Applications*, *141*, 112948. doi:10.1016/j.eswa.2019.112948

Chen, X., Mersch, B., Nunes, L., Marcuzzi, R., Vizzo, I., Behley, J., & Stachniss, C. (2022). Automatic labeling to generate training data for online LiDAR-based moving object segmentation. *IEEE Robotics and Automation Letters*, *7*(3), 6107–6114. doi:10.1109/LRA.2022.3166544 PMID:35832507

Chen, X., Zhang, H., Wu, C., Mao, S., Ji, Y., & Bennis, M. (2018). Optimized computation offloading performance in virtual edge computing systems via deep reinforcement learning. *IEEE Internet of Things Journal*, *6*(3), 4005–4018. doi:10.1109/JIOT.2018.2876279

Chiew, Y. M. (2008). Scour and scour countermeasures at bridge sites. *Transactions of Tianjin University*, *14*(4), 289–295. doi:10.1007/s12209-008-0049-z

Chiew, Y. M., & Melville, B. W. (1987). Local scour around bridge piers. *Journal of Hydraulic Research*, *25*(1), 15–26. doi:10.1080/00221688709499285

Childs, C. M., & Washburn, N. R. (2019). Embedding domain knowledge for machine learning of complex material systems. *MRS Communications*, *9*(3), 806–820. doi:10.1557/mrc.2019.90

Chitsaz, H., Shaker, H., Zareipour, H., Wood, D., & Amjady, N. (2015). Short-term electricity load forecasting of buildings in microgrids. *Energy and Building*, *99*, 50–60. doi:10.1016/j.enbuild.2015.04.011

Chiva, R., Grandıo, A., & Alegre, J. (2008). Adaptive and generative learning: Implications from complexity theories. *International Journal of Management Reviews*, *12*(2), 114–129. doi:10.1111/j.1468-2370.2008.00255.x

Chollet, F. (2019). On the Measure of Intelligence. *ArXiv*. https://10.48550/arXiv.1911.01547

Chou, J. S., & Pham, A. D. (2014). Hybrid computational model for predicting bridge scour depth near piers and abutments. *Automation in Construction*, *48*, 88–96. doi:10.1016/j.autcon.2014.08.006

Cioffi, R., Travaglioni, M., Piscitelli, G., Petrillo, A., & De Felice, F. (2020). Artificial intelligence and machine learning applications in smart production: Progress, trends, and directions. *Sustainability (Basel)*, *12*(2), 492. doi:10.3390/su12020492

Cipresso, P. (2015). Modeling behavior dynamics using computational psychometrics within virtual worlds. *Frontiers in Psychology*, *6*, 1725. doi:10.3389/fpsyg.2015.01725 PMID:26594193

Codex. (2023, September 15). *OpenAI Codex*. OpenAI. https://openai.com/blog/openai-codex

Cole, D. (2023). The Chinese Room Argument, The Stanford Encyclopedia of Philosophy (E. N. Zalta & U. Nodelman, Eds.; Summer 2023 Edition). Stanford. https://plato.stanford.edu/archives/sum2023/entries/chinese-room

Comert, G., Rahman, M., Islam, M., & Chowdhury, M. (2022). Change Point Models for Real-Time Cyber Attack Detection in Connected Vehicle Environment. *IEEE Transactions on Intelligent Transportation Systems*, *23*(8), 12328–12342. doi:10.1109/TITS.2021.3113675

Conole, G., Gašević, D., Long, P., & Siemens, G. (2011). Message from the LAK 2011 General & Program Chairs. *Proceedings of the 1st International Conference on Learning Analytics and Knowledge*. ACM.

Corno, L. (2008). On teaching adaptively. *Educational Psychologist*, *43*(3), 161–173. doi:10.1080/00461520802178466

Cowling, P., Kendall, G., & Soubeiga, E. (2001). A hyperheuristic approach to scheduling a sales summit. In *Practice and Theory of Automated Timetabling III: Third International Conference, PATAT 2000 Konstanz,* (pp. 176-190). Springer Berlin Heidelberg. 10.1007/3-540-44629-X_11

Craw, S. (2017). *Manhattan distance*. Springer.

Croce, F., Gowal, S., Brunner, T., Shelhamer, E., Hein, M., & Cemgil, T. (2022, June). Evaluating the adversarial robustness of adaptive test-time defenses. In *International Conference on Machine Learning* (pp. 4421-4435). PMLR.

Crowley, E. J., Turner, J., Storkey, A., & O'Boyle, M. (2018). *A closer look at structured pruning for neural network compression.* arXiv preprint arXiv:1810.04622.

Cruz-Duarte, J. M., Amaya, I., Ortiz-Bayliss, J. C., Conant-Pablos, S. E., Terashima-Marín, H., & Shi, Y. (2021). Hyper-heuristics to customise metaheuristics for continuous optimisation. *Swarm and Evolutionary Computation*, *66*, 100935. doi:10.1016/j.swevo.2021.100935

Cui, W. (2019). Visual analytics: A comprehensive overview. *IEEE Access : Practical Innovations, Open Solutions*, *7*, 81555–81573. doi:10.1109/ACCESS.2019.2923736

Dai, W., Tang, Y., Zhang, Z., & Cai, Z. (2021). Ensemble learning technology for coastal flood forecasting in internet-of-things-enabled smart city. *International Journal of Computational Intelligence Systems*, *14*(1), 1–16. doi:10.1007/s44196-021-00023-y

Dai, Y., Li, Z., & Wang, B. (2023). Optimizing Berth Allocation in Maritime Transportation with Quay Crane Setup Times Using Reinforcement Learning. *Journal of Marine Science and Engineering*, *11*(5), 1025. doi:10.3390/jmse11051025

Damassino, N., & Novelli, N. (2020). Rethinking, Reworking and Revolutionising the Turing Test. *Minds and Machines*, *30*(4), 463–468. doi:10.1007/s11023-020-09553-4

Danso-Amoako, E., Scholz, M., Kalimeris, N., Yang, Q., & Shao, J. (2012). Predicting dam failure risk for sustainable flood retention basins: A generic case study for the wider Greater Manchester area. *Computers, Environment and Urban Systems*, *36*(5), 423–433. doi:10.1016/j.compenvurbsys.2012.02.003

Dardikman G., Turko, N.A., & Shaked, N.T. (2019). Deep learning approaches for unwrapping phase images with steep spatial gradients: A simulation. *2018 IEEE Int Conf Sci Electr Eng Isr ICSEE*. IEEE. . doi:10.1109/ICSEE.2018.8646266

Dardikman-Yoffe, G., Roitshtain, D., Mirsky, S. K., Turko, N. A., Habaza, M., & Shaked, N. T. (2020). PhUn-Net: Ready-to-use neural network for unwrapping quantitative phase images of biological cells. *Biomedical Optics Express*, *11*(2), 1107. doi:10.1364/BOE.379533 PMID:32206402

Das, T., Zhong, Y., Stoica, I., & Shenker, S. (2014). Adaptive stream processing using dynamic batch sizing. In *Proceedings of the ACM Symposium on Cloud Computing* (pp. 1-13). ACM. 10.1145/2670979.2670995

Davidson, D. (1963). Actions, reasons, and causes. *The Journal of Philosophy*, *60*(23), 685–700. doi:10.2307/2023177

Davis, J., Malkani, H., Dyck, J., Korambath, P., & Wise, J. (2020). Cyberinfrastructure for the democratization of smart manufacturing. In *Smart Manufacturing* (pp. 83–116). Elsevier. doi:10.1016/B978-0-12-820027-8.00004-6

Dawson, S., Jovanovic, J., Gašević, D., & Pardo, A. (2017). From prediction to impact: Evaluation of a learning analytics retention program. *Proceedings of the Seventh International Learning Analytics & Knowledge Conference*, (pp. 474–478). ACM. 10.1145/3027385.3027405

Dayal, A., Aishwarya, M., Abhilash, S., Mohan, C. K., Kumar, A., & Cenkeramaddi, L. R. (2023). Adversarial Unsupervised Domain Adaptation for Hand Gesture Recognition Using Thermal Images. *IEEE Sensors Journal*, *23*(4), 3493–3504. doi:10.1109/JSEN.2023.3235379

Deaton, A., & Cartwright, N. (2018). Understanding and misunderstanding randomized controlled trials. *Social Science & Medicine*, *210*, 2–21. doi:10.1016/j.socscimed.2017.12.005 PMID:29331519

Demrozi, F., Jereghi, M., & Pravadelli, G. (2021, March). Towards the automatic data annotation for human activity recognition based on wearables and BLE beacons. In *2021 IEEE International Symposium on Inertial Sensors and Systems (INERTIAL)* (pp. 1-4). IEEE. 10.1109/INERTIAL51137.2021.9430457

Dey, S., Mondal, J., & Mukherjee, A. (2019, March). Offloaded execution of deep learning inference at edge: Challenges and insights. In *2019 IEEE International Conference on Pervasive Computing and Communications Workshops (PerCom Workshops)* (pp. 855-861). IEEE.

DhoniP.KumarR. (2023). Synergizing Generative AI and Cybersecurity: Roles of Generative AI Entities, Companies, Agencies, and Government in Enhancing Cybersecurity. TechRxiv.

Diao, E., Ding, J., & Tarokh, V. (2021). *Communication efficient semi-supervised federated learning with unlabeled clients.*

Dijkstra, E. W. (1970). *Notes on Structured Programming*. University of Texas. https://www.cs.utexas.edu/users/EWD/ewd02xx/EWD249.PDF

Dkhil, H., Diarrassouba, I., Benmansour, S., & Yassine, A. (2021). Modelling and solving a berth allocation problem in an automotive transshipment terminal. *The Journal of the Operational Research Society*, *72*(3), 580–593. doi:10.1080/01605682.2019.1685361

Dokeroglu, T., Deniz, A., & Kiziloz, H. E. (2022). A comprehensive survey on recent metaheuristics for feature selection. *Neurocomputing*, *494*, 269–296. doi:10.1016/j.neucom.2022.04.083

Donovan, R. P., Kim, Y. G., Manzo, A., Ren, Y., Bian, S., Wu, T., Purawat, S., Helvajian, H., Wheaton, M., Li, B., & Li, G. P. (2022). Smart connected worker edge platform for smart manufacturing: Part 2—Implementation and on-site deployment case study. *Journal of Advanced Manufacturing and Processing*, *4*(4), e10130. doi:10.1002/amp2.10130

Doshi, P., & Badawy, A. (2019). Machine Learning in Cybersecurity: A Review. *Journal of Cybersecurity and Mobility*, *8*(1), 1–27.

Dosovitskiy, A., Fischer, P., Ilg, E., Hausser, P., Hazirbas, C., Golkov, V., & Brox, T. (2015). Flownet: Learning optical flow with convolutional networks. In *Proceedings of the IEEE international conference on computer vision* (pp. 2758-2766). IEEE. 10.1109/ICCV.2015.316

Drachsler, H., & Goldhammer, F. (2020). Learning analytics and eAssessment—Towards computational psychometrics by combining psychometrics with learning analytics. In D. Burgos (Ed.), Radical solutions and learning analytics: Personalised learning and teaching through big data (pp. 67–80). Springer Singapore.

Dulebenets, M. A. (2020). An Adaptive Island Evolutionary Algorithm for the berth scheduling problem. *Memetic Computing*, *12*(1), 51–72. doi:10.1007/s12293-019-00292-3

Dulebenets, M. A. (2023). A Diffused Memetic Optimizer for reactive berth allocation and scheduling at marine container terminals in response to disruptions. *Swarm and Evolutionary Computation*, *80*, 101334. doi:10.1016/j.swevo.2023.101334

Dulebenets, M. A., Golias, M. M., & Mishra, S. (2018). A collaborative agreement for berth allocation under excessive demand. *Engineering Applications of Artificial Intelligence*, *69*, 76–92. doi:10.1016/j.engappai.2017.11.009

Du, S., Song, G., Han, L., & Hong, H. (2017). Temporal causal inference with time lag. *Neural Computation*, *30*(1), 271–291. doi:10.1162/neco_a_01028 PMID:29064787

Du, S., Zheng, N., Ying, S., & Liu, J. (2010). Affine iterative closest point algorithm for point set registration. *Pattern Recognition Letters*, *31*(9), 791–799. doi:10.1016/j.patrec.2010.01.020

Edureka! (2020). *How the collection size in blue prism is consumerd for memory.* Edureka. https://www.edureka.co/community/75067/collection-prism-consumed-memory-includes-count-columns-rows#:~:text=It%20is%20always%20advised%20to,Hope%20this%20helps

Eiben, A. E., & Smith, J. E. (2015). *Introduction to Evolutionary Computing*. Springer-Verlag Berlin Heidelberg. doi:10.1007/978-3-662-44874-8

Ellis, R. A., Han, F., & Pardo, A. (2017). Improving learning analytics – combining observational and self-report data on student learning. *Journal of Educational Technology & Society*, *20*(3), 158–169.

Elmi, Z., Singh, P., Meriga, V. K., Goniewicz, K., Borowska-Stefańska, M., Wiśniewski, S., & Dulebenets, M. A. (2022). Uncertainties in liner shipping and ship schedule recovery: A state-of-the-art review. *Journal of Marine Science and Engineering*, *10*(5), 563. doi:10.3390/jmse10050563

Elsaeidy, A., Munasinghe, K. S., Sharma, D., & Jamalipour, A. (2019). Intrusion detection in smart cities using Restricted Boltzmann Machines. *Journal of Network and Computer Applications*, *135*(January), 76–83. doi:10.1016/j.jnca.2019.02.026

Emirbayer, M., & Mische, A. (1998). What is agency? *American Journal of Sociology*, *103*(4), 962–1023. doi:10.1086/231294

Essa, S. G., Celik, T., & Human-Hendricks, N. E. (2023). Personalized adaptive learning technologies based on machine learning techniques to identify learning styles: A systematic literature review. *IEEE Access: Practical Innovations, Open Solutions*, *11*, 48392–48409. doi:10.1109/ACCESS.2023.3276439

Estivill-Castro, V. (2002). Why so many clustering algorithms: A position paper. *SIGKDD Explorations*, *4*(1), 65–75. doi:10.1145/568574.568575

Eteläpelto, A., & Lahti, J. (2008). The resources and obstacles of creative collaboration in a long-term learning community. *Thinking Skills and Creativity*, *3*(3), 226–240. doi:10.1016/j.tsc.2008.09.003

Everingham, M., Van Gool, L., Williams, C. K., Winn, J., & Zisserman, A. (2010). The pascal visual object classes (voc) challenge. *International Journal of Computer Vision*, *88*(2), 303–338. doi:10.1007/s11263-009-0275-4

Fallah, S. N., Deo, R. C., Shojafar, M., Conti, M., & Shamshirband, S. (2018). Computational intelligence approaches for energy load forecasting in smart energy management grids: State of the art, future challenges, and research directions. *Energies*, *11*(3), 596. doi:10.3390/en11030596

Fan, Z., Kalogridis, G., Efthymiou, C., Sooriyabandara, M., Serizawa, M., & McGeehan, J. (2010). The new frontier of communications research: smart grid and smart metering. *Proceedings of the 1st International Conference on Energy-Efficient Computing and Networking*, (pp. 115-118). ACM. 10.1145/1791314.1791331

Farhadi, A., & Redmon, J. (2018). Yolov3: An incremental improvement. *arXiv preprint arXiv*:1804.02767.

Fawns, T. (2019). Postdigital education in design and practice. *Postdigital Science and Education*, *1*(1), 132–145. doi:10.1007/s42438-018-0021-8

Fekri, M. N., Patel, H., Grolinger, K., & Sharma, V. (2021). Deep learning for load forecasting with smart meter data: Online Adaptive Recurrent Neural Network. *Applied Energy*, *282*, 116177. doi:10.1016/j.apenergy.2020.116177

Fernández, E., & Munoz-Marquez, M. (2022). New formulations and solutions for the strategic berth template problem. *European Journal of Operational Research*, *298*(1), 99–117. doi:10.1016/j.ejor.2021.06.062 PMID:35039709

Floridi, L., & Chiriatti, N. (2020). GPT-3: It's Nature, Scope, Limits and Consequences. *Minds and Machines*, *30*(4), 681–694. doi:10.1007/s11023-020-09548-1

Flynn, T.J. (1997). *Two-dimensional phase unwrapping with minimum weighted discontinuity.*

Fraser, J., Papaioannou, I., & Lemon, O. (2018). Spoken conversational AI in video games: Emotional dialogue management increases user engagement. *Proceedings of the 18th International Conference on Intelligent Virtual Agents*, (pp. 179–184). ACM. 10.1145/3267851.3267896

Frazier, P. I. (2018). *A tutorial on Bayesian optimization*. arXiv preprint arXiv:1807.02811.

Fredriksson, T., Mattos, D. I., Bosch, J., & Olsson, H. H. (2020, November). Data labeling: An empirical investigation into industrial challenges and mitigation strategies. In *International Conference on Product-Focused Software Process Improvement* (pp. 202-216). Cham: Springer International Publishing. 10.1007/978-3-030-64148-1_13

Gale, J., Alemdar, M., Boice, K., Hernández, D., Newton, S., Edwards, D., & Usselman, M. (2022). Student agency in a high school computer science course. *Journal for STEM Education Research*, *5*(2), 270–301. doi:10.1007/s41979-022-00071-9

Gallagher, M. A., Parsons, S. A., & Vaughn, M. (2022). Adaptive teaching in mathematics: A review of the literature. *Educational Review*, *74*(2), 298–320. doi:10.1080/00131911.2020.1722065

García-Escudero, L. A., Gordaliza, A., Matrán, C., & Mayo-Iscar, A. (2010). A review of robust clustering methods. *Advances in Data Analysis and Classification*, *4*(2), 89–109. doi:10.1007/s11634-010-0064-5

Garg, S., Wu, Y., Balakrishnan, S., & Lipton, Z. (2020). A unified view of label shift estimation. *Advances in Neural Information Processing Systems*, *33*, 3290–3300.

Gartner. (2022). *Adaptive AI.* Gartner. https://web.archive.org/web/ 20221130080642/https://www.gartner.com/en/information-technology/glossary/adaptiveai

Gartner. (n.d.). *How Markets and Vendors Are Evaluated in Gartner Magic Quadrants.* gartner Research. https://www.gartner.com/en/documents/3956304

Ghobakhloo, M. (2020). Industry 4.0, digitization, and opportunities for sustainability. *Journal of Cleaner Production*, *252*, 119869. doi:10.1016/j.jclepro.2019.119869

Gibson, S. A., & Ross, P. (2016). Teachers' professional noticing. *Theory into Practice*, *55*(3), 180–188. doi:10.1080/00405841.2016.1173996

Goh, G. B., Hodas, N. O., & Vishnu, A. (2017). Deep learning for computational chemistry. *Journal of Computational Chemistry*, *38*(16), 1291–1307. doi:10.1002/jcc.24764 PMID:28272810

Gollob, H. F., & Reichardt, C. S. (1987). Taking account of time lags in causal models. *Child Development*, *58*(1), 80–92. doi:10.2307/1130293 PMID:3816351

Gong, M., Zhang, K., Liu, T., Tao, D., Glymour, C., & Schölkopf, B. (2016, June). Domain adaptation with conditional transferable components. In *International conference on machine learning* (pp. 2839-2848). PMLR.

Granger, C. W. (1969). Investigating causal relations by econometric models and cross-spectral methods. *Econometrica*, *37*(3), 424–438. doi:10.2307/1912791

Groenewald, E., & le Roux, A. (2023). Student agency: Two students' agentic actions in challenging oppressive practices on a diverse university campus. *Higher Education Research & Development*, *42*(1), 48–61. doi:10.1080/07294360.2022.2052817

Grunschel, C., Patrzek, J., & Fries, S. (2013). Exploring different types of academic delayers: A latent profile analysis. *Learning and Individual Differences*, *23*, 225–233. doi:10.1016/j.lindif.2012.09.014

Gu, A., Goel, C., & Ré, C. (2022). Efficiently modeling long sequences with structured state spaces. *The Tenth International Conference on Learning Representations*. Open Review. https://openreview.net/pdf?id=uYLFoz1vlAC

Gyamfi, E., & Jurcut, A. D. (2023). Novel Online Network Intrusion Detection System for Industrial IoT Based on OI-SVDD and AS-ELM. *IEEE Internet of Things Journal*, *10*(5), 3827–3839. doi:10.1109/JIOT.2022.3172393

Hadidi, R., Cao, J., Ryoo, M. S., & Kim, H. (2019). Collaborative execution of deep neural networks on internet of things devices. arXiv preprint arXiv:1901.02537.

Haleem, A., Javaid, M., Singh, R. P., Rab, S., & Suman, R. (2021). Hyperautomation for the enhancement of automation in industries. *Sensors International*, *2*, 100124. doi:10.1016/j.sintl.2021.100124

Haleem, A., Javaid, M., Singh, R. P., Rab, S., & Suman, R. (2022). Perspectives of cybersecurity for ameliorative Industry 4.0 era: A review-based framework. *The Industrial Robot*, *49*(3), 582–597. doi:10.1108/IR-10-2021-0243

Hamouda, D., Ferrag, M. A., Benhamida, N., & Seridi, H. (2021). Intrusion Detection Systems for Industrial Internet of Things: A Survey. *2021 International Conference on Theoretical and Applicative Aspects of Computer Science, ICTAACS 2021*, (pp. 1–8). IEEE. 10.1109/ICTAACS53298.2021.9715177

Han, M., Zhang, T., Lin, Y., & Deng, Q. (2021). Federated scheduling for typed DAG tasks scheduling analysis on heterogeneous multi-cores. *Journal of Systems Architecture*, *112*, 101870. doi:10.1016/j.sysarc.2020.101870

Han, S., Pool, J., Tran, J., & Dally, W. (2015). Learning both weights and connections for efficient neural network. *Advances in Neural Information Processing Systems*, 28.

Hansen, L. D., Stokholm-Bjerregaard, M., & Durdevic, P. (2022). Modeling phosphorous dynamics in a wastewater treatment process using Bayesian optimized LSTM. *Computers & Chemical Engineering*, *160*, 107738. doi:10.1016/j.compchemeng.2022.107738

Harnad, S. (1990). The Symbol Grounding Problem. *Physica D. Nonlinear Phenomena*, *42*(1-3), 335–346. https://web-archive.southampton.ac.uk/cogprints.org/3106/. doi:10.1016/0167-2789(90)90087-6

Hassan, M. M., Huda, S., Sharmeen, S., Abawajy, J., & Fortino, G. (2021). An Adaptive Trust Boundary Protection for IIoT Networks Using Deep-Learning Feature-Extraction-Based Semisupervised Model. *IEEE Transactions on Industrial Informatics*, *17*(4), 2860–2870. doi:10.1109/TII.2020.3015026

Hauptman, A. I., Schelble, B. G., McNeese, N. J., & Madathil, K. C. (2023). Adapt and overcome: Perceptions of adaptive autonomous agents for human-AI teaming. *Computers in Human Behavior*, *138*, 107451. doi:10.1016/j.chb.2022.107451

Havard, N., McGrath, S., Flanagan, C., & MacNamee, C. (2018, December). Smart building based on internet of things technology. In *2018 12th International conference on sensing technology (ICST)* (pp. 278-281). IEEE. 10.1109/ICSensT.2018.8603575

Hayati, M., & Mohebi, Z. (2007). Application of artificial neural networks for temperature forecasting. *Iranian Journal of Electrical and Computer Engineering*, *1*(4), 662–666.

Heartfield, R., Loukas, G., Bezemskij, A., & Panaousis, E. (2021). Self-Configurable Cyber-Physical Intrusion Detection for Smart Homes Using Reinforcement Learning. *IEEE Transactions on Information Forensics and Security*, *16*, 1720–1735. doi:10.1109/TIFS.2020.3042049

He, F., Zhou, J., Feng, Z. K., Liu, G., & Yang, Y. (2019). A hybrid short-term load forecasting model based on variational mode decomposition and long short-term memory networks considering relevant factors with Bayesian optimization algorithm. *Applied Energy*, *237*, 103–116. doi:10.1016/j.apenergy.2019.01.055

Heilala, V. (2022). *Learning analytics with learning and analytics: Advancing student agency analytics* (JYU Dissertations 512) [Doctoral dissertation, University of Jyväskylä].

Heilala, V., Saarela, M., Jääskelä, P., & Kärkkäinen, T. (2020). Course satisfaction in engineering education through the lens of student agency analytics. *2020 IEEE Frontiers in Education Conference (FIE)*, (pp. 1–9). IEEE.

Heilala, V., Jääskelä, P., Kärkkäinen, T., & Saarela, M. (2020). Understanding the study experiences of students in low agency profile: Towards a smart education approach. In A. El Moussati, K. Kpalma, M. G. Belkasmi, M. Saber, & S. Guégan (Eds.), *Advances in Smart Technologies Applications and Case Studies* (pp. 498–508). Springer International Publishing. doi:10.1007/978-3-030-53187-4_54

Heilala, V., Jääskelä, P., Saarela, M., Kuula, A.-S., Eskola, A., & Kärkkäinen, T. (2022). "Sitting at the Stern and Holding the Rudder": Teachers' Reflections on Action in Higher Education Based on Student Agency Analytics. In L. Chechurin (Ed.), *Digital Teaching and Learning in Higher Education: Developing and Disseminating Skills for Blended Learning* (pp. 71–91). Palgrave Macmillan. doi:10.1007/978-3-031-00801-6_4

He, K., Kim, D. D., & Asghar, M. R. (2023). Adversarial machine learning for network intrusion detection systems: A comprehensive survey. *IEEE Communications Surveys and Tutorials*, *25*(1), 538–566. doi:10.1109/COMST.2022.3233793

He, K., Zhang, X., Ren, S., & Sun, J. (2016). Deep residual learning for image recognition. In *Proceedings of the IEEE conference on computer vision and pattern recognition* (pp. 770-778). IEEE.

Henderson, P., Islam, R., Bachman, P., Pineau, J., Precup, D., & Meger, D. (2018, April). Deep reinforcement learning that matters. *Proceedings of the AAAI Conference on Artificial Intelligence*, *32*(1). doi:10.1609/aaai.v32i1.11694

Hernandez, J., Muratet, M., Pierotti, M., & Carron, T. (2022). Enhancement of a gamified situational judgment test scoring system for behavioral assessment. *2022 International Conference on Advanced Learning Technologies (ICALT)*, (pp. 374–378). IEEE. 10.1109/ICALT55010.2022.00116

Hernández-Orallo, J. (2020). Twenty Years Beyond the Turing Test: Moving Beyond the Human Judges Too. *Minds and Machines*, *30*(4), 533–562. doi:10.1007/s11023-020-09549-0

He, W., Guo, S., Guo, S., Qiu, X., & Qi, F. (2020). Joint DNN partition deployment and resource allocation for delay-sensitive deep learning inference in IoT. *IEEE Internet of Things Journal*, *7*(10), 9241–9254. doi:10.1109/JIOT.2020.2981338

Hewage, P., Behera, A., Trovati, M., Pereira, E., Ghahremani, M., Palmieri, F., & Liu, Y. (2020). Temporal convolutional neural (TCN) network for an effective weather forecasting using time-series data from the local weather station. *Soft Computing*, *24*(21), 16453–16482. doi:10.1007/s00500-020-04954-0

He, Y., Yu, F. R., Zhao, N., Leung, V. C., & Yin, H. (2017). Software-defined networks with mobile edge computing and caching for smart cities: A big data deep reinforcement learning approach. *IEEE Communications Magazine*, *55*(12), 31–37. doi:10.1109/MCOM.2017.1700246

Hingmire, A. M., & Bhaladhare, P. R. (2022). A review on urban flood management techniques for the smart city and future research. In *International Conference on Intelligent Cyber Physical Systems and Internet of Things* (pp. 303-317). Springer.

Hochreiter, S., & Schmidhuber, J. (1997). Long short-term memory. *Neural Computation*, *9*(8), 1735–1780. doi:10.1162/neco.1997.9.8.1735 PMID:9377276

Ho-Huu, V., Nguyen-Thoi, T., Truong-Khac, T., Le-Anh, L., & Vo-Duy, T. (2018). An improved differential evolution based on roulette wheel selection for shape and size optimization of truss structures with frequency constraints. *Neural Computing & Applications*, *29*(1), 167–185. doi:10.1007/s00521-016-2426-1

Hong, Y., Zhou, Y., Li, Q., Xu, W., & Zheng, X. (2020). A deep learning method for short-term residential load forecasting in smart grid. *IEEE Access : Practical Innovations, Open Solutions*, *8*, 55785–55797. doi:10.1109/ACCESS.2020.2981817

Hosseini, K., Karami, H., Hosseinjanzadeh, H., & Ardeshir, A. (2016). Prediction of time-varying maximum scour depth around short abutments using soft computing methodologies-A comparative study. *KSCE Journal of Civil Engineering*, *20*(5), 2070–2081. doi:10.1007/s12205-015-0115-8

Hou, S., Jiao, D., Dong, B., Wang, H., & Wu, G. (2022). Underwater inspection of bridge substructures using sonar and deep convolutional network. *Advanced Engineering Informatics*, *52*, 101545. doi:10.1016/j.aei.2022.101545

Hou, X., & Fan Wu, L. Y. (2006). Stitching algorithm for annular subaperture interferometry. *Chinese Optics Letters*, *4*, 211–214.

Hsieh, K., Ananthanarayanan, G., Bodik, P., Venkataraman, S., Bahl, P., Philipose, M., & Mutlu, O. (2018). Focus: Querying large video datasets with low latency and low cost. In *13th {USENIX} Symposium on Operating Systems Design and Implementation ({OSDI} 18)* (pp. 269-286). IEEE.

Hu, C., Bao, W., Wang, D., & Liu, F. (2019, April). Dynamic adaptive DNN surgery for inference acceleration on the edge. In *IEEE INFOCOM 2019-IEEE Conference on Computer Communications* (pp. 1423-1431). IEEE. 10.1109/INFOCOM.2019.8737614

Hu, D., & Krishnamachari, B. (2020, April). Fast and accurate streaming CNN inference via communication compression on the edge. In *2020 IEEE/ACM Fifth International Conference on Internet-of-Things Design and Implementation (IoTDI)* (pp. 157-163). IEEE. https://software.intel.com/content/www/us/en/develop/tools/openvino-toolkit.html

Huang, Q., Zhou, H., Dong, S., & Xu, S. (2015). Parallel Branch-Cut Algorithm Based on Simulated Annealing for Large-Scale Phase Unwrapping. *IEEE Transactions on Geoscience and Remote Sensing*, *53*(7), 3833–3846. doi:10.1109/TGRS.2014.2385482

Huber, P. J. (1981). *Robust statistics*. John Wiley & Sons. doi:10.1002/0471725250

Huda, S., Miah, S., Hassan, M. M., Islam, R., Yearwood, J., Alrubaian, M., & Almogren, A. (2017). Defending unknown attacks on cyber-physical systems by semi-supervised approach and available unlabeled data. *Information Sciences*, *379*, 211–228. doi:10.1016/j.ins.2016.09.041

Hu, R. L., Granderson, J., Auslander, D. M., & Agogino, A. (2019). Design of machine learning models with domain experts for automated sensor selection for energy fault detection. *Applied Energy*, *235*, 117–128. doi:10.1016/j.apenergy.2018.10.107

Huyen, C. (2022). Data distribution shifts and monitoring. In C. Huyen, Designing machine learning systems (pp. 225-261). O'Reilly Media, Inc.

Ianculescu, M., & Alexandru, A. (2020). Microservices–A catalyzer for better managing healthcare data empowerment. *Studies in Informatics and Control*, *29*(2), 231–242. doi:10.24846/v29i2y202008

Ian, X. I. T., Ingzhou, X. T. U., Hang, J. U. Z., Pires, O. L. S., Eal, N., & Rock, B., & (2018). Snapshot multi-wavelength interference microscope. *Optics Express*, *26*(14), 18279–18291. doi:10.1364/OE.26.018279 PMID:30114009

Ifenthaler, D., & Schumacher, C. (2016). Student perceptions of privacy principles for learning analytics. *Educational Technology Research and Development. Educational Technology Research and Development*, *64*(5), 923–938. doi:10.1007/s11423-016-9477-y

Ifenthaler, D., Schumacher, C., & Kuzilek, J. (2023). Investigating students' use of self-assessments in higher education using learning analytics. *Journal of Computer Assisted Learning*, *39*(1), 255–268. doi:10.1111/jcal.12744

Ijaz, S., Ali, M., Khan, A., & Ahmed, M. (2016). Smart Cities: A Survey on Security Concerns. *International Journal of Advanced Computer Science and Applications*, *7*(2). doi:10.14569/IJACSA.2016.070277

Imhof, D. (2004). *Risk assessment of existing bridge structures* [Doctoral dissertation, University of Cambridge].

Issam, E. H., Azza, L., & Mohamed, E. M., kaoutar, A., & Yassine, T. (2017, March). A multi-objective model for discrete and dynamic berth allocation problem. In *Proceedings of the 2nd international Conference on Big Data, Cloud and Applications* (pp. 1-5). ACM. 10.1145/3090354.3090464

Jääskelä, P., Heilala, V., Vaara, E., Arvaja, M., Eskola, A., Tolvanen, A., Kärkkäinen, T., & Poikkeus, A.-M. (2022). *Situational agency of business administration students in higher education: A mixed methods analysis of multidimensional agency* [Conference presentation]. NERA22 Conference, Reykjavık, Iceland.

Jääskelä, P., Tolvanen, A., Marin, V., Häkkinen, P., & Poikkeus, A.-M. (2018). *Students' agency experiences in finnish and spanish university courses* [Conference presentation]. European Conference on Educational Research (ECER), Bolzano, Italy.

Jääskelä, P., Heilala, V., Kärkkäinen, T., & Häkkinen, P. (2021). Student agency analytics: Learning analytics as a tool for analysing student agency in higher education. *Behaviour & Information Technology*, *40*(8), 790–808. doi:10.1080/0144929X.2020.1725130

Jääskelä, P., Poikkeus, A.-M., Häkkinen, P., Vasalampi, K., Rasku-Puttonen, H., & Tolvanen, A. (2020). Students' agency profiles in relation to student-perceived teaching practices in university courses. *International Journal of Educational Research*, *103*, 101604. doi:10.1016/j.ijer.2020.101604

Jääskelä, P., Poikkeus, A.-M., Vasalampi, K., Valleala, U. M., & Rasku-Puttonen, H. (2017). Assessing agency of university students: Validation of the AUS scale. *Studies in Higher Education*, *42*(11), 1–19. doi:10.1080/03075079.2015.1130693

Jääskelä, P., Tolvanen, A., Marın, V. I., & Poikkeus, A.-M. (2023). Assessment of students' agency in Finnish and Spanish university courses: Analysis of measurement invariance. *International Journal of Educational Research*, *118*, 102140. doi:10.1016/j.ijer.2023.102140

Jaber, A., Kocaoglu, M., Shanmugam, K., & Bareinboim, E. (2020). Causal discovery from soft interventions with unknown targets: Characterization and learning. *Advances in Neural Information Processing Systems*, *33*, 9551–9561.

Jamieson, D. (2018). Animal agency. *The Harvard Review of Philosophy*, *25*, 111–126. doi:10.5840/harvardreview201892518

Jämsä-Jounela, S. L. (2007). Future trends in process automation. *Annual Reviews in Control*, *31*(2), 211–220. doi:10.1016/j.arcontrol.2007.08.003

Jeong, H. J., Lee, H. J., Shin, C. H., & Moon, S. M. (2018, October). IONN: Incremental offloading of neural network computations from mobile devices to edge servers. In *Proceedings of the ACM symposium on cloud computing* (pp. 401-411). ACM. 10.1145/3267809.3267828

Jia, L., Yuen, W. L., Ong, Q., & Theseira, W. E. (2023). Pitfalls of self-reported measures of self-control: Surprising insights from extreme debtors. *Journal of Personality*, *91*(2), 369–382. doi:10.1111/jopy.12733 PMID:35556246

Jiang, J., Ananthanarayanan, G., Bodik, P., Sen, S., & Stoica, I. (2018, August). Chameleon: scalable adaptation of video analytics. In *Proceedings of the 2018 Conference of the ACM Special Interest Group on Data Communication* (pp. 253-266). ACM. 10.1145/3230543.3230574

Jiang, J., Sekar, V., & Zhang, H. (2012, December). Improving fairness, efficiency, and stability in http-based adaptive video streaming with festive. In *Proceedings of the 8th international conference on Emerging networking experiments and technologies* (pp. 97-108). ACM. 10.1145/2413176.2413189

Jörg, T., Davis, B., & Nickmans, G. (2007). Towards a new, complexity science of learning and education. *Educational Research Review*, *2*(2), 145–156. doi:10.1016/j.edurev.2007.09.002

Jos, B. C., Harimanikandan, M., Rajendran, C., & Ziegler, H. (2019). Minimum cost berth allocation problem in maritime logistics: New mixed integer programming models. *Sadhana*, *44*(6), 1–12. doi:10.1007/s12046-019-1128-7

JPMorgan Chase & Co. (2018). *JPMorgan Chase to Use AI in Its Fight Against Fraud.* JP Morgan. https://www.jpmorgan.com/technology/news/omni-ai

Kadel, R., & Kadel, R. (2022). Impact of AI on Cyber Security. *International Journal of Scientific Research and Engineering Development, 5*(6).

Kalchbrenner, N., Danihelka, I., & Graves, A. (2015). *Grid long short-term memory*. arXiv preprint arXiv:1507.01526.

Kallel, L., Benaissa, E., Kamoun, H., & Benaissa, M. (2019). Berth allocation problem: Formulation and a Tunisian case study. *Archives of Transport*, *51*(3), 85–100. doi:10.5604/01.3001.0013.6165

Kang, Y., Liu, Y., & Chen, T. (2020). Fedmvt: Semi-supervised vertical federated learning with multiview training. *arXiv preprint arXiv:2008.10838.*

Kang, Y., Hauswald, J., Gao, C., Rovinski, A., Mudge, T., Mars, J., & Tang, L. (2017). Neurosurgeon: Collaborative intelligence between the cloud and mobile edge. *Computer Architecture News*, *45*(1), 615–629. doi:10.1145/3093337.3037698

Kärkkäinen, T., & Heikkola, E. (2004). Robust formulations for training multilayer perceptrons. *Neural Computation*, *16*(4), 837–862. doi:10.1162/089976604322860721

Kärner, T., Warwas, J., & Schumann, S. (2021). A learning analytics approach to address heterogeneity in the classroom: The teachers' diagnostic support system. *Technology Knowledge and Learning*, *26*(1), 31–52. doi:10.1007/s10758-020-09448-4

Karpathy, A. (2015, May 21). *The Unreasonable Effectiveness of Recurrent Neural Networks*. Karpathy. http://karpathy.github.io/2015/05/21/rnn-effectiveness

Kassem, H., Alapatt, D., & Mascagni, P., Karargyris, A., & Padoy, N. (2022). Federated cycling (FedCy): Semi-supervised Federated Learning of surgical phases. *IEEE Transactions on Medical Imaging*. PMID:36374877

Kaufman, A. S., & Lichtenberger, E. (2006). *Assessing Adolescent and Adult Intelligence* (3rd ed.). Wiley.

Kavoosi, M., Dulebenets, M. A., Abioye, O. F., Pasha, J., Wang, H., & Chi, H. (2019). An augmented self-adaptive parameter control in evolutionary computation: A case study for the berth scheduling problem. *Advanced Engineering Informatics*, *42*, 100972. doi:10.1016/j.aei.2019.100972

Kavoosi, M., Dulebenets, M. A., Abioye, O., Pasha, J., Theophilus, O., Wang, H., Kampmann, R., & Mikijeljević, M. (2020). Berth scheduling at marine container terminals: A universal island-based metaheuristic approach. *Maritime Business Review*, *5*(1), 30–66. doi:10.1108/MABR-08-2019-0032

Kavya Balaraman Utility Dive. (2020). *PG&E deploys machine learning to safeguard its grid against California wildfires.* Utility Dive. https://www.utilitydive.com/news/wildfires-pushed-pge-into-bankruptcy-should-other-utilities-be-worried/588435/

Kaytez, F., Taplamacioglu, M. C., Cam, E., & Hardalac, F. (2015). Forecasting electricity consumption: A comparison of regression analysis, neural networks and least squares support vector machines. *International Journal of Electrical Power & Energy Systems*, *67*, 431–438. doi:10.1016/j.ijepes.2014.12.036

Kent, M. D., & Kopacek, P. (2020, September). Social and ethical aspects of automation. In *The International Symposium for Production Research* (pp. 363-372). Springer, Cham.

Kerrigan, D., Hullman, J., & Bertini, E. (2021). A survey of domain knowledge elicitation in applied machine learning. *Multimodal Technologies and Interaction*, *5*(12), 73. doi:10.3390/mti5120073

Khan, A. R., Mahmood, A., Safdar, A., Khan, Z. A., & Khan, N. A. (2016). Load forecasting, dynamic pricing and DSM in smart grid: A review. *Renewable & Sustainable Energy Reviews*, *54*, 1311–1322. doi:10.1016/j.rser.2015.10.117

Khan, W. Z., Ahmed, E., Hakak, S., Yaqoob, I., & Ahmed, A. (2019). Edge computing: A survey. *Future Generation Computer Systems*, *97*, 219–235. doi:10.1016/j.future.2019.02.050

Khoei, T. T., Aissou, G., Hu, W. C., & Kaabouch, N. (2021). Ensemble Learning Methods for Anomaly Intrusion Detection System in Smart Grid. *IEEE International Conference on Electro Information Technology*, (pp. 129–135). IEEE. 10.1109/EIT51626.2021.9491891

Khosravi, H., Shum, S. B., Chen, G., Conati, C., Tsai, Y.-S., Kay, J., Knight, S., Martinez-Maldonado, R., Sadiq, S., & Gašević, D. (2022). Explainable artificial intelligence in education. *Computers and Education: Artificial Intelligence*, *3*, 100074.

Khosravi, K., Khozani, Z. S., & Mao, L. (2021). A comparison between advanced hybrid machine learning algorithms and empirical equations applied to abutment scour depth prediction. *Journal of Hydrology (Amsterdam)*, *596*, 126100. doi:10.1016/j.jhydrol.2021.126100

Khwairakpam, P., & Mazumdar, A. (2009). Local scour around hydraulic structures. *International Journal of Recent Trends in Engineering*, *1*(6), 59.

Kim, H. S., & Chen, H. C. (2014). Three-Dimensional Numerical Analysis of Sediment Transport Around Abutment in Channel Bend. *Coastal Engineering Proceedings*, *1*(24), 21. doi:10.9753/icce.v34.sediment.21

Kim, T. H., Ramos, C., & Mohammed, S. (2017). Smart city and IoT. *Future Generation Computer Systems*, *76*, 159–162. doi:10.1016/j.future.2017.03.034

Kim, Y. G., Donovan, R. P., Ren, Y., Bian, S., Wu, T., Purawat, S., Manzo, A. J., Altintas, I., Li, B., & Li, G. P. (2022). Smart connected worker edge platform for smart manufacturing: Part 1—Architecture and platform design. *Journal of Advanced Manufacturing and Processing*, *4*(4), e10129. doi:10.1002/amp2.10129

Kingma, D. P., & Ba, J. (2015). *ADAM: A method for stochastic optimization.* In *International Conference on Representation Learning*, San Diego.

Klemenčič, M. (2015). What is student agency? An ontological exploration in the context of research on student engagement. In M. Klemenčič, S. Bergan, & R. Primožič (Eds.), *Student engagement in Europe: Society, higher education and student governance* (pp. 11–29). Council of Europe Publishing.

Klemenčič, M. (2017). From student engagement to student agency: Conceptual considerations of European policies on student-centered learning in higher education. *Higher Education Policy*, *30*(1), 69–85. doi:10.1057/s41307-016-0034-4

Ko, J. H., Na, T., Amir, M. F., & Mukhopadhyay, S. (2018, November). Edge-host partitioning of deep neural networks with feature space encoding for resource-constrained internet-of-things platforms. In *2018 15th IEEE International Conference on Advanced Video and Signal Based Surveillance (AVSS)* (pp. 1-6). IEEE. 10.1109/AVSS.2018.8639121

Kocaoglu, M., Shakkottai, S., Dimakis, A. G., Caramanis, C., & Vishwanath, S. (2020). Applications of common entropy for causal inference. *Advances in Neural Information Processing Systems*, *33*, 17514–17525.

Kocarev, L., & Parlitz, U. (1996). Generalized synchronization, predictability, and equivalence of unidirectionally coupled dynamical systems. *Physical Review Letters*, *76*(11), 1816–1819. doi:10.1103/PhysRevLett.76.1816 PMID:10060528

Kosch, T., Welsch, R., Chuang, L., & Schmidt, A. (2023). The placebo effect of artificial intelligence in human–computer interaction. *ACM Transactions on Computer-Human Interaction*, *29*(6), 1–32. doi:10.1145/3529225

Kouw, W. M., & Loog, M. (2019). A review of domain adaptation without target labels. *IEEE Transactions on Pattern Analysis and Machine Intelligence*, *43*(3), 766–785. doi:10.1109/TPAMI.2019.2945942 PMID:31603771

Kratzert, F., Gauch, M., Nearing, G., & Klotz, D. (2022). NeuralHydrology---A Python library for Deep Learning research in hydrology. *Journal of Open Source Software*, *7*(71), 4050. doi:10.21105/joss.04050

Krizhevsky, A., Sutskever, I., & Hinton, G. (2012). ImageNet classification with deep convolutional neural networks. *Proc. Advances in Neural Information Processing Systems*, *25*, 1090–1098. doi:10.1145/3065386

Kuhn, M., & Johnson, K. (2019). *Feature engineering and selection: A practical approach for predictive models*. Chapman Hall/CRC. doi:10.1201/9781315108230

Ku, J.-H. (2018). A study on adaptive learning model for performance improvement of stream analytics. *Journal of Convergence for Information Technology*, *8*(1), 201–206.

Kumar, A., & Kumar, R. (2018). Adaptive artificial intelligence for automatic identification of defect in the angular contact bearing. *Neural Computing & Applications*, *29*(8), 277–287. doi:10.1007/s00521-017-3123-4

Kuncheva, L. I. (2008). Classifier ensembles for detecting concept change in streaming data: Overview and perspectives. In *2nd Workshop SUEMA* (pp. 5-10). ACM.

Kurt, M. N., Ogundijo, O., Li, C., & Wang, X. (2018). Online Cyber-Attack Detection in Smart Grid: A Reinforcement Learning Approach. *IEEE Transactions on Smart Grid*, *10*(5), 5174–5185. doi:10.1109/TSG.2018.2878570

Kwon, S., Yoo, H., & Shon, T. (2020). IEEE 1815.1-Based power system security with bidirectional RNN-Based network anomalous attack detection for cyber-physical system. *IEEE Access : Practical Innovations, Open Solutions*, *8*, 77572–77586. doi:10.1109/ACCESS.2020.2989770

LaFlair, G., Yancey, K., Settles, B., & von Davier, A. A. (2023). Computational psychometrics for digital-first assessments: A blend of ML and psychometrics for item generation and scoring. In V. Yaneva & M. von Davier (Eds.), *Advancing natural language processing in educational assessment* (pp. 107–123). Routledge. doi:10.4324/9781003278658-9

Laverghetta, A. Jr, & Licato, J. (2023). Generating better items for cognitive assessments using large language models. *Proceedings of the 18th Workshop on Innovative Use of NLP for Building Educational Applications (BEA 2023)*, (pp. 414–428). ACM. 10.18653/v1/2023.bea-1.34

Lee, C. Y. (2003). Entropy-Boltzmann selection in the genetic algorithms. *IEEE Transactions on Systems, Man, and Cybernetics. Part B, Cybernetics*, *33*(1), 138–149. doi:10.1109/TSMCB.2003.808184 PMID:18238164

Lee, D. H. (2013, June). Pseudo-label: The simple and efficient semi-supervised learning method for deep neural networks. In *Workshop on challenges in representation learning, ICML* (Vol. 3, No. 2, p. 896).

Leng, L., Zhang, J., Zhang, C., Zhao, Y., Wang, W., & Li, G. (2020). Decomposition-based hyperheuristic approaches for the bi-objective cold chain considering environmental effects. *Computers & Operations Research*, *123*, 105043. doi:10.1016/j.cor.2020.105043

Leng, L., Zhao, Y., Wang, Z., Wang, H., & Zhang, J. (2018). Shared mechanism-based self-adaptive hyperheuristic for regional low-carbon location-routing problem with time windows. *Mathematical Problems in Engineering*, *2018*, 1–21. doi:10.1155/2018/8987402

Le, T. D., Hoang, T., Li, J., Liu, L., Liu, H., & Hu, S. (2016). A fast PC algorithm for high dimensional causal discovery with multi-core PCs. *IEEE/ACM Transactions on Computational Biology and Bioinformatics*, *16*(5), 1483–1495. doi:10.1109/TCBB.2016.2591526 PMID:27429444

Le, X. H., Ho, H. V., Lee, G., & Jung, S. (2019). Application of long short-term memory (LSTM) neural network for flood forecasting. *Water (Basel)*, *11*(7), 1387. doi:10.3390/w11071387

Li, F., Yan, X., Xie, Y., Sang, Z., & Yuan, X. (2019). A Review of Cyber-Attack Methods in Cyber-Physical Power System. *APAP 2019 - 8th IEEE International Conference on Advanced Power System Automation and Protection*, (pp. 1335–1339). IEEE. 10.1109/APAP47170.2019.9225126

Li, J., Gao, H., Lv, T., & Lu, Y. (2018, April). Deep reinforcement learning based computation offloading and resource allocation for MEC. In 2018 IEEE wireless communications and networking conference (WCNC) (pp. 1-6). IEEE. doi:10.1109/WCNC.2018.8377343

Li, L., Wang, M., Ni, B., Wang, H., Yang, J., & Zhang, W. (2021). 3d human action representation learning via cross-view consistency pursuit. In *Proceedings of the IEEE/CVF conference on computer vision and pattern recognition* (pp. 4741-4750). IEEE.

Li, C., Tian, Y., & Tian, J. (2019). A method for single image phase unwrapping based on generative adversarial networks. *Elev Int Conf Digit Image Process*, *1117911*, 157. doi:10.1117/12.2540155

Li, G., Yuan, C., Kamarthi, S., Moghaddam, M., & Jin, X. (2021). Data science skills and domain knowledge requirements in the manufacturing industry: A gap analysis. *Journal of Manufacturing Systems*, *60*, 692–706. doi:10.1016/j.jmsy.2021.07.007

Li, H., Wang, Y., Wang, H., & Zhou, B. (2017). Multi-window based ensemble learning for classification of imbalanced streaming data. *World Wide Web (Bussum)*, *20*(6), 1507–1525. doi:10.1007/s11280-017-0449-x

Li, J., Kong, X., Yang, Y., Deng, L., & Xiong, W. (2022). CFD investigations of tsunami-induced scour around bridge piers. *Ocean Engineering*, *244*, 110373. doi:10.1016/j.oceaneng.2021.110373

Li, L., Ota, K., & Dong, M. (2018). Deep learning for smart industry: Efficient manufacture inspection system with fog computing. *IEEE Transactions on Industrial Informatics*, *14*(10), 4665–4673. doi:10.1109/TII.2018.2842821

Lim, F. V., & Nguyen, T. T. H. (2023). 'If you have the freedom, you don't need to even think hard' – Considerations in designing for student agency through digital multimodal composing in the language classroom. *Language and Education*, *37*(4), 409–427. doi:10.1080/09500782.2022.2107875

Lindgren, I. (2020). Exploring the Use of Robotic Process Automation in Local Government. In EGOV-CeDEM-ePart-* (pp. 249-258). Research Gate.

Linja, J., Hämäläinen, J., Nieminen, P., & Kärkkäinen, T. (2023). Feature selection for distance-based regression: An umbrella review and a one-shot wrapper. *Neurocomputing*, *518*, 344–359. doi:10.1016/j.neucom.2022.11.023

Lin, T. Y., Maire, M., Belongie, S., Hays, J., Perona, P., Ramanan, D., & Zitnick, C. L. (2014). Microsoft coco: Common objects in context. In Computer Vision–ECCV 2014: 13th European Conference, Zurich, Switzerland, September 6-12, 2014 [Springer International Publishing.]. *Proceedings*, *13*(Part V), 740–755.

Lin, Z., Shi, Y., & Xue, Z. (2022, May). Idsgan: Generative adversarial networks for attack generation against intrusion detection. In *Pacific-asia conference on knowledge discovery and data mining* (pp. 79–91). Springer International Publishing. doi:10.1007/978-3-031-05981-0_7

Lipponen, L., & Kumpulainen, K. (2011). Acting as accountable authors: Creating interactional spaces for agency work in teacher education. *Teaching and Teacher Education*, *27*(5), 812–819. doi:10.1016/j.tate.2011.01.001

Li, S., & Gu, X. (2023). Based on literature review and Delphi–AHP method. *Journal of Educational Technology & Society*, *26*(1), 187–202.

Liu, L., Li, H., & Gruteser, M. (2019, August). Edge assisted real-time object detection for mobile augmented reality. In *The 25th annual international conference on mobile computing and networking* (pp. 1-16). ACM. 10.1145/3300061.3300116

Liu, J., Shahroudy, A., Perez, M., Wang, G., Duan, L. Y., & Kot, A. C. (2019). Ntu rgb+ d 120: A large-scale benchmark for 3d human activity understanding. *IEEE Transactions on Pattern Analysis and Machine Intelligence*, *42*(10), 2684–2701. doi:10.1109/TPAMI.2019.2916873 PMID:31095476

Liu, M., & Cai, Z. (2022). Adaptive two-layer ReLU neural network: II. Ritz approximation to elliptic PDEs. *Computers & Mathematics with Applications (Oxford, England)*, *113*, 103–116. doi:10.1016/j.camwa.2022.03.010

Liu, M., Cai, Z., & Chen, J. (2022). Adaptive two-layer ReLU neural network: I. best least-squares approximation. *Computers & Mathematics with Applications (Oxford, England)*, *113*, 34–44. doi:10.1016/j.camwa.2022.03.005

Liu, P., Yuan, W., Fu, J., Jiang, Z., Hayashi, H., & Neubig, G. (2023). Pre-train, prompt, and predict: A systematic survey of prompting methods in natural language processing. *ACM Computing Surveys*, *55*(9), 1–35. doi:10.1145/3560815

Liu, Q., Huang, S., Opadere, J., & Han, T. (2018, April). An edge network orchestrator for mobile augmented reality. In *IEEE INFOCOM 2018-IEEE conference on computer communications* (pp. 756–764). IEEE. doi:10.1109/INFOCOM.2018.8486241

Liu, W., Anguelov, D., Erhan, D., Szegedy, C., Reed, S., Fu, C. Y., & Berg, A. C. (2016). Ssd: Single shot multibox detector. In Computer Vision–ECCV 2016: 14th European Conference, Amsterdam, The Netherlands, October 11–14, 2016 [Springer International Publishing.]. *Proceedings*, *14*(Part I), 21–37.

Liu, W., Xu, X., Wu, L., Qi, L., Jolfaei, A., Ding, W., & Khosravi, M. R. (2023). Intrusion Detection for Maritime Transportation Systems with Batch Federated Aggregation. *IEEE Transactions on Intelligent Transportation Systems*, *24*(2), 2503–2514. doi:10.1109/TITS.2022.3181436

Liu, X., Zhu, L., Xia, S.-T., Jiang, Y., & Yang, X. (2021). GDST: Global Distillation Self-Training for Semi-Supervised Federated Learning. In *2021 IEEE Global Communications Conference (GLOBECOM)* (pp. 1-6). IEEE. 10.1109/GLOBECOM46510.2021.9685700

Liu, Y., Han, Y., Li, F., & Zhang, Q. (2018). Speedup of minimum discontinuity phase unwrapping algorithm with a reference phase distribution. *Optics Communications*, *417*, 97–102. doi:10.1016/j.optcom.2018.02.025

Liu, Z., Zhang, H., Chen, Z., Wang, Z., & Ouyang, W. (2020). Disentangling and unifying graph convolutions for skeleton-based action recognition. In *Proceedings of the IEEE/CVF conference on computer vision and pattern recognition* (pp. 143-152). IEEE. 10.1109/CVPR42600.2020.00022

Livieris, I. E., Pintelas, E., & Pintelas, P. (2020). A CNN–LSTM model for gold price time-series forecasting. *Neural Computing & Applications*, *32*(23), 17351–17360. doi:10.1007/s00521-020-04867-x

Li, Y., Bao, T., Gao, Z., Shu, X., Zhang, K., Xie, L., & Zhang, Z. (2022). A new dam structural response estimation paradigm powered by deep learning and transfer learning techniques. *Structural Health Monitoring*, *21*(3), 770–787. doi:10.1177/14759217211009780

Li, Y., Wu, C. Y., Fan, H., Mangalam, K., Xiong, B., Malik, J., & Feichtenhofer, C. (2022). Mvitv2: Improved multiscale vision transformers for classification and detection. In *Proceedings of the IEEE/CVF Conference on Computer Vision and Pattern Recognition* (pp. 4804-4814). IEEE. 10.1109/CVPR52688.2022.00476

Longo, F., Nicoletti, L., & Padovano, A. (2022). New perspectives and results for Smart Operators in industry 4.0: A human-centered approach. *Computers & Industrial Engineering*, *163*, 107824. doi:10.1016/j.cie.2021.107824

Lu, J., Liu, A., Dong, F., Gu, F., Gama, J., & Zhang, G. (2018). Learning under concept drift: A review. *IEEE Transactions on Knowledge and Data Engineering*, *31*(12), 2346–2363.

Lundberg, S. M., & Lee, S.-I. (2017). A unified approach to interpreting model predictions. *NIPS'17: Proceedings of the 31st International Conference on Neural Information Processing Systems*, (pp. 4768–4777). ACM.

Luo, A. C. (2012). *Dynamical System Interactions. Discontinuous Dynamical Systems*, 623-683.

Lynch, P. (2006). *The emergence of numerical weather prediction: Richardson's dream*. Cambridge University Press.

Lyu, K., Tian, Y., Shang, Y., Zhou, T., Yang, Z., Liu, Q., Yao, X., Zhang, P., Chen, J., & Li, J. (2023). Causal knowledge graph construction and evaluation for clinical decision support of diabetic nephropathy. *Journal of Biomedical Informatics*, *139*, 104298. doi:10.1016/j.jbi.2023.104298 PMID:36731730

Madaan, A., Tandon, N., Clark, P., & Yang, Y. (2022). Memory-assisted prompt editing to improve GPT-3 after deployment. *ArXiv*. /arXiv.2201.06009 doi:10.18653/v1/2022.emnlp-main.183

Madakam, S., Holmukhe, R. M., & Jaiswal, D. K. (2019). The future digital work force: robotic process automation (RPA). *JISTEM-Journal of Information Systems and Technology Management, 16*.

Madni, A. M., Sievers, M., & Madni, C. C. (2018). Adaptive Cyber-Physical-Human Systems: Exploiting Cognitive Modeling and Machine Learning in the Control Loop. *Insight (American Society of Ophthalmic Registered Nurses)*, *21*(3), 87–93.

Magic leap one. (2020). https://www.magicleap.com/

Mahadevan, R., Jagan, A., Pavithran, L., Shrivastava, A., & Selvaraj, S. K. (2021). Intelligent welding by using machine learning techniques. *Materials Today: Proceedings*, *46*, 7402–7410. doi:10.1016/j.matpr.2020.12.1149

Malinsky, D., & Danks, D. (2018). Causal discovery algorithms: A practical guide. *Philosophy Compass*, *13*(1), e12470. doi:10.1111/phc3.12470

Mameli, C., Grazia, V., & Molinari, L. (2021). The emotional faces of student agency. *Journal of Applied Developmental Psychology*, *77*, 101352. doi:10.1016/j.appdev.2021.101352

Manowska, A., & Bluszcz, A. (2022). Forecasting Crude Oil Consumption in Poland Based on LSTM Recurrent Neural Network. *Energies*, *15*(13), 4885. doi:10.3390/en15134885

Mansouri, B., Roozkhosh, A., & Farbeh, H. (2021). A survey on implementations of adaptive AI in serious games for enhancing player engagement. *2021 International Serious Games Symposium (ISGS)*, (pp. 48–53). IEEE. 10.1109/ISGS54702.2021.9684760

Mao, J., Chen, X., Nixon, K. W., Krieger, C., & Chen, Y. (2017, March). Modnn: Local distributed mobile computing system for deep neural network. In Design, Automation & Test in Europe Conference & Exhibition (DATE), 2017 (pp. 1396-1401). IEEE.

Mao, H., Negi, P., Narayan, A., Wang, H., Yang, J., Wang, H., & Alizadeh, D. (2019). Park: An open platform for learning-augmented computer systems. *Advances in Neural Information Processing Systems*, 32.

Mao, H., Netravali, R., & Alizadeh, M. (2017, August). Neural adaptive video streaming with pensieve. In *Proceedings of the conference of the ACM special interest group on data communication* (pp. 197-210). ACM. 10.1145/3098822.3098843

Mao, H., Schwarzkopf, M., Venkatakrishnan, S. B., Meng, Z., & Alizadeh, M. (2019). Learning scheduling algorithms for data processing clusters. In *Proceedings of the ACM special interest group on data communication* (pp. 270-288). ACM. 10.1145/3341302.3342080

Marcus, G., & Davis, E. (2020). GPT-3, Bloviator: OpenAI's language generator has no idea what it's talking about. *MIT Technology Review*. https://www.technologyreview.com/2020/08/22/1007539/gpt3-openai-language-generator-artificial-intelligence-ai-opinion

Marmol, F. G., Sorge, C., Ugus, O., & Perez, G. M. (2012). Do not snoop my habits: Preserving privacy in the smart grid. *IEEE Communications Magazine*, *50*(5), 166–172. doi:10.1109/MCOM.2012.6194398

Martin, F., Chen, Y., Moore, R. L., & Westine, C. D. (2020). Systematic review of adaptive learning research designs, context, strategies, and technologies from 2009 to 2018. *Educational Technology Research and Development. Educational Technology Research and Development*, *68*(4), 1903–1929. doi:10.1007/s11423-020-09793-2 PMID:32837122

Matthews, A. (2019). Design as a discipline for postdigital learning and teaching: Bricolage and actor-network theory. *Postdigital Science and Education*, *1*(2), 413–426. doi:10.1007/s42438-019-00036-z

McCulloch, W., & Pitts, W. (1943). A Logical Calculus of Ideas Immanent in Nervous Activity. *The Bulletin of Mathematical Biophysics*, *5*(4), 115–133. doi:10.1007/BF02478259

McMahan, B., Moore, E., Ramage, D., Hampson, S., & Arcas, B. A. (2017). Communication-efficient learning of deep networks from decentralized data. In *Artificial intelligence and statistics* (pp. 1273–1282). PMLR.

Mehta, S. (2017). Concept drift in streaming data classification: Algorithms, platforms and issues. *Procedia Computer Science*, 804–811.

Melville, B. W. (1975). *Local scour at bridge sites* [Doctoral dissertation, researchspace@ Auckland].

Membrive, A., Silva, N., Rochera, M. J., & Merino, I. (2022). Advancing the conceptualization of learning trajectories: A review of learning across contexts. *Learning, Culture and Social Interaction*, *37*, 100658. doi:10.1016/j.lcsi.2022.100658

Microsoft hololens. (2020). https://www.microsoft.com/en-us/hololens/

Microsoft. (n.d.). *Power Automate*. Microsoft. https://powerautomate.microsoft.com/en-us/

MindMajix. (n.d.). *Key Differences*. MindMajix. https://mindmajix.com/uipath-vs-automation-anywhere

Mirchevska, V., Luštrek, M., & Gams, M. (2014). Combining domain knowledge and machine learning for robust fall detection. *Expert Systems: International Journal of Knowledge Engineering and Neural Networks*, *31*(2), 163–175. doi:10.1111/exsy.12019

Mirhoseini, A., Pham, H., Le, Q. V., Steiner, B., Larsen, R., Zhou, Y., & Dean, J. (2017, July). Device placement optimization with reinforcement learning. In *International Conference on Machine Learning* (pp. 2430-2439). PMLR.

Mislevy, R. J. (2019). On integrating psychometrics and learning analytics in complex assessments. In H. Jiao, R. W. Lissitz, & A. van Wie (Eds.), *Data analytics and psychometrics* (pp. 1–52). Information Age Publishing.

Mislevy, R. J., & Bolsinova, M. (2021). Concepts and models from psychometrics. In A. A. von Davier, R. J. Mislevy, & J. Hao (Eds.), *Computational psychometrics: New methodologies for a new generation of digital learning and assessment: With examples in R and Python* (pp. 81–107). Springer International Publishing. doi:10.1007/978-3-030-74394-9_6

Mitchell, R., & Chen, I. R. (2014). Adaptive intrusion detection of malicious unmanned air vehicles using behavior rule specifications. *IEEE Transactions on Systems, Man, and Cybernetics. Systems*, *44*(5), 593–604. doi:10.1109/TSMC.2013.2265083

Mnasri, S., & Alrashidi, M. (2021). A comprehensive modeling of the discrete and dynamic problem of berth allocation in maritime terminals. *Electronics (Basel)*, *10*(21), 2684. doi:10.3390/electronics10212684

Mnih, V., Kavukcuoglu, K., Silver, D., Rusu, A. A., Veness, J., Bellemare, M. G., & Hassabis, D. (2015). Human-level control through deep reinforcement learning. *nature, 518*(7540), 529-533.

Mnih, V., Badia, A. P., Mirza, M., Graves, A., Lillicrap, T., Harley, T., & Kavukcuoglu, K. (2016, June). Asynchronous methods for deep reinforcement learning. In *International conference on machine learning* (pp. 1928-1937). PMLR.

Mocanu, E., Nguyen, P. H., Gibescu, M., & Kling, W. L. (2016). Deep learning for estimating building energy consumption. *Sustainable Energy. Grids and Networks*, *6*, 91–99.

Mohammadpour, R., Sabzevari, T., & Mohammadpour, F. (2014). Investigation of Local Scour development around Abutment using Experimental and Numerical Models. *Caspian Journal of Applied Sciences Research, 3*(1).

Moishin, M., Deo, R. C., Prasad, R., Raj, N., & Abdulla, S. (2021). Designing deep-based learning flood forecast model with ConvLSTM hybrid algorithm. *IEEE Access : Practical Innovations, Open Solutions*, *9*, 50982–50993. doi:10.1109/ACCESS.2021.3065939

Montemayor, C. (2021). Language and Intelligence. *Minds and Machines*, *31*(4), 471–486. doi:10.1007/s11023-021-09568-5

Mosadegh, H., Ghomi, S. F., & Süer, G. A. (2020). Stochastic mixed-model assembly line sequencing problem: Mathematical modeling and Q-learning based simulated annealing hyper-heuristics. *European Journal of Operational Research*, *282*(2), 530–544. doi:10.1016/j.ejor.2019.09.021

Moshkovitz, M., Dasgupta, S., Rashtchian, C., & Frost, N. (2020). Explainable k-means and kmedians clustering. In H. D. Iii, & A. Singh (Eds.), *Proceedings of the 37th international conference on machine learning* (pp. 7055–7065). PMLR.

Mughal, A. A. (2018). The Art of Cybersecurity: Defense in Depth Strategy for Robust Protection. *International Journal of Intelligent Automation and Computing*, *1*(1), 1–20.

Mukul, E., & Buÿüközkan, G. (2023). Digital transformation in education: A systematic review of education 4.0. *Technological Forecasting and Social Change*, *194*, 122664. doi:10.1016/j.techfore.2023.122664

Naik, S., Patil, S. A., Verma, A., & Hingmire, A. (2020). Flood prediction using logistic regression for Kerala state. [IJERT]. *International Journal of Engineering Research & Technology (Ahmedabad)*, *9*(03).

Namaee, M. R., Sui, J., Wu, Y., & Linklater, N. (2021). Three-dimensional numerical simulation of local scour around circular side-by-side bridge piers with ice cover. *Canadian Journal of Civil Engineering*, *48*(10), 1335–1353. doi:10.1139/cjce-2019-0360

Narwane, V. S., Raut, R. D., Gardas, B. B., Narkhede, B. E., & Awasthi, A. (2022). Examining smart manufacturing challenges in the context of micro, small, and medium enterprises. *International Journal of Computer Integrated Manufacturing*, *35*(12), 1395–1412. doi:10.1080/0951192X.2022.2078508

Nasiri, H., Nasehi, S., & Goudarzi, M. (2019). Evaluation of distributed stream processing frameworks for IoT applications in Smart Cities. *Journal of Big Data*, *6*(1), 1–24. doi:10.1186/s40537-019-0215-2

Netravali, R., Sivaraman, A., Das, S., Goyal, A., Winstein, K., Mickens, J., & Balakrishnan, H. (2015, July). Mahimahi: Accurate Record-and-Replay for HTTP. In *Usenix annual technical conference* (pp. 417-429).

Nguyen, A., Ngo, H. N., Hong, Y., Dang, B., & Nguyen, B.-P. T. (2023). Ethical principles for artificial intelligence in education. *Education and Information Technologies*, *28*(4), 4221–4241. doi:10.1007/s10639-022-11316-w PMID:36254344

Nguyen, H., Dunne, N., Li, H., Wang, Y., & Wang, Z. (2019). Real-time 3D shape measurement using 3LCD projection and deep machine learning. *Applied Optics*, *58*(26), 7100. doi:10.1364/AO.58.007100 PMID:31503981

Nie, H., Liu, G., Liu, X., & Wang, Y. (2012). Hybrid of ARIMA and SVMs for short-term load forecasting. *Energy Procedia*, *16*, 1455–1460. doi:10.1016/j.egypro.2012.01.229

Niemelä, M., Kärkkäinen, T., Ayrämö, S., Ronimus, M., Richardson, U., & Lyytinen, H. (2020). Game learning analytics for understanding reading skills in transparent writing system. *British Journal of Educational Technology*, *51*(6), 2376–2390. doi:10.1111/bjet.12916

Nieminen, J. H., Tai, J., Boud, D., & Henderson, M. (2022). Student agency in feedback: Beyond the individual. *Assessment & Evaluation in Higher Education*, *47*(1), 95–108. doi:10.1080/02602938.2021.1887080

Nishi, T., Okura, T., Lalla-Ruiz, E., & Voß, S. (2020). A dynamic programming-based matheuristic for the dynamic berth allocation problem. *Annals of Operations Research*, *286*(1-2), 391–410. doi:10.1007/s10479-017-2715-9

OECD. (2019). *Concept note: Student agency for 2030*. OECD.

Open A. I. (2023, September 15). GPT-4. *OpenAI Documentation*. OpenAI. https://platform.openai.com/docs/models/gpt-4

Oppy, G., & Dowe, D. (2021). The Turing Test, The Stanford Encyclopedia of Philosophy (E. N. Zalta, Ed.; Winter 2021 Edition). Stanford. https://plato.stanford.edu/archives/win2021/entries/turing-test

Ota, K., Yamamoto, T., Fukuda, Y., Otaki, K., Nishiyama, I., & Okazaki, S. (2001). Advanced point diffraction interferometer for EUV aspherical mirrors. *Emerg Lithogr Technol V*, *4343*, 543–550. doi:10.1117/12.436686

Otaki, K., Ota, K., Nishiyama, I., Yamamoto, T., Fukuda, Y., & Okazaki, S. (2002). Development of the point diffraction interferometer for extreme ultraviolet lithography: Design, fabrication, and evaluation. *Journal of Vacuum Science & Technology. B, Microelectronics and Nanometer Structures : Processing, Measurement, and Phenomena : An Official Journal of the American Vacuum Society*, *20*(6), 2449–2458. doi:10.1116/1.1526605

Ouyang, F., & Jiao, P. (2021). Artificial intelligence in education: The three paradigms. *Computers and Education: Artificial Intelligence*, *2*, 100020. doi:10.1016/j.caeai.2021.100020

Pal, M. (2022). Deep neural network based pier scour modeling. *ISH Journal of Hydraulic Engineering, 28*(sup1), 80-85.

Pal, J., Sikdar, S., & Banerjee, S. (2022). A deep-learning approach for health monitoring of a steel frame structure with bolted connections. *Structural Control and Health Monitoring*, *29*(2), e2873. doi:10.1002/stc.2873

Paluš, M., Krakovská, A., Jakubík, J., & Chvosteková, M. (2018). Causality, dynamical systems and the arrow of time. *Chaos (Woodbury, N.Y.)*, *28*(7), 075307. doi:10.1063/1.5019944 PMID:30070495

Panimalar, A. (2018). ARTIFICIAL INTELLIGENCE TECHNIQUES FOR CYBER SECURITY. *International Research Journal of Engineering and Technology (IRJET),05*(03).

Park, H., & Zhang, J. (2022). Learning analytics for teacher noticing and scaffolding: Facilitating knowledge building progress in science. In A. Weinberger, W. Chen, D. Hernández-Leo, & B. Chen (Eds.), *Proceedings of the 15th international conference on Computer-Supported collaborative learning - CSCL 2022* (pp. 147–154). International Society of the Learning Sciences.

Park, Y., & Jo, I.-H. (2019). Factors that affect the success of learning analytics dashboards. *Educational Technology Research and Development. Educational Technology Research and Development*, *67*(6), 1547–1571. doi:10.1007/s11423-019-09693-0

Pasha, J., Nwodu, A. L., Fathollahi-Fard, A. M., Tian, G., Li, Z., Wang, H., & Dulebenets, M. A. (2022). Exact and metaheuristic algorithms for the vehicle routing problem with a factory-in-a-box in multi-objective settings. *Advanced Engineering Informatics*, *52*, 101623. doi:10.1016/j.aei.2022.101623

Paszke, A., Gross, S., Massa, F., Lerer, A., Bradbury, J., Chanan, G., & Chintala, S. (2019). Pytorch: An imperative style, high-performance deep learning library. *Advances in Neural Information Processing Systems*, 32.

Pathak, A. R., Pandey, M., & Rautaray, S. (2020). Adaptive framework for deep learning based dynamic and temporal topic modeling from big data. *Recent Patents on Engineering*, *14*(3), 394–402. doi:10.2174/1872212113666190329234812

Pearl, J. (2009). *Causality*. Cambridge university press. doi:10.1017/CBO9780511803161

Peeters, R. (2020). The agency of algorithms: Understanding human-algorithm interaction in administrative decision-making. *Information Polity*, *25*(4), 507–522. doi:10.3233/IP-200253

Pelikan, M. (2005). Bayesian optimization algorithm. In *Hierarchical Bayesian optimization algorithm* (pp. 31–48). Springer. doi:10.1007/978-3-540-32373-0_3

Pencheva, T., Atanassov, K., & Shannon, A. (2009). Modelling of a roulette wheel selection operator in genetic algorithms using generalized nets. *International Journal Bioautomation*, *13*(4), 257.

Peng, B., Quesnelle, J., Fan, H., & Shippole, E. (2023). YaRN: Efficient Context Window Extension of Large Language Models. *arXiv preprint*. https://10.48550/arXiv.2309.00071

Peng, Y., Wang, Y., Lu, X., Li, H., Shi, D., Wang, Z., & Li, J. (2019). Short-term load forecasting at different aggregation levels with predictability analysis. In 2019 IEEE Innovative Smart Grid Technologies-Asia (ISGT Asia) (pp. 3385-3390). IEEE. doi:10.1109/ISGT-Asia.2019.8881343

Peng, Y., Dong, M., Li, X., Liu, H., & Wang, W. (2021). Cooperative optimization of shore power allocation and berth allocation: A balance between cost and environmental benefit. *Journal of Cleaner Production*, *279*, 123816. doi:10.1016/j.jclepro.2020.123816

Penttilä, S., Kah, P., Ratava, J., & Eskelinen, H. (2019). Artificial neural network controlled GMAW system: Penetration and quality assurance in a multi-pass butt weld application. *International Journal of Advanced Manufacturing Technology*, *105*(7), 3369–3385. doi:10.1007/s00170-019-04424-4

Peregrin, J. (2021). Do Computers Have Syntax, But No Semantics? *Minds and Machines*, *31*(2), 305–321. doi:10.1007/s11023-021-09564-9

Pereira, E. D., Coelho, A. S., Longaray, A. A., Machado, C. M. D. S., & Munhoz, P. R. (2018). Metaheuristic analysis applied to the berth allocation problem: Case study in a port container terminal. *Pesquisa Operacional*, *38*(2), 247–272. doi:10.1590/0101-7438.2018.038.02.0247

Piadeh, F., Behzadian, K., & Alani, A. M. (2022). A critical review of real-time modelling of flood forecasting in urban drainage systems. *Journal of Hydrology (Amsterdam)*, *607*, 127476. doi:10.1016/j.jhydrol.2022.127476

Pinkwart, N. (2016). Another 25 years of AIED? Challenges and opportunities for intelligent educational technologies of the future. *International Journal of Artificial Intelligence in Education*, *26*(2), 771–783. doi:10.1007/s40593-016-0099-7

Pirbhulal, S., Abie, H., & Shukla, A. (2022). Towards a Novel Framework for Reinforcing Cybersecurity using Digital Twins in IoT-based Healthcare Applications. *2022 IEEE 95th Vehicular Technology Conference: (VTC2022-Spring)*. IEEE. 10.1109/VTC2022-Spring54318.2022.9860581

Pokhrel, S. R., & Choi, J. (2020). Federated learning with blockchain for autonomous vehicles: Analysis and design challenges. *IEEE Transactions on Communications*, *68*(8), 4734–4746. doi:10.1109/TCOMM.2020.2990686

Poli, M., Massaroli, S., Nguyen, E., Fu, D. Y., Dao, T., Baccus, S., Bengio, Y., Ermon, S., & Ré, C. (2023). Hyena Hierarchy: Towards Larger Convolutional Language Models. ArXiv. https://10.48550/arXiv.2302.10866

Poojitha, S., Kalyani, Likitha, & Venkatesh, K. (2023). ML framework for efficient assessment and prediction of human performance in collaborative learning environments. [TURCOMAT]. *Turkish Journal of Computer and Mathematics Education*, *14*(2), 527–536.

PR Newswire. (2022). Alitek Launches Flowatcher365™ for Microsoft Power Automate - Advanced Flow Monitoring, Management, and Notification PaaS. PR Newswire.

Prencipe, L. P., & Marinelli, M. (2021). A novel mathematical formulation for solving the dynamic and discrete berth allocation problem by using the Bee Colony Optimisation algorithm. *Applied Intelligence*, *51*(7), 4127–4142. doi:10.1007/s10489-020-02062-y

Pritt, M. D. (1995). Unweighted least squares phase unwrapping by means of multigrid techniques. *Synth Aperture Radar Passiv Microw Sens*, *2584*, 289–300. doi:10.1117/12.227138

Prosperi, M., Guo, Y., Sperrin, M., Koopman, J. S., Min, J. S., He, X., Rich, S., Wang, M., Buchan, I. E., & Bian, J. (2020). Causal inference and counterfactual prediction in machine learning for actionable healthcare. *Nature Machine Intelligence*, *2*(7), 369–375. doi:10.1038/s42256-020-0197-y

Pu, J. H., & Lim, S. Y. (2014). Efficient numerical computation and experimental study of temporally long equilibrium scour development around abutment. *Environmental Fluid Mechanics*, *14*(1), 69–86. doi:10.1007/s10652-013-9286-3

Qadar, A. (1981). The Vortex Scour Mechanism at Bridge Piers. *Proceedings - Institution of Civil Engineers*, *71*(3), 739–757. doi:10.1680/iicep.1981.1816

Qian, W., Chai, J., Xu, Z., & Zhang, Z. (2018). Differential evolution algorithm with multiple mutation strategies based on roulette wheel selection. *Applied Intelligence*, *48*(10), 3612–3629. doi:10.1007/s10489-018-1153-y

Qi, J., Kim, Y., Chen, C., Lu, X., & Wang, J. (2017). Demand response and smart buildings: A survey of control, communication, and cyber-physical security. *ACM Transactions on Cyber-Physical Systems*, *1*(4), 1–25. doi:10.1145/3009972

Qiu, C., Li, K., Li, B., Mao, X., He, S., Hao, C., & Yin, L. (2022). Semi-supervised graph convolutional network to predict position-and speed-dependent tool tip dynamics with limited labeled data. *Mechanical Systems and Signal Processing*, *164*, 108225. doi:10.1016/j.ymssp.2021.108225

Qiu, H., Ahmad, F., Bai, F., Gruteser, M., & Govindan, R. (2018, June). Avr: Augmented vehicular reality. In *Proceedings of the 16th Annual International Conference on Mobile Systems, Applications, and Services* (pp. 81-95). ACM. 10.1145/3210240.3210319

Qiu, H., Dong, T., Zhang, T., Lu, J., Memmi, G., & Qiu, M. (2020). Adversarial attacks against network intrusion detection in IoT systems. *IEEE Internet of Things Journal*, *8*(13), 10327–10335. doi:10.1109/JIOT.2020.3048038

Radford, A., Narasimhan, K., Salimans, T., & Sutskever, I. (2018). *Improving language understanding by generative pre-training*. Amazon. https://s3-us-west-2.amazonaws.com/openai-assets/research-covers/language-unsupervised/language_understanding_paper.pdf

Radford, A., Wu, J., Child, R., Luan, D., Amodei, D., & Sutskever, I. (2019). Language models are unsupervised multitask learners. *OpenAI blog, 1*(8), 9. https://insightcivic.s3.us-east-1.amazonaws.com/language-models.pdf

Rajalakshmi, R., Sivakumar, P., Prathiba, T., & Chatrapathy, K. (2023). An energy efficient deep learning model for intrusion detection in smart healthcare with optimal feature selection mechanism. *Journal of Intelligent & Fuzzy Systems*, *44*(2), 2753–2768. https://content.iospress.com/articles/journal-of-intelligent-and-fuzzy-systems/ifs223166. doi:10.3233/JIFS-223166

Rajpurkar, P., Jia, R., & Liang, P. (2018). Know What You Don't Know: Unanswerable Questions for SQuAD. *ArXiv*. / arXiv.1806.03822 doi:10.18653/v1/P18-2124

Ramírez-Sanz, J. M., Maestro-Prieto, J.-A., Arnaiz-González, Á., & Bustillo, A. (2023). Semi-supervised learning for industrial fault detection and diagnosis: A systemic review. *ISA Transactions*, *143*, 255–270. doi:10.1016/j.isatra.2023.09.027 PMID:37778919

Ranjbar, I., & Toufigh, V. (2022). Deep long short-term memory (LSTM) networks for ultrasonic-based distributed damage assessment in concrete. *Cement and Concrete Research*, *162*, 107003. doi:10.1016/j.cemconres.2022.107003

Ravi, V., Pham, T. D., & Alazab, M. (2022). Attention-Based Multidimensional Deep Learning Approach for Cross-Architecture IoMT Malware Detection and Classification in Healthcare Cyber-Physical Systems. *IEEE Transactions on Computational Social Systems*, *10*(4), 1597–1606. doi:10.1109/TCSS.2022.3198123

Raza, A., Tran, K. P., Koehl, L., & Li, S. (2023). AnoFed: Adaptive anomaly detection for digital health using transformer-based federated learning and support vector data description. *Engineering Applications of Artificial Intelligence*, *121*, 106051. doi:10.1016/j.engappai.2023.106051

Redmon, J., Divvala, S., Girshick, R., & Farhadi, A. (2016). You only look once: Unified, real-time object detection. In *Proceedings of the IEEE conference on computer vision and pattern recognition* (pp. 779-788). IEEE. 10.1109/CVPR.2016.91

Redmon, J., & Farhadi, A. (2017). YOLO9000: better, faster, stronger. In *Proceedings of the IEEE conference on computer vision and pattern recognition* (pp. 7263-7271). IEEE.

Ren, S., He, K., Girshick, R., & Sun, J. (2015). Faster r-cnn: Towards real-time object detection with region proposal networks. *Advances in Neural Information Processing Systems*, 28.

Ren, Y., & Li, G. P. (2022). A contextual sensor system for non-intrusive machine status and energy monitoring. *Journal of Manufacturing Systems*, *62*, 87–101. doi:10.1016/j.jmsy.2021.11.010

Ren, Y., & Li, G. P. (2022). An interactive and adaptive learning cyber physical human system for manufacturing with a case study in worker machine interactions. *IEEE Transactions on Industrial Informatics*, *18*(10), 6723–6732. doi:10.1109/TII.2022.3150795

Ren, Y., Yen, A. H., & Li, G. P. (2023). A Self-Labeling Method for Adaptive Machine Learning by Interactive Causality. *IEEE Transactions on Artificial Intelligence*, 1–10. doi:10.1109/TAI.2023.3311782

Rhee, H. G., Yang, H. S., Moon, I. K., Kihm, H., Lee, J. H., & Lee, Y. W. (2011). Eight-axis-polishing machine for large off-axis aspheric optics. *Journal of the Optical Society of Korea*, *15*(4), 394–397. doi:10.3807/JOSK.2011.15.4.394

Richens, J. G., Lee, C. M., & Johri, S. (2020). Improving the accuracy of medical diagnosis with causal machine learning. *Nature Communications*, *11*(1), 3923. doi:10.1038/s41467-020-17419-7 PMID:32782264

Rodrigues, F., & Agra, A. (2022). Berth allocation and quay crane assignment/scheduling problem under uncertainty: A survey. *European Journal of Operational Research*, *303*(2), 501–524. doi:10.1016/j.ejor.2021.12.040

Roh, C. (2022). Deep-Learning-Based Pitch Controller for Floating Offshore Wind Turbine Systems with Compensation for Delay of Hydraulic Actuators. *Energies*, *15*(9), 3136. doi:10.3390/en15093136

Roman, R., Lopez, J., & Mambo, M. (2018). Mobile edge computing, Fog et al.: A survey and analysis of security threats and challenges. *Future Generation Computer Systems*, *78*, 680–698. doi:10.1016/j.future.2016.11.009

Rooney, D., & Boud, D. (2019). Toward a pedagogy for professional noticing: Learning through observation. *Vocations and Learning*, *12*(3), 441–457. doi:10.1007/s12186-019-09222-3

Royakkers, L., & van Est, R. (2015). A literature review on new robotics: Automation from love to war. *International Journal of Social Robotics*, *7*(5), 549–570. doi:10.1007/s12369-015-0295-x

Saarela, M., Heilala, V., Jääskelä, P., Rantakaulio, A., & Kärkkäinen, T. (2021). Explainable student agency analytics. *IEEE Access : Practical Innovations, Open Solutions*, *9*, 137444–137459. doi:10.1109/ACCESS.2021.3116664

Saarela, M., & Jauhiainen, S. (2021). Comparison of feature importance measures as explanations for classification models. *SN Applied Sciences*, *3*(2), 1–12. doi:10.1007/s42452-021-04148-9

Safdari, M., Serapio-García, G., Crepy, C., Fitz, S., Romero, P., Sun, L., Abdulhai, M., Faust, A., & Matarić, M. (2023). *Personality traits in large language models*. arXiv. https://doi.org//arXiv.2307.00184 doi:10.48550

Sarıkaya, A., Kılıç, B. G., & Demirci, M. (2023). RAIDS: Robust Autoencoder-Based Intrusion Detection System Model Against Adversarial Attacks. *Computers & Security*, *135*, 103483. doi:10.1016/j.cose.2023.103483

Satyanarayanan, M. (2017). The emergence of edge computing. *Computer*, *50*(1), 30–39. doi:10.1109/MC.2017.9

Savi, M., & Olivadese, F. (2021). Short-term energy consumption forecasting at the edge: A federated learning approach. *IEEE Access : Practical Innovations, Open Solutions*, *9*, 95949–95969. doi:10.1109/ACCESS.2021.3094089

Saxena, D., & Singh, A. K. (2022). Auto-adaptive learning-based workload forecasting in dynamic cloud environment. *International Journal of Computers and Applications*, *44*(6), 541–551. doi:10.1080/1206212X.2020.1830245

Scardapane, S., Scarpiniti, M., Baccarelli, E., & Uncini, A. (2020). Why should we add early exits to neural networks? *Cognitive Computation*, *12*(5), 954–966. doi:10.1007/s12559-020-09734-4

Schepler, X., Absi, N., Feillet, D., & Sanlaville, E. (2019). The stochastic discrete berth allocation problem. *EURO Journal on Transportation and Logistics*, *8*(4), 363–396. doi:10.1007/s13676-018-0128-9

Schlosser, M. E. (2015). Agency. In E. N. Zalta (Ed.), *Stanford encyclopedia of philosophy*.

Schneider, S., Rusak, E., Eck, L., Bringmann, O., Brendel, W., & Bethge, M. (2020). Improving robustness against common corruptions by covariate shift adaptation. *Advances in Neural Information Processing Systems*, *33*, 11539–11551.

Schölkopf, B. (2022). Causality for machine learning. In Probabilistic and Causal Inference: The Works of Judea Pearl (pp. 765-804). ACM. doi:10.1145/3501714.3501755

Schumacher, C., & Ifenthaler, D. (2018). Features students really expect from learning analytics. *Computers in Human Behavior*, *78*, 397–407. doi:10.1016/j.chb.2017.06.030

Schunk, D., & Zimmerman, B. (2012). Competence and control beliefs: Distinguishing the means and ends. In P. A. Alexander & P. H. Winne (Eds.), *Handbook of educational psychology* (pp. 349–368). Routledge.

Shapley, L. S. (1953). A value for n-person games. In H. W. Kuhn & A. W. Tucker (Eds.), Contributions to the theory of games (AM-28), volume II (pp. 307–318). Princeton University Press. doi:10.1515/9781400881970-018

Sharma, A., Jain, A., Gupta, P., & Chowdary, V. (2020). Machine learning applications for precision agriculture: A comprehensive review. *IEEE Access : Practical Innovations, Open Solutions*, *9*, 4843–4873. doi:10.1109/ACCESS.2020.3048415

Shen, C., & Lawson, K. (2021). Applications of deep learning in hydrology. *Deep Learning for the Earth Sciences: A Comprehensive Approach to Remote Sensing, Climate Science, and Geosciences*, 283-297. Research Gate.

Shen, H. W., Schneider, V. R., & Karaki, S. S. (1966). *Mechanics of local scour*.

Shen, C. (2018). A transdisciplinary review of deep learning research and its relevance for water resources scientists. *Water Resources Research, 54*(11), 8558–8593. doi:10.1029/2018WR022643

Shen, S., Yu, C., Zhang, K., & Ci, S. (2021). Adaptive artificial intelligence for resource-constrained connected vehicles in cybertwin-driven 6G network. *IEEE Internet of Things Journal, 8*(22), 16269–16278. doi:10.1109/JIOT.2021.3101231

Sheppard, D. M. (2004). Overlooked local sediment scour mechanism. *Transportation Research Record: Journal of the Transportation Research Board, 1890*(1), 107–111. doi:10.3141/1890-13

Shi, H., Xu, M., & Li, R. (2017). Deep learning for household load forecasting—A novel pooling deep RNN. *IEEE Transactions on Smart Grid, 9*(5), 5271–5280. doi:10.1109/TSG.2017.2686012

Shi, W., Cao, J., Zhang, Q., Li, Y., & Xu, L. (2016). Edge computing: Vision and challenges. *IEEE Internet of Things Journal, 3*(5), 637–646. doi:10.1109/JIOT.2016.2579198

Shortliffe, E. H., Davis, R., Axline, S. G., Buchanan, B. G., Green, C. C., & Cohen, S. N. (1975). Computer-based consultations in clinical therapeutics: Explanation and rule acquisition capabilities of the MYCIN system. *Computers and Biomedical Research, an International Journal, 8*(4), 303–320. doi:10.1016/0010-4809(75)90009-9 PMID:1157471

Shreyas, N., Venkatraman, M., Malini, S., & Chandrakala, S. (2020). Trends of sound event recognition in audio surveillance: a recent review and study. *The Cognitive Approach in Cloud Computing and Internet of Things Technologies for Surveillance Tracking Systems*, 95-106. Research Gate.

Shute, V., & Towle, B. (2003). Adaptive E-Learning. *Educational Psychologist, 38*(2), 105–114. doi:10.1207/S15326985EP3802_5

Sikström, P., Valentini, C., Sivunen, A., & Kärkkäinen, T. (2022). How pedagogical agents communicate with students: A two-phase systematic review. *Computers & Education, 188*, 104564. doi:10.1016/j.compedu.2022.104564

Silvast, A., & Virtanen, M. J. (2023). On Theory–Methods packages in science and technology studies. *Science, Technology & Human Values, 48*(1), 167–189. doi:10.1177/01622439211040241

Silver, D., Schrittwieser, J., Simonyan, K., Antonoglou, I., Huang, A., Guez, A., & Hassabis, D. (2017). Mastering the game of go without human knowledge. *nature, 550*(7676), 354-359.

Simonyan, K., & Zisserman, A. (2014). *Very deep convolutional networks for large-scale image recognition.* arXiv preprint arXiv:1409.1556.

Singh, A., Chatterjee, K., & Satapathy, S. C. (2023). TrIDS: An intelligent behavioural trust based IDS for smart healthcare system. *Cluster Computing, 26*(2), 903–925. doi:10.1007/s10586-022-03614-2 PMID:36091662

Singh, P., Yadav, A. K., & Singh, K. (2017). Phase image encryption in the fractional Hartley domain using Arnold transform and singular value decomposition. *Optics and Lasers in Engineering, 91*, 187–195. doi:10.1016/j.optlaseng.2016.11.022

Siriwardhana, Y., Porambage, P., Liyanage, M., & Ylianttila, M. (2021). *AI and 6G Security: Opportunities and Challenges.* 2021 Joint European Conference on Networks and Communications & 6G Summit (EuCNC/6G Summit), Porto, Portugal. 10.1109/EuCNC/6GSummit51104.2021.9482503

Sobieszek, A., & Price, T. (2022). Playing games with AIs: The limits of GPT-3 and similar large language models. *Minds and Machines, 32*(2), 341–364. doi:10.1007/s11023-022-09602-0

Song, H., Du, S., Yang, J., Zhao, Y., & Yu, M. (2022). Evaluation of hydraulic fracturing effect on coalbed methane reservoir based on deep learning method considering physical constraints. *Journal of Petroleum Science Engineering, 212*, 110360. doi:10.1016/j.petrol.2022.110360

Soong, C. J., Rahman, R. A., Ramli, R., Manaf, M. S. A., & Ting, C. C. (2022). An Evolutionary Algorithm: An Enhancement of Binary Tournament Selection for Fish Feed Formulation. *Complexity*, *2022*, 2022. doi:10.1155/2022/7796633

Spoorthi, G. E., Gorthi, S., & Gorthi, R. K. S. S. (2019). PhaseNet: A deep convolutional neural network for two-dimensional phase unwrapping. *IEEE Signal Processing Letters*, *26*(1), 54–58. doi:10.1109/LSP.2018.2879184

Šprogar, M. (2018). A ladder to human-comparable intelligence: An empirical metric. *Journal of Experimental & Theoretical Artificial Intelligence*, *30*(6), 1037–1050. doi:10.1080/0952813X.2018.1509897

Srivastava, V. (2023). Adaptive Cyber Defense: Leveraging Neuromorphic Computing for Advanced Threat Detection and Response. *2023 International Conference on Sustainable Computing and Smart Systems (ICSCSS)*, Coimbatore, India. 10.1109/ICSCSS57650.2023.10169393

Stahl, R., Zhao, Z., Mueller-Gritschneder, D., Gerstlauer, A., & Schlichtmann, U. (2019). Fully distributed deep learning inference on resource-constrained edge devices. In Embedded Computer Systems: Architectures, Modeling, and Simulation: 19th International Conference. Springer.

Standen, P. J., Brown, D. J., Taheri, M., Galvez Trigo, M. J., Boulton, H., Burton, A., Hallewell, M. J., Lathe, J. G., Shopland, N., Blanco Gonzalez, M. A., Kwiatkowska, G. M., Milli, E., Cobello, S., Mazzucato, A., Traversi, M., & Hortal, E. (2020). An evaluation of an adaptive learning system based on multimodal affect recognition for learners with intellectual disabilities. *British Journal of Educational Technology*, *51*(5), 1748–1765. doi:10.1111/bjet.13010

Stankovski, T., Pereira, T., McClintock, P. V., & Stefanovska, A. (2019). Coupling functions: Dynamical interaction mechanisms in the physical, biological and social sciences. *Philosophical Transactions. Series A, Mathematical, Physical, and Engineering Sciences*, *377*(2160), 20190039. doi:10.1098/rsta.2019.0039 PMID:31656134

Staudemeyer, R. C., & Morris, E. R. (2019). *Understanding LSTM—a tutorial into long short-term memory recurrent neural networks*. arXiv preprint arXiv:1909.09586.

Stenalt, M. H. (2021). Researching student agency in digital education as if the social aspects matter: Students' experience of participatory dimensions of online peer assessment. *Assessment & Evaluation in Higher Education*, *46*(4), 644–658. doi:10.1080/02602938.2020.1798355

Stenalt, M. H., & Lassesen, B. (2021). Does student agency benefit student learning? A systematic review of higher education research. *Assessment & Evaluation in Higher Education*, *47*(5), 1–17.

Su, K., Liu, X., & Shlizerman, E. (2020). Predict & cluster: Unsupervised skeleton based action recognition. In *Proceedings of the IEEE/CVF Conference on Computer Vision and Pattern Recognition* (pp. 9631-9640). IEEE. 10.1109/CVPR42600.2020.00965

Sun, C., Ma, M., Zhao, Z., Tian, S., Yan, R., & Chen, X. (2018). Deep transfer learning based on sparse autoencoder for remaining useful life prediction of tool in manufacturing. *IEEE Transactions on Industrial Informatics*, *15*(4), 2416–2425. doi:10.1109/TII.2018.2881543

Sun, X., Yang, S., & Zhao, C. (2022). Lightweight Industrial Image Classifier based on Federated Few-Shot Learning. *IEEE Transactions on Industrial Informatics*.

Sun, Y., Yin, X., Jiang, J., Sekar, V., Lin, F., Wang, N., & Sinopoli, B. (2016, August). CS2P: Improving video bitrate selection and adaptation with data-driven throughput prediction. In *Proceedings of the 2016 ACM SIGCOMM Conference* (pp. 272-285). ACM. 10.1145/2934872.2934898

Suresh Babu, C. V., Abirami, S., & Manoj, S. (2023). AI-Based Carthage Administration Towards Smart City. In C. Chowdhary, B. Swain, & V. Kumar (Eds.), *Investigations in Pattern Recognition and Computer Vision for Industry 4.0* (pp. 1–17). IGI Global. doi:10.4018/978-1-6684-8602-3.ch001

Suresh Babu, C. V., & Srisakthi, S. (2023). Cyber Physical Systems and Network Security: The Present Scenarios and Its Applications. In R. Thanigaivelan, S. Kaliappan, & C. Jegadheesan (Eds.), *Cyber-Physical Systems and Supporting Technologies for Industrial Automation* (pp. 104–130). IGI Global.

Suresh Babu, C. V., & Yadav, S. (2023). Cyber Physical Systems Design Challenges in the Areas of Mobility, Healthcare, Energy, and Manufacturing. In R. Thanigaivelan, S. Kaliappan, & C. Jegadheesan (Eds.), *Cyber-Physical Systems and Supporting Technologies for Industrial Automation* (pp. 131–151). IGI Global.

Sutton, R. S., & Barto, A. G. (1999). Reinforcement learning: An introduction. *Robotica*, *17*(2), 229–235.

Sutton, R. S., McAllester, D., Singh, S., & Mansour, Y. (1999). Policy gradient methods for reinforcement learning with function approximation. *Advances in Neural Information Processing Systems*, 12.

Szegedy, C., Liu, W., Jia, Y., Sermanet, P., Reed, S., Anguelov, D., & Rabinovich, A. (2015). Going deeper with convolutions. In *Proceedings of the IEEE conference on computer vision and pattern recognition* (pp. 1-9). IEEE.

Tang, J. H., & Puspasari, A. D. (2021). Numerical Simulation of Local Scour around Three Cylindrical Piles in a Tandem Arrangement. *Water (Basel)*, *13*(24), 3623. doi:10.3390/w13243623

Tang, S., Zhu, Y., & Yuan, S. (2022). Intelligent fault diagnosis of hydraulic piston pump based on deep learning and Bayesian optimization. *ISA Transactions*, *129*, 555–563. doi:10.1016/j.isatra.2022.01.013 PMID:35115164

Tedre, M., & Vartiainen, H. (2023). K-12 computing education for the AI era: From data literacy to data agency. *Proceedings of the 2023 Conference on Innovation and Technology in Computer Science Education*. ACM. 10.1145/3587102.3593796

Teerapittayanon, S., McDanel, B., & Kung, H. T. (2016, December). Branchynet: Fast inference via early exiting from deep neural networks. In *2016 23rd International Conference on Pattern Recognition (ICPR)* (pp. 2464-2469). IEEE.

Tempelaar, D., Rienties, B., & Nguyen, Q. (2020). Subjective data, objective data and the role of bias in predictive modelling: Lessons from a dispositional learning analytics application. *PLoS One*, *15*(6), e0233977. doi:10.1371/journal.pone.0233977 PMID:32530954

Thai, H. T. (2022, April). Machine learning for structural engineering: A state-of-the-art review. In *Structures* (Vol. 38, pp. 448–491). Elsevier.

Tharewal, S., Ashfaque, M. W., Banu, S. S., Uma, P., Hassen, S. M., & Shabaz, M. (2022). Intrusion Detection System for Industrial Internet of Things Based on Deep Reinforcement Learning. *Wireless Communications and Mobile Computing*, *2022*, 1–8. doi:10.1155/2022/9023719

Thomas, M. L., & Duffy, J. R. (2023). Advances in psychometric theory: Item response theory, generalizability theory, and cognitive psychometrics. In APA handbook of neuropsychology, volume 2: Neuroscience and neuromethods (vol. 2) (pp. 665–680). American Psychological Association.

Thomas, G., & Sule, M.-J. (2023). A service lens on cybersecurity continuity and management for organizations' subsistence and growth. *Organizational Cybersecurity Journal: Practice, Process and People*, *3*(1), 18–40. doi:10.1108/OCJ-09-2021-0025

Török, G. T., Baranya, S., Rüther, N., & Spiller, S. (2014, September). Laboratory analysis of armor layer development in a local scour around a groin. In *Proceedings of the International Conference on Fluvial Hydraulics, RIVER FLOW* (pp. 1455-1462). ACM.

Tramer, F., Carlini, N., Brendel, W., & Madry, A. (2020). On adaptive attacks to adversarial example defenses. *Advances in Neural Information Processing Systems*, *33*, 1633–1645.

Tran, K., Bisazza, A., & Monz, C. (2016). Recurrent Memory Networks for Language Modeling. *ArXiv*. /arXiv.1601.01272 doi:10.18653/v1/N16-1036

Tran, D.-P., & Hoang, V.-D. (2019). Adaptive learning based on tracking and ReIdentifying objects using convolutional neural network. *Neural Processing Letters*, *50*(1), 263–282. doi:10.1007/s11063-019-10040-w

Turing, A. (1950). Computing Machinery and Intelligence. *Mind*, *59*(236), 433–460. doi:10.1093/mind/LIX.236.433

Tzimas, D., & Demetriadis, S. (2021). Ethical issues in learning analytics: A review of the field. *Educational Technology Research and Development. Educational Technology Research and Development*, *69*(2), 1101–1133. doi:10.1007/s11423-021-09977-4

Uher, J. (2021). Psychometrics is not measurement: Unraveling a fundamental misconception in quantitative psychology and the complex network of its underlying fallacies. *Journal of Theoretical and Philosophical Psychology*, *41*(1), 58–84. doi:10.1037/teo0000176

UiPath. (2023). *UiPath Community 2023.12 Release*. UiPath. https://forum.uipath.com/t/what-is-the-maximum-number-of-rows-in-an-excel-sheet-that-works-with-uipath/206349

UiPath. (n.d.). *Home*. UiPath. https://www.uipath.com/solutions/technology

Van Engelen, J. E., & Hoos, H. H. (2020). A survey on semi-supervised learning. *Machine Learning*, *109*(2), 373–440. doi:10.1007/s10994-019-05855-6

Vandewaetere, M., Desmet, P., & Clarebout, G. (2011). The contribution of learner characteristics in the development of computer-based adaptive learning environments. *Computers in Human Behavior*, *27*(1), 118–130. doi:10.1016/j.chb.2010.07.038

Vartiainen, H., Pellas, L., Kahila, J., Valtonen, T., & Tedre, M. (2022). Pre-service teachers' insights on data agency. *New Media & Society*. doi:10.1177/14614448221079626

Vaswani, A., Shazeer, N., Parmar, N., Uszkoreit, J., Jones, L., Gomez, A. N., Kaiser, Ł., & Polosukhin, I. (2017). Attention is all you need. *Proceedings of the 31st International Conference on Neural Information Processing Systems*, (pp. 6000–6010). IEEE.

Vaughn, M. (2020). What is student agency and why is it needed now more than ever? *Theory into Practice*, *59*(2), 109–118. doi:10.1080/00405841.2019.1702393

Vellenga, K., Steinhauer, H. J., Karlsson, A., Falkman, G., Rhodin, A., & Koppisetty, A. C. (2022). Driver intention recognition: State-of-the-art review. *IEEE Open Journal of Intelligent Transportation Systems*, *3*, 602–616. doi:10.1109/OJITS.2022.3197296

Venkatraman, S., & Surendiran, B. (2020). Adaptive hybrid intrusion detection system for crowd sourced multimedia internet of things systems. *Multimedia Tools and Applications*, *79*(5–6), 3993–4010. doi:10.1007/s11042-019-7495-6

Verdonck, T., Baesens, B., Oskarsd'ottir, M., & vanden Broucke, S. (2021). Special issue on feature engineering editorial. *Machine Learning*. doi:10.1007/s10994-021-06042-2

Vieira, C., Parsons, P., & Byrd, V. (2018). Visual learning analytics of educational data: A systematic literature review and research agenda. *Computers & Education*, *122*, 119–135. doi:10.1016/j.compedu.2018.03.018

von Davier, A. A., Mislevy, R. J., & Hao, J. (2021). Introduction to computational psychometrics: Towards a principled integration of data science and machine learning techniques into psychometrics. In A. A. von Davier, R. J. Mislevy, & J. Hao (Eds.), *Computational psychometrics: New methodologies for a new generation of digital learning and assessment: With examples in R and Python* (pp. 1–6). Springer International Publishing. doi:10.1007/978-3-030-74394-9_1

Wadiwala, R. (2019). *The good, the bad and the ugly of Power Automate in 2021.*

Wang, A., Singh, A., Michael, J., Hill, F., Levy, O., & Bowman, S. R. (2018). GLUE: A Multi-Task Benchmark and Analysis Platform for Natural Language Understanding. *ArXiv.* /arXiv.1804.07461 doi:10.18653/v1/W18-5446

Wang, Y., Chen, H., Heng, Q., Hou, W., Fan, Y., Wu, Z., & Xie, X. (2022). Freematch: Self-adaptive thresholding for semi-supervised learning. arXiv preprint arXiv:2205.07246.

Wang, H., Li, Z., & Wang, H. (2021). Few-shot steel surface defect detection. *IEEE Transactions on Instrumentation and Measurement*, *71*, 1–12.

Wang, K., Li, Y., Kemao, Q., Di, J., & Zhao, J. (2019). One-step robust deep learning phase unwrapping. *Optics Express*, *27*(10), 15100. doi:10.1364/OE.27.015100 PMID:31163947

Wang, L., Kubichek, R., & Zhou, X. (2018). Adaptive learning based data-driven models for predicting hourly building energy use. *Energy and Building*, *159*, 454–461. doi:10.1016/j.enbuild.2017.10.054

Wang, M., Yang, N., & Weng, N. (2023). Securing a Smart Home with a Transformer-Based IoT Intrusion Detection System. *Electronics (Basel)*, *12*(9), 1–19. doi:10.3390/electronics12092100

Wang, P., & Gao, R. X. (2020). Transfer learning for enhanced machine fault diagnosis in manufacturing. *CIRP Annals*, *69*(1), 413–416. doi:10.1016/j.cirp.2020.04.074

Wang, P., & Govindarasu, M. (2020). Multi-Agent Based Attack-Resilient System Integrity Protection for Smart Grid. *IEEE Transactions on Smart Grid*, *11*(4), 3447–3456. doi:10.1109/TSG.2020.2970755

Wang, R., Ji, F., Jiang, Y., Wu, S. H., Kwong, S., Zhang, J., & Zhan, Z. H. (2022). An adaptive ant colony system based on variable range receding horizon control for berth allocation problem. *IEEE Transactions on Intelligent Transportation Systems*, *23*(11), 21675–21686. doi:10.1109/TITS.2022.3172719

Wang, R., Nguyen, T. T., Li, C., Jenkinson, I., Yang, Z., & Kavakeb, S. (2019). Optimising discrete dynamic berth allocations in seaports using a Levy Flight based meta-heuristic. *Swarm and Evolutionary Computation*, *44*, 1003–1017. doi:10.1016/j.swevo.2018.10.011

Wang, T., Qiao, M., Zhang, M., Yang, Y., & Snoussi, H. (2020). Data-driven prognostic method based on self-supervised learning approaches for fault detection. *Journal of Intelligent Manufacturing*, *31*(7), 1611–1619. doi:10.1007/s10845-018-1431-x

Wang, Z., Leng, L., Wang, S., Li, G., & Zhao, Y. (2020). A hyperheuristic approach for location-routing problem of cold chain logistics considering fuel consumption. *Computational Intelligence and Neuroscience*, *2020*, 2020. doi:10.1155/2020/8395754 PMID:32405298

Wari, E., & Zhu, W. (2016). A survey on metaheuristics for optimization in food manufacturing industry. *Applied Soft Computing*, *46*, 328–343. doi:10.1016/j.asoc.2016.04.034

Webb, G. I., Lee, L. K., Petitjean, F., & Goethals, B. (2017). Understanding concept drift. *arXiv preprint arXiv:1704.0036.*

Westerfield, G., Mitrovic, A., & Billinghurst, M. (2015). Intelligent augmented reality training for motherboard assembly. *International Journal of Artificial Intelligence in Education*, *25*(1), 157–172. doi:10.1007/s40593-014-0032-x

Wigfield, A., Cambria, J., & Eccles, J. S. (2019). Motivation in education. In R. M. Ryan (Ed.), The oxford handbook of human motivation (second, pp. 443–462). Oxford University Press.

Williams, S., Waterman, A., & Patterson, D. (2009). Roofline: An insightful visual performance model for multicore architectures. *Communications of the ACM*, *52*(4), 65–76. doi:10.1145/1498765.1498785

Wilson, G., & Cook, D. J. (2020). A survey of unsupervised deep domain adaptation. [TIST]. *ACM Transactions on Intelligent Systems and Technology*, *11*(5), 1–46. doi:10.1145/3400066 PMID:34336374

Wingate, D., Shoeybi, M., & Sorensen, T. (2022). Prompt Compression and Contrastive Conditioning for Controllability and Toxicity Reduction in Language Models. *ArXiv*. /arXiv.2210.03162 doi:10.18653/v1/2022.findings-emnlp.412

Winstein, K., Sivaraman, A., & Balakrishnan, H. (2013, April). Stochastic forecasts achieve high throughput and low delay over cellular networks. In NSDI (Vol. 1, No. 1, pp. 2-3).

Wolfram, S. (2023a, March 23). ChatGPT Gets Its "Wolfram Superpowers". *Stephen Wolfram Writings*. writings.stephenwolfram.com/2023/03/chatgpt-gets-its-wolfram-superpowers/

Wolfram, S. (2023b, February 14). What Is ChatGPT Doing … and Why Does It Work? *Stephen Wolfram Writings*. writings.stephenwolfram.com/2023/02/what-is-chatgpt-doing-and-why-does-it-work/

Wu, C., Qiao, Z., Zhang, N., Li, X., Fan, J., Song, H., Ai, D., Yang, J., & Huang, Y. (2020). Phase unwrapping based on a residual en-decoder network for phase images in Fourier domain Doppler optical coherence tomography. *Biomedical Optics Express*, *11*(4), 1760. doi:10.1364/BOE.386101 PMID:32341846

Wu, X., Liang, Z., & Wang, J. (2020). Fedmed: A federated learning framework for language modeling. *Sensors (Basel)*, *20*(14), 4048. doi:10.3390/s20144048 PMID:32708152

Xia, S., Huang, Y., Peng, S., Wu, Y., & Tan, X. (2017). Robust phase unwrapping for phase images in Fourier domain Doppler optical coherence tomography. *Journal of Biomedical Optics*, *22*(3), 036014. doi:10.1117/1.JBO.22.3.036014 PMID:28353689

Xing, S., & Guo, H. (2017). Temporal phase unwrapping for fringe projection profilometry aided by recursion of Chebyshev polynomials. *Applied Optics*, *56*(6), 1591. doi:10.1364/AO.56.001591 PMID:28234364

Xin, M., Li, B., Yan, X., Chen, L., & Wei, X. (2018). A robust cloud registration method based on redundant data reduction using backpropagation neural network and shift window. *The Review of Scientific Instruments*, *89*(2), 024704. doi:10.1063/1.4996628 PMID:29495860

Xu, M., Qian, F., Zhu, M., Huang, F., Pushp, S., & Liu, X. (2019). Deepwear: Adaptive local offloading for on-wearable deep learning. *IEEE Transactions on Mobile Computing*, *19*(2), 314–330. doi:10.1109/TMC.2019.2893250

Xu, R., Hao, R., & Huang, B. (2022). Efficient surface defect detection using self-supervised learning strategy and segmentation network. *Advanced Engineering Informatics*, *52*, 101566. doi:10.1016/j.aei.2022.101566

Xu, Z., Tang, J., Meng, J., Zhang, W., Wang, Y., Liu, C. H., & Yang, D. (2018, April). Experience-driven networking: A deep reinforcement learning based approach. In *IEEE INFOCOM 2018-IEEE conference on computer communications* (pp. 1871–1879). IEEE. doi:10.1109/INFOCOM.2018.8485853

Yan Jiang, F. H. (2017). A Hybrid Algorithm of Adaptive Particle Swarm Optimization Based on Adaptive Moment Estimation Method. *Lecture Notes in Computer Science*, *10361*, 658–667. doi:10.1007/978-3-319-63309-1_58

Yan, H., Guo, Y., & Yang, C. (2021, December). Augmented self-labeling for source-free unsupervised domain adaptation. In *NeurIPS 2021 Workshop on Distribution Shifts: Connecting Methods and Applications*. IEEE.

Yang, T., Andrew, G., Eichner, H., Sun, H., Li, W., Kong, N., & Beaufays, F. (2018). Applied federated learning: Improving google keyboard query suggestions. *arXiv preprint arXiv:1812.02903.*

Yang, K., Yang, M., & Anderson, J. H. (2016, October). Reducing response-time bounds for dag-based task systems on heterogeneous multicore platforms. In *Proceedings of the 24th international conference on real-time networks and systems* (pp. 349-358). ACM. 10.1145/2997465.2997486

Yang, Q., Liu, Y., Chen, T., & Tong, Y. (2019). Federated machine learning: Concept and applications. [TIST]. *ACM Transactions on Intelligent Systems and Technology*, *10*(2), 1–19. doi:10.1145/3298981

Yang, X., Song, Z., King, I., & Xu, Z. (2022). A survey on deep semi-supervised learning. *IEEE Transactions on Knowledge and Data Engineering.*

Yang, Z., Al-Dahidi, S., Baraldi, P., Zio, E., & Montelatici, L. (2019). A novel concept drift detection method for incremental learning in nonstationary environments. *IEEE Transactions on Neural Networks and Learning Systems*, *31*(1), 309–320. doi:10.1109/TNNLS.2019.2900956 PMID:30932852

Yan, K., Yu, Y., Sun, T., Asundi, A., & Kemao, Q. (2020). Wrapped phase denoising using convolutional neural networks. *Optics and Lasers in Engineering*, *128*, 105999. doi:10.1016/j.optlaseng.2019.105999

Yan, X., Xu, Y., Xing, X., Cui, B., Guo, Z., & Guo, T. (2020). Trustworthy Network Anomaly Detection Based on an Adaptive Learning Rate and Momentum in IIoT. *IEEE Transactions on Industrial Informatics*, *16*(9), 6182–6192. doi:10.1109/TII.2020.2975227

Yao, L., Long, W., Yi, J., Li, T., Tang, D., & Xu, Q. (2021). A novel tournament selection based on multilayer cultural characteristics in gene-culture coevolutionary multitasking. *Soft Computing*, *25*(14), 9529–9543. doi:10.1007/s00500-021-05876-1

Yao, S., Zhao, Y., Shao, H., Liu, S., Liu, D., Su, L., & Abdelzaher, T. (2018, November). Fastdeepiot: Towards understanding and optimizing neural network execution time on mobile and embedded devices. In *Proceedings of the 16th ACM Conference on Embedded Networked Sensor Systems* (pp. 278-291). ACM. 10.1145/3274783.3274840

Yildiz, B., Bilbao, J. I., Dore, J., & Sproul, A. B. (2017). Recent advances in the analysis of residential electricity consumption and applications of smart meter data. *Applied Energy*, *208*, 402–427. doi:10.1016/j.apenergy.2017.10.014

Yin, C. T., Xiong, Z., Chen, H., Wang, J. Y., Cooper, D., & David, B. (2015). A literature survey on smart cities. *Science China. Information Sciences*, *58*(10), 1–18. doi:10.1007/s11432-015-5397-4

Yin, J., Deng, Z., Ines, A. V., Wu, J., & Rasu, E. (2020). Forecast of short-term daily reference evapotranspiration under limited meteorological variables using a hybrid bi-directional long short-term memory model (Bi-LSTM). *Agricultural Water Management*, *242*, 106386. doi:10.1016/j.agwat.2020.106386

Yin, X., Jindal, A., Sekar, V., & Sinopoli, B. (2015, August). A control-theoretic approach for dynamic adaptive video streaming over HTTP. In *Proceedings of the 2015 ACM Conference on Special Interest Group on Data Communication* (pp. 325-338). ACM. 10.1145/2785956.2787486

Yiu, E., Kosoy, E., & Gopnik, A. (2023). Transmission versus truth, imitation versus innovation: What children can do that large language and language-and-vision models cannot (yet). *Perspectives on Psychological Science*, 17456916231201401. doi:10.1177/17456916231201401 PMID:37883796

Yoo, S., & Jeong, O. (2020). Automating the expansion of a knowledge graph. *Expert Systems with Applications*, *141*, 112965. doi:10.1016/j.eswa.2019.112965

Younes, S. S. (2021). Examining the effectiveness of using adaptive AI-enabled e-learning during the pandemic of COVID-19. *Journal of Healthcare Engineering*, *2021*, 3928326. doi:10.1155/2021/3928326 PMID:34567481

Yousefpour, N., Downie, S., Walker, S., Perkins, N., & Dikanski, H. (2021). Machine learning solutions for bridge scour forecast based on monitoring data. *Transportation Research Record: Journal of the Transportation Research Board*, *2675*(10), 745–763. doi:10.1177/03611981211012693

Yu, H., Sun, S., Yu, H., Chen, X., Shi, H., Huang, T. S., & Chen, T. (2020). Foal: Fast online adaptive learning for cardiac motion estimation. In *Proceedings of the IEEE/CVF conference on computer vision and pattern recognition* (pp. 4313-4323). IEEE. 10.1109/CVPR42600.2020.00437

Yu, J., Zhang, H., Jin, C., Ma, D., Wang, H., & Lu, Z. (2016). Ultra-high accuracy point diffraction interferometer: development, acccuracy evaluation and application. *8th Int Symp Adv Opt Manuf Test Technol Opt Test, Meas Technol Equip*. Spie. 10.1117/12.2246269

Yu, X., Shi, S., Xu, L., Liu, Y., Miao, Q., & Sun, M. (2020). A novel method for sea surface temperature prediction based on deep learning. *Mathematical Problems in Engineering*, *2020*, 1–9. doi:10.1155/2020/6387173

Yu, Y., Si, X., Hu, C., & Zhang, J. (2019). A review of recurrent neural networks: LSTM cells and network architectures. *Neural Computation*, *31*(7), 1235–1270. doi:10.1162/neco_a_01199 PMID:31113301

Zador, A., Escola, S., Richards, B., Ölveczky, B., Bengio, Y., Boahen, K., Botvinick, M., Chklovskii, D., Churchland, A., Clopath, C., DiCarlo, J., Ganguli, S., Hawkins, J., Körding, K., Koulakov, A., LeCun, Y., Lillicrap, T., Marblestone, A., Olshausen, B., & Tsao, D. (2023). Catalyzing next-generation Artificial Intelligence through NeuroAI. *Nature Communications*, *14*(1), 1–7. doi:10.1038/s41467-023-37180-x PMID:36949048

Zavadskas, E. K. (2010). Automation and robotics in construction: International research and achievements. *Automation in Construction*, *19*(3), 286–290. doi:10.1016/j.autcon.2009.12.011

Zehner, F., Eichmann, B., Deribo, T., Harrison, S., Bengs, D., Andersen, N., & Hahnel, C. (2021). Applying psychometric modeling to aid feature engineering in predictive log-data analytics: The NAEP EDM competition. *Journal of Educational Data Mining*, *13*(2), 80–107.

Zeylikman, S., Widder, S., Roncone, A., Mangin, O., & Scassellati, B. (2018, October). The HRC model set for human-robot collaboration research. In *2018 IEEE/RSJ International Conference on Intelligent Robots and Systems (IROS)* (pp. 1845-1852). IEEE. 10.1109/IROS.2018.8593858

Zhang, H., Li, W., Gao, S., Wang, X., & Ye, B. (2019, April). ReLeS: A neural adaptive multipath scheduler based on deep reinforcement learning. In *IEEE INFOCOM 2019-IEEE Conference on Computer Communications* (pp. 1648-1656). IEEE. 10.1109/INFOCOM.2019.8737649

Zhang, Z., Flora, K., Kang, S., Limaye, A. B., & Khosronejad, A. (2022). Data-Driven Prediction of Turbulent Flow Statistics Past Bridge Piers in Large-Scale Rivers Using Convolutional Neural Networks. *Water Resources Research*, *58*(1), e2021WR030163.

Zhang, B., Jin, X., Ratnasamy, S., Wawrzynek, J., & Lee, E. A. (2018, August). Awstream: Adaptive wide-area streaming analytics. In *Proceedings of the 2018 Conference of the ACM Special Interest Group on Data Communication* (pp. 236-252). ACM. 10.1145/3230543.3230554

Zhang, B., Wang, Y., Hou, W., Wu, H., Wang, J., Okumura, M., & Shinozaki, T. (2021). Flexmatch: Boosting semi-supervised learning with curriculum pseudo labeling. *Advances in Neural Information Processing Systems*, *34*, 18408–18419.

Zhang, C., Liu, Z., Gu, B., Yamori, K., & Tanaka, Y. (2018). A deep reinforcement learning based approach for cost- and energy-aware multi-flow mobile data offloading. *IEICE Transactions on Communications*, *101*(7), 1625–1634. doi:10.1587/transcom.2017CQP0014

Zhang, D., Westfechtel, T., & Harada, T. (2023). Unsupervised Domain Adaptation via Minimized Joint Error. *Transactions on Machine Learning Research.*

Zhang, H., Ananthanarayanan, G., Bodik, P., Philipose, M., Bahl, P., & Freedman, M. J. (2017). Live video analytics at scale with approximation and delay-tolerance. In *14th USENIX Symposium on Networked Systems Design and Implementation*. ACM.

Zhang, J. E., Wu, D., & Boulet, B. (2021). Time Series Anomaly Detection for Smart Grids: A Survey. *2021 IEEE Electrical Power and Energy Conference. EPEC*, *2021*, 125–130. doi:10.1109/EPEC52095.2021.9621752

Zhang, J., Tian, X., Shao, J., Luo, H., & Liang, R. (2019). Phase unwrapping in optical metrology via denoised and convolutional segmentation networks. *Optics Express*, *27*(10), 14903. doi:10.1364/OE.27.014903 PMID:31163931

Zhang, P., Wu, X., Wang, X., & Bi, S. (2015). Short-term load forecasting based on big data technologies. *CSEE Journal of Power and Energy Systems*, *1*(3), 59–67. doi:10.17775/CSEEJPES.2015.00036

Zhang, W., Han, B., & Hui, P. (2017, August). On the networking challenges of mobile augmented reality. In *Proceedings of the Workshop on Virtual Reality and Augmented Reality Network* (pp. 24-29). ACM. 10.1145/3097895.3097900

Zhang, W., & Zhang, Y. (2022). Intrusion Detection Model for Industrial Internet of Things Based on Improved Autoencoder. *Computational Intelligence and Neuroscience*, *2022*, 1–8. doi:10.1155/2022/1406214 PMID:35669645

Zhang, X., Zhou, X., Lin, M., & Sun, J. (2018). Shufflenet: An extremely efficient convolutional neural network for mobile devices. In *Proceedings of the IEEE conference on computer vision and pattern recognition* (pp. 6848-6856). IEEE. 10.1109/CVPR.2018.00716

Zhang, Y., Deng, B., Jia, K., & Zhang, L. (2020, August). Label propagation with augmented anchors: A simple semi-supervised learning baseline for unsupervised domain adaptation. In *European Conference on Computer Vision* (pp. 781-797). Cham: Springer International Publishing. 10.1007/978-3-030-58548-8_45

Zhang, Y., Ding, K., Hui, J., Lv, J., Zhou, X., & Zheng, P. (2022). Human-object integrated assembly intention recognition for context-aware human-robot collaborative assembly. *Advanced Engineering Informatics*, *54*, 101792. doi:10.1016/j.aei.2022.101792

Zhang, Z., Qiu, J., Huang, X., Cai, Z., Zhu, L., & Dai, W. (2021). Comparing and Evaluating Macao Flood Prediction Models. [). IOP Publishing.]. *IOP Conference Series. Earth and Environmental Science*, *769*(2), 022001. doi:10.1088/1755-1315/769/2/022001

Zhan, Z., Zhou, J., & Xu, B. (2022). Fabric defect classification using prototypical network of few-shot learning algorithm. *Computers in Industry*, *138*, 103628. doi:10.1016/j.compind.2022.103628

Zhao, L., Chen, Z., & Yang, Y. (2017). Parameter-free incremental co-clustering for multi-modal data in cyber-physical-social systems. *IEEE Access : Practical Innovations, Open Solutions*, *5*, 21852–21861. doi:10.1109/ACCESS.2017.2758798

Zhao, Z., Barijough, K. M., & Gerstlauer, A. (2018). Deepthings: Distributed adaptive deep learning inference on resource-constrained iot edge clusters. *IEEE Transactions on Computer-Aided Design of Integrated Circuits and Systems*, *37*(11), 2348–2359. doi:10.1109/TCAD.2018.2858384

Zhao, Z., Li, B., Kang, X., Chen, L., & Wei, X. (2019). Precision optical path alignment system for point diffraction interferometer based on image information. *Applied Optics*, *58*(14), 3703. doi:10.1364/AO.58.003703 PMID:31158181

Zhao, Z., Zhang, H., Xiao, Z., Du, H., Zhuang, Y., Fan, C., & Zhao, H. (2019). Robust 2D phase unwrapping algorithm based on the transport of intensity equation. *Measurement Science & Technology*, *30*(1), 015201. doi:10.1088/1361-6501/aaec5c

Zha, W., Liu, Y., Wan, Y., Luo, R., Li, D., Yang, S., & Xu, Y. (2022). Forecasting monthly gas field production based on the CNN-LSTM model. *Energy*, *260*, 124889. doi:10.1016/j.energy.2022.124889

Zheng, L., Niu, J., Zhong, L., & Gyasi, J. F. (2021). The effectiveness of artificial intelligence on learning achievement and learning perception: A meta-analysis. *Interactive Learning Environments*, 1–15.

Zhong, H., Tang, J., Zhang, S., & Chen, M. (2011). An Improved Quality-Guided Phase Unwrapping Algorithm Based on Priority Queue. *IEEE Geoscience and Remote Sensing Letters*, *8*(2), 364–368. doi:10.1109/LGRS.2010.2076362

Zhou, L., Samavatian, M. H., Bacha, A., Majumdar, S., & Teodorescu, R. (2019, November). Adaptive parallel execution of deep neural networks on heterogeneous edge devices. In *Proceedings of the 4th ACM/IEEE Symposium on Edge Computing* (pp. 195-208). ACM/IEEE. 10.1145/3318216.3363312

Zhou, C., Liu, T., Si, S., Xu, J., Liu, Y., & Lei, Z. (2015). An improved stair phase encoding method for absolute phase retrieval. *Optics and Lasers in Engineering*, *66*, 269–278. doi:10.1016/j.optlaseng.2014.09.011

Zhou, P., Xiong, C., Yuan, X., & Hoi, S. C. H. (2021). A theory-driven self-labeling refinement method for contrastive representation learning. *Advances in Neural Information Processing Systems*, *34*, 6183–6197.

Zhou, Z., Chen, X., Li, E., Zeng, L., Luo, K., & Zhang, J. (2019). Edge intelligence: Paving the last mile of artificial intelligence with edge computing. *Proceedings of the IEEE*, *107*(8), 1738–1762. doi:10.1109/JPROC.2019.2918951

Zhu, X., & Ghahramani, Z. (2002). Learning from labeled and unlabeled data with label propagation. *Tech. Rep., Technical Report CMU-CALD-02–107.* Carnegie Mellon University.

Zliobaite, I., Pechenizkiy, M., & Gama, J. (2016). An overview of concept drift applications. *Big data analysis: new algorithms for a new society*, (pp. 91-114). Research Gate.

Zliobaite, I., Bifet, A., Pfahringer, B., & Holmes, G. (2011). Active learning with evolving streaming data. In *Machine Learning and Knowledge Discovery in Databases: European Conference, ECML PKDD 2011*, Athens, Greece, September 5-9, 2011 [Springer.]. *Proceedings*, *22*(Part III), 597–612.

Zliobaite, I., & Gabrys, B. (2012). Adaptive preprocessing for streaming data. *IEEE Transactions on Knowledge and Data Engineering*, *26*(2), 309–321. doi:10.1109/TKDE.2012.147

Zuo, G., Luo, J., Wang, N., Lian, Y., & He, X. (2020). Decomposition ensemble model based on variational mode decomposition and long short-term memory for streamflow forecasting. *Journal of Hydrology (Amsterdam)*, *585*, 124776. doi:10.1016/j.jhydrol.2020.124776

About the Contributors

Nawaf Abdulla holds a Master of Science in Computer Science from the Jordan University of Science and Technology in Amman as well as a Bachelor of Science in Computer Science and Engineering from the University of Aden in Yemen. His research interests include data mining, machine and deep learning, adaptive learning, federated learning, and smart city applications. He is currently pursuing a doctorate in Information Systems at Gazi University in Turkey. Moreover, he has recently demonstrated a significant interest in data science, particularly the energy management industry.

C.V. Suresh Babu is a pioneer in content development. A true entrepreneur, he founded Anniyappa Publications, a company that is highly active in publishing books related to Computer Science and Management. Dr. C.V. Suresh Babu has also ventured into SB Institute, a center for knowledge transfer. He holds a Ph.D. in Engineering Education from the National Institute of Technical Teachers Training & Research in Chennai, along with seven master's degrees in various disciplines such as Engineering, Computer Applications, Management, Commerce, Economics, Psychology, Law, and Education. Additionally, he has UGC-NET/SET qualifications in the fields of Computer Science, Management, Commerce, and Education. Currently, Dr. C.V. Suresh Babu is a Professor in the Department of Information Technology at the School of Computing Science, Hindustan Institute of Technology and Science (Hindustan University) in Padur, Chennai, Tamil Nadu, India. For more information, you can visit his personal blog at .

Ning Chen is currently pursuing the PhD degree in the Department of Computer Science and Technology, Nanjing University, under the supervision of Prof. Sheng Zhang. His research interests include edge computing, deep reinforcement learning, and video streaming. To date, he has published several papers, including those appeared in INFOCOM, TPDS, TON, SECON, Computer Network, ICPADS, et al.

Yu Chen is a PhD Student in Nanjing University

Abhijit Chirputkar works as an Associate Professor and Director at SIDTM in Symbiosis International (Deemed University), India. His academic chronicles include Ph, D. in Accounting and Finance and C.A. His research interests include Inclusion of Technology in Finance domain.

Mehmet Demirci received his B.S. degree in computer science and mathematics (double major) from Purdue University, West Lafayette, Indiana, USA in 2006, and his M.Sc. and Ph.D. degrees in computer science from Georgia Institute of Technology, Atlanta, Georgia, USA, in 2009 and 2013, respectively. He is currently an associate professor at the Department of Computer Engineering, Faculty of Engineering, Gazi University, Ankara, Turkey. His current research interests are software-defined networking (SDN), programmable networks, 5G/6G, edge computing, network security, network architecture, and future Internet.

Sedef Demirci is an assistant professor at the Department of Computer Engineering, Faculty of Engineering, Gazi University, Ankara, Turkey. She completed her Ph. D. at the same department in 2020. Her research interests include network functions virtualization (NFV), software-defined networking (SDN), 5G and beyond, smart grids, green computing, cybersecurity, and machine learning.

Akshata Desai is a PG scholar from Symbiosis Institute of Digital and Telecom Management of Symbiosis International University, Pune. She did her B.E. in Information Technology at University of Mumbai. Her research interests include Hyper Automation, 5G, Internet of Things.

Giri. G. Hallur is working as an Associate Professor and Deputy Director in Symbiosis Institute of Digital and Telecom Management, Symbiosis International (Deemed University), Pune. His interests include Digital and Telecom Management, Telecom Policy and Regulations.

Ville Heilala received a Ph.D. in Mathematical Information Technology from the University of Jyväskylä in 2022. He also holds an M.A. degree in Education and a B.A. in Music. He works as a postdoctoral researcher at the University of Jyväskylä, focusing on learning analytics, artificial intelligence in education, and future perspectives of digitalization. In his dissertation research, Heilala developed and examined a learning analytics process for analyzing learning experiences using machine learning and computational psychometrics. Before his research career, Heilala worked for over a decade as a teacher in Finnish primary education.

Päivikki Jääskelä (PhD in Education) was hired as the Senior Researcher by the Finnish Institute for Educational Research, University of Jyväskylä (JYU) in 2017 and is currently the PI of the StudyAgent research project funded by the Academy of Finland (2023-2026). From 2009-2016, she worked at the Department of Teacher Education (JYU) as the University Teacher for Educational Sciences and the Postdoctoral Researcher in university-level projects on the development of higher education pedagogy and guidance. During 1995-2008, she worked as the University Teacher for Education and Adult Education and the Coordinator for university studies at the Open University Units of JYU. She received her PhD in 2005 and the title of Docent (Adjunct Professor) 2019 from the JYU. She is the main developer of the Agency of University Students (AUS) scale. She has published widely on issues of higher education pedagogy, including student agency, teacher development, and curriculum work.

Tommi Kärkkäinen received a Ph.D. degree in Mathematical Information Technology from the University of Jyväskylä (JYU) in 1995. Since 2002, he has been serving as a full professor of Mathematical Information Technology at the Faculty of Information Technology (FIT), JYU. TK has led 50 different R&D projects and has been supervising over 60 PhD students. He has published over 200 peer-reviewed articles. TK received the Innovation Prize of JYU in 2010. He has served in many administrative positions at FIT and JYU, currently leading a Research Division and a Research Group on Human and Machine based Intelligence in Learning. The main research interests include machine learning, learning analytics, brain research, and nanotechnology. He is a senior member of the IEEE.

Bokang Li is a Doctoral Student and Graduate Research Assistant in the Department of Civil & Environmental Engineering at Florida A&M University-Florida State University (FAMU-FSU) College of Engineering. He holds a B.S. degree in Engineering with concentration in Harbor, Waterway and Coastal Engineering from Wuhan University (Wuhan, China). His research interests include, but are not limited to, operations research, machine learning, artificial intelligence, metaheuristics, hybrid algorithms, hyper-heuristics, transportation engineering, freight terminals, and marine container terminals.

G. P. Li, professor at the University of California, Irvine (UCI) with appointments in Electrical Engineering and Computer Science, and Biomedical Engineering. He is director of California Institute for Telecommunications and Information Technology (Calit2) at UCI and director of the Integrated Nanosystems Research Facility. Prior to UCI, Li worked at IBM's T. J. Watson Research Center on VLSI technology. Li holds 41 U.S. patents and has published 425 research papers involving microelectronic devices&circuits, communication and biomedical MEMS, IOT and data analytics for edge intelligence in sustainability, manufacturing, and e-health. A member of numerous technical committees at professional conferences, Li was chair of the Taiwan VLSI Technology, Circuit, and System Conference and chair of the executive committee for electronics manufacturing research and new materials at the University of California. Li is fellow of IEEE and AAIA and received IBM outstanding research contribution award, two outstanding engineering professor awards, UCI Innovators Award, and UCI Chancellor's Award for Excellence in Fostering Undergraduate Research.

Sanglu Lu received her BS, MS, and PhD degrees from Nanjing University in 1992, 1995, and 1997, respectively, all in computer science. She is currently a professor in the Department of Computer Science and Technology and the State Key Laboratory for Novel Software Technology. Her research interests include distributed computing, wireless networks, and pervasive computing. She has published over 80 papers in referred journals and conferences in the above areas. She is a member of IEEE.

N.A. Natraj is an Assistant Professor at SIDTM in Symbiosis International University, India. His academic chronicles include Ph, D. in Electronics and Communication Engineering. He has 11 years of Academic experience in various Countries. His research interests include Wireless Sensor Networks, the Internet of Things, 5G and Communication Networks. He holds publications in reputed Journals and has published patents in the mentioned research fields. He has completed certifications in domains like 5G, IoT, Digital Forensics and Blockchain from various organizations like Stanford, Europe Open University, Qualcomm, University of London, etc.

Suat Ozdemir is with the Department of Computer Engineering at Hacettepe University, Ankara, Turkey. He received his MSc degree in Computer Science from Syracuse University (August 2001) and PhD degree in Computer Science from Arizona State University (December 2006). His current research interests include Internet of Things, Data Analytics, Artificial Intelligence, and Network Security.

Tao Peng received his Ph.D. degree in the Department of Computer Science and Technology at Soochow University in 2019. From 2020 to 2022, he was a postdoctoral researcher in the Department of Health Technology and Informatics at Hong Kong Polytechnic University, and Department of Radiation Oncology at University of Texas Southwestern Medical Center, Dallas, TX, USA, successively. During this period, he obtained the "Research Talent" award from Hong Kong government. Currently, Dr. Peng is an Associate Professor in School of Future Science and Engineering, Soochow University, Suzhou, China. He has published 37 peer-reviewed journal/conference papers, where the total impact factor (IF) of all the journal publications as the first author is IF > 67. He now serves as Guest Associate Editor of Medical Physics journal, a Co-Editor of Special Topic at Frontiers in Signal Processing journal, and a reviewer of some high-quality journals/conferences, including IEEE Trans. Intell. Transp. Syst., Med. Phys., Quant. Imaging. Med. Surg., Secur. Commun. Netw., Imaging Sci. J., J. Health Inform., IEEE Consum. Electron. Mag., Biocybern. Biomed. Eng., IEEE Access, IEEE ISBI, IEEE SMC, MMM, MICCAI. His main research interests include medical image processing, pattern recognition, machine learning, and their applications. His homepage is or .

Mirka Saarela is an Academy of Finland Research Fellow in the Faculty of Information Technology at the University of Jyväskylä, Finland. She holds a Ph.D. in Mathematical Information Technology (2017, JYU). Her research lies at the intersection of learning analytics, machine learning, education, and artificial intelligence. She is especially interested in explainability and fairness in algorithmic decision-making. Her research was supported by Otto A. Malm, the Finnish Foundation for Share Promotion, and the Academy of Finland (project no. 356314).

Salaar Saraj is an undergraduate student at the University of California, Irvine. He is currently a double major pursuing BS degrees in Computer Science and Mathematics, with a specification focus on intelligent systems and data science. He has a hands-on background in AI development, having previously collaborated on a lifestyle application that utilizes AI to provide daily health recommendations. Salaar's current research interests encompass machine learning, human-robot collaboration, data analysis, and data annotation techniques.

Aaron Yen is an undergraduate Electrical Engineering and Computer Engineering student at the University of California, Irvine (UCI). His research focuses on adaptive architectures in Machine Learning and Digital Signal Processing for communications applications.

Sheng Zhang is an associate professor in the Department of Computer Science and Technology, Naning University.He is also amember of the State Key Lab. for Novel Sotware Technology. He received the BS and PhD degrees from Nanjing University in 2008and 2014, respectively. His research interests include cloud computing and edge computing. To date, he has published more than 80papers, including those appeared in TMC, TON,TPDS, TC, MobiHoc, ICDCS, and INFOCOM. He received the Best Paper Award ofEEE ICCCN 2020 and the Best Paper Runner-Up Award of EEE MASS 2012. He is the recipient of the 2015 ACM China DoctoralDissertation Nomination Award. He is a member of the IEEE and a senior member of the CCF.

Index

A

Adaptive AI 21, 25, 29-32, 34, 36-38, 40-41, 52-54, 58-59, 62, 64, 69, 71, 74-78, 81, 83-87, 89-90, 92-93, 196, 199, 222
Adaptive AI model 222
Adaptive Artificial Intelligence 20-21, 58
adaptive configuration 151-152, 154, 157-159, 168, 173-174
Adaptive Machine Learning 179-183, 199
AI Integration 64, 71
ANN learning 116
ANN Parameters 117
ANN Training 116
Artificial General Intelligence 103, 117, 122
Artificial Intelligence 20-21, 25-30, 32, 39, 52, 58-60, 62, 64-65, 69, 81, 91, 102, 104, 117, 122, 209, 214
Artificial Neural Networks 82, 112
Augmented reality 151-152, 157
Auto Encoder 222, 224-225, 238
automation 63, 180, 188, 263-265, 267-269, 271
autonomous driving 76, 92, 199

B

Bayesian optimization 207, 210-212, 214, 216
Benchmark 77, 82, 102-103, 105-107, 117, 194, 198-199
Bridge Pier 208, 210, 214

C

Causal Machine Learning 182
civil engineering 210, 216
CNN Inference 123-127, 129-130, 139-140, 145-146
CNN Structure 139
Cognitive Skills 106, 117
Computational Psychometrics 20, 26-27, 35, 37, 39-41
contextual information 181, 190
Cyber Physical Systems 179-181
Cyber Threats 55, 58-59, 62, 64, 71, 84
Cybersecurity 52-55, 57-64, 68-71, 76, 84, 92

D

Deep Learning 68, 75, 77-80, 82-83, 88, 90, 107, 124, 127, 139, 209-211, 216, 223, 225
Deep Neural Network 210, 223-225, 229, 260
deep reinforcement 90, 152, 157, 174
Digital Landscapes 52-54, 71
digital transformation 21, 38, 90
Dynamic Cybersecurity 52-54, 71

E

Edge Computing 82-83, 91, 124, 126, 140, 147, 152
energy consumption 73, 75-76, 81-82, 147
Energy Consumption Forecasting 73, 76, 81-82
Ethical Considerations 22, 25-26, 34, 39-40, 69-70
Evolving Threats 52-54, 71
Explainability 28, 68

F

Flood Forecasting 76, 78-81

G

Goldstein branch 223, 236-238

H

heuristics 4, 6-7, 14-15
Higher Education 20-22, 24, 38, 41
human intervention 30, 181, 183, 189, 191, 268
hyperheuristics 1, 4, 14-15

I

In-Context Learning 104, 107-108, 111-112, 117
Inference Latency 123-124, 129, 141, 143, 145
Intelligence Metrics 104, 112, 117
Interferometry 223-224, 232
Internet of Things 73-74, 78, 83, 124
Iterative Closest Point 222, 224, 229, 231, 238

L

Ladder Metric 106-107, 110, 122
Learning Analytics 20-22, 24-27, 33, 35, 38, 41
LSTM 66, 75, 77, 79, 82-83, 86, 88, 107, 122, 207, 210-214, 216

M

Machine Learning 21, 25-28, 31, 34, 39-40, 52, 54, 60-62, 64-67, 73-79, 82-83, 85, 91-92, 104, 117, 179-183, 198-199, 242, 260, 265, 268
Maritime transportation 1-2, 15, 88
Memory Footprint 123, 125-127, 130, 138-139, 141-142, 144-146
ML applications 181, 190

O

Optical metrology 223

P

PDI system 224, 233-234, 238
pedagogical decision-making 21, 25-26, 36, 38, 40
Phase unwrapping 222-224, 229, 235, 238

R

Real-time Threat Detection 52, 59
reinforcement learning 86-87, 90, 146, 151-152, 157, 174
Robotic process automation 264-265

S

Self-labeling 179, 181-182, 184-188, 190, 192-194, 197-199
Smart Grid 84
Smart Manufacturing 180, 199
Stream Processing 74, 77
Student Agency 20-29, 31, 34-41
Student-Centered Learning 21, 36-37, 41
Symbol Grounding Problem 111, 117, 122
Synchronization 123, 125-127, 129, 137, 139-143, 145

T

Turing Test 103-107, 112, 117

W

Weather Forecasting 76-77
workflows 264, 267-270

www.ingramcontent.com/pod-product-compliance
Lightning Source LLC
LaVergne TN
LVHW080640011026
849160LV00014B/1273
* 9 7 9 8 3 6 9 3 0 2 3 1 6 *